A PSYCHOLOGY SERIES

Edited by

J. McV. Hunt, Ph.D.

PROFESSOR OF PSYCHOLOGY
UNIVERSITY OF ILLINOIS

PSYCHOLOGY

OF

PERSONALITY

Hubert Bonner

PROFESSOR OF PSYCHOLOGY

OHIO WESLEYAN UNIVERSITY

THE RONALD PRESS COMPANY • NEW YORK

Library of Congress Catalog Card Number: 61-5656
PRINTED IN THE UNITED STATES OF AMERICA

Preface

The purpose of this volume is to present a description of the personality as seen from the holistic, field-psychological, and perceptual points of view. These views when applied to the study of personality form an image of the person which is at once both humanistic and supported by recent developments in the natural sciences.

While this book explicitly challenges the mechanistic view of human behavior it does not lose sight of its achievements. I am fully aware that the stimulus-response approach to the study of human behavior has not only become increasingly self-corrective, but has built a substantial foundation for a more organismic theory of personality. I follow the behaviorist as far as I can, but the path which he treads does not, I believe, take psychology far enough. The fact is, most stimulus-response psychologists have shown astonishingly little interest in the psychology of the whole personality. The general tone of the book, accordingly, expresses dissatisfaction with much of the current mechanistic investigation of the psychology of personality. I am strongly, but I hope not irrevocably, convinced that a theory of personality based on the animal model does not come to grips with the living person but tends to obscure him, if not to lose him to view.

While the view of personality presented in this volume is relatively simple, it is a product of many and complex influences. I have vividly felt the "shock of recognition" which every writer must surely experience in the course of delineating his ideas. The seminal ideas of my late and revered teacher, Alfred North Whitehead, particularly his philosophy of the organism and his inexpressible sensitivity to the uniqueness of the human person, have shaped my own ideas about man. Edwin G. Boring sensitized me early in my psychological training to the role of the *Zeitgeist* in the growth of science, particularly psychology, as well as to the intensely personal nature of the history of psychology. To Gordon

W. Allport I am indebted not only for a creative view of human nature but also for concrete suggestions regarding the fascinating problem of expressive behavior. Gardner Murphy's views have stirred my own thinking, and his words of encouragement have increased my confidence in my own ideas. I owe much to A. H. Maslow's constant freshness of approach to old problems, the insights of his several unpublished manuscripts, and his helpful suggestions. To Carl R. Rogers, to whose views I have hardly done justice in this book, I owe more than he can realize. My indebtedness to Kurt Lewin is obvious. J. McV. Hunt's balanced editorial help has rescued the book from the exaggerations of overenthusiasm, and has made the manuscript into a better book. To my family go the unsung tributes that only an author spending many solitary hours in daily writing can truly appreciate. Mrs. Mary Alter, the typist of the manuscripts of my other books, has shown herself to be a highly perceptive reader of the manuscript of the present book. I am grateful to Mrs. Mary H. Cox for her expert help with the manuscript at a time when I found myself hard-pressed for time. My special thanks go to the Committee on Grants-in-Aid of Ohio Wesleyan University, particularly Dean George W. Burns, for substantial financial assistance while I was preparing my manuscript. Such errors and defects as may mar the quality of this book, must be attributed solely to myself.

HUBERT BONNER

Delaware, Ohio
  January, 1961

Contents

PART IV

Conclusion: Summary and Interpretation

PSYCHOLOGY
OF
PERSONALITY

Introduction

Contemporary psychologists evidence a strong need to impress upon their readers the scientific status of every area or important problem concerning human behavior. They tend to be much concerned that their thinking and research conform to the methods and results of scientific investigation. They often seek respectability for their science, especially as it concerns those areas which are least scientific, such as social psychology and the psychology of personality, by showing that these disciplines use the methods of the natural sciences. This emulation of the natural sciences is a noticeable characteristic of contemporary psychology.

In view of the scientific contributions of many contemporary psychologists, this anxiety about the scientific status of psychology is not necessary. Moreover, many personality psychologists are insufficiently aware that the S-R (stimulus-response) psychologists have been for the most part their own strongest critics. Behavioristic methodology is itself demonstrating the inadequacy of S-R theory. The conceptual scheme of Miller and Dollard, which is described in detail in Chapter 8, points to the inadequacies of S-R theory. In the work of Osgood, for instance, especially in his meaning systems, S-R theory becomes almost the equivalent of cognitive schemata in recent cognitive theories of learning. Again, most psychologists are coming to realize that careful measurement of the various minutiae which are readily available for measurement will not automatically lead to an explanation of all psychological phenomena.

While there is much to be said in favor of the scientific approach to the study of personality, it is obvious that this approach has not altogether clarified the nature of the subject matter nor given us a dependable definition of personality. On the contrary, it has produced little or no agreement among the investigators, even among those who are most vocal in their demand that the study of personality be scientific.

Accordingly, while the foregoing observations reflect great credit on the rigor of the behavioristic approach, this stress on strict scientism has meant that the methods which are advocated and the conclusions which are drawn frequently do not touch, but instead are quite independent of each other. The reader of many "scientific" investigations of personality is thus left with the feeling that the field abounds in attempts at scientific explanations but provides us with too few plausible solutions of important problems in the psychology of personality.

It should be pointed out that the effort to cast personality psychology in the mold of an exact or experimental science is largely a contemporary trend. In the past, personality theorists were seldom dependent on the central tendencies of contemporary academic psychology, and even today there are many who rebel against its formalism and rigidity. Hall and Lindzey have made explicit note of this historical fact in their assertion that *"personality theory has occupied a dissident role in the development of psychology. Personality theorists in their own times have been rebels."* [1]

In view of the disagreements regarding both the importance of scientific method in personality psychology and the definition of personality itself, it is only realistic to choose our data from any appropriate source, use whatever technique permits us to formulate a plausible view of personality, and follow every promising lead sympathetically yet open-mindedly. Only in this way may we arrive at a view of personality that will do justice to its complexity and permit us to delineate it in its totality. Of all the areas of psychology, the psychology of personality can least afford the practice of partition and segmentalization.

The reader may very well wonder why these pages are being devoted to a discussion of the nature of science, inasmuch as this is a book on the psychology of personality. The reason is simple and pragmatic. Since the view of personality in this book stems not from a mechanistic but from a holistic view of science, not from a rigid S-R conception of behavior, it is necessary to make our position clear at the very outset. Briefly, this view of science, while not rejecting the mechanistic approach entirely, holds that it has been largely outgrown in the physical sciences, and that there is no convincing reason why it will not in brief time be outgrown by psychology itself.

[1] C. S. Hall and G. Lindzey, *Theories of personality* (New York: John Wiley & Sons, Inc., 1957), p. 4.

SCIENCE AND PSYCHOLOGY

Commitment to preconceptions and stereotypic thinking is a besetting weakness of investigators in any field. This is evident in science, especially as it concerns the scientific method, much more than is commonly recognized by scientific investigators. Yet, if any one fact clearly emerges from the history of science, it is that science and scientific method are always changing. Besides, the work of the best scientists demonstrates that there is no one scientific method, but that it varies not only with the times but also with the problems that are being scientifically investigated. Successful, productive scientists always adapt their methods to the materials on which their methods are to be exercised.

PSYCHOLOGY: AN OBJECTIVE-SUBJECTIVE SCIENCE. In light of the view of many distinguished scientists that subjective elements cannot be eliminated from science, one would think that the fruitless controversy over objectivity vs. subjectivity would by now have abated. Nevertheless, many psychologists are still battling the old straw man. In describing their science they unfailingly stress its objective character and show unjustified pride in comparing it with subjective descriptions, which they usually condemn. The comparisons generally take the form of showing that the psychologist's view of human behavior is based on experimentation, or at least on careful empirical observation, and that it is quantitative, in contrast to the poet's or the humanist's descriptions, which are evaluative and subjective.

There are three sources of this narrow view of science. One source is found in a negative and fallacious view of the nature of philosophy. Too many psychologists still condemn or eschew the philosophical element in all science, particularly in psychology. Their hostility toward philosophy is actually a hostility toward the procedures of mediaeval philosophers who believed that reason alone could describe facts even without regard to the observed facts themselves. This objection to mediaeval philosophy, while fully justified, is inapplicable to contemporary philosophy, especially as the latter relates to modern science. In contemporary philosophy facts and logic are inseparable, as they are in science.

A second reason for the psychologist's tendency to condemn as unscientific whatever does not meet his own criterion of objectivity is his belief that the scientific method is largely a fact-gathering process. However, facts alone never lead to valid generalizations, and by themselves they are meaningless. The great scientists of today are not too insistent in their demand for a large number of validating instances of a particular event. A few crucial confirmatory instances are often sufficient to meet their demand for certainty. They incline to an "unhesitating acceptance of a theory after it has been subjected to a number of tests which are wholly inadequate statistically." [2] The productive scientist is no mere empiricist, but a creative individual who can freely play with facts in his imagination as well as accumulate them.

The justification for regarding a small sample of validating instances as adequate lies in the great care that natural scientists take to establish the logical coherence of their constructs before they subject them to verification. In other words, before the natural scientists put their conceptions to an empirical or experimental test, they engage in extensive rational or logical study and analysis, with little concern at the moment for the empirical and quantitative aspects of their investigations. In fact, the design of experiments or the selection of crucial tests of hypotheses are themselves largely rational procedures.

From the standpoint of the most up-to-date natural science, our view of the physical world is determined at least in part by the scientist who investigates it. Man is not a passive being but an active participant in his own universe. In a sense, man creates his own universe. As an observer, man must be included in any scientific view of the world. The theories of the physicist and the formulations of the psychologist are both human inventions. Both are products of the interrelation between given facts and particular scientists at a given time in a specific cultural milieu.

The third source, and probably the most important one, of the narrow view of science held by many psychologists is the uncritical belief that physics is the most objective science. Scientific method is frequently equated with its mathematical form in theoretical physics. Scientists working in less rigorous and less exact sciences than mathematical physics are easily beguiled by the latter's success and prestige. Psychologists in particular are prone to yield to the view that objectivity always lies in rigorous hypotheses and experimental verification. (Ironically, this is to misread physics, too, since physics is not afraid of imaginative attempts to order knowledge.) However, psychology has thus far been rather deficient in rigorous and testable hypotheses. Its search for the *experimentum crucis*, so indefatigably stressed in psychological methodology, has largely been a lost cause. Science has produced

2 H. Margenau, *The nature of physical reality* (New York: McGraw-Hill Book Co., Inc., 1950), p. 107.

few really *crucial* experiments.[3] If an important function of verification is to enable any qualified research worker to check the
conclusions of other competent investigators as a means of arriving
at objective knowledge, then psychology has been singularly unsuccessful in extending publicly verifiable knowledge of human
behavior. The psychology of personality, as well as those fields of
investigation which are closely affiliated with it, such as social
psychology and psychotherapy, is proliferated by differences.
Omitting its lesser offshoots or deviations, there are no fewer than
a dozen major theories of personality, each offering its own version of what personality is and how it comes to be.

In the field of psychotherapy the results are even less dependable. Every technique of psychotherapy has chalked up many
successes to its credit, even though both the assumptions on which
the techniques rest and the techniques themselves are quite different. The crucial test, if it could be performed, would be to
determine how many of the persons treated by the various methods might have recovered without benefit of the method of treatment. In reviewing the effects of psychotherapy Eysenck found
that there was no difference between the effects of psychotherapy
and estimates of spontaneous remissions.[4]

The role of theory. In the preceding section we called attention
to the importance of rational procedures in scientific investigation.
Logic, thinking, rational analysis—these must be placed on an
equal footing with measurement, experimentation, and other empirical methods. The great makers of science often advanced their
special field by means of penetrating theories. A good theory often
throws new light upon accepted facts and established laws. The
history of science shows that the great moments in scientific discovery were ushered in by theories. Although a large amount of
empirical observation lies at their base, the great theories which
have changed the course of human knowledge were born in contemplation and philosophical analysis. They were products of the
effort "without further experiment at the moment, merely by *think-*

---

[3] For an elaboration of this point see P. Duhem, *The aim and structure of physical
theory* (Princeton, N.J.: Princeton University Press, 1954), Ch. 6.

[4] H. J. Eysenck, The effects of psychotherapy: an evaluation, *J. consult. Psychol.*,
16 (1952), 319–24. See also H. J. Eysenck, *The dynamics of anxiety and hysteria*
(New York: Frederick A. Praeger, Inc., 1957), Ch. 1. While Eysenck's disclosure
is interesting and important, his explanation of the difficulty lies in the same narrow
view of scientific methodology which we have already briefly stated. Although he
does not wholly condemn the clinical method which is basic in psychotherapy, he attributes its failure mostly to the clinician's rejection of the experimental method and
statistical analysis. Psychotherapy, according to him, can attain the status of a science
only when it becomes an experimental and mensurative discipline.

ing about what was already known, to put together the pieces of a puzzle that might reveal an order in nature never before envisaged. Any discipline in which theory in this sense is neglected, or in which theoretical obscurities never haunt us, is a poor science indeed." [5]

We believe that the most important goal of the psychologist is to formulate, on the basis of empirical data and logical postulates, general laws of behavior. But he cannot achieve this end as long as his theories remain primitive, that is, as long as they fail to integrate the existing low-order laws. In contemporary physics, where there is no timidity regarding the use of constructive thinking, matters are very different. The physicist is constantly formulating abstract principles that will integrate low-order laws into a unified system. Einstein's unified field theory, for example, while not yet empirically established, aims to integrate into a coherent system several realms of law, namely, the law of gravitation and the principles governing light quanta, electromagnetic phenomena, and subatomic events.

In psychology, by contrast, theory has not played the same important role. This is due to two reasons: skepticism regarding the value of theory, and the presence of a plurality of variables even in the simplest psychological experiment. Accordingly, up to now the psychologist has introduced theory largely in the form of hypothetical constructs of limited and temporary value. But even if the theoretical formulations of psychology are primitive by contrast with those of physics, they show, as all scientific investigations show, that science may be less the product of painstaking experimental research than of creative thinking.

The foregoing observations have an important bearing on the psychology of personality. They show that instead of trying to deduce the basic characteristics of personality from the results of empirical investigation, the psychologist must initially hypothesize what the basic characteristics might be and then design an experiment to test his hypothesis. The history of science, including psychology, has shown that a complete reliance on experimental or other purely empirical procedures always involves hidden assumptions which, unless they are explicitly formulated, result in ambiguous conclusions.

Moreover, the empirical approach of itself can never yield a science, be it a knowledge of physical events or of human behavior. Empiricism may help us to produce facts, but the facts in them-

[5] F. H. Allport, *Theories of perception and the concept of structure* (New York: John Wiley & Sons, Inc., 1955), p. 5.

selves can produce neither laws nor predictions. Facts must always be related to one another, lest they remain meaningless. In order to be related to one another, to be meaningful, facts must be ordered to some scheme, system of concepts, or rational plan which, though suggested by the facts already established, is nonetheless independent of them.

In order to illustrate the assertion that the psychology of personality cannot be primarily empirical in its methodology, we call attention to an example in an excellent paper by Churchman and Ackoff.[6] According to them, in order to set up an experimental situation for testing any theory of personality we must begin with a workable definition of personality. Accordingly, they suggest that personality be provisionally defined as "the characteristic ways an individual has of solving his problems."[7] In other words, personality is initially conceived as a form of purposive or goal-integrated behavior.

However, problem-solving behavior itself demands a definition. Since categories for describing goal-integrated behavior already exist in the psychological literature, namely, "means" and "ends," a definition of problem-solving behavior can be easily formulated. Thus the individual who is trying to solve a problem "selects a certain means to accomplish a certain end."[8] In actual experience ends and means are inseparable; neither is meaningful without the other. Means are actions taken toward the attainment of an end. Any action which increases the probability of attaining the end is an "efficient" action. But in order to attain any end there must exist at least two distinct means, for "no means is a necessary condition for attaining the end." We must assume, furthermore, that in any pursuit of an end there are external or environmental conditions which, though not in themselves aspects of the individual's behavior, nevertheless aid him in the achievement of his goal. Again, an individual's means to an end can be increased through repetition or learning. The learning factor is thus an important aspect of the means-end relationship, and this observation relates the subject of personality to some well-established facts in the psychology of learning. On the background of our discussion thus far, therefore, personality may be provisionally described as a measure of the effectiveness with which an individual solves a problem or attains a goal.

It should be noted that the foregoing statements concerning

[6] C. W. Churchman and R. L. Ackoff, Towards an experimental measure of personality, *Psychol. Rev.*, 54 (1947), 41–52.

[7] *Ibid.*, p. 43.

[8] *Ibid.*

personality are largely suppositional. They are based on assumptions and on widely accepted definitions of such terms as "means" and "ends." The latter may be considered as provisional confirmations, as is also the attempt to relate the means-end schema to learning theory. While this is good as far as it goes, it does not go far enough. What we now need is the design of an experiment that will measure or test the proposed definition of personality. Churchman and Ackoff provide us with two such experiments, and we shall describe them here very briefly.

In the first experiment, the experimenter gives the subject problems whose most efficient solution is *independent* of any environmental changes over a particular interval in the environmental scale. He next changes the environment over this interval and notes whether or not the subject varies his method. This process is repeated for changes in means and ends. In more exact terms, "the three types of stimuli are varied while the most efficient method of solution is kept invariant." [9]

In the second experiment, the experimenter gives the subject problems whose most efficient solution is *dependent* upon changes over a particular interval in the environment. He next changes the environment over this interval and observes whether the subject changes his methods. A similar procedure is used in studying the changes in means and ends.

The experimental procedures outlined above are applied to several well-known personality problems, two of which we shall now examine, namely, introversion and extraversion.

The authors define *introversion* as "the degree of insensitivity an individual exhibits to environmental changes when the most efficient solution is a function of such changes." [10] In testing the degree of introversion, the subject is instructed to choose from a variety of means the one which is most efficient for performing the assigned task. The environment is then changed by introducing new individuals. The degree of change toward greater complexity continues until the subject chooses the more efficient means. The assigned task, however, remains the same. The subject's choice of the more efficient means is the measure of his insensitivity to change, or the degree of his introversion.

Extraversion is defined as "the degree of sensitivity an individual exhibits to environmental changes when the most efficient solution remains invariant with such changes." [11] In testing the degree of

[9] *Ibid.*, p. 48.
[10] *Ibid.*, p. 49.
[11] *Ibid.*, p. 49.

extraversion, the subject is instructed to use the most effective means accessible to him for performing the assigned task. The environment is changed by introducing other people, thus "complicating" it beyond its original state. The subject's end or task, however, has not been changed. If, as a consequence of the changed environment, the subject changes his means for a less efficient one, he shows extraversion. The degree of extraversion is determined by how much change or complication of the environment has to be made before the subject chooses a less efficient means.

This brief description shows clearly the cogency of our emphasis on the empirical *and* the conceptual nature of scientific investigation, and that the two are inseparable. Beginning with a set of definitions and assumptions, some of which are purely conceptual and some of which are derived from prior empirical research, Churchman and Ackoff designed experiments by means of which the assumptions and their implications were either confirmed or invalidated. Our discussion has shown not only that theory is one of the chief objectives of science but that it is absolutely essential. A good theory, as distinguished from the undisciplined speculation with which it is sometimes confused, explains and generalizes facts. It can give us important hints of what will happen under given conditions. Finally, a good theory is an effective pointer in scientific research, for it can serve as a guide for further investigation. There can be no empirical or mensurative study of personality without benefit of basic theoretical constructs and hypotheses. Without a theory no scientist can progress beyond the patient collection of facts which in themselves have neither explanatory nor predictive value. With a sound theory the scientist can penetrate the surface of the observable phenomena to discover their hidden explanatory properties. A theory is useless only when it leads to no verifiable conclusions, or when it has no logical or empirical bearing upon the events which it purports to explain. In the light of these considerations there is nothing so practical as a good theory, as Kurt Lewin has remarked.

HUMANISTIC ASPECTS OF SCIENCE. It is not enough to show that science is not wholly empirical simply because it is based on abstract and theoretical formulations. The greatness of science is due not only to its formal and empirical achievements but also to its profoundly aesthetic qualities. In their haste to demonstrate its experimental and mensurative nature too many writers have been remiss regarding the artistic and creative character of science. Because of the psychologist's preoccupation with adaptive, adjustive, and coping mechanisms in the explanation of behavior, psychology is particularly vulnerable to this criticism. Not until recently has the professional psychologist paid serious attention to the creative and expressive features of the human personality.[12] However, our attention at the moment is directed not to the problem of creative personality but to science as an art.

The division of ideas into scientific and artistic is an old one. This artificial and arbitrary division of art and science is related to the fallacious notion that science deals with facts whereas art deals with imaginary constructions or fictions; or that the former deals solely with objective reality whereas the latter describes the subjective world of the artist. However, both the great artists and the eminent scientists have long recognized the basic inseparability of art and science. Each in his own particular idiom has shown by means of belief and practice that every productive scientist is something of a poet and every creative artist is something of a scientist. No great scientist is wholly "tough-minded" and factual and no distinguished artist is fully "tender-minded" and nonlogical.

Furthermore, the scientist, as we have already shown, has no monopoly on objectivity, nor can the artist or the poet be charged with unrestrained subjectivity. Both science and art are the consequences of our ways of thinking; both are forms of idealization, of transforming "what is" into "what might be." An illuminating and instructive instance of the inseparability of the objective and the subjective, or of the factual and the imaginative, is found in the quantum theory of contemporary physics. Heisenberg, the distinguished Nobel Prize-winning physicist, as well as other famous scientists, asserts that quantum theory precludes a completely objective description of the physical world. In quantum theory, "man as the subject of science is brought in through the questions which are put to nature in the *a priori* terms of human science." [13] In the biological and behavioral sciences this truth stands out even more sharply. In order to understand human behavior the psychologist, who himself belongs to the category of behaving men, must already know what human behavior is before he has formulated it objectively. He cannot get outside his own nervous system in order to see man "as he really is"; he is always limited in his observations

[12] This criticism does not apply to Gordon Allport, who for many years was the single protesting voice against psychology's neglect of the creative and expressive elements in human behavior. More recently, Gardner Murphy and A. H. Maslow have vigorously argued for the creative aspect of personality.

[13] W. Heisenberg, *Physics and philosophy* (New York: Harper & Bros., 1958), p. 106.

and idealizations by the verbal or conceptual interaction between the world and himself—by the "human response to the challenge of nature."[14]

Heisenberg makes a plausible comparison between the conceptualizations or idealizations of science and the different styles of art. An art style can be formalized as a set of abstract rules which are applied to the materials of a special art—say, painting or music. While these rules cannot yet be denoted by mathematical concepts, their fundamental properties, such as repetition and symmetry or equality and inequality, are mathematical in character. Nor can one say of these art styles that they are arbitrary fabrications of the artist. The illusion that they are capricious inventions lies partly in the difficulty of determining how well the styles describe the reality which they are intended to represent. This cannot be determined from an examination of the styles themselves, for, like the mathematical representation of nature, they are idealizations which the artist creates in order to make intelligible the reality that he is trying to portray.

Accordingly, the forms of idealization which the artist and the scientist invent in order to represent objective reality are not wholly different from each other. "Both science and art form in the course of the centuries a human language by which we can speak about the more remote parts of reality, and the coherent sets of concepts as well as the different styles of art are different words or groups of words in this language."[15]

S. S. Stevens, writing in a similar vein, points out that "science is an art." Since *the* scientific method does not exist, the scientist, like the artist, is free to devise whatever procedure will best accomplish the end which he has set up for himself. "There are no *ab initio* principles to tell us how to be clever in devising procedures of measurement," Stevens tells us. "The way to empirical discovery," he writes, "lies not through mathematics, even, but through the exercise of uncommon experimental sense and ingenuity. We invent mathematical models, but we discover measures in the laboratory."[16]

However, the foregoing is not yet the whole story. Ideas are not generated in a vacuum, be they scientific concepts or styles of art. They are products of an individual's interaction with his social environment. Important sociological investigations have

---

[14] *Ibid.*, p. 109.

[15] *Ibid.*, p. 109.

[16] S. S. Stevens, Measurement and man, *Science,* 127 (1958), 383–89, on p. 387.

pretty well demonstrated that ideas in both art and science are socially conditioned. They reflect the spirit of the time in demonstrable ways. There are styles in thought. Scientific, aesthetic, philosophical, and other ideas are subject to the influence not only of preceding developments in these fields of thought but to the influence of suggestion and prestige-value which temporarily crystallize them into conventions and fashions. The ultrabehaviorism of John B. Watson was dominant in psychology until about 1930, but today it is in eclipse. Technocracy swept the country in the 1930's, almost reaching the proportions of a cult, but today it looks like an aberration of a fear-ridden decade. It is likely that the current demand for operational definitions of concepts will be modified in psychology, as it has been in physics where it was stimulated by the writings of Bridgman.[17] The spirit of a time, the *Zeitgeist,* is as real as any fact in science and affects the course of scientific development as it does philosophical ideas and styles or art. Science has not been and cannot be wholly scientific.

Our discussion of the relatedness of science and art has been a way of calling attention to the convergence of the scientific and the humanistic modes of thought in contemporary views of objective nature and behaving man. The humanist who understands modern science need no longer protest against nineteenth-century scientism's lifeless formalization of nature nor its dehumanization of man. The scientist, on the other hand, is learning against his own professional bias, because his data are forcing it upon him, that a scientific view of reality must include the creative acts of man. Ruesch and Bateson describe this convergence as follows:

The physicist found that he could understand his data only when he realized that they were collected by his own activities interfering in some degree with the external world which he was attempting to study. Therefore he was compelled to include the observer within the system studied. Similarly he found that he could understand his own ideas only when he accepted the fact that they were his, and therefore in part determined by the culture and epoch in which he was living. Thenceforward he was forced to accept the reflexive nature of his theoretical constructions—i.e., to include the theorist as well as the observer within the system studied.[18]

[17] See P. W. Bridgman, *The logic of modern physics* (New York: The Macmillan Co., 1928). It is an historical error to attribute the formulation of operationism to the physicist Bridgman. C. S. Peirce, the American philosopher and mathematician, expounded the basic idea of operationism several decades before. See C. S. Peirce, How to make our ideas clear, in *Chance, love and logic* (New York: Harcourt, Brace and Co., 1923), pp. 32–60. This paper was originally published in *Popular science monthly,* January, 1878.

[18] J. Ruesch and G. Bateson, *Communication: the social matrix of psychiatry* (New York: W. W. Norton & Co., Inc., 1951), p. 263.

In the light of these changes the traditional antagonism between the scientific and humanistic views of the world have become anachronistic. The humanist cannot with impunity describe the world and man vaguely or incorrectly; and the scientist must become ever more sensitive to the risk that "to do a task *correctly* destroys the impulse to do it stylistically." [19]

There is nothing in our discussion thus far to suggest that we are trying to appease the outraged feelings of poets, philosophers, or theologians against the rigorous formulae of the natural scientists. The convergence of scientific explanations with the value-relations of the humanist, we have said, has been forced upon the scientist by the ineluctable results of his own investigations. Neither are we so much as hinting for a return to the obsolescent view that the methods and conclusions of science destroy man's creativeness and sense of freedom. We are suggesting, rather, that the scientist must and that the creative scientist does recognize the close affinity between the image of the poet and the causal formula of the scientist. Although both sides of the human enterprise will have to move closer to each other, the humanist's will have to be the greater accommodation. The humanist has the more difficult task of reorienting his image of man and incorporating in his view of life the indubitable disclosures of contemporary science.

The scientist, on the other hand, must become increasingly dissatisfied with the additive and segmentalized description of the world which until recently has dominated the scientific scene. He must realize that science is not a piling of data on still more data. He must become even more aware than he already is of the fact that science deals with complex wholes. In the realm of human phenomena the principle of parsimony or simplicity may very well have to give way increasingly to the principle of prodigality or complexity which stresses larger and larger wholes. The psychologist who is bent on preserving the fiction that psychology is a rigorous experimental science which investigates only limited segments of human experience will not find this easy to accept. Nevertheless, the weight of evidence and informed opinion is rising up against him. The time is not far distant when the psychologist will cease to preoccupy himself with the traditional segments of behavior, such as learning, attention, and perception, and concentrate on the personality as an indivisible and functional whole. If this should come to pass, then the psychology of personality, which

[19] G. W. Allport, *Personality: a psychological interpretation* (New York: Holt, Rinehart & Winston, Inc., 1937), p. 467.

deals with the whole individual, is in some respects more advanced than the more "rigorous" divisions of psychology.[20]

CLOSED AND OPEN VIEWS OF SCIENCE. Our discussion thus far suggests that there are two compatible but different views of the method of science. We shall call these the *closed* and the *open* views. The closed view has a long and respectable history and has been exclusively associated with the natural sciences, especially physics. We have already called attention to this by pointing out that it employs highly rigorous mathematical and causal formalizations. It investigates the logical and empirical relationships between hypotheses and their verifications. It constructs experimental situations in which hypotheses are tested. Its results can be publicly verified under the same or similar conditions by other investigators. Its truths are said to have been *established*, rather than *created*.

The open view does not deny the effectiveness and usefulness of the closed approach. It simply denies that the closed view is the whole of the scientific method. This is the position held by an increasing number of scientists. From the open point of view the essence of the scientific approach is not only experimentation or proof, but also a critical and nondogmatic spirit. It prefers scientific skepticism to cognitive closure. It follows every argument logically but skeptically to what Whitehead eloquently described as its final unravelment. It has a wholesome distrust of certainty. It can tolerate ambiguity without fear. Unlike the psychologist who adheres to the closed approach and who feels uncomfortable when he ventures too far from his empirical data, the scientist who follows the open method feels no uneasiness in their absence. Finally, the open view will employ a variety of methods—any method, in short, that will help the scientist reach his goals of explanation, prediction, and above all, understanding. He will trust naive experience, or systematic constructs, or experimental verification if they are relevant to his problems and if they aid him in realizing his aim of attaining dependable knowledge. Since he knows that there is no knowledge apart from a knower, and that the knower himself can have no direct knowledge of the events which he is observing, he will be free of the fruitless concern with whether his conclusions are subjective or objective.

Certainly, as applied to the study of personality the controversy over objectivity and subjectivity is artificial and academic. Objec-

---

[20] For a recent and very convincing argument to show that scientific ideas are products of the same kind of creative imagination as those of art, see J. Bronowski, *Science and human values* (New York: Julian Messner, Inc., 1958).

tivity consists of agreement on relevant matters, but it does not exclude subjectivity regarding hypotheses before they are publicly verified. Just as quantum theory does not permit a completely objective description of nature, so the unique qualities of an individual make a wholly objective picture of personality impossible. There are neither a priori nor empirical restrictions on what can be investigated scientifically. When it is conceived too narrowly the scientific approach becomes authoritarian and intolerant. When this happens, science becomes scientism, a form of dogmatism as dangerous as any other unshakable set of beliefs.

NOMOTHETIC AND IDIOGRAPHIC APPROACHES. As early as 1883 German scholars made what they considered to be a profound distinction between the natural and the mental sciences.[21] Dilthey, especially, stressed the uniqueness of the mental or social sciences—the *Geisteswissenschaften*. The natural sciences were described as the *generalizing* disciplines, in contrast to the *individualizing* character of the social sciences. The difference between the two, they believed, was fundamental. Later, Windelband distinguished them by naming the social sciences *idiographic* and the natural sciences *nomothetic*. In his well-known book on personality Gordon Allport applied these distinguishing terms to the study of psychology.[22]

The nomothetic sciences, of which the well-established natural sciences are the best examples, try to establish general laws of phenomena, to state the universal and invariant occurrence of events. The law of gravitation, for instance, which obtains for all falling bodies, is such a general principle. Psychology, which strives to be an exact science, has been attempting to formulate similar general principles concerning human behavior. Many psychologists believe that through the use of exact methods, such as experimentation and statistical analysis, students of personality will be able to arrive at general laws of personality.

The idiographic sciences, of which history is the best example, seek to describe the single or unique event. A historical occurrence, for example, can take place in exactly the same form only once. It cannot be repeated: it is unique. Those, like Allport, who stress the idiographic approach in psychology hold that personality is a unique phenomenon. Exact measurements or descriptions of traits, while having value in showing how different

[21] See the following: W. Dilthey, Einleitung in die Geisteswissenschaften in *Gesammelte Schriften* (Berlin: B. G. Teubner, 1921–1922), Vol. 1, 1922 (originally published in 1883); H. Rickert, *Die Grenzen der Naturwissenschaftlichen Begriffsbildung* (Tübingen und Leipzig: Mohr, 1902); W. Windelband, *Geschichte und Naturwissenschaft* (3d ed.; Leipzig: Breitkopf und Härtel, 1904).

[22] G. W. Allport, *Personality, passim*, especially Ch. 20.

individuals are similar, do not touch the unique qualities which distinguish one human person from all others. Individual traits are the basic properties, the primary units of behavior, and they cannot be generalized, for they are uniquely determined. The psychology of personality is thus a study of the single case.

Furthermore, Allport believes that psychology will become more, rather than less, scientific when it studies the single person in all his complexity. As long as psychology investigates only universals and not particulars, it tends to deal too much with the inconsequential—certainly not with personality.[23] When it has carefully observed and evaluated single tendencies in individuals, psychology's predictive power will be greatly increased. If prediction is one of the most important goals of science, then psychology will become more scientific as it is able to anticipate the individual's behavior by knowing his single trends.

However, it would be misleading to suppose that in his predilection for the idiographic approach and in his stress on the uniqueness of personality Allport closed his mind to the value of the contrasting view. From the time he initially proposed his individualistic view he has recognized the values of both. The dichotomy, he pointed out, is too sharp. "It is more helpful," he then said, "to regard the two methods as overlapping and as contributing to one another. . . . A complete study of the individual will embrace both approaches."[24]

Likewise, his belief in the uniqueness of each person is not absolute. In one of his recent and most eloquent writings on the subject, he shows full perceptiveness of the problem and a clear indication of its solution. "Each person," he writes, "is an idiom unto himself, an apparent violation of the syntax of the species. . . . Yet at the same time, idioms are not entirely lawless and arbitrary; indeed they can be known for what they are only by comparing them with the syntax of the species."[25]

This way of conceiving the interrelations of the nomothetic and idiographic views is compatible with our contention that the scientific and the humanistic approaches in the natural and behavioral sciences are not antithetical. Each possesses some characteristics of the other. The synthesis is made possible in the proposal of the open view of science. Thus, both the idiographic and the nomothetic methods use logic, follow the rules of evidence, are disin-

[23] G. W. Allport, Geneticism *versus* ego-structure in theories of personality, *Brit. J. educ. Psychol.*, 16 (1946), 57–68.

[24] G. W. Allport, *Personality*, p. 22.

[25] G. W. Allport, *Becoming: basic considerations for a psychology of personality* (New Haven: Yale University Press, 1955), p. 19.

terested and objective, and eschew dogmatism and bias. In short, the scientific spirit of pursuing truth wherever it may be found characterizes both. Eysenck's self-assured pronouncement that *"the science of personality must by its very nature be nomothetic"*—that is, nomothetic *only*—is in our view an unjustified overstatement.[26]

Our discussion, we believe, points to an important conclusion regarding scientific methodology, especially as it applies to the study of personality. It should now be clear that the division of scientific research into the closed and the open, the objective and the subjective, the nomothetic and the idiographic, the experimental and the clinical, the peripheralist and the centralist,[27] while historically informative, is neither necessary nor fundamental. Each has its place and usefulness; each can contribute something of value to the construction of a picture of man. The experimentalist must realize that the study of behavior in the artificial setting of the laboratory and the statistical manipulation of his data have to date yielded only fragments, and too often unilluminating fragments, of the total personality. The clinician or "centralist" must also take a critical look at his approach.[27] He is too often inexcusably repelled by laboratory findings and statistical quantifications. In this attitude he has been biased and irrational. The full stature of psychological man will be measured only by the intelligent and sympathetic cooperation of the clinician and the experimentalist, not by either one alone.

SCIENCE AS A DESCRIPTION OF INTERFERENCE WITH NATURE. There is a growing recognition among quantum physicists that the investigating scientist, when probing for nature's "secrets," is unlikely to find them because, while probing nature for answers to his questions, he is in actuality interfering with it.[28] Heisenberg discovered thirty years ago that the measurement of the position and velocity of electrons required the focusing of powerful light rays upon matter, and that in the process of doing so he changed the behavior of the electrons in their elliptical movement around their proton. He was interfering with the state of nature so much, in fact, that he found it impossible to measure at the same instant

---

[26] For his discussion of this problem and the above quotation see H. J. Eysenck, The science of personality: nomothetic! *Psychol. Rev.,* 61 (1954), 339–42.

[27] The terms "centralist" and "peripheralist" are objectionable because they imply, respectively, an honorific and a derogatory attitude. The "peripheralists" confine their research to what is measurable; the "centralists" investigate the "inner" man— his loves, hatreds, anxieties, and aspirations. For this distinction see H. A. Murray, *Explorations in personality* (New York: Oxford University Press, 1938), pp. 6–8.

[28] See E. Persico, *Fundamentals of quantum mechanics* (Englewood Cliffs, N.J.: Prentice-Hall, Inc., 1950).

the velocity and position of the electrons.[29] The act of investigating a physical phenomenon and the instrument used in its investigation tend to modify the phenomenon.

If this be the true state of affairs in quantum physics—and there can no longer be any doubt that it is—then science may also be conceived as a system of laws or principles regarding the scientists' interpositions in the stream of natural events. As a knower, as a probe-body, the scientist changes the object of his knowledge, and this change must be incorporated into his knowledge as an important addition to it. Accordingly, not only is an experiment an interference in the alleged order of nature, but, as London and Poltoratzky have recently affirmed, the theory resulting from this interposition is "a theory of *interferences,* as it were, rather than one of a so-called objective world whose composition, after interference effects have been 'canceled out' or 'adjusted for,' can be pieced together mosaic-like from the data of experiments." [30]

If this interference in nature modifies nature and constitutes our theory of its operation, a similar interference is even more characteristic of the investigation of psychological phenomena. When a rat has once learned the instrumental value of depressing a lever which releases a food pellet, or when it has learned to run a maze efficiently, it is no longer the same rat. The instrument and the psychologist's design of the experiment are both interferences in the behavior of the naive rat. They have interfered to the extent of modifying the rat's behavior in such a way that what was once focal, such as the walls and the corners and turns, are now peripheral rather than focal.

THE PERSONAL NATURE OF SCIENCE. The foregoing observations are in agreement with an increasing tendency to view science as not wholly objective, but as a product of the active participation by the scientist in the phenomena which he investigates. Positivism, in both its naive nineteenth-century form and its sophisticated physicalist development of the 1920's, is no longer completely tenable. While intersubjectivism is still a criterion to be vigorously applied, the inescapabality of subjectivism must be frankly recognized and incorporated into our philosophy of science. Indeed, as Bridgman has recently argued, science is "something essentially private," and it is characteristic of all knowledge "to be subject to uncertainty." When we can no longer pursue the operations which

[29] W. Heisenberg, *The physical principles of quantum theory* (Chicago: University of Chicago Press, 1930).

[30] I. D. London and N. P. Poltoratzky, The problem of contemporary analysis in history and psychology, *Behavioral Science*, 3 (1958), 269–77, on p. 273.

Bridgman so forcefully advocated in the 1920's, "we are pretty much driven to accept our primitive operations on the basis of feelings in our bones that we know what we are doing." [31]

Recognition of the private and personal nature of science has far-reaching implications for psychology, especially the psychology of personality. It at least restores to psychology what Watson and the whole behavioristic tradition have deprived it of: *the role of the observer in psychological investigations.* If the observer's own formal instruments affect the results of his observation in the physical sciences, then the psychologist's instruments of knowing, judging, inferring, perceiving, and so forth, have an even more profound effect on his description and understanding of psychological phenomena. This is the more true in face of the fact that, unlike the nature of physical events, psychological processes—at least those on the human level—have a profound valuational orientation.

CONCLUSION

The discussion of the nature of science, particularly its more recent developments, has made clear that it is no longer a closed, rigid, and mechanistic system of concepts, laws, and conclusions. Complete objectivity in science cannot even be an ideal, for we know it to be a fallacy and an illusion. We see both man and nature through human experience; and any attempt to describe either one by eliminating the human equation must lead to absurdity. Man's beliefs about himself and the universe are inescapably anchored in himself. We may construct psychological man on the pattern of a machine, an automaton, or a neurological model, and these things may simulate thinking, judging, and perceiving so closely that they may easily deceive us; but as Polanyi, addressing himself to the same subject, has remarked, "a deception, however compelling, does not qualify thereby as a truth," for the designer of machines and models knows from the start that they differ in their nature from the living human being.[32] A false notion of scientific rigor, objectivity, and impersonal knowledge must eventually endanger the nature of science itself.

Even more remarkable is the growing consensus, from Max Planck to Heisenberg, that randomness is a property of nature, not

[31] These statements express the general tone of Bridgman's revisions of his earlier views. See P. W. Bridgman, *The way things are* (Cambridge, Mass.: Harvard University Press, 1959). For his earlier views see his book, *The logic of modern physics* (New York: The Macmillan Co., 1927).

[32] M. Polanyi, *Personal knowledge: towards a post-critical philosophy* (Chicago: University of Chicago Press, 1958), p. 263. See also, M. Polanyi, *The study of man* (Chicago: University of Chicago Press, 1959).

a function of man's intellectual limitations. Chance is not due to human ignorance of the order and uniformity of nature, but is a plain fact. "The absence of random elements in nature would imply a purely mechanical universe," and such a universe would fall to pieces, for there would be no way for it to recover from disturbances "by switching from chains of cause and effect leading perhaps to unavoidable disaster." In other words, "nature employs indeterminateness, randomness, chance, or probability to keep things running smoothly." [33]

The main considerations in the view of science expounded in this Introduction have a direct bearing upon the image of man described in this book, and justify our rather extended discussion of its dominant characteristics. We seriously doubt that individuality, uniqueness, and creativeness, so characteristic of man at his healthiest and best, can be explained by means of the principles and categories of orthodox science; for orthodox science, pretending to an impersonality which it has never demonstrated, does not recognize persons, but presents us with a picture of the psychological world in which man is omitted. In such a world, as Polanyi has profoundly observed, there is no one capable of creating and upholding scientific values; hence there can be no science.

The account of personality presented in this book rests squarely on the nature of science as we have here described it. We hasten to add that the psychologist studying personality, like the physicist exploring nature, wants to attain dependable knowledge. However, if in his pursuit of testable hypotheses the psychologist distorts or trivializes the integrity of the human person, then he has traded the science of man for a sterile scientism. An unpardonable attitude in a scientist is the dogmatic conviction that there is only one path to reliable knowledge—his own. The realm of personality is full of challenging uncertainties.

Our criticism has been reserved for those who would hold fast to only one interpretation of human conduct, especially insofar as it denies the inner nature of man. "For narrow systems, dogmatically held," says Allport, "tend to trivialize the mentality of the investigator and of his students. Sad to relate, we have examples of such trivialization in psychology today." [34]

[33] S. T. Bornemisza, *The unified system concept of nature* (New York: Vantage Press, Inc., 1955), pp. 3–4.
[34] G. W. Allport, *Becoming*, p. 17.

Part I

THE STUDY
OF PERSONALITY:
AN OVERVIEW
OF THE PROBLEM

CHAPTER 1

What Is Personality?

Since the subject matter of this book is personality, it is only natural that the reader should want to know at the very outset what personality is. As we shall soon see, however, no simple definition is possible; our knowledge of personality must be the end-product of extensive theoretical and empirical investigation. Accordingly, in this chapter we shall first examine the major approaches taken by personality theorists—the behavioral approach, the mechanistic-adjustive view, and the holistic-dynamic approach—and then outline a provisional sketch of the general nature of personality as conceived in this book. The details of a full portrait of the human individual will then be developed throughout the book and drawn together in a final chapter.

THE BEHAVIORISTIC APPROACH

Behaviorism is a distinctly American contribution to psychology. The polemical nature of early behaviorism had much to do with helping to establish it as the dominant American psychology in the second decade of this century. More important than the assertiveness of its founder, John B. Watson, was his determination, as he said, to study behavior "with the human animal before me." [1] The appeal of the animal model was all the more effective because of the increasing importance of animal psychology which was already under way in England in the investigations of C. Lloyd Morgan in

[1] J. B. Watson, *Psychology from the standpoint of a behaviorist* (Rev. ed.; Philadelphia: J. B. Lippincott Co., 1919), Preface, p. xi. See also, Psychology as a behaviorist views it, *Psychol. Rev.*, 20 (1913), 158–77.

the 1890's, in this country in the work of E. L. Thorndike at the turn of the century, and in the writings of Margaret Washburn at about the same time. Accordingly, while an unrelenting protest against "classical" psychology animated the origin of behaviorism, Watson's attempt to study human beings as biologists studied other animals was probably its most sustained motivation. With this scientific impetus Watson was sure that man is an organic machine, and that the infant and child, regardless of his native equipment, could be molded into whatever the limits of animal conditioning permitted. In this view, unconditioned responses could easily be built into conditioned responses into an organized system of habits. On this view, one personality differed from another one only as the habit systems of each differed, and personality itself was conceived as being nothing more than the sum-total of all the habit systems or hierarchies of an individual.

While Watson wrote some discussions of personality in his early views, the sum-total of what he had to say about it, as is clear from our brief exposition of his most important ideas, hardly added up to a theory or view of personality. He could have said all that he did without using the term "personality" at all; for what was important to him in psychology was the concept of a habit hierarchy. Even the most distinctive features of the human personality, namely, language and thought, were reduced to laryngeal habits, just as motions were conceived as visceral habits and skills as motor responses.

Although the behaviorism of Watson was modified and vastly enriched by the stimulus-response psychologists of the past thirty years, notably by the researches of Hull, Tolman, Guthrie, and Skinner, they largely neglected the human personality. Clark L. Hull envisaged the day when he might apply his knowledge of animal behavior to human conduct; but at his death he had not yet made a beginning. E. R. Guthrie wrote a chapter on personality in *Personality and the Behavior Disorders;* [2] but the view which he presents there is not one of personality, but of the learning process in the language of association.

E. C. Tolman's view, which we discuss in detail in Chapter 8, while taking a cognitive view of learning, comes much closer to giving us a basis for the conceptualization of personality. However, it fails to come to grips with personality as a unique entity, for Tolman's view of psychology is derived from the study of rats and, as he himself regretfully admits, has no place for introspec-

[2] J. McV. Hunt, ed. (2 vols.; New York: The Ronald Press Co., 1944), Vol. 1, Ch. 2.

tion and consciousness.[3] Yet man, as a psychological person, is uniquely a self-conscious and self-evaluating individual.

Skinner's original, and in many ways remarkable, contributions to psychology scarcely touch the problem of personality. While he writes about the latter in one of his important books, it is always with the feeling that it is not a psychological structure in its own right.[4] Personality is conceived as an end-product of reinforcement and operant learning. His conclusions about learning are convincing, and the experimental work by means of which he has established them are impressive; but they offer us a very thin program for a psychology of personality. His exclusion of the concept of the self from the study of personality makes this program more anemic still; for, despite their admirable qualities, Skinner's experimental researches banish from psychology its central problem—the psychology of personality. The person is thus deleted from psychology altogether.

The similarities among the general-behavior views of personality, as found in the work of Hull, Tolman, Guthrie, and Skinner, are evident. None of them emphasizes the importance for psychology of individual behavior, the true characteristic of personality. Their chief—indeed, their only—concern is with the uniformities of behavior. Being deeply concerned with making psychology scientific, they aim to formulate *general laws of behavior*. While this aim is to be highly commended, it has been carried to the point where personality is simply omitted. Accordingly, there cannot be a separate field for the study of personality. For this reason, although we discuss the stimulus-response view of personality in detail in Chapter 8, we do so as a means of showing the strengths and limitations of the learning-theory approach. Logically, there is no reason for discussing it as a view of personality at all, and for this reason we omit it from our survey of the views of personality in Chapter 2. We do not subscribe to the view that a general theory of overt behavior is also a theory of personality, and we hope to demonstrate in this volume, against the excellent work of Miller and Dollard—and incidentally of Mowrer—all of whom we highly respect, that personality is something more than the learned behavior of individuals.[5] We do not believe that the researches of

[3] See his own admission of the role of the animal model in his Kurt Lewin Memorial Lecture, The psychology of social learning, *J. soc. Issues*, 5 (1949), No. 3.

[4] See B. F. Skinner, *Science and human behavior* (New York: The Macmillan Co., 1953).

[5] See N. E. Miller and J. Dollard, *Personality and psychotherapy: an analysis in terms of learning, thinking, and culture* (New York: McGraw-Hill Book Co., Inc., 1950); O. H. Mowrer, *Learning theory and personality dynamics* (New York: The Ronald Press Co., 1950).

the stimulus-response psychologists, however exact and fruitful they may have been for the psychology of learning, have demonstrated that personality traits, conceived as individual differences, are but the unsystematic variations of the general laws of learning.

In any broad review of the work of the learning theorists and the relevance of their investigations to the study of personality, one is always compelled to view the work of Tolman separately. While his approach, too, is a form of learning theory, it differs from the views of Hull, Guthrie, and Skinner, among other ways, in attributing purpose to individual behavior. Behavior from this standpoint is not merely the reaction of an organism to a stimulus or a pattern of stimuli, but the adaptation of means in the pursuit of a desired end. In this way Tolman transcends the *mechanistic* foundations of his behavior theory by attributing foresight, purpose, and the intelligent selection of means for the attainment of selected ends. Man is thus not merely impelled by drive-reductive needs, but by future-oriented goals. As it relates to personality, therefore, Tolman's behavior theory implicitly makes room for a view of individual differences—and hence of personality—which are not expressions of chance variations in the general laws of behavior, but which are dependable indicators of individual *purposes*. Man is thus conceived by Tolman, and by ourselves throughout this book, as a forward-looking organism, even though the grounds for this conception are distinctly different.

PERSONALITY AS AN ADJUSTIVE MECHANISM

American psychology, from the functionalism of William James and John Dewey to the current preoccupation with *adjustment*, has been deeply cast in the mold of Darwinian principles. Despite his opposition to the elementarism of classical psychology, and his stress on mind as a process, James' psychology was nevertheless partly mechanistic in an important sense. The pursuance of future ends, which he deemed to be the mark of the human mind, was purely "functional": the means by which the mind adapted the the individual to his surroundings. This is the Darwinian notion: mind in use, or mind as an "organ" whose function is to enable the individual to survive. The keynote in James' psychology is not "mind" or "consciousness," but the effective *adaptation* of the organism.

The psychology of John Dewey, despite our close kinship with it, was but a more rigorous elaboration of the principle of adaptation. In view of Dewey's lifelong preoccupation with the individual and individual differences, it is surprising that his psychology falls short of a holistic view of personality. Despite his relentless criticism of the reflex-arc concept which dominated the psychological scene when he first came upon it, and despite his substitution for it of the highly important concept of "coordinations," the key to the unity of behavior in his psychology was the *biological* function of an act. Coordinations were conceived as *adaptations* of the individual to his environment, as means of survival in the Darwinian sense. It is a significant fact that Dewey, who was second to no one in his emphasis on the creative nature of human acts, should have stressed the importance of social adjustment all out of proportion to what his philosophical and pedagogical works would lead one to expect. The clue to this paradox, if paradox it be, lies in the fact that by the 1920's he had ceased to investigate psychological phenomena as such, and had turned his great mind instead to the philosophical examination of the vital problems of the day: society, politics, and education.

By 1925, when Harvey A. Carr formulated the functional psychology of Dewey in what probably is its final form, American psychology had become a more or less integrated mixture of behaviorism and functionalism. Most psychology in America was a combination of these not unlike approaches, and its abiding interest has been the problem of adjustive behavior. Through the integration of functionalism and behaviorism mental acts, which could still be entertained in the early functionalist approach of James, became manipulations of experience as a means of attaining a more effective adjustment to the environment.

The *functionalist-adjustive* psychology has become the "standard" approach to the study of personality, beginning with Shaffer's *Psychology of Adjustment* and running through most writings in the field up to the present time.[6] This approach to personality is not strictly speaking concerned with personality as such, but with the mechanisms by which the person tries to cope with the problems of his experience, and the means by which he may preserve his integrity. In this way a personality is doubtless implied, but the adjustment psychologist, especially Shaffer, is more concerned with establishing the conditioned nature of the coping mechanism, than with the maintenance by the person of his identity and individual integrity. Shaffer's theory is a mechanistic-behavioristic account

[6] L. F. Shaffer, *The Psychology of adjustment* (Boston: Houghton Mifflin Co., 1936; 2d ed. with E. J. Shoben, 1956); see also H. C. Lindgren, *The psychology of personal and social adjustment* (New York: American Book Co., 1953); W. F. Vaughan, *Personal and social adjustment* (New York: Odyssey Press, Inc., 1952); L. H. Steckle, *Problems of human adjustment* (New York: Harper & Bros., 1949).

of the way in which the human machine learns to cope with its environment. The view is largely unconcerned with the purposive, creative, and expressive nature of the human personality. Where it does touch upon this issue, as when Shaffer examines the Freudian view of personality, it conceives it largely in negative terms. This it does despite Shaffer's free use of psychoanalytical mechanisms in accounting for human adjustment.

Again, there is no explicit recognition of the self as that aspect of the total personality in the employment of which the mechanisms of adjustment get their meaning. This is inevitable, for on behavioristic grounds the conception of the self is a vitalistic one which has no place in scientific psychology. However, the mechanisms of self-defense imply the existence of a self-process: an active psychological agency by means of which the safety and integrity of the personality are achieved and preserved. Reinforcement, conditioning, operant or other forms of learning are not sufficient as explanatory principles for the nature and use of the mechanisms of adjustment.

Finally, the mechanisms of adjustment, as they are defined in strictly behavioristic psychology, tend to neglect the important process of self-enhancement. Man wants not only to preserve himself, to cope with a threatening environment, but even more to enhance and actualize himself. Not being primarily a machine, but a purposive being, man sets up goals which he strives to achieve by means of his own creative acts. He is not a passive recipient of external stimuli only, but an active agent in his own transformation. He is not merely a coping and adaptive mechanism, but a self-actualizing person. More time and energy in each of us goes into efforts at self-enhancement and self-actualization than the adjustment psychologists would ever lead us to expect. Like the theory that personality can be explained by the principles of learning, the psychology of personality, basing itself on the same principles, tries to account for human behavior on the basis of a mechanistic view of human behavior.

The beguiling fact about both the learning theory and the adjustment approaches to the study of personality is that both have come up with "decisive proofs" of what we learn—in the one case, habits, in the other, modes of adjustment. But once we look at them critically we find that both views, especially since they are in fact the same, are based on *inferences* from observed behavior. These inferences can no more be directly verified in the behavioristic approach than in the one which informs the theory of personality expounded in this book. The choice of theory, therefore, con-

trary to a widespread belief, depends largely on systematic preferences.[7]

THE HOLISTIC-DYNAMIC VIEW

The rejection of the mechanical model in psychology does not
commit us, any more than it does the physicist, to the view that
there is a supermechanical principle operative in the human organism. Sad to relate, this is the conclusion that some critics of
the holistic approach in psychology have reached.[8] The holistic
approach is *not* a species of vitalism. While it stresses the importance of what is unique in the human personality, as vitalism
does, unlike the latter, it does not account for human behavior by
means of an *entelechy* or *psychoid*, that is, by means of inherent
tendencies, in the language of Hans Driesch.[9]

In Chapter 2, where we discuss the holistic view in detail, we do
not imply that no other psychologists have recognized the holistic
character of behavior. A glance at the history of American psychology will quickly dispel this erroneous view. Even the structuralism, or elementarism, of Titchener recognized the ordered
nature of psychological phenomena; and behaviorism from the day
of its inception described behavior as the response of the total
organism to its environment. However, in fairness to the critics
of both views, it should be said that both structuralism and behaviorism only paid lip service to the conception of behavior as a
total act. There is little evidence that in their researches they paid
serious attention to their occasional reference to the organism as
a whole.

In contrast, the holistic view, which is often mistakenly referred
to as a school, bases its entire view of the personality on the concept
of the integrated whole. This is no mere fiction, no verbal convenience, but serves as the foundation for a view which never seg-

[7] Despite the foregoing strictures, it is only fair to point out that all American
psychology today is to some extent behavioristic and functional in the adjustive sense,
even the point of view which lies at the basis of the view of personality expounded in
this book. The holistic, organismic, field-dynamic view, to which we subscribe, works
with behavioristic and adjustive concepts, but goes extensively beyond them.

[8] Even Kurt Lewin, in his criticism of the vitalistic mode of thought in psychology,
carelessly suggests this. See K. Lewin, *Dynamic theory of personality* (New York:
McGraw-Hill Book Co., Inc., 1935), Ch. 1.

[9] It is possible to agree with many aspects of Driesch's vitalism without the use of
his supermechanical concepts. We are of the opinion that Driesch's important ideas,
seen in the light of recent developments in biology, can be incorporated by holistic
psychology without falling into the error of mysticism which has characterized the history of vitalism. See H. Driesch, *The science and the philosophy of the organism*
(Gifford Lectures, Aberdeen, 1908), Vols. 1 and 2.

mentalizes behavior into sensations, reflexes, responses, and habits. Whether the exponent be a biologist who conceives the whole in bio-organismic terms, as in the case of Kurt Goldstein; or a psychiatrist describing the human "mind" as an organized being in action, as in the case of Adolf Meyer; or a psychologist basing a science of psychology on the view of the individual as a unique whole, as in the case of Gordon Allport, the emphasis is, without a flicker of doubt, on the total, structured individual.

Moreover, the "personalistic" phase of holistic psychology always includes a conception of the self. To the self-psychologist the self is as "real" as reflexes or habits are to the behaviorist, and it has the additional merit of serving as an explanatory principle for the consistency and continuity of the individual personality which do not characterize reflexes and habits. In the psychology of Gordon Allport, this stress on the self, individuality, and uniqueness which characterizes the holistic approach is organized into a science, or psychology, which recognizes not only the descriptive nature of science but even more its understanding function. This places the psychology of personality in the frame of reference of *Verstehende-psychologie*—the psychology of understanding—and thereby brings together the scientific and the humanistic, the nomothetic and the idiographic, approaches to the study of personality. These combined approaches, which also inform the view of personality expounded in this book, present us a portrait of the person as a living whole which the professions of behaviorism and other segmental approaches have not achieved.

Again, the achievements of the holistic-dynamic approach, like the behavioristic approach, have been effected without recourse to dubious and superfluous metaphysical conceptions. Likewise, it has given us a view of man without denying the value of the experimental and statistical approaches. As we affirm in various places in this book, the holistic-dynamic view of personality encourages experimentation, and will follow its lead as long as it throws light upon the nature of human behavior. We object and complain only when the "objectivists" mislead us into believing that formal and controlled experiments constitute the only scientific study of personality. There are many roads to the understanding of human behavior, and the experimental one is not always the most satisfactory. No psychologists of any consequence advocate that we cast the nomothetic laws aside; what some of them insist on, however, is that we be always mindful that these laws do not account for all behavior, and more particularly, that they fail to account for the uniqueness of the individual. As we tried to show in the Introduction, the nomothetic and the idiographic, the generalizing and the particularizing, phases of psychology are not antithetical, but can be made to work in harmony toward the construction of a view of man that is in accord with both the laws of science and the aspirations of the human spirit.

A PROVISIONAL VIEW OF PERSONALITY

Since the subject matter of this book is personality, it may be useful to begin our discussion by offering a preview of what personality is. In doing so, however, we would warn the reader that a real understanding of the human personality must await the extensive theoretical and empirical analyses contained in subsequent chapters. Nonetheless, an advance outline of the psychological organization we call personality may help us to better understand the various dimensions that constitute the whole.

WHAT PERSONALITY IS NOT. In the interest of clarity it is sometimes useful when defining a concept to show what it is not. This is particularly true of personality, for it is easy for the reader to lose his way in the multiplicity of current definitions.

Personality is not completely a habit-hierarchy. The belief that man is largely, if not entirely, a reactive organism has a respectable history. Its modern form is rooted in British empiricism—in the philosophies of Locke, Berkeley, and Hume. Its contemporary expression is found in the psychological position of behaviorism, extending from John B. Watson to Clark L. Hull.[10] Strictly speaking, this position has been investigating general behavior, not personality as such. The approach is almost wholly nomothetic. When behaviorists speak of personality they define it as the learned behavior of an individual, as a system of responses to stimuli, or as a habit-hierarchy. This description is the more true in view of the fact that many behaviorists, with a few exceptions, see no fundamental difference between the behavioral characteristics of animals and of human beings. Even such complex processes as language behavior, for example, are thought to be subject to the same general laws of behavior which govern an animal in the laboratory. Individual differences do not make a separate category called personality; they are but chance variations in the general laws of behavior. Accordingly, personality does not form a distinct subject

[10] We are fully mindful of the fact that few contemporary psychologists describe their positions by the conventional appellations of "behaviorism," "functionalism," and so on. They are interested in the problems of behavior with little concern for the "system" or "school" to which the problems, together with their solutions, might be oriented.

matter, and its laws are not distinct from the laws of behavior in general.

However, it is interesting and instructive to note that even such ardent general-behavior theorists as Miller and Dollard had to go outside the limits of the stimulus-response explanation of animal behavior to account for the highly complex behavioral structure which we know as personality. Finding the precise description of animal behavior insufficient for an account of the origin and development of personality they freely borrowed concepts and principles from psychoanalysis and cultural anthropology.[11] It is to their credit that they have been aware of the serious limitations of the stimulus-response explanation of complex human behavior. Indeed, their own work points up the poverty of the general-behavior theory, for when it is applied to the problems of personality the explicitness and rigor which are its prized features give way to principles, concepts, and procedures which are as lax as those of the opposing theory which many psychologists condemn. It is a tribute to psychoanalysis and cultural anthropology that Dollard and Miller were impelled to appeal to these disciplines to rescue their theory from the narrow limitations and atomizations of general-behavior theory.

In view of the fact that general-behavior theory asserts that the concept of personality is unnecessary because it adds nothing to our knowledge of behavior that is not already implicit in the stimulus-response formula, its conclusions are of very limited value for understanding the nature of personality. Since it usually prefers to describe behavior as a stimulus-response pattern, as largely the organization of learned behavior, or as a habit-hierarchy, all of which descriptions are valid and useful mostly in the narrow field of animal behavior in a rigidly controlled environment, this view is not altogether satisfactory. Personality is not only a set of habits; it is not merely a pattern of learned behavior; these are forms of behavior through which personality manifests itself, but they do not combine to form it.

Personality is not a mechanical structure of molecular units. There is a long history in psychology of dissecting the total individual into more or less separate and static parts. Mechanistic theories account for behavior by asserting that it is the effect of an antecedent cause. In psychology this principle has taken the form of affirming that an individual acts only when he is stimulated. From our point of view a stimulus does not always initiate a response; it often only modifies or directs a behavior that has already

[11] See Dollard and Miller, *Personality and psychotherapy.*

begun. In personality theory the most banal example of this practice is the description of the person in terms of the mechanisms
of adjustment. Like other mechanistic explanations this view is
based on the uncritical premise that the individual is only a reactive organism. His behavior is conceived too largely as a response to stimuli, and too seldom as the striving of a self-propelling
individual. Moreover, such mechanisms of adjustment as rationalization and projection, for example, often tell us less about the
behavior of a given individual than about the person who uses them
to describe another. In any case, the mechanisms are not separable
units of adjustment; rather they are "elements in the functioning of
a total individual as perceived and dissected by another individual
(the scientist)." [12]

Personality conceived as a totality of integral acts cannot be derived or predicted from a consideration of elemental responses,
even though the latter form a part of or are continuous with the
whole. Personality is not determined by external pressure alone,
but far more assuredly by the internal pressures of the total organism. In any event a complete knowledge of the stimulus-response
relationship—which, incidentally, is impossible, since psychologists
cannot always define the nature of the stimulus—does not of itself
give us a convincing description of psychological man. In modern
physics, as we have seen, one cannot predict the behavior of an
event from a knowledge of the mechanical connection between
antecedent and consequent. Paradoxically, causal relationships
seem to be "nondetermined." How much more true this must be
in the human realm where the participant person, far more profoundly than in the events of nature, is an effective cause of his own
behavior.[13]

It is generally forgotten that John B. Watson, the arch-mechanist
and supreme atomist in psychology, was not wholly committed to
his own position. It is not clear whether Watson asserted the contrasting views because he thought they were compatible, or whether
he unwittingly shifted from one to the other without being aware
that he was positing divergent views of behavior. At any rate, he
seems not to have been aware of their difference. In one context
he described behavior in terms of stimuli as the physicist defines

[12] J. Ruesch and G. Bateson, *Communication: the social matrix of psychiatry* (New
York: W. W. Norton & Co., Inc., 1951), p. 69.

[13] The principle of indeterminacy, which occupies an important place in contemporary physical theory and which is implied in the above statement, does in no way commit us to the traditional doctrine of free will. While this doctrine comes readily to
mind when the problem of determinism is discussed, it is wholly irrelevant to the present issue.

them and responses as they are viewed by the physiologist; but in a later context he defines behavior in terms of the *acts* of the *whole man*.[14]

The upshot of our brief discussion of the mechanistic and the molecular views of human behavior is that when they are used as a basis for defining personality, they have many shortcomings. We shall see throughout this book that personality is not the sum of its individual parts, but the whole behaving man. To use the terms fashionable today, personality is "molar," not "molecular." [15]

SOME CHARACTERISTICS OF PERSONALITY. It is easier to describe personality than to define it. In our description personality is the organized needs and abilities of an individual, or the characteristic manner in which he satisfies his needs and actualizes his potentialities. It is characterized by stability in change. A strain of consistency gives direction to man's behavior and sustains the individual in the face of shifting experience. Consistency refers to the enduring, but not unchanging, qualities of personality. Consistency gives to the behavior of a person a measure of predictability. The individual is thus seen to be a dynamic agent in the sociocultural process. He is not only conditioned by the customs and institutions of his culture but he transcends them and creates new ones. He is an active force in his own development. He sets up his own goals and either fails or succeeds in achieving them.

Furthermore, personality is not a thing possessed but a process of growth and experience. For this reason it cannot be measured like a physical object. What we measure is its flux, its change, its successive approaches to an end. It cannot always be described in terms of the organism's response to stimuli, although this formulation gives us knowledge of its elemental habit structure. For a penetrating understanding of personality a knowledge of the individual's responses to stimuli is not only inadequate but intellectually destitute. Learning is only a slender portion of the total person's behavior. What we need to know in trying to understand any person is the degree of his self-awareness, the intensity of his striving for self-actualization, and the self-consistent intentions and values which serve to guide his conduct.

This general description of personality has several merits. It recognizes the place of learning, habit formation, problem-solving,

[14] See J. B. Watson, *Psychology from the standpoint of a behaviorist;* and *Behaviorism* (New York: W. W. Norton & Co., Inc., 1930).

[15] This distinction was initially made by the English philosopher C. D. Broad and its use is now being overworked by American psychologists. See C. D. Broad, *The mind and its place in nature* (New York: Harcourt, Brace, and Co., 1929).

motivation, and adjustment in individual behavior. Since these properties have been extensively investigated on an empirical and experimental level their use in personality theory is compatible with the scientific enterprise in psychology. To this extent our view of personality is in accord with the desideratum of making the study of personality scientific. On the other hand, our definition of science in the broad or open sense opens the door to an unbiased consideration of those creative aspects of personality which elude exact measurement. Purely empirical descriptions of personality do not come to grips with the complexity of individual behavior. Learning theory tends to be indiscriminate. It squeezes behavior into a narrow mold wherein all stimulations and reinforcements have an equal status in the organization of personality. The learning process has, of course, as we shall see, an important place in the structuring of personality. However, while learning tells us much about an individual's adjustment and survival, it sheds only a dim light on his persistence in a chosen direction even in the face of unbelievable obstacles. If the learning psychologist is all too eager to describe the person's determination as an index of unadaptability, or of learning deficiency, he is, of course, free to do so; but he is thereby devaluating the very essence of personality: its thrust into the future. We live not by habits only, but even more by presuppositions and intentions. We seek not only the satisfaction of our needs or the reduction of our tensions, but even more a steady growth toward maturity. The major criticism of experimental psychology in its narrow but popular form is that it makes peripheral and subsidiary what is in fact central, namely, man as a striving and creative organism. In doing so, it ignores the role of the scientist in creating his own universe. Unlike the great contemporary physicists, the modern psychologist is rarely aware of the constitutive nature of what he knows. Unlike some pioneer sociologists, too many present-day psychologists are oblivious of the extent to which both man and culture define the human situation.[16]

SOME WORKING PROPOSITIONS. To help the reader to form a clearer image of personality at the outset and to acquaint him with some of the guiding principles which make up the conceptual scheme for the study of personality, we present in the following few paragraphs some provisional assumptions or propositions in the study of personality. If, because of what we have already

[16] W. I. Thomas early called attention to the "definition of the situation" by the person and by the culture. See W. I. Thomas, *The unadjusted girl* (Boston: Little, Brown & Co., 1923).

asserted in this chapter, some of these propositions now appear obvious through repetition, their importance is not, however, diminished.

1. *Human behavior consists of* acts. In our criticism of the atomizing tendency in psychology we argued that the stimulus-response couplet is inadequate to account for complex behavior. Consequently we posit the *total act* of the individual as the fundamental "unit" of behavior. Our object of investigation is the total personality, not an isolated modality, be it learning, motivation, cognition, or whatever. The modalities in themselves have no meaningful place outside the whole of which they are integral parts; they are derived from the whole by a process of differentiation; they are episodes, albeit important ones, in the total act called the personality.

2. *Personality conceived as a whole actualizes itself in a determinate environment.* Just as the separate acts of an individual cannot be understood apart from the whole person, so the total person cannot be fully understood if he is abstracted from his environment. Some of the most important characteristics of the total individual are derived from his environment, especially from the sociocultural matrix of customs and institutions. Differences in personality are expressions not only of inherent tendencies but even more of events in the social environment. The individual and his environment form a more or less coherent structure, namely, the person-in-his-environment.

Because of its familiarity this principle appears to be less vital than it is. However, it helps us to bridge the artificial gap between the subjective and the objective which the history of psychology has needlessly established. In our view, what was once outside the organism has been internalized and transformed by the intentions of the individual, and what was once inside it has been extraverted or actualized in response to the need for growth and self-realization. Internal and external, the organism and the environment, together constitute an indivisible whole of human experience.

3. *Personality is characterized by self-consistency.* We are quite aware of the strong tendency in some quarters to exaggerate the unity of the personality. This exaggeration appears to be a reaction against the molecularization of behavior which we already have noted. It is also partly based on a misunderstanding of the nature of self-consistency, on the erroneous belief that it means rigidity and freedom from change. It rests, finally, on the disproportionate concern of many psychologists with the pathological features of

personality, such as mental and emotional conflicts, hysterical phenomena, neurotic ambivalence, and schizoid behavior.

Nevertheless, there is much confirming evidence for the principle of consistency. There is a strong tendency in every healthy individual to react similarly in corresponding situations. To say this is not to affirm the regnancy of habits merely, but to stress the driving forces of self-integrity. A mark of the mature yet growing person is the strong tendency to organize his behavior into a changeable but consistent pattern called the self.[17]

4. *Personality is goal-directed behavior.* This principle is logically related to the preceding one. Self-consistency is not only the determination to maintain one's self; it also implies and involves the direction of acts toward a goal set up in advance. The unity of the personality is derived in large measure from the persistence of effort toward the attainment of a system of ends. Indeed, it is the properties of goal-integration and purpose that lend personality its distinguishing mark of identification. Were it not for the individual's constant choice among a variety of means toward previsioned ends, we could not distinguish one person from another; for general behavior, such as learning, is very much the same in all people. Individual behavior, in short, is *intentional*.[18]

5. *Personality is a time-integrating structure.* In traditional behavioristic psychology man is largely a creature of habit. Having been conditioned to respond in a given way the individual tends to persist in a mode of behavior until he has been "reconditioned," or until rewards and punishments compel him to surrender to a newly conditioned response. Psychoanalysis says very much the same thing. After the child's ego is fully structured in adolescence he largely recapitulates earlier forms of conduct in a contemporary setting. That this is true is not disputed, but the description is woefully incomplete. From our point of view, although the individual conserves much of the past and is deeply bound to the present, he

[17] See such notable self-psychologies as are found in the following: G. H. Mead, *Mind, self and society* (Chicago: University of Chicago Press, 1934); P. Lecky, *Self-consistency: a theory of personality* (New York: Island Press, 1945); C. R. Rogers, *Client-centered therapy* (Boston: Houghton Mifflin Co., 1951); G. W. Allport, *Becoming: basic considerations for a psychology of personality* (New Haven: Yale University Press, 1955).

[18] While this view has much in common with the theory of cognitive maps and of expectancy, it differs from the latter in its unfailing stress on the *act*. With all his emphasis on expectancy, purpose, and the organism as a whole, Tolman's view still operates too much within the static frame of reference of stimulus-response psychology, rather than the conceptual scheme of acts and intentions. For a good statement of Tolman's view, see E. C. Tolman, *Purposive behavior in animals and man* (New York: The Century Co., 1932).

foreshadows and anticipates the future. It is this future orientation that we define as growth, self-enhancement, and creative conduct. The psychologist who ignores this aspect of personality because it eludes his demand for operational rigor and experimental validation is capitulating to a sterile principle. Allport described this deplorable situation accurately and eloquently when he pointed out that "the sparseness that results from the application of operational criteria discourages the investigation of consciousness as a datum, as well as of personality as a complex structure, for in these domains relatively few concrete operations can be performed, few are repeatable, and few are public.[19]

6. *Personality is a process of becoming.* Personality is not, we have said, a mechanical process; it is not even a system of energy, merely, as one might be tempted to say. Rather, personality is an organization of potentialities striving to actualize themselves. The extent of this actualization will be helped or hindered by obstacles or facilitating conditions in the individual's social environment. This view of personality as becoming is reminiscent of the philosophical idea of *potentia*, without its mystical overtones. Like the tendency for becoming which has been posited in the quantum theory of modern physics, personality is a process standing halfway between the idea of an event and the event itself; a kind of reality "just in the middle between possibility and reality." [20]

CONCLUSION

In this chapter we have presented an introductory view of personality by describing the main lines of development of the subject and by a provisional statement regarding the nature of personality as developed in this book.

The discussion has shown that the chief emphasis at the turn of the century was upon a rigorous account of human behavior based on the animal model. In this connection Watson's behaviorism not only was an innovation in psychology but had a lasting influence upon it. The latter-day behaviorism of Hull, Guthrie, Tolman, and Skinner continued the tradition, but in a much more sophisticated and rigorous manner. The application of the latter approach in the study of personality was made by Dollard, Miller, and Mowrer. This approach is playing an important role in contemporary personality theory.

The second important contribution to personality theory, closely

[19] G. W. Allport, *Becoming*, p. 11.

[20] W. Heisenberg, *Physics and philosophy* (New York: Harper & Bros., 1958), p. 41.

related to the foregoing, was the conception of personality in the framework of "adjustment," a point of view already explicit in the functionalist psychology of Dewey and his followers. It represents an effective integration of behaviorism and the view that mental phenomena are adaptations by the organism of means in the pursuit of desired ends.

A third important development in personality psychology was the holistic, field-dynamic approach. This view, while not denying a limited value to the animal model of behaviorism, nor to the adaptive character of human behavior as posited by the adjustive psychology, stresses the integrated and creative features of the human personality.

The provisional view presented in this chapter is intended to bring out the nonmechanistic, configurational, and intentional nature of personality which informs this book, and which is discussed in detail in Chapter 17.

CHAPTER **2**

Theory of Personality:
Points of View

By now the reader must be conscious of the fact that personality is an exceedingly complex and dynamic psychobiological and psychosocial structure. This complexity is particularly apparent, as we shall see, in the fact that many views have been offered to account for the origin, nature, and development of personality, but none of them has found general acceptance.

The many views of personality are indiscriminately described as *theories;* [1] yet we question the validity of describing the various approaches as theories in the strict sense of the term. A theory is the formalization of data and observations into postulational form. The result of this formalization is a coherent group of general propositions regarding a class of phenomena which are testable and predictable. In this sense a theory is a more or less verified explanation of the group of general propositions or hypotheses with which the theorist begins his investigations.

The views which have dominated the psychology of personality are not theories in this sense. Rather, they are systematized and coherent, frequently illuminating statements regarding the nature of personality based on observational, experimental, and clinical data. This in part accounts for the large variety of views. If a theory is a more or less verified explanation of a class of objects,

[1] The latest example is the lucid and scholarly volume by Hall and Lindzey. See C. S. Hall and G. Lindzey, *Theories of personality* (New York: John Wiley & Sons, Inc., 1957).

then there should be much more agreement among the proposed accounts of personality. Since there is far less agreement than one has a right to expect, it is better to call the explanations leading approaches or *points of view*.[2] Consequently, we shall do so in this and the following chapters.

In the earlier period of inquiry into the psychology of personality the individual was seldom studied as a coherent and indivisible whole. He was viewed, rather, as a coordination of sensations, drives, motor responses, and habits. These are important components of personality, but before they can function as characteristics of a total person they must be organized into a dynamic and coherent structure.[3]

The earlier atomization of the personality was not a total waste, however. It was partly through the awareness of the segmental nature of earlier views, and partly through rebellion against traditional psychology, that contemporary psychology has "discovered" the organized nature of human personality. A consistent view of the total personality must, of course, be formulated in terms of a detailed investigation of sensations, drives, learned behavior, and other processes. Personality in its most elementary form is the organization of these processes into a unified structure. What was conspicuously lacking in the early views of human behavior was the integration of the separate processes into a functional whole.

At the turn of the present century, psychological systems were still largely views of *mind*, not of personality. Structural psychology, the psychology imported from Germany, was interested in the generalized mind. It focused on mental elements—sensations, memory, imagery, thought. It was not much concerned with patterned behavior, despite Wundt's "creative synthesis" and the doctrine of psychological compounding. Functional psychology, which suffuses all contemporary psychology in one way or another, did not examine personality as such, but studied mind as an adaptive mechanism, as a means of survival in the struggle for existence. As indicated in Chapter 1, John Dewey demolished the centrality of the reflex arc and criticized elementarism relentlessly; still, his

[2] We are not unmindful of some of the attempts at theory-building, such as the recent efforts of Rotter and Kelly; but it would be premature to evaluate their endeavors adequately. Rotter's is basically a learning-theory approach, whereas Kelly's is not. See J. B. Rotter, *Social learning and clinical psychology* (Englewood Cliffs, N.J.: Prentice-Hall, Inc., 1954); G. A. Kelly, *The psychology of personal constructs* (2 vols., New York: W. W. Norton & Co., Inc., 1955).

[3] This has not been true of twentieth-century psychiatry and psychoanalysis. Both disciplines have from the beginning focused their attention on the whole man. This is particularly true of Freudian psychoanalysis, despite its preoccupation with the libido.

own emphasis on *coordinations, integral acts,* and *transactions* left little room in his approach for the total individual. Of the early functionalists, Harvey Carr, in the 1920's, explicitly postulated a self as the coordinating principle of adjustive behavior. He conceived the self as "the unitary organization of the totality of life's experiences." [4]

From its very beginning the behavioristic approach in psychology showed very little interest in the problem of personality. While John B. Watson mentioned personality, as we pointed out in Chapter 1, it was peripheral to his view of behavior, and the concept of self had no place in his system. While he showed interest in man as a whole, he conceived him as an organic machine. Personality was described as a structure consisting of stimulus-response connections, as the end-product of habit-systems.[5]

With this background in mind, we turn now to an all-too-brief delineation of the leading views of personality.

THE PSYCHOANALYTIC APPROACH

It goes without saying that an extended exposition of the psychoanalytic view of personality in a section of a single chapter is wholly impossible. Freud's system alone cannot be adequately summarized, for it is not only exceedingly complex but the product of extended revision in his own lifetime. Moreover, we are interested only in the normal personality, which was not Freud's chief concern, and we shall refer to the neurotic individual, the focus of Freud's study, only in passing.

When one speaks of the psychoanalytic approach it is necessary to distinguish which "branch" of the psychoanalytic school we have in mind. Although "orthodox" psychoanalysts recognize only their own point of view as truly psychoanalytic, the historical facts clearly contradict them. Shortly after its inception, psychoanalysis gave rise to schisms and unresolved controversies which eventually developed into new schools and opposing systems. Our major attention will be directed to the Freudian point of view, but we shall also note briefly some of the other psychoanalytic approaches.

FREUD'S VIEW OF PERSONALITY. At the outset, three facts concerning Freud and his school must be noted. First, Freud was a

[4] H. A. Carr, *Psychology: a study of mental activity* (New York: Longmans, Green & Co., Inc., 1925), p. 346. Although this view is still essentially sound, it has been superseded by contemporary self-psychology.

[5] Our purpose here is not to criticize behaviorism. It must be recognized that it is no longer a school or a movement, but a method of investigating behavior scientifically. Some of its conclusions have been absorbed by most of contemporary psychology, and there is a strain of behaviorism in all of us.

biological scientist who was influenced by his training in medicine and by the dominant evolutionary point of view of nineteenth-century biology. Second, while he was a practicing psychoanalyst deeply involved with the problems and techniques of psycho-therapy, he was throughout his entire career concerned with de-veloping a scientific theory of human behavior. Third, all criticism to the contrary notwithstanding, psychoanalysis was changed and revised throughout Freud's active career as a scientist.

Basic drives and behavior. Unlike Breuer, his early and close senior associate, who concerned himself with objective factual descriptions, Freud was interested in the *interpretation* of man's behavior. Like all creative scientists, Freud was trying to formulate hypotheses to account for what he observed in his practice. These hypotheses are theoretical constructs, the purpose of which is to integrate the various facts and interpretations into a consistent view of human conduct.

The most important of Freud's constructs is that of *basic drives* or urges.[6] Freud postulated that our behavior is motivated by two basic urges: the *life-urge* and the *death-urge.* The life-urge impels an individual toward the preservation of self and of others, and it is expressed in constructiveness, creativity, love, and sociability. A vital aspect of the life-urge is the *libido,* a term which unfortu-nately has generated misunderstanding and undeserved merriment. The term refers to that expression of the life-urge which draws people into close psychological interaction with one another. It refers to nothing more mysterious than sociability, a concept needed by every personality psychologist in order to account for human behavior. It differs, however, from the current conception of so-ciability in the fact that Freud *seemed* to regard it as a native, rather than an acquired, tendency. Libido, or psychosexual energy, as it may also be called, is expressed not only in coitus, but in all close human relationships, from the sexual embrace of two lovers, or the tender ministrations of parents to their children, to the devotion of good friends to each other.

While Freud was impressed by the importance of the life-urge, he was also deeply stirred by the aggressive and destructive char-acter of man. In this he was reinforced by what he saw in World

[6] Unfortunately, the German word *Trieb,* which Freud employed, was translated as *instinct* in all the early translations. The terms *drive, urge, impulse,* and *tendency* are generally more adequate renderings. The most satisfactory translations are those published by the Hogarth Press. Parenthetically, the student who knows German ade-quately should read Freud in the original, for the latter's style, unlike the pompous *akademische Deutsch* of German university professors, is attractive, simple, and lucid.

War I. Accordingly, he found it necessary to posit the existence of a death-urge. Man not only loves, but hates; he not only builds and creates, but kills and destroys; he not only enjoys close relationships with others, but is also aggressive toward them. The death-urge may be turned inward upon oneself in the form of suicide and other forms of self-punishment; or outward upon others in the form of violence, injury of others, homocide, and war. In its milder manifestations it is found in all forms of aggressiveness, either toward oneself or others, such as guilt, self-punishment, self-criticism, jealousy, hostility, criticism of others, including some of the disputes and polemics of scholars and scientists.[7]

In the last decade of his life, Freud emphasized the death-urge increasingly. The suppression and repression of the sex-drive was no longer envisioned as the chief source of man's mental ills. Instead, he saw the chief source of maladjustment in society's control of man's aggressive impulses.[8]

Interdependence of the basic urges. Although the life-urge and the death-urge seem to work in opposite directions, they are not mutually exclusive. On the contrary, they interpenetrate and neutralize each other. This interpenetration of the two impulses is known as *ambivalence,* whereby an individual may harbor for the same person both love and hate, friendliness and hostility, acceptance and rejection. Human relations are characterized by conflicts, compromises, and conciliations. Human personality arises out of this conflict and fusion of the basic impulses. From this point of view, personality is that organization of behavior which results from the struggle for ascendancy by the life-urge and the death-urge.

With poetic sensitivity, Freud describes and analyzes the polarity of the basic urges in the rich variety of its forms. The most dramatic of these conflicts—at least in our own society—is the *Oedipus complex.* In this situation the child feels hostility or hatred toward the parent of the same sex, who frustrates him in his striving for libidinal gratification. Thus, a boy, being attached to his mother, finds himself to be his father's competitor and rival. He resents his father's favored place in the latter's relation to the mother; and so while he loves him, he yet hates him. Lovers and friends are fond of each other and yet feel jealousy, resentment, or hatred one for the other. In extreme situations,

[7] For a full discussion of these urges and their interrelationships, see S. Freud, Beyond the pleasure principle, in *The standard edition of the complete psychological works,* ed. J. Strachey (London: Hogarth Press, Ltd., 1955), Vol. 18.

[8] S. Freud, *New introductory lectures on psycho-analysis* (New York: Carlton House, 1933), pp. 141–52.

which are typically neurotic, the lover can consummate his affection only when he can also humiliate or debase his beloved. The ambivalences may go on in this manner endlessly, every expression being a blend of the basic urges of love and hate.[9]

Psychosexual development. In the very beginning of his psychoanalytical researches, Freud was impressed by the role of sexuality in neurosis, particularly in hysterical reactions. The theory of psychosexual genesis refers to the course of development of the personality as it is affected by the frustrations of the life-urge and the death-urge. Both the normal and the abnormal personalities are products of the frustrations of the basic urges. The major phases of psychosexual development are infancy, latency, and puberty. The normal adult personality results from the successful elaborations and expressions of these phases.

Infancy is the period of egoistic self-seeking, the stage of psychosexual development from birth to approximately the end of the fifth year. It is also referred to as the period of *narcissism*, when the child is largely absorbed in himself and seeks to gratify his impulses and wishes without regard for others. In the earlier phase of this period *oral* pleasures are predominant. The young child obtains pleasure from sucking and from appropriating objects for the mouth. By the eighth month, more or less, the infant is weaned. This experience is deeply frustrating and ungratifying. However, there are other pleasures in store for him, particularly *anal* and *phallic*. He derives pleasure from fecal elimination, and he soon discovers that his genitals are sources of pleasure and satisfaction. However, in the phallic stage the genital pleasures are not yet explicitly sexual. They are derived not only from manipulations of the sexual organs, but from nakedness, from the mystifying erotic and affectional interactions of his parents, from observing the genitals of the opposite sex, and so forth. While oral and anal pleasures do not cease at this time, the masturbatory and other forms of sexual excitement are now the child's chief sources of pleasure.

This infantile sexuality soon meets rebuffs and frustrations. Like weaning, it too must come to an end, or at least be controlled and inhibited, if not yet repressed. Clearly, custom in our society does not permit a prolongation of these infantile indulgences, and so by the sixth year, approximately, the child has learned to *repress* them. This period, normally lasting to the end of the twelfth year in our culture, is called the *latency* period, the period when the

[9] For a description of the drama of conflict one must turn to Freud's metapsychological work: *Civilization and its discontents* (London: Hogarth Press, Ltd., 1930).

earlier pleasures associated with oral, anal, and genital activities are variously frustrated. During this period the child learns to identify himself with his parents. At this time children are highly conscious of members of the opposite sex in their own age groups, but usually avoid them in their daily activities. Boys, particularly, are embarrassed by kissing and embracing, and put on an air of unconvincing masculinity during which they avoid or renounce affectional display. Children seek and enjoy outside playmates, usually members of their own sex.[10] Identification, which continues beyond the latency period, is now intensified. In this relationship the boy's father becomes an ideal to be imitated, and the mother becomes the little girl's leading model. Explicit sexual interests become increasingly dormant. At any rate, autoerotic and heterosexual interests do not dominate the child's activities. He has more things to occupy him now, and his little world expands almost daily. He goes to school, makes new friendships, and finds fresh adventures. While it is still present, his earlier sexuality is largely repressed out of fear of disapproval, or out of the embarrassment which children in our society experience over erotic activities and interests.

Latency is also the period when the child needs to renounce or repress his Oedipal strivings. This repression represents the child's fear of disapproval or punishment for his erotic interest in his opposite-sexed parent. Out of this repression the child's ego, which we shall discuss later, develops, impelling him to adapt to and live more in accordance with reality instead of his wishes. Out of the fear of parental disapproval of his sexual and Oedipal interests, the beginning of conscience, or the superego, emerges.

With the appearance of the superego, the child enters the period of *puberty*, or adolescence, which continues from the thirteenth to the eighteenth or nineteenth year. This period is also called the genital stage, for sexuality, which was largely repressed during the latency period, now reasserts itself with particular force. While the adolescent must continue to control his sexual strivings, there is less repression and more inhibition than during the latency period. The pubertal stage is also the period in psychosexual development when other repressed impulses are revived. Kissing, fondling, and related forms of erotic behavior are among the most common of these activities. Anal interests are reactivated in the form of stories and epithets describing anal expulsion. Masturba-

---

[10] If recent sociological reports and impressionistic observations are correct, this pattern of interchild relations is changing. "Dating" has frequently been observed between ten-year-olds.

tion, either individually or mutually with another, is a common form of behavior. Homosexual attachments are not uncommon in this period. The adolescent's need to satisfy his sexual urges is very strong, although the desire still has narcissistic elements in it: that is, it is still highly self-seeking and very little governed by considerations for the love object.

Adult genital satisfaction is sanctioned only in marriage in our society, even though the statistical figures contradict this moral expectation. Since marriage usually takes place only after adolescence, true "object-love," or adult heterosexuality, is delayed. The pubertal period is thus still in some ways phallic rather than genital, for the earlier forms of sexual expression constitute a modest proportion of the adolescent's erotic life. In the "true" genital stage sexuality is merged with tender affection, wherein the individual not only receives but gives, and where sexual relations are engaged in for mutual happiness and, generally speaking, eventual procreation. This is the stage of adult heterosexuality, when the psychosexual development of the individual has reached its full maturity.[11]

Structure of the personality. Although Freud divided the total personality into "parts," he stressed its essential unity without closing his mind to its division. In this he avoided the common errors of either overemphasizing its unity, or minimizing the situational factors which stimulate its disunity. It is not difficult to see why Freud's critics seized upon the partitions of personality and not its unity. Freud's literary style and poetic proclivity led him to dramatize what a less creative and original mind would have described prosaically. Thus, in one of his writings Freud speaks of the ego serving "three harsh masters"—the id, the external world, and the superego. However, he is quick to add a warning: "When you think of this dividing up of the personality into ego, superego and id, you must not imagine sharp dividing lines such as are artificially drawn in the field of political geography. . . . After we have made our separations, we must allow what we have separated to merge again." [12]

The *id* is that aspect of the total personality which aims at an immediate and direct satisfaction of the basic urges.[13] It is the

11 For Freud's full discussion of psychosexual development see his Three essays on sexuality, in *The standard edition of the complete psychological works* (1953), Vol. 7.

12 Freud, *New introductory lectures,* p. 110. Apparently, some expositors of Freud's psychology took his *Topographie der Seele* (topography of the mind) too literally. It was used by Freud as a figure of speech.

13 The term *id* has been the butt of much ridicule. It is the Latin form of the German *das Es,* which is eminently sensible in its original form. The Latin version avoids the awkward English rendering of it into *the it.*

obscure and directly inaccessible province of the personality—"a chaos, a cauldron of seething excitement. It satisfies its impulses in accordance with the 'pleasure principle'" (*der Lustprinzip*). It knows no logic, and contradictory impulses may coexist within it without neutralizing one another. It knows no values, and no good or evil. It has no conscience, and is completely nonmoral.

The *ego* seeks the satisfaction of its wishes in conformity with objective opportunities and limitations. It is the "reality principle" in human behavior. The ego protects the id from destruction, for it directs the latter's blind impulses along lines of expression which are in keeping with external reality, as when it eventually "informs" the child that the moon for which he is crying is wholly beyond his reach. It interposes between blind desire and its un-inhibited satisfaction a delaying action in the form of logic and the lessons of experience. As Freud states the contrast, "the ego stands for reason and circumspection, while the id stands for the untamed passions." [14]

The *superego* is that dimension of the total personality which imposes restrictions on the id, not by making it conform to objective reality, as the ego does, but by pressing it to live in accordance with the established moral principles. It is "the advocate of the impulse toward perfection;" and it impels the individual to regulate his behavior by the customs and traditions which are imposed on the child by his parents. As we have said before, the parents normally serve as ideals for the child in the process of identifying himself with them. The parents' own superegos are the models which the child tends to follow; that is, their own moral and ex-pected behavior, handed down as customs and traditions from the past, is the fountainhead for the child's own individual and social character. Man's moral behavior cannot be understood apart from his superego. Because it imposes moral restrictions on man, it prevents him from engaging in antisocial conduct, such as dis-honesty, delinquency, or crime. It inclines man to think of the consequences of his present conduct, aiding him to live in the emerging future as well as in the immediate present. The beliefs which constitute the superego "perpetuate the past, the traditions of the race and the people, which yield but slowly to the influence of the present and to new developments, and, as long as they work through the super-ego, play an important part in man's life. . . ." [15]

Loci of conflict situations. As part of his hypothesis of basic urges, Freud advanced the idea that these urges are in conflict with

---

[14] *New introductory lectures*, p. 107.
[15] *Ibid.*, p. 96.

each other, as we have already stated. The normal personality develops from the conflicts between the id, the ego, and the superego. Freud had now to explain "where" these dynamic processes take place. Accordingly, he posited the existence of the unconscious, preconscious, and conscious areas of the personality. In so doing, he also brought the id, the ego, and the superego into relation with the "topographical" aspects of the total personality.

The *unconscious* mind is one of Freud' important but controversial contributions to the study of human behavior. Its postulation is necessary in order to account for various psychological phenomena, both normal and abnormal. The unconscious mind is the "seat" of most of the strivings of the id, and of all the memories and experiences which cannot be voluntarily recalled, but which may suddenly appear in consciousness without any apparent reason. Furthermore, the unconscious is the locus of all those thoughts and wishes which have been repressed because they are incompatible with the individual's ideals, or with the practices and beliefs of society. Thus, any wish or desire that is socially or morally unacceptable tends to be consigned to the unconscious dimension of the personality. In short, as someone has remarked, the unconscious mind is the reservoir of what we must forget.

The *preconscious*, or foreconscious, is that dimension of the person in which those experiences, ideas, and memories are stored which, though unconscious much of the time, are only latent, and can be recalled at will. Thus, I have in my mind many bits of knowledge, such as the fact that Columbus discovered America in 1492, or that I received a wristwatch on my twenty-first birthday. These and thousands of similar facts seldom come into my field of consciousness; but although they are not before my mind at the moment, I can recall them when I have the occasion or need for so doing. Meanwhile, they lie dormant in the preconscious dimension of my mind. The difference between unconscious and preconscious materials is that the preconscious are temporarily unconscious experiences which can be transformed into conscious ones when the need arises.

The *conscious* is the seat of immediate awareness. Freud was not much concerned with it, and he assumed that its meaning "is beyond all doubt." Unlike the unconscious mind, whose existence is assumed because it helps to account for certain effects, the conscious mind is known to exist because we experience it from moment to moment.[16]

16 *Ibid.*, pp. 99–102.

The foregoing dimensions are related to the total structure of the personality. As we have already pointed out, the id is largely confined to the unconscious orbit of experience, although on occasions, particularly during psychoanalytic therapy, it may reach consciousness. The ego is found largely in the conscious mind, thus causing us to act in accordance with reason and our knowledge of reality. The superego overlaps with the others more extensively than either the ego or the id, for conscious, preconscious, and unconscious experiences are held within it. Likewise, the ego may interact with all three areas, for it often mediates between the id and the superego in their conflicts with each other.

In summary, the adult personality is a product of the adequate resolution of the conflicts between the basic urges as they are expressed in the id, the ego, and the supergo of the conscious, preconscious, and unconscious dimensions of the total psychobiological individual.[17]

It would take us far beyond our purpose here to attempt a critique of Freud's psychoanalysis. Suffice it to say that although it has given us interesting and valuable insights into the nature of human personality, it has been difficult to test its validity. On the other hand, much of the scorn which has been heaped upon Freud's system is ill-deserved. Our own chief objection to it is that (1) it has invented concepts, such as libido, which are neither necessary nor illuminating; and (2) its stress upon infantile and other past motivations, especially the belief that adult personality is largely a recapitulation of archaic and childhood experiences, is controverted by empirical facts. However, to argue, as some have done, that Freud was an artistic genius whose works have no scientific value and will one day be forgotten, is an unconvincing and unscientific estimation of some profound observations by a scientifically dedicated man.[18]

VARIANTS OF THE PSYCHOANALYTIC VIEW. The psychoanalytic approach to personality was revised not only by Freud himself, but very drastically by his followers and critics as well. The course of this modification is too intricate to record in these pages. Accordingly, we present here only those fundamental ideas which

[17] Freud's discussion of the normal personality is found in his *The ego and the id* (London: Hogarth Press, Ltd., 1935).

We might say to the student who confuses the terms "unconscious" and "subconscious" when he finds the latter used in the psychological literature, that the term "subconscious" may be used as a more general term to cover the foreconscious and the unconscious.

[18] For one such assessment see C. C. Pratt, *The logic of modern psychology* (New York: The Macmillan Co., 1948), p. 164 f.

have contributed to the divergences from the Freudian point of view.

Alfred Adler. The first of Freud's followers to challenge some of his fundamental ideas was Alfred Adler. He called his view of human nature *individual psychology.* Aside from personal reasons, the break with Freud was based on Adler's rejection of the sexual origin of psychoneuroses. However, of interest to us here is Adler's theory of normal personality. He believed that personality is largely a product of the manner in which the individual adjusts to his feeling of inferiority, a feeling which Adler believed to exist in everyone. This universal sense of inferiority, he held, stems from the feeling of helplessness in all infants and children. This helplessness and its resulting sense of inferiority are either mitigated or aggravated by parental attitudes of acceptance or rejection.

In order to compensate for this feeling of inferiority the individual will seek ways of feeling superior. As we have indicated, compensation may serve as one of the most constructive modes of human adjustment. A person may compensate in multitudinous ways, particularly by striving for power and self-assurance in the form of complete *masculinity.* This is true of both men and women. The *will-to-power*, arising from feelings of inferiority, rather than the sexual drive, is the basic determinant of personality. In this lies the first, and earliest, distinction between the views of Freud and Adler.

Again, from the need for superiority the child develops the "masculine protest," a rejection of his inferiority and a determination to achieve adulthood, which is to say, adequacy as a man or as a woman. Whether an individual becomes a neurotic or a normal person depends on the outcome of the struggle between the masculine protest and social reality. Thus, if he strives to achieve his goals despite a limited endowment, or in the face of insuperable social and economic barriers, he may fail and thus be forced to compensate through neurotic—that is, unrealistic—means. As Adler would describe it, the individual will compensate through neurotic illness.[19]

However, like Freud, Adler subjected his ideas to frequent and occasionally fundamental revisions, especially in response to frequent and severe criticism. By the late 1930's he had broadened his view considerably by stressing man's social nature. In his interesting volume, *Social interest,* he stressed man's devotion to the

[19] This is, in essence, Adler's view in its early stages. See A. Adler, *A study of organ inferiority and its psychical compensations* (New York: Nervous and Mental Disease Publishing Co., 1917).

betterment of society as the fundamental compensation for all man's deficiences and weaknesses.[20]

According to Adler, man's social interest is innate, not acquired through interaction with other social beings. Interaction with others externalizes and directs it into constructive channels. The innate character of the social interest helps to explain man's uniqueness; for although through social interaction man's social interest is guided toward constructive ends, his modes of realizing them are uniquely his own. This unique way of expressing his social interests, or of striving for perfection, as Adler conceived it, he called the individual's *style of life*. This style of life represents each man's uniqueness and determines his entire conduct. This style of life is, indeed, an expression of man's *creative self*, and bestows on all of life whatever meaning it can formulate in the light of man's native endowments and experience.[21]

Carl G. Jung. Jung was the second important figure to break with Freud. "Analytical psychology," the term Jung used to describe his viewpoint, differed from Freud's ideas in important ways. Jung broadened Freud's concept of libido to encompass all drives and emotions, not only sexual needs, and since the first formulation of his views, he has held that it resides not only in the individual but in the human race as a whole. Libido is not only sexual, but a force which opposes sexuality. The sexual aspect of libido is man's animality; its moral aspect is his spirituality: it is antisexual. Again, just as there is an individual and a racial libido, so there is a personal unconscious and a collective unconscious, wherein the conflict between the two phases of the libido takes place. The personal unconscious is the repository of forgotten, repressed, and subliminal processes; the collective unconscious refers to the phylogenetic, or racial, modes of thinking and feeling. For example, dreams, while taking place in the individual, are really manifestations of the collective unconscious. Owing to this fact, individual dreams mean the same thing in every culture, no matter who the dreamer may be.

Rational thought, on the other hand, takes place in the conscious mind. It selects what is relevant to the immediate situation

[20] A. Adler, *Social interest: a challenge to mankind* (London: Faber & Faber, Ltd., 1938).

[21] For the discussion of "style of life," see A. Adler, *What life should mean to you* (Boston: Little, Brown & Co., 1931); for a brief statement of his concept of the creative self, see his article, The fundamental views of individual psychology, *Int. J. indiv. Psychol.*, 1 (1935), 5–8. A good over-all introduction to his view of personality is found in his *The practice and theory of individual psychology* (New York: Harcourt, Brace and Co., 1927).

and relegates to the unconscious whatever has no bearing upon man's thinking at the moment. The conscious and the unconscious are thus antithetical, and create conflicts between themselves. The normal, conscious mind is expressed either during serious tensions when intelligent discriminations have to be made, or in rational and logical thinking. When one or the other predominates, the individual is either a thinking type, or *introvert*, or an emotional type, or *extravert*. Introverts and extraverts are in turn divided into subtypes, depending on whether thinking, sensation, feeling, or intuition is the prevailing mode of expression. Since these are discussed in detail in the next chapter, we need say no more about them here.[22]

As the professional reader can see, this is but the barest preface to Jung's inordinately complex view of the nature of psychological man. We have omitted any discussions of the separate segments of the total personality, such as the persona, the animus, the archetypes of the collective unconscious, the shadow, and the self. With the exception of the self, which seems to be the whole personality and which therefore is a questionable addition to his already overburdened view, these concepts have a doubtful value for the psychology of personality. Indeed, it is these ideas, as well as his concepts of a universal libido and a racial unconscious which imply the doctrine of the inheritance of acquired characteristics, that have generally repelled academic psychologists and account for the fact that Jung's influence on the psychology of personality has been negligible. His viewpoint is so suffused with occult, mystical, and theological ideas that it has no attraction to the empirically-minded psychologist.[23]

The Neo-Freudians. There is a growing number of psychoanalysts, not co-workers of Freud, who diverge in more or less important ways from orthodox psychoanalysis. This group of revisionists have been labeled Neo-Freudians. All of them have a strong orientation toward sociology and anthropology, rather than toward biology. They account for human personality not in terms of biological heredity, but on the basis of the sociocultural conditions in which the individual is reared. Human motives and human

---

[22] C. G. Jung, *Collected papers on analytical psychology* (London: Bailliere, Tindall & Cox, 1920); *Psychological types* (New York: Harcourt, Brace and Co., Inc., 1933); *Psychology of the unconscious* (New York: Dodd, Mead, & Co., Inc., 1925).

[23] The eighteen-volume *Collected works*, financed by the Bolingen Foundation, attest not to the scientific vigor of Jung's ideas, but to their religious and theological appeal. These volumes are being published by the Pantheon Press, of which about six volumes have come off the press since 1953.

personality are, accordingly, different in divergent cultures. This view has been most consistently developed by Fromm, Horney, Sullivan, and Kardiner.[24]

Erich Fromm is a social scientist well trained in the practice of psychoanalysis. Throughout all his writings, beginning with publications in Germany in the late 1920's to his recent book on Freud, he emphasizes the social nature of man.[25] Man is what he is, not because of innate urges, but largely because of the manner in which he is treated as a child by others, especially his parents. Man's problems, his normality and neurosis, grow out of culturally produced needs and desires. Man functions not by instinct, but by means of social learning and cultural conditioning; his "nature, his passions, and anxieties are a cultural product. . . ."[26]

Fromm believes that man's personality problems arise from the dominant trends in the culture, not primarily from sexual or aggressive urges. If the culture values power and destructiveness, the individual will more likely than not pursue these ends. If he develops neurotic reactions, it is because the institutions or practices of his culture stifle his "productive orientations"—his needs to actualize his own potentialities and to relate himself creatively to others.[27]

While man's problems arise in his response to society's demands, he is not initially a social being. His problems and his attempts to solve them are both products of his inborn nature and society's frustrations of his basic needs. While Fromm thinks such a society could be devised, none has yet permitted man to adequately satisfy his need to relate himself to others in productive love—the kind of relatedness that will give him a sure sense of belonging and at the same time permit him to be a unique person. Relatedness to others and individual uniqueness are man's greatest desires, and their full realization would make for a healthy and complete personality.[28]

Karen Horney, who acknowledged Fromm's influence on her own views, also rejected most of Freud's biological premises and

[24] For the beginner, we recommend the excellent but brief discussion of these revisionists in C. Thompson, *Psychoanalysis: evolution and development* (New York: Hermitage House, Inc., 1950), Ch. 10.

[25] See particularly the following: *Escape from freedom* (New York: Farrar & Rinehart, Inc., 1941); *Man for himself* (New York: Farrar & Rinehart, Inc., 1947); *The sane society* (New York: Farrar & Rinehart, Inc., 1955); *The art of loving* (New York: Harper & Bros., 1956); *Sigmund Freud's world mission* (New York: Harper & Bros., 1959).

[26] Fromm, *Escape from freedom,* p. 13.

[27] Fromm, *Man for himself,* pp. 82–96.

[28] Fromm, *The sane society.*

put greatest stress upon cultural influences and the current life situation of the individual. While as a practicing psychoanalyst she was much more interested in the neurotic person, she also shed important light upon the normal individual.

A normal person pursues realistic goals—goals that are within his reach. On the other hand, it is characteristic of the neurotic person to pursue overidealized goals. In effect this means that he has an overidealized and distorted image of himself—himself not as he actually is, but as he unrealistically thinks he is. He strives for the realization of false values.

Like Fromm, Horney stressed the importance of the child's treatment by his parents in the development of personality. She rejected, or at least greatly minimized, Freud's idea of a "repetition compulsion"; that is, the view that a person's present characteristics are repetitions of his infantile drives. In opposition, she stressed the principle that present behavior is a complex of infantile and current experiences. This complex makes up the individual's "character structure." This character structure strives to realize the individual's potentialities and a more adequate self. The present character structure is much more important than infantile strivings. If the child is adequately treated by his parents and other adults, he will have a good chance of realizing his selfhood; if he is unfavorably treated by them, he is in danger of developing neurotic anxiety, from which he will ineffectually try to escape.[29]

Harry Stack Sullivan, like Fromm and Horney, stresses the impact of culture upon the individual. However, Sullivan differs from both in his far greater emphasis of the role of *interpersonal relations* in both normal and abnormal personalities. Our personalities, he believed, are significantly shaped by the success or failure in achieving security, or a feeling of belonging and acceptance. If the parents show attitudes of acceptance and approval of the child, he develops security and well-being; if they disapprove of or reject him, he develops anxiety and insecurity. Anxiety restricts the growth of the self, whereas approval and acceptance are conducive to its growth and enhancement. Taking man as a whole, we find that he is everywhere molded by his culture. Whenever he tries to break away from the culture and the people in it, he feels anxious and lonely. Culture and its effect upon the individual can be changed only by other individuals. If the culture produces anxiety, this can be allayed by the kindness and approval of others,

[29] K. Horney, *New ways in psychoanalysis* (New York: W. W. Norton & Co., Inc., 1939), Introduction and Ch. 12; *Neurosis and human growth* (New York: W. W. Norton & Co., Inc., 1950), Introduction.

especially the parents. If the parents lack these traits, the child's anxiety can be mollified by other individuals, such as friends, companions, teachers, or therapists. The individual's personality is thus molded by both the culture and interpersonal relations.[30]

Abram Kardiner, despite his extensive use of Freudian terminology, is less Freudian than he seems to be. He has been engaged in tracing the role of cultural forces in the shaping of personality for more than twenty years. According to him, personality is the resultant of the impress of cultural factors upon the individual's biological substructure. The cultural forces are numerous, but the most important is the prevailing method of child-rearing. In our society, the pattern of child-rearing is largely determined by the class structure, so that parents bring up their children largely in accordance with their class status. The personality is deeply molded by the family structure; and since this varies in the world between the monogamous, polygynous, and polyandrous, people's basic personalities differ in accordance with these types. The basic disciplines, which we shall discuss in Chapter 6, are crucially important. A given society's economic ethic, its competitiveness, rivalry, or cooperativeness, as the case may be, as well as actual economic and social conditions, all have important effects on our attitudes and personalities. The ideals and life-goals, as determined mostly by a person's class membership, also aid in determining the personality. These goals vary from culture to culture, and consist of such values as economic success, prestige, spiritual salvation, immortality, and the like. In short, for Kardiner cultural conditions are the most effective determinants of personality.[31]

GESTALT AND FIELD THEORIES

The early *Gestalt* psychologists were largely interested in the problem of perception, which they investigated experimentally. However, *Gestalt* psychology has some very important things to say concerning the personality as a whole. This is particularly true of field theory, a special form of *Gestalt* psychology which has been investigating the total personality. The *Gestalt* point of view naturally led investigators into the field of personality psychology,

[30] H. S. Sullivan, *Conceptions of modern psychiatry* (Washington, D.C.: The William Alanson White Psychiatric Foundation, 1947); *The interpersonal theory of psychiatry* (New York: W. W. Norton & Co., Inc., 1953).

[31] See A. Kardiner, *The individual and his society* (New York: Columbia University Press, 1939); *The psychological frontiers of society* (New York: Columbia University Press, 1945). For an interesting study of the effect of the caste system on the personalities of American Negroes, see A. Kardiner and L. Ovesey, *The mark of oppression* (New York: W. W. Norton & Co., Inc., 1951).

because of its basic tenet that behavioral phenomena are organized wholes, rather than aggregates of stimulus-response phenomena. The emphasis on organized wholes, or *Gestalten*, stands in sharp contrast to the atomistic approach of early behaviorism.

THE PROBLEM OF ORGANIZATION. A crucial problem of field-theoretical, as of *Gestalt*, psychology has been from the very beginning the question of the organization of experience. Of course, the problem of organization is bound to present itself to almost any contemporary psychologist, but it has been particularly important for the field theorist. According to *Gestalt* and field psychology the various "parts," be they attitudes, traits, motives, or whatever, interlock to form a whole in which they constantly affect one another. However, it is possible to have an interrelation of traits and other personality variables, without genuine organization. The concept of correlation, for example, may be used to study the interrelationships of personality units, but the end result is not necessarily an organized whole, for the interconnections may be random or "accidental." For instance, a person may be a gifted musician and a highly skilled chess player. The two are correlated but not necessarily functionally interconnected. It is characteristic of a *Gestalt*, or configuration, that the interconnections are internally determined. Parts do not stand in isolation—that is, without being mutually affected by one another. Their nature and behavior are determined by their position in the web of interconnections which we call personality. Knowing the organization of the personality we can roughly predict the behavior of its units, for their action is largely determined by the character of the whole. The latter is not a mere summation of parts, but a dynamic unity characterized by a reciprocal and moving relationship of parts to one another.

Viewed in terms of the history or biography of the individual, personality is the product of an individual's past and present behavior, with the present events as the more crucial. It is not the *sum* of its traits, attitudes, values, and motives, but a *configuration* which differs from the parts yet includes them. Consequently, personality has properties which are different from the properties of its constituent units. In and of themselves the parts or units have no intelligible meaning; they derive their meaning only from the whole.

This description holds that the personality, like any unimpaired organism, is a self-regulating whole. Clearly, this is true only of a healthy personality, for as in any sick organism, defective parts become isolated and autonomous and are no longer effectively related to the larger whole. The mentally disordered personality is no longer what it was before. It is a different organization; indeed, mental disorder is somewhat of a negation or privation as Goldstein points out. The personality is no longer bearing its defect, but is mentally sick.[32]

FIELD-THEORETICAL VIEW OF PERSONALITY. We can present only the barest outline of this view in the present section. It is an extension and elaboration of the *Gestalt* point of view, with special reference to the personality, by Kurt Lewin.

In our judgment, all behavior sciences which study man as a total organism-in-environment take a field-theoretical view, even though they do not explicitly acknowledge or label it by this term. The modern psychiatrist, who seldom develops a systematic view of the normal personality, is a field theorist insofar as he studies the whole personality. Progressive psychiatry and practically all current psychologies which have been influenced by the field concept emphasize the wholeness of the human personality in a defined social situation. Murphy states the matter clearly in writing on the subject. *"We cannot define the situation operationally,"* he says, *"except in reference to the specific organism which is involved; we cannot define the organism operationally, in such a way as to obtain predictive power for behavior, except in reference to the situation. Each serves to define the other; they are definable operationally while in the organism-situation field."* [33] In other words, personality is a *biopsychosocial totality*.

From our discussion of the chief aspects of personality in this book, it should be clear that no particular determinant *alone*—heredity, family, community, or economic status—can explain the patterned growth of the personality, but only all of them together in their total impact upon the biological organism. This is the meaning of field theory when applied to the study of personality.

In contrast to "orthodox" *Gestalt* psychology, which is largely perceptually oriented, Lewin's field dynamics stresses the importance of motivation.[34] The behavioral environment of an individual is not only the environment as he perceives it, but even more the field in which his desires, aspirations, and needs are frustrated and satisfied. His behavior is deeply affected by the positive and

[32] K. Goldstein, *The organism* (New York: American Book Co., 1939), pp. 392–93. For a more psychological discussion of the part-whole relationship, see W. Köhler, *Gestalt psychology* (New York: Liveright Publishing Co., 1947); K. Koffka, *Principles of Gestalt psychology* (New York: Harcourt, Brace and Co., 1935).

[33] G. Murphy, *Personality: a biosocial approach to origins and structure* (New York: Harper & Bros., 1947), p. 891. Italics in the original.

[34] It should be pointed out that Koffka formulated a systematic *Gestalt* psychology, including motivation, based on Lewin's experimental investigations. See Koffka, *Principles of Gestalt psychology*.

negative valences of the objects toward which he is striving. Objects having a positive valence attract the individual, causing him to move in the direction of satisfying his need for them; objects having negative valence repel him, causing him to withdraw from them in order to avoid displeasure or injury. Lewin called this attraction and repulsion *locomotion,* that is, movement through a social-psychological field toward or away from a goal.

The construct of barrier is important in the development of personality. A barrier is the degree of resistance which the individual encounters in his locomotion toward a goal; it creates blockages or frustrations in his pursuit of goals. A knowledge of how the individual meets the barriers to locomotion throws important light upon the individual's personality. If a person successfully meets or overcomes the barriers to a goal, he tends to become a self-confident and balanced individual; if he fails too frequently, he may become bitter, self-doubtful, or abnormal, depending substantially on his frustration tolerance. But blockages there will be, since some frustration is inescapable. Some blocking of effort, we know, is indispensable for the development of personality. As we have said before, without any barriers and blockages, if such a condition can be said to prevail, the individual tends to be contented and mediocre, whereas in the face of too many barriers his personality tends to become warped and distorted.

Structure of the personality. In Chapter 15 we shall show in considerable detail that every normal adult personality is a dynamic structure, and that this structure is similar and variable in different individuals, thus making them alike and yet different. Lewin's analysis of the personality structure is largely concerned with contrasting the adult, child, and mentally defective in the degree of structuring. Differences in structure consist in the degree of differentiation, psychical properties, and meaningful content.

Lewin's comparison of the personality structures of the child and the adult disclosed a much more extensive differentiation of need, activity, attitude, and so forth in the adult. The child's personality is more simply unified because he participates in fewer life-spheres, or psychological spaces. As he develops and participates in an ever expanding life space, his personality becomes at once more differentiated and more unified. This fact suggests that there are degrees of differentiation and integration, depending on a person's experience and the degree of interconnection among the different units. For example, the individual who participates in different groups among whom there are few differences and cleavages, and whose behavior patterns are harmoniously executed, will be highly differentiated yet relatively integrated. Intelligence also plays a part in this matter, as we shall see in Chapter 15.

Individuals differ from one another also in their *psychical properties*, even though they may be similar in their structure or organization. Thus, as we said before, some individuals are more resilient than others, some more plastic, some more skillful in changing their roles. The child's personality is more plastic, more subject to the molding force of the environment, whereas the adult's is more elastic, being able to shift its perspectives freely when objective circumstances demand it.

Finally, persons differ in the manner in which they internalize experience. The experiences of individuals and the meaning which they attach to them differ with individuals. This is the more true the more the culture which generates them also differs. Thus, to use one of Lewin's examples, a boy living in the Russian steppes would be substantially different in his ideals and aspirations from a boy living in the Chinese quarter of San Francisco.[35]

In summary, from the field-theoretical standpoint personality is a product of the field properties which act upon the individual from within (the organic make-up) and from without (the socio-cultural environment). As the field properties acting upon the individual change, his personality also changes. Personality is thus not something which an individual *has*, but which he *is* within a spatio-temporal-cultural matrix. It is dynamic, not static. The interconnections which constitute it are changing and adjusting as new needs and different environmental variables are brought into play. Personality, in short, is a field of psychobiological and social properties, a *Gestalt* whose units are constantly changing in their relation to one another.[36]

THE HOLISTIC APPROACH

The holistic approach is not a systematic theory of personality, but a way of looking at the developing structure as a totality.[37] Its primary and continuous interest is *the person* as a whole. In this respect it differs from the *Gestalt* and field-theoretical views only

[35] For a detailed discussion of personality structure from the field-theoretical view, see K. Lewin, *A dynamic theory of personality* (New York: McGraw-Hill Book Co., Inc., 1935), Chs. 2 and 7.

[36] For additional references on Lewin's field-theoretical view, see his *Principles of topological psychology* (New York: McGraw-Hill Book Co., Inc., 1936) and his *Field theory in social science*, ed. D. Cartwright (New York: Harper & Bros., 1951).

[37] The term "holistic" was used by Jan Smuts, the South African philosopher and statesman, to describe his view of man and the world. He was particularly concerned with the resolution of human conflicts and the attainment of the *wholeness* of being. See J. C. Smuts, *Holism and evolution* (New York: The Macmillan Co., 1926).

in its more relentless emphasis on the wholeness of the complete human organism.

The holistic approach to psychological problems is a modern attitude toward an old problem, namely, the body-mind problem. Its modern germinal source is the study of mass activity and differentiation in the field of experimental embryology. In Coghill's well-known experiments it was shown that organisms develop by a process of specialization from a mass of undifferentiated protoplasm. Thus, the movements of an organism are not built up additively—not, that is to say, by a combination of local or specific reflexes—but by a process of individuation or differentiation from a larger whole. Mass action precedes specific movement. The organism reacts to stimuli as a whole; only as maturation takes place do specialized parts, like hands, fingers, feet, and toes, appear and react to stimulation.[38]

Some of the views which we have described, and the underlying tone and theme of this book, are holistic in this sense. Lewin's description of the structure of the person is clearly holistic. Coghill's developmental principle is basic to all of them. From the standpoint of this principle the adult's personality differs from the child's somewhat as specialized or discriminating behavior differs from mass action. As we have already indicated, the child's personality lacks extensive differentiation or individuation. As maturation proceeds, his personality becomes more differentiated, individualized, complex, and "rich." By the time he has reached adulthood, if his growth meanwhile is not impeded, he has developed into a highly individuated person, different from the child that he was, while yet remaining the same individual.

Although the following classification will not please everyone, we believe that we can legitimately and usefully divide holistic psychology into the *organismic,* the *personalistic,* and the *biosocial.*

THE ORGANISMIC APPROACH. Modern organismic theory in biology was most fully and systematically developed by the great German biologist Hans Driesch. While Driesch combatted the mechanistic position in biology, his view was considered by his critics as a species of vitalism, rather than a dynamic theory of the organism.[39] The vitalistic view holds that the parts and the whole

[38] G. E. Coghill, *Anatomy and the problem of behavior* (New York: The Macmillan Co., 1929).

[39] See H. Driesch, *Philosophie des organischen* (3d ed.; Leipzig: W. Engelmann, 1921). See also his interesting book, *The crisis in psychology* (Princeton, N.J.: Princeton University Press, 1925). This interpretation might be challenged, for Driesch argued that the development of a cell is a function of its position in the whole—a field-dynamic view. See further, R. S. Lillie, *General biology and philosophy of organisms* (Chicago: University of Chicago Press, 1945).

are held together by a vital principle, and that the whole organism is more than the sum of its parts. In contrast, the modern dynamic point of view conceives the total organism as different from but including the separate parts. The whole in Driesch's point of view is supersummative and posits the existence of an *élan vital,* something like that which is posited by the French philosopher, Henri Bergson.[40]

The organismic view of personality is fundamentally *psychobiological.* It deals with the individual as a *psychosomatic whole.* There are several representative statements of this point of view, but we need mention only two influential examples, the *psychobiological* standpoint of Adolf Meyer and the *unimotivational* position of Kurt Goldstein.

A leading figure in American psychiatry, Adolf Meyer from the beginning of his career held to the view that the study of personality is the investigation of the functions and activities of the total human organism. He thought the proper role of psychology and psychopathology to be "the study of the *total behavior of the individual and its integration as it hangs together as part of a life history of a personality in distinction from the life history of a single organ. . . ."* [41] A smooth functioning of the entire organism characterizes the normal, healthy individual, whereas a conflict among its constituent parts indicates a condition of abnormality.

Again, the organism is a unit or whole from the beginning. It is not separated into a mind and a body, even though for certain practical reasons we sometimes have to make the division. The person is always a psychobiological organism. By "common-sense psychiatry" Meyer wished only to suggest that therapy must be dominated by the practical demands of understanding and treating the individual. That is, the construct of whole personality should serve, not hinder, our understanding of the individual. Accordingly, if an individual's illness is physical we do not shut our eyes to the psychical aspects of his behavior; and if his illness is mental we do not suppose that there is no underlying somatic pathology responsible for it. The individual must always be seen as a *person* trying to adjust himself to a life situation. This can be effected only by knowing him in his total life history.

Kurt Goldstein has given us the most detailed and systematic statement of the organismic point of view. Although he is a

[40] H. Bergson, *L'évolution créatrice* (Paris: F. Alcan, 1925).
[41] A. Lief (ed.), *The commonsense psychiatry of Dr. Adolf Meyer* (New York: McGraw-Hill Book Co., Inc., 1948), p. 492. Italics in the original.

biological scientist and a physician, his contributions have an important relevance to the study of personality.

Goldstein's view of personality is a powerful argument against the atomization of the person which characterizes much of contemporary experimental research in psychology. Indeed, it has cogently demonstrated the fallaciousness of partial views of behavior. Goldstein has found that the whole organism reacts to stimuli, or participates in any reaction. "*With any change in one locality in the organism,*" he writes, "*simultaneous changes occur in other localities.*" [42] In other words, an individual's behavior is not a bundle of reflexes, or a pattern of reactions, but a unit, and the reacting individual is a global personality.

On the basis of this global view of the individual Goldstein differentiates between a normal and a mentally disordered person. Every organism, he tells us, engages in a constant effort to come to terms with its environment. "Certainly all creative activity originates from the living impulse of the organism to cope productively with the environment," he writes.[43] The needs and strivings of a normal or healthy individual are well-balanced and integrated. The healthy person acts holistically; he is motivated by a single, all-inclusive need: the need to achieve optimal performance of the total organism, which Goldstein calls the drive of *self-actualization.*[44]

The neurotic individual, on the other hand, lacks balance and integration of his impulses. He is swayed by isolated needs which, by virtue of their unrelatedness to the rest of his personality, produce segmental and unyielding behavior. Accordingly, he cannot come to terms with reality but rigidly persists along the same line of action even though it does not materially aid him in gratifying his needs. He is motivated by the "drive for self-preservation," which, according to Goldstein, is a pathological phenomenon. Whereas the normal or mature person comes to terms with reality, the sick person seeks only to escape it, and to find release from the need-tensions which it produces. A neurotic person experiencing tension in the sexual sphere, for instance, is forced before all else to relieve it. In sick people, "the discharge of tension is in the foreground, the tendency to *remove* any arising tension prevails." However, in healthy life, Goldstein asserts, "the result of the normal equalization process is the *formation* of a certain level

[42] K. Goldstein, *The organism* (New York: American Book Co., 1939), p. 213. Italics in the original.

[43] *Ibid.*, p. 335.

[44] *Ibid.*, p. 197; also K. Goldstein, *Human nature in the light of psychopathology* (Cambridge, Mass.: Harvard University Press, 1940), p. 146.

of tension, namely, that which makes possible further ordered activity." [45] For this reason Goldstein rejects Freud's contention that life is dominated by the need to release tension. The healthy individual can enjoy the "pleasure of tension." [46] His point of view also contrasts sharply with the explanation of human behavior in terms of need-reduction, the basic tenet of stimulus-response psychology.

THE PERSONALISTIC APPROACH. The chief proponents of this approach to personality are William Stern in Germany and Gordon Allport in the United States. Stern's discussion is heavily freighted with metaphysical ideas, in contrast to Allport's psychological interpretation (though one rich in penetrating philosophical overtones). [47]

According to Stern, psychology must begin with the whole person, not a particular aspect such as mind or emotion. But this whole person is an organized totality in varying degrees; it is a mistake to think of him as a completely unified structure. Personality is not only a *Gestalt* but also an *Ungestalt* (formlessness). Order or integration is achieved slowly, and it is never complete, for every individual is to some extent characterized by inconsistencies. Thus, Stern does not commit the frequent error of holistic psychology of overestimating the unity of the personality.

Still more important is Stern's emphasis on the spontaneous and creative capacity of every individual. As he perceives him, the individual does not react passively to the environment; rather, every normal person makes constructive and creative adjustments, especially in the form of conscious planning of and striving for previsioned ends. Conscious goal-striving is an important attribute of the human person. His creative quality is most characteristically manifested in human *thought*. While Stern recognizes the adjustive value of thought and stresses the rational character of man, he is much more deeply impressed by what he believes to be an *active need* for thinking. This fact again calls attention to the active nature of the person, in contrast to his passive and largely adjustive character, as he is described in purely reaction psychologies. [48]

[45] *The organism*, pp. 195–96.

[46] *Ibid.*, p. 333.

[47] The very ambitious student with a good command of the German language will find Stern's three-volume discussion absorbing in *Person und Sache: System der philosophischen Weltanschauung* (3 vols.; Leipzig: S. A. Barth, 1924).

[48] See W. Stern, *General psychology from the personalistic standpoint*, trans. H. D. Spoerl (New York: The Macmillan Co., 1938). For an excellent brief statement of Stern's personalistic psychology see G. W. Allport, The personalistic psychology of William Stern, *Char. &. Pers.*, 5 (1937), 231–46.

Although we include Gordon Allport's approach to personality in the personalistic category, it has the enduring quality of defying satisfactory classification. In this respect it represents the fundamental spirit of Allport's whole psychological position, namely, an uncompromising emphasis on the uniqueness of every personality. His view also resembles *Verstehendepsychologie*, which aims to *understand* and not merely to describe the personality of another. Contrary to those psychologists who affirm that uniqueness cannot be studied scientifically, Allport has based many of his observations on empirical evidence. Whether his position is scientific or not depends mostly on the conception of science which one espouses. If our exposition of the dominant outlook of modern science is valid, as we think it is, then Allport's idiographic approach to psychology is valid. At any rate, Allport has shown a fine discernment in combining humanistic insight with scientific detachment.

Although something of Allport's spirit is found in practically every one of his publications, his full-bodied view of personality is developed in two of his well-known volumes: *Personality: a psychological interpretation*, and *Becoming: basic considerations for a psychology of personality*.[49]

Allport states his position clearly when he writes: "Somewhere in the interstices of its nomothetic laws psychology has lost the human person as we know him in everyday life. To rescue him and to reinstate him as a psychological datum in his own right is the avowed purpose of the psychology of personality." [50]

We can properly begin with Allport's well-known and frequently quoted definition of personality. "Personality," he says, "is the dynamic organization within the individual of those psychophysical systems that determine his unique adjustments to his environment." [51] The psychophysical systems are the psychobiological dispositions, or *traits*, which "provoke those adjustive and expressive acts by which the personality comes to be known." However, man's adjustive acts are not merely reactive. Adjustive acts are also, and even more importantly, spontaneous and creative. Adjustment to the environment "involves *mastery* as well as passive adaptation." [52]

Finally, personality is also unique. The adjustive and creative acts of every person differ in time, place, and quality. Every trait of an individual is concretely and uniquely his own. In this emphasis on the uniqueness of individual traits Allport differs markedly

49 G. W. Allport, *Personality* (New York: Henry Holt & Co., 1937); *Becoming* (New Haven: Yale University Press, 1955).

50 *Personality*, p. 558.

51 *Ibid.*, p. 48.

52 *Ibid.*, pp. 49, 50.

from most of his professional colleagues. However, it attests to the vitality and influence of this formulation to note that an increasing number of personality psychologists have come around to the same view.

The dynamic and creative character of personality is also brought out in Allport's theory of functional autonomy, to which we refer on several occasions in this book. He takes issue with all those psychologists who attribute all present behavior to past conditioning. In his view, this approach reduces every act, no matter how individual and unique, to a limited number of universal drives, or to behavior learned in the process of need reduction. He agrees that motives are products of antecedent events, but he holds that they may become functionally independent of them. (See Chapter 9.) In contrast to the Freudian view in particular, Allport maintains that a motive cannot be understood solely on the basis of a child's early experience of need-gratification or need-frustration, but also needs to be studied in the light of knowledge of his present experience. Adult motives are thus not merely later expressions of infantile satisfactions and frustrations. A person can and does continually recreate himself; he is not merely the passive and inevitable victim of his past; his adult personality is not archaic, but consciously intentional and future-oriented. This "propriate striving," which is a unique trait of the human personality, makes the unification of personality possible. To quote Allport's own summary of the intentional nature of personality: "the most comprehensive units in personality are broad intentional dispositions, future-pointed." [53]

Allport's view points up the incongruity of the contemporary emphasis on antecedent conditions when it is contrasted with the vitality of man's determination to move into the future. In this connection he wisely observes: "People, it seems, are busy leading their lives into the future, whereas psychology, for the most part, is busy tracing them into the past." [54]

THE BIOSOCIAL APPROACH. Despite his broadly eclectic position Gardner Murphy's view of personality is fundamentally holistic in its consistent emphasis on the total personality. It is, as a matter of fact, a deft combination of the basic tenets of field theory, which also stresses the wholeness of the personality, and the holistic approach. This is seen in the concept of *biosocial:* the integration of the biological organism and the social field in which it func-

[53] *Becoming,* p. 92.
[54] *Becoming,* p. 51.

tions.[55] Since Murphy's exposition of personality is many-sided, requiring more than nine hundred pages to develop, we can hardly do justice to it here. Accordingly, we shall select those features which call attention to the holistic nature of the personality.

Murphy's view is first of all a *motivational* psychology. But motives are not as specific in Murphy's system as in many other points of view. They are, broadly, any energizing process in the *biosocial* organism. Accordingly, it is artificial to draw a sharp line between biological drives and social motives. "We can make no use . . . of the convenient suggestion that there are *biological* needs and social needs"; he writes, "for the social proves to be just as biological a reality as anything else in the world." [56]

Canalization is an important factor in the growth and development of personality. Although Murphy does not neglect the role of the conventional conditioning process, a more important learning feature in personality formation is canalization, the process whereby the child's biological energies are invested in increasingly specific modes of expression. Thus, using his own example, while milk tends to gratify an infant's hunger practically everywhere, the kind of food which will later satisfy it will depend on the food habits of the family or community. This canalizing process is a progressive narrowing of the infant's hunger drive into socially-conditioned modes of satisfaction.

This fact calls attention to the force of *socialization* in the formation of personality, or the role of culture in shaping it. In this respect, Murphy's discussion does not differ from our analysis of the place of cultural conditioning in personality formation in Chapters 6 and 10.

Another important element in Murphy's conceptualization of personality is *role behavior*. As we pointed out in several places in this book, personality may be conceived as a more or less consistent configuration of roles. These roles are largely prescribed by the group in which we live. They are ways of behaving in the light of other people's expectations and are important factors in the development of sympathy and regard for others. We are socialized in no small degree to the extent that we play our roles well and skillfully.

Finally, personality can be conceptualized most adequately in the language of *field theory*. Since we have already expounded this theory, it is unnecessary to add more to what we have already

[55] See G. Murphy, *Personality: a biosocial approach to origins and structure* (New York: Harper & Bros., 1947).

[56] *Ibid.*, p. 769.

written.[57] It is sufficient to point out that, conceived in terms of motivation, canalization, role behavior, and field influences, *personality is a dynamic continuum of biosocial events.*

OTHER "HOLISTIC" VIEWS. We must also at least mention three other figures who are representative, each in his own distinctive way, of the holistic approach to personality. They are Prescott Lecky, A. H. Maslow, and Carl R. Rogers. We do not expound their views with the fullness which they clearly deserve because, first, Lecky's view has not been widely assimilated in personality psychology, even though his concept of self-consistency is being freely borrowed; second, Maslow's ideas, while seminal and hence exceedingly important, are so fluid and ever growing that they obscure his important contributions to personality theory; and third, Roger's view is so much a part of his technique of therapy that one cannot write about one without writing about the other.

Personality is the central fact of psychology, according to Lecky, and the source of all unity in human behavior. It might be said that, just as Goldstein postulated the existence of a single unifying drive of self-actualization, so for Lecky there is only one basic need of self-consistency. Man does not basically seek pleasure, or the gratification of physical desires, but the satisfaction which comes from the attainment of wholeness and unity of the self. Therefore, he will reject all forms of value and experience which impair his personal identity, and aspire for those satisfactions that attain and secure it. If man does not always succeed in attaining personal unity, it is not because he is not constantly striving for that unity, but because the forces of enculturation too often inhibit it.[58]

Maslow's view of personality does not differ fundamentally from other holistic views, but it is, nevertheless, essentially his own. Perhaps more than any other American psychologist except Allport, Maslow stresses the growth and self-actualizing features of the personality. Like Allport, Maslow is much more interested in the healthy than in the sick person, even though he is coauthor with Mittelmann of a textbook of abnormal psychology.[59] His central ideas regarding the nature of personality are found in a collection of articles recently published.[60] At the same time, some of his

[57] See the section, Field-theoretical View of Personality, above, including Murphy's phrasing of field theory on p. 60.

[58] P. Lecky, *Self-consistency: a theory of personality* (New York: Island Press, 1945).

[59] A. H. Maslow and B. Mittelmann, *Principles of abnormal psychology* (Rev. ed.; New York: Harper & Bros., 1951).

[60] A. H. Maslow, *Motivation and personality* (New York: Harper & Bros., 1954).

most arresting and stimulating ideas are found in his occasional papers, informal and unpublished.

Maslow conceives personality as the organized striving of a person to be himself: to grow and actualize himself. This striving is a process of maturation, of the continuous, never-ending assertion of man's potentialities. This striving for self-actualization is potentially present in all people, but is greatly inhibited by the forces of socialization. Thus, the sick personality is one which has ceased to resist enculturation, has become conventional and noncreative in his attitude toward himself and in his relationship with others. He has become more defensive than actualizing, more self-impairing than self-enhancing; he has stopped growing, become smug and self-satisfied. The following statement describes this situation eloquently: "The lack of meditativeness and inwardness, of real conscience and real values, is a standard American personality defect; a shallowness, a superficial living on the surface of life, a living by other people's opinions rather than by one's own native, inner voice." [61]

In summary, the healthy, mature personality lives in accordance with its inborn tendencies which it is continuously trying to actualize in thought and overt behavior. These native tendencies are positive, constructive, and good. The unhealthy and immature personality inhibits his own growth motive, or is prevented by the dispiriting and negative forces of a defective socialization from giving it full expression.

One of the major and most penetrating contemporary theories of the self is that of Carl R. Rogers. The complexity of his view of the self is at once obvious in the fact that it is both a theory of the self and of psychotherapy; and that it is similar to the holistic views which we have delineated and yet is at the same time original.

The phenomenological character of the self is seen in Rogers' stress on the view that the individual can know himself only within the framework of his own perceptual organization. *The self exists as it is perceived by the individual in his own perceptual field.* Again, the self is an organismic structure, a totality, never a mere arrangement of parts. It is biosocial in that Rogers believes that while the self is a product of its perceptual and social environment, the manner in which it actualizes itself is determined by the organism's heredity. The self, finally, is conceived holistically, not only because it is an organism, but even more because it responds to its ambient world as an *ordered whole striving to reach the goals*

[61] A. H. Maslow, Personality problems and personality growth (unpublished manuscript), p. 7.

of its own choosing. The self is thus no mere reacting organism, but a goal-directed being; it is not a stimulus-response configuration, but a pattern or field in which changes in one part initiate changes in all other parts, and therefore in the entire organism.

The self is formed in the individual's "evaluational interactions with others" . . . "an organized, fluid, but consistent conceptual pattern of perceptions. . . ." This process begins in infancy, when the baby develops sufficient discrimination to identify himself as an object and to differentiate himself from other objects in his environment. In this process of discrimination between self and "not-self," the child also internalizes or introjects the values of those around him and makes them his own. The values of the environment and of the persons who constitute it form an important aspect in the growth and development of the self. Furthermore, these values are important in Rogers' system of psychotherapy, for an essential element in the treatment of a disturbed or distorted self is the recognition that conflict of values between children and their parents is a vital source of psychological ill health. According to Rogers, good psychotherapy consists in the sympathetic recognition by the therapist of the distortions of experience that characterize the unsoundly structured self.[62] Client-centered therapy is thus a form of psychological treatment which places the self at the very core of the attempt to "reorganize" or "restructure" the total personality. Thus client-centered therapy is also a diagnostic technique. In client-centered therapy both the therapist and the client learn to classify the latter more correctly, and to diagnose him in veridical as opposed to distorted terms.

CONCLUSION

We have presented to the reader summaries of a considerable variety of views regarding the nature of personality. While the experience of reading so many different versions of the same phenomenon may be disheartening to the beginner, it has its compensations, too. He should have found in this chapter further demonstration of the oft-repeated observation that human personality is too complex and variable to be pressed into a neat little formula or a tight little theory. He should by now have become aware that the men who have labored to bring order into the complex and seemingly unrelated aspects of human nature are men of exceptional ability seriously bent on disclosing the mainsprings of human behavior—an exciting scientific enterprise. Their for-

[62] C. R. Rogers, *Client-centered therapy* (Boston: Houghton Mifflin Co., 1951), p. 503.

mulations attest to the breadth and richness of personality and to
the keenness of the minds which are continuously attempting to
penetrate the so-called "mysteries of the human mind."

At the same time, our exposition has revealed that beneath the
rich variety of views, and the individual predilections of the
authors, there is a much more substantial core of agreement than
a superficial acquaintance with the theories would lead one to believe. When they are stripped of the special verbiage, particular
emphases, and misinterpretations which time has accumulated, all
the approaches are to a large degree concerned with the personality as a whole. In this respect it is not altogether improper to
describe them as holistic. Freud's topographical division of the
person is more a heuristic device than an actuality. As we have said
before, Freud was always interested in the whole man rather his
subdivisions. If he found conflicts and cleavages in man's personality, that fact only confirmed what everyone must agree to be
true—that the whole man is also torn by conflicting interests and
desires.

Gestalt psychology, and more particularly its field-theoretical
variant, has been concerned with totality or wholeness from the
time of its inception. Field theory stresses the wholeness of man
in a total social-psychological life space. It does not account for
personality in terms of original drives only; its focus is on the
organism's interaction with other organisms in a field. Freud, too,
in his later rethinking of the doctrine of instincts, gave increasing
importance to the influence of environmental forces. Although he
never developed the idea beyond an occasional bare assertion, in
the last major revisions of his system Freud conceived the innate
urges as convenient scientific fictions. In so doing he brought
his ideas in line with the dominant trend in contemporary psychology, namely, the hypothesizing of "entities" or "forces" as *constructs* for testing an hypothesis. In this connection Freud wrote
clearly and unequivocally: "The theory of the instincts is, as it
were, our mythology. The instincts are mythical beings, superb in
their indefiniteness. In our work we cannot for a moment overlook
them, and yet we are never certain that we are seeing them
clearly." [63]

In view of what we have said concerning the holistic approach
it is superfluous to repeat that the total personality is central in
Freud's formulation. Both the organismic and the personalistic,
and also Murphy's, Lecky's, and Maslow's views, deal not with
aspects of the total individual but with the entire person. They

[63] *New introductory lectures*, p. 131.

deal with people, not with abstractions. Allport perhaps more than the others, is deeply impressed by man's individuality and uniqueness. Many other psychologists are now recognizing the importance of man's uniqueness, even though they do not always recognize or acknowledge their indebtedness to Allport.

CHAPTER **3**

Theory of Personality: Typologies

In Boris Pasternak's novel, *Doctor Zhivago*, Zhivago makes the following observation: "It's a good thing when a man is different from your image of him. It shows that he isn't a type. If he were, it would be the end of him as a man. But if you can't place him in a category, it means that at least a part of him is what a human being ought to be. He has risen above himself, he has a grain of immortality." [1]

This statement sets the stage at once for our own view and for the predicament which faces every psychologist when he tries to do justice to the uniqueness of man and to the need to organize our knowledge about him into relatively stable categories. The problem of personality types is a controversial subject. The controversy is an aspect of the larger dispute over the specificity and generality of behavior, over traits and syndromes, over idiographic and nomothetic explanations of behavior. There are, clearly, no "pure" types; and some of the forms described in this chapter are not generally recognized as being psychological types.

Some of the objections to the theory of types are based on misconceptions regarding its objectives. Typology does *not* affirm the existence of isolable personality categories, but only of dominant trends within some personalities which are very similar to the dominant trends in other personalities. Thus, an introvert does not differ from an extravert in *kind,* but in the degree of the

[1] B. Pasternak, *Doctor Zhivago* (New York: Pantheon Books, Inc., 1958), p. 296.

dominant expression of the personality of each. Every introvert resembles an extravert in differing ways, but his introversion overshadows his outgoing tendencies.

We believe that typologies, with all their faults, have a useful function to perform in the psychology of personality. The theory of wholes or *Gestalten,* of the organization of parts into structured fields, suggests the existence of more or less stable types. A type, from this point of view, is an interconnection of traits, attitudes, sentiments, and so forth. Traits are not distributed in a random fashion; and as we shall see in Chapter 15, they tend to cluster into larger patterns or structures. These relatively orderly arrangements of the parts into wholes are what we mean to express by the concept of types. Just as field theory does not, contrary to some misconceptions, deny the importance of parts, so it does not reject the notion of specific traits. It does, however, argue that the parts do not stand in isolation but attain meaning and function only in an organized whole. In the same manner it claims that specific traits in and of themselves do not give us a complete view of personality. Personality type may be thought of as the larger whole of which specific traits are concrete manifestations.

A REVIEW OF SOME TYPE THEORIES

The problem of personality types, of "character" and "temperament," is very old. Greek philosophers, notably Plato and Aristotle, were interested in delineating different types of men. Perhaps the earliest, and certainly the best known, classification of men into types was that of the Greek physician, Hippocrates. His division of men into sanguine, phlegmatic, choleric, and melancholic, while scientifically worthless, was a serious effort to develop a typology, and shows that men then as now tried to classify persons into general categories on the basis of physical characteristics.[2] Theophrastus, a pupil of Aristotle, is well known for his vivid verbal portraits of a large variety of character types based upon a keen observation of people over a long period of time.

Gnostic philosophy, according to Jung, established three types which corresponded roughly to the three basic psychological processes: thinking, feeling, and sensation.[3] Mediaeval philoso-

[2] It should be noted in passing that Hippocrates' typology finds a modern counterpart in the scientific work of Pavlov, the Russian physiologist, and his associates. See I. P. Pavlov, *Conditioned reflexes* (London: Oxford University Press, 1927); J. S. Rosenthal, Typology in the light of the theory of conditioned reflexes, *Char. & Pers.,* 1 (1932), 56–69.

[3] C. G. Jung, *Psychological types* (New York: Harcourt, Brace and Co., 1923), p. 18.

phers and theologians, too, tried their hand at describing different types of character or temperament. Later, outstanding literary figures, such as Chaucer, Ben Jonson, Joseph Addison, Richard Steele, and Samuel Johnson, engaged in writing descriptions of character types.[4] German poetry, according to Jung, has been deeply preoccupied with the problem, and German psychiatry from the very beginning has given it serious attention.[5]

While Francis Galton was probably the first to offer a quantitative scientific theory of individual differences, a great deal of objective work on this problem was being carried on by psychiatrists and psychiatrically oriented psychologists at the end of the nineteenth century.[6] Although most of the contributions were on personality types in abnormal people, they had considerable relevance to the problem of normal psychological types.

Kraepelin, the "father" of modern psychiatry, early made a distinction between the psychoses of manic-depression and dementia praecox. This dichotomy led to Bleuler's division into manic-depressive and schizophrenic types. Janet established a dichotomy for the psychoneuroses, dividing them into hysteria and psychasthenia.[7] Although these dichotomies are no longer in vogue, they have given rise to "a rather elaborate scheme of typological formulations which has influenced, often directly but more often in indirect and subtle ways, the development of psychiatric and psychological thought about problems of personality."[8] Some of these we shall discuss later.

PSYCHOANALYTIC TYPES. Psychoanalysts, particularly Freud, have made some interesting, if not widely acceptable, formulations of personality types. The *oral-erotic* type is one in which the libido, or psychosexual energy, is discharged through oral activities. There are two forms of the oral-erotic type: the oral-passive and the oral-sadistic. The *oral-passive* type is a product of frustration of the sucking impulse in the infant, who remains fixated at the sucking stage. When he reaches maturity he persists on a level of infantile dependency in his strivings, depending on his parents or other adults instead of on himself. He is basically an immature

---

[4] D. W. Mackinnon, The structure of personality, in J. McV. Hunt, ed., *Personality and the behavior disorders* (New York: The Ronald Press Co., 1944), Vol. 1, p. 13.

[5] Jung, *Psychological types*, Chs. 2–6. For a comprehensive discussion of psychological types see A. A. Roback, *The psychology of character* (New York: Harcourt, Brace and Co., 1931.

[6] For Galton's work see his *Inquiries into human faculty and its development* (London: The Macmillan Co., 1883).

[7] Mackinnon, The structure of personality, p. 16.

[8] *Ibid.*, p. 17.

individual. The *oral-sadistic* type also owes his make-up to frustration of the sucking impulse in infancy, but instead of compensating for it passively he develops an active outlet. He becomes pessimistic, bitter, and suspicious, exploits others for his own good, and treats them cruelly. Sarcastic and malicious people are usually of this type.

The *anal-erotic* is a second main type posited in psychoanalytical writings. He is a product of the fixation of the libido upon the anal functions resulting usually from faulty toilet training, particularly oversevere demands by the parents for early sphincter control by the child. As a consequence of excessive concern by the parents for the child's toilet activities, the individual develops an obsessive demand for order and meticulousness and grows up into a stubborn and stingy adult. The preoccupation with order and cleanliness is derived from the praise or blame which the child received during bowel movements, and the stubbornness and stinginess is related to the child's pleasure in withholding his feces in order to please his parents. If his reaction to the demand for anal continence was resentment and anger, he tends to develop an aggressive attitude which is described as *anal-sadistic*. The Japanese and the German basic personalities have been given by some writers as illustrations, if not confirmations, of the Freudian concept of the anal-erotic personality type.

The *phallic* type is a product of fixation at the phallic stage of libidinal development, the stage which we described in the preceding chapter as the latency period, the period of childish and immature sexuality. The phallic individual is a self-centered, self-absorbed, and exhibitionistic person. Freud calls him the *narcissistic* type. The narcissistic individual is invariably overambitious and highly conceited. His egocentrism and conceit create an imperious demand for adulation and attention. If the attention is not forthcoming, he becomes moody and fretful and his feeling of self-esteem suffers deflation.[9]

CONSTITUTIONAL TYPES. Kretschmer's and Sheldon's types, based on the correlations between constitutional make-up and psychological patterns of reaction, are discussed in Chapter 5. Their works are more properly described as primarily correlational studies, rather than studies of psychological types. That is, while their investigations have been used to illustrate, if not to corroborate, the existence of psychological types, they were mainly concerned with establishing correlations between constitutional structures and

[9] For a detailed and interpretive discussion of the foregoing types see S. Freud, *Collected papers* (London: Hogarth Press, Ltd., 1950), Vol. 2.

personality organization. For these reasons they are not included in the present chapter on personality types. However, the reader should profit from a review of these types and should try to relate them to the general discussion of the present chapter.

VALUE-MOTIVATED TYPES. In the preceding chapter we made passing reference to *Verstehendepsychologie*—the psychology of understanding. This view, it will be recalled, strives not only to describe personality, but even more, to understand it—to grasp the uniqueness of every individual. The point of view represented by this school is the wholeness and uniqueness of the personality. Despite the emphasis on the uniqueness of the person the psychology of understanding posits the existence of ideal types of individuals motivated by a consistent set of philosophical or ethical values.

Spranger's types. The best-known formulation of this point of view is that of Eduard Spranger.[10] It is an interesting fact which should not be overlooked, that Spranger's value-types, although philosophical constructions, have served as a basis for an important and well-known empirical study of values and their relation to personality.[11] Spranger's value-types were considered as ideal types or hypothetical extremes to which different individuals approximated in various degrees.

Spranger posited the existence of six value-systems which serve as philosophies along which personalities may be unified: theoretic, economic, aesthetic, social, political, and religious.[12]

The theoretic man is fundamentally motivated by the search for truth. When the theoretical attitude dominates an individual, he views the world as an ordered whole. He has only one passion: the desire for objective knowledge; he has only one kind of longing: "to solve a problem, explain a question or formulate a theory." Spranger writes about him feelingly, even rapturously. The theoretically motivated man "despairs when ignorant and rejoices over a purely theoretic discovery even if it should be an insight which would mean his death. He exhausts himself as a physical being to give birth to a purely intellectual world based on reason." He cares for nothing but the truth. He dwells in an eternal world, his eyes gazing into the distant future and sometimes comprehending whole epochs of the world's history.[13] While the theoretic man is fundamentally an intellectual, he need not necessarily be a professional

---

[10] See E. Spranger, *Types of men: the psychology and ethics of personality*, trans. P. J. W. Pigors (Halle: Max Niemeyer Verlag, 1928).

[11] See P. E. Vernon and G. W. Allport, A test for personal values, *J. abnorm. soc. Psychol.*, 26 (1931), 231–48.

[12] These are fully discussed in Spranger, *Types of men*, Pt. 2, pp. 109–246.

[13] *Ibid.*, pp. 111–12.

philosopher or scientist. He is not judged solely by his intellectual achievements but by his basic attitudes. It is only necessary that he view life "with the eyes of a reflective observer." [14]

The economic man is motivated by practical and utilitarian interests. While the theoretic man seeks truth for itself, the economic man is interested in truth only insofar as it can be used. The economic man seeks only such truth or wisdom as can be utilized or applied to the business of production and consumption. Even his interest in other people is utilitarian rather than unselfish and charitable. He sees them as producers, consumers, or buyers. Moral qualities are appraised economically: they are important only in the form of thrift, industry, or efficiency—in short, in the form of vocational-economic abilities. The behavior of the economic man is determined by the satisfaction of his wants and needs. Even his religious attitudes are colored and suffused by the economic motive. The economic man's god is "the owner of all wealth," "the giver of all useful gifts." Mammon is the highest god. Moreover, the religious beliefs of the economic man, especially the speculator or the stockbroker, is dominated by superstitious beliefs in fate and chance. He secretly worships a power which he thinks is in control of "the great world-lottery." Just as the theoretic man need not be a formal scientist or philosopher, so the economic man need not engage in purely economic activities. It is only necessary that he prefer utility to other values, and that he see everything as a means for self-preservation and for rendering life more pleasant.[15]

The aesthetic man enjoys every value for its own sake. He looks at life through "form," or aesthetic standards. In contrast to the theoretic man, who views life through abstract concepts, the aesthetic man looks at it through the "mythological" method. Compared with the economic man who values aesthetic objects for their utility, the aesthetic man values them as pure beings, for their beauty, symmetry, and form. He approaches life from a highly individualistic point of view; "he sees everywhere that which enlarges his own inner power." He interprets experience not according to concepts of general validity, as the theoretic man does, nor according to practical considerations, as does the economic man, but according to individual standards of fitness. Unlike either of them, he questions the conventional picture of reality and sees it "originally," that is, in its natural color and plasticity—in his own unique way. Although he is highly individualistic, the aesthetic man is not unsocial; rather, he tends to be eccentric and self-

---

14 *Ibid.*, p. 124.
15 *Ibid.*, pp. 133–39.

important in his social relations. Individualism, not self-denial, is his attitude. His relation to others is not so much sympathy as empathy: his response to them is not a desire to help them but to enjoy them as aesthetic objects. Finally, just as the theoretic man need not be a scientist or philosopher nor the economic man a toiler for his daily bread, so the aesthetic man need not be an artist or poet; it is only necessary that his inner life be organized on the basis of beauty and aesthetic harmony.[16]

The social man is characterized by selflessness. The organizing principle of his life is sympathy. In its highest reaches this sympathy is love. The social man finds his self in and enriched by the self of another. He lives through others rather than through himself. This may attain such heights that the social man sees his own value only as it is reflected in others. "In perfect love," writes Spranger, "the limits of individuation disappear. The ego feeling and the alter feeling, self-hood and self-sacrifice, liberty and renunciation coincide." [17] The social man differs from the theoretic, economic, and aesthetic individuals in his view of other people. The theoretic man views others predominantly in the cold light of objectivity and impartiality. The economic man sees them largely as means to an end. The aesthetic man perceives them through aesthetic self-enjoyment. The social man forgets his self and is ready to renounce life "for the sake of loving." In Orientals, this attitude encompasses all living things, including plants and animals, "as a veneration of the sanctity of life on every level." Love is the highest law. Accordingly, the social man, when he carries his attitude to its ultimate expression, recognizes no legal state and no formal justice, only "an anarchism of love and fraternity." [18]

The political man realizes himself most fully in power relations, in relations of domination over others. While the term "political" has been used to describe him, the German *Machtmensch* describes him more adequately, for he need not confine his power activities to the political arena alone. It is only necessary that he affirm his own ego, vitality, and energy as an "original life urge" rather than as a rational purpose. Nor is the person who finds expression for his power needs solely in political activity necessarily crass and despotic. Modern political liberalism has enhanced the ethics and justice of the political leader in his relations to the masses. The "good" politician is the man who takes human beings for what they are rather than for what they ought to or might be.

16 *Ibid.*, pp. 148–56.
17 *Ibid.*, p. 173.
18 *Ibid.*, pp. 174–77.

Like the economic man, the political man uses others as means to an end, but for a different reason. The political man is not usually interested in others as consumers, but as persons whom he can dominate and manipulate for the enjoyment and satisfaction he gets from his influence over them. Unlike the theoretic man who seeks truth for its own sake, the political man uses it as a political weapon. To the political man, truth and falsehood may become mere expediencies; they may be equated, if that is necessary, to serve the desire for power. The aesthetic is only "a link in the chain of means which are to serve the development of power." Thus the symbol of power—an eagle, a sword, or a swastika—always embodies something resplendent and awe-inspiring. Music may be used in the service of martial glory. Constructive imagination—the imagination of the artist—can conceive "great designs or world-reforming thoughts." Finally, while love and power are not mutually exclusive, unlike the social man who controls and influences others through the power of love, the political man tries to control them through domination or coercion. Everything must serve his will to power.[19]

The religious man is one who seeks absolute unity with the highest values. In his mind, every experience is related to the total value of life. The need for oneness or unity dominates his entire being. He is restless and dissatisfied, and unless he is searching for the highest value in his experience, he is "homeless, torn, and despairing." But whoever finds the highest value in himself experiences "salvation and blessedness."[20] Again, the religious man is fundamentally a mystic, of which there are three types, according to Spranger. The *immanent* mystic makes an absolute affirmation of life. He finds something divine in every aspect of life and enters into each with great vitality and enthusiasm. "He rejoices in the infinite divine beauty of the universe and feels himself like God as a world-reflecting monad."[21] The *transcendental* mystic finds the highest value in "utter negation of the world." He has no interest in finite and sense experiences. He mortifies the flesh and cultivates "the capacity for ecstasy"—the ability to see the imperceptible and to communicate with God. He is forever striving for inner vision and for the love of God. He is the truly holy man who scorns everything that is not divine. The third type of mystic is an *intermediate* one, in whom the search for unity and the divine is present but less extreme than in the other two.

[19] *Ibid.*, pp. 190–95.
[20] *Ibid.*, p. 212.
[21] *Ibid.*, p. 214.

Morris' "Paths of Life." Charles W. Morris, an American philosopher with keen interest in the problems of human behavior, has found that men can be classified on the basis of their choice of a particular "design for living," or "path of life." Using Sheldon's somatotypes, he has made the interesting discovery that the path of life which a person follows is related to his constitutional type. According to him, there are seven ways of life, which we shall describe briefly.[22]

Path 1 is that in which the individual actively participates in the social life of his community. He seeks to understand life but not primarily to change it. He cherishes order, refinement, and clarity. Vulgarity, indulgence, and irrationality are avoided. He believes in slow and careful social change. Moderation in all things is an essential element of this way of life, and this can be obtained by intelligence and restraint.

Path 2 is a way of life in which self-sufficiency, meditation, and self-knowledge are man's chief aspirations. The individual so motivated seeks privacy and tries to reduce or moderate all desires which require dependence on physical and social factors outside himself. He tends to shy away from intimate associations with social groups and has little interest in the control of his environment. He finds the center of life within himself.

Path 3 is a style of life in which a sympathetic concern for other persons is central. Affection is the basic motive and gives significance to life. The individual so motivated is free from greed, from emphasis on sexual passion, from the desire for power over persons and things, and from an excessive emphasis upon intellect, for these are barriers to sympathy and love for others.

Path 4 is characterized by abandonment to the sensuous enjoyment of life. A person who follows this path lets himself go and is deeply receptive to things and persons. He takes delight in life, avoids self-sacrifice, and seeks both sociality and solitude, for they are both necessary for the good life.

Path 5 is a design for living which affirms the need for man to merge himself with society and actively to join with others for the realization of common ends. Restraint, concern for oneself, solitude, and meditation are avoided, for they hinder the attainment of social solidarity. A person works with others to achieve a pleasant

[22] See C. W. Morris, Individual differences and cultural patterns, in C. Kluckhohn and H. A. Murray (eds.), *Personality in nature, society, and culture* (New York: Alfred A. Knopf, Inc., 1948), pp. 141–43. Regrettably, this article is omitted in the second edition of 1953.

social life, and even brings pressure on those who do not share these goals.

Path 6 stresses the need for activity. Man's fate depends on action, not on feelings and thoughts. Man must solve his problems as they arise, and he must continually improve the world if he is to progress. He relies on science and technology to change the world, not on wishes and pious hopes. "The good is the enemy of the better."

Path 7 combines in balanced form the attractive features of the other six ways of life without being dominated by any one of them. Each mode of life is appropriate at different times, and one lives in accordance with that mode which fits in with the demands of the occasion, but they interact dynamically. The goal of life, in short, is found in the "dynamic integration of enjoyment, action, and contemplation."

Morris tried to see what relationship existed in a sample of 59 persons (27 men and 32 women) between path of life and mesomorphy (physiques dominated by bone, muscle, and connective tissue development).[23] He found a general direction for the first six paths of life. Paths 5 and 6 stress the importance for the individual of power and control over others and his desire to change society. Path 6 emphasizes the reconstruction of society by means of science and technology. Both are thus "strongly power-oriented." These two paths appeal very strongly to the highly mesomorphic individual, but have little or no appeal to the person who rates low in mesomorphy. The latter finds Paths 2, 1, and 4 most attractive. Morris concludes that the path of life which expresses the power ideal seems to be in proportion to the amount of mesomorphy.

Paradoxically, however, he found that Path 3, which stresses sympathy for others, eschews aggressiveness, and devaluates the power ideal, is preferred by those high in mesomorphy. This is contrary to expectation. Morris argues that it is possible that if more data had been on hand those who chose Path 3 would be lower in mesomorphy. He gives several explanations of the inconsistency and consoles himself by the assertion that Path 3 "is not so far from the power ideal as appears on the surface. For in advising sympathetic helpfulness to other persons it opens the door to power tactics. To do things for other people slips easily into attempts to make other persons do what one believes they should

[23] Something of the relationship between path of life and the other somatotypes (endomorphic and ectomorphic) can be learned from this study by inference. See the discussion of Kretschmer's and Sheldon's constitutional psychology in Chapter 5.

do. Advocating that other persons give up the ideal of power is one way of enhancing one's own power over them." [24]

SOCIOLOGICAL TYPES. Sociologists who have been concerned with the problem of types have been less prone to commit the error of thinking of types as if they described consistent behavior. They have thought of types of individuals in terms of role behavior. A person is introverted, say, whenever he assumes a certain role in his relation to other persons. In the presence of strangers he might be shy and reserved; in the presence of his intimate friends he might be relaxed and friendly. In each situation he acts a different role, but he is not *consistently* an introvert.

The sociologist's approach to types thus involves a distinction between *personality* types and *social* types. Personality type refers to the characteristic organization of traits which develop early and are more persistent. It changes markedly more during the early years when it is being formed than later, although it may be somewhat changed by the individual himself when he becomes aware of and dissatisfied with it. Personality type is more effectively determined by heredity, constitution, and early sociocultural conditioning. Social type is derived entirely from the status which a person has in his group and the roles he plays therein. The dramatic changes in personality which are sometimes reported are changes in attitude rather than personality type. Thus, when Saint Paul on the road to Damascus was converted from a critic of Christianity to an ardent proselyter for it, he changed not his personality but his attitudes.[25]

Social type is the more changeable aspect of the total personality. It is changeable because it is not a pattern of traits which are early stamped into the person, but a set of roles which he plays and which are recognized by members of his group. One study, for example, showed that Chicago Negroes designated members of their own race by the set of attitudes which they assumed, or the roles which they played in the community. Some were known as "the white man's 'nigger,' "; others, as "barfly," "mammy," or "the uppety"; still others were called "the jive cat," "the striver," or "the club woman." [26] These were classified on the basis of a set of values which the Negroes of Chicago maintained and by which they judged or evaluated one another.

[24] Morris, Individual differences, p. 136.
[25] See E. W. Burgess and H. J. Locke, *The family* (New York: American Book Co., 1945), p. 245.
[26] S. M. Strong, Social types in a minority group, *Am. J. Sociol.*, 48 (1943), pp. 563–73.

These highly impressionistic examples show that social types are roles assigned to the individual by society and enacted by the individual. They consist of "attitudes, values, and philosophy of life derived from copies presented by society." [27]

One of the best-known but also least satisfactory classifications of social types is that of Thomas and Znaniecki. These authors describe three social types: the Bohemian, the Philistine, and the creative man. [28]

The *Bohemian* is a mercurial, role-changing, and unformed individual. He lives almost exclusively in and for the present. Because of his changeability he is usually inconsistent and gives the impression of superficial adaptability. Being unformed in character, he is opportunistic. His adaptability is seldom constructive or productive of new adjustments, for he is too restless and impulsive to exert the necessary effort. The *Philistine* is the practical man. He is rigid and unwilling to change or to make new adjustments. Unlike the mercurial Bohemian who is typically a rebel, the Philistine is essentially a conservative conformist. He is motivated by the need for security and safety, and therefore tends to live by rules and precepts, rather than by new definitions and interpretations. The *creative man* differs from both the Bohemian and the Philistine. Although he is relatively stable, he is able to change his attitudes and aims to create new values and develop new interests. Instead of passively adjusting himself to the social world about him, he tries to modify it more in accordance with his own set of values. Instead of simply living in his world, he tries to recreate it. He may do this in constructive relatedness to others, in artistic creations, or in reformist or revolutionary readjustments.

Social type, then, is a pattern of attitudes and behavior which results from and changes with the social role of the individual and the social status which he holds in his group. In contrast with psychological type proper, it is more changeable, more dependent upon the individual's status in his group. It may be designated, as is done by Linton, by the term "status personality." [29] The status personality, or social type, is not congruent with the whole personality, but only with those aspects of the total personality which are directly concerned with the successful enacting of an individual's roles. Thus, while one psychological type may be better equipped

[27] E. W. Burgess, in C. R. Shaw, *The jack-roller* (Chicago: University of Chicago Press, 1930), p. 193.

[28] W. I. Thomas and F. Znaniecki, *The Polish peasant in Europe and America* (Boston: Howard G. Badger, 1918–20), Vol. 3.

[29] R. Linton, *The study of man* (New York: D. Appleton-Century Co., Inc., 1936), Ch. 26.

to play certain roles than another, these roles may be taken by more than one psychological type.

Linton illustrates the foregoing statements by the status personality of the businessman. The businessman in American society is characterized by such traits as vitality, shrewdness, competitiveness, and friendly social contacts. Generally speaking, the psychological type known as the extravert is found among businessmen and is more likely to be successful in his work than the introvert. Nevertheless, there are many successful businessmen who are introverts—that is, less sociable, less energetic, and less competitive in business relationships. They manage to play the required role of the extraverted businessman fairly well without surrendering their introverted personality after working hours. "Where the extravert spends his spare time in meeting more people and enjoys the crowds and noise of night clubs, the introvert prefers to go home after business and to spend his time reading or working at some hobby." [30]

Social type is thus seen to be a more superficial dimension of the total personality, to go less below the surface, than the deeper layers of the personality type. The psychological type is, as Linton points out, an individual phenomenon, whereas the status personality, or social type, is a social phenomenon.[31] The influence of the social type on the personality is comparatively small for, while an individual may through conscious effort or training make himself a businessman, an engineer, or a salesman, he cannot easily make himself an extravert. Personality type is psychogenic; it is a more enduring system of traits developed early in the growth of the individual, and cannot be easily acquired through deliberate cultivation. Many traits which are conventionally described as introverted or extraverted are probably expressions of social adjustment rather than psychological dispositions, and so are indicative of social rather than strictly psychological types. However, insofar as social roles are part of the total personality organization they must be reckoned with in any study of personality type. Personality type and social type are interrelated, not separate, aspects of the global individual.

EXTRAVERSION AND INTROVERSION

Jung's typology of introversion and extraversion, because it is well known and influential, deserves a separate consideration. Whatever its merits and deficiencies may be, it has become almost

[30] *Ibid.*, p. 477.
[31] *Ibid.*

a byword for type-designation by laymen and scholars alike. However, its continued use and discussion in psychology is puzzling, for practically all reliability and validity studies, as well as its employment in clinical practice, have failed to establish its dependability.

Jung's typology is a part of his system of analytical psychology. In the preceding chapter it was pointed out that Jung believed that the normal or conscious mind is expressed during either serious tension or rational thinking. When one or the other modality predominates, the individual is said to be either a thinking type or an emotional type. Generally speaking, the thinking type is introverted, the emotional type, extraverted. The introvert, as we shall see, tends to retreat from the external world and to engage in meditation, is absorbed in his own thoughts, and generally approaches life from the standpoint of his own personal or "subjective" values. The extravert, on the other hand, is oriented toward the external world of objects and people. He is a "doer" rather than a "thinker." His subjective life is oriented by and related to the object, rather than to himself.

In this loose, rather impressionistic description, the two types are easily recognized by most people, even though they may not attach the overworked labels to them. "Who does not know," Jung remarks, "those taciturn, impenetrable, often shy natures, who form such a vivid contrast to these other open, sociable, serene maybe, or at least friendly and accessible characters, who are on good terms with all the world, or, even when disagreeing with it, still hold a relation to it by which they and it are mutually affected." [32]

EXTRAVERTED TYPES. Extraversion and introversion, we saw, are ways of orienting oneself to the world of objects, values, and experiences. When a person's orientation is determined primarily by objective conditions or facts, he is said to be extraverted. When there is a cautious interposition of delayed response between the individual and the objective world, the person so oriented is said to be introverted. If a man thinks, feels, and acts so that his whole mode of living corresponds *directly* with objective conditions, he is extraverted. [33] His consciousness, his thinking, his whole subjective life are determined largely by objective factors. His inner life is controlled by external conditions. He lives in the immediate environment, and his attention and interest are directed almost solely by conditions outside himself. His inner life is largely affected by

[32] Jung, *Psychological types*, p. 413.
[33] *Ibid.*, p. 417.

outer or objective determinants because his attention is fundamentally riveted on the external world. He is interested in persons and things. Accordingly, his actions are determined by them, rather than by ideas or abstractions, as in the introvert.

In his moral life the extravert displays the same objective orientation. His moral actions correspond with society's expectations. Accordingly, the extravert is largely conventional: he behaves as he is expected to behave; he finds society's moral demands congenial and is not ordinarily inclined to transcend or to rebel against them. In fact, the extravert is deemed normal in his moral as well as other forms of behavior because he fits into existing conditions easily. He acts as he is expected to act, and seldom attempts innovations which would disturb those in his surroundings.

Although the extravert may thus be socially adjusted, he tends to close his eyes to his subjective needs. According to Jung, this is his weak point. The behavior of the extravert is so strongly outward that he tends to neglect both his body and mind. The body, not being sufficiently "external," is too often neglected, and the extravert becomes aware of it generally only when its impairment forces it upon his attention. In the same manner, the extravert is negligent of his subjective life. His objective orientation causes him to ignore and leave uncultivated many emotions, wishes, needs, and thoughts. Continued adjustment to objective conditions hinders undesirable subjective impulses from becoming conscious. These impulses, accordingly, become the more regressive and infantile, the more they are denied awareness or conscious expression.

Extraverts and introverts are divided further on the basis of how the intellectual functions express themselves. A person's libido, or life-energy, may be manifested in rational or irrational forms. The rational may be dominated in turn by thinking or feeling, and the irrational by sensation or intuition. On the basis of the relative dominance of any one of these modalities, Jung has divided both the extravert and the introvert into four different kinds: the thinking, feeling, sensation, and intuition types of extravert and the thinking, feeling, sensation, and intuition types of introvert. In this section we shall examine the extraverted types.[34]

Extraverted thinking type. The extravert who is dominated by reflective thinking is said to be the extraverted thinking type. His aim is always to orient his life to intellectual conclusions based either on objective facts or generally valid ideas. He lives by an intellectual formula, and he measures his own life and that of others

[34] These are described at length by Jung, *ibid.*, pp. 434–71. We draw heavily on Jung's discussion in this and the next sections.

by means of it. Whatever agrees with this formula is right, good, and beautiful; whatever fails to correspond to it is wrong, evil, and ugly. Because everything must correspond to his intellectual formula, he does not easily tolerate exceptions. He is thus basically rigid in his thinking and intolerant of differences of opinion. If in some cases the formula is wide enough to permit divergences, he may become a useful reformer or innovator; but the more rigid it is, the more likely is he to be merely a "self-righteous critic, who would like to impress both himself and others into one schema." [35]

Since the intellectual formula is all-encompassing and all-absorbing, the rigid extraverted thinking type will inhibit and disparage his feeling tendencies. Concretely, this involves the repression and denial of aesthetic sensitivity, sympathy, friendship, and the like. If this repression is carried far enough, it may disturb the individual's conscious conduct, and in extreme cases it may lead to neurosis. If he permits feelings any play at all, they must support the intellectual formula and adapt themselves to its aims. Because he subordinates feeling and personal sympathy to the intellectual formula, he is usually considered by his family and friends as an unyielding tyrant. Because he cannot brook opposition, he becomes unduly sensitive to the views of others, which he falsely construes as ill-will against himself. He is thus inclined to be rigidly dogmatic and to attack the views of others with hostility and invective.

When the intellectual formula of the extraverted thinking type is more flexible, it is productive. It leads to new facts or generalizations; it advances beyond analysis to a new synthesis, and for every idea or value that it criticizes or destroys it substitutes a fresh and new one. These qualities, however, as Jung with a not-too-rigid consistency admits, are found only in "a thinking that is not given priority in consciousness." [36]

Extraverted feeling type. In this type the feelings are not purely subjective experiences but are also determined by objective phenomena, by concrete objects. Whereas the extraverted thinking type represses his feelings, the extraverted feeling type represses his thinking. This is more particularly true when the thinking is incompatible with feeling. The thinking of the feeling type is largely unconscious, for in this form it cannot seriously affect the feelings. But in this form the thinking is infantile and negative. When it reaches consciousness it is usually negative and obsessive, full of prejudice and depreciation.

[35] *Ibid.,* p. 436.
[36] *Ibid.,* p. 442.

According to Jung, "feeling is, incontestably, a more obvious peculiarity of feminine psychology than thinking." This is an expression of a typical cultural prejudice. Because of their feminine psychology women are the best and most pronounced exemplars of the feeling types. Jung believes that these types are almost without exception women. The feelings of this type usually correspond with objective conditions and values. A woman feels "correctly" about most things because her feelings are in harmony with things as they are, or as society expects them to be. However, this congruence between feelings and objective situations can exist only when feeling is undisturbed by thought. Since nothing disturbs feeling so much as thinking, the extraverted feeling type will eschew or repress thinking as much as possible. This does not mean that this type does not think at all; she may think a great deal, but the thinking is subordinated to feeling and is carried on in such a manner as not to disturb her feeling; it is mostly unconscious.

Extraverted sensation type. This is the supreme example of the realist who is dominated to an extraordinary degree by objective facts. He uses sense experience to attain more sensations. He seeks concrete enjoyment, piling sensation upon sensation. However, he is not necessarily gross or sensual, for he may have sense-satisfaction of the highest aesthetic purity. He is usually a man.

The sensation type is hardly aware that he is ruled by his senses; he does not feel them as compulsive forces. On the contrary, he takes his sensuous life for granted, something not apart from life, but life itself—"simply the fullness of actual living." When sensation becomes the all-absorbing reason for being, the sensation type degenerates into a crude and pleasure-seeking voluptuary. The object of his pleasure, although necessary, is now condemned and violated; its sole function is to produce more sensations. In its pathological manifestation, it consists of projections and anxiety states and, in the case of a sexual object, unfounded jealousies.

Extraverted intuitive type. The intuitive extravert is objectively oriented, but his experience of the external world of objects and people is gained through direct and naive awareness, where neither thought, feeling, nor sensation are effective mediating factors. He is particularly attuned to the potential, the about-to-be. "He has a keen nose for things in the bud pregnant with future promise." [37] Because he is forever hungering for new possibilities he feels uncomfortable in the face of the stable, the old, and the conventional. His morality is shaped by the same restless search for the new or

---

[37] *Ibid.*, p. 464.

the possible, and discontent with the accepted and stable. His morality is fundamentally his own; it demands loyalty to its own spontaneous and unconscious view of the world.

The intuitive type, Jung believes, is found more frequently in women than in men. When it is found in women it manifests itself most normally and effectively in the area of social relationships. Such women have a spontaneous perception of social fitness and unusual skill in making the desired social contacts. However, in their social contacts they seek relationships which will provide them with possibilities for further relationships. When they seek lovers they do so only to abandon them for new possibilities and newer experiences.

If the intuitive type is well-intentioned he can be very valuable to society. He is especially skillful in the intuitive diagnosis of men and their abilities. He can inspire others with confidence and initiate enthusiasm for a cause. But in this very capacity there lurks danger to himself. In his zeal to inspire others he spends himself. He creates an abundant life which others live. He does not pluck the fruits of his labor, for he is too bent on abandoning the present actuality for a future possibility. "In the end he goes empty away." [38]

INTROVERTED TYPES. The introvert is motivated predominantly by subjective factors. Although he is not blind to objective conditions, he assimilates them in a more personal manner than the extravert. He is much more influenced in his thoughts and actions by the world as it appears to him than "as it really is." In contrast to the extravert, in whom the objective world is given almost exclusive importance, the introvert finds the inner world of thought, feeling, sensation, or intuition most appealing and convincing. In extreme form, the form bordering on neurosis, the introvert recoils from the external world and protects himself from it by a variety of defense mechanisms which will preserve for him his sense of aloneness in the face of stark reality. However, since he cannot entirely succeed in shutting out the external world, he experiences a constant struggle to preserve himself.

As a consequence of a rather depreciatory attitude, direct or implied, toward introversion, the view is widespread that introversion is undesirable or even abnormal. This is an erroneous view of the matter and has created unjustified prejudice toward introversion. Introversion is not synonymous with egocentrism, peculiarity, unsociableness, and the like. Jung certainly did not equate introversion with incipient neurosis, as Freud apparently did; nor

[38] *Ibid.*, p. 466.

did Jung believe that lack of sociability is necessarily a mark of introversion.[39] The introvert is an individual with a predominantly subjective outlook, has a higher degree of cerebral activity than the extravert, and shows a marked tendency to inhibition or self-control.[40] These characteristics are in themselves neither undesirable nor abnormal; they are merely one way of coping with the world in which the individual lives.

Not only is introversion not necessarily undesirable, but under certain conditions, or in terms of psychic economy, it may be an index of superiority. Introversion, by virtue of the capacity of imaginative elaboration which characterizes it at its best, can lead to new adjustments, even though it may entail restricted social participation. In the absence of healthy introversion the individual often forms only "superficial attachment to the externals of living," and his capacity for expression in the forms of poetry, religion, folklore, and so on, becomes blunted.[41] Introversion is not necessarily a product of frustration. "It is not the outwardly frustrated individual who discovers the greatest riches in his own world of fantasy or creation; it is a Shelley, a Wordsworth, a Goethe, rich in the outer world of persons and beautiful things, whose *inner* world is most deeply rewarding."[42] This is not even to mention the protective function of introversion; for in the face of external difficulties which cannot be resolved directly, the introvert, through his constructive imagination, can find relaxation from the stresses which difficulties beget.[43]

The best contemporary opinion holds that both introverts and extraverts are needed by society, but that better understanding and evaluation of the introvert is overdue. Our society, by virtue of its pragmatic and other-directed orientation, over-extols the quality of extraversion and the herd-mindedness which is often associated with it, while it disparages introversion because it does not truly understand it. Even the psychologist, though he understands the introvert, not infrequently compares him unfavorably with the extravert. There is insufficient awareness of the fact that the person who develops introversion very early responds more to himself than to others, and that this self-responsiveness is a product of his greater valuation of the inner world—the world of thought and

---

[39] H. J. Eysenck, *Dimensions of personality* (London: Routledge & Kegan Paul, Ltd., 1948), pp. 52–55.

[40] *Ibid.*, p. 58.

[41] See A. Kardiner, *The psychological frontiers of society* (New York: Columbia University Press, 1945), pp. 255, 348.

[42] G. Murphy, *Personality* (New York: Harper & Bros., 1947), p. 599.

[43] *Ibid.*, p. 348.

aesthetic appreciation. The richness of his inner experience is preferred to the objects of the external world, which are to him more commonplace.

Introversion and extraversion are both means by which persons, each in his own way, enhance their living. Furthermore, introversion and extraversion are not inherent dispositions, but biosocial characteristics. Each is acquired in interaction, especially in the child's early interpersonal relations. Thus, while they are relatively enduring qualities they can be modified, especially when objective conditions and the qualities of interpersonal contacts change. An introvert with an adequate self-regard may be more healthy, normal, and happy—all rather subjective terms, we know—than an extravert whose self-feeling is poorly developed. The introvert's self-regard should not be mistaken for a narcissistic self-love, for some narcissism exists in both types of individuals, especially in childhood. Normal narcissism is in actuality a mode of self-evaluation, not self-fixation. If the introverted individual is much more preoccupied than the extraverted one in evaluating his selfhood, it is because his self-image is the anchorage point of his experience, and hence more important to him than the objective frame of reference to which the extraverted person is more strongly bound.

Finally, and most important of all, the tendency to equate introversion with neuroticism, as is done, for instance, by Berneuter, is wholly misguided, particularly in view of the fact that the measures of Berneuter's *Personality Inventory* have not been satisfactorily validated.

It is quite possible that many attractive children become introverted because the norms of our culture place a high premium upon them. Being liked by others, even though it may be based on the child's physical attractiveness only, tends to generate liking for himself. His resulting self-image is positive, not necessarily narcissistic. Since self-love is preferable to self-hatred and the sense of inadequacy which it engenders, it does not deserve the condemnation which it usually receives. It follows, then, that there is a healthy as well as a morbid introversion, a gloomy and cynical as well as a joyous and self-confident extraversion.

Jung divides introverts on the basis of the four modalities which we have described: thinking, feeling, sensation, and intuition. To these we now turn.

Introverted thinking type. The life of the introverted thinking individual is motivated by ideas; but, unlike the ideas of the extraverted thinking type, they are not primarily determined or controlled by external objects, but by inner stimulation and elaboration. "Intensity is his aim, not extensity," Jung points out. The introverted thinker is usually indifferent to, and often even repelled by, external reality. Not feeling at home in the presence of the external object, he becomes uneasy upon exposure to it. Accordingly, he is impelled to disarm others whom he looks upon as opponents and disturbers of his pseudo-equanimity. This attitude usually leads to his being misunderstood by others and compels him to redouble his effort to develop a mask of urbanity. Like the extraverted thinker, the introvert tends to be dogmatic, but for a different reason. If his subjective elaboration of the objective world is correct in his own mind, others must accede to his own conception. He will make little effort to verify it to others; on the contrary, he tends to alienate them by his lack of appreciation of their judgment. But to his close friends who know him intimately and who know how to respect his privacy, he is highly valuable. When his introversion and dogmatism become extreme, he hovers between normality and abnormality, and at long last his ideas become irrelevant and mythological and get lost in themselves.[44]

Introverted feeling type. Jung believes that this type is found principally in women. The individual so constituted is taciturn, inaccessible, and inscrutable. Outwardly she appears composed, but when she is confronted by upsetting realities or rebuffed by others she becomes disturbed and melancholic. Because she controls her feelings excessively she appears cold and insensitive. The truth is that her feelings, though restricted to a narrow range of objects, are deep and intense. Her apparent coldness is a failure of expression, and her feeling has a "passionate depth that embraces the misery of a world and is simply benumbed." It finds outlets in "a concealed religiosity anxiously shielded from profane eyes, or in intimate poetic forms equally safeguarded from surprise." This make-up especially imbues a woman with a mysteriousness which casts a magic spell over the extraverted male who is easily caught by its insidiousness. However, the mysteriousness may also be transmuted into vanity, ambition, and petty tyranny, leading at last to neurosis—a neurasthenic state of utter exhaustion.[45]

Introverted sensation type. This type is fundamentally irrational, for the individual is motivated by the subjective stimulation of the moment. There is little or no relationship between his subjective state and objective condition; what stimulates him, therefore, may be arbitrary and capricious. In its extreme form this alienation of subject from object readily leads the individual to

[44] Jung, *Psychological types*, pp. 484–89.
[45] *Ibid.*, pp. 492–95.

believe that all his sensations happen without an external cause. He is thus led to believe further that the object has no value and that it is in the final analysis illusory. In morbid cases this condition impairs the individual's capacity to discriminate between reality and its subjective distortion. When the distinction between object and subject disappears entirely, the individual is frankly psychotic.[46]

Introverted intuitive type. This type of individual is motivated by autistic imagery. He lives intensely in his own fantasies. In the eyes of others, therefore, he is enigmatic and peculiar. The mystical dreamer, the seer, the crank, and a certain type of artist are examples of this type. Because there is no intelligible relation between the object and his subjective attitude toward it, he expresses contradictory trends within his own experience. Jung portrays this disjointed tendency very clearly. If the person is an artist, Jung writes, "he reveals extraordinary, remote things in his art, which in iridescent profusion embrace both the significant and the banal, the lovely and the grotesque, the whimsical and the sublime. If not an artist, he is frequently an unappreciated genius, a great man 'gone wrong,' a sort of wise simpleton, a figure for 'psychological' novels." [47]

This completes our survey of introversion and extraversion—two types of personality which have been talked and written about at length in both psychological and popular literature. For the extravert the objective situation, and for the introvert the self, are the central reference points of experience. In these designations, it is necessary to bear in mind that each is a form of expression, not regarding a specific situation but regarding situations in general. Also, no individual is completely or exclusively one or the other type; every extraverted individual manifests introverted characteristics in some situations, and every introverted person shows extraverted tendencies. In between the two extremes are various gradations of introversion and extraversion.[48]

The question of the existence of extraverted and introverted types has been much debated, both by armchair psychologists and by statisticians interested in the validation of tests of introversion-extraversion. Thus far there is no general agreement among them. Meanwhile, however, with less logic than one should expect, especially from those who do not accept the typology, most students

---

[46] *Ibid.*, pp. 500–502.

[47] *Ibid.*, p. 509.

[48] We have omitted from our discussion a type designated by the term "ambivert" —that individual who is a more or less harmonious blend of introversion and extraversion. This type is a recent addition.

of personality continue to use it in conversation, teaching, and writing. It has proved to be useful and convenient, if not very scientific. It has stimulated a large body of research and been helpful in clinical practice. Its virtues are probably as many as its defects, and one cannot go altogether wrong in using it as a technique for personality study and research.

THE SELF-ACTUALIZING PERSON

The concept of self-actualization has not yet found a wide use in psychological literature. There is just enough evidence on hand, however, to justify and encourage a brief discussion of this type in the present chapter.[49]

On the basis of the empirical study of 49 individuals, some contemporary, some historical and public figures, as well as others who give evidence of falling into this type of expression, Maslow has found "important and useful whole-characteristics of self-actualizing people" which we shall briefly describe. Among the famous persons are such figures as Beethoven, Jefferson, Lincoln, Walt Whitman, Einstein, and Eleanor Roosevelt. The contemporary individuals, except the well-known public figures, were mostly unselected students. The historical figures may have been selected without full consciousness that they had the trait of self-actualization, and so tend to bias the selection in favor of the concept of self-actualization with which Maslow began. The present writer, on the basis of the study of eight cases, has found the same characteristics to a large degree. Six of these subjects have been studied over a period varying from five to twenty years. The sample consists of a designer, a painter, an architect, a former college teacher turned industrial consultant, the director of a learned society, and a university professor. Of these, one is a woman and five are men. These were chosen because they were—and are—close friends of the writer's, and therefore accessible, not because they were thought to be self-actualizing persons initially. The seventh subject is Albert Schweitzer, studied on the basis of his writings and biographical data; and the eighth is Goethe, studied on the basis of his life and works.

Self-actualizing people are neither introverted nor extraverted, neither "normal" nor neurotic in the conventional meanings of

[49] A first extensive discussion of the self-actualizing type is found in A. H. Maslow, Self-actualizing people: a study of psychological health, in W. Wolf (ed.), *Values in personality research*, Symposium No. 1 (New York: Grune & Stratton, Inc., 1950), pp. 11–34. This article is reprinted in A. H. Maslow, *Motivation and personality* (New York: Harper & Bros., 1954), pp. 199–234.

these terms. They are people who, generally speaking, "seem to be fulfilling themselves and to be doing the best that they are capable of doing." [50] More specifically they are described by the traits to be listed and analyzed.

SUPERIOR REALITY PERCEPTION AND RELATIONS. The self-actualizing person has an unusual ability to judge people and situations efficiently and correctly. He is quick to detect the spurious and the dishonest in people, in the arts, in scientific matters, and in politics and public affairs. This ability is based on a healthy personality, thus making the self-actualizing individual base his judgment less on wish, anxiety, and temperamental disposition than either the "normal" or the insecure person. The self-actualizing person perceives the world more as it is than as his desires might impel him to see it.

His relations to the world, especially to its unknown and ununderstood aspects, are comfortable and free of the anxiety and fear that the unknown tends to beget. Often he is even more attracted to it than to the known. He can be, when necessary, "*comfortably* disorderly, anarchic, chaotic, vague, doubtful, uncertain." These conditions may actually stimulate and challenge the self-actualizing individual. He has a high *tolerance of ambiguity*, to use Frenkel-Brunswik's well-known term.[51]

ACCEPTANCE. Unlike the neurotic or even the normal individual, the self-actualizing person accepts himself without unnecessary shame or guilt, without unrealistic complaint or anger. He is not self-satisfied, but accepts himself as he is as he accepts nature or anything else as it really is. This is part of his strong tendency to see things as they are rather than as he might wish they were. He can accept himself as a healthy animal and as a refined, honorable, and self-respecting person. In the same way he can accept others. Since he can accept his own shortcomings realistically he has little or no reason or need to be defensive about himself, no need to pose or erect an attractive façade. Hypocrisy, playing the game, and trying to impress—these traits are practically absent in the self-actualizing person, for these are crutches which he does not need.

SPONTANEITY. The self-actualizing person is simple, natural, and unaffected. He is spontaneous in his behavior, and particularly so in his "inner life" and thoughts. Spontaneity often results in unconventionality, and the self-actualizing person is unconventional,

[50] Maslow, Self-actualizing people, p. 12. In what follows we draw heavily upon Maslow's *Symposium* article.

[51] T. W. Adorno *et al.*, *The authoritarian personality* (New York: Harper & Bros., 1950), Ch. 11.

again more in his thoughts and ideas than in his overt behavior. His unconventionality is not like the Bohemian's, a rebellion against authority or much ado about nothing; it is concerned with basic issues and important things.

His basic spontaneity or unconventionality leads him to construct codes of ethics which are individual rather than tribal. His behavior is ethical, not in the sense of being conventional, but in being based on principles.

PROBLEM-CENTERING. The self-actualizing person's interest is focused on problems outside himself, not on himself. He is usually not a problem to himself and he is not very introspective, unlike the insecure individual, who is usually self-centered. Instead, he is occupied with some ambition or some objective problem that must be solved, with some basic issue, or philosophical or ethical problem. He is in many ways a philosopher (in the informal sense of this word) whose horizon is always broad and cast in the widest frame of reference.

DETACHMENT AND PRIVACY. The self-actualizing person not only can be solitary without suffering adverse effects but he positively likes solitude and privacy much more than the average individual. This fact does not make him an introvert, for as we said earlier, the introversion-extraversion dichotomy does not apply to him. Maslow describes this love of privacy and solitude as "detachment." The self-actualizing person is not very dependent upon other people; he can be quite self-sufficient. He finds it easy to be reserved, even aloof. He is not seriously disturbed by personal reverses or misfortunes. This is related to the problem-centered quality of his outlook on life. Because he is not easily upset by untoward events he can concentrate on what he is doing far more intensely than the ordinary person. His detachment seems by ordinary standards cold, unfriendly, snobbish, or even hostile. For this reason he is not readily understood and accepted by the average individual.

The foregoing characteristics suggest that the self-actualizing person is autonomous and relatively independent of his environment. Because this type is basically motivated by the need for growth and self-actualization he is not, as we said, very dependent on others or on his culture. He depends rather on his own potential resources. This high degree of autonomy, this independence from his environment, explains in part his serenity in the face of upsetting events. Not only does he not need other people, but he may frequently find them an obstacle to the attainment of the good life. The source of the good life for him is not social but "inner-

individual." This detachment from the love and respect of others
is a product of his deep capacity for love and respect for others.

CONTINUED FRESHNESS OF APPRECIATION. The self-actualizing
person has the unusual capacity for repeated and fresh enjoyment of "the basic goods of life." While for the ordinary individual
repeated experiences of the same pleasures and satisfactions become
washed-out and commonplace, for the self-actualizing person they
produce the same wonder and exhilaration that they had at the
first encounter. He displays the characteristic found by Goldstein,
of positively enjoying and even increasing his tensions. For him,
as Maslow describes him, "every sunset is as beautiful as the first
one, any flower may be of breath-taking loveliness even after he
has seen a million flowers. The thousandth baby he sees is just
as miraculous a product as the first one he saw." While the choice
of beautiful objects may be different, the self-actualizing person
derives happiness and inspiration, and therefore strength, from
the basic goods of life. Maslow found that none of his subjects
derived this same ecstatic enjoyment from attending a night club,
getting a lot of money, or having a good time at a party; our own
findings confirm this observation.

THE "OCEANIC FEELING." The freshness of appreciation and
ecstatic enjoyment of the self-actualizing person is capable of reaching a stage involving self-forgetfulness. His ecstatic experiences
have unlimited horizons and cause him to feel at once more powerful and more helpless than he was before. This "oceanic experience," as William James called it, is a feeling that something extremely important and precious has happened to the individual,
transforming and strengthening him in his daily living. He may
feel this ecstacy and self-forgetfulness in any experience from a
sexual orgasm to the beauty of music or art.

IDENTIFICATION WITH MANKIND. While the self-actualizing person may occasionally be impatient and disgusted with human
beings, he nevertheless identifies himself with them and feels deep
sympathy or compassion for them. He is sincerely interested in
the welfare of mankind and desirous of improving its lot. Although
he may be exasperated by men's shortcomings and even consider
them a nuisance sometimes, he nevertheless feels a kinship with
them. He is rarely impatient or arrogant; rather his attitude is
that of an "older brother" toward his less-favored, less-able, or less-
wise fellow human beings.

INTERPERSONAL RELATIONS. The self-actualizing person has a
greater capacity for identification with other people than most

individuals. In this respect he is probably surpassed only by children. While his capacity to lose himself in others is great, it is also highly selective.[52] His circle of friends is small, and the number of those whom he can love are very few. This must be so, because for him "devotion is not a matter of a moment." This highly selective expression of devotion exists alongside the capacity for identification with mankind, his kindness toward almost everyone. The writer knows a self-actualizing university professor who not only associates with his colleagues, but has frequent "hearing sessions" with farmers, truck-drivers, merchants, a trash-collector, as well as lawyers, dentists, and physicians. They talk with him freely while he mostly listens. The self-actualizing person has an especially tender love for children and is easily touched or moved by them. He usually does not hate those who irritate him although he may be momentarily angered by them.

DEMOCRATIC CHARACTER STRUCTURE. In his relations with others the self-actualizing person is essentially and thoroughgoingly democratic. He can establish a natural relatedness to anyone irrespective of class position, education, or race. He can learn from anyone and can be genuinely humble before anyone who has something to teach him. He asks only that the other person be a master of his own craft. Although he is selective in his relations with others, his selection is based on the character and talent of the individual, rather than on the conventional and invidious distinctions of birth, race, name, or fame. He respects human beings because he is himself a human being.

MEANS SUBORDINATED TO ENDS. A high degree of certainty concerning ethical issues marks the self-actualizing individual in his daily living. He is virtually free of the confusion and conflict which characterize the average individual regarding moral issues. He is strongly ethical, but his notion of right and wrong often differs from conventional standards. In this sense he might be described as broadly religious. This religious attitude is in no sense orthodox; even his god, if he believes in one, is conceived in metaphysical rather than personal terms. His attention is focused on ends or purposes, to which the means are decidedly subordinated. An end, or the pursuit of an end, is enjoyed for itself.

PHILOSOPHICAL SENSE OF HUMOR. The self-actualizing person's sense of humor differs from that of most individuals. He does not laugh at what the average man thinks is funny. He does not laugh

[52] About two-thirds of the individuals selected for identification in Maslow's sample are themselves self-actualizing persons.

at things that involve other people's miseries or inferiorities. He does not indulge in smutty jokes. His humor is philosophical in the broad sense: a compassionate poking of fun at man's foibles. It consists in a keen perception of incongruity, as when the puny individual tries to be big and powerful. The self-actualizing person is humorous less often than the average individual, and punning and joking are not to his taste. His humor is "spontaneous rather than planned," and the average man, "accustomed as he is to joke books and belly laughs," considers him too serious.

CREATIVENESS. According to Maslow, this characteristic is found in every subject whom he studied. It was also present in the subjects of our own study. While one would expect to find this trait in Beethoven, Whitman, Einstein, and Goethe, the same expectation cannot have been predicted in the different students, nor in the college and university teachers and the director of a learned society in our own sample. However, the creativeness of the self-actualizing person is not necessarily of the "special-talent" type. It is a creativeness which "arises out of the nature of the character of the person performing the act"—a naive or fresh way of looking at life. In this sense the tailor or the cobbler may be creative if the coat or the shoe that each makes has something of his own natural and spontaneous being in it. Maslow likens it to the "universal creativeness of unspoiled children," which most people lose through the inhibitedness with which enculturation saddles them.

The verbal picture which we have drawn in the foregoing pages sounds flattering because it is an ideal type. In real life, the self-actualizing person is by no means a *completely* good human being. On the contrary, he displays many of the weaknesses of common "human nature." He, too, is capable of pride and vanity, of prejudice and partiality. He may even on occasion be extraordinarily ruthless and show a "surgical coldness" which is quite at variance with his essential humanity. He can turn down a friend who betrays a trust without any feeling. He may recover so quickly from the death of a beloved that he seems positively heartless. Finally, not every self-actualizing individual is wholly free from gnawing fears, anxieties, conflicts, and feelings of guilt. While he is not neurotic he can nevertheless be distressed and unhappy.

CONCLUSION

Students of personality generally have not taken kindly to the typological approach to personality. They have argued that personality traits are distributed on a continuum, and that it is therefore impossible to separate personality into specific types. Traits, attitudes, and other characteristics, they hold, are distributed on a quantitative scale. These characteristics overlap, spill over, run into one another.

While we agree with this version of the difficulty of typing individuals we also recognize the advantages derived from the classification of types. Typing is a form of classification, and classification has an important economic function in science. In this connection Chein made an important observation when he wrote: "If there are . . . dangers in the typological approach, such as that of forgetting that an individual who has been 'typed' is still an individual and not a type, or of assuming that once an individual has been 'typed' he is no longer subject to change, these dangers inhere in the ineptness of the typologist rather than in the typological approach." [53]

Moreover, as we remarked in the opening paragraph of this chapter, if personality psychology is to attain something of the stature of a science, it must try to formulate nomothetic as well as idiographic formulations of behavior. It cannot rest entirely on the single case, the unique, or the exception. Typology is an effort in the direction of developing a workable classification of people on the basis of oft-recurring traits, attitudes, and emotional reactions. It is a heuristic device whose value and adequacy must be judged by its economy, by the extent to which it is able to reduce a proliferation of traits to a workable scheme. In this sense the typological approach is both valid and useful. If we think of a psychological type, not as an actual entity, nor even as the average of many instances, but as a hypothetically pure case, then the process of typing individuals becomes a valid enterprise. So conceived, a type, say an introvert, is an ideal or pure case toward which a concrete individual approximates in varying degrees. Typing is then more than a process of pigeonholing; it is a process of psychological analysis which can lead to valid and illuminating insights into human personality.

With all its shortcomings, then, the theory of psychological types is valuable as an "anchorage point" for "reference frames regarding personalities." It serves as a landmark by which the personality psychologist may orient himself by comparing any personality to the known types. "He can thus achieve," as Stagner notes, "a fuller and more complete description of the personality than would be possible without such reference points." Stagner adds wisely "that none of the type theories help toward under-

53 I. Chein, Personality and typology, *J. soc. Psychol.*, 18 (1943), 89–109, p. 97.

standing the origin of the personality structure, or in planning advice or therapy." [54]

The most serious weakness of the theory of psychological types, which is increasingly being rectified, especially by field theory, is the erroneous belief that every individual fits exactly into a specific type. As we said before, no person is, for example, wholly an introvert or an extravert. There are traits of both in each of us. If we bear this in mind and at the same time conceive of the whole process of typing as one which is motivated by the need for economy and the desire for simplicity, the theory of personality types becomes a useful and illuminating approach to the study of personality.

[54] R. Stagner, *Psychology of personality* (Rev. ed.; New York: McGraw-Hill Book Co., Inc., 1948), p. 255.

CHAPTER **4**

How Personality Is Studied

There are at least two reasons why the student of personality must concern himself with the methods by which the subject is investigated. First, the techniques which the psychologist has devised are the tools with which he hopes to design a more accurate and reliable explanation of personality than he has been able to obtain by simple observation and common sense. It is erroneous, of course, to disparage the usefulness of common sense, but the history of science has shown that in scientific matters it has too often been an unreliable guide. "Scientific procedure is above all things self-corrective," and unlike common sense with its deep-rooted preconceptions, it "reacts to every refutation of its conclusions with a feeling of triumph in having discovered its own errors. Every admission of error is but a vindication of its spirit of objectivity, tentativeness, and cautious inquiry." [1]

On the other hand, we do not wish to imply that the scientific approach is either infallible or completely objective. In the Introduction we called attention to the subjective elements in science. To this we must add the fact that the scientist is not wholly free from the current prejudices, especially in psychology. Too often he is oblivious to the cultural and intellectual forces that shape his thinking and observation. This fact has been extensively documented by sociologists of knowledge.[2]

The second reason why one must be familiar with the tools of

[1] H. Bonner, *Social psychology: an interdisciplinary approach* (New York: American Book Co., 1953), p. 17.

[2] See, for example, K. Mannheim, *Ideology and utopia* (New York: Harcourt, Brace and Co., 1936).

105

science in psychology is neither obvious nor always recognized by psychologists themselves. It refers to the fact that the conclusions derived from the use of various methods sometimes tell us less about the nature of man than about the instruments themselves. This is true not only in the study of human subjects but of animals in the laboratory as well. Every instrument, be it a laboratory maze or a personality inventory, limits the actions of the subject whose behavior is to be measured. As Snygg astutely phrased the situation, inasmuch as "the behavior of the subject in most experiments is pretty well limited by the nature of the apparatus that is used, what we may actually be doing is studying the limitations of our apparatus." [3]

With these critical cautions in mind we can proceed to examine the methods or techniques by means of which the psychologist studies the nature of personality. As a practical aid in simplifying the classification of techniques we shall use Rosenzweig's tripartite division into *objective, subjective,* and *projective.* [4]

As the name suggests, the *objective* techniques purport to describe only that behavior which is subject to direct measurement. The psychologist who uses them will demand that the characteristics which he intends to measure be operationally valid, experimentally verifiable, or statistically measureable. A behavior variable is said to be operationally valid when it is defined without surplus meaning, that is, when it can be stated entirely in terms of what a person *does* without positing any internal factors to account for the behavior. It is experimentally verifiable when it has been tested under rigidly controlled laboratory conditions. It is statistically measurable when it can be stated in the form of a central tendency, a variability, or a coefficient of correlation.

Subjective techniques, on the other hand, are those which tap the individual's inner states or attitudes by requiring him to observe himself. The most widely used subjective technique is the questionnaire.

Projective techniques permit each individual to externalize his inner trends in response to ambiguous or neutral and allegedly culture-free stimulus situations. In the "ink-blot" or Rorschach test,

[3] D. Snygg, Learning: an aspect of personality development, in *Learning theory, personality theory, and clinical research*. The Kentucky Symposium. (New York: John Wiley & Sons, Inc., 1954), p. 133. See also, G. W. Allport, *Becoming: basic considerations for a psychology of personality* (New Haven: Yale University Press, 1955), p. 18.

[4] S. Rosenzweig, Levels of behavior in psychodiagnosis with special reference to the picture-frustration study, *Amer. J. Orthopsychiat.*, 20 (1950), 63–72.

for example, every subject will perceive what, presumably, he is predisposed to see.

In the following pages of this chapter we shall describe in detail, with critical comments when we consider them helpful, the specific techniques in accordance with the three-fold classification described above.

OBJECTIVE TECHNIQUES

We must reiterate that by objective methods we refer to those techniques which measure behavior which is expressed in overt responses. We do not refer to objectivity as a set of attitudes, for the attitudes of those using any of the three categories of personality measurement may be equally objective. Objectivity is conceived as a condition in which the results of measurement are, under ideal conditions, independent of the observer. Objective methods, as distinguished from objectivity as an attitude of impartiality and freedom from bias, are techniques designed to give valid measures of what can be overtly explored.

THE EXPERIMENTAL METHOD. Many psychologists, because of their emulation of the natural sciences, have come to look upon experimentation as the method *par excellence* for studying behavior. Owing to its success in the investigation of animal behavior in the laboratory, most experimental psychologists believe that it can also be effectively used in the study of personality. Some psychologists, on the other hand, believe that the experimental method is unsuitable for investigating so complex a structure as the human person. In their opinion the exact procedures of the laboratory are artificial and eliminate the psychological individual altogether. If this has in fact often been true, it may have been the fault of the experimenter rather than of the experimental method itself. In the last analysis, the experimental method, like any tool, is only as good as the skill and understanding of the individual who employs it is able to make it.

The behavioristic approach. To the extent that experiments have revealed uniformities in the behavior of men they have added to our knowledge of the individual. We know from experience, if not from laboratory research, that people are not only different from one another but similar as well. When similarities can be observed and formulated into general principles they add to the body of dependable knowledge of the human person. The nomothetic and idiographic approaches, as we have said, need not be antithetical, and in actual practice never are. Accordingly, the fault lies not entirely with the experimental method, but with the fact that the human individual declines to remain put.

Although Galton was the first scientist to advocate and apply the experimental method to the study of human nature, its rigorous development took place some forty years later.[5] Some years after the first flush of the victory of the behavioristic approach to the study of behavior, John B. Watson proposed and adapted the conditioning technique to the study of children.[6] By discarding the traditional assumptions regarding mind, consciousness, and other "mentalistic" conceptions, Watson believed that personality could be described as the end-product of our habit systems as they are developed in the process of conditioning. While this point of view has been very much refined by succeeding psychologists, the fundamental principle of redirecting responses under controlled conditions which result in certain habits is still basic in most experimental investigations of personality. The aim of these experiments is to identify and locate differences in response which are due to differences in the stimulus situation to which the individual is exposed.

Although the experimentalist employs the term "personality," he does not regard personality as having an independent existence. Personality is an attribute of behavior, not behavior itself. Those who do not regard it as a mere attribute *identify* it with behavior. Personality, in this view, is an individual's acquired behavior. Those who show concern for individual differences buttress their theory further by holding that an adequate theory of behavior must also formulate principles which will predict individual differences in behavior.[7]

Thus from the Watsonian conditioned response, through Guthrean S-R contiguity, to Hullian reinforcement theory, personality is learned behavior as it has been investigated in the laboratory.[8]

Physiological indicators. Although psychologists are ready to admit that physiological processes play a part in the making and expressing of personality, they tend generally not to interest themselves in this area. Because physiological factors are not readily

[5] For the earliest proposal of experimentation with human beings see F. Galton, Measurement of character, *Fortnightly Rev.*, 42 (1884), 179–85.

[6] J. B. Watson, *Behaviorism* (New York: W. W. Norton & Co., Inc., 1925).

[7] See G. S. Klein and D. Krech, The problem of personality and its theory, *J. Pers.*, 20 (1951), 2–23.

[8] See C. L. Hull, *Principles of behavior* (New York: Appleton-Century-Crofts, Inc., 1943); E. R. Guthrie, Personality in terms of association learning, in J. McV. Hunt (ed.), *Personality and the behavior disorders* (New York: The Ronald Press Co., 1944), Vol. 1, Ch. 12.

apparent, their importance is either minimized or totally neglected. Recent behaviorists, like Skinner, for example, have investigated the overt behavior of animals, and lately of men, without consideration of the functioning of physiological processes.[9] For this neglect Skinner's point of view has been facetiously described as the psychology of "the empty organism." Nevertheless, even common-sense observation of such emotional states as love, hate, and fear informs us that they are anchored in internal physiological conditions. Cannon's well-known investigation of bodily changes during emotional states comes readily to mind.[10] Landis and Hunt experimentally established the physiological source of the startle pattern.[11] This reaction can be elicited by any unexpected stimulus situation, such as a loud or sudden noise. The more noticeable forms of this pattern are such physiological reactions as sweating, cardiac palpitation, dilated pupils, and in extreme cases, panic.

An interesting example of the use of physiological indicators, although its relevance to human behavior has not been well established, is the method of experimental induction of neurosis in animals. When a cat, sheep, or dog is subjected to a monotonous repetition of stimuli, such as electric shock applied to its foreleg, while at the same time it is conditioned to assume a quiet position, so that conflictual needs are pitted against each other, the animal eventually is unable to discriminate between signals indicating shock and signals indicating no shock. The resulting state is one of agitation resembling neurosis, as well as of physiological responses such as prolonged increase in the animal's heart rate.[12] This method, varied in different ways, gives an account of behavior—in this case experimental neurosis—in terms of central nervous system action and of effect or response patterning.[13]

The chief criticism of the physiological approach is that, like the early behavioristic approach, it segmentalizes behavior and throws very little light on the behavior of the total human individual. The physiologically oriented psychologists, like the reflex-

[9] See B. F. Skinner, *The behavior of organisms* (New York: Appleton-Century-Crofts, Inc., 1938); also *Science and human behavior* (New York: The Macmillan Co., 1953).

[10] W. B. Cannon, *Bodily changes in pain, hunger, fear and rage* (2d ed.; New York: Appleton-Century-Crofts, Inc., 1936).

[11] C. Landis and W. A. Hunt, *The startle pattern* (New York: Farrar & Rinehart, Inc., 1939).

[12] H. S. Liddell, Conditioned reflex method and experimental neurosis, in Hunt, *Personality and the behavior disorders*, Vol. 1, Ch. 12.

[13] For a less reflexological and more holistic inducement of animal neurosis, see J. H. Masserman, *Behavior and neurosis* (Chicago: University of Chicago Press, 1943); also *Principles of dynamic psychiatry* (Philadelphia: W. B. Saunders Co., 1946).

ologists, show too great a predilection for the experimental methodology of the physical sciences. So far there has been very little evidence to show that the nature of personality has been clarified or that psychology has been dignified by this attitude of reverence for the strict laboratory methods. As Murray pointed out, "if physical appliances do not give results which lead to conceptual understanding, it is not scientific to use them. For the all-important characteristic of a good scientific method is its efficacy in revealing general truths." [14]

EXPERIMENTAL DYNAMICS. Not all experimental work on personality begins with the premise that man is a reactive organism. The learning process, be it conceived as simple conditioning, association, or reinforcement, is only one experimental approach to human behavior. Significant experimental research has also been performed on the structural level in which personality is measured by the investigation of dynamic processes, as distinguished from learning, such as traits, capacities, motives, and levels of aspiration. These processes are dynamic yet consistent determining tendencies in behavior. These variables have been investigated not only in the form of controlled experiments but also by means of factor analysis and miniature life situations.

Factor analysis. This is a psychometric technique by which various trait measurements can be arranged into common factors, called clusters. Suppose, for example, the psychologist wants to investigate fear. He can do this by administering a questionnaire containing a large number of items pertaining to fear. One person may indicate that he fears snakes, another, scholastic examinations, another, financial debts, and so on. Other persons will similarly report their individual fears. Statistical treatment in the form of intercorrelations of the fears of all the individuals will show that fears fall into clusters or matrices. Because these clusters are found together, each one being connected with all the others, they reveal the covert or hidden determinants of personality.

We have included factor analysis under experimental investigation because it resembles experimental procedure in a crucial way. It is a technique for holding constant the influence of specific factors while it investigates the effects of other characteristics.

Although factor analysis is a promising experimental device, the traits which it purports to factor into clusters have thus far been inadequately defined. Thurstone and Guilford consider them measurable functional unities, whereas Allport, who does not employ

[14] H. A. Murray, *Explorations in personality* (New York: Oxford University Press, 1938), p. 26.

factor analysis, conceives them as statistical artifacts.[15] However, Allport's criticism of factors as statistical artifacts is logically indefensible. All scientific laws are statistical or methodological artifacts. A scientific construct or law is independent of the reality which it was designed to explain. It is a shorthand way of conceptualizing man or nature. Spearman's g (general intelligence) and Newton's g (gravitational force) are both, and for the same reasons, as Eysenck has remarked, mathematical artifacts.[16] Furthermore, a factor is not only a functional unity but *"a hypothetical causal influence underlying and determining the observed relationship between a set of variables."* [17] So conceived, a factor can bring to light the concealed determinants of behavior.

Because factor analysis has concentrated on abstracted elements like traits and dimensions, it has created the erroneous impression in the minds of many critics that the method is essentially atomistic and narrowly empirical. It is true that Eysenck, who indefatigably stresses dimensions and scorns non-empirical methods, has by his attitude and critical phrasing encouraged this impression. Yet even he is deeply conscious of the need to understand personality in all its aspects. He candidly admits that "partial approaches are liable to lead only to partial understanding." [18]

Of all the factor analysts, Cattell puts greatest emphasis on the total individual and bases his view of personality on both overt and internal characteristics. The goal of psychology, he believes, is to formulate laws which will permit us to predict the behavior of people in a multiplicity of environmental situations. From this standpoint, personality is that pattern of traits which permits the prediction of an individual's behavior in a given environmental condition.[19]

Cattell's factorial approach thus nullifies the charge of those

[15] See L. L. Thurstone, *The vectors of mind* (Chicago: University of Chicago Press, 1935); L. L. Thurstone, *Multiple-factor analysis* (Chicago: University of Chicago Press, 1947); J. P. Guilford, Human abilities, *Psychol. Rev.*, 47 (1940), 367–94; G. W. Allport, *Personality: a psychological interpretation* (New York: Holt, Rinehart & Winston, Inc., 1937). For an excellent introduction to the method of factor analysis the reader should carefully study the following: R. B. Cattell, *Factor analysis: an introduction and manual for psychologist and social scientist* (New York: Harper & Bros., 1952).

[16] H. J. Eysenck, The logical basis of factor analysis, *Amer. Psychologist*, 8 (1953), 105–14. This lucid article helps to clear up the confusion about the aims and techniques of factor analysis.

[17] *Ibid.*, p. 108.

[18] H. J. Eysenck, *The structure of human personality* (New York: John Wiley & Sons, Inc., 1953), p. 319.

[19] R. B. Cattell, *Personality: a systematic, theoretical, and factual study* (New York: McGraw-Hill Book Co., Inc., 1950); also *Personality and motivation structure and measurement* (Yonkers-on-Hudson, N. Y.: World Book Co., 1957).

critics of factor analysis who hold that this method segmentalizes personality into independent elements. In Cattell's view, the molecules of personality can be understood only in their relationship to the total functioning individual. The holistic nature of personality factors also contributes to the unified view of Cattell's analysis. Traits are unified and consolidated when they are all directed toward a single goal to form a dynamic trait unity. Persons may be described as honest, sociable, religious, dishonest, or selfish. Any one of these trait unities may be expressed by a variety of behaviors. Thus, the person who is described as honest will tell the truth, return a lost article to its owner, avert his eyes from his neighbor's examination paper, report his exact age, and so on. Whereas each of these acts is significantly different from the others, all together they form a unity because they are directed toward the same goal.

It is impossible in this chapter to consider the variety of criticisms of factor analysis as a technique for studying personality. Most of the criticisms concern highly involved and specialized matters.[20] For this reason we shall call attention to only two of its weaknesses.

First is the surprising amount of disagreement among the experts of factor analysis themselves. For a method that purports to be objective and mathematically based, that is, designed to find quantitative scores for denoting personality traits, factor analysis has come up with few generalizations that receive universal assent. Yet factor analysts have been critical of the reluctance of other investigators to propose generalizations; and this inconsistency has been emphasized when factor analysts attack those investigators whose approach is not based on mathematical formulations.

A second criticism is that the "revisionists" of factor analysis, who laudably attempt to correlate individuals instead of traits through "inverted factor analysis," have not been very successful either.[21] Instead of factoring out one quality at a time within a specified population, this method deals with one *person* at a time for a complex of factorial variables. Instead of comparing many people on a single trait, the technique of inverted factor analysis concentrates on the presence of various traits within a single individual. The results show that two persons may share certain traits

[20] For an early and still largely valid critique of factor analysis, see Allport, *Personality*, pp. 242–48.

[21] For a discussion of inverted factor analysis, see W. Stephenson, Some recent contributions to theory of psychometry, *Char. & pers.*, 4 (1935), 295–304; Introduction to inverted factor analysis, *J. educ. Psychol.*, 27 (1936), 353–67. See further, W. Stephenson, *The study of behavior: q-technique and its methodology* (Chicago: University of Chicago Press, 1953).

and yet be described as different types. On the other hand, two individuals might be classified in the same type yet be markedly different in the strength of given traits when these are compared with a standard population. Accordingly, unlike standard factor analysis which argues for the normal distribution of individual traits, inverted factor analysis has shown that traits tend to form clusters which do not conform to the normal distribution curve. Instead of correlating single traits within a given population, this technique correlates single individuals with a normative person who represents a given type. However, just as clusters of traits give us no knowledge of the specific individual, so inverted factor analysis substitutes the individual for a general type. But the individual case whom the factor analyst studies is not the person whom we have in mind in speaking of the unique individual.

The miniature social situation. To our knowledge this descriptive term was initially used by Vinacke.[22] The method is experimental in that the principles of control and manipulation are exercised in its use. It is a social situation in that it reproduces on a miniature scale conditions as they might be encountered in real life situations. What it sacrifices of the precision of the animal laboratory it compensates for by the reality of the human situation which it studies. We shall briefly examine a few experiments belonging in this category.

Zeigarnik's experiments on the effect of the *interruption of a task* on an individual's performance is one of the many investigations which were carried on under the influence or guidance of Kurt Lewin in Berlin in the late 1920's, and fully reported in *Psychologische Forschung* over a period of several years.[23] Lewin and other field-theorists investigated personality in a framework of tensions in a psychological field. All behavior, whether it is of a single motivation or of the total person, takes place in response to psychological tensions. One way to account for an individual's behavior is to observe him in a carefully designed miniature situation where tensions can be carefully controlled. Thus, Zeigarnik instructed her young subjects to perform a series of some twenty simple tasks. She permitted the subjects to complete half of the tasks but interrupted them on the others. Upon completing the experiment Zeigarnik asked the subjects to indicate in writing the tasks on which they had been working. This notation served as a

---

[22] W. E. Vinacke, *The miniature social situation* (Honolulu: University of Hawaii Psychological Laboratory, February, 1954). See also Allport, *Personality*, p. 383, where he calls it a "miniature life situation."

[23] B. Zeigarnik, Über das Behalten von Erledigten und Unerledigten Handlungen, *Psychol. Forsch.*, 9 (1927), 1–85.

test of the subjects' memory for the interrupted and uninterrupted tasks. The results of the experiment showed that almost twice as many of the interrupted tasks were recalled. The explanation of this memory differential, supported by experiments designed to test the hypothesis, is that the psychological tensions associated with the interrupted tasks continued to activate the individual subjects, whereas in the completed task the tensions were discharged. In a similar experiment by Ovsiankina the subjects returned to complete the interrupted task at the first opportunity, and she was thus able to further substantiate the hypothesis that tensions persist until they can be adequately discharged.[24]

Another example of experiment in a miniature life situation is the study of the *level of aspiration*. This term was introduced by Dembo, another worker in Lewin's laboratory.[25] It has an important place in the psychology of personality because it is intimately related to the human self, especially the individual's self-picture, which gives us knowledge of a person not only as he is but as he would like to be. This self is further complicated by the individual's perception of and expectancies toward others, and by his success or failure in achieving his goals. These factors are difficult to study objectively, but the level of aspiration technique is a simple way to their better understanding.

A typical situation for determining the level of aspiration is to assign a task to a subject for which he has no special skill, such as shooting at a target. In performing this task the subject will exhibit a sequence of typical events. Suppose the subject has scored 6 in aiming darts at a target with ring 10 at the center. Since his score does not please him he decides to try for 8, but, to his disappointment, he scores only 5. Accordingly, he reduces his level of aspiration to his initial level of 6.

In this experiment the subject's "ideal goal" is to hit the center of the target. Having discovered that this goal is, for the time at least, unobtainable, he lowers his level of aspiration for the next attempt. This is referred to as his "action goal," that is, the goal he tries for at that time. The action goal then becomes the standard for the level of aspiration of the subject at a given time. How-

[24] M. Ovsiankina, Die Wiederaufnahme Unterbrochener Handlungen, *Psychol. Forsch.*, 11 (1928), 302–79. See further, A. F. Zeller, An experimental analogue of repression. I. Historical Summary. *Psychol. Bull.*, 47 (1950), 39–51. For a good recent example of this technique, see M. Horwitz, The recall of interrupted group tasks: an experimental study of individual motivation in relation to group goals, *Hum. Relat.*, 7 (1954), 3–38.

[25] T. Dembo, Der Ärger als dynamisches Problem, *Psychol. Forsch.*, 15 (1931), 1–144.

ever, setting the goal below the level of the desired hit does not mean that the subject has given up his original goal. Both the ideal goal and the action goal must be seen in the whole aspiration framework of the individual. The distance between the ideal goal and the action goal is called "inner discrepancy." There is also a difference between the action goal and the level of "expected performance." This difference is called the "goal-expectation discrepancy." This discrepancy is determined in part by the "subjective degree of probability" which the subject feels regarding his chances of attaining his action goal, and is expressed in his level of confidence.[26]

Studies of the level of aspiration show that this phenomenon is not an isolated expression of the personality. In describing a person's level of aspiration we are in fact describing *him*. It is inalienably an expression of the self, of the subject's future or past orientation, his confidence in himself, his fear of failure, his optimism or pessimism, his ambition, and his courage to face reality. For these and other reasons investigation of an individual's level of aspiration is an effective way of learning to understand his personality.

However, the level of aspiration, like personality itself, cannot be isolated from the rest of reality. Striving for a goal is not completely an individual or subjective event. There are many social and cultural influences determining a person's degree of goal-integration. The scales of reference which help to determine the attractiveness of a goal are influenced by the dominant values of the society in which the person lives. Whether he will experience satisfaction from performing a task below his level of aspiration will depend not only on his own ambition but upon the valuation of his level of performance by others. That group standards affect the aspiration of an individual has been extensively demonstrated. Miniature life-situation experiments have shown that other individuals and the norms of the group play an important part in determining the level at which we aim and the achievement with which we are satisfied. Pressures toward social conformity and competition with others are very strong. In Zuñi society, for instance, where a high premium is placed on inconspicuousness and lack of ambition, the level of aspiration plays no significantly functional role in the development of personality. In our own culture, where the need to get ahead is firmly implanted, the level of aspira-

[26] K. Lewin, T. Dembo, L. Festinger, and P. S. Sears, Level of aspiration, in Hunt, *Personality and the behavior disorders*, Vol. 1, Ch. 10.

tion is an important expression of the whole striving individual.[27]
There is a superabundance of recent experimental work which confirms the important role of group influences on the level of individual aspiration and performance.[28]

The level of aspiration is thus a conspicuous index of the person
as an individual and as a member of society. In an earlier work
we summarized this dual reference of the individual's aspiration
level as follows:

The level of aspiration which a person sets up for himself is frequently determined by the amount of self-esteem which he needs to maintain. A person
whose self-image is wavering and unstable will go to extreme lengths to prop
it up. He may deliberately set his sights low to convince himself that he
has succeeded; or aim so high that, although failure is in the cards, he gains
prestige in his own eyes by impressing others with his high aspirations. The
self conceals poor performance from itself in order to protect itself from the
unfavorable judgment of others. . . . Self-defense and self-enhancement are
closely intertwined.[29]

The study of the effect of barriers is another illustration of the
miniature situation technique of investigating personality. Like the
two preceding examples, this method was conceived within the
Lewinian theoretical framework. It has the additional advantage
that it takes social learning into account, for experiments have
shown that the preference for more difficult goals induced by barriers to their attainment is affected by the degree of socialization
and training of the individual. While Wright found that children
will prefer a toy that is less accessible to one that is readily available, Child, on the other hand, discovered that this preference for
goals not readily obtainable is greater in adults than in children.[30]
Both experiments, and a variety of similar ones, confirm Lewin's
earlier observation that barriers enhance the "positive valence,"
or attractiveness, of a goal or an object. Many parents of small
children can testify to the fact that children can perform their
school work better while the radio or television is turned on. We

[27] See D. W. Chapman and J. Volkmann, A social determinant of the level of
aspiration, *J. abnorm. soc. Psychol.*, 34 (1939), 225–38; P. S. Sears, Levels of aspiration in academically successful and unsuccessful children, *J. abnorm. soc. Psychol.*, 35
(1940), 498–536; E. R. Hilgard, E. M. Sait, and G. A. Magaret, Level of aspiration
as affected by relative standing in an experimental social group, *J. exp. Psychol.*, 27
(1940), 411–21; L. Festinger, Wish, expectation, and group performance as factors
influencing level of aspiration, *J. abnorm. soc. Psychol.*, 37 (1942), 184–200.

[28] See H. Bonner, *Group dynamics: principles and applications* (New York: The
Ronald Press Co., 1959).

[29] Bonner, *Social psychology*, p. 143.

[30] H. F. Wright, *The influence of barriers upon strength of motivation.* Contributions to Psychological Theory (Durham, N. C.: Duke University Press, 1937); I. L.
Child, Children's preference for goals easy or difficult to attain, *Psychol. monogr.*, 60
(1946), No. 4.

all know that prohibition of an act and threat of punishment often serve as strong inducements to perform the prohibited act. If the barriers to learning are not too great they tend to stimulate effort and produce better results. However, if the obstacles are perceived by the learner as insurmountable, he tends to give up and attend to something else.

SUBJECTIVE TECHNIQUES

In using the term "subjective," one opens himself to attack from those who hold that psychology cannot deal with the inner life of man. However, we wish to point out that subjective techniques have been designed to elicit and objectify internal processes in order to make them amenable to interpretation and measurement. For example, by administering a questionnaire regarding an individual's attitude toward racial segregation, we can extract and thereby make overt what is initially a subjective tendency. Recent investigations by Smith, Bruner, and White have found a close relationship between opinions and personality.[31] Opinions are usually not deeply buried characteristics but are in close contact with the world of external events. By permitting a subject to externalize his inner trends on well-designed questionnaires and inventories, in autobiographies, life histories, and the like, these techniques can give us an understanding of the individual as a whole far more adequately than the instruments of the animal laboratory.

We shall now describe the most widely used of the subjective techniques: namely, the diagnostic method, the life history, the autobiography, the questionnaire, the rating scale, and the interview.

THE DIAGNOSTIC METHOD. This is an intensive study of the individual case. While the diagnosis of many cases has produced widely applicable generalizations it is nevertheless concerned primarily with the individual characteristics of a single person. Although the method is fundamentally utilitarian and was developed largely within the framework of psychotherapy, it is, nevertheless, also a means of studying the normal individual. Because it has not been and perhaps cannot be formalized in such a way as to permit every diagnostician to proceed in exactly the same manner, the diagnostic method leaves a wide latitude for individual judgment and intuitive skill. This means that the probing individual in the person of the psychologist is an important instrument in psy-

[31] M. B. Smith, J. S. Bruner, and R. W. White, *Opinions and personality* (New York: John Wiley & Sons, Inc., 1956).

chological research. Whereas the diagnostician is as dedicated as any scientific student to the attainment of valid knowledge, he believes that this knowledge should be put far ahead of the artificial techniques which are sanctioned by the methodological fashions of the day. "Nothing can be more important," says Murray, "than an understanding of man's nature, and if the techniques of other sciences do not bring us to it, then so much the worse for them." [32]

In order to obviate the subjective nature of an individual diagnosis it can be submitted to the assessment of other competent judges. An encouraging aspect of the procedures of some diagnosticians is their readiness to consult the judgment of others. In this connection Murray early subjected his diagnoses to multiple assessment. His *diagnostic council* consisted of several judges whose *individual* and *weighted* evaluations were the source of the final estimates. The need for the diagnostic council was indicated not only because one judge could not carry out all the examinations, nor because the experimenter should check his own interpretations, but also because in order to vary conditions adequately it is necessary to vary the judges or experimenters themselves. [33]

In the interests of scientific reliability it would be more advantageous to present Murray's systematic procedures than Freud's psychoanalytic method. However, even the obscurities of Freudian psychoanalysis can be more easily recounted and compressed than Murray's multifaceted technique. This holds also for Roger's nonmethodical yet very fruitful diagnostics. We shall briefly describe three forms of the diagnostic method: the psychoanalytic method, the client-centered technique, and the diagnostic interview.

Psychoanalytic technique. Whatever the shortcomings of psychoanalysis may be—and they are many and serious—as a method it has led to an important theory of personality. Before we describe the psychoanalytic method of Freud, its originator, it is necessary to write a thumbnail sketch of the factors underlying the formation of personality.

On the basis of his observation of many individuals who came to him with neurotic disturbances, Freud concluded that the frustration of childhood needs and impulses results in enduring personality characteristics. The child's reactions to these frustrations tend to become fixed and to continue in adulthood. The frustrations result from the conflict of the sexual impulses, which are bent on uninhibited expression, and the ego impulses, which impel the individual to curb his sexual impulses in accordance with the reality

[32] Murray, *Explorations in personality,* p. 26.
[33] *Ibid.,* Ch. 4.

of society's demands and prohibitions. The conflict between these two sets of impulses causes the sexual ones to be repressed, or driven into the unconscious dimension of the mind. Since the repressed impulses frequently fail to be integrated into the total personality, they become the sources of conflicts which often lead to maladjusted behavior. The undischarged tensions which are generated by the many frustrations seek an outlet in the mechanism of dreaming and other modes of adjustment. In order to uncover the repressed or concealed impulses and wishes the Freudian psychoanalyst will use the methods of *free association* and *dream analysis*. These we shall now briefly examine.

1. *Free association.* The method of free association is simple, but the interpretation of the associations themselves is difficult and subject to legitimate criticism. Although psychoanalysts have done their best to standardize the interpretation of both free associations and dreams, their translation is still too dependent on the individual analyst.

The free association method requires the subject to verbalize or report to the analyst anything that comes to mind, no matter how illogical or absurd it may be. The analyst listens but does not interfere with the flow of words and images of the subject. The analyst eventually finds meaningful associations in the subject's verbalizations. The associated productions are invariably found to be connected with the childhood experiences of the subject. Eventually the analyst is able to fit together the seemingly unassociated ideas and to get a glimpse of the subject's personality structure. Thus, whereas the chief goal of the analyst was to uncover the subject's crippling symptoms as a means of leading him to a more realistic and healthy understanding of himself and his relation to others, an important end-product of the process is a better understanding of the individual's total personality.

2. *Dream analysis.* Save for the vehement reactions to Freud's emphasis on sexuality in the growth of personality, no aspect of his theory has been more severely criticized than the role of dreams in the explanation of personality. Fundamentally, dream analysis does not differ from the method of free association. In his use of free association Freud discovered that his subjects often used their dreams as the starting point in free association. He soon came to realize that even the most fantastic dreams are functionally connected with the individual's childhood fears and current problems. Accordingly, Freud came to look upon dreams as expressions of a person's repressed desires and as symbolic fulfillments of his

dominant wishes. He worked on the premise, which is not widely accepted by academic psychologists, that the symbolic meanings of the dreams are universal, so that in discovering their meanings we can arrive at a view of personality that is applicable to all mankind.

From the standpoint of current psychological research dreams may be indicative of unconscious trends in a given person, but their meanings cannot be generalized to hold for every individual. On the contrary, every dream must be interpreted in the light of the past and present experiences of the total personality.[34]

3. Word association. This technique was developed by C. G. Jung and is not an integral part of Freudian psychoanalysis, but of Jung's "analytical" psychology.[35] Because of its frequent use in interviews it may also be classified in the latter category, which we shall describe later. It is also sometimes identified with free association, but the two are not the same.

In using this technique the investigator presents, one at a time, a standard list of words to which the subject is instructed to respond as promptly as possible with the first word that comes into his mind. Also, the individual's reaction time is measured with a stop watch. The rationale behind this procedure is that when the response does not normally follow the stimulus word it is an indicator of a complex or an emotional problem. The most important indicators are delayed or prolonged responses, failure to respond, irrelevant responses, especially when associated with a "trigger" reaction time, and anxiety symptoms such as blushing, changes in respiration, palpitation, and cardiac acceleration, all of which can be measured by appropriate instruments, such as a pneumograph and a psychogalvanometer.

The word-association test, mostly because of its quantitative and "experimental" nature, has appealed to many psychologists and has been one of Jung's lasting and influential contributions to the science of psychology.

Client-centered diagnosis. This technique is uniquely associated

---

[34] For the original discussion of dreams and their interpretation, first published in 1900, see S. Freud, *The interpretation of dreams* (New York: The Macmillan Co., 1933).

[35] See C. G. Jung, *Studies in word-association* (New York: Dodd, Mead, & Co., Inc., 1918). A recent comprehensive discussion of the word-association test is found in S. Levy, Sentence completion and word association tests, in D. Brower and L. E. Abt (eds.), *Progress in clinical psychology* (New York: Grune & Stratton, Inc., 1952), Vol. 1, pp. 191–208. See also J. B. Rotter, Word association and sentence completion methods, in H. H. Anderson and G. L. Anderson (eds.), *An introduction to projective techniques* (Englewood Cliffs, N.J.: Prentice-Hall, Inc., 1951), Ch. 9.

with Carl R. Rogers, who originated it and gave it its name.[36] As in the case of psychoanalysis, our concern with the client-centered approach is not in its method of psychological treatment, but with the light it throws upon the nature of personality. In this connection it is instructive to note that while Rogers' interest in psychotherapy has in no wise diminished, his interest in the total personality has remarkably increased. One so deeply responsive to the psychological state of another as Rogers could hardly perceive his anxious and troubled clients as other than individuals seeking to become whole persons. His therapeutic practice led him to formulate a justly respected view of personality.

Rogers' technique is quite simple, even if its results are highly complex. In a typical therapeutic "movement" from its initial stages to its completion, the subject begins to talk about his problems and symptoms, but as therapy progresses he talks less about these and shows instead increased understanding of the connection between his past and present behavior and an enlarged self-understanding. These changes are induced by the individual's own self-propelling needs, not by the suggestion or persuasions of the therapist. The latter directs the client hardly at all, but serves rather as a sensitive organism who reflects back to the client the latter's own deepened self-understanding. Rogers astutely describes the process as "movement from *symptoms to self*." [37] The method of therapy is put in the service of the individual's basic tendency to maintain and enhance the self. It does not use the elaborate form of analysis and interpretation that characterizes psychoanalysis; it needs no esoteric language, no dream interpretation, no seeking for infantile sexuality in disguise. All that is necessary is to create a favorable psychological climate in which the constricted and harassed person can take "further steps in a direction which has already been set by his growth and maturational development from the time of conception onward." [38]

The essential fact regarding Rogers' technique is that it is used to understand behavior from the "internal frame of reference of the individual himself." By the internal frame of reference he means the individual as he reports or reveals himself to the psychologist in their mutual relatedness. The individual learns to

[36] See C. R. Rogers, *Client-centered therapy* (Boston: Houghton Mifflin Co., 1951). Rogers' method is not a form of diagnosis in the clinical, but in a purely descriptive sense. Rogers studies the individual in order to understand him as a whole person, not in order to classify him into a type.

[37] *Ibid.*, p. 135. Italics are in the original.

[38] *Ibid.*, p. 196.

know himself and the psychologist learns to know him not by external signs, nor simple observation, nor inferences made from tests, but by the self which the subject reveals in the permissive therapeutic relationship.

THE LIFE HISTORY. This technique, also called the case history method, has been widely used by psychiatrists, clinical psychologists, guidance experts, and social case workers. It rests on the premise that a full-bodied knowledge of personality cannot be obtained without a detailed knowledge of an individual's past history. Inasmuch as life histories have become considerably standardized by the use of such data as family life, social and economic status, education, and the like, some writers have classified this device with the objective techniques. The point may be argued, however, for life histories also elicit the more subjective aspects of personality. Their objectivity is weakened by the fact that, since many of the data are subject to the memory distortions of both the subject and other informants, their reliability is greatly diminished. Nevertheless, since unconscious distortions often throw light upon the subject's beliefs, what he *believes* about himself can become an important datum in studying his personality. If skillfully and cautiously used, therefore, the life history can serve as a valuable record of the growth of the personality. Jones has made the most pertinent statement regarding the life or case history. "The case student at best," he writes, "differs from the experimental scientist mainly in that he does not bring a person into a laboratory but follows his activities and the impressions he has made on others in a natural life setting." [39]

THE AUTOBIOGRAPHICAL APPROACH. There is no sharp division between the life history and the autobiographical technique. Although most of the data in a life history are obtained from other persons and from the records of social service and other agencies, some of them are also drawn from autobiographies and other sources closely allied with the latter, such as diaries and personal correspondence. Because it touches so intimately the inner ruminations of an individual, his hopes and aspirations, his conception of himself and his relation to others, a good autobiography can

---

[39] E. S. Jones, Subjective evaluations of personality, in Hunt, *Personality and the behavior disorders*, Vol. 1, Ch. 4. For a richer, less restricted conception of the life history than is found in most accounts, see G. W. Allport, *The use of personal documents in psychological science*. Social Science Research Council Bulletin 49 (New York: Social Science Research Council, 1942). For a critique of the case-history technique, see P. Horst, *The prediction of personal adjustment*. Social Science Research Council Bulletin 48 (New York: Social Science Research Council, 1941), especially Part Two, Supplementary Study A, by Paul Wallin, pp. 181–239.

be an effective instrument for plumbing some of the individual's deepest reactions and experiencies. When the confidential nature of the autobiographical material is assured in advance, as it indeed is by all conscientious investigators, the autobiography yields some of the most significant and complex characteristics of an individual. Since autobiographers and diarists more often than not will record the important events of their lives—their difficulties, tragedies, triumphs, and failures, including their own reactions to and appraisals of these events—their reports are valuable exercises in self-revelation.

The chief defects of the autobiographical method are, first, that it is practically impossible to determine the consistency or stability of its data short of requiring the autobiographer to write still another self-revealing document, with which to compare the first. Second, there is no criterion for evaluating the subject's internal attitudes and feelings regarding the crucial events of his life. We have to take his revelations as they are, and his evaluations of the important events of his life as he perceives them. Unwitting retrospective falsifications and the "halo effect" may distort his observations, and these are difficult to discover. In that event we can only hope, as in the case of the life history, that the subject's false beliefs about himself will throw light upon him as a person.

THE QUESTIONNAIRE. Although the questionnaire did not come into its own until shortly after the First World War, simple forms of it were used long before. Charles Darwin and Francis Galton distributed them to hundreds of people in England. Writing in 1890, William James refers to them as "circulars of questions," and adds in typical Jamesian fashion and on a somewhat prophetic note, that "it will be well for us in the next generation if such circulars be not ranked among the common pests of life." [40]

The questionnaire, as its name indicates, is a list of carefully prepared questions constructed to elicit certain kinds of knowledge regarding an individual or a group of individuals. The fact that questionnaires in use today are self-administering, that is, that they do not require any special skill to administer, is an important factor in their popularity.

A well-designed questionnaire is essentially impersonal. The wording of its questions, their order, and the instruction for recording answers increase its uniformity for many persons and situations. The uniformity may be further secured by testing it on a small population before it is administered to a specific person or group

[40] W. James, *Principles of psychology* (New York: Holt, Rinehart & Winston, Inc., 1890), Vol. 1, p. 194.

for a given purpose. Sometimes this is the quickest and most effective way for discovering whether the questions have the same meaning to every respondent.

As in the case of other psychological methods, the questionnaire should be tested for reliability and validity. The reliability of a questionnaire refers to the self-consistency of its items. A questionnaire is said to be reliable when after repeated administrations the individual's responses remain fairly constant. This is usually determined by means of a test-retest technique in which the questionnaire is used twice and its results are carefully compared. Once its validity has been established, however, it is inadvisable to administer the questionnaire to the same subject more than once, for experience has shown that repetition introduces a memory factor into the second administration which may crucially affect the results.

The items on a questionnaire are valid when they measure what they are purported to measure. For example, a questionnaire on communistic beliefs is valid when it measures the latter only and not radicalism in general. There are several ways of testing for validity, but the most crucial is to compare an individual's verbal responses with his actual behavior with reference to the items being tested. A test of an individual's attitude toward Negroes, for example, is valid when it permits us to predict how he will behave in a situation where his relations to Negroes is involved.[41]

The value of the questionnaire for the study of personality lies in the abundance of information it elicits from the subject. This information, or "question content," can be classified into types. Jahoda, Deutsch, and Cook have classified the information into six types.[42] One type aims mainly to find out "facts." This includes information on such items as age, education, religion, occupation, desires, and intentions. Another type seeks to find out beliefs, in the form of the respondent's prejudices, the amount of discrimination he believes exists in his community, beliefs about minority groups, and the kinds of stereotypes which he has observed in those around him. A third type aims to find out a person's feelings toward such items as minority groups, criminals, and homosexuals. Still another type aims to discover standards of action, such as a person's view of appropriate behavior in various social situations and toward persons. A fourth type aims at present or past behavior. For example, knowledge that an individual in the past behaved in a prejudiced manner in a certain situation is, in the absence of

41 See Bonner, *Social psychology*, pp. 28–29.
42 M. Jahoda, M. Deutsch, and S. W. Cook, *Research methods in social relations* (New York: The Dryden Press, Inc., 1951), Part One, pp. 160–70.

contrary evidence, predictive of how he will behave in the future in the given type of situation. Finally, there is a type of information which is aimed at eliciting the *conscious reasons* for the individual's beliefs, behavior, and attitudes. *Why* does a given individual feel as he does about Negroes or homosexuals?

THE RATING SCALE. Despite the fact that ratings of personality have been unpopular with many psychologists, they have nonetheless been widely used. However, like most instruments for measuring personality they are useful provided great care is taken in their construction and provided that they be appropriate to the purpose for which they were designed. The skill of the rater has much to do with the dependability of the rating. The correlations yielded by an expert psychologist in rating a person are bound to be more reliable than those of a college student just beginning to use rating scales. Perhaps the greatest success in the use of rating scales has been in the measurement of attitudes.

Most scales are based on either *rankings* or *ratings*. *Ranking* is the arrangement of the units of a measurable trait in the order of *amount*. Thus, on such a scale subject A is more prejudiced toward Jews than subject B, subject B is more prejudiced than subject C, and so on. Since these rankings are based on individual *judgments* they are subject to the degree of impartiality and accuracy of the individual judge. *Rating,* on the other hand, is the arrangement of the units of a measurable trait into *ascending classes,* as when we describe one person as more prejudiced toward Negroes than another one. This rating may be performed by others or by oneself. If performed by oneself it is called a *self-rating.* Almost from its inception, however, the self-rating technique has been so severely criticized that few psychologists have been willing to recommend it. Nevertheless, when it is compared with the ratings of an individual by others it can be a useful technique. As we pointed out in our discussion of life histories and biographies, even the distorted views an individual has of himself will reveal important knowledge about him. Thus the inconsistency between a self-rating and the rating made by another may tell us something about the lack of insight in the self-rating individual.

The defects of rating scales are apparent to anyone engaged in the assessment of personality. Neither their reliability nor validity are statistically adequate. This situation is made worse by the fact that they vary perceptibly for different traits. Judges of personality differ in the meaning they attach to the same trait. Psychological tension, for example, may be viewed by one judge in terms of physiological indicators, such as an increased respiration rate or excessive perspiration, whereas another may describe it in terms of emotional symptoms, such as anxiety or irritability. They may agree on the presence of a given trait but differ widely in their estimate of its intensity and on its effect on the behavior of the individual. They are likely to rate a trait which they admire favorably, and one which they dislike adversely. This "halo effect," as it is called, tends to envelop the evaluated person as a whole, not merely his separate characteristics. While these defects can with effort and ingenuity be partly eradicated, the rating of personality is even at best a precarious task.

THE INTERVIEW. Considerably more valuable than questionnaires and rating scales is the interview. Unlike the questionnaire, which too often touches only the superficial layers of the personality, the interview, especially in skilled hands, can elicit concealed and vital feelings and attitudes. Referring to the success of the Kinsey interviews regarding sexual behavior, Jahoda, Deutsch, and Cook remind us that a skillful interviewer can elicit information which an individual is ordinarily not likely to report to anyone but a psychiatrist.[43]

Unlike the questionnaire, the interview, because it can be controlled by the interviewer in the act of interrogating his respondent, can establish the congenial and permissive atmosphere which is necessary in effectively persuading people to discuss themselves. Also, since most people talk better than they write, and since they are either unable or unwilling to expend the effort to write at length about themselves, the interview can elicit information much more freely. In any case, it is the more practical device when one remembers that, "for purposes of filling out even a simple written questionnaire, at least 10 percent of the adult population of the United States is illiterate." [44]

The intrusion of the interviewer's bias and predilection into the interviewing situation is a common and deplorable defect. This situation can be remedied in part by using the "framed" interview containing specific questions, and by the interviewers' conference. The framed interview is one in which the course of interrogation is controlled by an extensive series of prepared questions and by preparing the attitudes of respondents to make them ready for the interview. The latter may consist of nothing more than setting the subject at ease regarding delicate questions.

The interviewers' conference is similar to and has the same objectives as Murray's diagnostic council which we discussed in

[43] *Ibid.*, p. 158.
[44] *Ibid.*, p. 159.

connection with the diagnostic method, namely, to compare the observations of two or more interviewers in order to eliminate the bias and projecting tendency of a single judge.[45]

Because of its nonquantitative character, the interview is held in low esteem by many psychologists. Nevertheless, it is, despite its defects (some of which we have called attention to but briefly) a very useful method of studying personality. Experienced interviewers *have* brought to light covert personality characteristics. At all events, it is noticeably superior to common-sense evaluations, more reliable than some of the methods we have already described, and assuredly better than no method at all. Finally, what is too often overlooked, the interview is more than a systematic interrogation of a person, for it synthesizes many different data from a variety of sources. In this sense it combines some features of the questionnaire, the rating scale, and the informal case history.

PROJECTIVE TECHNIQUES

The construction and use of projective techniques can be traced to Rorschach as early as 1921. In that year he published a book describing the method, its rationale, and the technique for scoring and interpreting its results.[46] Since 1939 they have been extensively used and widely discussed, partly because of a comprehensive description and evaluation of them by Frank, who first used the term "projective" and showed their application to the study of personality.[47]

[45] Limitation of space prohibits any discussion of the *psychiatric interview* developed and used by psychiatrist H. S. Sullivan. While his technique has not been extensively evaluated it is not premature to say that it taps deeply the interpersonal processes in which the individual reveals himself. See H. S. Sullivan, *The psychiatric interview* (New York: W. W. Norton & Co., Inc., 1954).

For a comprehensive review of the different types of interviews, see E. E. Maccoby and N. Maccoby, The interview: a tool of social science, in G. Lindzey (ed.), *Handbook of social psychology* (Reading, Mass.: Addison-Wesley Publishing Co., Inc., 1954), Vol. 1, Ch. 12. For a discussion of the clinical approach in interviewing, see F. Deutsch and W. F. Murphy, *The clinical interview* (New York: International Universities Press, Inc., 1955).

[46] H. Rorschach, *Psychodiagnostik: Methodik und Ergebnisse Eines Wahrnehmungs-diagnostischen Experiments* (Leipzig: Ernst Bircher Verlag, 1921).

[47] L. K. Frank, Projective methods for the study of personality, *J. Psychol.*, 8 (1939), 389–413. See also H. Sargent, Projective methods: their origins, theory, and application in personality research, *Psychol. bull.*, 5 (1945), 257–93. For the most up-to-date, comprehensive, and detailed survey of the field of projective techniques, see H. H. Anderson and G. L. Anderson (eds.), *An introduction to projective techniques* (Englewood Cliffs, N.J.: Prentice-Hall, Inc., 1951). Although the bulk of the book deals with projective techniques, it also describes and evaluates other devices for the study of personality, as indicated by its subtitle: *And other devices for understanding the dynamics of human behavior.*

We have already suggested that there is often only an arbitrary demarcation line between some of the techniques for studying personality. This is especially true when we compare some of the subjective with some of the projective methods. It is difficult, if not impossible, to say whether free-association and word-association techniques are to be classified with the subjective or the projective methods. Although we have placed them in the former category, a number of psychologists have classified them with the latter. While this cross-classification may not make for clarity and certainty it calls attention to their essential similarity.[48]

The rationale of all projective tests is the postulate that personality is a *Gestalt,* or structured whole. Accordingly, projective methods seek to investigate the organizational trend of personality, not its more or less independent traits. Although Frank applied the term "projective" to this form of personality study, its meaning is derived from Freud's defense mechanism of that name. Most psychologists who use this term to denote the projective tests have this meaning in mind. As conceived by Freud, projection is the tendency to attribute to others those characteristics in ourselves which are too painful or too threatening to our egos, and whose presence in ourselves must therefore be denied. However, psychologists have extended Freud's original meaning to include methods not only for studying other personality dynamisms, but for describing a person's distortions or deformations of others and the outside world as well.[49] Thus, instead of projecting my fright to another's face, as in "true" projection, I may call the other person's face *frightening.* In that case, as Van Lennep points out, my fear has created its "correlate object in the outer world." [50] This mixture of categories, Van Lennep believes, is not a gain, but a loss. However that may be and however desirable a single meaning would be, and owing to the fact that the term "projection" is used in its broader or extended sense by an increasing number of psychologists, it must be included in the present-day conception of projective techniques.

A second factor in the rationale of projective tests is that, because they are purposely unstructured or ambiguous, every person

---

[48] R. W. White, for example, places both free association and word association in the projective category. See R. W. White, Interpretation of imaginative productions, in J. McV. Hunt (ed.), *Personality and the behavior disorders,* Vol. 1, Ch. 6. See also the work already cited by Jahoda, Deutsch, and Cook, who describe the word-association test as a projective form (pp. 212 f).

[49] See D. J. van Lennep, The four-picture test, in Anderson and Anderson, *An introduction to projective techniques,* ch. 6.

[50] *Ibid.,* p. 150.

will project himself into a test situation in a different manner. Each will see in the stimulus situation what he is predisposed to see, or interpret it in accordance with his own private view of its meaning.[51] He will organize or interpret a stimulus situation, such as an un-labelled picture which has no inherent meaning, into an organized structure. This individually unique structure, when interpreted by a properly qualified expert, is thought to reveal the subject's idea-tional trends without the latter's awareness that he has disclosed his innermost predispositions.

The number of projective tests has grown remarkably since their inception and earliest use. A partial list includes such forms as the Rorschach Test, the Thematic Apperception Test, the Bender-Gestalt Test, the Make A Picture Story, the Rosenzweig Picture-Frustration Study, the Drawing of the Human Figure, and the Szondi Test. Since we cannot describe and evaluate all the tests in this list in any detail, we shall concentrate here on the Rorschach and the Thematic Apperception tests.

THE RORSCHACH TEST. Named after its originator, Hermann Rorschach, this is the most widely used projective technique. Orig-inally described by its author in a brilliant yet tedious monograph, it has become the favorite diagnostic instrument of many psy-chiatrists and clinical psychologists.[52]

The test consists of ten cards each containing a symmetrical "ink-blot" design. The figures on five of the cards are in varying shades of gray. On two cards the figures or blots are bright red. Three of the cards contain color blots only, with a tinge of gray on one of these. The order of presenting the cards to the subject is always the same, for this has the effect of inducing neurotic and anxiety shocks. Theoretically, each ink-blot is free from cultural influences, thereby permitting each subject to interpret them ac-cording to his own predisposition. The subject is simply asked to report what he perceives on each card, or what the blot suggests to his mind. When he has responded to all ten cards, the tester has to determine what factors influenced the subject's responses. Some of these factors are the location of every item on the card and the effect of color, form, and shading. The perception of ink-blots as global masses, the perception of small or large details, and the number of color responses are considered important. For ex-ample, if the subject reports numerous color responses, the indi-

51 Bonner, *Social psychology*, p. 25.
52 For the original discussion of this technique, see Rorschach, *Psychodiagnostik*, translated by P. Lemkau and B. Kronenberg as *Psychodiagnostics* (New York: Grune & Stratton, Inc., 1942).

vidual is said to be emotionally outgoing; if he sees the blots as global masses, he is given to abstract thinking; if he responds frequently to small details, he is considered critical-minded; if kinesthetic responses (sensation of muscular movement and strain) are reported frequently, the subject is thought to be highly imaginative and creative. Strangely enough, attention to details may indicate the subject's preoccupation with trifles, and perception of wholes or masses is sometimes a symptom of brain injury. Such surface inconsistencies underline the fact that only the interpretation of *all the responses in their interrelationship* can yield a dependable delineation of the individual personality.

The Rorschach test "measures" personality along three important dimensions, namely, intellectual activity, internal emotional operations, and fantasy response.[53]

Intellectual activity is revealed when *form* in the ink-blots is accurately perceived. Clear perception, the ability to center one's attention, the power to select from the remembered perceptions, all indicate accurate perception of form. Intellectual activity—"height of intelligence"—is revealed also in the perception of *wholes*. Whole responses are, as we have said, indicative of abstract thinking and theoretical powers. Intellectual activity is measured, further, by the subject's capacity to organize his perceptions, which is indicative of an ability to grasp new relations between segments of the figures which are not organized in this particular manner. "It appears consistently related to intelligence in the *height* dimension," as Beck points out.[54] *Sequence* is another property of intellectual activity. It indicates intellectual control. The latter is a "central directive function of personality," and is dependent on the subject's ability to see the items of a perceptual whole in their proper sequence. This is additionally confirmed by the fact that certain mentally disturbed persons' perceptions are confused, that is, they lack an ordered sequence.

Other intellectual activity indicators, which we shall merely enumerate, are excessive *perception of animals* in the ink-blots, which indicates sterility of the thought process; seeing *original forms* in the figures, which shows creative thinking; the *variety of content*, great variety suggesting high intellectual activity; *popular response*, indicating surface interest rather than a sincere desire to conform. On the latter point, excessive or infrequent popular responses are both undesirable, for the first is indicative of ob-

---

[53] S. J. Beck, The Rorschach test: a multidimensional test of personality, in Anderson and Anderson, *An introduction to projective techniques*, ch. 4.
[54] *Ibid.*, p. 107.

eisance and conventionality and the second of rebellion and lack of sociability. Finally, *high productivity*, or "liberated associated potential," is an important index, and it may reflect either a neurotic need to be thorough, narcissism, or the enthusiasm of a healthy person.[55]

Although man communicates with others both verbally and emotionally, his emotional communications are often more important. He "speaks" with looks, gestures, ambiguous words, and accusing silences. A test of personality must elicit this deep inner life of the individual, and the Rorschach is considered by its advocates to be a fit instrument for this purpose. Color responses to the ink-blots are considered keys to an individual's inner life, particularly his emotions. Color is also combined with form, and when so combined projects something different from pure color alone. The more pure the color, the more egocentric and self-gratifying is the experience associated with it. When a response combines color and form it indicates "allocentric" behavior, that is, the ability to sympathize with others. Anxiety, feelings of inadequacy, depression, and the like are revealed in "light-determined" responses along the gray-black continuum. Texture responses, as represented by such tactual elements as hardness or smoothness, are expressions of free-floating or vague anxiety and, in some recent researches, probably of affect hunger and a feeling of deprived love. Finally, the white space response indicates resistiveness, negativism, and stubborness.

The third dimension measured by the Rorschach test is the role of *fantasy*. The movement response, which is revealed when the subject sees the blot or some portion of it as if it were moving, indicates a strongly felt wish. Wishes that are not particularly screened or concealed by the subject are usually expressed by moving *human* figures, such as "two children, with caps on, on top of two piles of snow." Wishes that are considerably disguised in order to keep them from reaching consciousness, are usually projected in the form of *animal* behavior, such as "a big gorilla reaching for you."

What can one say in a short space regarding the reliability and validity of the Rorschach test? Many of the studies of its reliability, especially those that have made statistical analyses of single scores, have been made by unsympathetic critics. Be that as it may, the fact is that most statistical studies have found the reliability to be low. When more holistic or molar measures of the Rorschach responses are made, the reliability is so high that it generates doubt

[55] *Ibid.*, pp. 108–9.

in the minds of Rorschach critics. This doubt exists in the minds of many psychologists because of the conviction that there is no one-to-one correspondence between two variables. Even when several examiners compare the same records the average correlation between them is only about .65.

The validity of the Rorschach test has also been widely questioned. It is perfectly right, on logical and statistical grounds, to question the propriety of generalizing about the total personality from a small number of reactions to ink blots. It may be going too far, however, to question with Cattell, the actual existence of some of the traits reported on Rorschach diagnoses.[56]

Increasingly, the validation of the Rorschach test is being pursued with greater scientific sophistication. Many more diagnoses are now being validated by means of "blind" interpretations and rating by several judges. A "blind" interpretation is one in which two or more investigators are working on the same problem without either having access to the other's data. One of the most interesting and confirmatory examples of this procedure is the combined ethnological study of people on the East Indian island of Alor by DuBois and the diagnosis of these same individuals with Rorschachs by Oberholzer.[57]

The Rorschach technique has also been subjected to direct experimental conditions. A promising technique which has thus far been used on too few cases, however, is the use of hypnosis, sodium amytal, and electric shock treatment. In one experiment the Rorschach scores of a subject in a waking state were compared with her responses under hypnotically induced moods like fear, anxiety, and depression. The results confirmed some of the original Rorschach interpretations.[58]

To the present writer the fairest observation on the validity of the Rorschach test is that, since neither validity nor lack of validity have been established, most of the criticisms which have been leveled against it are unjustified. As important as establishing the

[56] See R. B. Cattell, An objective test of character temperament. II, *J. soc. Psychol.*, 19 (1944), 99–114.

[57] C. DuBois, *The people of Alor* (Minneapolis: University of Minnesota Press, 1944), Ch. 22.

[58] K. N. Levine, J. R. Grassi, and M. J. Gerson, Hypnotically induced mood changes in verbal and graphic Rorschach: A Case Study, *Rorschach res. exch.*, 7 (1943), 130–44.

For a study each of the use of sodium amytal and of electric shock, see the following: D. M. Kelly and K. Levine, Rorschach studies during sodium amytal narcoses (abstract), *Rorschach res. exch.*, 4 (1940), 146; D. M. Kelley, H. Margulies, and S. E. Barreva, The stability of the Rorschach method as demonstrated in electric convulsive therapy cases, *Rorschach res. exch.*, 5 (1941), 35–43.

validity of the test is establishing the technical competence of the individual tester. As important as having the technical competence to administer and interpret the test is a profound formal and intuitive knowledge of the human personality. Until these desiderata have been met, claims and counterclaims, praises and condemnations, will not advance the scientific and practical usefulness of the Rorschach test. However, there can be no doubt that it has been one of the most useful techniques for the study of personality.

THE THEMATIC APPERCEPTION TEST. This technique, generally referred to as the TAT, is a multidimensional test developed in 1935 by H. A. Murray in collaboration with C. D. Morgan.[59] In contrast to the Rorschach test, which frequently reveals only the structural or relatively static dimensions of personality, the TAT elicits the dynamic images, sentiments, and strivings of the individual. However, as in the Rorschach test, the rationale of the TAT is that an individual who is faced by an ambiguous or unstructured stimulus situation will unwittingly reveal the dominant trends of his inner life and show how he perceives himself, other people, and the world around him. While he is engaged in describing the pictures presented to him by the investigator, he discards his habitual circumspection and self-consciousness and freely develops themes about the pictures which articulate his inner preoccupations.

The test consists of thirty pictures. Ten pictures are designed for men, ten for women, and ten for both men and women. These are presented to the subject one at a time, and he is instructed to invent "a theme or plot suggested to him by the picture—what the character in the picture is doing, thinking, or feeling, what motives the subject imputes to him, what the outcome of the story will be, and so on. The imagination of the subject is quite free to fabricate any plot, logical or illogical, probable or improbable; it is controlled only to the extent that the subject reacts to the concrete pictures themselves." [60]

The description of a single picture might help the reader derive a more concrete understanding of the operation of the TAT. This picture presents a woman standing at an open door. Her head is bowed and her face is hidden in her right hand. Her left hand touches the open door, but there is no way of knowing whether

[59] C. D. Morgan and H. A. Murray, A method for investigating fantasies: the thematic apperception test, *Arch. neurol. Psychiat.*, 34 (1935), 289–306. For the set of thirty cards and manual, see H. A. Murray, *Thematic apperception test* (Cambridge, Mass.: Harvard University Press, 1943). For its concrete use in clinical settings, see Murray, *Explorations in personality*.

[60] Bonner, *Social psychology*, p. 27.

she has emerged from another room or is going outdoors. What does it mean? That is to say, what story or theme does it suggest? Is she leaving the room where someone—her husband, perhaps, or her child—lies ill? Or is she leaving the room after an unhappy encounter with her husband? Is she just entering her house in tears after a lover's quarrel? Is she perhaps ill herself, and does her bowed position indicate her suffering? There can be as many themes built around this ambiguous picture as there are individuals responding to it, but each theme exposes the personality of the narrator as much as the events which he is describing. "To one with double hearing . . . he is disclosing certain inner tendencies and cathexes: wishes, fears, and traces of past experience." [61]

While a number of investigators have attempted to test the validity and reliability of the TAT, these attempts have been regrettably few. Since the test is not a precise measuring instrument but a method of clinical analysis and interpretation, the principles of reliability and validity have only a limited applicability. What the tests disclose about an individual is greatly dependent on inferences regarding a large variety of his personal characteristics. These are no more amenable to validation than is behavior in general, for no psychologist would think of attempting to validate the latter. Recurrent themes are most likely indicative of inner trends, just as repeated dreams are usually more significant than transient ones. This fact lends some reliability to the instrument. Finally, the clinical experience of those who have used it extensively has proved that it yields a multiplicity of propositions that are confirmed by independent sources of data.

CONCLUSION

In this chapter we have shown that the general methodology of the psychology of personality is in principle the same as that of other disciplines. This is evident in the fact that it follows the same logic, subscribes to the same rules of evidence, and strives for the same attitude of impartiality as the other sciences. However, because its subject-matter is not time quanta or atomic particles, but viable human beings, the psychology of personality has found it necessary to invent instruments that have application to the active and intentional human person. These techniques, as is surely evident, do not lend certainty to the principles of psychology; but considering their limitations, they far surpass the speculative guesswork in which psychology had its origin.

[61] Murray, *Explorations in personality*, p. 531.

Our survey of the methods of personality psychology shows that of the three categories of methods, the subjective and the projective have the greater relevance, applicability, and meaningfulness. Despite its resemblance to natural science procedure, the objective method, with its formal experimental laboratory, its trappings of instruments and apparatus, and its emulation of a somewhat erroneous view of quantification and measurement, has investigated problems that are largely irrelevant to an understanding of human personality.

At the same time, the subjective and projective techniques are disappointing to those who cannot tolerate imprecision, uncertainty, and ambiguity. They must live on the uncertain hope that refinement and sharpening of our instrument, while possible, are not directly around the corner. We are thus impaled on the horns of a dilemma from which we can free ourselves only by making a radical choice. The choice was suggested, if we remember correctly, by Henry Murray a quarter of a century ago: we must choose to work on unimportant problems with adequate tools, or on important problems with inferior instruments.[62]

[62] Many psychological problems today are handled by the sharp tool of statistical analysis. However, *statistics is not a distinct method* in the sense that the other techniques are. It is used extensively in connection with some of the methods which we have discussed in this chapter. In the determination of the reliability and validity of many of the tests of personality, in the study of the correlation of variables, in the establishment of statistic norms, etc., the method of statistical analysis adds certainty, objectivity, and quantitative rigor to a large number of psychological problems.

Part II

THE FORMATION
OF PERSONALITY:
ITS DETERMINANTS

CHAPTER **5**

Organic Foundations

Because personality is an elusive form of being and becoming, the role of genetic and organic factors in its formation is not readily apparent. Unless one subscribes to the discarded view that the personality *is* the biological organism and nothing more, it is tempting to conclude that the organism is unimportant. To some extent the latter course is a rationalization of the psychologist's deficiency in the area of biological knowledge; but to a greater extent it is based on the theoretical and experimental position that behavior can be described as a learning process with little or no reference to or assumption about an underlying organic basis. It is an unhappy fact, however, that some personality psychologists base their position here on quite different considerations; indeed, some seem not to be aware of the relevance of biological and other organic data to the study of personality.

Those who like the present writer are deeply impressed by the unique nature of personality should be sensitive to the role of organic factors for this very reason. From its very beginning the science of genetics has stressed the individual *differences* between related organisms, not their similarities.

Again, those students of human behavior who consign the learning process to a secondary place in the formation of personality, and at the same time are unimpressed by the importance of organic factors, tend to overvalue the determining force of the social environment. In their minds, personality is an organization of socially acquired traits. However, they fail to recognize that what is acquired is not an accumulation of socially conditioned characteristics but a modification of existing potentialities by specific environmental pressures. Potentialities cannot be observed because they cannot be fixed. We are obliged to study them as they become actualized in specific social circumstances.

The implication of the foregoing paragraphs is clear: both the biological organism and the social environment in their dynamic interrelationship must enter into any theory of personality which is to be scientifically and humanistically adequate. A well-balanced and believable likeness of man requires information from both biology and sociology. Neither biological processes nor social conditions are independent of each other. This conclusion is not motivated by personal preference but is forced upon us by the scientific facts themselves, as we shall see in this and subsequent chapters.

THE ROLE OF HEREDITY

We shall not take time to discuss the *mechanisms* of inheritance conceived as the transmission of genetic traits from parent to offspring. By the mechanisms of heredity we refer to the complicated process by which the sperm cells of the male and the egg cells of the female unite to form a new organism. We assume an elementary knowledge of this process by the reader, especially of the fact that the cell emerging from the fertilization of the egg cell by the sperm holds the entire hereditary potential of the individual. Our interest lies in the *inherited traits* which contribute to the development of the personality.

MORPHOLOGY. Morphology is that branch of genetics which studies the form or structure of the body and its organs. Its method of investigation is *anthropometry,* or the measurement of the human body, its organs, and their interrelationships. Since most morphologists believe that there is a close correlation between an individual's physical make-up and his personality, their claim is naturally of great interest to psychologists.

Physique. From the standpoint of common-sense observation few characteristics of the human person seem more obviously inherited than his physique. The size and shape of his body, the contour of his head and face, the color of his hair and eyes are plain to see. Being accustomed for many centuries to view a reproduction of himself in his offspring, man could hardly deny that a "part" of himself was transmitted to the next generation, even though he was wholly ignorant of the genetic process by which the miracle took place. Furthermore, folklore fortifies the belief that character and personality are dependent on the physical structure of the individual. It is still popularly believed that a low or receding forehead betokens a low intelligence; a sloping or diminutive chin, a weak character; and a fat body, the essence of good nature. Again, while few psychologists are much impressed by the morphological argument, there are many notable exceptions. Kretschmer in Germany and Sheldon in the United States have, on the basis of anthropometric and psychometric investigations, found fairly consistent correlations between body build and psychological make-up. Since constitutional factors will be examined in detail in a later section of this chapter, it need only be pointed out here that such morphological features as physique and color of hair and eyes are known to follow Mendelian principles, that is, they are fixed by heredity.[1]

The effect of the physique on personality, when it exists, is in any case *indirect*. Physical defects, such as deformity, a diminutive stature in men, and physical ugliness in women, to cite only the most obvious examples, may have serious consequences for the personality. A well-known theory of personality is largely based on the hypothesis that physical or organic deficiencies have adverse effects on the individual's attitude toward himself.[2] The individual's effort to overcome or compensate for his physical shortcomings was thought by Adler to be the source of the now well-known "inferiority complex." This powerful sense of inadequacy is thought to be the source of many personality characteristics, including exceptional individual achievements as well as psychological disorders.

Musculature. Although the muscular system can be modified by exercise, disease, and other conditions, its basic structure is inherited. Muscles play an important part not only in the obvious area of physical locomotion but also in the realm of personality. The degrees of tension and repose are to a great extent functions of muscle tonus. When the muscles maintain a normal tonus or tension, a person feels relaxed. When he is excited or afraid, his muscles, particularly those of the stomach and intestines, increase their activity. For this reason, many "objective" psychologists consider these emotions as roughly equivalent to the muscular activities themselves.

The nervous system. Despite the enormous amount of research

[1] We recognize, of course, that specific physical traits like color of eyes and hair are subject to modification in the course of maturation and growth. Nevertheless, the potentials underlying this modification are determined by the genes, or units of heredity.

[2] See A. Adler, *Study of organ inferiority and its psychical compensations,* trans. S. E. Jelliffe (New York: Nervous and Mental Disease Publishing Co., 1917).

in the field of neurology there has been but a slight advance in our understanding of the higher neural activities in man. The brain, whose role in intellectual functions has been known for centuries, is still not well understood. The battle is not yet over between the advocates of cerebral functional *localization,* which localizes intellectual abilities within the cerebral cortex, or within groups of synapses and conductors, and the proponents of *equipontiality,* who deny localization and hold that the nervous system is an unorganized network, capable only of random responses. In fairness to those experimentalists who have worked indefatigably on higher mammals, it should be remarked that in lower animals, such as the rat, there seems to be less localization and more equipontiality, whereas in man the opposite condition prevails.[3]

The point of greatest importance is not the battle between the localizationists and the equipontialists, but the recognition of a growing tendency in recent neuroanatomical research to attribute an inherent organization to neural and cortical phenomena. Most of the evidence to date points to the conclusion that "the basic patterns of synaptic association throughout the vertebrate nervous system are organized for the most part by intrinsic forces of development without the aid of learning. . . ." Consequently, for the purpose of our brief statement, it is sufficient to recognize that "the basic integrative architecture of the nervous system is organized directly in the growth process itself," that is, in the factors of inheritance, not in the learning process.[4]

ABILITIES. In the area of human abilities, more than in any other, the controversy between the hereditarians and the environmentalists has been lively, even acrimonious. Reading some of the earlier controversies, one gets the impression that the proponents on each side had a personal stake in the outcome. We suggest that, since there was no crucial evidence on either side, those who took pride in inherited abilities were on the side of heredity, whereas those redoubted individualists who had more pride in self-achieve-

[3] See K. S. Lashley, *Brain mechanism and intelligence: a quantitative study of injuries to the brain* (Chicago: University of Chicago Press, 1929); H. Klüver and P. C. Bucy, Preliminary analysis of the functions of the temporal lobes in monkeys, *Trans. Amer. neurol. Assoc.,* 65 (1939), 170–80. For citation of numerous studies dealing with this problem, see J. Deese and C. T. Morgan, Comparative and physiological psychology, *Annu. Rev. Psychol.,* 2 (1951), 193–216.

[4] R. W. Sperr, Mechanisms of neural maturation, in S. S. Stevens (ed.), *Handbook of experimental psychology* (New York: John Wiley & Sons, Inc., 1951), p. 237. For a brief review of the role of inheritance in the nervous system, see W. S. Hunter, Summary comments on the heredity-environment symposium, *Psychol. Rev.,* 54 (1947), 348–52. Reviews of the latest research on the nervous system are found in the *Annual Review of Psychology,* Vols. 1–9.

ment sided with environment. Today we are far less sure of the extent of hereditary and environmental factors and more patient in waiting for tangible evidence. Some abilities are no doubt functions of the combined operation of both heredity and environment, many are products of cultural influence and learning, and a few are hereditarily determined.

Intelligence. It is generally agreed by psychologists that the more specifically an ability is defined, the more easily its hereditary features can be investigated and measured. When we come to the investigation of intelligence, however, the problem of specificity and generality is not always clearly defined. Since Spearman's early definition of intelligence, the latter has been conceived as a *general* ability.[5] Viewed as a single measurable characteristic, intelligence is, no doubt, a general ability. However, viewed in the framework of the total personality, it must be recognized as a specific trait.[6]

The most widely used technique for studying the inheritance of intelligence is the method of correlation. Correlations of intelligence may be determined between parents and their children, between siblings, and between twins.

The study of the intelligence of parents and children, while shedding much light on the hereditary component of intelligence, is difficult because the intelligence of the children must be tested very early in order to reduce, if not to eliminate, the influence of the home environment. But the measures of the intelligence of infants, despite some well-constructed scales, are inadequate, for they do not permit us to predict their scores on later tests.[7] It is only when the child is about two years old that tests will tell us anything certain about his intelligence. Before the age of two we can estimate the child's intelligence more accurately by testing his parents than by testing him. The insignificant correlation between the results of tested infants and their later intelligence scores, recently confirmed at the Yale child development clinic, highlights the difficulty of comparing parents and children on the hereditary element in human intelligence.[8]

[5] C. Spearman, "General intelligence" objectively determined and measured, *Amer. J. Psychol.*, 15 (1904), 201–93. See also C. Spearman, Theory of General Factor, *Brit. J. Psychol.*, 36 (1946), 117–31.

[6] See L. S. Penrose, Heredity, in J. McV. Hunt (ed.), *Personality and the behavior disorders* (New York: The Ronald Press Co., 1944), Ch. 16.

[7] N. Bayley, Consistency and variability in the growth of intelligence from birth to eighteen years, *J. genet. Psychol.*, 75 (1949), 165–96.

[8] For a report of the results of the Yale study see J. R. Wittenborn *et al.*, A study of adoptive children: II. The predictive validity of the Yale developmental examination of infant behavior, *Psychol. Monogr.*, 70 (1956), No. 409.

The well-known studies at Stanford University, the University of Minnesota, and the University of Iowa throw additional light on the role of heredity in the determination of intelligence. These are studies of the correlation between the intelligence of children with that of their true parents and with that of their foster parents.[9] With complete awareness of the fact that the extensive data and the statistical correlational studies do not lend themselves well to generalization, we can nevertheless clearly state that the studies show that heredity is a significant, but far from exclusive, factor in intelligence. More specifically, these studies reveal that in studies of intelligence a child resembles his true parents more than his foster parents even when the child has not grown up with his true parents. On the other hand, the *level* of intelligence of foster children (rather than the relative ranks measured by coefficients of correlation) is higher than would be expected from their hereditary antecedents. This increase in the intelligence level must be attributed to the superior background of the foster home. It would appear that intelligence, like personality as a whole, is positively affected by a favorable home in which potential intelligence can develop freely. But even this gain in intelligence level argues for the importance of heredity, for in these studies the greatest improvement was made by those children who had the brightest true mother. All in all, a good home tends to stimulate hereditary potentialities to their highest level, thus confirming once more the dynamic interaction between heredity and environment.

Special abilities. There is a paucity of reliable data on the source of special aptitudes and skills. By special abilities we refer to such capacities as mechanical and inventive aptitudes, artistic gifts, and musical imagination and performance. Musical ability often runs in families, but most of our knowledge regarding the hereditary factor here is literary, biographical, or purely anecdotal. Moreover, traditional attempts to trace musical and artistic abilities are often misleading, for they are examined mostly in families where these capacities are very outstanding. Children who come from the same families but who show no aesthetic interests or

[9] For the Stanford Study, see B. S. Burks, The relative influence of nature and nurture upon mental development: a comparative study of foster parent-child resemblance and true parent-child resemblance, *Yearb. nat. Soc. Stud. Educ.*, 27 (1928), 219–316. For the Minnesota Study, see A. M. Leahy, Nature-nurture and intelligence, *Genet. Psychol. Monogr.*, 17 (1935), 235–308. For the Iowa Study, see M. Skodak and H. M. Skeels, A final follow-up of one hundred adopted children, *J. genet. Psychol.*, 75 (1949), 3–19.

capacities are conveniently overlooked; and relatives of the gifted families who show no special talent are ignored.[10]

Of the abilities enumerated above, mechanical aptitude is generally the easiest to measure. Some of the tests require the subject to assemble the various parts of a machine into an operating unit. Others test the individual's manual skills, such as placing parts into a complicated formboard. According to those who employ them, these and similar tests have been found to be valuable in selecting persons for various tasks in industry. While this may be so, these tests tell us nothing regarding the genetic source of the capacities which they purport to measure. Since the design of these tests was purely utilitarian, we should not, of course, criticize them for failing to do what they were not constructed to perform.[11]

Artistic and musical talents are well known for their resistance to scientific measurement. They are widely used in our public schools to detect hidden abilities which might be amenable to direct training. A pioneer test of musical aptitude is Seashore's Measures of Musical Talents.[12] Seashore conceived of music as a complex of interrelated attributes, some of which his test could identify and measure. By means of phonograph records this test searches out the subject's tonal memory and his ability to discriminate differences in time interval, intensity, pitch, consonance, and rhythm. Since there is a wide range of differences in the subjects' discriminations which cannot be readily attributed to training or learning, one may assume the existence of a hereditary basis.

Our brief discussion of a few personality components which are partially determined by heredity reveals the basic weakness of investigations in this area. First, because of its inaccessible nature, personality cannot be easily studied by the rigid genetic methods which have proved to be successful in research on the morphology and the hereditary components of lower animals. Second, there are no scientifically adequate scales for measuring the qualitative characteristics of personality, and there is as yet no way for investigating the relationships among the elementary properties of the total personality structure. This is a serious methodological

[10] See Penrose, Heredity, p. 513.

[11] For a detailed discussion of these tests see D. G. Patterson et al., Minnesota mechanical ability tests (Minneapolis: University of Minnesota Press, 1930); W. V. Bingham, Aptitudes and aptitude testing (New York: Harper & Bros., 1937).

[12] C. E. Seashore et al., Measures of musical talents (Rev. ed.; Camden, N.J.: Education Department, R. C. A. Manufacturing Co., 1939). For a psychological analysis of music see C. E. Seashore, Psychology of music (New York: McGraw-Hill Book Co., Inc., 1938); P. R. Farnsworth, The social psychology of music (New York: Holt, Rinehart & Winston, Inc., 1958).

limitation, for the relationship among the elementary characteristics is greatly responsible for the baffling complexity of the human personality. Measuring these components one at a time, no matter how accurately, tells us very little about the personality as a whole; for the latter is, as we have remarked before, a configuration or *Gestalt*. Finally, the primitive state of our knowledge of the hereditary components of personality can be attributed in part to the fact that some of our leading personality psychologists either have not paid sufficient attention to the genetics of human behavior or have too greatly minimized its importance.

SOME PHYSIOLOGICAL DETERMINANTS OF PERSONALITY

We have already touched on some of the physiological aspects of human behavior. The nervous system, including the brain which is its most vital organ, is technically classified with the neurophysiological structure of the human organism. The understanding of basic reaction patterns like feelings and emotions is dependent upon a knowledge of physiological processes. Homeostatic drives, such as hunger, thirst, and sexual needs, are important physiological characteristics. Visceral responses and endocrine functions add to our understanding of human behavior, especially of temperament and the emotions.

Now, while psychologists have access to an enormous amount of physiological information, they have availed themselves of only a small portion. Moreover, when students of personality are confronted by physiological data they find themselves in the difficult position which we have already described: they do not have adequate measuring instruments to permit them to investigate the relation of the known physiological factors to the complex personality structure which they are trying to understand. Also, it is regrettably true that not infrequently, impressed by the importance of a single physiological component, some psychologists will employ it to account for a very complex form of behavior. This being the case, the student of personality should know at the very beginning of his adventure into the field that *a single physiological factor never explains a complicated psychological pattern*. This assertion has been convincingly demonstrated in a series of studies by Beach on the maternal and sexual behavior of rats.[13]

PHYSIOLOGICAL DRIVES. No other physiological aspect of behavior has been more extensively used in psychology than the physi-

[13] See, for example, F. A. Beach, Jr., Effects of cortical lesions upon the copulatory behavior of male rats, *J. comp. Psychol.*, 29 (1940), 193–245.

ological or homeostatic drives, especially in the psychology of motivation and learning. A physiological drive arises from the bodily condition of the organism which initiates a sequence of behavior that, if it is fully achieved, results in need-satisfaction or the avoidance of painful, dangerous, or noxious stimuli.

In denoting physiological drives as *homeostatic*, we call attention to the fact that they are basically need-reductive. Their "goal" is to return the physiologically agitated organism to a state of equilibrium. Thus when an organism is hungry, or in a state of physical discomfort, the body initiates forms of behavior whose function is to restore the state of equilibrium by consumption of food or removal of the source of physical discomfort. The process is described as a *cycle of activity*, involving a *need* (say, hunger), a *mechanism* to satisfy the need (say, looking for food), *consummatory behavior* (attaining food), and *homeostasis*, or the pleasure and satisfaction experienced in satisfying the need.

The hunger drive. Since hunger is probably the most elemental physiological drive, we shall discuss it first. Hunger is caused by the reduction of food energy in the blood. The stomach contractions which invariably follow prolonged food deprivation set the cycle of activity into motion, which comes to an end only when food is ingested by the stomach.

As in so many apparently simple physiological processes the situation is not quite so uncomplicated. Experiments with animals have shown that the chemical conditions of the body, not only stomach contractions, influence the hunger drive.[14] The hunger drive is further complicated by the fact that some hungers can be satisfied only by specific foods. Preferences for certain foods are largely culturally induced, but not entirely so. In his experiment on the food preferences of infants, Davis found that, if left to themselves, infants prefer some foods to others. Especially dramatic was the case of the infant suffering from rickets who selected cod liver oil, but only until he recovered.[15]

The sex drive. In the framework of cycles of activity sex need does not differ basically from hunger; the end state or goal differ-

[14] C. T. Morgan and J. D. Morgan, Studies in hunger: II. The relation of gastric denervation and dietary sugar to the effect of insulin upon food-intake in the rat, *J. genet. Psychol.*, 57 (1940), 153–63.

[15] C. M. Davis, Self-selection of diet by newly-weaned infants, *Amer. J. Dis. Child.*, 36 (1928), 651–79; C. M. Davis, A practical application of some lessons of the self-selection of diet and the feeding of children in hospitals, *Amer. J. Dis. Child.*, 46 (1943), 743–50. For a survey of researches on food preferences, up to 1935, see A. H. Maslow, Appetites and hungers in animal motivation, *J. comp. Psychol.*, 20 (1935), 75–83. For a brief review of recent research on hunger and thirst, see J. Brozek, Physiological psychology, *Annu. Rev. Psychol.*, 9 (1958), 71–98.

entiates them essentially. The sexual drive, like the hunger drive, is a state of restless activity; each is described by the need to release tensions, to attain the condition of homeostasis. The sexual drive as a form of restless activity is, however, much more characteristic of lower animals than of man. Experiments on rats have shown that during the *estrus* cycle the female is extremely restless and attempts copulation the moment she is placed near a male rat. An interesting fact about the rat's sexual behavior is the fact that injection of ovarian hormones advances the female's sexual behavior, showing that hormones play an important part in the sexual life of lower animals, but a much less significant one in human beings.[16]

In the area of human sex drives we are once more reminded that physiology alone does not account for even the primary drives. In the human being the sex drive is intertwined in intricate ways with the whole personality, with all of selfhood; so that, as Murphy has wisely observed, "ego psychology and the psychology of sex are bound to become interwoven." [17] The hereditary nature of the sex drive, like that of hunger, throws only a tiny ray of light on personality. Neither hunger nor sex as innate patterns help us to understand the *individual* person, for these drives are common to all normal men. It is the problem of individuality that is controlling here, for individuals differ in the intensity of their hunger and sex drives, and the specific goals toward which each is directed. In one man's life, food and sexual intercourse may be central and dominating; in another one's, these needs may become fused with other aspects of a total pattern of living. Human drives, despite their physiological bases, are not explained by physiological factors alone.

The maternal drive. The maternal impulse has been romanticized and sentimentalized in poetry and song. Tradition has it that the desire for and impulse to care for infants are inborn. There are clear evidences of this in the observation of and experiments on lower animals. Apparently prolactin, a hormone regulating the secretion of milk, plays an important role in maternal behavior. It has been found that if this hormone is injected into either male or female rats they build nests and care for infant rats around them.[18]

[16] F. A. Beach, *Hormones and behavior* (New York: Paul B. Hoeber, Inc., 1948); F. A. Beach, Characteristics of masculine 'sex drive,' in M. Jones (ed.), *Nebraska symposium on motivation* (Lincoln: University of Nebraska Press, 1956).

[17] G. Murphy, *Personality: a biosocial approach to origins and structure* (New York: Harper & Bros., 1947), pp. 106–7.

[18] O. R. Riddle, R. W. Bates, and E. L. Lahr, Maternal behavior in rats induced by prolactin, *Proc. Soc. exp. Biol.*, 32 (1935), 730–34; M. McQueen-Williams, Maternal behavior in male rats, *Science*, 82 (1935), 67–68.

In the human species, maternal care is not so simply explained. There is no doubt a physiological basis for it, for the length of the menstrual flow has been found to be an influencing factor.[19] Nevertheless, the far more important factor in the human maternal drive is the force of custom. As in the acquisition of all customs, there is a large element of learning in the maternal impulse of the human mother.

Owing to the psychologist's justified aversion to anecdotal and folk explanation of sex differences in behavior, he sometimes closes his eyes to information on this subject which merits his serious attention. A number of recent researches strongly support the claim for the biological determination of differential interests and activities of the sexes. In an investigation of drawing completions of college students it was found that the men showed a strong preference for locomotion, towers, and angular lines, whereas the women preferred containers, fruits, and flowers.[20] Another study shows a tendency toward motor agression in males and toward holding and carrying by females. In both cases these differences seem to be related to the muscular development of the sexes.[21] Like Franck, Erikson found a distinct preference for movement, height, and descent by boys, and for static representations by girls.[22]

Seward, remarking on the sexual differences found in various activities, also points out these variations in ethnic groups. Because these distinctions occur so regularly she believes that they probably have a biological substratum. "Boys seem to be consistently oriented toward motion, daring, and power; girls, toward serving and conserving. . . . Underlying the surface variations in custom and code among preliterate peoples, males have been found consistently preoccupied with achievement, and women with nurturing." [23]

ENDOCRINE FUNCTIONING. In several places in this chapter we remarked on the overlapping nature of physiological phenomena. In describing the organic drives like the sexual and maternal, we were in fact speaking of hormonal secretion. Lactation and menstruation are controlled by the endocrine system. The endocrine or ductless glands are the organs of internal secretion. They dis-

[19] D. M. Levy, Psychosomatic studies of some aspect of maternal behavior, *Psychosom. Med.* 4 (1942), 223–27.

[20] K. Franck, Preference for sex symbols and their personality correlates, *Genet. Psychol. Monogr.*, 33 (1946), 73–123.

[21] P. Greenacre, Anatomical structure and superego development, *Amer. J. Orthopsychiat.*, 18 (1948), 636–48.

[22] E. H. Erikson, Sex differences in the play configurations of preadolescents, *Amer. J. Orthopsychiat.*, 21 (1951), 667–92.

[23] G. Seward, *Psychotherapy and culture conflict* (New York: The Ronald Press Co., 1956), p. 196.

charge their chemical substances, called hormones, directly into the blood stream. While the evidence is not sufficiently convincing, a reasonably good case can be made out in support of the belief that endocrine secretions may predispose a person to be calm or excitable, tense or unharried, active or sluggish. Although we are not concerned in this book with the abnormal personality, there is clear evidence that endocrine dysfunctions produce abnormalities in behavior. There is no reason to deny, therefore, that inherited differences in glandular reactions and secretions may result in differences in normal individual dispositions and temperaments.

The literature on the role of endocrine factors in behavior is truly enormous. Worse yet, from the standpoint of a simple exposition of the subject, this field is overrun with contradictory experimental results, almost all of which can muster at least some respectable supporting evidence. In the face of this trying state of affairs, we shall select for discussion only a very few important items.

Role of the endocrine glands. While it is necessary to describe these glands separately, they do not function individually. Rather, they form an interlocking system in which each influences every other. The chemical compounds which they produce are essential to normal life. When any one of them secretes either too little or too much of a specific chemical compound, it produces noticeable changes in the personality.

The *thyroid* gland, whose action is probably best known of all the endocrine glands, produces a hormone of iodine. A certain amount of it is essential for health, although there are slight differences in individual tolerance. If the gland is deficient in producing iodine, it causes dullness and sluggishness. If the deficiency is serious it results in a form of feeble-mindedness called *cretinism.* If the gland is overproductive, the person becomes tense, overactive, and excitable. In severe overproduction, the individual develops exophthalmic goiter, which is easily recognized by a noticeable bulging of the eyeballs.

The *parathyroid* glands, of which there are two, regulate the calcium content of the blood. Deficient secretion of their content results in overexcitability of the nervous system, which in turn decreases a person's self-control. Oversecretion of their content gives rise to physical pains and weakness, but its effect on the personality is not understood.

The *pituitary* gland regulates the growth of the body. The giant and the dwarf are products of pituitary dysfunction. This gland also controls the other endocrine glands by either stimulating or inhibiting their functions.

The *adrenal* glands produce a chemical known as adrenalin, which regulates the sugar in the blood, blood pressure, and muscular energy. It has been referred to as the "emergency gland," because it mobilizes extra effort when the individual is confronted by a crisis or emergency, such as fear, flight, or combat.

The *pancreas*—or more accurately, the parts of the pancreas known as the *islands of Langerhans*—secretes insulin. A deficiency in insulin secretion makes it difficult for the body to assimilate carbohydrates, and results in diabetes. The relation between diabetes and personality is not well known, and so far it has been impossible to differentiate cause and effect in the relationship. Some researches have found mental confusion in diabetics, but others have discovered no difference between normal and diabetic cases regarding important intellectual functions, particularly on intelligence test scores.[24] Emotional maladjustment in diabetic children has been reported in some investigations, but the condition was complicated by other factors, especially social conditions.[25]

The function of the *gonads*, or sex glands, is generally best understood. They regulate the differential sex characteristics, especially in adolescence. Accordingly, they are particularly important in the development of the obvious physical differences between men and women, such as facial hair, breasts, voice, and musculature. Maldevelopment in these areas affects the personality in various ways. However, the effect of these maldevelopments is considerably affected by the norms of the society in which a person lives. Feminine characteristics in a man, for instance, are not evaluated similarly in all societies, just as homosexuality is ignored in one culture, despised in another, and esteemed in still another.

The emotions. The "classical" work of Cannon, which we have already cited, has neatly demonstrated the role of the emotions in behavior.[26] Emotions serve at once to adjust the individual to his environment and to interfere with his adjustment. Whether they help or hinder in adjustment depends largely on their intensity and consequent disorganizing effect upon the individual's behavior.

[24] G. D. Brown, The development of diabetic children, with special reference to mental and personality comparisons, *Child Developm.*, 9 (1938), 175–84.

[25] A. P. McGaven, E. Schultz, G. W. Peden, and B. D. Bowen, The physical growth, the degree of intelligence and the personality adjustment of a group of diabetic children, *New Engl. J. Med.*, 223 (1940), 119–27. (Abstract.)

[26] W. B. Cannon, *Bodily changes in pain, hunger, fear, and rage* (2d ed.; New York: Appleton-Century-Crofts, Inc., 1929).

This statement, like so many others, must be qualified so as to account for the fact that an intense emotion, such as fright, may protect a person from danger or destruction. An intense emotion in a different situation may be exceedingly disruptive. It is known to disorganize learning and problem-solving. It has been shown, for example, that intelligence scores on a second test drop as a consequence of intense emotional upset due to disappointment over the results of the first test.[27]

The physiological aspects of the emotions have been measured extensively in the laboratory. Among the physiological indicators which have been studied are changes in the blood pressure and in its composition, such as blood sugar and adrenalin content, the rate and depth of respiration, the heart rate, electrical changes on the skin, gastro-intestinal disturbances such as vomiting and diarrhea, pupillary dilation, and muscle tensions.

Emotions also affect our perceptions in discernible ways. When angry, a person perceives the actions of others in a different light than he perceives them when he is calm. The suspicious person interprets another's behavior as hostile or unfriendly, even though these conditions do not realistically describe the other's attitudes. The tendency to project our fears is well known in chronic anxiety and insecurity. In order to understand a person we must know how he perceives his world; and in order to know why he perceives it in a certain way, we must be informed of his dominant and enduring emotional states. A person who derives joy from reading good books and hearing great music differs from one whose happiness depends upon betting on horses and viewing a prize fight. Each perceives life from a different emotional perspective.

The upshot of the foregoing remarks is that while there is unquestionably a physiological basis for our emotions, physiology alone cannot explain them. It has been found that when hormone substances are injected into the blood a human being will experience the typical organic reactions associated with them, such as increased blood pressure and blood-sugar content, without experiencing emotions in a meaningfully human sense. "To experience 'emotion' there must be something more than the physiological upheaval in which the adrenal glands participate."[28] One of these additional elements is the manner in which we perceive our experience.

[27] B. Lantz, Some dynamic aspects of success and failure, *Psychol. Monogr.*, 59 (1945), No. 271.
[28] N. W. Shock, Physiological factors in behavior, in Hunt, *Personality and the behavior disorders*, p. 582.

In view of the uncertain reliability of research in the field of the psychological effects of physiological conditions, and the variety of authoritative opinion on the subject, much of the work on this problem is irrelevant. Most certainly, it has not been very fruitful. Even the results of investigations in psychosomatic conditions are geared too much to the physiological effects of emotional states and not enough to gaining a more penetrating understanding of the human personality. A hopeful sign on the psychological horizon is the increasing attention to the conception of emotions as a state of excitement, and less to what is sometimes largely an arbitrary distinction between the different modalities. This view stresses emotional intensity, ranging from the absence of emotions, as in sleep, to diffuse excitement, as in anticipation of a coming event.[29]

In conclusion, most existing evidence points to the fact that physiological states are only minor determinants of human behavior. Hence it follows that behavior cannot be explained on the basis of any particular organic condition, be it the nervous system, physiological drives, or endocrine functioning. The endocrinologists, particularly, have asserted more than the facts seem to justify. To describe the endocrine glands as the regulators of personality is to push an illuminating idea very much farther than the evidence permits. The dependable evidence suggests the conclusion that the higher we go in the phyletic scale, the less marked is the influence of physiological conditions on behavior. When we come to man, we find that much is acquired but little is inherited.

CONSTITUTIONAL FACTORS IN PERSONALITY

Attempts to show a relationship between personality and constitutional make-up can be traced to ancient times. Hippocrates, the "father" of medicine, argued for a connection between temperament and the cardinal "humors," or bodily fluids of blood, phlegm, yellow bile, and black bile. Interest in this problem seems never to abate, and one psychobiologist, William Sheldon, has been devoting his career for more than thirty years to the investigation of this recurring topic.

Although contemporary constitutional theories are described as typologies, which would logically place the subject in Chapter 3, where we take up the theory of types, they are in fact *correlational* studies of the relation between constitution and behavioral characteristics. Kretschmer, the first rigidly scientific investigator of this association, has been widely misunderstood and unfairly

[29] R. S. Woodworth and H. Schlosberg, *Experimental psychology* (Rev. ed.; New York: Holt, Rinehart & Winston, Inc., 1954).

maligned, but it is grossly inaccurate to dismiss his work as merely a typology. That his findings led him to a theory of constitutional and psychological types is obvious, but it is of secondary importance when compared with the centrality of his remarkable empirical and correlational studies.[30]

KRETSCHMER'S CHARACTEROLOGY. Kretschmer's work on "character" or "temperament" as conditioned by constitutional make-up, has been partly corroborated. It has implications for normal, prepsychotic, and psychotic individuals. The prepsychotic and psychotic forms of character are the *cycloid* and the *schizoid*. The first characterizes the manic-depressive patient; the second, the schizophrenic. In a less clearly marked form these two are also found in the prepsychotic personality, that condition of temperament which hovers between normality and abnormality. Kretschmer used the terms *cyclothymia* and *schizothymia* to describe the same conditions of sociability and unsociability in the normal individual. It is the cycloid and schizoid types, however, that have been most fully described.

The cycloid temperament is essentially sociable, outgoing, and good-natured. A cycloid individual may fluctuate between elation and depression. When elated, he displays in exaggerated form those emotional traits which we associate with the good-natured individual: he is cheerful, facetious, and impulsive. When depressed, he presents a picture of dejection, reticence, and psychomotor inertia.

The schizoid temperament, on the other hand, is fundamentally unsociable, withdrawn, morose, and "peculiar." This peculiarity stems largely from the bipolar nature of his temperament, for he is at once receptive and indifferent, hypersensitive and unfeeling. His receptiveness and hypersensitivity are expressed in shyness and an exaggerated concern for the opinions of others. His indifference and coldness are revealed in moroseness and taciturnity. Since this pattern of traits tends to convey a picture of eccentricity, the schizoid's social relationships are correspondingly constricted, and for this condition he compensates through autistic reveries.

Like many investigators before him, Kretschmer was interested

[30] For the original edition of his book on this subject, see E. Kretschmer, *Körperbau und Charakter* (Berlin: Springer Verlag, 1921). An English translation, *Physique and character* (New York: Harcourt, Brace and Co., 1925), was made by W. J. H. Sprott. The twentieth German edition of this work appeared in 1951, and contains Kretschmer's latest thinking and research on this problem. Unfortunately, Kretschmer's mature and more definitive views have, judging by the wearisome repetition of his earlier researches in our textbooks, scarcely reached the American professional audience.

in relating the two basic dispositions to physique. On the basis of extensive observations, as well as familiarity with the work of his French and German predecessors on the problem of constitutional types, Kretschmer initially described three main physical types. These he called *pyknic, asthenic,* and *athletic.* Later he added a new, mixed type, which he called *dysplastic.*

The *pyknic* type has a large head, full thorax, and ample abdomen. The body as a whole is rounded, with a tendency toward obesity. The face is round and broad, and the hands are wide and pudgy. The *asthenic* type is thin and long, flat-chested, with lean and long arms and narrow shoulders. His face is long, thin, and angular. The *athletic* type has a strong body-build, powerful muscles, deep chest, and large hands and feet. The *dysplastic* physique is a mixture of types, characterized mostly by asymmetry.

Corresponding to these physical types, Kretschmer claims, are personality or character types, both normal and psychotic. The pyknic type is largely cyclothymic, that is, sociable and jolly, realistic and outgoing. In the psychotic state, he is manic-depressive. The asthenic and athletic individuals tend toward schizothymia: they are withdrawn, unsociable, idealistic, and reserved. This is particularly true of the asthenic individual. In the psychotic state the asthenic and athletic persons tend strongly toward schizophrenia, particularly the aesthenic individual. While the dysplastic is a mixed form, he leans heavily toward the withdrawn and schizophrenic end of the distribution scale.[31]

Although the work of Kretschmer has interested many psychologists, most of them in this country have been unsympathetic toward both his typology and his methodology. American psychologists are, as a rule, repelled by such vague terms as "character" and "temperament," which have considerable vogue in Europe, especially in Germany. The partly correct view that Kretschmer's study of character is a typology causes many students to ignore his meticulous research in favor of superficial digests in textbook chapters. Had Kretschmer used the words "matrix," "cluster," or "factor," his work would probably find a more sympathetic audience.

Again, those psychologists who believe that statistical analysis is the *sine qua non* of psychological research have been too impatient with Kretschmer's failure to provide a rigorous statistical treatment for his correlational studies. This weakness, while ad-

[31] For a brief summary of the literature and the main conclusions on this subject, see H. J. Eysenck, *Dimensions of personality* (London: Kegan Paul, Trench, Trubner & Co., Ltd., 1947), pp. 83–94; H. J. Eysenck, Cyclothymia and schizothymia as a dimension of personality. I. A historical review. *J. Pers.,* 19 (1950), 123–52.

mittedly regrettable, blinds Kretschmer's critics to the importance of his experimental techniques and the originality of his psychological insights. We remind the reader of Murray's dictum regarding the relative merits of meticulous techniques and the urgency of psychological problems. With all its statistical defects, Kretschmer's investigations are rich in psychological interest and pregnant with valuable implications for the study of man. These are no small achievements.

SHELDON'S CONSTITUTIONAL PSYCHOLOGY. As in Kretschmer's case, Sheldon's work is usually described as forming a typological system; and as in Kretschmer's case, this is partly true, but is only of secondary relevance. The basic fact regarding Sheldon's researches is that they form a basis for the study of *individual differences,* as well as of general types. Only by noting this important truth can Sheldon's investigations be justly evaluated.

On the basis of his study of the photographs of several thousand individuals by a special technique of bodily measurement, Sheldon found statistically significant tendencies toward certain bodily configurations which he called *somatotypes.* These measurements were made only on men. However, during the past few years Sheldon has been using the same technique in measuring the physical dimensions of women.[32]

Emerging from the extensive measurements of the male physique are three somatotypes, namely, endomorphic, ectomorphic, and mesomorphic.

In the *endomorphic* constitution the digestive viscera is large and highly developed, while the body structure of bone, muscle, and connective tissue is relatively weak and undeveloped. Endomorphs are generally obese, soft, and spherical. In the *ectomorphic* constitution, the body is linear and fragile, the chest is flat, and both viscera and body structure are undeveloped. A stooped posture and restrained movement are conspicuous characteristics of the ectomorph. In the *mesomorphic* constitution the body structure is relatively strong, hard, well-developed, and tough. Blood vessels, especially the arteries, are large. The skin is thick and its pores

[32] For a full-scale discussion of the problem, methods, and conclusions, see the following: W. H. Sheldon *et al., The varieties of human physique: an introduction to constitutional psychology* (New York: Harper & Bros., 1940); W. H. Sheldon and S. S. Stevens, *The varieties of temperament: a psychology of constitutional differences* (New York: Harper & Bros., 1942). For the technique of somatotyping, see W. H. Sheldon *et al., Atlas of men: a guide for somatotyping the adult male at all ages* (New York: Harper & Bros., 1954). For a brief but comprehensive review of the subject, see W. H. Sheldon, Constitutional factors in personality, in Hunt, *Personality and the behavior disorders,* Ch. 17.

are large. An upright and sturdy posture are the most noticeable features of the mesomorphic individual.

Some psychological correlates of constitutional types. Sheldon has been interested, we pointed out, in ascertaining what associations or correlations, if any, are to be found between somatotypes and personality. He found a high congruence between somatotypes and their temperamental or personality correlates—a correlation, however, which has not been duplicated or confirmed by other, independent investigators. Corresponding to the endomorphic, ectomorphic, and mesomorphic constitutions he found, respectively, visceratonic, cerebrotonic, and somatotonic temperaments.

The *visceratonic* is sociable, convivial, loves comfort, and is a glutton for food. Eating and digestion seem to be the most important activities in his life. He likes physical and social proximity with others, like sheep rubbing wool against wool. As Sheldon put it: "The motivational organization is dominated by the gut and by the function of anabolism. The personality seems to center around the viscera." [33] The *cerebrotonic* is dominated by restraint and inhibition, unsociableness, and withdrawal. His restraint reaches even the somatic and visceral expressions, which he tends to repress. The *somatotonic* is characterized by vigorous muscular and bodily activity. He is largely motivated by bodily self-assertiveness, vigor, and push. Action, ambition, love of power, together with a thoughtless disregard of others, make up the flywheel of his life.

Although Sheldon studied some four thousand individuals, his initial reports on correlations between physique and temperament are based on an analysis of about two hundred cases. The correlations between the constitutions and their corresponding temperaments are given below.

Endomorphy–Visceratonia	+.79
Ectomorphy–Cerebrotonia	+.83
Mesomorphy–Somatotonia	+.82

Clearly, this is a correlation of the order of +.81, which is statistically a very reliable relationship. If this correlation should be confirmed by many independent investigators—and we have indicated that this confirmation has not been made, the coefficients found by others being much lower—we might indeed have important proof of the organic basis of human personality. However,

[33] Constitutional factors in personality, in Hunt, *Personality and the behavior disorders,* Vol. I, p. 543.

it is a commonplace in the logic of statistical analysis that a high correlation between two events tells us nothing concerning their fundamental connectedness. Sheldon's correlations shed no light on the structural interconnectedness of constitution and personality. It may be there are factors mediating between the constitutional and psychological dimensions which are not elicited by the correlation technique.

Again, the role of expectancy and the subtle influence of stereotypes should not be ruled out. Sheldon is himself aware of the insidious effect of rater bias, but he has to date made little attempt to eliminate it in his own work. Sheldon made both the constitution and temperament ratings himself. The likelihood that his own preconceptions unwittingly slipped into his ratings must be seriously entertained.

Ratings made by others than Sheldon himself are subject to the same criticism. Their ratings were made with full knowledge of Sheldon's morphological findings and his view of the psychological correlates of the constitutional types. It need not be surprising, therefore, if their ratings were contaminated by a set of expectations in the direction of Sheldon's own conclusions. Thus the logic of research design demands replications of Sheldon's measurements by many others under conditions of "blind" procedure. This will not eliminate subjective factors altogether, but it will considerably reduce them on the one hand, and put Sheldon's methodology above justly deserved criticism on the other.

Further, the well-known stereotypes regarding the fat man and the thin can affect a Sheldon as well as a Shakespeare. The fat man is widely believed to be relaxed and jolly, and the thin man anxious and suspicious. "Let me have men about me that are fat," says Caesar, in Shakespeare's famous tragedy. "Yon Cassius has a lean and hungry look . . . such men are dangerous."

Finally, Sheldon's methods, while good on numerous grounds, may very well affect the nature of the results which he obtained. We have already called attention to the fact that in psychological research particularly, the methods may tell us more about themselves than about the subject which they were designed to investigate. Another researcher, using different techniques for assessing temperament, may arrive at different conclusions regarding the relation between morphological factors and personality.

These critical comments are intended as a warning to the student of personality whose knowledge of characterological research is very limited. They are not to be construed as a complete rejection of either the methods or the findings of constitutional psychology.

Research in the area leaves no doubt that there is an important correlation between constitutional organization and personality structure. The moot question concerns the *magnitude* of the association, not the association itself. The trend of authoritative opinion is against Sheldon's extreme claim on both methodological and theoretical grounds. His methodological procedures are subject to the user's preconception and bias, whereas his results are insufficiently supported by present knowledge of the nature of personality. When these considerations are taken into account we have to conclude that constitutional psychology has made a valuable contribution to our understanding of personality.

CONCLUSION

Although this chapter is relatively brief, it covers an enormous territory. The section on heredity shows that much is known about the genetic transmission of physical characteristics, but very little regarding the role of heredity in the human personality. The morphology of the body, musculature, and the nervous system must be reckoned with in the study of behavior, but so far our knowledge of them has been barren of psychological understanding. Intelligence and special abilities probably have genetic bases, but the results of research are contradictory and inconclusive. The controversy over the relative effects of heredity and environment is largely fruitless. Even the geneticists, who naturally emphasize the great importance of heredity, do not see the problem simply. Heredity is a complex process of transmission of biophysical traits from parent to offspring, and demands a respectful hearing even by environmentalists.

The physiological determinants of personality are too often given more weight than they deserve. This is particularly true regarding the homeostatic drives and the role of endocrine functioning. Because of the high status of learning theory in contemporary psychology, personality psychologists have tended to ignore other approaches to the investigation of personality. While it is true that the learning of laboratory animals has been investigated almost exclusively by the technique of food deprivation, the results of this mode of investigation have thrown little light upon the character of the human personality. Human beings learn and seek and solve their problems, not only to restore their equilibrium, but for reasons which elude the probing techniques of the animal laboratory.

Again, although the human emotions are embedded in the endocrinological system of the organism, their role in the human personality is not completely physiological. How an individual feels is also determined by his perception of the world around him —by what it *means* to him. The emotions in turn affect his perception of the world. The happy and the miserable person do not perceive a tragedy or misfortune in identical ways.

The student of personality must guard himself against the beguiling force of constitutional psychology. What is more natural than seeing a linkage between an individual's physical appearance and his personality structure? Common-sense observations and popular psychology are replete with plausible instances of constitutional properties and their corresponding psychological characteristics. The student of personality must, however, be able to view untested conclusions sympathetically, yet skeptically. This applies with special force to the tendency to be disproportionately impressed by coefficients of correlations, or by statistical indices. Since in our view psychological truth must be computed not only by means of technical skill but even more by wisdom derived from the use of scientific imagination, the psychologist has the moral obligation to defer judgment until there is little cause for serious doubt. We do not hesitate to say that in the realm of the organic foundations of personality there is sufficient reason for maintaining an unyielding skepticism.

Personality, we have frequently remarked, is an intricate psychological system. It is inordinately difficult to factor out those attributes which have a genetic, neurophysiological, or constitutional origin. This should be a sufficient warning to all of us to regard organic agencies not as determining but as *limiting* factors in the growth of personality. Genetic and organic components place a limit on the degree and extent to which environmental forces can direct the course of psychological development. Claims that go beyond this simple observation are, in the present stage of our knowledge, based on unsupported speculation.

CHAPTER 6

The Human Group

In the preceding chapter we contrasted heredity with environment without specifying the meaning of the latter. In the present chapter we shall describe the environment of the social group in detail, and trace its effect on the developing human organism. The human group, composed of people in interaction, and human culture, comprised of the social heritage of customs, codes, and rules of behavior, make up the society in which every individual's personality is formed. The social heritage we shall defer to the next chapter; the human group and the process of socialization which takes place in it are the subject matter of the present chapter.

It is a commonplace that under normal conditions man is nowhere a solitary creature. From the moment he issues from his mother's womb to the time when he draws his last breath, man is dependent on others in his group. He grows and matures into an independent individual as the range of his interactions increases and the dimension of his participation in the lives of others deepens. To a great extent man derives his individuality as a person in the being of others. This is, as we shall see, no sentimental notion but an indisputable fact. The early responses of the infant, which he would make even in complete isolation because they are biological in nature, are patterned into increasingly specific forms by the coacting behavior of others. The child's socially patterned relationships mold his future attitudes and actions until at last he is recognized as having his own unique individuality. His personality is a dynamic product of group pressures upon his biological heritage. Outside these group pressures human beings as we know them could not originate and develop. "The raw materials of adjustment—the reflexes, glands, drives, and other elements of the infant's biological heritage—are transformed, by a long process of social and cultural conditioning, into attitudes, habits, and modes of behavior demanded by the group."[1] The student of personality who is intent on understanding human nature must, accordingly, pay careful attention to the socializing forces of group life.

Of the groups that shape man's personality we shall single out for detailed discussion the family, the school, anchorage groups, and the work group. In the family the child forms important identifications and attachments and acquires his fundamental habit patterns. In the school he extends his interactions beyond the family circle to include a variety of other persons. In his anchorage groups he expresses preferential relationships, seeking out those individuals who supply him with contacts and satisfactions that he can obtain neither in the family nor in the school. In the work group he seeks economic independence.

THE FAMILY MATRIX

Sociologists describe the family as a *primary* group. A primary group is one in which the interactions of its members are intimate, face-to-face, and personal. It is distinguished from other groups by its characteristic psychological structure. This structure impels the group members to identify themselves closely with one another, and to feel a direct and intimate concern for the group as a whole. In this mutual identification human sympathy develops. Indeed, sympathy *is* the psychological structure of the primary group, especially the family. Personality itself is formed within the matrix of sympathy, so that in its maturity it is a way of behaving, as G. H. Mead would say, which we attribute to others because we perceive it in ourselves.[2]

GROUP CHARACTERISTICS OF THE FAMILY. Despite the radical changes that have taken place in the American family, and despite the expressed fears that it has ceased to be the chief molding force of human character, it is still the most profound socializing agency in our lives. In order to understand more clearly the role of the family in the development of personality, it will be helpful if we first examine its important group-psychological characteristics.

Interdependence. This characteristic is nonetheless important

[1] H. Bonner, *Social psychology: an interdisciplinary approach* (New York: American Book Co., 1953), p. 83.

[2] See G. H. Mead, *Mind, self and society* (Chicago: University of Chicago Press, 1934).

for being so obvious. Interdependence is a social state often confused or identified with mutual dependence, which it resembles. However, mutual dependence, which looms large in the early months of a child's life, is essentially a passive trait. Although the infant depends wholly on the responses made to him by others, as he develops his relations with others become increasingly interactional or interdependent. Family life can be said to exist only when each family member depends on and has concern for the welfare of the whole group. The similar attitudes, objectives, and interests which characterize the unified family are products of the interdependence of its members. Through their interaction with one another they learn to participate in joint activities. Despite the decrease in mutual identification in the modern family, brought about by the conditions of modern life, a unity of interests is still one of its leading attributes. We are, of course, describing the organized family, not the family divided by dissension and intense conflicts of interest. When, through interdependence, the family achieves relative unity, it enables the individual to share a common value system, a common heritage. In this common heritage the individual escapes isolation and yet is able to develop his own individuality. In the unified family the individuals can adjust their differences because they are deeply conscious of the social and individual consequences of inimical behavior.

Sympathy. We have already described this group characteristic by saying that it forms the psychological structure of the primary group. An individual acquires sympathy because he lives in a primary group in which the fortunes or misfortunes of one of its members become the intimate concern of all. This psychological structure is inherent in the primary group, for group togetherness demands that people act in certain common ways. It requires that we take one another's roles; and in taking one another's roles we acquire the sentiment which the particular role represents. Thus, we have a human nature, a personality, to the extent that we can imagine ourselves doing what another person is doing. From this standpoint, personality is not explained in terms of either biological or cultural factors alone but must include the kind of experience which an individual has when he interacts with others and participates in intimate personal relationships in a primary group. The universal similarity of people is less a biological than a social fact. Men are alike because they possess the feeling of sociability or sympathy, which is generated in the primary group, the family. Sympathy, a property of the group structure, is internalized to form an individual's sentiments and attitudes.

Social control. As a set of established rules, social control is a universal group phenomenon. In every society the individual is required to subordinate his own interests to those of the group if they are inimical to the welfare of the latter. Its purpose in all groups, whether primary or secondary, is to provide its members with a common set of expectations whereby unity and consensus is made possible, and to secure for the group the continuity of its own existence. In the absence of common expectations no one could anticipate the behavior of others. Without continuity no group could safeguard its own stability and survival. The regulation of the child's behavior in the home is necessary not only in the interests of his own humanization, but also because it vouchsafes the stability and permanence of the family as a whole.

The role of language in social control is obvious. When he communicates his needs to his parents, the growing child is utilizing language to influence their behavior, just as they are controlling his own actions by their verbal commands and entreaties. The sound of his voice and the rudimentary verbal gestures made by the child modify the behavior of other family members. It is reasonable to assume that the chief stimulus to the origin and growth of language lies in "its utility in influencing organisms which are similarly constituted. . . . From its beginning, language must have served one fundamental purpose: *to influence the thinking and behavior of men in relation to one another.*" [3]

This brief account of the role of social control in the group not only makes it clear that the group patterns behavior, or molds the individual along certain lines, but also calls attention to the group's restraining and regulatory functions. Since every primary group, including the family, exercises coercive power over its members and requires conformity to its demands, social control acts as a conservative and stabilizing influence. Excessive control in this sense tends to discourage variation and individuality and to stifle creativeness and the impulsion to self-actualization. The implications of the restraining force of social control for good and evil are obvious.

INTERPERSONAL RELATIONS IN THE FAMILY. It must be clearly understood that we are not using the term "interpersonal relations" in Sullivan's limited sense. In the latter's interpersonal theory of psychiatry, the interpersonal condition, or set of relations between persons, and not the individual himself, is the unit of investigation.[4]

---

[3] Bonner, *Social psychology*, p. 70.

[4] See H. S. Sullivan, *The interpersonal theory of psychiatry* (New York: W. W. Norton & Co., Inc., 1953).

We are using the term to denote any intimate or personal interaction of two or more individuals. At the same time, in using the term as here indicated we do not mean, as should be clear from our preceding remarks, that the personality exists apart from an individual's relations to other people. The person, we said, does not live in isolation. He is a system of intrapsychic traits, but he is inseparable from others who are also systems of intrapsychic events.

Early interpersonal contacts. The infant's earliest contact is obviously with his mother. She provides the first important satisfactions in the infant's life, and exercises the first important restrictions. These controls are prescribed by the customs of the group, of course, but their psychological feeling-tone is generated almost entirely by the mother. Our interest in this section is not with the controls as such, but with the manner in which they are exercised by adults.

Of first importance are the *basic disciplines* which in most societies are largely controlled by the mother. These are the forms of child training which prepare the infant and young child in the performance of the acceptable ways of bodily and organic behavior.[5]

The *oral* disciplines are those forms of control which center around gratification of needs by way of the mouth. The earliest oral activity is nursing. The nursing activity is not a simple process of ingesting milk into the baby's mouth and stomach. It involves the pleasant sensations afforded by holding the nipple in the mouth, satisfying of the sucking impulse, and relieving hunger. These satisfactions are completely physical. However, a sound and beneficial nursing activity is always accompanied by important psychological benefits. The close contact with his mother arouses feelings of warm acceptance and security in the child. Many pediatricians and child psychologists have frequently noted that infants who receive insufficient attention in the nursing act, or who are left alone too much, do not thrive as well physically and psychologically as those whose mothers are psychologically more involved in the performance of the feeding process. One can hardly avoid speculating on the psychological effect on the child of the increasing practice of bottle feeding in our own society. It is not unreasonable to suppose that this practice may deprive the growing infant of the all-important feeling of security. Since the *quality*

[5] The most comprehensive and detailed survey of the basic disciplines and their psychological import is found in O. S. English and G. H. J. Pearson, *Emotional problems of living* (2d ed.; New York: W. W. Norton & Co., Inc., 1955).

of the interpersonal contact between mother and child is important, the increasingly depersonalized regime of infant-feeding must be taken into account in assessing its consequences for the later adult personality.[6]

The oral disciplines are not restricted to eating as such. They include any family- or group-prescribed expectation associated with it, such as regularity, table manners, and food preferences. For example, in one society good etiquette requires one to smack one's lips, or emit a resounding belch, in expression of appreciation, whereas in another these same actions would violate the rules of etiquette. The oral activities extend to the area of speech, and include instruction in the use or rejection of words, pronunciation, and tone of voice.

The *anal* and *urethral* disciplines, generally called toilet training, are regulated by the family largely in accordance with the practices of the social group. Although toilet training is significantly influenced by the class status of the parents, there is a latitude in which the feelings and attitudes of a particular parent, most often the mother, has an important effect upon the child. The age at which sphincter control is initiated varies with the education and social status of the mother, but the manner of effecting it depends upon her own disposition and temperament. This is equally true regarding the child's bladder control. The mother who finds ministration to the child's toilet needs unpleasant or disgusting may readily transmit her reactions to her child. The *quality* of her interpersonal contacts in the training is very crucial. The anxious and impatient mother, who hurries the child to perform his toilet acts, tends to create anxiety and irritability in him. If she responds to his unavoidable lapses with anger or punishment, the child, by a simple process of conditioning, may learn to associate unpleasantness or anxiety with elimination for the rest of his life. Activities that are not only normal but pleasant, to the child are associated with resentment. And ironically, parental anxieties here are self-defeating. The parent who inculcates shame or disgust in the child will not by these attitudes make him a refined adult, but more likely a prude or a neurotic.

Where the relations between mother and child are warm and accepting, the process of toilet training becomes an important

[6] It is well known that infant-feeding practices, being influenced by the prevailing social climate of the group, are subject to considerable fluctuation. However, the *quality* of the interpersonal contacts, the specific *feeling tone* of the mother's behavior toward the child, are not greatly affected by the changes in styles of discipline. For a comprehensive review of child-training practices from 1914 to 1940, see M. Wolfenstein, The emergence of fun morality, *J. soc. Issues*, 8 (1951), 15–25.

method of learning. Patience and sympathy by the parent will give the child time to learn that his present effort to control his bowel and urethra will result in future reward in the form of love and approval. The child will learn that self-control leads to the best results in the long run. He will have sufficient opportunity to acquire what the psychoanalysts call the "reality principle," which enables a person to defer immediate pleasures for future rewards. "A parent," we have written elsewhere, "who muffs the opportunity during toilet training of letting the child acquire the reality principle will deprive him of one of the most important principles for achieving a mature personality." [7]

The child's potential for learning the acceptable toilet habits is greater than most parents know. If parents are unaware of this, it is usually because they do not, in the first place, realize the drastic change involved when the child is stimulated to surrender his former irresponsibility and to acquire a measure of control over his natural functions. In the second place, the parents are seldom cognizant of the child's own eagerness to please them by doing what they request. Despite his resistance to socialization, the healthy child *wants* to conform to the expectations of his parents and, given love and encouragement, will do so in time. A third consideration is the failure of parents to realize that every child has his own rhythms of bowel and urethral elimination. Children differ in these functions, and it is a grave mistake to use as a model the child of the envied parents next door. Life is too short and the stability of the growing child too important, to saddle parents and children with the anxiety borne of a slight difference in maturation.

The *genital* disciplines occupy a special position in the American family. Preoccupation with the child's sexual activities is still, despite an enlightened attitude toward them, a marked characteristic of child rearing. Furthermore, even though an enormous amount of reliable evidence now exists in support of the presence of sexuality in young children, conceived as a part of the more inclusive complex of pleasurable experience, too many parents are still ignorant of its place in the total psychic economy of the developing infant. However, authorities on the psychosexual development of the child know that before the latter is two years old he has already discovered that his genital organs are sensitive to touch and manipulation, and that he can obtain sensual pleasure by self-stimulation. While this condition causes anxiety in many parents, it is perfectly normal for the healthy child. Indeed, the

[7] Bonner, *Social psychology,* p. 104.

consensus of expert medical and psychological opinion is that it is essential to human psychosexual growth and personality development. Existing evidence points to the conclusion that sexual behavior, consisting of genital play and later masturbation, aids in the development of the individual. Parental interference, especially if it is punitive and depreciatory of the child's ego and self-esteem, may have serious consequences. It may cause excessive dependence upon others and encourage hostility toward the offending parent. Psychiatric and psychological opinion is that masturbation *in itself* has no harmful mental or physical effects upon the child. In those cases where injurious results take place, it consists in the form of mental and emotional conflict arising from the *feelings of guilt and unworthiness* which are generated by the outraged and interfering parent. The belief that masturbation leads to mental disorder, impotence in men, and frigidity in women has been thoroughly discredited. On the contrary, the evidence supports the view that sexual deficiencies in men and women are often caused by the failure of individuals thus afflicted to focus their diffuse sexual curiosity and feeling upon their genital organs through early sexual play.

Some psychological effects of the basic disciplines. We have cited some of the consequences of the quality of the interpersonal relations of mother and child in the use of the basic disciplines. Love, acceptance, patience, encouragement, and a tender forgiveness of lapses and failures in the child's behavior usually have healthful consequences. The person grows into a stable adult, and for the most part he is free of the crippling anxieties and inhibiting pruderies which accompany faulty training in the basic disciplines.

On the other hand, the child whose parents, either through ignorance or their own immaturity, use the disciplines ineptly may grow into an unhappy, anxious, and hostile adult. Clinical evidence and case studies have shown that if a child is weaned too suddenly he may later show symptoms of anxiety. Mild apprehensions and restless sleep are not uncommon consequences of the drastic cessation of nursing. These conditions are even more in evidence if the child is toilet trained too early, or if the training is suffused with parental hostility. The ambivalence arising from resistance to training and the fear of loss of love in case of failure may persist in the form of conflictual and hostile parent-offspring relations. Psychosomatic researches demonstrate that constipation in children and adults may often be traced to faulty toilet training. In a young child, constipation may result from the fear of the mother's reproval, from the wish to take revenge on her, or from his aggrandizing need to get sensual pleasure from her.[8]

Mismanagement of the basic disciplines frequently has effects which, to those who scorn psychoanalysis, seem remote and farfetched. Many children enjoy the sounds and odors of elimination which offend or disgust their parents. Thus, the child who is hurried to empty his bowels or is reproved for enjoying the passage of flatus may transfer his enjoyment to the upper end of the gastrointestinal tract and use obscene speech instead. In this way the child gets even with his punitive mother by shocking her with his indecent language.[9] English and Pearson cite the case of a child who, as a consequence of anal mismanagement by his mother, suffered apprehension lest he shout during the church service. Actually his fear was not that he might shout in church but lest he pass flatus, for which he had on many occasions been severely criticized.[10] In the absence of contradictory experimental or other "objective" evidence, who is to say that the habitual use of profanity and obscenity in some adults may not be scatological in origin? In the face of extensive case history material psychoanalytically interpreted, who can deny that excessive meticulousness and compulsive cleanliness may have its source in childhood anxiety about anal incontinence?

The psychoanalytical evidence in proof of the intimate linkage between early sexual conditioning and adult personality structure is so extensive that only the existence of unreasonable prejudice can account for its persistent denial. Clinical and diagnostic evidence abounds in support of the basic contention. Unbridled condemnation of, or severe punishment for, normal sexual feelings in the child, are known to have injurious consequences in adult life. In the area of sexual behavior, rejective and harsh treatment of the child too often brings disaster in its wake. We have already cited impotence and frigidity as well-known examples. Experts in family life and marriage counseling have shown that rigid sexual discipline in childhood not only affects the marriage relationships of a person, but weakens or destroys that dimension of his personality which gives life buoyancy, zest, and meaning. As English and Pearson have stated the matter, "if the sexual feeling that is struggling to express itself through the child's masturbation is dammed back and the development inhibited, that child will grow into a person with

8 See English and Pearson, *Emotional problems of living*, Ch. 4.
9 *Ibid.*
10 *Ibid.*

little interest in marriage, or one who, marrying reluctantly, will have a rather lukewarm interest in marriage and get an early divorce, or drift on through an unhappy married life. . . ." [11]

Earlier in this chapter we stated that our interest in the basic disciplines is not in the controls themselves, but in the manner in which they are exercised by the child's parents. We referred to the *quality* of the interpersonal contacts of parents and children, the *feeling-tone* expressed in their interrelationship. Two mothers may use the same punitive technique; but one uses it tenderly while at the same time she conveys to the child some notion of the goal of her action, whereas the other uses it in a harsh and unfeeling way and unwittingly underscores her resentment and hostility toward the offending child. In the first case, the child is given an opportunity to learn to view the disciplinary situation realistically, to renounce or to curb his present needs for future compensations. He can do this because his experience with his mother has assured him of love and acceptance. In the second case, having experienced nothing but rebuffs and reminders of his unworthiness, the child has no recourse but to fear and hate his cruel parent. The first child learns to look forward expectantly and with confidence; the second one, either rebelliously or with submissiveness and hurt feelings. Although these outcomes are not necessarily fixed and immutable, since feelings and motives are characterized by functional autonomy, they may persist through an individual's life and place their distinctive cast upon his personality.[12] The psychologically injured child, believing that other people are like his parents, since he can judge them only by the measuring rod of his own familial experience, thus tends in his adulthood to behave antagonistically or submissively in the presence of others.

The basic disciplines are highly interrelated. This fact largely accounts for the relative consistency with which most parents use them in practice. The mother who nurses her infant in a hurried and depersonalized manner tends to behave in a similar fashion regarding his toilet training. His sexual curiosity and genital play distress or disgust her, and she reacts to these in typical irritation and anger. In the child himself, the activities which the parent is trying to regulate and direct are united by a common affective bond: *the desire for sensual pleasure.* Thus, as we have indicated elsewhere, the parent, especially the mother, "who can in a tender and sympathetic manner help her child step by step to gratify his

[11] *Ibid.*
[12] The principle of functional autonomy is discussed in Chapter 9.

pleasure needs will in all probability aid her child to develop naturally, gracefully, and with economy of psychic expenditures, into a happy and well-integrated adult." [13]

Parental relations. There is no longer any doubt that the relation of parents to each other, or the quality of their marital adjustment, deeply affects not only the spouses themselves but even more the personalities of their children. Marital harmony, characterized by affection and concern for the happiness of each partner, generally affects the children positively. Marital dissension, typified by quarreling and bickering, tends to affect children adversely. The broken home, whether effected by separation, divorce, or the death of a parent, is known to have undesirable effects on growing children. Inasmuch as the child identifies himself with the parents, their conflictual behavior almost invariably produces emotional disturbances in him. There probably is no child who can daily witness his parents' resentments toward each other without suffering intense emotional insecurity. For this reason divorce, although unfortunate in many other respects, frequently eliminates the child's emotional tensions by removing their source from his home. Intact but unhappy homes are frequently worse than broken but happy ones.[14]

Since our concern in this chapter is not exclusively with the personality of the child, but the whole trajectory of an individual's life, we must also consider the effect of parental disharmony on his own future marital adjustment. There are numerous studies, especially those of Terman, Burgess and Cottrell, and Locke, which give us information on this subject. They show that the marital happiness or adjustment of an individual's parents is significantly related to the marital happiness of the individual himself. Happy and mutually loving parents tend to produce children who, as adults, have a better than chance likelihood of becoming happily married persons themselves.[15]

Sibling relations. The relation between children in the family has been investigated theoretically and statistically, but the conclusions are unreliable and uncertain. Much is made of the birth order of a child in the family by some researchers, and of the

[13] Bonner, *Social psychology,* p. 106.
[14] See F. I. Nye, Child adjustment in broken and unhappy unbroken homes, *Marr. Fam. Liv.,* 19 (1957), 356–61.
[15] See the following well-known studies: L. M. Terman, *Psychological factors in marital happiness* (New York: McGraw-Hill Book Co., Inc., 1938); E. W. Burgess and L. S. Cottrell, *Predicting success or failure in marriage* (Englewood Cliffs, N.J.: Prentice-Hall, Inc., 1939); H. J. Locke, *Predicting adjustment in marriage* (New York: Holt, Rinehart & Winston, Inc., 1951).

conflict and rivalry between siblings. The youngest, oldest, middle, and only child have been subjected to scrutiny, but aside from some inconsequential temporary effects of their positions, rivalries, and animosities, no important effects on their personalities have been discovered. The child who is loved and accepted by his parents can weather any emotional storm stirred up by the inescapable rivalries, quarrels, and hostilities between himself and his siblings. The only child is not necessarily self-centered and spoiled, for every observant person can cite enough cases to show that the claim is untrue.[16]

THE SCHOOL

Although the school has some of the features of the primary group, especially those relating to teacher-pupil contacts, it is primarily an institution organized along secondary-group dimensions. This is seen most clearly in the impersonal authoritarian administration which reaches down into the classroom, but which, on the basis of a more enlightened philosophy of human relations, could be the center of a deeply sympathetic communication.

The school too often fails to realize its full potentials of democratic learning and living because of the public's own attitudes. Too often the school is looked upon as an institution for absolving parents of their responsibility for the continued socialization of the child. When the child is in school, the parents sigh with relief that another burden has been removed from their harried lives. The school tends increasingly to become a depository for bothersome children. We cannot complain, accordingly, if the school comes to be looked upon by a fast-growing number of children, especially adolescents, as a place for biding their time until they reach the legal age to escape from its control.

As a consequence, much of the teacher's time and energy is absorbed in acting as a surrogate parent, a task which she tends to resent and neglect. When the job becomes too irksome or too specialized for her qualifications, she will probably transfer it to the school counselor who will try to diagnose, if not solve, the child's disturbing problems.

THE TEACHER-CENTERED SCHOOL. Despite the great strides that have been made in classroom teaching, it is still very much a teacher-oriented practice. In this situation the child is too dependent upon the teacher, both on her skill and her personality. He

[16] For a summary and evaluation of fifty studies on sibling relations, see G. Murphy, L. B. Murphy, and T. M. Newcomb, *Experimental social psychology* (Rev. ed.; New York: Harper and Bros., 1937).

is expected to think and act largely in ways that are pleasing and acceptable to the teacher. The teacher has traditionally had three functions, and these are still prominent in American school education. She must first of all maintain *discipline,* for without it the classroom cannot perform its functions quietly and uninterruptedly. Next, she must steer the child's thinking and shape his attitudes along *conformist patterns,* since recalcitrance or deviance is not only a challenge to the teacher but to the whole established social order as well. Finally, she must concentrate largely on content or *subject matter,* for knowledge will be the crucial test in future evaluations of the pupil's achievement.

The demand for conformity on the part of both teachers and pupils is particularly pronounced in the average school system. It is not cynical to observe that the American school is extensively regulated by the dominant minority, not by the representative groups, of the community. This minority controls in both subtle and direct ways the thinking and attitudes of the school's participants, from the top administrator to the lowly pupil. (Interestingly enough, the custodian may think and act as he pleases, but others must conform to the established philosophy.) The danger in this demand for conformity lies in the fact that it pays very little heed to the value of independent thinking and altogether too much to the preservation of deep-rooted prejudices. It inculcates a pernicious self-righteousness in the minds of immature students, and cultivates the kind of blindness which believes that in controversial issues there is but one point of view. Education for democracy often turns out to be indoctrination for a political ideology. Instruction in ethnic sympathy and understanding can hardly be consummated by a teacher who has shed few of her own prejudices regarding peoples and classes.

It is not easy to tell whether intolerance breeds authoritarianism or authoritarianism generates intolerance. We do have some information showing that a genuinely democratic education encourages acceptance and understanding of viewpoints and attitudes that differ from one's own; and in this fact lies a glimmer of hope for producing a generous and democratic personality. In the well-known researches on the authoritarian personality it was found that "ethnocentrism shows a slight negative correlation with amount of education. It is likely, though far from a demonstrated fact, that college graduates are less ethnocentric than high school graduates, who are in turn less ethnocentric than those who did not complete high school." But, as Levinson adds in reflecting upon the slight negative correlation, to those who consider education per se "as a kind of panacea, the smallness of the correlation ought probably to be stressed." Indeed, "it emphasizes that our educational system, college as well as public school, is still far from realizing its potential strength as a social force in the service of democratic values." [17]

Social climate of the classroom. Can the effect of the social atmosphere of the classroom on the pupils be determined? The answer is in the affirmative. Since the by now well-known and much-quoted experiment of Lewin, Lippitt, and White was first made, their technique has been widely applied to the study of the classroom situation. These investigators organized ten-year-old boys into three groups with different types of leaders. In the *democratic* group, the leader was objective in his relation with the boys and participated in their activities as if he were one of them. The boys were given every opportunity to work out their own problems, but were free to consult the leader, who was always ready to help them. In the *authoritarian* group, practically all activities and policies governing the group were dictated by the leader. In the *laissez-faire* group, the leader did almost nothing, and the boys were completely at liberty to do their work in their own way.

Omitting descriptions of the democratic atmosphere, which had psychologically favorable effects on the boys in the above group, and the *laissez-faire* group which seemed to produce uncoordinated and unproductive but relaxed behavior, we wish rather to stress the effects of the authoritarian atmosphere on the boys. Generally speaking, the effect of the authoritarian group was found to be psychologically negative or harmful. It aroused aggressiveness and ill feeling. The boys in this atmosphere were uncooperative, self-centered, frustrated, and most of all, dissatisfied with their work and with one another and their leader. The nonaggressive boys were for the most part submissive, lifeless, and apathetic. They were not given to smiling and joking, as in the democratic group, and they showed very little initiative in setting up new projects. Bodily tensions were frequently manifested by the boys.[18]

The comparative effects of democratic and authoritarian forms of classroom management have been studied by a number of individuals. The results follow closely those of the experiment we have just described. The authoritarian teacher engages frequently in scolding and preaching. She compels her pupils to follow closely

[17] D. J. Levinson, Ethnocentrism in relation to intelligence and education, in T. W. Adorno *et al., The authoritarian personality* (New York: Harper & Bros., 1950), Ch. 8, p. 287.

[18] K. Lewin, R. Lippitt, and R. K. White, Patterns of aggressive behavior in experimentally created "social climates," *J. soc. Psychol.*, 10 (1939), 271–99.

a fixed pattern of conduct, which inhibits the children's interest and enthusiasm. These effects are further confirmed by the fact that the child's classroom behavior tends to vary with the personality of the teacher.[19]

In a study dealing with the effect of the social-emotional climate of the classroom on learning, Withall gives further support to the importance of social climate. The study shows that a dominating and repressive, or authoritarian, teacher has the effect of dispiriting and discouraging the student and thereby appreciably interferes with the effectiveness of his learning.[20] Corroborating this, a study by Flanders showed that the dominating teacher causes anxiety and aggressiveness in pupils, whereas the accepting and supporting one generates socially constructive behavior.[21] And in a cooperative pupil-teacher planning program, Rehage found that the democratic and cooperative group created better working relations between teacher and pupils than the traditional authoritarian classroom.[22]

These and many other investigations show that, generally speaking, the traditional teacher-oriented classroom, which still dominates a large area of our public school education, affects adversely the child's attitudes, learning efficiency, and personality. It compels the child to depend too much upon the teacher for her help and her good will toward him. He is expected to think and act in accordance with her own expectations. The teacher conceives her function to be—because the educational system as a whole conceives it to be—that of a disciplinarian. "In this process the guidance of the child toward an independent but socially responsible citizen is adventitious rather than central." [23]

THE GROUP-CENTERED SCHOOL. The foregoing strictures notwithstanding, the American school system is in some ways performing admirably. In no other group in American life, except the family, is the concern for the welfare of the growing child and youth more important than in the school, however poorly it may be realized at times. Certainly, nowhere else is there the same determination to help the child to acquire an understanding of the group and

[19] H. H. Anderson, Studies in dominative and socially integrative behavior, *Amer. J. Orthopsychiat.*, 15 (1945), 133–39.

[20] J. Withall, *The development of a technique for the measurement of social-emotional climate in the classrooms* (Ph. D. dissertation, The University of Chicago, 1948).

[21] N. A. Flanders, Personal-social anxiety as a factor in experimental learning situations, *J. educ. Res.*, 45 (1951), 100–110.

[22] K. J. Rehage, A comparison of pupil-teacher planning and teacher-directed procedures in eighth grade social studies classes, *J. educ. Res.*, 45 (1951), 111–15.

[23] H. Bonner, *Group dynamics: principles and applications* (New York: The Ronald Press Co., 1959), p. 251.

his functional place in' it. Thanks to the researches and practices of group dynamics, education in our schools is not only teaching the democratic way of life but trying to live it as well. Group sharing and collective learning, in contrast to persuasion and coercion, are becoming increasingly practiced in the group-centered school. Teaching is becoming more an instrument of guidance, of promoting the child's continued socialization, and less a process of rote learning and a process of behavioral compulsion. It is a way of stimulating and guiding the learning and thinking of a group—including the teacher's—along such lines of change as organized society deems necessary or desirable.[24]

The teacher occupies a very important position in the educative process of the classroom. She is in a position where she can create its social climate and by means of the latter affect the emotional and intellectual growth of the child. The teacher can, by arbitrary authority, create fear or resentment in her pupils, or by encouraging them to disagree and challenge, develop personal independence and group responsibility. By a deft combination of firmness and respect for the dignity of the individual, the group-centered teacher can aid the child to develop his own personality.[25]

The constructive value of group-centered education for the child's personality is its encouragement of *self-discipline*. Discipline is conceived, not in terms of punishment, but as a means of helping the child to internalize the norms of his group in such a way as to make them truly his own. The feeling of coercion and of arbitrary external social pressure is thus reduced to a minimum. The child learns to follow the rules of society because he sees the advantages of doing so, and because he feels that they are at least in part his own. The individualism which emerges from self-discipline as we have defined it is neither "rugged" nor rebellious, but a personal autonomy within the group framework.

Psychologically speaking, group-oriented education is conceived as a condition of human relations. It consists of transactions with people and although the subject matter is never minimized, the latter cannot take precedence over respect for human personality.

Uncritical enthusiasm for anything is always unwise, and group-centered education has perhaps received an undue share of indiscriminate loyalty. It is neither a lofty ideal nor a panacea. But insofar as it embodies the principle of free discussion and of mutual respect of teachers, pupils, administrators, and parents, it can serve as a valuable educational experience for all of them. Its

[24] *Ibid.*, Ch. 8.
[25] *Ibid.*

technical superiority aside, group-centered education is preferable to other kinds because it humanizes learning and instruction by making people the focus of its attention.

THE TEACHER'S PERCEPTION OF BEHAVIOR PROBLEMS. The negative effect of a teacher upon her pupils is revealed not only in the type of social climate she creates in the classroom but also by the way she perceives their behavior problems. Although the American schoolteacher has acquired a considerable knowledge of the elements of mental hygiene and the psychology of personality, she is still swayed too much by custom, prejudice, and her own sense of propriety in dealing with behavior problems. Her attitudes in this phase of the educative process still reflect her own moral disposition and society's traditions more than scientific knowledge of the determinants of human behavior.

More than thirty years ago Wickman compared teachers and mental hygienists on what they considered the most and the least serious behavior problems in school children.[26] He found an important difference in the ratings of teachers and mental hygienists. The teachers' attitudes very largely reflected their own dispositions and the expectations associated with the authoritarian approach. Thus the teachers rated as most serious such problems as obscene language, masturbation, smoking, stealing, heterosexual activities, and the like, whereas the experts in mental hygiene rated them least important. On the other hand, such traits as unsociableness, shyness, hypercriticism of others, and sensitiveness, which the mental hygienist rated as most serious, were considered least important by the teachers. Apparently teachers judged the behavior of pupils by the standard of traditional morals rather than by psychological principles. They were motivated by the strong demand for conformity and by the need to maintain their own authority and self-esteem. The "deviant" could no more be tolerated in the classroom than in the community as a whole.

The study, we said, was made more than thirty years ago. Have teachers during the intervening years changed in their attitude toward misbehavior? A recent investigation of this problem by Stouffer using Wickman's technique generally confirms the results of the earlier study, but at the same time shows that teachers are using the mental hygiene point of view more than in the first study.[27] While the teachers' approach to behavior problems is

[26] E. K. Wickman, *Children's behavior and teachers' attitudes* (New York: Commonwealth Fund, 1928).

[27] See G. A. W. Stouffer, Jr., Behavior problems of children as viewed by teachers and mental hygienists, *Ment. Hyg.*, 36 (1952), 271–85.

slowly improving, they continue to evaluate the problems by the extent to which they disturb the teachers emotionally or by their variance with the outmoded folk-attitudes of the community in which they teach.

The long-range effect on the children of the teacher's treatment of their behavior problems is neither clear not conclusive. The immediate effects are observable, but their permanent influence has not been objectively demonstrated. Mistreatment of the misbehaving child by means of punishment tends to magnify the very behavior which mental hygienists and psychologists rate as most serious, such as aggressive and antisocial behavior. Punishment attacks the symptoms but seldom the underlying cause of misbehavior. It is known to increase the child's difficulty of adjusting to the autocratic and often arbitrary demand for obedience and conformity. Whether the child's rebelliousness is generated in the home or the school is of no great consequence, but its reinforcement in the classroom may very well cause it to become chronic. The child whose integrity and self-respect are hurt by the teacher's authoritarian attitudes may come to hate authority even more. In another child, his sense of unworthiness in the face of his treatment by the teacher may only impair his capacity for continued adjustment. In either case, the teacher's standard of acceptable behavior and self-control tends to increase unacceptable behavior by evaluating the child's rebellion and failure as antisocial. The primary function of any discipline, even that which we disapprove, is to aid the child in his personal growth, not to assuage the anger or aggrieved sensibility of the disciplinarian.

The teacher's personality. From data of the foregoing type we can often learn more about the personality of the teacher than about the dereliction of her students. We learn that she defines a behavior problem in terms of her own disposition and experience. This fact explains in part the disagreement of teachers on what undesirable conduct is. The teacher inevitably brings into the classroom her own perception of life and people. This perception, which makes up her own personality, reflects itself in her attitudes toward her pupils. If her perception is deformed, she will tend to distort the meaning of the children's conduct. Chronic distortion of the behavior of others is an important symptom of personality maladjustment. A maladjusted teacher may contribute to the maladjustment of her immature pupils. Although the evidence for this is inconsistent, the maladjusted teacher's tendency to compensate for her disability by dominating her pupils is sufficient in itself to disqualify her for the task of shaping the personalities of others.[28]

We do not have enough facts to justify a positive assertion that maladjusted teachers contribute to the maladjustment of their pupils. Neither do existing facts substantially support the opposing view. Nevertheless, it is reasonable to suppose that, just as many "nervous" and unstable parents tend to produce neurotic children, many chronically unsatisfied and emotionally disturbed teachers are prone to deform the personalities of their pupils. The conclusion gains credence in the face of the fact that several investigations of teachers' personalities have revealed a high incidence of mental disorder among teachers before the age of forty.[29] One can only speculate on the adverse effect they may have had on the growing children in their classes. At all events the anxiety, rebelliousness, and resentment which many children suffered under many teachers' classroom management must have been appreciable. A school system in which these conditions prevail must be adjudged a failure.

It is not our wish to stress the maladjustive aspects of the teacher's influence upon students. The emotionally stable teacher has ample opportunity to determine the direction of her pupils' psychological development. Yet we should not underestimate her role in forming compliant, submissive, and uncritically conforming individuals. Being herself largely recruited from the lower middle class, in which conformity is a cardinal virtue, she is playing a role that is congenial to her nature and propagating a set of values with which she is deeply identified. She acts in the classroom in accordance with the responsibilities dictated by the public school system and by the ends set up for her by formal education in our society. We have summed up this situation elsewhere as follows:

The teacher to a great extent reflects the attitudes and values of the public schools and the community in which she lives. She is expected to function within the framework of goals and values in the cultivation of which she plays almost no effective part. She is a "public servant" whose attitudes and practices must correspond largely with those of the school system and of those who administer its operation. The behavior problems of school children are fundamentally the problems of the educational system. The teacher is largely

[28] For contrasting conclusions regarding the maladjustive effect of unstable teachers upon school children, see the following: W. U. Snyder, Do teachers cause maladjustment? *J. except. Child.*, 14 (1947), 40–46; R. Gladstone, Do maladjusted teachers cause maladjustment? *J. except. Child.*, 15 (1948), 65–70.

[29] For an early study of this incidence, see F. V. Mason, A study of seven hundred maladjusted school teachers, *Ment. Hyg.*, 15 (1931), 576–99. For a study of poor emotional adjustment in teachers, see W. S. Phillips, Analysis of certain characteristics of active and prospective teachers, *Peabody Coll. Contrib. Educ.* (Nashville, Tenn., 1935), No. 161.

an instrument for putting its expectations into concrete practice. It is the school as a whole, and not only its teachers, that puts its stamp upon the growing child's personality.[30]

ANCHORAGE GROUPS

Current studies of the effect of group relations upon the individual's personality place a great deal of emphasis on *frames of reference*. A frame of reference is the system of functionally related perceptions which operate in a group at a given time. Within a frame of reference we judge our position in the group, interpret our social environment, and evaluate our experience. Any person, object, event, or personal experience is organized into an intelligible whole by the frame of reference which is embedded in the group. Thus, although we are unique individuals in important ways, our personality is always *anchored* in a social matrix determined by the groups with which we closely identify ourselves. This is but another way of saying what *Gestalt* psychologists, who are mostly responsible for this concept, have said from the beginning of their investigations a half century ago, namely, that no object, person, or event exists in isolation. The meaning of any experience is defined by the whole of which it is a part. If different people perceive the same object or event similarly, it is because they perceive or judge it from the same perspective; if they perceive it dissimilarly, it is because they view it in a different frame of reference. If a person dislikes Negroes, it is because he perceives them in the frame of reference of those who reject Negroes. Frames of reference are thus seen to be shared ways of perceiving and interpreting the world around us. When a person has ceased to dislike Negroes, for example, he has not been reformed or regenerated; rather, the social matrix through which he perceives Negroes has undergone important alterations.

When frames of reference are shared in such a manner as to cause every individual in a group to perceive and understand a social event in the same way, we propose to call the assemblage of persons an *anchorage* group. We shall discuss several of these below.

REFERENCE GROUPS. A reference group may be defined as an informal collection of persons with which an individual closely identifies himself. However, since close identification is a characteristic of all primary groups, particularly the family, the definition must be amended to differentiate it from other primary groups. A reference group, then, is an association of persons that an indi-

[30] Bonner, *Social psychology*, p. 332.

vidual freely elects to join because he *wants* to belong to it. A person has no voice in choosing his family: he is a captive member. Although under normal circumstances the person wants to be a member of his family, his wishes obviously played no part initially. An individual may like his school, but his membership is determined by the legal codes of his society. The same is largely true of his church.

Again, a reference group gives to its members satisfactions which they normally cannot achieve in other groups. This is an important source of its attraction. For example, an individual may obtain numerous pleasures and satisfactions from his family, such as love and affection, security and safety, but the family cannot give him the camaraderie and sense of excitement of his neighborhood club. The reference group performs functions and engages in activities that cannot be satisfied as effectively in other groups. The person who finds his social anchorage in a reference group usually feels strongly devoted to it, and it gives him devotion in return. He relates his attitudes to it, and it approves or modifies them in accordance with the spirit and consensus of the group as a whole.

In contemporary social psychology the concept reference group has two different meanings, thus causing confusion in the mind of even the most critical and reflective reader. The first stresses the individual's desire or aspiration for membership in it. The individual who aspires for affiliation with such a group will conform his attitudes to what he perceives to be the group's values.[31] An example will illustrate this. In a combat unit almost half of the unseasoned members were ready to go into an actual battle zone, whereas only 15 per cent of the veterans expressed a readiness to begin combat. Before long, however, the inexperienced soldiers absorbed the attitudes of the veterans and expressed an increasing unwillingness to engage in combat. The aspirations of the unseasoned soldiers were being influenced by the prestige of the veterans, whose values became the norms of the group. In short, the person who aspires to be accepted by the group to which he wants to belong shifts his attitude to conform with it. This group has become his reference group, in that he is influenced by the norms which he imagines he shares with it. Aspiration or motivation is seen to play an important part in a person's act of relating himself to it. In view of this fact, a reference group may be either

[31] See H. H. Kelley, Attitudes and judgments as influenced by reference groups, in G. W. Swanson, T. M. Newcomb, and E. L. Hartley (eds.), *Readings in social psychology* (Rev. ed.; New York: Holt, Rinehart & Winston, Inc., 1952), pp. 410–14.

positive or negative. A *positive* reference group is one in which
a person wants to be accepted and considered as a member. A
negative reference group is one which the person opposes and
of which he does not want to be considered as a member.[32]

The second meaning of reference group denotes a collection of
persons in which an individual makes evaluations of himself in the
eyes of others. In this sense the collection of persons becomes a
reference group for him "because *other persons* compare the individual with it."[33] Thus to a person seeking a desired position it
is unimportant what his friends think of his qualifications for the
job; what is relevant is the reference group of employers who will
judge his fitness for the position.

For the psychology of personality the importance of a reference
group lies in the fact that this group is an important source of
attitude formation, attitude change, the conception of one's status,
one's level of aspiration, and the degree of one's self-esteem.

MEMBERSHIP GROUPS. In a complex and rapidly changing society
there is a multiplicity of groups to which a person can relate himself. Multiple group membership is a noticeable feature of American life. An individual may belong to a church, a political party,
a fraternal lodge, a recreational club, and other associations. His
relation to them is generally less ego-involved than that to his
reference groups, and his attitudes are not so readily formed or
changed by his membership in them. However, this is always a
matter of degree difficult to determine. Insofar as membership
groups provide their members with anchorage points or frames of
reference, they serve a function similar to that of reference groups.
Informal observation as well as empirical research demonstrates that
attitudes and behavior are influenced by the values of groups in
which one not only aspires for membership but in which one
actually belongs, for whatever reason.

It may be seriously questioned whether anything truly significant
is gained by saying that a reference group is one to which the individual *aspires*, whereas the membership group is one to which he
belongs.[34] Belongingness is a characteristic of all group relations,

[32] *Ibid.*, p. 411.

[33] *Ibid.*, p. 412.

[34] When it differs from a reference group, a membership group is said to be one
"in which a person is recognized by others as belonging," irrespective of his member-
ship *aspiration*. See T. M. Newcomb, *Social psychology* (New York: The Dryden
Press, Inc., 1950), p. 225. For an experiment on a membership group as defined by
Newcomb, see W. W. Charters, Jr., and T. M. Newcomb, Some attitudinal effects of
experimentally increased salience of a membership group, in E. E. Maccoby, T. M.
Newcomb, and E. L. Hartley (eds.), *Readings in social psychology* (3d ed.; New
York: Holt, Rinehart & Winston, Inc., 1958), pp. 276–81.

and does not truly distinguish one group from another. A person *aspires* to belong to a gang or a club, but once having been granted membership in it he obviously *belongs* to it. The relevance of reference and membership groups for the study of personality is not the distinction between these groups but the light it throws upon group influences on attitudes and behavior. Modern social psychologists are of one mind in believing that attitudes and behavior are effectively molded by reference and membership groups.

THE WORK GROUP. The role of occupational pursuits in the formation of attitudes and other personality characteristics has been extensively studied by social and personality psychologists. The mode in which an individual makes his living, especially in our society, where important prestige values are attached to a person's vocation, has been demonstrated to be important in accounting for human behavior. We do not wish to suggest that machine production, with its repetitive monotony, is evil. It has obviously made possible the unparalleled standard of living which all but the cynics consider a blessing. Nor do we wish to suggest that the highly competitive nature of modern business and industrial life has produced a nation of unconscionable self-seekers. Nevertheless, insofar as modern modes of production, whether in factory, trade market, or business office, are characterized by ruthless exploitation of others, man's occupations make for considerable psychological impoverishment. The inhumanness of industrial society no longer consists in low wages, long hours, and predatory business enterprise, but in a growing insensitivity in every functioning person to the welfare of all.

Desire for recognition. A deeply entrenched fallacy in industry, now happily on the way out, is the belief that men will work only for money. Although it is sentimental and romantic to believe that men are not deeply desirous of earning money and amassing wealth, it is extremely unperceptive to disregard other important motives that impel men to enjoy and stick to their jobs. One of these motives is the desire for recognition in one's vocation. Numerous experiments show that not only wage increases, but also the opportunity to participate in directing the work group's management can be an effective incentive to increased production. Many investigations have shown that production increases when workers are permitted to set up their own quotas. The goal of production cannot be established by the management alone, for the worker, out of the need to maintain respect for his own person, will not wholly submit to orders from above. A worker is moved much more strongly toward goals which he himself has a part in setting

up.[35] He takes understandable pride in his own achievement. He
is more likely to strive for higher productive goals when management accords him the recognition that he rightfully deserves. It
is not necessary to amass impressive figures to show that all normal
people want to be liked and to know that what they are doing
is important. Even the so-called "man in the street" considers it
commonplace knowledge. A recent survey of 2,500 skilled workers by I. C. Ross and A. Zander revealed that the desire for recognition was a crucial motive on their job. The greatest difference
between the men who quit and those who remained on the job
was the amount of recognition received by the latter.[36] Satisfaction or discontent, self-esteem or self-devaluation, in short, are
determined by the character of the work group, as well as by other
human associations. Man's sense of dignity and well-being are
enhanced when people in his work group appreciate and understand him. His personality is enriched when he can enjoy meaningful human associations on the job.

Satisfaction in work. Students of human nature have known for
a long time that work, when stripped of its crippling and dispiriting
features, is a source of keen satisfaction. Idleness, as distinguished
from leisure and constructive recreation, is a source of escape only
for the irresponsible drifter. Man does not normally have to be
forced to work. He is not inherently lazy. Neither does he normally work merely in order to survive. Thorstein Veblen, the
bête noire of American social economy, was fond of describing
workmanship as an instinct.[37] While no psychologists today consider workmanship as an instinct, they agree that work can be a
source of a great deal of personal-emotional satisfaction.[38] The
pursuit and enjoyment of productive work are socially induced, and
work is normally performed only in a group. To the extent that
modern industry has discarded the "stick and carrot" conception
of what makes workers work, it has discovered that men are motivated by the enjoyment that their jobs can provide them.[39]

It is widely recognized by medical authorities, psychologists,

[35] See W. F. Whyte, *Patterns for industrial peace* (New York: Harper and Bros.,
1951), p. 191.

[36] Reported in *The New York Times*, March 24, 1957.

[37] T. Veblen, *The theory of business enterprise* (New York: Charles Scribner's
Sons, 1904).

[38] For a convincing discussion of the satisfying nature of productive work, see
H. DeMan, *Joy in work* (London: George Allen & Unwin, Ltd., 1929), translated
from the German by E. Paul and C. Paul.

[39] See F. H. Blum, *Toward a democratic work process* (New York: Harper & Bros.,
1953), pp. 163–64.

and gerontologists that satisfying work makes for better adjustment and well-being in old people than the enforced idleness made necessary by retirement. Again, many executives who ascribe workers' discontents to personality maladjustments in the latter are perpetuating a prejudice. Dissatisfaction is usually due to the dullness of the job, to the conditions of work, and to the autocratic and arbitrary behavior of the managers and supervisors, rather than to the emotional instability of the worker. Neuroticism and other forms of maladjustment, when they occur, may be the consequences rather than the causes of job dissatisfaction. Prolonged exposure to depressive working conditions, especially when they inhibit any opportunity to redress the abuses of an insensitive management, can lead to neurotic behavior. A worker who is habitually forced to submit to the arbitrary will of another finds the experience degrading. In this situation he tends to react in the only ways that are accessible to him, namely, uncooperativeness, rebelliousness, demoralization, and in severe cases, hysterical outbursts.

Our brief discussion of the work group thus shows that satisfying work breeds feelings of dignity and self-respect. On his job, man wants both his employer and his fellow workers to appreciate him as a person and as a productive worker. He rightfully anticipates meaningful human associations on the job. When an industrial organization is aware of the worker's needs and acts to put them into practice, his personality will be positively affected by its perceptive attitude.

GROUP STRUCTURE AND PERSONALITY

We have now reviewed the nature and the influence of several important groupings and their relation to personality. The family is the group in which the infant has his first social contacts. In it are laid down for his gradual internalization the basic disciplines, and in it, through his interactions with his parents and siblings, he acquires the important skill of relating himself to others. In the school he has the opportunity to extend his social relationships to an everexpanding group of people, where his social skills may be enhanced or warped, depending in part on his native propensities, but for the most part on the character of the school group itself. In the anchorage groups, finally, the individual obtains gratifications and recognitions that he could not fully satisfy in other groups.

In our discussion of the foregoing groups we have focused attention on description and analysis of specific groups and concrete group characteristics. In the next few pages of this chapter we shall attempt to conceptualize more abstractly the group factors that influence our attitudes and personality.

PRESSURE OF GROUP NORMS. Almost since the inception of their science, sociologists have stressed the directing and constraining power of the group. Durkheim, the distinguished French sociologist, conceived the group as essentially a coercive or restraining force in the lives of people.[40] He held that human behavior can be explained only by a consideration of the collective structure of the group. The group both supersedes and transcends the individual; through the collective representations which are its essence, the group imposes the stamp of the social codes on the individual's thinking, feeling, and memory. The ways of acting, thinking, and feeling do not originate in the individual's consciousness. They are *external* to the individual. The "collective consciousness," as Durkheim calls it, is the highest form of psychic life.[41] While this extreme collective determinism has been discredited, and while Durkheim himself later modified his position, all social psychologists are agreed that the group forms an important framework for the individual's perceptions and actions.[42] They believe that we are in no small way what we are because the groups in which we have our being make us so.

Pressure toward conformity. The foregoing statements may be generalized by saying that an important mark of social groups is their pressure upon the individual to conform to its standards. The rebel or bohemian who withdraws from "conventional" society to join a deviant group, soon finds that his new association, too, imposes on him its own norms which he cannot violate with impunity. Extensive empirical research and experimental investigations with small groups in the last two decades have established the fact that conforming behavior in groups is due to their norms and standards. This is especially true of cohesive groups. Indeed, the evidence clearly demonstrates that the degree of conformity to group standards is positively related to the cohesiveness of the group.[43] This conclusion suggests, what has been substantiated,

[40] É. Durkheim, *The rules of sociological method* (Chicago: University of Chicago Press, 1938). This was originally published in Paris, in 1895.

[41] *Ibid.*, pp. 19 ff. See also, É. Durkheim, *Les formes élémentaires de la vie religieuse* (Paris: F. Alcan, 1912), p. 365.

[42] For Durkheim's qualification of his views, see his *The rules of sociological method*, Preface.

[43] See L. Festinger, S. Schachter, and K. Back, *Social pressures in informal groups* (New York: Harper & Bros., 1950).

that much of the failure in familial socialization of the child results from lack of family solidarity or cohesiveness.[44]

Effect of group pressures on attitudes. Most students of personality and social behavior have found that attitudes are less affected by propaganda and appeals to good will than is widely supposed. Significant changes in attitudes are much more easily effected by the pressures toward conformity which exist in groups. Festinger and Thibaut found that the *degree* of pressure toward conformity makes a noticeable difference in attitudinal change. In the groups where the pressure toward uniformity was greatest the subjects' responses changed most, whereas in the groups where the pressure was lowest the subject's responses changed least.[45]

Effect of group pressures on performance. The effect of the group on personality can also be demonstrated by its differential effect upon individual performance. Since performance is influenced not only by hereditary ability and acquired skill, but very significantly by the motivation of individuals and the expectations of others, one would reasonably expect performance to be influenced by the pressures of group norms. This expectation was confirmed in a recent experiment by Brehm and Festinger.[46]

Brehm and Festinger set up 60 groups of individuals to participate in a training session designed to teach people to make accurate judgments about others. Of the 60 groups, 30 groups—the experimental groups—were required to perform in two conditions of "High Importance" and "Low Importance." The groups were divided equally by sex, were randomly chosen, and friends were not placed in the same group. In the High Importance Condition groups the subjects were falsely told that several students in the university where the experiment was being conducted were to be selected for a paid tour through England as good-will ambassadors. They were told that they would be chosen on the basis of their sensitivity to other people. In the High Importance Condition this sensitivity was strongly emphasized. In the Low Importance

---

[44] This was confirmed by some well-known studies of the fate of the family during the Depression of the 1930's. Cohesive and well-integrated families were much less subject to breakup and disorganization than families in which the opposite condition prevailed. The personalities of its members were also adversely affected by the condition of the family. See the following: R. C. Angell, *The family encounters the depression* (New York: Charles Scribner's Sons, 1936); M. Komarovsky, *The unemployed man and his family* (New York: The Dryden Press, Inc., 1940); E. W. Bakke, *Citizens without work* (New Haven: Yale University Press, 1940).

[45] L. Festinger and J. Thibaut, Interpersonal communication in small groups, *J. abnorm. soc. Psychol.*, 46 (1951), 92–99.

[46] J. Brehm and L. Festinger, Pressure toward uniformity of performance in groups, *Hum. Relat.*, 10 (1957), 85–91.

Condition, on the other hand, the above instructions were omitted.
Accordingly, the importance of the ability in question was left
unchanged in half of the groups.

In the training session the subjects were directed to form judgments of how the different individual might behave in specified
hypothetical situations, and to discuss their judgments with one
another. Each subject was asked to rate from 0 to 100—that is,
from completely wrong to completely right—each judgment made
of him by the others. Three judgments were made in this manner.
When all the judgments were scored, the experimenter wrote prearranged scores on the blackboard. In this prearranged set of
scores, one subject always scored high, one low, and the remaining
clustered between the others. The subjects were next asked to
complete a questionnaire, the purpose of which, unknown to the
subjects, was to evaluate their capacity of judging others.

The result of the experiment showed that high scorers would
rate other people higher and low scorers would rate them lower
"in order to bring others close to their own level." It also revealed
that "the stronger the pressure toward uniformity the more marked
this effect would be, and that the pressure toward uniformity
would be stronger in the high-importance condition. . . ." [47]

In sum, the experiment showed that the pressure toward conformity (or uniformity) was effective in the given situation, and
it further suggested that the degree of the pressure tended to
increase with the increasing importance to the person of the ability
in question.

In addition to the data which we have submitted in proof of
the group's effect on the person, there is a large body of evidence
which we have had to omit. We have not even cited the valuable
material concerning the effects on persons of cliques and gangs,
of the street-corner society, of the adolescent activities of Elmtown,
of the Bank Wiring Room in the Western Electric plant, and of
numerous other social groupings.

Finally, a word of warning, which we shall elaborate extensively in later chapters, is here in order. The stress on the role of
the group in the development of personality might mislead the
reader into believing that the individual does not count for much
in the process of human development. This is manifestly not true.
Resistance to socialization is a pronounced feature of every human
organism, especially in its formative years, and in many it is as
powerful as the desire to conform. In the struggle for humanizing
the growing infant, both the individual and the group win only a

[47] *Ibid.*, p. 88.

partial victory. Although opposition to the molding force of the group can lead to strange deviations, yielding to the group's pressure for conformity often results in pernicious complacency.

CONCLUSION

Our objective in this chapter has been to demonstrate, by means of a large body of evidence, that the group, conceived as a body of interdependent and interactive persons, molds an individual's attitudes, behavior, and personality as a whole. In the process of conditioning the individual along certain dimensions, the group is consciously or unconsciously motivated by two powerful forces. On the one hand, every group forces an individual into a certain mold because the process of socialization is conceived as acting in behalf of his own welfare. The infant and child can grow into the image of man only if he gets sympathetic and loving care from members of his group, especially his family. On the other hand, every group imposes its standards upon the individual in order to vouchsafe its continued existence. Obviously no group can survive as such if it is riddled with conflicts and antagonisms. Conformity and consensus are warrants of a group's survival. Without them there is a state of *anomie*, a veritable social vacuum, devoid of the norms and standards which add direction and meaning to every person's life. Neither the individual nor the group can maintain itself in the face of perilous divergences and divisive disputes. While it may, as in the case of democratic or self-directing groups, encourage differences, it does so with its eyes focused on the larger consensus that promises to follow when all persons and ideas have had an audience.[48]

Of the groups that mold human personality, the family is still pre-eminent. While the school affects the attitudes of children, its psychological function is much more the continuation and reinforcement of habits initiated in the home. Although the peer group— a kind of amorphous reference group—is increasingly competing with the home and setting up rigid standards of expectation of its own, it captures the child too late and sustains him too briefly to effectively aid or hinder his personality structure.

In describing the techniques of child training in the home we stressed the importance of the psychological quality of the interpersonal relations between parents and children. The manner in which the parents relate themselves emotionally to their children and to each other can in the long run transcend the value of their

[48] Bonner, *Group dynamics,* Ch. 13.

formal knowledge of human psychology and child behavior. A mother who is untutored in the ways of repressions and complexes can by her attitude of acceptance, love, and tender forgiveness of mistakes instil more confidence and trust in her offspring than the psychologically sophisticated mother who has not a single drop of the proverbial milk of human kindness.

The group is only as good as the benefits which it generates. Its pressure on the individual to conform to standards is excellent when it leads to productive human relationships—to stability, order, and the psychological continuity of the individual. When by its rigid demand for conformity it stifles human individuality, it is malevolent. The growing attitude, unwittingly encouraged by some devotees of group dynamics, that the group can do no wrong, that togetherness is always preferable to apartness, has no acceptable place in human psychology.

Finally, despite his sometimes magnificent struggle to resist change and socialization, the biological individual is at last, but not with undignified finality, transformed into a human person. Part of this transformation we briefly described in the present chapter, the rest we shall discuss in the next one.

CHAPTER **7**

Enculturation

The study of the effect of culture on personality is to a great extent a continuation of the investigation of socialization begun in the preceding chapter. We defined the group as a collection of people in various degrees of interaction. However, people in groups are invariably carriers of culture. When people interact with others in a group they not only relate themselves to these others in required ways, but they act in accordance with rules and customs that are in various degrees shared by all. In the preceding chapter we indicated, without elaboration, that the mode of child training is dictated by the culture, although there are wide latitudes in which the personalities and emotional tone of the family can operate freely. The school as an educational group is not only a form of teacher-pupil interaction but a complex of norms and values inherited from the past, as well as those determined by present needs. The anchorage groups are not only associations of people which gratify certain needs, but social forms whose being and behavior are partly regulated by custom and tradition.

These brief observations underline the inseparability of group processes and cultural values. There are no functional groups without a culture, and no culture exists outside a group. This inseparability is not a mere interrelatedness, but an overlapping of functions and a deep structural-functional interpenetration. The chief purpose in separating them is the recognition that the elementary fact regarding group structure is interpersonal *contacts*, whereas the essence of culture is a complex of *values*.

191

THE NATURE OF CULTURE

Although our interest in this chapter is culture as an important tool for the investigation of personality, we must first understand its meaning as defined by contemporary anthropologists. Before so doing it might be well to consider briefly some popular misconceptions.

When an anthropologist speaks of culture he does not refer to it in the popular sense of education or refinement. To be sure, these traits are elements in a culture, but they are not culture itself. While refinement and education are evaluated on the basis of cultural standards, they are largely individual attributes. The English language does not have words for defining the difference. Thus culture may refer to the extent of one's education or to the set of values which defines a society's behavior. The German language permits no such confusion. The word *Bildung*, meaning education and instruction, never denotes culture in the anthropologist's sense, which is denoted by the term *Kultur*. This distinction divests the concept of culture of the popular evaluational overtone implicit in the expression "the finer things of life." Culture in its scientific meaning also includes the "coarser" things of life, such as menial labor or the commission of crimes. Thus a person is "cultured" not only when he knows English poetry or enjoys classical music, but whenever he participates in a group's way of life.

A second misconception is to think of culture as something existing apart from people in interaction. Culture does not *act* upon people like an external force; it is a prescribed way of behaving in a given group. One never participates in culture, but only in a specific culture. When anthropologists use the term *culture,* they are using it as an abstract concept, or as a generalization derived from their knowledge and comparison of several cultures. No custom or tradition or way of life is anchored in culture in general. When we consider the individual himself we must specify culture even more rigidly, for no person internalizes the whole culture in which he lives. His group membership, especially his class status, his intelligence and education, his age and sex, determine what segment of his total culture will shape his personality. Other parts of one's culture may also affect a person, but only indirectly, as in the case of the dime-store clerk emulating members of the upper class by wearing simulated jewelry.

DEFINITION OF CULTURE. A definition of culture which adheres to anthropological usage and at the same time is relevant to the study of personality, has been given by a distinguished anthropologist as "the configuration of learned behavior and results of behavior whose component elements are shared and transmitted by the members of a particular society.[1]

This definition is useful for several reasons. First, it shows that culture is not a static structure, but a dynamic process. It denotes that culture is not only the sum of accumulated traditions, but even more the transmission of ideas, values, artifacts, and ways of doing things. Further, it implies the organic nature of culture, its togetherness, by stressing its distributive character: culture is mutually shared. Next, culture is a form of learned behavior, thus making it compatible with modern social psychology which denies the instinctive origin of universal social patterns. Again, the term *results of behavior* allows room for innovation and individual creativeness. While in themselves the results of behavior, by virtue of their individuality and idiosyncrasy, are noncultural, their sharing by others makes for their eventual cultural integration. Finally, the definition has a special relevance for the psychology of personality by conceiving culture as a *behavioral* configuration, and not wholly a determinate social structure. Culture, in short, is a way of *behaving*, a way of doing things, rather than a static social structure.[2]

CONTENT OF CULTURE. Although culture is a dynamic process, it is, nevertheless, a structure composed of institutions and practices that tend to remain relatively stable. These relatively stable cultural forms serve as marks of its identification. A culture is recognized over a period of time—in other words, by the institutionalized ways of life of a people in a group. These institutionalized ways of life, while differing among various cultural groups, seem to be universal. The family we have already partially described in our account of the basic disciplines—showing once more, parenthetically, that the group and its culture commingle in intimate ways. Other institutions and practices are the integrative systems and language.[3]

The family. In this section we shall not repeat the socializing functions of the family, but view it as a form of social organization.

[1] R. Linton, *The cultural background of personality* (New York: Appleton-Century-Crofts, Inc., 1945), p. 32.

[2] For a similar analysis, see *ibid.*, pp. 32–38.

[3] Any good textbook on cultural anthropology will help the reader to get a detailed knowledge of the content of culture. See, for example, J. Gillin, *The ways of men: an introduction to anthropology* (New York: Appleton-Century-Crofts, Inc., 1948), Ch. 20; M. J. Herskovits, *Man and his works* (New York: Alfred A. Knopf, Inc., 1948), Ch. 15.

An account of family organization includes such characteristics as the marriage bond, the biological relationship among the family members, and the specific functions of the family.[4]

The *marriage bond* is the form of relationship existing between the spouses. This may be *monogamous,* as in our own society, where the bond exists between a husband and wife; or *polygynous,* where one husband may have more than one wife; or *polyandrous,* where one wife may have more than one husband. The marriage bond is important for the attitudes and values that it imposes upon the child growing up in any one of the three types we have mentioned. The parental fixations, for example, which are common in the monogamous family, are seldom possible in a family where the marriage bonds are plural in nature. The child's attachments are made to several parents, so that the relationship between the parents and children tends to be diffused. The case of the Marquesan family, in which the marriage bond is polyandrous, illustrates rather clearly the effect of the family organization upon the children.[5] Because of the polyandrous marriage bond the mother's first concern is not the welfare of her infant but the sexual gratification of her husbands. Her breasts are not feeding organs for the child, but sexual objects for her husbands. In order to enhance the erotic quality of her breasts she does not breast feed her infant. Therefore the child is deprived of the tenderness of breast feeding and is left with a feeling of frustration. Consequently, the child grows up being either indifferent or hostile toward his mother.[6] The so-called Oedipus complex, in which a child's emotions are unduly fixated upon the opposite-sexed parent, seems to be absent in the Marquesan family. This complex, according to most psychoanalytically oriented ethnologists, is not universal, as Freud thought, but exists only in those families where the child's sexual aim is seriously blocked.[7] However, whatever the verdict of future research on the Oedipus complex may be, there is enough theoretical and empirical evidence to justify the claim that the form of marriage bond characterizing a family structure affects the personalities of its members.

[4] See Gillin, *The ways of men,* pp. 419–21.

[5] The Marquesans are a Polynesian people who inhabit the Marquesas Islands in the central Pacific.

[6] For a detailed discussion of the effect of maternal neglect upon the maturing child in Marquesan society, see A. Kardiner, *The individual and his society* (New York: Columbia University Press, 1939); also, *The psychological frontiers of society* (New York: Columbia University Press, 1945).

[7] The view of the limited distribution of the Oedipus complex has been challenged by Roheim. See G. Roheim, *Psychoanalysis and anthropology* (New York: International Universities Press, 1950).

The *biological relationship* among family members refers to the blood bond between children and parents, and other members of the family. Normally, the family unit is based on such a biological relationship; but sometimes it is not, as in the case of families with adopted children and stepchildren or in childless marriages. A child who reacts unfavorably to the knowledge that he is adopted may develop anxiety and self-doubt. Some stepchildren, either through actual mistreatment by or antagonism toward their new parent, suffer personality disturbances. In some cultures a marriage is terminated if the wife cannot give birth to an offspring. That this state of affairs can have serious consequences for the stability of the person is demonstrated by the recent case of the Shah of Iran and his infertile wife. Reliable reports, and not sensational newspaper accounts merely, attest to the deep psychological wounds, especially for the former Iranian queen, resulting from a divorce that was legally sanctioned because of childlessness.

The *functions* of the family, while differing in explicit details, are similar in every culture. They not only conserve and perpetuate the family group itself, but in important ways pattern the personalities and outlook of its members. According to Gillin, there are four specific functions of the family. The first concerns the *physical care* of the members. This care is directed toward protection from bodily harm and illness and assuring the provision of food, shelter, and clothing. The second involves the transmission of the *cultural patterns* to the children, such as the basic disciplines, speech, the use of clothing, and, in some cultures, training for adult occupations. The third function consists of *economic pursuits*, which involves such conditions as the division of labor, usually according to sex and age, and ownership of property. The fourth includes *social care*, such as the granting of status, protection from humiliation and insult, the patterning of courting and marital activities, and the direction of vocational, religious, political, and recreational interests.[8]

Language. There is no aspect of human culture which more profoundly reveals its essential nature, and no characteristic of man which more truly sets him apart from other animals, than language. Although the capacity for speech is an inherited characteristic of man, language as a system of sounds and symbols for communicating the accumulated traditions of the group to others is a thing of culture and invention. It has a triple nature: it is the basic medium of interaction, it is the sole transmitter of culture, and its use permits people in a group to create a common universe

[8] J. Gillin, *The ways of men*, 420–21.

of discourse. Little do we appreciate in our daily living the extent
to which man "lives in a symbolic universe." Man has so "enveloped
himself in linguistic forms," as Cassirer has profoundly observed,
"that he cannot see or know anything except by the interposition
of this artificial medium" of language.[9] There are other indices of
culture than language, such as its body of customs, but even man's
customs can be comprehended only in the form of a symbolic
system, or language. The meaning which man attaches to his
experience is conditioned by the language which he uses to give
it utterance. Language is thus at once a culture-building agent
and a personality-forming process. The personality of every individual, no matter what his symbolic limitations may be, is a
product of the enculturating force that takes place largely by
means of his language. Enculturation through the linguistic process differentiates man's socialization from that of every other
animal.[10]

Integrative systems. Every society has means whereby its collective experiences are interpreted and made coherent to its members. These basic cultural frames we have called integrative systems.[11] They permit an individual to organize his behavior around
relatively stable ideas and practices. Some of these systems, such
as economic, religious, and political behavior, overlap with a few
of the functions already described. However, as in other forms
of overlapping this again only serves to demonstrate that group
life and culture are deeply interpenetrated.

There are three main types of integration of man's psychological
life, namely, the rational systems, the belief systems, and the social
ideologies. The *rational systems* integrate man's experience in the
natural or physical world. They aid man in manipulating the forces
of nature in the service of his physical survival. Typical examples
are tools, technology, science, and other practical means for enabling
man to exploit nature for his own use. Contemporary man's science
and technology, compared to those of other periods in Western
culture, have vastly modified his conception of the physical world
and of his own place in it. The impact of man's view of the physical
world, and the large-scale use of technology for improving his
living conditions, has changed Western man's personality in discernible ways.

[9] E. Cassirer, *An essay on man: an introduction to a philosophy of human culture*
(New Haven: Yale University Press, 1944), p. 25.

[10] Language as symbolic behavior is discussed in detail in Chapter 11.

[11] H. Bonner, *Social psychology: an interdisciplinary approach* (New York: American Book Co., 1953), Ch. 8; "Culture et personnalité," *Connaiss. de l'homme*, 1955,
Nos. 12 and 13, pp. 13–26.

Changes in personality and man's outlook on life following changes in the mode of production have also been investigated in primitive societies. The study of Tanala and Betsileo, two cognate cultures on the island of Madagascar, is particularly illuminating.[12] The Tanala economy is founded on the method of dry rice cultivation. This method permits the easy exploitation of their physical environment and accordingly assures its people a fairly steady subsistence. Anxiety concerning their food supply is accordingly almost nonexistent. This freedom from anxiety concerning their subsistence is confirmed not only by their confidence, but by the fact that they do not rely upon ritual and magic, or other supernatural appeals, to cause their crops to grow.

The Betsileo people, on the other hand, practiced wet rice cultivation, which was made necessary by the swampy land they occupied when they left the uplands and moved down into the valleys. Wet rice cultivation, however, produced a shaky food economy, required the dogged determination of the individual, and permitted no cooperation among the Betsileo people. Instead, competition among the members became pronounced. Cunning and treachery took the place of cooperative effort. Appeals to supernatural power and superstitious practices replaced their Tanala neighbors' confidence and realistic approach to making a living. As a consequence of the mad scramble for land and intense interpersonal and interfamilial rivalries, the personalities of the Betsileo people suffered hostility, aggression, and anxiety.

The contrast between the Tanala and Betsileo modes of production shows that when the rational system—in this case the mode of production—is adequate, its effect on the personality is positive; when it is decidedly inadequate, the effect is negative. Self-confidence and neurotic conflict and anxiety are both products of the method of making a living.[13]

The *belief systems* are all the conceptual, particularly magical and ritualistic, schemata and contrivances which man uses when his rational or technological skills fail him in attaining his ends. Even a modern state like Soviet Russia, which professedly has renounced all bourgeois or "decadent" values, is constantly employing ritualistic double-talk along with its technological know-how. It relies on

---

[12] See Linton's ethnological report and Kardiner's psychological analysis of these cultures, in Kardiner, *The individual and his society*, Chs. 7 and 8.

[13] Bonner, Culture et personnalité, p. 17. A more detailed discussion of the rational system than we have here given would examine the important cultural features of the division of labor and of property and its meaning in different cultures. Extensive discussions of these subjects can be found in good textbooks in cultural anthropology. We again refer the reader to the books of Gillin and Herskovits.

an outmoded Marxist ideology to inspire, cajole, or lull the faithful into a belief in the magical quality of verbal commands and entreaties. While no Marxist prays for rain or for victory on the battlefield, he has a consuming faith, nonetheless, in the ultimate triumph of his creed—very much like the religious devotee who is certain of attaining the kingdom of heaven.

The most typical and enduring form of belief system is religion. In this form it consists of the belief in a suprahuman and suprasocial power which, in propitious circumstances, works for man's ultimate good. In primitive society it is an integral part of man's daily life; whereas in Western civilization it is mostly a technique for protecting man in extremities and crises, when his rational systems— that is, his knowledge, science, and practical skills—are insufficient to ward off catastrophies and failures. However, even in Western society, the integrative and consoling power of religion, despite its external expression in swollen church attendance, is waning. Its place is rapidly being taken by the vicarious but very real satisfactions of modern sensuous pleasures and entertainments, especially the motion picture, radio, television, and phrenetic popular music.[14]

The *social ideologies* are the set of ideas and practices which are designed to control both the rational and belief systems in the interests of man's social and economic welfare. Like the belief systems, the social ideologies are practical myths, but unlike them, they vouchsafe man's well-being here and now. The rewards proffered by the belief system, especially religion, are always deferred, whereas the promises of the social ideologies may be realized in the present.

Furthermore, the social ideologies manifest themselves in the form of political systems and national states. As such they constitute power relationships within groups and between states. In mediaeval society a close bond existed between the social ideologies, the belief systems, and the rational systems. The Church was not only a sacred but a highly secular institution which regulated both science (the rational system) and political states (social ideologies). A similar development has been taking place in contemporary culture in the form of increasing control of both science and human welfare by the political state. While it is too early to say what the effect of these changes will be on personality, it would hardly be rash on *a priori* grounds to expect important changes in men's attitudes and values.

A social ideology in the form of political organization seems to

[14] *Ibid.,* p. 18.

be universal. As a form of political organization it regulates and orders all affairs that concern the welfare of the group as a whole. The political organization may be informal and amorphous, as in many primitive societies where, by virtue of this fact, it seems to be nonexistent, or highly structured, as in modern political states. It is an interesting commentary on the bias of social scientists when in many instances neither anthropologists nor political scientists will acknowledge as forms of government the generalized and informal regulating structures of some primitive societies. Apparently, for such observers a government exists only when they can indicate the presence of a formal legal machinery. The fact is that the universal characteristic of political organization is not an established legal apparatus, but some form of leadership. This may range from primitive chieftainship to contemporary dictatorship. In any case, a society's political organization is controlled by a leader, or a hierarchy of leaders in the interests of the welfare of the whole group. This is true, but with very unequal degree, of both a dictatorship and a democracy. Even the most dictatorial autocrat has the delusion that his leadership will benefit others as well as himself.

The relevance of the integrative systems to the study of personality need be but briefly stated. Since the different aspects of culture are known to affect personality, it would be most extraordinary if so important areas of human living as the modes of production and material subsistence, religion and folklore, and the sociopolitical institutions which minister to man's social welfare should not leave their impress on the human personality. We have already demonstrated the role of vocational activity and modes of production, and the differential effects of democratic and authoritarian social climates, in the development of man's nature. These conditions are manifestations of the integrative systems, and hence whatever is true of them is true of the integrative systems as they influence attitudes and behavior. These points will be considered in detail in later sections of this chapter.

CULTURAL CHANGE. Customs, mores, traditions, and institutions are generally thought to be relatively fixed and static. In preliterate societies, especially when they are viewed in short-term perspective, this is largely true. But from an evolutionary point of view even the simplest society changes to meet altered environmental conditions; and in highly complex societies the impulsion of the leading institutions and practices to assume new forms is both startling and extraordinary.

Sociologists and anthropologists generally account for cultural

changes by attributing them to inventions and diffusion. There is
a third source of change which, although recognized by all social
scientists, is seldom sufficiently stressed. We refer to the psychological motivation for change.

Invention. The term "invention" has a much wider meaning
in social science than is the case in popular thought. In the widest
sense an invention is any addition to or improvement of existing
practices. This definition implies what is of course well-known—
namely, that significant inventions tend to be rare; most of them are
modifications of earlier contrivances.

Inventions are said to be technological or social. When they
refer to material culture, such as economic development and technological improvement, they are called technological inventions.
When they refer to the nonmaterial culture, such as a marriage
counseling agency or a new theory of education, they are known
as social inventions.

Diffusion. The circulation or transmission, through borrowing
and imitation, of culture traits beyond the group in which they
originated is labeled "diffusion." Diffusion is the most common,
though not necessarily the most far-reaching, source of culture
change. This is confirmed by the fact that whereas an important
invention may initiate revolutionary changes in social life, it appears only occasionally, while many more ideas and practices are
borrowed than are invented. Finally, the concept of diffusion helps
to account for cultural similarities, as well as cultural changes, inasmuch as most inventions are largely variations from a common
cultural heritage.

Cultural changes, especially in fundamental and deeply-rooted
institutions and beliefs, affect the personalities of people. The
attitudes and disposition of the Betsileos, we saw, came about as
a result of moving from the uplands to the valleys, an experience
which produced fundamental changes in the modes of making a
living. The changed modes of living, with their dislocations of
family life and division of labor, were followed by mutual antagonism, mistrust, and individual anxiety. Since fundamental and far-
reaching changes in accustomed social practices tend to create—
or are perceived by many members as creating—anxiety-provoking
crises, they invariably produce new patterns of behavior.

Psychological motivations. As we have pointed out, these
powerful impulses for cultural change are too often ignored. Institutions frequently change because society's needs are not being
adequately served under prevailing conditions. Often the ac-

ceptance or rejection—which is to say, the success or failure—of an innovation depends on people's evaluation of it: if they want or need it, its success is more certain than if they do not. If they perceive it as a means for enhancing their pleasure or comfort, or as affording a release from drudgery or distress, or as enhancing their prestige, they readily incorporate the innovation into the matrix of their daily lives. The Zuñi Indians, for example, are loath to adopt the white man's ways on the basis that these ways are carriers of prestige. Their highest values are prudence and inconspicuousness, on which the white man's vanity and ambition have made no inroads at all.[15]

Those Americans who never cease to be dismayed by the unwillingness of many people throughout the world to accept the blessings of democracy are oblivious to the motivational factor in cultural change. A custom that is rewarding to the people who practice it will not be eagerly supplanted by another whose need-gratification has not been demonstrated. The Navahos have even astounded some field ethnologists by their inability to understand and their consequent failure to assimilate Christianity, which has been taught to them by missionaries for more than seventy years.[16] Christianity, particularly its stress on the Resurrection, is abhorrent to the Navaho psychology, in which contact with the dead amounts to a tribal phobia. Again, since the Navaho believes that "reproduction is the ultimate human and supernatural purpose," he rejects as totally unworthy Christianity's belief that man is conceived in sin for which he must be punished.[17]

Acculturation, or change in a people's social practices in favor of new ones, is thus seen to be profoundly a matter of motivation. If a new belief or practice does not gratify people's needs better than their accustomed ways, they will resist it, for it challenges the very meaning of their customs, and is conceived as bent on destroying them. Adjustment and resistance to acculturation is to no small extent a function of human motivation.

INTEGRATION OF CULTURE. Years ago Lowie, a distinguished ethnologist, described culture as a thing of "shreds and patches."[18] Malinowski, an equally eminent anthropologist, on the other hand, described culture as "an integral in which the various elements are

[15] See R. Benedict, *Patterns of culture* (Boston: Houghton Mifflin Co., 1934), Ch. 4.

[16] See G. A. Reichard, The Navaho and Christianity, *Amer. Anthropologist*, 51 (1949), 66–71.

[17] *Ibid.*, p. 67.

[18] R. H. Lowie, *Primitive society* (New York: Boni & Liveright, 1920), p. 441.

interdependent." [19]   This is a cardinal principle of the *functionalist* view of human culture. What it means is that every society is characterized by some degree of integration, or wholeness. Unless a culture is integrated, there can be no consistent pattern of individual thought and action, for much of the unity of personality is provided by the relatively consistent values which energize all social behavior. The content of culture, which we discussed at length in a preceding section of this chapter, is everywhere organized into a relatively consistent structure. If it were not organized it would breed its own destruction and decay.[20] Even if it survived for a considerable period of time, the personality molded by such a condition would be marked by limited means for self-security. In a condition of destructive conflict or social disorganization, no individual could establish dependable and trusting relations with others. In the absence of such relationships security and confidence cannot thrive.

When considering the nature and importance of cultural integration one should not consider it the converse of cultural heterogeneity. Relatedness does not exclude differences and variety. Even the most highly integrated society makes room for individual differences. Besides, it is doubtful that complete connectedness of all parts of a cultural configuration exists anywhere in human society. A condition of complete relatedness would preclude the separate activity of any part of the cultural system. Individual autonomy, that priceless attribute of every mature personality, would be impossible in a culture where integration was all-pervasive. This qualification aside, in the absence of a consistent set of cultural definitions—which is another way of describing an integrated culture—there cannot be much integration of the personality. Cultural integration and unity of personality are closely related. This way of viewing the matter recognizes the fact, stressed by all contemporary ethnologists, that the structural and psychological aspects of culture are closely interwoven. It is also conscious of the fact that cultural integration is "the manifestation of certain deeper psychological drives that give ultimate significance to the formal elements of cultural structures," thus permitting "a way of life to achieve its final unity." [21]

[19] B. Malinowski, *A scientific theory of culture and other essays* (Chapel Hill: University of North Carolina Press, 1944), p. 150.

[20] It is true, of course, that too much fixity and organization are also inimical to cultural survival.

[21] Herskovits, *Man and his works*, p. 216.

CULTURE AND PERSONALITY STRUCTURE

The purpose of our discussion of the nature of culture was not to acquaint the reader with culture as such, but to help him to understand the nature of personality itself. Even anthropology, as should now be clear, does not investigate culture only, but studies the human beings who create culture and are created by it. The anthropological approach to psychological problems permits us to discover the similarities of people who have been conditioned by a similar way of life, and it enables us to understand their uniqueness and differences as products of their resistance to enculturation and their deviation from the cultural norms. It helps us to understand that personality is neither a baffling internal mechanism nor an assemblage of overt actions, but a way of behaving demanded by the conventional understandings and expectancies of the group. This is not, be it noted, a definition of personality, for that is reserved for later discussion, but a statement of its cultural character. The cultural analysis of personality shows that it is not present at birth, but is largely a social structure that originates in human experience. Personality is the biological individual who has been socialized by the prevailing values and norms of his culture.

ASPECTS OF THE TOTAL PERSONALITY. Because of the complexity of personality when it is viewed as a whole, it might be helpful at this point to consider briefly its separate yet related dimensions. Awareness of these aspects has been made possible largely by the cultural approach to the study of personality. These aspects also reveal the special emphases of psychology, sociology, and anthropology. We shall call these distinct dimensions the *nuclear personality*, the *social personality*, and the *role personality*.

The nuclear personality. This is the unique, or individual, psychological dimension. It is the subjective organization of organic, interpersonal, and cultural factors. Every individual is a structure composed of hereditary and other characteristics described in detail in Chapter 5. He is also the structure which emerges from his internalization of the acts of others, as described in the preceding chapter. He is, finally, an individual who reflects in his behavior and attitudes the values and norms of his group—the subject matter of the present chapter. The specific way in which these three aspects—the organic, the personal-social, and the cultural—are assimilated by the individual, distinguishes him from other individuals and makes him unique. This nuclear personality is an important topic in psychology.

The term "unique" is a troublesome one. Many psychologists are reluctant to use it, since it suggests that generalizations and laws regarding personality cannot be formulated. This concern is unnecessary, for other scientists, particularly biologists, are constantly stressing that no two organisms are exactly alike. This emphasis upon the uniqueness of every organism has not prevented biologists from generalizing about a species as a whole. In the same manner, while the nuclear personality is individualized and unique, it has not deterred psychologists from formulating principles which generally hold for all similarly constituted individuals. Although the theory of personality types is in disfavor with many psychologists, nothing is lost but much is gained if we acknowledge the fact that personality, while unique with every individual, is nevertheless widely distributed typologically. No society patterns individuals exclusively into introverts, or into extraverts, into geniuses or dullards, or into ascendant or submissive individuals.

Moreover, no two environments are identical. This fact alone, if we were to ignore the organic features of personality, would result in different life experiences and this in itself would lead to differences in personality. Cultural uniformity does not necessarily make for identical specific environments, and within each specific environment the individual is relatively free to assimilate whatever values are congenial with his basic biological nature. On the other hand, uniqueness does not imply that the individual is impervious to the expectations of his group. Every individual, if he is to be socially accepted and socially adjusted, must regulate his behavior by cultural imperatives—that is, by his social personality and his role personality.

No segment of personality holds within itself more of its totality than the nuclear personality. This is true because, being the core of a person's psychological being, it must contain essential elements of the others. Paradoxically, it is the unique nuclear personality which helps us to understand uniformities in an individual's behavior, and accounts for its enduring features. This fact was described in a different way when we discussed the element of consistency or integrity in Chapter 1. The *enduring personality structure*, by means of which we can identify a person, or differentiate him from other persons, is largely derived from the unique nuclear personality. Even individual idiosyncrasies make sense within the deeper unity of the nuclear personality. Strange as it may seem, individual behavior is more adequately predicted from the nuclear personality than from the mores of the group. This is true because the mature person acts more by the wisdom of his own experience than by the incompatible dictates of his culture.

The social personality. Just as the nuclear personality has been the primary concern of the psychologist, so the social personality has been most extensively investigated by the sociologist. As a result of the sociologist's contribution, the psychology of personality has been greatly enriched.

Predilections for the uniqueness of personality do not justify the neglect of the social personality. As the preceding chapter has demonstrated, socialization in the home and school, in reference and membership groups, with its ubiquitous pressures toward conformity, causes every individual to bow to the demands of some social organization. The relatively consistent submission or adherence to the expectations of others constitutes an individual's social personality. Social personality may thus be defined as the pattern of responses made by an individual with a view to social or public approval. The individual in whom the social personality is highly developed tends to be less individualized in his behavior, less determined to be himself on most occasions, and more ready to adapt his behavior to what others expect. He behaves to a great extent as he believes others expect him to behave.

Control by the social personality does not necessarily mean that the individual who follows its imperatives is necessarily more sensitized to the opinion of others. Like most persons, including the individual in whom the nuclear personality is dominant, his perception of right conduct is conditioned by the norms of the group, to which it is easier to submit than to resist. Even the most individualistic person needs social acceptance and approval. This is true because, as we have already noted, the nuclear, the social, and the role personalities are interrelated to form the total mature personality. Nevertheless, the social personality is generally more responsive to social approval and disapproval, is a better "mixer," and is quicker to size up social situations than the personality less susceptible to public opinion. The "ideal" personality, of course, has both qualities well-developed.[22] In the introverted individual, and certainly in the isolated and withdrawn person, the social personality is less developed—or perhaps only less overtly manifested— than in the more outgoing individual.

Burgess' definition of the social personality, which is none the less adequate for being old, describes it in terms of "social effective-

[22] The concept of the ideal personality more appropriately belongs in a discussion of role personality, which we shall take up shortly.

ness." [23] Interestingly enough, in Burgess' view, in contrast to recent definitions, the social personality *determines* the role and status of the person in his culture, whereas contemporary anthropologists hold that the social personality is largely *determined by* the individual's role and status. Another definition, widely accepted by both sociologists and psychologists, was early given by May, a psychologist. He defined personality as "the responses made by others to the individual." [24] This is the same as our definition of the social personality.

These definitions make the social personality an objective phenomenon, although its objectivity is differently conceived by different psychologists. McClelland defines it as that which is observable. [25] However, by observable he means observable by the scientist, thus giving his definition only a limited range. Other investigators interpret its observability broadly in terms of its stimulus-value to anyone. From this point of view the most defensible definition, since it is also in harmony with the views of sociologists and anthropologists, is the one that conceives social personality as "the qualities of a person's thought and conduct as they are apprehended by another person." [26]

However, it is regrettable that the definitions of Burgess, May, McClelland, Raven, and others apply to personality as a whole instead of to social personality, which is but one aspect of the total personality.

The role personality. In his interesting and attractive discussion of personality, Allport examines some ancient meanings of *persona.*[27] A recurrent meaning of the term, according to him, is that of a *mask,* that is, the person as he appears externally, as not the true self. The modern extension of this meaning, with an important reservation, is the role personality. A role is a position or attitude which a person assumes in response to the expectations of others. Personality is thus manifested in the various roles which we play at different times and in different situations. The roles which we play are determined by our status in the group.

Does this mean that the role personality is a *persona,* a mask which we wear and which may be devoid of a necessary connection

[23] E. W. Burgess, in *Proc. of the Second Colloquium on Personality Investigation* (Baltimore: Johns Hopkins University Press, 1930), p. 149.

[24] M. A. May, The foundations of personality, in P. S. Achilles (ed.), *Psychology at work* (New York: McGraw-Hill Book Co., Inc., 1932), Ch. 4.

[25] D. C. McClelland, *Personality* (New York: The Dryden Press, Inc., 1951), p. 69.

[26] J. C. Raven, The comparative assessment of personality, *Brit. J. Psychol.*, 60 (1950), 115–24, on p. 115.

[27] G. W. Allport, *Personality: a psychological interpretation* (New York: Holt, Rinehart & Winston, Inc., 1937), pp. 25–29.

with the nuclear or "true" personality? Doubtless in many cases this is so, for one can, for opportunistic or other reasons, falsely assume a role or play a part which is at variance with his personal integrity. However, role personality, as we use the term here, is a "mask" or a mode of behavior specifically *sanctioned by the mores* of the group. Hence, its enaction is not a mark of insincerity or hypocrisy, but of social compliance and good adjustment. So conceived, role personality is an important dimension of a healthy being. Modern clinical psychology has demonstrated that deficiency and failure in role behavior is an important source of personality maladjustment.[28]

Every society has a large list of roles which it expects its members to learn and enact. They are manifested in age and sex roles, marriage roles, avoidance roles, occupational roles, and so forth. Boys are expected to be brave and adventurous, and eventually become breadwinners. Girls must learn to cook, keep house, and minister to their husbands and children. In most societies there are institutionalized avoidance roles which regulate the social relations between men and specified women such as mother-in-laws, or between women and their father-in-laws. In many societies women must be demure and submissive, and men competitive and aggressive. A good servant adopts an ingratiating air; and a modern business executive cultivates a taste for dry martinis. These are role-expectations of the group, and are important in shaping the personalities of its people.

The concept of role behavior, or role personality, discloses the intimate relation between the individual, society, and culture. It binds together the three fundamental ways of conceptualizing human behavior: psychology, which deals with the individual; sociology, which investigates the social personality, or the individual's status in his group; and anthropology, which studies role behavior. The psychology of personality can ignore these other disciplines only at the risk of being extremely one-sided and incomplete.

Every individual, because of the status he occupies and the roles which he plays, gradually becomes a unified person. As a child the individual looks to others for his survival and growth. By a process of social learning he develops a set of expectations about the actions of others and the awareness that others expect certain modes of behavior from him. In this way he comes to acquire a

[28] For an excellent discussion of this subject, see N. Cameron, *The psychology of behavior disorders* (Boston: Houghton Mifflin Co., 1947), Ch. 4; N. Cameron and A. Magaret, *Behavior pathology* (Boston: Houghton Mifflin Co., 1951), pp. 114–22.

certain well-defined position in his group. This position is called his *status*. The position, once established, carries with it the obligation to play certain roles; as, for instance, the child who must learn to obey his parents, and the parents who in turn must discharge their obligations to the dependent offspring. The interpersonal relations between the child and his parents form a pattern of interlocking roles which regulate their behavior toward each other. From this pattern of interlocking roles, both the child and his parents emerge as enculturated and mature individuals. Each has become aware of his status, each is responsive to the roles which his status requires him to enact, and each has become conscious of himself as a person. Role, status, and self—or role personality, social personality, and nuclear personality—are thus seen to commingle and form the total personality.[29]

CULTURE AND COMPLEX PSYCHOLOGICAL MODALITIES. Personality is a general term which organizes into a relatively coherent scheme all the modalities of human behavior, such as learning, thinking, perception, problem-solving, concept-formation, and emotions. We call these processes *complex* modalities to distinguish them from the *sense* modalities, such as seeing, hearing, and tasting, which are by contrast simple and largely neurophysiological in character.

In the preceding chapter we indicated that the determination of thinking and other cognitive activities by the social structure has been recognized at least since the end of the nineteenth century, especially in the writings of Durkheim and his followers in the present century. The ways of acting, thinking, remembering, and feeling, we pointed out, are noticeably affected by the norms of the group. (See Chapter 6, pp. 185–86.) Lévy-Bruhl, an early follower of Durkheim, held that the ways of thinking are not inherent, but are determined by collective representations, or value frames of reference. On the basis of his analysis of primitive cultures, he attempted to show that primitive people do not cognitively discriminate between the real and the imagined world. They think, not in terms of causal relations, but on the basis of the "law of participation" (*participation mystique*); on the basis, that is, of the belief that they are an integral part of the "unseen" world. In this in-

---

[29] For an excellent comprehensive discussion of the concept of role, including an extensive bibliography, see T. R. Sarbin, Role theory, in G. Lindzey (ed.), *Handbook of social psychology* (Reading, Mass.: Addison-Wesley Publishing Co., Inc., 1954), Vol. 1, Ch. 6. For a pioneer study of the function of role behavior in the rise and growth of the self, see G. H. Mead, *Mind, self and society* (Chicago: University of Chicago Press, 1934), Pts. 3 and 4.

visible world logical contradictions, as Western man understands this term, are nonexistent or inoperative.[30]

Following the leads of Durkheim and Lévy-Bruhl, Blondel examined the affective life of people. His investigations led him to believe that the affective life—the life of feelings and emotions—is not universally identical. Feelings and emotions are products of the cultural life of a group, and they can be understood only by knowing the social structure in which they manifest themselves. Emotions like love and hate are denoted by appropriate words, and these words serve as criteria for judging and understanding the emotions. Accordingly, the emotion will differ in different groups in accordance with the affective vocabulary which they have at their command. Grief over the death of a loved one may be expressed by means of profuse tears, hopeless wailing, stunned silence, or happy celebration. In short, emotions are cultural, not individual, forms of expression.[31]

Halbwachs, another follower of Durkheimian thought, was one of the earliest investigators of the social nature of memory. According to him, memory is not an individual or unique phenomenon, but is always embedded in a social framework. If he did not belong to a cultural group, if he were not anchored in a social frame of reference, an individual would not be able to remember. Memory is always localized in a cultural milieu, and can function only by using the language and experience of a group. In the absence of a cultural reference frame one could not distinguish a memory from a dream, and it would have the disjointed and meaningless character of a dream. In order to recall a past event in a new situation one has to place oneself mentally into the old framework.[32]

Our purpose in expounding the foregoing investigations is to show that interest in tracing the social and cultural conditions of complex psychological modalities is fairly old. Although a critical evaluation of these studies would expose a number of cardinal weaknesses, they are, nevertheless, fundamentally right in their general line of argument. Recent investigations of an empirical and experimental nature confirm the earlier belief that thinking, feeling, emotion, perception, and similar complex modalities are in a con-

---

30 L. Lévy-Bruhl, *Les fonctions mentales dans les sociétés inférieures* (Paris: F. Alcan, 1910); also *L'âme primitive* (Paris: F. Alcan, 1927).

31 C. Blondel, *Introduction à la psychologie collective* (Paris: A. Colin, 1928).

32 M. Halbwachs, *Les cadres sociaux de la mémoire* (Paris: F. Alcan, 1925). For experimental investigations of the social nature of memory, see F. C. Bartlett, *Remembering: a study in experimental and social psychology* (Cambridge: Cambridge University Press, 1932).

siderable measure conditioned by cultural expectations. Indeed, this is so patently true from the standpoints of modern anthropology and social psychology that one may for practical purposes consider culture and the psychological modalities as largely identical. Insofar as culture is, as we said, a way of life, it is a way of perceiving, thinking, and feeling about men's experience. One can hardly explain the behavior of men toward one another in a group without knowing how they perceive themselves and others.[33]

Let us, then, re-examine this problem in the light of recent scientific research.

The cognitive process. This process refers to all those intellectual functions which psychologists refer to as perception, learning, thinking, problem-solving, and concept formation. We are not at the moment suscribing to any specific cognitive theory. Therefore, when we view learning and problem-solving, for example, we are committing ourselves neither to reinforcement theory nor to the view that they form a process of perceptual reorganization. Our understanding of the term in any case is compatible with present usage. In its widest meaning, the term includes "all the means whereby the individual represents anything to himself or uses these representations as a means of guiding his behavior."[34] This definition has the merit of including in the realm of cognition such important processes as learning, perceiving, thinking, and concept formation. However, we shall examine only the subject of thinking.

Its very commonplaceness makes *thinking* appear to be a simple phenomenon. It varies all the way from undirected reverie to the critical and creative symbolic manipulations of artists, scientists, and philosophers. Rather than being a simple act of conjoining words and ideas, it is a highly complex process of conceptualizing, categorizing, and ordering the events of our world into a meaningful system. The infant apparently feels no anxiety in not comprehending the events which occur all around him, for his needs are at once simple and easily gratified by others. An intelligent adult, however, were he suddenly deprived of the categories which help him to identify the objects of his experience, would be overcome with terror by the strange and complex world which his words and ideas help him to order and simplify. It might well once again become, like the child's in William James' description, a big, booming, and buzzing confusion.

[33] See D. D. Lee, Notes on the conception of the self among the Wintu, *J. abnorm. soc. Psychol.*, 45 (1950), 538–43.

[34] R. Leeper, Cognitive processes, in S. S. Stevens (ed.), *Handbook of experimental psychology* (New York: John Wiley & Sons, Inc., 1951), Ch. 19.

We have no way of knowing what *pure* thinking might be—
thinking, that is, which is untouched by social and cultural categories. Since all thinking is performed by cognitive beings, and
all cognitive beings are conditioned by the society into which they
are born, their thinking is profoundly influenced by the symbolic
systems of their cultural group. Thinking in lower animals consists
of conditioned activities whose direction is determined by antecedent stimuli and remembered responses. The learned cues on
which the animal's thinking is based are direct *signal* reactions.
Nothing external to the stimulus-response structure is interposed
between the cue which the animal perceives and the action which
it takes. In man, however, there is always the interposition of the
abstract or linguistic symbols of his culture. Anecdotal descriptions of thinking in dogs notwithstanding, it is safe to say that
canine thinking is the same the world over. It is characteristic of
man's thinking, however, that it profoundly reflects the linguistic
and other categories of his culture. Cultural groups differ remarkably in the way in which they categorize or perceive different
human activities. Anthropologists have extensively documented
the different ways in which ethnic groups conceptualize such commonplace phenomena as sex, intelligence, sickness, good and evil,
time, measurement, and the like. Hallowell, an anthropologist with
a lifelong interest in personality, has amassed a great amount of
evidence to confirm the cultural basis of cognitive processes.[35] So
extensively is human thinking conditioned and enveloped by cultural categories that custom and thought seem to be almost identical. Man is the only creature who thinks with his customs.

Philosophical reflections on the nature of man have long recognized the molding force of *language* in human thought. No one,
to be sure, can be certain that thinking can take place without
language, but today no psychologist doubts that they are intrinsi-
cally related. But language, we have said, is an important human
artifact—a thing of culture and invention. No animal besides man
has invented a language, and man's cognitive superiority to other
animals lies in his use of meaningful symbols. It is a well-known
fact that the chimpanzee, who is man's closest non-human "relative,"

[35] See the following works by A. I. Hallowell: Temporal orientation in Western
civilization and in preliterate society, *Amer. Anthropologist*, 39 (1937), 647–70; Sin,
sex and sickness in Saulteaux belief, *Brit. J. med. Psychol.*, 18 (1939), 191–97; Some
psychological aspects of measurement among the Saulteaux, *Amer. Anthropologist*, 44
(1942), 62–77; Cultural factors in the structuralization of perception, in J. H. Rohrer
and M. Sherif (eds.), *Social psychology at the crossroads* (New York: Harper & Bros.,
1951), pp. 164–95; Culture, personality, and society, in A. L. Kroeber (ed.), *Anthropology today* (Chicago: University of Chicago Press, 1953), pp. 597–620.

is unable to develop a language. While he may be man's equal in the latter's childhood, he soon falls behind him. Indeed, judging by the well-known experiment of the Kelloggs, who reared their five-month-old child in the company of a chimpanzee, the latter may show himself superior to the young child in mental development, but the child quickly surpasses him when he begins to acquire a language.[36] The chimpanzee, on the other hand, with all the opportunities of acquiring a language in the Kelloggs' household, never learned to speak.

Again, the previsioning of future courses of action is a conspicuous trait of man. This setting up of future goals depends upon man's capacity of imaginative construction, or more specifically, his potentiality for dealing with the world *indirectly*. Man's indirect control of his environment is effected to a large extent by his abstract and symbolic system, his language. Language is the conceptual tool by which man transforms both the world of nature and himself. *Concepts* are thus the effective means by which man comprehends and controls his environment, albeit indirectly. Words and concepts are thus seen to be inseparable.

The conceptual nature of language is most evident in the language of science and philosophy. Generally speaking, the more highly developed the language, the more numerous are its abstractions, and the better discriminations between objects and events it affords. Thus the Klamath Indians, whose culture is quite primitive, have no general word for "run." Hence, in trying to denote this form of locomotion, they must use a specific word for the running of every animal. The German language differentiates between the eating by a human being and by an animal; and in the same manner distinguishes between the death of an animal and that of a man. Accordingly, when a German wishes to show deep contempt for someone, he may describe the latter's eating or dying by the words that are reserved only for the description of these events in an animal. There are cultural groups that have no general term for "tree," but must specify the kind of tree they are denoting, such as "maple tree," or "willow tree." According to Boas, the Greenland Eskimos discriminate ice into more than thirty kinds, such as "fresh-water ice," or "salt-water ice." [37]

Obviously these differences, and hundreds more, are not biologically or racially determined. They are examples of widely

[36] W. N. Kellogg and L. A. Kellogg, *The ape and the child* (New York: McGraw-Hill Book Co., Inc., 1933).

[37] F. Boas, *General anthropology* (Boston: D. C. Heath & Co., 1938), pp. 129 f.

scattered cultural variations. People conceptually discriminate or generalize because their cultural life makes it either necessary or unimportant. Americans, unlike the Arabs, who have some 6,000 discriminating terms for camel, are content with a single word for the animal, but they easily need a dozen to differentiate their evening cocktails.

In comparing man biologically with the species below him the scientist observes that all are characterized by a common possession: they all act within a framework of receptors and effectors, of stimuli and responses. In man, however, the polar ends of the behavioral continuum are joined by a symbolic complex which has been interposed by millennia of cultural development. There is a sense of poetry in this scientific fact, for nothing more eloquently illuminates the fateful transformation of man from the brute that he was than the language and customs which he has painfully wrought. Through language, man at once comes closer to reality and yet moves away from it. He comes closer to it because only through language can he truly comprehend reality; he is removed from it because what he sees is not the world itself but its verbal symbolization. What he knows of reality and how he feels about it are wrapped up in the symbolic and cultural matrix of the society in which he moves and lives. Man is, in short, not only a rational animal but a symbolic being.

While in the present state of psychological and anthropological research it is impossible to state precisely and definitively the interpenetrating relationship between thought, language, and culture, there is no doubt that the relationship exists and that it is crucial. The grammatical categories may not determine cultural reality, but they doubtless condition the manner in which men in divergent cultures perceive and comprehend it. The reality itself may be of no great consequence, especially since we cannot know it directly, but man's cognitive structuring of it tells us much about his culture and his thinking. Perhaps it is no mere coincidence or historical accident that the ancient Greeks excelled in science and philosophy, whereas their Roman neighbors were primarily pragmatic and legalistic. It is, possibly, no mere chance that the Germans have been superior in technological enterprise and the Americans in business inventiveness. The symbolic structure favored by each has led them to perceive the world from different perspectives. At all events these possibilities deserve serious attention, with a view to future confirmation or disqualifica-

tion. The testable hypotheses deserve to be teased out and investigated.[38]

In this analysis of the cognitive process as it is affected by
cultural categories we have been obliged to omit discussion of
learning, perception, problem solving, and intelligence as well as
of other intellectual functions. These, too, reflect the culture in
which they originate and are used. Intelligence, which is a general
ability rather than a strictly cognitive function, has also been
extensively investigated from a cultural point of view. We include
it here because intelligence is thought by some investigators to be
influenced by culture. In actuality, however, the effect of culture
on intelligence is manifested not fundamentally, if at all, in the
capacity itself, but in the prevailing techniques for its measurement. The "culture-free" intelligence tests have not been adequately validated, so that cultural loading is still present in current
assessments of intelligence. The most balanced treatment of this
difficult subject, as it applies to the American scene only, shows
that the differences on the test performances of "Old Americans"
and other ethnic groups *when status in both cases is held constant,*
are statistically insignificant.[39]

Bruner and his associates have stated the matter discerningly in
their recent volume on thinking. "The categories in terms of which
man sorts out and responds to the world around him," they write,
"reflect deeply the culture into which he is born. The language,
the way of life, the religion and science of a people: all of these
mold the way in which a man experiences the events out of which
his own history is fashioned. In this sense his personal history
comes to reflect the traditions and thought-ways of his culture,
for the events that make it up are filtered through the categorical
systems he has learned." [40]

---

[38] For fruitful comments on linguistic categories and their relation to cultural experience, see C. Lévi-Strauss, R. Jakobson, C. F. Voegelin, and T. A. Sebeok, Results
of the conference of anthropologists and linguists, *Int. J. Amer. Linguistics,* 19 (1953),
No. 2, Memoir 8. See also, E. H. Lenneberg, Cognition in ethnolinguistics, *Language,*
29 (1953), 463–71.

[39] K. Eells, A. Davis, R. J. Havighurst, V. E. Herrick, and R. Tyler, *Intelligence
and cultural differences* (Chicago: University of Chicago Press, 1951).

[40] J. S. Bruner, J. C. Goodnow, and G. A. Austin, *A study of thinking* (New York:
John Wiley & Sons, Inc., 1956), p. 10.

Experiments also support Halbwachs' semiphilosophical observations on the cultural determination of memory. An interesting experiment by Yuker, while not dealing with the influence of *culture* on memory, but with the effect of a contrived group
atmosphere, shows that group recall is superior to individual recall, and that a cooperative group atmosphere is superior to a competitive one as they relate to memory.
See H. E. Yuker, Group atmosphere and memory, *J. abnorm. soc. Psychol.,* 51 (1955),
17–23.

The affective process. The emotions are generally thought to be physiologically determined. That they are basically physiological processes originating in the hypothalamus is now accepted as an established fact. The work of Cannon, cited in Chapter 5, has demonstrated that the hypothalamic activities regulated by the sympathetic nervous system and the adrenal glands are the physiological correlates of what we ordinarily call the emotions.[41] The physiological basis of the emotions is also confirmed by the universal distribution of such well-known reactions as anger, joy, sorrow, and laughter.

Emotional behavior may possibly be determined by the anatomical structure of the human face. Klineberg, reporting the observations of a Chinese medical officer, states that the Chinese facial anatomy differs in certain respects from that of the white European.[42] A certain facial muscle in the European is divided into three, semi-independently acting, parts, whereas in the Chinese face they are much more rigidly connected. This seems to permit a freer play to the muscular contractions in the white man's face, and gives an appearance of immobility to the Chinese face. This fact may account for the popular view of the Chinese as inscrutable.

It is also true, nevertheless, that the objects or circumstances which evoke emotions, and the manner in which they are expressed, vary with the cultural circumstances. Thus, as Klineberg points out, the impassive face of the Chinese may well be due to the type of restrained behavior which their culture expects of them. A Chinese girl is taught that she must not display unhappiness, and a Chinese boy is admonished not to lose his temper or be boisterous.[43]

Since the time of Blondel's observations on the cultural nature of the emotions, cited earlier in this chapter, a number of interesting but not always convincing investigations have lent support to the general hypothesis that the emotions are culturally conditioned. The best way to conceptualize these emotional expressions is to consider them as important aspects of the *role personality* —that is, as standard and expected ways of behavior, as elements of the *persona,* as we have defined this term. There was a time when a woman could display her femininity by swooning at the sight of a mouse. Today the same behavior is seldom indulged in

[41] W. B. Cannon, *Bodily changes in pain, hunger, fear, and rage* (2d ed.; New York: Appleton-Century-Crofts, Inc., 1929).

[42] O. Klineberg, *Social psychology* (Rev. ed.; New York: Holt, Rinehart & Winston, Inc., 1954), pp. 174–75.

[43] O. Klineberg, Emotional expression in Chinese literature, *J. abnorm. soc. Psychol.,* 33 (1938), 517–20.

and is evaluated otherwise. How one reacts to emotion-provoking circumstances is partly dependent on how the culture defines the situation for us. Emotions thus in part reflect the manner in which we perceive a situation and in part are based on cultural prescriptions. Emotions accordingly contain cognitive elements, as well as a physiological basis. Whether we perceive a social event as sad or amusing will depend in no small degree upon how culture has caused us to view it. In the land of the Kwakiutl death is a calamity which demands revenge on him who is thought to be responsible. In a society where death is a journey to a happier abode, its occurrence is cause for rejoicing. In one group a person responds to insults with wrath or indignation; in another, by turning the other cheek.[44]

Feelings of love and tenderness are expressed or inhibited in accordance with existing mores. Among the Kaska Indians affection after the third year is almost completely repressed. The warm emotional responses which the Kaskan mother showed toward her child before he was three years old is suddenly terminated. This treatment makes for emotionally constricted adults.[45]

The affective life of the Balinese is similar in this respect to that of the Kaska Indians. The mother's attention to her infant is withdrawn when the latter is a year old. She teases her child, leads him on, and then rebuffs him. Stimulation is chronically followed by frustration. The child soon learns not to give himself to anyone, and by the time he is an adult he is a constricted and withdrawn individual. The capacity for love and affection was there, but it was snuffed out by the repressing spirit of the Balinese culture.[46] Among the Pilaga Indians love is completely unrewarded. They are best described as an unloving and hostile people, devoid of warmth and friendship. Life is oriented around the emotion of mutual rejection.[47] Love and warmth, understood as acceptance of and sympathy for people, is nonexistent. The Henrys, who made a detailed study of Pilaga people and society, suggest that perhaps

[44] See descriptions of these differences in the following references: Benedict, *Patterns of culture;* J. W. M. Whiting, *Becoming a Kwoma* (New Haven: Yale University Press, 1941); O. Lewis, *Life in a Mexican valley* (Urbana: University of Illinois Press, 1951).

[45] J. J. Honigmann, *Culture and ethos of Kaska society* (Yale University Publications in Anthropology, No. 40 [New Haven: Yale University Press, 1949]).

[46] M. Mead, Educative effects of social environment as disclosed by studies of primitive societies, in E. W. Burgess *et al., Environment and education* (University of Chicago Supplementary Education Monographs, No. 54 [Chicago: University of Chicago Press, 1942]), pp. 48–61.

[47] J. Henry and Z. Henry, *Doll play of Pilaga Indian children,* in C. Kluckhohn and H. A. Murray (eds.), *Personality in nature, society, and culture* (New York: Alfred A. Knopf, Inc., 1953), pp. 292–307.

the Pilaga's obsession with sexuality is a disguised affect hunger, a compensation for ungratified affection.[48]

SOCIAL CLASS MEMBERSHIP AND PERSONALITY. The problem of social class influences on personality has received a large share of attention from students of culture and personality. The reason for this interest is not hard to find, for anthropologists have demonstrated that culture for the most part filters through to the individual through his class position in the community. (We called attention to this fact in the preceding chapter in connection with the child-rearing practices of parents.) The importance of class position here stems from the fact that there are perceptible differences in the use of basic disciplines in different classes. A number of good studies show that feeding, toilet training, sexual control, aggression, and so forth, differ in the different classes—or in caste relations, where these exist—and that these differences are reflected in the personalities of its members.[49]

Anthropologists do not generally think of class stratification in terms of occupation and income, but on the basis of the rank or social position of persons in the community. People of similar rank are in closer communication with one another than with people of other ranks, and their behavior is affected, or made similar, by this access to one another. Thus, while most Americans are very much alike, they differ distinctly, nevertheless, as a consequence of their social positions in the class structure. Such homogeneity as exists in modes of living and behavior in the United States is not diffused throughout its culture. Homogeneity characterizes the various classes, not our culture as a whole.

Some researchers have found pronounced class differences in attitudes toward sex and eating, anxieties regarding food and shelter, sentiments and beliefs, and so forth. Davis found that, owing to the greater certainty regarding their food supply, middle-class Americans eat more regularly and more sparingly than people in the lower class. They are also much concerned with obesity, especially the women, whereas the lower-class people tend to overeat when they have plenty of food available. Children of

[48] For a comprehensive review of the cultural basis of emotions, including those which we have omitted, and with copious illustrative examples, see W. La Barre, The cultural basis of emotions and gestures, *J. Pers.*, 16 (1947), 49–68.

[49] A. Davis and R. J. Havighurst, Social class and color differences in child-rearing, *Amer. sociol. Rev.*, 11 (1946), 698–710; A. Kardiner and L. Ovesey, *The mark of oppression* (New York: W. W. Norton & Co., Inc., 1951); R. J. Havighurst and A. Davis, A comparison of the Chicago and Harvard studies of social class differences in child rearing, *Amer. sociol. Rev.*, 20 (1955), 438–42; R. R. Sears, E. E. Maccoby, and H. Levin, *Patterns of child rearing* (Evanston, Ill.: Row, Peterson & Co., 1957).

middle-class parents are anxiously concerned about getting good grades in school, whereas children of lower-class parents, particularly those living in the slum areas, are not worried by poor scholarship, and even tend to conceal good grades when they attain them. Middle-class people tend to control or sublimate their aggressions, whereas lower-class persons express them directly in quarreling and fighting.[50]

Ethical values of honesty, truthfulness, and justice have also been found to differ among the classes. Both the middle and the lower classes in a community studied by Havighurst and Neubauer subscribe in principle to the common virtues, but in practice they express them differently. Thus, people in the lower class have little compunction about dealing unfairly or dishonestly with persons outside their families and neighborhoods. Moral virtues are conceived as operating more within the primary group; as regards others, lower-class persons are far less meticulous.[51]

All in all, middle-class persons are more strongly inclined toward obedience of social taboos, ambition, restraint in individual behavior, symbolic gratification (such as good grades in school), good adjustment, and social approval, whereas these values have less importance to lower-class people.[52]

The effect of caste membership within the American class-stratified society has also been extensively studied by psychologists and anthropologists. There can be little serious doubt that the American Negro's personality is seriously constricted, if not warped, by his caste position—by the fact, in other words, that he is born into a group with an inferior social status from which he cannot effectively escape, whatever his individual gifts and abilities may be. The study by Davis and Havighurst which we have already cited, as well as others, document this effect extensively. The interesting investigation by Kardiner and Ovesey, which we have also cited, is worth describing, despite some of its serious methodological weaknesses. The results are based on the psychoanalyses of 25 American Negroes. While these results reveal little or nothing that was not already known regarding the personalities

[50] A. Davis, *Social class influences on learning* (Cambridge, Mass.: Harvard University Press, 1948). We are fully aware of the fact that there are too few studies of this kind, and that other studies might not find these characteristics as pronounced as Davis describes them. The value of Davis' study lies in calling attention to class differences, which until recently were practically neglected.

[51] R. J. Havighurst and D. Neubauer, Community factors in relation to character formation, in R. J. Havighurst and H. Taba, *Adolescent character and personality* (New York: John Wiley & Sons, Inc., 1949).

[52] See W. L. Warner, *American life—dream and reality* (Chicago: University of Chicago Press, 1953).

of Negroes, they are valuable for the support they give to the psychoanalytical study of culture and personality. The authors found that in his caste-restricted contacts with the white man and his culture the Negro almost inevitably forms a devaluated image of himself. This devaluation causes him to idealize and emulate the white man, only to be frustrated by the caste barriers. The affability and apparent good humor which even the untutored perceive in most Negroes is partly an unconscious means of concealing his repressed antipathy toward the white man's privileged position. The Negro child grows up into a person with little genuine trust in human relationships. As Kardiner and Ovesey point out, the Negro "must operate on the assumption that the world is hostile." [53]

Moreover, the Negro's caste membership gives rise to negative relationships among Negroes themselves. These relationships begin early in the home and continue to operate outside it. The Negro, according to Seward, is nurtured on inconsistent punishment by an overworked and frustrated mother who is usually employed outside the home. He has little training in relating himself to others except through hostility and suspicion. For this reason, as she points out, the Negro seldom internalizes the group mores successfully. Hence, he tends to rely on magical aid, or to win the white man's esteem by proving himself superior within the white man's own domain. However, as might be expected, too often the Negro fails in this aspiration, and pays the price of anxiety and emotional stress. [54]

Seward goes on to point out, justifiably, indeed, that the Negro church regrettably missed a supreme opportunity to compensate for its people's domestic defects by failing to establish a meaningful contact with the individual's daily life. "The atmosphere of otherworldliness and the adoption of a white god and white angels was more hindrance than help to the Negro in his down-to-earth struggle for existence in a society where the white man is already god." [55]

The Negro's caste position has reached into his sexual life as well. Although the Negro is usually singled out for his moral laxity, clinical evidence shows a high rate of frigidity and impotence. These conditions are probably symptomatic, as Seward suggests, of the emotional impoverishment and of the inverted sexual

[53] Kardiner and Ovesey, *The mark of oppression*, p. 308.
[54] G. Seward, *Psychotherapy and culture conflict* (New York: The Ronald Press Co., 1956), Chs. 6 and 7.
[55] *Ibid.*, p. 126.

roles of the Negro man and woman. Kardiner and Ovesey likewise call attention to the lack of sexual interest in Negroes—a fact which shatters the average white man's image of the Negro as being over-sexed. Seward, as well as Kardiner and Ovesey, ascribe this sexual poverty to the Negro woman's role as the family provider, and to the consequent feeling of dependence on the part of the man. The woman in effect becomes masculinized and a threat to the man's masculinity. This is not even to mention the figure of the Negro mother as the severe disciplinarian who, because of her frustrating and punitive behavior toward her child, conditions his relations with women for the rest of his life.[56]

The foregoing are but samples of class relations as they affect the human personality. The complex influence of the class struc-ture as an important segment of culture is being vigorously pursued in the study of personality today. It is too early to say how reliable this mode of study is, for the methods are open to serious criticism and the results are frequently inconsistent. Yet, all in all, these investigations have added to our understanding of the origin and growth of personality. When the data which they have accu-mulated are critically sifted and assimilated to the existing body of psychological knowledge they should enlarge our insight into human nature.

CONCLUSION

In this chapter we have attempted to show how the human personality comes to be by describing and analyzing the cultural conditions and pressures which play a part in molding it into a definite form. The essence of what we have been saying is fairly simple, albeit the exact mechanisms which are at work in the process of enculturation are very complex. We have been saying in effect that, *while the individual comes into the world as a biological organism, he is gradually transformed into a human being by the customs of his group.* Furthermore, to the extent that customs are finite, social structures are universally similar, and the ways in which people can relate themselves to one another are limited, it may be said that personality is very much the same universally. On the other hand, since cultural diversity character-izes human associations everywhere, thereby creating different mo-tivations and expectations, personality is significantly different in different cultures. Beginning with the family unit and extending throughout the variety of customs and institutions, the social roles

56 *Ibid.*, p. 125; Kardiner and Ovesey, *The mark of oppression*, pp. 307–8.

and positions, and the complex class arrangements found in either bold or attenuated forms in all societies, it is every person's fate to be shaped by the molding force of each of them. Combined and integrated in various ways, these molding forces shape the personalities of every human organism.

The psychological process, however, is complex and never-ending. While it is breaking an organic process into separate dimensions, we can denote the different forces without destroying the integrity of the whole. These dimensions were discussed in detail in the pages of this chapter. They can be conveniently listed into three groups.

(1) *The organic needs are canalized into specific modes of gratification.* The basic disciplines, for example, are given expression along the lines required by the culture. An infant must learn when and under what circumstances he may eat, and the kinds of foods which he may consume as an adult. His disposition to eliminate excreta is gradually curtailed, so that eventually he learns to dispose of them in accordance with cultural prescriptions.

(2) *Personality patterning is greatly extended and deepened by the symbolic complex of one's culture.* Through a culture's language man learns to deal with the world around him; by means of it he is able to grasp the world conceptually and in a meaningful order. Without symbols, man could not have risen above the beasts. As we have said before, while we do not know if linguistic categories themselves determine cultural reality, there is no doubt that they condition the way men perceive it.

(3) *Personality is shaped by the systems of integration*—by the rational and belief systems and by the prevailing social ideology. These systems, which are wholly cultural, structure the perception of reality through language and the process of canalization. Even the conflicts and discontinuities which exist in all men and in all cultures are explained by the integrative systems. The conflicts which lead to maladjustment and deviant behavior can be partially explained by the breakdown in any or all the integrative systems, as witnessed by the example of Betsileo's social disorganization and conflictual behavior. Canalization, symbolic structuring of reality, and the integration of human experience are thus seen to be fundamentally interrelated.

Lest the reader infer from the data and arguments of this chapter that culture is a reality existing by itself, a structure removed from the flow of human relationships, we hasten to add that this cannot be true. We have in no way reified culture. Culture does not exist apart from the generations of men who have created it. Man and culture, we have said, form a more or less organized whole in which neither exists in isolation from the other. Yet, when all is said and done, it is man, the striving human organism, who is the fundamental causal agent in the cultural patterning of the living personality.

Part III

ORGANIZATION
AND DYNAMICS:
PSYCHOLOGICAL
ANALYSIS OF
PERSONALITY

CHAPTER 8

Personality and Learned Behavior

In the preceding two chapters we discussed in great detail the molding force of social groups and culture. The patterning processes by means of which the group and culture together shape the human personality are known as socialization and enculturation. By means of interaction with members of his group, especially the family in the child's early development, the individual's interpersonal patterns are established. His dispositions, attitudes, and emotional responses, while always subject to change, are grounded in the affectional bonds of the primary group. *So profoundly is this true that even individual uniqueness and autonomy are characteristics that the individual learns in his interactions with others.* How else can one account for the differences in these traits from person to person? We all know that some persons are more individualized and autonomous than others. Yet what causes this difference? The answer must be that, while basic biological components play a part, it is also in part acquired from contact with people and the cultural heritage. Assuming that the tendency of every organism is to become more and more what it already potentially is, the process of becoming is promoted or hindered by aids or obstacles in the social environment. One person is unique and autonomous because of encouragement and loving care during his childhood; another is similarly constituted because of a deep and abiding rebellion against unreasoning restraints by stupid or hostile adults. Each acquired his uniqueness and autonomy in response to social conditions external to himself.

The implication of the foregoing remarks is that the learning aspect of personality, which is the subject matter of the present chapter, has already been described by other names. In a broad sense, socialization and enculturation are forms of learning. Like the learning process which the psychologist investigates in the laboratory, socialization and enculturation are modifications in behavior. These modifications are much more profound and far-reaching than the temporary changes wrought in an animal in the formal laboratory. Nevertheless, in principle they are very much the same.

This last observation is not to say that personality can be—or some day will be—explained wholly in terms of the principles of animal learning. One shortcoming of much research in the field of learning is the implicit assumption that learning theory is the best way to a scientific account of human behavior. The great variety of learning theories alone makes one doubtful. Nevertheless, learning is important. It is important, not because all behavior can best be analyzed in terms of learning categories, but because, first, one cannot fully appreciate the leading ideas in psychology—even those that may turn out to be untrue—without a knowledge of the psychology of learning; and, second, if one does not press the claims of learning theory too far, it helps us to see that personality is the most significant learning product.

In this chapter we shall examine the learning process with two questions in mind: (1) How does an organism, particularly a human being, learn? (2) What are the possibilities and the limitations of the learning process in accounting for the formation and growth of the human personality?

THE NATURE OF LEARNING

If for some curious reason a person were to assemble all the published writings on learning in our society, they would easily fill an average-size classroom; and he would surely be impressed by the quantity of the work performed. If, however, he were then to ask what men have learned about learning from this prodigious labor, the answer he received would be all the more surprising. He would be told that we know little for certain about learning, and that the most imaginative and productive scholars in this field are in lively—and sometimes intense—disagreement. One of the best-informed learning theorists has passed perhaps the most critical judgment of all: "There are no laws of learning which can be taught with confidence. Even the most obvious facts of improvement with practice and the regulation of learning under reward and punishment are matters of theoretical dispute." [1]

There are two salutary reasons for burdening the nonprofessional reader with so adverse a judgment. First, it should give him a sense of the complexity of learning, especially in human beings. Second, it should fortify him against the critics of personality theory, many of whom are psychologists of learning, who severely criticize it on the ground that it is perforated by irreconcilable differences. The difficulty inherent in the psychology of learning should not, however, deter us from examining it impartially. It will even bring us a special reward, for in studying it in the context of personality we shall learn to understand its human relevance. This will be no small gain.

Although there are almost as many distinct theories of learning as there are psychologists who propound them, they can be classified into two major views. Technically these approaches are known as *stimulus-response* theory and *cognitive* theory. In the stimulus-response group are all the views beginning with Thorndike's in 1890's, to such contemporary figures as Hull, Guthrie, and Skinner. The so-called "functionalists"—men like Woodworth, Melton, McGeoch, Underwood, and others—are also stimulus-response (S-R) theorists. In the group of cognitive theorists are such outstanding psychologists as Köhler, Koffka, Lewin, and Tolman. Since it is neither necessary nor possible to expound the separate contributions of each of these men, we shall select as most representative and rigorous the theory of Hull, as modified and expanded by Miller and Dollard, among the S-R psychologists, and of Tolman among the cognitive theorists.

STIMULUS-RESPONSE LEARNING. In its most general form, S-R theory aims to explain behavior by attempting to predict measurable correlations between a stimulus and its manifestation in an overt response. In Hull's rigorous (but difficult and often extremely technical) writings, learning is conceived as the establishment or reinforcement of connections between stimuli and responses. The connection between the two ends of the behavioral continuum, if made often enough, results in a habit. Indeed the connection *is* the habit. The habit or connection is established by the contiguity of a stimulus, a response, and a reinforcement. In a dog, for instance, reward or reinforcement may satisfy either a basic tissue need, like hunger, or a need regularly associated with the original reinforcement, such as pleasure at the sight of the master who

[1] E. R. Hilgard, *Theories of learning* (2d ed.; New York: Appleton-Century-Crofts, Inc., 1956), pp. 457–58.

feeds him. The first example illustrates *primary* reinforcement; the other, *secondary* reinforcement. As the number of reinforcements increases, the habit is continuously strengthened. When the effects of learning or habit forming are transferred from one learning situation to others which are not identical with the earlier learning situation, the process is called *stimulus generalization*. The amount of generalization always depends on the degree of similarity between the different learning situations. Although Hull never extended these principles to more complex learning situations, like the formation of personality, he was convinced that it could be done without introducing any additional learning principles.[2] It is known that he had planned to write a book on social behavior before his death.

This is but the barest abstract of Hull's learning theory. Since his theory has been much more lucidly expounded and reworked with social behavior in mind by two of his associates at Yale, Miller and Dollard, we shall follow the latter's version, especially as it applies to the study of personality.[3] Their theory takes us much nearer to an understanding of personality as a form of learned behavior. At crucial points, however, as we shall see, their theory fails to come to grips with personality, and they are obliged to seek the help of psychoanalysis and anthropology.

Drive-reduction theory. This is the Hullian theory as it has been elaborated and reworked by Miller and Dollard. According to this view, learning takes place by means of four interrelated factors: drive, cue, response, and reinforcement. A *drive*—hunger, for example—serves as a stimulus to action. In the absence of a drive there can be no learning, for learning takes place in the act of satisfying a need. A *cue* determines the selection of responses that the learner makes. In the case of an infant's feeding, for example, such conditions as the sight of the mother's breast or the odor of her milk prepares the child to act in ways appropriate for obtaining the food. Without a cue the child could not anticipate the source of his hunger satisfaction, and therefore he could not learn. However, the cue itself is not sufficient for learning; the child must

[2] See C. L. Hull, *Principles of behavior* (New York: Appleton-Century-Crofts, Inc., 1943). Although Hull published a number of excellent papers after the publication of this book, and two volumes in which his earlier postulate sets were refined, his *Principles* is still the maturest expression of his entire view. See further Hull's posthumous work, *A behavior system: an introduction to behavior theory concerning the individual organism* (New Haven: Yale University Press, 1952).

[3] See N. E. Miller and J. Dollard, *Social learning and imitation* (New Haven: Yale University Press, 1941); J. Dollard and N. E. Miller, *Personality and psychotherapy* (New York: McGraw-Hill Book Co., Inc., 1950).

also *respond* to the cue, for unless he responds he cannot learn. The mother may help to direct the child's responses by touching his mouth with her breast or by turning his head in its direction. The responses will take place, finally, provided they are also rewarded, or *reinforced*. In the absence of a reward responses will not be repeated. Any act which reduces a drive tends to be repeated because reduction of tensions is accompanied by pleasure. The attainment of pleasure is satisfying, and hence the child will repeat his response in anticipation of a reward.[4] These four phases of the integrated learning act we shall now describe in some detail.

1. *Drive: the energizing function.* We shall have ample occasion to discuss drive or motivation in the next chapter. Here our first concern is to show its place in the stimulus-response association. Fundamentally, a drive is a stimulus, but a stimulus of sufficient intensity to arouse the organism to action. It is thus any condition which prepares the organism to initiate a sequence of behavior. It is the first segment of the cycle of activity which we discussed in Chapter 5. It is what makes the organism "go," or causes it to become responsive to conditions of upset inside itself, and to objects and situations in the environment. It energizes, or arouses, the organism to satisfy its needs or to pursue goals outside itself. It is a state of irritability or perturbation initiated by physiological and social deprivations.

There are two major categories of drives: physiological drives, the so-called *primary* drives, and social motives, or *secondary* drives. Some of the physiological drives were described in Chapter 5. The most common of these, the reader will recall, are hunger, thirst, sex, and pain-aversive drives. Their function is to preserve and protect the organism. The effect of drives on personality is largely determined by the individual's access to their satisfaction. For example, the Marquesan's personality, especially those features described by anxiety and interpersonal hostility, is in no small degree determined by an unstable and insecure food supply. Owing to droughts of two or three years' duration, the Marquesan's obsession with food is so intense that he develops deep anxiety and even cannibalistic proclivities. A middle-class American, on the other hand, is free of fears and obsessions in this connection, but may be intensely anxious regarding his social status and vocational success. The Marquesan's behavior stems from uncertain reduction of hunger tensions, whereas the American's is due to anxiety engendered by precarious social conditions.

[4] H. Bonner, *Social psychology: an interdisciplinary approach* (New York: American Book Co., 1953), pp. 98–99.

Having stressed the functions of physiological or primary drives in Chapter 5, we can hardly be charged with derogating their importance. Yet the fact is that except in extreme or cataclysmic conditions the primary drives, especially in our own efficient and protected society, more often than not affect personality indirectly. The taboos placed on the sex drive, and the inhibitions imposed upon their premarital and extramarital expressions, affect the individual far more enduringly than the urgencies and stresses of the drive itself. In the study of personality, therefore, the secondary or acquired drives take on much greater importance. These drives are based on the primary drives and represent elaborations of them. Furthermore, the secondary drives, as Miller and Dollard point out, "serve as a façade behind which the functions of the underlying innate drives are hidden." [5] In our own terminology, they make up an important dimension of the *persona*, or role personality, which we have already described.

Every society has a large repertory of secondary drives which clamor for efficient reduction. The desire for approval and acceptance, for power and riches, for prestige and fame, and so forth, are well-known energizers of human behavior. These secondary drives are learned in the long and complex processes of socialization and enculturation. They are not innate, but acquired.

The important thing to bear in mind concerning both the innate and the acquired drives is that in their absence the organism cannot learn. They make up the first segment in the complete cycle of activity, the first step in the learning process. Lack of motivation can make the most able person end up as a mediocrity. The child who has no desire to learn tends to be a poor learner, irrespective of his intellectual endowments; just as one with modest abilities who is strongly motivated to learn may surpass all expectations.

The reader who is not sufficiently acquainted with learning theory might well be confused by the statement that the drive is the first step in the learning process, for he may have learned that the initial item is always the stimulus. This is, of course, true, but does not offer any difficulty once we are aware that any stimulus can become a drive provided it has sufficient magnitude or intensity. A drive is frequently defined as a stimulus which is strong enough to arouse an organism to action. Accordingly, the greater the magnitude of the stimulus, the greater is the drive that

[5] Miller and Dollard, *Social learning and imitation*, p. 19; Dollard and Miller, *Personality and psychotherapy*, p. 32.

leads to action. Action is a form of behavior by means of which the individual reduces his drive stimuli. When he has succeeded in reducing his drive stimuli the individual is said to have learned. Learning, then, may be conceived as the most effective way in which an individual reduces his drive stimuli.

2. *Cue: the directive function.* In the absence of a guiding principle a drive would largely be a random form of need-satisfaction. This guiding principle is known as a cue. Its function is to direct a drive into the channels that will reduce the disequilibrium of the organism until the need is satisfied. While a drive arouses the organism and gets it set to gratify a need, a cue *impels* the organism to respond in a certain way. It determines the time, the place, and the selection of the response. The ringing of the dismissal bell, for example, is a cue to the bored student that his ordeal has come to an end.

The nature and function of the cue are better understood if we examine the relationship between the drive and cue functions of stimuli. Stimuli, as is well known, may vary in kind and in magnitude or strength. They may be strong or weak, and they may have distinctive cue values. For example, an individual may be trained to make differential responses to weak sounds of high pitch and weak sounds of low pitch. The more the two sounds differ in pitch, the more distinctive they are as cues. As the magnitude of a stimulus increases, its drive value also increases. If the intensity of a sound, for example, becomes too great it serves as a cue to motivate the person to escape from it, in which case the escape is a form of drive reduction, or reward.

The foregoing relationship between stimulus-drive and cue may be summarized by saying that a stimulus varies in kind and intensity, has a distinct drive value, and a specific cue value.[6]

Again, the significance of cues in the learning process becomes clear in cases in which learning fails to take place because of the absence of cues. Dollard and Miller describe an experiment on a young child in which candy was hidden under a red book in the middle of a row of black books. At the third trial in the experiment the child responded perfectly. However, when the candy was concealed under a dark book in a long row of books of similar color, he learned to select books in that general region during the first few trials, but for the subsequent ten trials he did not improve at all. As the authors point out, if the cues are vague or obscure

[6] Miller and Dollard, *Social learning and imitation*, p. 22; Dollard and Miller, *Personality and psychotherapy*, p. 34.

an individual cannot make the appropriate responses accurately. "Noticing a cue," they add, "can in itself be a response which may be learned. This is called learning to pay attention." [7]

Finally, the occurrence of a specific response does not always depend upon a single stimulus alone, but upon intricate configurations of stimuli. A speeding driver may respond differently to the stimulus pattern of a warning sign to reduce speed and a police car seen in the rear-view mirror, than he would to either the warning sign without the police car or the police car without the warning sign, perceived separately.[8]

3. *Response: the behavioral function.* The perception of a cue, we said, is necessary before behavior can take place. Before behavior can occur—that is, before learning can take place—a response must also occur. This is the impelling reason why, if effective and correct learning is to take place, the learner's first response must be correctly made. In the teaching-learning process half the battle has already been won when the person makes the first correct response. If the first response is not made he obviously cannot learn; and if the first response is faulty or incorrect, the error may be difficult to eradicate from the learner's behavior pattern. The elimination of a response, and the changing of a habit once established, require more numerous reinforcements or rewards in order to extinguish them. The establishment of appropriate responses is thus a critical step in the total learning process.

In every learning situation some responses are more likely to occur than others. The initial order or tendency of a stimulus to elicit a response, or more correctly, the probability of the occurrence of a response, is called the *initial hierarchy* of responses. The response most likely to occur in the initial hierarchy is called the *dominant* response; whereas the one least likely to occur is called the *weakest* response. The dominant and weakest responses describe the causal sequence between the stimulus and the dominant response, and a weak causal sequence between the stimulus and the weakest response. The causal sequence is not described in terms of neurological connections, however, but in terms of a complex nexus the details of which are at the present time practically unknown.

Response hierarchies are subject to change with every new learning. Because the new learning, like all learning, was a consequence of reinforcement or reward, it tends to take precedence over former learnings. Thus, the newly rewarded response, though it may

---

[7] Dollard and Miller, *Personality and psychotherapy*, p. 35.
[8] *Ibid.*, p. 34.

formerly have been weak, now assumes the dominant position in the hierarchy. This new hierarchy is called the *resultant hierarchy*. If we return to the case of the child learning to select the hidden candy, we can see that at the beginning the correct response was a late response in the initial hierarchy. It occurred after looking under many books, and after the occurrence of other responses, such as asking questions. At the completion of the experiment, the correct response had become the dominant response in the resultant hierarchy.

Not all learning sequences in an initial hierarchy are the results of previous learning in similar situations. In other words, the order of response is not always determined by previous learning, but may be due to hereditary conditions. In the latter case, the initial hierarchy is called an *innate hierarchy*. For example, in very young children, crying and rage have a superior position in the innate hierarchy to words for expressing them.[9]

4. Reinforcement: the rewarding function. The place of reward and punishment has long been known as influencing factors in learning. In 1911 Thorndike formulated this influence into the "law of effect," which states that a stimulus-response connection is strengthened by a reward or punishment that accompanies it.[10] Later the emphasis was shifted almost exclusively on reward as the source of the stimulus-response connections. Today, the term "reinforcement" has largely displaced the word "reward." [11]

We have shown that a drive is a stimulus of sufficient magnitude to arouse an organism to respond to cues and impel it to action. This is important as a starting point in the learning process, but it is no guarantee that the elicited response will be repeated and that learning will continue. A response is repeated only when it is reinforced or rewarded; or at best, the response is critically weakened in the absence of reward, so that extinction takes place sooner. A reward thus strengthens the stimulus and, paradoxically, reduces the drive. That is, the individual is impelled to satisfy a need as the stimulus for its production increases. The reward strengthens the stimulus in the sense that the individual desires to continue experiencing the same stimulus; but it reduces the strength of the

[9] *Ibid.*, p. 36.

[10] E. L. Thorndike, *Animal intelligence* (New York: The Macmillan Co., 1911).

[11] The reinforcement function is roughly equivalent to *operant conditioning*, a term which is widely used today. We think it is correct to say that the term "reinforcement" is much more compatible with present-day usage of the law of effect. Miller and Dollard employ the term "reward" in their 1941 publication and "reinforcement" in their 1950 work. See Miller and Dollard, *Social learning and imitation* (1941) and Dollard and Miller, *Personality and psychotherapy* (1950).

drive in proportion to the latter's satisfaction. As long as reinforcement or reward continues the organism learns; when reward is absent its learning of the unrewarded response ceases. Reinforcement is thus a crucial element in the learning process.

Reinforcement takes two forms in the learning process. *Primary reinforcements* are innate. They refer to rewards associated with the satisfaction of hunger, thirst, and sex, and avoidance of pain. But as we have made clear in various places, most drives and their reinforcement are social in character. These *secondary reinforcements* are learned. The child who learns to eat spaghetti or beefsteak to reduce his hunger drive is acting on the basis of secondary reinforcement. To an American accustomed to eating steaks, snails may present either aversive or neutral cues, and hence reinforcement and learning to eat them will not take place. A large repertory of our most important reinforcements are social or secondary. Many of the failures in school or in other situations may be attributed to the absence of secondary reinforcements. Davis and Dollard, and Davis and Havighurst, as well as other researchers, have convincingly demonstrated that the apparent mental inferiority and poor intellectual achievements of lower-class children can be traced to the paucity or absence of rewards, such as praise and recognition, by the teachers; rewards which, however, are freely bestowed upon middle-class pupils.[12]

While reinforcement is a good guarantee for continued learning, it does not necessarily assure new learning. Indeed, reinforcement strengthens existing stimulus-response bonds, thus making the appearance of new responses less likely to occur. In order to establish new responses the learner must often be placed in a potential learning situation where his old responses will not be reinforced. The person must be confronted, in other words, with a *learning dilemma*, a situation where he is impelled to make new associations because the old ones are inappropriate. The present writer can cite a case almost identical with one described by Dollard and Miller.[13] The case is that of a five-year-old boy who until recently spoke very little, and when he did, articulated so poorly that most of his speech was unintelligible to his parents. The child's needs were usually anticipated before he made them known by means of verbal utterances. Being a bright child he quickly learned that his wants would be satisfied by his parents without any verbal

[12] A. Davis and J. Dollard, *Children of bondage* (Washington, D.C.: American Council of Education, 1940), A. Davis and R. J. Havighurst, *Father of the man* (Boston: Houghton Mifflin Co., 1947); A. Davis, *Social class influences on learning* (Cambridge, Mass.: Harvard University Press, 1948).

[13] Dollard and Miller, *Personality and psychotherapy*, pp. 45–46.

efforts on his own part. He was thereby deprived of opportunities for vocal behavior which normally leads to true social speech. A remedial-speech teacher did not reinforce the child's indistinct and monosyllabic verbalization, and the child was for the first time placed on his own. This exasperating situation soon impelled the child to acquire the vocabulary and speech control which were necessary for his being understood by others. He was placed in a learning dilemma which compelled him to acquire new verbal habits.[14] In short, we tend to learn and to acquire new habits most readily when we are placed in problem situations that serve as strong drive-stimuli which impel us to seek ways for resolving our dilemmas or reducing our drives. Dollard and Miller state the matter vividly when they write:

> The absence of a dilemma is one of the reasons why it is often difficult to teach successful people new things. Old, heavily rewarded habits must be interrupted before new learning can occur. When the accustomed rewards are withdrawn by unusual circumstances such as revolution, new responses may occur and, if rewarded, may be learned; Russian counts can learn to drive taxicabs and countesses to become cooks.[15]

Principles governing the four learning functions. The four learning functions of drive, cue, response, and reinforcement make up the frame of reference of the drive reduction theory. For a better understanding of their operation in the learning process which we have been describing, it is necessary to consider briefly their complications and implications—in short, the principles which govern them. These principles are seven in number: extinction, spontaneous recovery, generalization, discrimination, gradient of reinforcement, anticipatory response, and short-circuiting.

1. *Extinction.* It should now be clear that when an acquired response is not reinforced or rewarded the impulsion to repeat it is progressively reduced. This progressive reduction is called *extinction.* It is effected by repeating the conditioned stimulus without reinforcement. Extinction is not, however, a passive cessation of response but an active inhibition of it. Neither is it a destruction of the conditioned response, as we shall see in a moment, for otherwise it could never be recovered. The child in Dollard's and Miller's example, for instance, tended not to pick up a book in her search for candy if she did not find a piece under it. Past learning had taught her to avoid looking under certain books when her efforts were unrewarded. We say that her habit of looking

---

[14] It is a tribute to Dollard and Miller that they are the only learning theorists who explicitly acknowledge John Dewey's early ideas in this connection. See J. Dewey, *How we think* (Boston: D. C. Heath & Co., 1910).

[15] Dollard and Miller, *Personality and psychotherapy,* p. 46.

under certain books was extinguished. However, extinction is not the same thing as forgetting. In forgetting, a response is not repeated; in extinction, a response is repeated without reinforcement. [16]

2. *Spontaneous recovery.* In the foregoing paragraph we stated that extinction does not mean the annihilation of the conditioned response, for otherwise it could no longer be recovered. Laboratory experiments have amply demonstrated the fact that, after an interval of time, the extinguished response returns without additional reinforcement. This condition is known as spontaneous recovery. The function of extinction is to induce the individual to perform new responses; but it functions only in those situations in which the absence of reward is only temporary. Frequent extinctions without subsequent reinforcement, however, may so enfeeble an old habit that the tendency for its recovery would be seriously impaired.

3. *Generalization.* The principle of generalization makes it possible for us to react to new situations because they resemble those with which we are already familiar. This is also known by the older term of *transfer of training.* The more two learning situations resemble each other, the greater will be the generalization or transfer from one to the other, and vice versa. The well-known example of the child who is frightened by a furry dog and who transfers his fear to all furry objects illustrates this principle. The variation of transfer between more and less similar learning situations is called a *gradient of generalization.*

4. *Discrimination.* Since this principle is the complementary of generalization it refers to the differential reaction to two stimuli. Whereas in generalization we react to similar situations, in discrimination we react to different ones. A commonplace example of discrimination is that of a child who, after calling all women "Mamma," finds that only a specific woman responds to him. In this discovery he has learned to discriminate between a certain woman and all women. It follows the principle of reinforcement, so that if a generalized response is unrewarded it tends to become extinguished. Its chief value to the organism is that it helps to prevent false generalizations.

5. *Gradient of reinforcement.* The effects of reinforcement tend to spread from a particular response sequence directly associated with a reward to responses less directly associated with the reward. It accounts for increase in response tendencies the nearer the goal is approached. A cue-response connection near the reward is

[16] *Ibid.,* pp. 48–49.

strengthened more than a connection far removed from the reward, as when, for instance, a hungry man quickens his pace on approaching his house. The adaptive value of a gradient of reinforcement lies in its tendency to "force the subject to choose the shortest of alternative paths to a goal and to eliminate unnecessary responses from the sequence." [17]

The principle of gradient reinforcement illuminates the problem of human motivation, especially the feeling of ambivalence. Experiments have shown that (a) the nearer a person is to a positive goal the stronger is his desire to approach it; (b) the nearer he is to a negative goal the stronger is his wish to avoid it; (c) the magnitude of avoidance increases more rapidly with nearness to the goal than does the strength of approach; and (d) approach or avoidance tendencies vary with the magnitude of the drive on which they rest.[18]

6. *Anticipatory response.* This principle, derived from the principles of gradient reinforcement and generalization, states that "responses near the point of reinforcement tend, wherever physically possible, to occur before their original time in the response series." In other words, they become *anticipatory.*[19] In the case of the child looking for candy under the books, the selection of the correct book moved up in the response series and tended to eliminate the prior selection of the wrong book. Generalization did not occur because the same cue—the bookcase within reach—elicited both responses. The cues from the bookcase when it was beyond reach and when the child was removing a book were similar. Therefore the act of reaching generalized from the near to the farther cues, so that the child tended to start reaching before she arrived at the bookcase.[20]

7. *Short-circuiting.* All efficient learning is marked by the elimination of useless acts from a response sequence. Dollard and Miller illustrate this principle with the case of the hungry boy who returns from play at dinnertime. After a workout on the playground the boy came home hungry, dirty, and dishevelled. Instead of directly proceeding to eat, he performed a series of acts such as wiping his shoes, brushing his clothes, washing his face and hands, and combing his hair. But eating the food was the

---

[17] *Ibid.,* p. 56.

[18] N. E. Miller, Experimental studies of conflict, in J. McV. Hunt (ed.), *Personality and the behavior disorders* (2 vols.; New York: The Ronald Press Co., 1944), Vol. I, pp. 431–65; N. E. Miller, Comments on theoretical models illustrated by the development of a theory of conflict, *J. Pers.,* 20 (1951), 82–100.

[19] Dollard and Miller, *Personality and psychotherapy,* p. 57.

[20] *Ibid.,* p. 57.

reinforcing response to all the other activities. On subsequent occasions, however, he began to eliminate more and more of these
acts and went directly into the dining room. This last act tended
to crowd out the preceding responses because the connection to
it had been strengthened by being nearer to the point of reward.
The food the boy obtains will more strongly reinforce the anticipatory responses and these will tend more likely to occur on later
occasions. The response sequence has in effect been short-circuited.

The parsimony in learning which short-circuiting makes possible should be apparent.

This, then, is in bare outline the drive-reduction theory of learning. Its principles are thought to apply in the higher mental
functionings of reasoning and problem solving, symbolic behavior,
and the learning and "forgetting" of neuroses. We shall return
to the drive-reduction theory when we examine its place in the
explanation of personality formation. Meanwhile, we must turn
to the cognitive theory of learning.

COGNITIVE THEORY OF LEARNING. The cognitive theory of learning utilizes many of the same principles as stimulus-response theory.
It is the most recent and systematically rigorous development of
Gestalt and field theories. Its basic concept is not drive-reduction
but *field-cognition*, or *cognitive structure*. In stimulus-response
theory the product of learning is a habit or response; whereas in
cognitive theory it is alternate means to the same end. In stimulus-
response theory there is always a direct bond between stimulation
and specific behavior by means of reinforcement—or by means of
contiguity in time, if one follows other versions of this theory,
such as that of Guthrie. In cognitive or field theory, the individual
associates external events directly to form "hypotheses," "field
expectancies," or "cognitive maps" (insights). The mind has an
organizing property by means of which, through contiguity of time
and place, it binds together the somewhat loosely interdependent
cognitions.[21]

Although Lewin and Tolman are both distinguished contemporary psychologists, and although both belong in the general
category of field theorists, we shall choose for exposition the view
developed by Tolman. Despite his lively interest in the psychology
of learning, Lewin produced primarily a psychology of motivation,

[21] Unlike the stimulus-response theorists who hold that all learning can be explained by drive-reduction or reinforcement, Tolman, whose view we have in mind,
acknowledges that different types of learning may require different explanatory principles. See E. C. Tolman, There is more than one kind of learning, *Psychol. Rev.*, 56
(1949), 144–55.

rather than of learning.[22] Also, his theory has been consistently couched in an imaginative but unconvincing quasi-mathematical form whose logical relevance is questionable. Stripped of its topological nomenclature, Lewin, like Tolman, asserts that learning is basically a change in the individual's cognitive structure, or a change in his knowledge, in his valences (attraction and repulsion of goals), and in the value system, with its rewards and punishments. With this broad acknowledgment of Lewin's contribution to learning theory, we can now proceed directly to an examination of Tolman's view.

Beginning with his earliest publications during World War I and extending to his most recent studies up to 1956, Tolman has steadfastly maintained his fundamental ideas of learning. These ideas, it should be added, are thoroughly grounded on animal experimentations in the formal laboratory. This does not mean that Tolman's ideas have not changed, but rather that nothing in them of any great moment has been contradicted by later investigations. This may in part be due to the fact that they lack the logical rigor and inflexible systemization of Hull's theory, for example, in which the incompatibility of one element with any of the others would seriously damage the whole theory.[23]

Sign learning. The drive-reduction theory of Hull, as reformulated by Dollard and Miller, it will be recalled, conceives learning as a process in which an organism learns because its responses to drive-stimuli are accompanied by reinforcement or reward, by the gratification of a need. In sign learning, on the other hand, the organism learns in the act of following signs to a goal. It follows a "cognitive map," or a set of meanings, which directs it toward the goal. The connection between the need and its consummation is effected by several important "mechanisms," namely, cathexis, equivalence beliefs, field expectancy, field cognition, drive discrimination, and motor patterns.

1. *Cathexis.* This term refers to the valence, or attractive properties, of an object. It connects a drive with a satisfying goal-object. When a hungry individual reaches for a piece of nourish-

---

[22] For a full statement of Lewin's learning theory, see K. Lewin, Field theory and learning, in *The psychology of learning* (Washington, D.C.: Natl. Soc. Study, Educ., 41st Yearbook, 1942), Part II, pp. 215–42.

[23] For Tolman's "finished" and compactly stated views on learning see E. C. Tolman, Principles of performance, *Psychol. Rev.*, 62 (1955), 315–26. For his discussion of goal-directed behavior, see E. C. Tolman, *Purposive behavior in animals and men* (New York: Appleton-Century-Crofts, Inc., 1932). For a good and comprehensive secondary source, see K. MacCorquodale and P. E. Meehl, Edward C. Tolman, in W. K. Estes *et al.*, *Modern learning theory* (New York: Appleton-Century-Crofts, Inc., 1954), pp. 177–266.

ing food, we call the connection between the act and the goal a *positive* cathexis; when he is repelled by it, it is described as a *negative* cathexis. A cathexis is thus seen to be an acquired or learned connection between a drive and a goal-object.

2. *Equivalence beliefs.* These play an important role in social learning. They refer to a learning situation in which a previously neutral cue plays the same role in the performance of new responses as other rewards. For example, money is a neutral cue to a primitive individual who has neither knowledge nor need of it. In American society, on the other hand, where everyone soon learns the "meaning" of money, it may be used as an incentive or reinforcement to acquire new habits and maintain old ones. Equivalence beliefs correspond to secondary or learned reinforcements in stimulus-response psychology.

3. *Field expectancy.* This learning function is roughly equivalent to short-circuiting in drive-reduction theory. It enables the individual to devise short cuts to the achievement of a goal. Field expectancy is present in lower animals as well as in human beings. The principle maintains that with repeated experience of a chain of events leading to a goal the animal tends to discriminate the probability that a given act will produce the expected results: for example the rat comes to avoid the blind alleys in a maze. Experiments have shown that both animals and men have expectancies of, or directional orientations to, specific goal-objects. Because the learner cannot always reach a goal without intervening steps, he tends to rely on cue-producing responses which enable him to move toward its attainment. This is but another way of describing Hull's concept of *anticipatory goal responses.* Reasoning and planning for future events would be impossible in the absence of field expectancies.

4. *Field cognition.* This is of a higher order of complexity than field expectancy. While it is partly an innate capacity it is largely based on already established field expectancies in the areas of perception, memory, and reasoning.

5. *Drive discrimination.* It is a well-known fact that cues, especially verbal cues, can cause similar stimulus configurations to appear different, and dissimilar ones equivalent. The individual who does not easily form adaptive discriminations learns poorly, and the content of his learning lacks clarity and precision. Many irrational fears are consequences of maladaptive discriminations. A person who was not permitted to think and make discriminations in his childhood cannot be expected to do so successfully in his adulthood. He has never *learned* to discriminate, because the

tendency to do so was usually inhibited. Animals in the laboratory can be taught adaptive discrimination, as seen in the case of animals who learn to turn in one direction when hungry, and in another direction when thirsty.

6. *Motor patterns.* The acquisition of motor-habit patterns is difficult to explain in terms of sign-learning. Accordingly, Tolman relied on stimulus-response conditioning of the contiguity type to account for them. In this way he had to step out of the cognitive framework to borrow concepts from other points of view—a task not too distasteful for him, since he has not been averse to a discriminating eclecticism.

Latent learning. This form of learning has been the source of lively debate, of experimental proof and counterproof. It is also called "incidental learning." Simply stated, latent learning is any acquisition which takes place without reinforcement, and comes into evidence only when the time arises for using it. Experiments on rats have shown that the animal will run a maze without any reward. If the experiments on latent learning should prove to be substantially correct, as Tolman thinks they are, they would offer further confirmation of Tolman's sign-learning theory.[24] If experiments challenging Tolman's views did not exist, latent learning would indeed be a powerful support of his cognitive theory. There have been a number of experiments on latent learning, most of which deny latent learning. Nevertheless, many instances of learning without drive and reinforcement have been reported, so that to deny it would not be altogether warranted. The argument, based mostly on observations of daily life, that examples of latent learning are "merely instances of faulty analysis of obscure conditions of learned drive and reward," as Dollard and Miller believe, is insufficiently supported.[25] Working within the stimulus-response framework of Hull, who denied latent learning, Dollard and Miller would have to admit a fundamental inconsistency if latent learning could be established. The verdict at the present time is that the evidence favors the supporters of latent learning.[26]

Place learning. Drive-reduction theory asserts that what the organism learns is responses to stimuli—that is, it learns reinforced locomotion sequences, or movement habits. Sign-learning, on the other hand, holds that in some situations the organism learns spatial

[24] E. C. Tolman, Cognitive maps in rats and men, *Psychol. Rev.*, 55 (1948), 189–208.

[25] Dollard and Miller, *Personality and psychotherapy*, p. 46.

[26] J. Deese, *The psychology of learning* (New York: McGraw-Hill Book Co., Inc., 1952). Hull, in his *Principles of behavior*, argues against it.

relationships, such as paths and places. The well-known experiment of Maier and Schneirla established this fact almost a quarter of a century ago. They placed three tables, one of which was used as a feeding station, in a room. When a rat was fed on one of the tables and then was removed by the experimenter to either one of the other tables, the rat was able to select the correct path back to the feeding station even though it had never taken the path in this particular order. It learned by the *location* of a path or place, rather than by reinforced locomotion sequences. In a similar experiment conducted by Oakes, similar results were obtained.[27]

CONCLUDING REMARKS. The controversy between the stimulus-response theorists and the sign-learning theorists is not yet settled. The issue is a lively one, and until the reinforcement theorists can either settle the issues of latent and place learning with crucial experimental evidence against them, or satisfactorily account for them by means of the principle of reinforcement itself, the disagreement will continue to flourish. The distinction between drive-reduction learning and sign-learning will continue to be important as long as learning theorists cannot agree on the question whether what we learn is a response or a cognitive structure.

Both the stimulus-response theorist and the cognitive theorist make good sense, and the explanations of both are often experimentally and logically convincing. It may well be—indeed we very much suspect that it is true—that learning is a manifold and not a single process. This is, as we have already pointed out, a point made by Tolman at least a decade ago. There are in all probability different types of learning with different principles governing them. Hilgard summed up the matter well in saying that "we cannot choose between the theories by coming up with 'decisive' illustrations of what we learn, for both groups of theorists will offer explanations of all our examples. The competing theories would not have survived thus far had they been unable to offer such explanations."[28]

PERSONALITY AS A RESPONSE PATTERN

What light does the tiny fragment of learning theory we have discussed throw upon the nature of personality? This question is difficult for at least two reasons, not to mention the all-round

[27] See N. R. F. Maier and T. C. Schneirla, *Principles of animal psychology* (New York: McGraw-Hill Book Co., Inc., 1935); W. F. Oakes, Latent learning in the three-table apparatus, *J. exp. Psychol.*, 51 (1956), 287–89.

[28] Hilgard, *Theories of learning*, p. 10.

difficulty due to the plurality of learning theories. First, personality is, among other things, a *product*, a structure derived from the native equipment of the organism and from the latter's interaction with similarly constituted organisms in a meaningful or value-laden cultural environment. Since learning is almost universally conceived as a process, it begets only more learning, rather than a patterned structure which we call personality. Second, no learning theory, *qua* learning theory, has yet explained the origin and development of personality. Tolman's theory does not pretend to, whereas the view of Dollard and Miller goes outside the learning process and borrows concepts and principles from psychoanalysis and cultural anthropology. In the case of neither reinforcement theory nor cognitive theory is there a systematic or logically necessary connection between the theory and explanations of personality. Indeed, Dollard and Miller, while stressing the belief that their drive-reduction theory of reinforcement is an adequate account of learning, admit that their view is not essential to the main line of argument regarding personality and psychotherapy. "All we need to assume," they say, is that "a sudden reduction of strong drive acts as a reinforcement; we do not need to make the more controversial assumption that all reinforcement is produced in that way." [29] This leaves ample room for the introduction of other than strictly reinforcement principles.

DEVELOPMENT OF PERSONALITY. At birth, the human infant is endowed, like other animals, with a biological substratum of reflexes, primary drives, and an innate hierarchy of responses, to which we have already called attention. In themselves, these innate mechanisms account for the simple and somewhat segmental behavior that characterizes all higher animals before specific learning occasions arise. Learning, as we have defined it thus far, is initiated when the reflexes, primary drives, and the innate hierarchy of responses are transformed into secondary drives and a resultant hierarchy by means of social cues and secondary reinforcement. It is in this transformation that personality arises. Stated in another way, *personality as a pattern of learned responses can arise only in a social-cultural matrix.*

In the development of personality, psychology supplies us with knowledge of the fundamental learning processes which apply universally in animals and men. Psychoanalysis as a system of psychology supplies us with additional knowledge of the mechanisms of early emotional conditioning, especially the role of conflict and the unconscious in the early stages of the child's development.

[29] Dollard and Miller, *Personality and psychotherapy*, p. 42.

Sociology, on the other hand, furnishes us with knowledge of the set of relationships or interpersonal conditions in which human learning takes place. Finally, cultural anthropology provides us with knowledge of the materials of learning, that is, the more or less consistent set of customs, values, and institutionally sanctioned behaviors existing in a specific culture. In short, psychology provides us with knowledge of the *abstract principles*, psychoanalysis with the *emotional determinants*, sociology with the *social conditions*, and anthropology with the *cultural content* of the process of acquiring a personality.

Unconscious conflicts. A thoughtful glance at the history of psychology reveals that traditional, especially academic, psychology has overstressed the conscious and problem-solving aspects of human behavior and until recently neglected its unconscious and conflictual functions.[30] However, no one doubts that every individual has many desires and wishes that express themselves only in unconscious and indirect ways. There are conflicting and incompatible wishes in all of us, and ambivalence is a commonplace phenomenon. Society imposes incompatible and conflicting roles on each of us, and these make for conflicting behavioral demands. If we do not press the hypothesis too far we can affirm that these conflicts vary with the degree of complexity of the personality. A highly organized or integrated person is usually subject to a greater variety of conflictual situations, especially in the world of ideas and symbols, than a less complex individual who lives more completely in the world of concrete reality.[31]

Clinical evidence supports the view that, while emotional conflict exists and disorganizes behavior at all stages of development, it is probably most acute in childhood. The intensity of his emotions and the inability to control them adaptably are largely due to the child's helplessness. He has, as Dollard and Miller well put it, "few skills at evading the effects of unfavorable circumstances." [32] Understanding neither people nor his environment, the young child is unable to wait for his wants to be satisfied, but is impelled to seek immediate gratification. Freud's pleasure principle, restated as the principle of reinforcement in drive-reduction learning theory, dominates the child's life. The child, propelled from the extreme of wish-fulfillment on one side to the remoteness of need-frustration

[30] Today, complaints are made by some investigators that psychology is too much obsessed with emotional conflict and irrational behavior.

[31] See G. Murphy, *Personality: a biosocial approach to origins and structure* (New York: Harper & Bros., 1947), p. 319.

[32] Dollard and Miller, *Personality and psychotherapy*, p. 130.

on the other, becomes disoriented and confused. So impressed are
Dollard and Miller by the Freudian emphasis on the tyranny of the
Id, or the pleasure principle, that they describe the emotional conflicts in infancy as "a period of transitory psychosis" during which
the child is disoriented, deluded, and hallucinated.[33]

The unconscious conflicts arising in child training are particularly significant. Since we described these in detail in Chapter 6,
we shall touch upon the subject only briefly. The situations of
nursing and feeding, of toilet training, of sexual control, and of
acceptable discharge of aggression are frought with conflicts, apprehensions, even traumas; or they can produce gratification, well-
being, and a sense of trust of the ministering adults. The quality
of the interpersonal relations between parents and children and the
design of the culture for inculcating disciplines are, as we have
shown, of critical importance. Extreme aggressiveness, neurotic
anxiety, and psychosis are reflections of the degree of humanization
of the parents and of the wisdom of the culture which produced
them. From the standpoint of learning theory, "the existence of
neuroses is an automatic criticism of our culture of child rearing." [34]

In an earlier work, Dollard and Miller explicitly distinguish between learning as a *process*, defined by the learning principles of
psychology already described, and as a social *condition*, defined by
the interpersonal relations in the primary group, viewed socio-
logically. However, while they greatly stress the importance of
culture, they do not distinguish it from the social conditions of
learning already cited. From our point of view, every process also
has a *content*. The content, or *what* is learned, is the culture, particularly the prevailing modes of child training. Thus, while a person at the top of the cultural pyramid may look very much like the
one at the bottom, they are distinguished by different customs and
habits. "No personality analysis of two such people," they write,
"can be accurate which does not take into account these cultural
differences, that is, differences in the types of responses which have
been rewarded." [35]

Even repression, which is generally considered to be an individual act, is culturally determined. The individual learns what to
repress and under what conditions, on the basis of what acts are
punished and what acts are reinforced. Repression probably does
not begin in the cradle, but in the larger social context of the pri-

[33] *Ibid.*, p. 130.
[34] *Ibid.*, p. 8.
[35] Miller and Dollard, *Social learning and imitation*, p. 6.

mary group, when the child's actions involve conflicts with the established mores. Whether sex behavior is repressed or not will depend upon the presence or absence of anxiety-producing taboos against it. In some societies children do not repress their sexual interests and activities, and so they are free of the anxiety that stern measures tend to beget.

The act of repression has been more thoroughly investigated in connection with abnormal than with normal psychological phenomena. It is important in everyday thinking. If a person tends to avoid thinking about certain objects or events, his capacity to see connections between them is impaired. "Not-thinking" becomes a response, like other responses, although we cannot denote it in the same way that we can "not-talking." Who has not caught himself and stood still in his verbal tracks lest he utter a thought he should later come to regret? Thinking, like other forms of avoidance behavior, can be blocked, inhibited, and prevented by repression, and like them, it is a learned response. The value of "not-thinking" to the organism lies in its capacity to prevent fear-provoking thoughts and memories.

There are three ways in which repression may prevent a thought from reaching active consciousness. First, a *response labeling the drive may be inhibited*. The drive in such a case is present but unverbalized. An individual may be sexually stimulated but not put it into words. He may even mislabel it by calling it "nervousness." Everyone has experienced fear but refused to recognize it as such. The reinforcement for nonverbalization and mislabeling of the fear is another fear—that of ridicule by others. Second, *the response producing the drive may be inhibited*. A response can always be inhibited, and therefore the drive itself will disappear. Third, *the responses mediating the drive are inhibited*. For example, a person might not be angry in a given situation until he reflected on the thought that someone insulted him. From a practical point of view, stopping to think about an insult can reduce the anger which it normally evokes.[36]

Conflicts are inescapable facts of life. They may be very intense or relatively weak. When they are both strong and unconscious, the person experiencing them may go through life "making the same old mistakes and getting punished in the same old way." This is why naming or labeling them is important, for in the process of labeling they reach consciousness where new ways of dealing with them may be established. In this way the individual moves from a primitive intellectual level to a level where the process of ver-

[36] Dollard and Miller, *Personality and psychotherapy*, pp. 211–13.

balization and discrimination will enable him to deal with his anxieties more effectively.[37]

EVALUATION OF THE DOLLARD-MILLER VIEW. Can drive-reduction learning theory account for personality? It can do so, but only partially and then only if we define personality as a set of responses, a view which deprives it of its dynamic and self-propelling qualities. The theory gives us only a partial view—its outward manifestations. It makes no provision for the "inner" man—a concept which has been mostly scoffed at and little understood. We believe it is high time for those psychologists who scorn the concept of the inner man, or the self, to divest themselves of the fiction of the self as some kind of homunculus embedded in the biosocial organism. We like to believe that even those who subscribe to the latter criticism do not believe that their fellow psychologists are so naive as to believe in mystical entities. It is often a pose which they assume in order to court the appelation of being scientific.

Learning is as much a function of personality as it is its cause. A child gradually becomes good, bad, submissive, or self-confident not only because he is rewarded or punished for his behavior but even more because he is grimly determined to live up to his image of himself as a certain kind of person—an image which grows out of his personal-social interactions and his contacts with a social heritage. This mode of explanation posits a self which binds the individual's experience into an intelligible sequence. If the imperious drives of the infant are confused and hallucinated, it is because he has as yet no established self. The "higher mental processes," which Dollard and Miller equate with the self, cannot function, for the infant has no symbolic system by means of which he can order his world into a meaningful system. Only "with the aid of his language can he learn to wait, hope, reason, and plan." [38]

The combat soldier who breaks down in the face of extreme threat to his life, and who *at the same time finds it unbearable to admit that he might be a coward,* is in a situation similar to that of the young child. Whereas the infant as yet has not achieved selfhood, the soldier's self has been shattered or seriously weakened. The soldier's *image of himself* suffers from the implied stigma of cowardice in the eyes of his fellows. While the infant has no symbolic system with which to make his life intelligible, the soldier represses his symbols and ideas because his awareness of them would jeopardize his ego. Both learning and ego-development are necessary for the explanation of this behavior.

[37] See *ibid.,* p. 154.
[38] *Ibid.,* p. 131.

We have already expressed the view that the concept of the self does not make psychology mystical. On the other hand, we believe that the term "higher mental processes," which seems to be roughly equivalent to the self, is a nineteenth-century terminology which sounds quaint, if not anachronistic. It is certainly an evaluative term, and as such it has no acceptable place in psychology. In drive-reduction and reinforcement theory there can be no "higher" and "lower" dimensions, for the stimulus-response principles are the same in all learning.

The provision for new learning in drive-reduction theory is far from satisfactory. We saw that reinforcement strengthens established stimulus-response connections and makes the appearance of new responses less likely to occur. Consequently, in order to establish new responses the individual must be placed in a learning dilemma, or a learning situation where his old responses will not be reinforced. In illustration of this condition we cited the case of the five-year-old boy who learned to speak when his speech teacher and his parents refused to pay attention to—which is to say they ceased to reinforce—his monosyllabic behavior.

While this explanation undoubtedly accounts for some types of learning—and we agree with Tolman that there are many kinds— it does not necessarily explain all learning. There is nothing in the speech-learning situation of the little boy that would challenge or deny the role of the self. The boy learned to speak, not only because his teacher and parents confronted him with a learning dilemma, but also, and even more importantly, because he was made self-conscious. The image of himself as a helpless child gave way to the image of himself as a speaking individual, and henceforth this image had to be defended. He now speaks because his image of himself as a speaking person has become an important motivating force in his life, even though he is no longer placed in the former learning dilemmas.

Furthermore, the concept of learning dilemmas, which we consider very important, makes no provision for self-initiating and self-propelling behavior. People learn in situations where no problems exist and solve problems when no needs are involved.

Finally, there is an important self-contradiction in tension-reduction learning theory. As originally proposed, the theory holds that tension reduction is reinforcing, and hence responsible for learning. At the same time, tension reduction cannot strengthen the bond between the cue and the response-produced tension; for if it did, tension reduction would reinforce the tension-producing response. The reduction of tension, in other words, would increase tension. Miller tried to meet the challenge, but his explanation, which would take too long to recount, is an ingenious way of patching up a theory to make it appear invulnerable.[39]

PERSONALITY AS PURPOSIVE SIGN BEHAVIOR

In sign learning, it will be recalled, an individual learns in the act of following signs toward a goal. Rats as well as men are guided in their behavior toward an end by cognitive maps, or a set of meanings. Purposive behavior is a mark of all striving beings, and is especially important in accounting for both learning as a process and personality as a product of learning. The word "purposive" does not permit metaphysical teleological explanations, for not even personality as an effect or product is given priority over its source.

PERSONALITY AS GOAL-DIRECTED BEHAVIOR. Cathexis, we have shown, refers to the valence-properties of an act. It connects a drive or need with a satisfying goal-object. Valences are, of course, either positive or negative. We *want*, or *positively value*, some things; and we *do not want*, or *negatively value*, other things. When we are hungry we want food, and will seek to obtain it. We do not want to experience the pain of an electric shock, and so we try to avoid it.

Role of cognitive maps. Neither animals nor men pursue a goal in complete blindness, as it were. Each learns to go there in the act of following a sign, a cognitive map, or a set of meanings. The conditions underlying the formation of a cognitive map are the following: (1) the laws of frequency, recency, and emphasis; (2) the autochtonous or native factors which govern perception; and (3) the perceptual readiness factors derived from the drives, beliefs, and values which operate at the particular moment of learning to find the goal.[40]

This may be illustrated by the performance of a rat in a physical maze and by a man in a "social" maze. Each is directed by innate mechanisms controlling perceptual and motivational factors, by a cognitive map of the maze, and by the locations within it of specific means-objects and goal-objects. The learning of the cognitive map is determined by the stimulus configuration of the environment, by the frequency and recency with which the stimulus configuration

[39] For his attempt to meet the objection, see N. E. Miller, Learnable drives and rewards, in S. S. Stevens (ed.), *Handbook of experimental psychology* (New York: John Wiley & Sons, Inc., 1951), Ch. 13.

[40] E. C. Tolman, The psychology of social learning (Kurt Lewin Memorial Award Lecture), *J. soc. Iss.*, 5 (1949), No. 3, p. 18.

has been explored, and by the individual's perceptual readiness at the moment. "This," says Tolman, with disarming finality, "is all there is to it." [41]

The psychological person. The psychological person, like everything else that is not innate, is learned in the manner just described. The psychological person is composed of two related dimensions, namely, the *personality structure* and the *behaving self.*

Personality structure is conceived in terms of the acquisition of new drives, beliefs, values, and perceptual readiness. Doubting, but not rejecting, Woodworth's contention that means or mechanisms may become drives, and Allport's conception of functional autonomy of motives, which we shall discuss in the next chapter, Tolman contends that new drives are cases where what were orignally mere means-objects attached to one or more basic drives become sucked back into the inner drive-system itself—and in this way they themselves become drives. These new drives would thereafter establish direct contact with the "libido" and would be able to derive energy directly from it.[42]

The learning of beliefs is less easily explained, and it probably does not obey the simple laws of frequency, recency, and emphasis by which cognitive maps are explained. The question pertains to the manner in which a rat or a human being acquires general beliefs after learning particular ones. For instance, how does a rat or a child, from having learned one or a few mazes, acquire such general beliefs as "food-cans lead to food" or "kitchens lead to mothers"? Reinforcement is probably important in the acquisition of such beliefs.

Values and perceptual readiness do not have to be learned separately. Values result from beliefs, so that the principles which account for beliefs also explain values. Perceptual readiness, in turn, results from values.

The *behaving self* is that dimension of the psychological person in which the *need-pushes* operate.[43] Need-pushes are drives which are closely related to, but not identical with, appetites and aversions. There are four need-pushes in the behaving self: sex, aggression, pain aversion, and affiliation. Of these, sex is perhaps the only one that resists neutralization. Nevertheless, because of existing values and perceptual readinesses, the culture imposes perceptual

---

[41] *Ibid.*, p. 11.

[42] *Ibid.* Tolman's use of the term "libido" is neutral, not Freudian. He disclaims any preconceptions as to the basic nature of libido other than that it stems from some general physiological energy.

[43] *Ibid.*, p. 9.

blindness on the cognitive map for the original sex goal and for the barriers on the way to it. This is one reason, no doubt, why sexual "maladjustments" are so common.

We might close this description of purposive sign behavior with an illuminating reflection by Tolman himself. He writes:

> . . . unfortunately, I myself have learned most of my psychology from rats. Rats may show anger to the extent of biting the hand that feeds them, but I doubt if they are living up to a level of aspiration or trying to enhance their egos when they do so. I am, therefore, very hesitant and apologetic in proposing to talk . . . about the social learning of men. Yet, if we accept the assumption of some basic social drives in man which act in much the same manner as do the viscerogenic hungers in rats, then our studies of the hunger—and thirst-driven activities of these latter animals may after all contribute something to our understanding of the social behavior and social learning of *homo sapiens.*[44]

Evaluation of Tolman's view. The principal merits of Tolman's system can be summed up briefly. First, it conceives behavior as *molar.* This means that all behavior has a purpose, or goal-direction, and consists of total acts rather than segmental responses. The concept of cathexis, or positive and negative attractions, is pretty well established in learning-motivation psychology. Second, behavior is also *cognitive:* the organism makes use of the means-end schema to solve problems, reduce tensions, or reach goals. In short, behavior—or personality conceived in its broadest term—is the holistic, nonmechanical striving of the individual to achieve ends in a social environment.

However, the theory is subject to the limitations inherent in its animal-experimental framework. Despite Tolman's faith in the basic assumption of human and animal viscerogenic similarities, he has not made quantitative predictions from his theory. In this connection it should be recalled that, while Hull's system has been put to the test of predictiveness regarding animal behavior, Dollard and Miller, who applied a simplified version to the study of human behavior, did not consider their view of learning essential to the main line of argument regarding personality and psychotherapy. To the present writer this fact is of no great moment; but viewed in the light of the learning theorist's demand for scientific rigor in psychology, it is an obvious weakness.

Reflecting on Tolman's concept of the psychological person one approaches it with great expectation. One leaves it, however, with the feeling of "almost, but not quite." Personality seems to be waiting around the corner, but on getting there one finds only the

[44] *Ibid.,* p. 5.

familiar emphasis on drive-reductive learning. Stimulus-response theory and cognitive theory, while theoretically widely apart, seem to join hands in an uneasy alliance.

CONCLUSION

The reader who has carefully followed the discussion in this chapter must surely be impressed by the rigorous nature of contemporary learning theory, as well as discouraged by its differences. The beguiling simplicity of stimulus-response theory, and its apparent readiness to meet all criticism of its major tenets and assumptions with more of the same arguments, is marvelous to behold. The ingenuity of its experimental designs, which we have almost entirely omitted, and the logical rigor of its theoretical constructions, especially those of Hull, which we have also omitted, are admirable and deserve the envy of the personality psychologist. From all this, one certainty emerges: the findings of learning theorists, on the whole, seem to hold for animals under carefully controlled laboratory conditions. There is no doubt that the learning process as described by learning theorists of whatever persuasion accounts for the behavior of organisms. And man is an animal first and a human person only after the processes of socialization and enculturation have taken effect.

However, whether social learning is subject to the principles of drive-reduction and reinforcement is, to say the least, highly debatable. Learning in human beings cannot be separated from social interaction and symbolic patterning. A human individual does not respond to stimuli, but to events. His behavior is not a set of responses, as we have repeatedly pointed out, but of interrelated acts. These acts are not bare acts, but *meaningful* events determined by the dominant values of the culture in which the person lives. As Gibson discerningly pointed out, current learning theories "do not account for the astonishing prevalence of *moral* behavior among human adults." [45] Moral behavior cannot be wholly explained by the principles of need-reduction and reinforcement. Rather, it calls for a concept of the self. A mature adult is good or honest or law-abiding because these forms of behavior are compatible with his image of himself as a moral being. As a socially developed self he has internalized the social and moral values of his cultural group, and he behaves morally because he has made these social and moral values his own. The formation of moral

[45] J. J. Gibson, The implications of learning theory for social psychology, in J. G. Miller (ed.), *Experiments in social process: a symposium on social psychology* (New York: McGraw-Hill Book Co., Inc., 1950), p. 152. Italics added.

habits is regulated not only by need-reduction but by the influence of significant others, such as parents, teachers, and other individuals who form an important part of his social context. The developing child is not isolated, like an animal in an experimental situation. As Gibson rightly observes, "to assume that a parent is a stimulus object like any other, or that the social situation is a more complex maze situation, is to lose sight of the unique function of *the other organism* as a reinforcing agent. . . . If behavior is inescapably related to the mores, the assumption about human reinforcing agents should be explicit." [46] Thus, both the concept of a self and the child's identification with those who stimulate him to perform appropriate acts must be explicitly taken into account when we attempt to describe the origin and growth of his personality.

If we proceed on the assumption that you get out of a theory only what you put into it, the learning theories which we have discussed, as well as others like them, leave us approximately where we started. We are, in other words, dealing with learning as a process and neglecting the social situation which results in a unique *product,* which we call personality. A response is not, strictly speaking, a product, but the terminus of a stimulus-response process. To say that the product of the stimulus-response process is a habit, or a set of habits, or a cognitive structure is correct for descriptions of animal behavior in the laboratory, but inadequate for conceptualizing a complex personality. It is at once illogical and an unwarranted oversimplification to say that, because all adult behavior has learned components, therefore all adult behavior is learned. A chess player, for instance, makes some of his moves in the light of his previous learning, "but it would be silly to think that all chess moves are merely learned and that we would be able to deduce a chess player's moves simply from information about his previous 'reinforcements'. At least some information about his perceptions and expectations would be relevant. And, it may be added, to the theory of perception and cognition, learning theory of the Hullian type has thus far made no major contribution." [47]

For these and other reasons, Hullian learning theory, despite its many outstanding merits, and its elaboration by Dollard and Miller, cannot survive in its present form. A theory of learning that will account for personality in all its subtle complexities is waiting to be born.

All in all, then, personality theory has not been greatly helped

[46] *Ibid.,* pp. 154 and 157. Italics in original.
[47] S. Morgenbesser, Role and status of anthropological theories, *Science,* 128 (1958), 285–88, on p. 286.

or deeply enriched by learning theory. The main efforts of apply-
ing learning theory to personality problems have been made by
stimulus-response theorists, but, as Leeper put it, stimulus-response
theories have been meager and undernourished theories. "They
have been so afraid of eating anything except the most tangible
looking kinds of food that they are suffering from severe qualitative
food deficiencies." [48]

[48] R. Leeper, Current trends in theories of personality, in W. Dennis *et al., Current
trends in psychological theory* (Pittsburgh: University of Pittsburgh Press, 1951),
p. 48.

CHAPTER 9

Motivation and
Personality Dynamics

A striking feature of the contemporary view of psychological man is that he is an active being, not merely a passive spectator; a striving person, not only an adaptive animal. The shift from passivity to activity in the account of human behavior has been brought about in large measure by the increasing emphasis on *growth* motivation instead of *deficiency* motivation.[1]

The subject of motivation was discussed in Chapter 5, where we described the nature and some of the kinds of physiological drives; and again in Chapter 8, where it was found to be inseparable from the learning process as this is conceived by most contemporary learning theorists. Since most of current psychology centers around adaptive or adjustive behavior—unfortunately for the fate of psychology, we believe—it follows that the subject of drive or motive holds a central position in the study of behavior. The conception of motivation as almost wholly an adaptive function is not justified, however. Both animals and men perform acts which are not technically adaptive, but seem to be indulged in for their own sake—at least without any tangible or measurable reward. Man obviously not only adapts himself to his world, but changes it, and creates new ones as well. Manipulation of the environment and solutions of problems seem to carry their own rewards, even for animals. How

[1] This distinction is largely Maslow's. See A. H. Maslow, Deficiency motivation and growth motivation, in the *Nebraska symposium on motivation* (Lincoln: University of Nebraska Press, 1955).

much more this is true, as the history of civilization shows, of man who takes particular delight in shaping his environment in accordance with his own dreams, and often at a cost to himself that is unintelligible if we view his behavior wholly in the framework of individual rewards.[2]

One aspect of motivation is so commonplace that we seldom observe it. Man alone, of all the animals, is motivated to inquire into his own motives and the motives of other men and of animals. That is why he writes books about them, and sets up experiments to investigate their nature and function. This interest is not mere curiosity, for animals other than man display curiosity; it is, rather, an attempt to *understand* himself and his fellow beings. Again, man alone has shown interest in unconscious motives—the driving forces of his life which are hidden from direct observation. He has even constructed an elaborate intellectual machinery for sounding them out and interpreting their indirect expression.

The subject of motivation is important for psychology not only in its own right but also because of its intimate relation to the process of learning. The reader who has followed the discussion in the preceding chapter carefully and critically must have been impressed by how little learning theory stands on its own feet, so to speak, and how helplessly it leans on the shoulders of drive theory. Both reinforcement theory and cognitive theory—indeed all learning theories derived from associationism, old or new—are "successful" to the degree that they are intimately involved in a theory of motivation.

The usefulness of a motivation theory does not lie, however, in its function of buttressing an uncertain theory of learning, but in its contribution to a better account of the nature of personality. Insofar as motivation theory injects unity, order, and integration into the psychology of personality, and does not merely connect discrete events in the learning process, it makes a signal contribution to a theory of human nature. It is with the integrative function of motives in mind that we approach the subject matter of the present chapter.

THE NATURE OF HUMAN MOTIVATION

The study of motivation is concerned with the dynamic character of human behavior, with the directional properties of per-

[2] The individual who has been thoroughly indoctrinated with the reward-value of motivated behavior might achieve new insight into the nature of motivation by carefully studying the results of Harlow's experiments with rhesus monkeys. See, for example, H. F. Harlow, Learning motivated by a manipulation drive, *J. exp. Psychol.*, 40 (1950), 228–34.

sonality. When barriers to a person's achievement arise, as they inevitably do, he redoubles his effort to surmount them in order to reach his goal. He feels *driven*, as it were, and until he either succeeds or fails in his effort, he normally persists in the pursuit of his goal.

However, human motives tend to be highly discriminatory and selective. No person strives for everything, perhaps not even for many things, but only for certain things. The process of selection is intensified by social pressures as well as by individual desires. Animals and human infants, on the other hand, are strikingly less selective in the choice of ends. Their major interest is to reduce their basic physiological tensions, such as hunger, thirst, and elimination. Consequently it is a grave error to base the study of human motivation on a knowledge of animal drives only.[3] The psychology of personality must emphasize what Maslow calls the "human-centering" of motivation. Too many generalizations regarding animal drives are not relevant to human motivation. Accordingly, it is a mistake to assume that it is "more 'scientific' to judge human beings by animal standards," and on this basis to exclude the study of purposive behavior from motivational psychology.[4]

In this connection perhaps the venerated practice of using animals might well be reversed and human beings be used instead, particularly if the reluctance to accept purpose or goal-direction is largely a vivid expression of the desire to appear "scientific" at any price. In reacting to P. T. Young's arbitrary exclusion of the concept of goal or purpose from motivation theory on the ground that we cannot ask a rat about its purpose, Maslow pointedly remarked that we *can* ask a human being about his purpose. "Instead of rejecting purpose or goal as a concept because we cannot ask the rat about it," Maslow retorted, "it would seem much more sensible to reject the rat because we cannot ask him about his purpose."[5]

WAYS OF CONCEIVING THE PROBLEM OF MOTIVATION. When we ask questions like, What impels people to continue along certain lines of action, often in the face of seemingly insurmountable barriers, until they reach a desired goal? or, Why does the organism strive at all? we have no universally accepted answer. The questions are difficult to answer, among other reasons, because motives cannot be observed *directly*. Nevertheless, answers have been for-

[3] H. Bonner, *Social psychology: an interdisciplinary approach* (New York: American Book Co., 1953), p. 146.

[4] A. H. Maslow, A dynamic theory of motivation, *Psychol. Rev.*, 50 (1943), 370–96.

[5] A. H. Maslow, *Motivation and personality* (New York: Harper & Bros., 1954), p. 72n.

mulated, and the student of personality should become acquainted with some of them.

Motives conceived as instincts. One of the oldest answers to the question, What makes the organism go? is that it is impelled by innate predispositions called instincts. Darwin had already in the middle of the nineteenth century explained an organism's adaptation to its environment in terms of inherited mechanisms similar to instincts. It was McDougall, another Englishman, transplanted to America, who made instinct the center of his account of human nature. An instinct, according to him, is an inherited "psychological disposition" which causes an individual to perceive and react to certain objects in his environment, to experience an emotion in his reaction to them, and to act with reference to them. He isolated instincts into more than a dozen varieties, such as curiosity, self-assertion, pugnacity, and the like.[6]

The most important instinct-like theory, if not the most influential account of motivation in any form, is that of Sigmund Freud. Neither McDougall's nor Freud's view, however, is an unqualified instinct theory. It would take us beyond the limits of the present discussion to consider this problem, but it should be noted, nevertheless, that the central disposition in McDougall's view is *sentiment.* In Freud's case, the German word *Trieb*, which is basic in his system, has been questionably translated by the English term "instinct." Literally, the term means "drive" or "impulse." The German technical term for instinct is *Instinkt*, a term which Freud did not employ. In fairness to Freud, it should also be pointed out that in the last revision of his work before his death, he conceived *Trieb* as a kind of informal methodological construct—a *mythische Wesen*, or "mythical being." [7]

According to Freud, man is actuated by two basic urges, namely, the life-urge and the death-urge. The first impels men to love, construct, and create; the second, to hate, fight, and destroy. The man who devotes himself to unselfish causes, who builds or discovers, is motivated by the life impulse; whereas the man who strives for selfish or unworthy ends, such as the exploitation or destruction of someone else, is motivated by the death impulse. In this mode of analysis Freud made room for the force of customs and institutions, for he was aware that whether man was self-

[6] W. McDougall, *An introduction to social psychology* (Boston: J. W. Luce & Co., 1908).

[7] See in English translation, S. Freud, *New introductory lectures on psychoanalysis* (New York: W. W. Norton & Co., Inc., 1933), p. 131: "The theory of instincts is, as it were, our mythology. The instincts are mythical beings, superb in their indefiniteness."

seeking or altruistic depended a great deal on whether the pressures of society inhibit or facilitate these forms of behavior.

Motives conceived as drives. Although the instinct hypothesis had a wide appeal, American psychologists were early skeptical of its scientific validity. The behaviorists, who were bent on making psychology into an objective science, did much to force the concept of instinct from the psychological scene. Aided by important biological research in the 1920's, psychologists adopted the concept of *drive,* the *energy* behind the biogenic needs of the organism. Biogenic needs have been conceived as conditions of disequilibrium of the organism which impel it to action. For example, when the infant is hungry he will engage in a variety of movements, such as crying and moving his head toward his mother's breasts, until his hunger is satisfied. The condition which initiates the activity of feeding is muscular contractions of the stomach. This condition is described as a state of disequilibrium, upset, or tension which is unpleasant, and which can be terminated only when the infant has ingested food into his stomach. The adjustive habits formed in the process of need-reduction are called *mechanisms*—acquired techniques for reducing or temporarily de-activating a drive. The condition of equilibrium which results from the satisfaction of the drive is called *consummation.* The movement from need through mechanism to consummation is a cycle of activity by which the individual adjusts himself to the recurring alterations in his daily living (see Chapter 5).

Motives conceived as acquired habits. Psychology could not have progressed beyond a biological account of motivation if it concerned itself only with physiological drives. The biological view of drives is sufficient for a description of universal organic needs, but wholly inadequate for explaining socially conditioned wants. The psychology of personality, as well as other branches of the science of behavior, is primarily interested in impulsions aroused by the social environment. These are known to vary with both individuals and groups. The word "motive" describes these impulsions much better than the term "drive," which, by virtue of its historical context, stresses its organic character. Thus, motives are conceived as habits learned by the individual in early and continuous exposure to social and cultural demands and expectancies. An individual seeks to satisfy such wishes as security, self-esteem, affection, success, and so forth, not because he is a biological animal, but because he is a social *person* responsive to the attitudes of and evaluations made of him by other persons.

The whole process may be stated succinctly by saying that motives are determinants of personality in two ways. First, they are modifications of drives by social expectancies; and second, they are derived needs to reach individually and culturally established goals. Thus, in contrast to drives, which are determined by specific tissue needs of the organism, motives may be independent of the latter, and therefore independent also of drives. The latter point will be discussed in detail in a later part of this chapter.

SOCIAL CHARACTER OF MOTIVES.[8] Instincts and simple homeostatic drives, we see, do not account for man's behavior. Man is molded and remolded by the values and the patterned behavior forms of his society. Accordingly, in order to understand man's behavior, we must search not only for the fundamental physiological urges, but even more for the social circumstances which impel him to act in a specific way. The physiological drives help us to account for the basic similarities in human behavior, since they are determined by the universal physiological structure of the human organism. But while these physiological drives are important, their chief value for the study of personality lies in the fact that their expressions are determined by social customs. Our interest lies not in biological but in personality dynamics. This makes our task vastly more difficult, for we cannot measure the strength of human desires as we can animal drives under controlled conditions in the laboratory. We must derive our explanations and hypotheses from the study of the individual in his rarely simple interactions with other individuals, and from a knowledge of the effect of culture on the growing person.

Role of frustration. No animal but man is subject to the variety, intensity, and subtlety of needs and desires. Man not only seeks to satisfy his needs but is constantly creating new ones when the old ones for whatever reason have lost their appeal. When an animal's nurturing and sexual needs are gratified, his physiological equilibrium is restored, and until the next cycle begins, seems to be satisfied. He does not, so far as can be known, dream of more and better food to consume, or of more delectable females to subdue. Man, on the other hand, appears to be in a chronic state of want, even if all his physiological needs have been satisfied. No sooner does he satisfy one desire or wish when another, or several others, are aroused by the pressure of social living. A being so beset by needs and desires is bound to court many frustrations.

A frustration is a state of tension resulting from barriers to goal-

8 This section is adapted, with modifications, from the author's *Social psychology: an interdisciplinary approach*, pp. 148–56.

achievement. In this blocked state the individual tends to redouble his efforts either in the direction of the blocked goal, or toward a suitable substitute. He expends an enormous quantity of time and energy to achieve his desired goals. Speaking generally, the greater the frustration, the greater the amount of energy expended, until the person either withdraws, defers, or surrenders the goal-object. The important point, however, is this: in human beings *frustration itself can become one of the strongest motives to action.* Probably all the good and noble things in life, as well as the evil and base, derive in part at least from unfulfilled wants and frustrated efforts. Accordingly, one of the most important things about a person is the way he meets obstacles to achievement or how he reacts to frustration. His reaction to frustration not only reveals his immediate reactions but also illuminates his manner of adjustment and his personality as a whole. Frustrations or unresolved tensions may not be a threat to one individual; whereas for another, they may be a source of chronic emotional distress; and for still another, they may act as stimuli toward renewed effort to resolve his tensions.

The concept of *frustration tolerance* aids in understanding the effects of frustration on the individual. This term refers to an individual's capacity to endure blocked need-gratification without resorting to defensive or other inadequate modes of adjustment. The person with a high frustration tolerance withstands the blocking of wishes and desires adequately. In this case he may utilize other means of satisfying his wishes, such as a realistic assessment of himself and of the frustrating situation, or by engaging in behavior that promises the eventual solution of his problem. On the other hand, the person with a low frustration tolerance tends to resort to unsatisfactory techniques of response to a frustrating situation, such as excessive daydreaming, emotional outbursts of anger and aggressiveness, helplessness, neurotic symptoms, and similar forms of behavior.

Experimental and clinical evidence shows that, whatever the fate of a frustrated wish short of its satisfaction may be, it tends to remain much more active in behavior than a wish that has been satisfied. Experiments on the perseveration of effort by Lewin, Zeigarnik, and others illustrate this principle.[9] In these experiments, the reader will recall, children were permitted to finish some tasks but were interrupted before completing others. When later the children were permitted to work with the toys again, they re-

[9] See the experiments on interrupted and uninterrupted tasks, discussed in the section on miniature life situations, in Chapter 4.

turned more frequently to the tasks in which they had been interrupted than to those they had completed. These findings are supported by various studies that show that, generally speaking, frustration enhances the attractiveness of a goal. Some experiments, however, have revealed that if a goal is distinctly unattainable, its attractiveness declines.

Unfortunately, the term "frustration" carries with it overtones of opprobrium. It is frequently associated with maladjustment and even abnormality. Thus, in our daily conversation when we describe someone as being a frustrated person, we do so reproachfully rather than descriptively. Viewed objectively, the term refers to a condition of interruption of or interference with an individual's efforts to reach a goal. The term "tension" also has a popular negative connotation. It conveys the idea of nervous strain, or a state of psychological stress. However, it also means a state of readiness or expectancy, or a preparation for action. Consequently, both frustration and tension may have positive value as sources of human achievement, for they serve as stimuli for increased effort and for reorganizing a person's self-perceptions with reference to his goals.

Experiments in the role of frustration in human motivation challenge the Freudian stress on the permanent effect of childhood experiences on the adult personality. Psychoanalysis, as is well known, asserts that a person's present behavior is largely a product of his past pleasures and pains, successes and failures, satisfactions and frustrations. The views of Allport and Lewin, and of others who stress the contemporaneity of motives and actions, oppose the Freudian theory. Lewin's view stresses the importance of contemporary events in the individual's behavior; whereas Allport's theory shows the important role of the person—that is, the individual's conception of himself as an active instead of a passive being. But both Lewin and Allport assert that motivation is always contemporary. The motives of an adult are not merely later expressions of infantile desires or frustrations, as Freud believed. Thus a child who, because he was bitten by a dog, feared all dogs, may in later years not only like dogs but become an expert dog fancier as well.[10]

The theories of Freud, Lewin, and Allport seem more divergent than they are. This is due to the overemphasis by each of its basic tenets. Freud exaggerates the determining effects of infantile experiences; yet, infantile experiences are important. Lewin is too

[10] For Lewin's and Allport's views see K. Lewin, *Dynamic theory of personality* (New York: McGraw-Hill Book Co., Inc., 1935); G. W. Allport, *Personality: a psychological interpretation* (New York: Holt, Rinehart & Winston, Inc., 1937).

impressed by the overwhelming force of the immediate situation; yet, the situational factor plays a vital role in human behavior. Allport imputes an importance to the autonomy of the self which is difficult to demonstrate; yet, one's image of one's self, as we have said before, is a potent factor in every goal-integrated act. Viewed in this light, the three points of view are complementary rather than antagonistic.

Transformation of drives. We have defined drives as the energy behind biological needs which disturb the equilibrium of the organism and induce activities aimed at restoring its balance. Every organism reacts to needs, and we can within certain limits predict its behavior with reference to them in advance. If a man is hungry, he will seek food; if thirsty, he will seek water; if sexually aroused, he will seek coitus.

But everywhere—except in imagination and fiction, perhaps—he will satisfy his needs in accordance with the practices of the group in which he lives. If we have detailed and reliable knowledge of the cultural values of his group, we can also in a general way predict his behavior in eating, drinking, and coitus. If, in addition, we also have a perceptive understanding of his self, particularly his self-image, we will also know better why he prefers one food to another, why he drinks tea or wine instead of water, and why he selects one sexual object rather than another one in gratifying his genital needs—even though all these are profoundly shaped by his culture.

The individual's effort to harmonize his drives with his own propensities and with the expectancies of his group is fundamentally learned. *Human* motives are derived in the act of satisfying basic needs. They are learned by the individual through three interrelated processes: cross-conditioning, anticipation, and cultural patterning. The latter we shall discuss in detail in the next chapter.

Cross-conditioning refers to the tendency for drives to become generalized through continuous reinforcement. In the infant, for example, the hunger drive is very specific. Only food in the form of milk, let us say, will satisfy it. The infant's reaction to his mother in the act of feeding is to an object which reduces his hunger tensions. He "wants" her for that reason only. However, the mother *herself* gradually becomes an object of interest to him. He associates pleasure with her not only because she satisfies his hunger but also because she pets and fondles him. These associated feeding activities are linked with the pleasure of eating and increase the child's sense of well-being. In time these activities in themselves will arouse a positively toned response toward the mother, *even if they are not accompanied by food.* With further maturation and learning by the child, the mother's *presence* alone is sufficient to arouse the same responses. As he gets older the child comes to associate other expected forms of conduct with eating, such as good manners. This behavior is a response to approbation from the mother, and it thus too becomes linked with her as a source of satisfaction. (We leave out for the moment the role of the self in this process.)

Clearly, the primary goal of reducing hunger tension has slowly given way to forms of behavior which have no immediate connection with the original urge. These forms of behavior are secondary or derived goals. By the time the individual has reached maturity, the derived goals may increase in number and variety, depending on the expectancies of the group and the manner in which the individual has internalized them in his self-organization. The derived or learned goals become progressively more independent of the basic drives which served as the original impetus to action.

Cross-conditioning also applies to negatively toned responses. If the mother should react to the child's hunger with impatience or irritability, if she spoke harshly or punished him for his unacceptable manners, he would probably find his mother to be generally undesirable, even though she satisfied his immediate hunger tensions. Painful experiences, like pleasurable ones, are linked to the original drive and, like the latter, become generalized and pervasive in their functioning.

Anticipation is implicit in cross-conditioning. The hungry child who has been gratified by his mother anticipates similar gratification in the future. At the sight of her he "gets set" to receive food. His locomotions become more numerous and vigorous; his mouth is set to receive the mother's nipple; and a profuse excitement marks his actions. When he is older the same mechanism operates. If his table manners are not what they should be, he may anticipate reproof, for on similar occasions in the past his mother reacted in the same way to his unacceptable behavior. As Dollard and Miller have shown, in social learning, reactions near the point of reward tend to move forward in the series, or to become anticipatory.[11]

Anticipation of reward or punishment is an important determinant of behavior, as we have repeatedly shown. We act not only on the basis of memory of past rewards or punishments, but often with even greater force on the basis of future expectations. Man

[11] J. Dollard and N. E. Miller, *Personality and psychotherapy* (New York: McGraw-Hill Book Co., Inc., 1950), Ch. 4.

is a goal-integrating being; he sets up prospective lines of action in his over-all behavior.

Man's goal-directed behavior is anticipatory in two ways. First, he behaves in accordance with the expectancies of others. Social pressure in the form of approval or disapproval impels him to conform to the demands of the group. Second, he acts in accordance with goals that he has himself established. Expectancies in the form of ideals and ambitions, especially in the form of a level of aspiration, are powerful forces directing the course of his actions. Healthy adult behavior is not, strictly speaking, "purposeless." Every mature person is described by directionality. He guides his actions toward selected goals, toward what on the basis of his self-image is a worthy objective. He may lower his level of aspiration, or grimly persevere in the face of insurmountable obstacles. He may be bound to life only by indignation, as Allport eloquently describes it, but even then his "emotional focus serves as a goal for combat." [12]

The anticipatory nature of motivation adds to adult behavior a moral attribute, the character of social responsibility. A person is socially responsible not only because he sets up goals for his own seeking, but because he can anticipate the consequences of his own success or failure in their achievement. A life plan is only as good as the capacity of the individual to perceive the probable issue of his own efforts. Anticipation provides man with the instrument for making his life more intelligible or with a perspective afforded by long-range planning. The consequences of the underdevelopment or absence of a life plan, or of poorly motivated behavior, are etched deeply in the lives of those men who have no sense of direction— in despondent individuals, derelicts, drifters, and psychopaths. Not being moved even by indignation, they have no meaningful tie with life, and they live only in the present. They have no pointers to the future, and so they can live only in the blank vacuity of the moment.

Viewed in the light of the concept of role perception, anticipation is the capacity of playing the role of another. One individual knows something of the psychological state of another because he can in his imagination see the other person as an individual like himself. By seeing another as someone like himself, the individual can anticipate the acts of the other and thus make constructive adjustments to him. Anticipation makes role-taking possible and human behavior within limits predictable. Devoid of this anticipatory function man can neither be deeply social nor can he make his

[12] Allport, *Personality*, p. 219.

group life be significantly ordered. Therefore, it is no exaggeration
to say that in the absence of anticipation human personality is deprived of one of its most remarkable characteristics.

Cultural patterning will be discussed in detail in the next chapter. Here we shall examine the problem in its barest outline. In
view of our discussion of culture and personality in Chapter 7, we
may unhesitatingly assert that our motives are critically determined
by the society in which we live. Although all of us come into the
world possessed of roughly the same fundamental biological heritage, our interests and goals vary remarkably from society to society,
and even from group to group in the same society. As a simple
illustration, let us consider the motive of acquisitiveness. Not so
long ago acquisitiveness was thought to be a native characteristic
of man. However, there are too many instances which contradict
this simple explanation. For example, the Zuñi Indians show no
interest in acquiring property. The economic security which cooperation vouchsafes them makes the desire for possessions unnecessary. Should we argue (with dubious evidence to support us)
that they have acquisitive desires but inhibit or repress them, we
would not invalidate the assertion that acquisitiveness is a culturally
patterned phenomenon. Whether or not a motive is checked or
inhibited is largely decided by the culture. On the other hand,
should acquisitiveness be an organic drive, it is so profoundly modified by cultural expectancies that it loses its identity. Moreover,
the form of expression which acquisitiveness takes must be acceptable to members of the group; where it goes counter to their
expectancies it brings criticism or punishment upon the doer.
There is an approved manner for the expression of acquisitiveness
as there is an acceptable manner for ingesting one's food, imbibing
one's liquid, or satisfying one's sexual needs.

We have simplified the process of transforming drives into
motives by describing the process as one of channelization. But
this process is complex in itself, and it considers only one segment
of the global behavior which we call personality. We should bear
in mind a point we shall discuss at great length in later chapters,
namely, that when an individual seeks a goal he acts as a *total*
striving person, not as a segmental being. When a person strives
to satisfy his hunger, he is not merely trying to reduce the tensions
produced by muscular contractions in his stomach; he is trying to
satisfy *himself*, and the energy discharged in the effort is the energy
of the total individual. The whole set of attitudes, emotions, beliefs, and conations of the individual are engrossed in the task of

reaching a desired end. Further yet, his perception of things and his outlook toward the future tend to change as he reaches out toward his goal. A starving man's whole life is defined in terms of eating, as Maslow put it, and such a man "may fairly be said to live by bread alone." [13]

VARIETIES OF MOTIVES

Taxonomy is a respected and necessary function of science. Its aim is to inject order into the proliferation of single events by classifying them on the basis of their common properties. In the field of drives and motives it has become a difficult if not an impossible task. Unless he is a professional psychologist, the student of human behavior is invariably baffled by the large variety of proposals for classifying motives. He is perplexed to find the classificatory schemes ranging all the way from some twenty drives or needs, as proposed by Murray to the breathtakingly simple proposal of a single motive of "self-actualization," by Goldstein.[14] In reality, the number of motives or how they are classified is not a matter of great importance. What matters is their nature and the understanding they give us of the human personality. It seems clear that they afford such insights most effectively when we realize their profoundly social nature; even those that are indubitably organic gain their relevance to the personality by the manner in which they fit into our perceptions, or by the way which society defines them for each of us.

Attempts to arrange motives according to their prepotency are also ineffective. Maslow, who has done some of the best writing on motivation, believes that there is a hierarchy of motives and that each motive becomes impelling only when the one before it has been satisfied. Thus, the physiological needs like hunger or thirst must be satisfied first, but once satisfied they give way to other needs. While this is generally true, it cannot be formulated into a universal principle. There are instances when men must satisfy other needs before they will ingest food when they are hungry. As Mitya in *The Brothers Karamazov* poetically expressed it, we want not only bread, but answers to our questions. Experimental psychologists are discovering that not even very hungry rats will be-

---

[13] Maslow, A dynamic theory of motivation, p. 374.

[14] For a multiplicity of motives, see H. A. Murray, *Explorations in personality* (New York: Oxford University Press, 1938). For a single, all-inclusive motive of self-actualization, see K. Goldstein, *The organism* (New York: American Book Co., 1939).

have according to the prepotency principle. Rats have even been found to repeatedly perform an act which produces no reward.[15] Hungry rats have been known to refuse food until exploration and curiosity are satisfied. Small children drive their parents to exasperation and anxiety by their unconcerned dawdling at meals even though they have been unfed for several hours.[16] Referring to Harlow's well-known researches on motivational and problem-solving studies with monkeys, Cattell humorously remarks that "monkeys, like professors, will put in a sixteen-hour day without such gross rewards as food and drink." [17] Nor must we overlook the role of cultural factors in considering the alleged prepotency of physiological over other drives. There have been cases reported of Orthodox Jews in Nazi concentration camps who died of starvation rather than violate the food prohibitions of their religion.

These examples confirm the belief that motives have many sources, that they are highly individualized, and that, especially in man, the prepotency of exploration, curiosity, and the like over the hunger drive occurs frequently.

Since we believe that a knowledge of the variety of motives is more important than their classification, we shall briefly discuss the motives that instigate human beings to action. For convenience we shall order them into four main groupings: security, affiliation, mastery, and status.

THE SECURITY MOTIVE. Without claiming prepotency for this group of motives, that is, without saying that it must be satisfied before all others, we can say that the need for security is deep-rooted and basic. Research, especially clinical studies, has shown it to be extremely important in the development and expression of personality. Men as well as animals must protect themselves against dangers and threats to their existence and integrity. It is apparent in the avoidance of danger and risk, and in the human attitudes of conservatism and caution. The important security needs are (1) physiological needs, (2) safety needs, and (3) belief and conformity.[18]

[15] See W. M. Schoenfeld, J. J. Antonitis, and P. J. Bersh, Unconditioned response rate of the white rat in a bar-pressing apparatus, *J. comp. physiol. Psychol.*, 43 (1950), 41–48.

[16] For a witty but informative discussion of the exaggerated emphasis on home-ostatic drives in contemporary psychology, see H. F. Harlow, Motivational forces underlying learning, *Kentucky symposium* (New York: John Wiley & Sons, Inc., 1954), pp. 36–53.

[17] R. B. Cattell, Personality structures as learning and motivation patterns—a theme for the integration of methodologies, *Kentucky symposium*, p. 99.

[18] See Bonner, *Social psychology*, pp. 157–61. The following descriptions draw substantially on this reference.

Physiological needs. Such physiological needs as hunger, thirst, sex, and elimination are essentially emergency conditions and occur only periodically. As we shall see in the next chapter, although these are basically tissue needs they are substantially affected by cultural pressures. There are, as we saw in Chapter 7, regulations covering proper ways of eating, disposal of excreta, and other organic functions. The stimulus to eating is determined less by the rhythmic actions of the stomach wall, or the energy level of the human body, than by the customs of the group. Whether we eat one meal or three, dine whenever the spirit moves us or at designated times, are socially prescribed ways of behaving.

Safety needs. These security needs initiate all those forms of behavior which safeguard the individual from various internal and external threats, such as dangers to the person, illness, pain, loss of love, and rejection. Some safety needs are now better satisfied, some less so, than in the past. The consequences of unemployment, illness, accidents, and old age are less disastrous today than a generation or more ago; whereas the insecurity generated by threats of annihilating wars is far greater. Also, man's security is increasingly threatened by the abrogation of individual freedom at the hands of tyrants, dictators, and professional patriots.

Belief and conformity. These, too, are powerful motivating forces and effective guarantees for the security of the individual. People have a strong need to believe in something. Whereas all people find a measure of security in belief, it is extraordinarily important to the individual whose life is dominated by the need for security. Belief is characterized by a high degree of confidence and certainty, which contribute to the believer's feeling of security. Man clings to his beliefs, often against damaging evidence, because they provide him with psychological safety.

The motivating force of conformity is similar to that of belief. The person who conforms with the customs of his society is acting on the basis of the safe and the familiar. Receiving the sanction of his group carries also the assurance of acceptance and belongingness, both of which are important sources of security and safety. In most people the desire to conform is much stronger than the wish for change and novelty. This may be in part responsible for the fact that most people tend to be conservative and unproductive. The need for security inhibits the wish for novelty and change, so that originality in thought or behavior tends to be impaired.

Clearly, when the individual's physiological drives, his need to conform with the mores of the group, and his desire for acceptance by others have been satisfied, his security motive poses no serious problem.

THE AFFILIATIVE MOTIVE. This motive is closely related to, yet independent of, the security motive. Affiliation, or the need to belong, is obviously similar to the desire for acceptance and the wish to conform, which mark the security motive. The affiliative motive may thus strengthen the security motive. A person may gain security from affiliation with others, but in so doing his desire for affiliation with others is not necessarily satisfied; he may acquire a sense of security even if his contacts are limited. A person may have a strong need for affiliation even when his security motive has been adequately gratified.

The affiliative motive impels people to relate themselves to others, to seek their company, to belong to a person or to a group, to desire intimate and friendly contact with others. It thus includes more than what is implied by the term "sociability," though the latter is a form of the desire for affiliation. It ranges from the need to cooperate with others to the desire for the most intimate embrace of another. Unlike the sexual drive, which is fundamentally physiological, and which can be gratified through the reduction of its physiological tensions, the affiliative motive can be expressed only in close identification with others. Unconditional *love* is the supreme example of this motive. Wise people, especially perceptive parents, have probably always known, in a mute, inarticulate way, that love is necessary to human growth.

Belongingness and cooperation. These are universal expressions of the affiliative motive. Man long ago learned that he can survive only in a group, and that the group can survive only if he cooperates with others in the pursuit of a common end. Through belonging and cooperating man can best satisfy other needs and desires, especially love and friendship. Indeed, not only the so-called derived needs, but even the basic ones associated with self-preservation and survival, can be satisfied only in belonging to and cooperating with others. "Being a social animal, man derives satisfaction from *belongingness* as such. Isolation is a myth, whereas belongingness is a fact." [19] Belongingness and cooperation are elemental community feelings.

The "tender" sentiments. Affiliative need satisfactions are most obvious in the interactions of the family group. Affection between parents and children, between a husband and his wife, and be-

[19] H. Bonner, *Group dynamics: principles and applications* (New York: The Ronald Press Co., 1959), p. 47. Italics in original.

tween siblings are the most obvious examples of the affiliative need characterized by tender regard of one for the other. The desire for offspring and the sexual bonds between spouses have a physiological basis, but beyond this elementary fact these needs are enhanced and reinforced in the affiliative relations within a group.

Romantic love. This is a motive that is not only lived but brutalized and dramatized in erotic fiction. In our own society it is glamorized by the *romantic complex*—a pattern of attitudes and emotions in which the physiological sex drive is sublimated and idealized to such an extent that most often it no longer corresponds to reality. A consequence of this romantic complex is that romantic love serves, in our society, as a criterion for evaluating the success or failure of a marriage. Be that as it may, the need for the romantic expression must be satisfied, and when it is satisfied the individual tends to be, on the whole, a happy and well-adjusted person.

THE MOTIVE OF MASTERY. Security, as we saw, is the need of self-defense, of preserving the physical and psychological being. It is characterized by conservatism and caution. The need for mastery, on the other hand, is the desire for growth and enhancement, for novelty and adventure. It is seen early in the prowling and exploring activities of children and in the intense curiosity of most people to understand and control at least some segment of the world around them. The child who indefatigably persists in trying to turn the knob of a closed door, and who shows unmistakable signs of satisfaction in its final accomplishment, is impelled by the need for mastery. The man who is propelled by the need to be what potentially he *can* be, is moved by the need for self-actualization, a form of self-mastery. The individual who aspires not only to belong but even more to influence or lead others is motivated by the need for dominance, or the form of mastery over others.

Cognitive needs. Also termed the noetic impulse, cognitive need is roughly equivalent to what was formerly called the instinct of curiosity. It is the desire to know and to understand. In the form of inquisitiveness it seems to be present in all people. Researches in comparative animal psychology strongly support the claim that it is also found in animals—certainly in those high in the phyletic scale. Harlow's valuable researches on monkeys leave no doubt in our minds that that these primates are motivated by curiosity. In one of his characteristic witticisms, Harlow remarks that all primates, including man, "spend a large amount of time just 'monkeying around' and that monkeying around is an activity often leading to invention and creativity." [20] The "wish for new experience," as Thomas called it, is strong in all of us.[21]

One should, perhaps, distinguish between the desire to know and the desire for knowledge. The first, we said, is present in all people, like the "instinct of curiosity." The desire for knowledge, however, refers to the wish to master or to accumulate organized knowledge, such as the pursuit of science and scholarship, and to philosophize over it. If this distinction is valid, then the desire for knowledge seems to be found, according to Maslow's researches, only in people of considerable intelligence. However, it is interesting to note that in the revised form of his article on the subject, Maslow no longer makes the differentiation, but attributes the desire for knowledge to all healthy people.[22] This would seem to be more congruent with his mature position.

Self-actualization. As has been pointed out already, self-actualization is a form of self-mastery. It probably exists in its most uninhibited form in all children, but it is subject to a great deal of stunting and inhibiting by adults and by cultural pressures. The person in whom the motive of self-actualization is not inhibited has a strong tendency to persist along lines of action which permit him the greatest degree of self-enhancement, of becoming more and more what he potentially already is. Resistance to enculturation, which is another way of describing the same process, is an expression of the desire for self-mastery, for self-actualization. The need to be himself overshadows the need for security, even of affiliation and status needs, if these are conceived by him as obstacles to the flowering of his selfhood. The motive of self-actualization impels the individual to grow in the realization of his selfhood. In this striving to be himself, and with the assistance of the other motives, the person more nearly achieves a full individuality and selfhood than in any other way.

This pressure toward self-mastery through self-actualization must not be confused with stubborn rebelliousness, nor with lack of social sensitivity. On the contrary, the person who has mastered his self and has enhanced it to the full is a highly socialized individual; for, as we shall show in detail in a later chapter, his self is always sensitive to the selves of others.

Leadership and domination. The need for mastery is also expressed in leadership and domination. Whereas all healthy people

[20] Harlow, Motivational forces underlying learning, p. 39.
[21] See W. I. Thomas, *The unadjusted girl* (Boston: Little, Brown & Co., 1923).
[22] Maslow, *Motivation and personality*, Ch. 5.

desire to belong to a person or a group, some do not find full satisfaction from belongingness as such. Some desire even more to persuade, influence, or lead others in a group. The latter motives exceed the need for acceptance, and belongingness is primarily a means whereby some people may direct and influence others.

When the need to dominate is all-powerful, authoritarian control becomes the central gratification. When it is softened by a consideration for the well-being of others, democratic leadership is a normal consequence. In the latter case, dominance loses its aggressive properties, and the individual finds satisfaction in being an instrument for the achievement of goals collectively.[23]

Clearly, not every desire for mastery over others is expressed in the form of leadership or domination. Most persons in some situations may merely be *self-assertive*, and this self-assertiveness may be nothing more than the need to control the routines and barriers of daily living. It may, indeed, be a healthy enthusiasm which causes our motivational energy to spill over into efforts which are not demanded by the task immediately before us. It may express itself in a wholesome effort to overcome the obstacles which restrain our healthy energy. Domination may serve as a technique of self-defense, for it may be a form of self-assertiveness which is expressed to contain the self-assertiveness of others. Of the forms of domination in daily life, pugnacity is most undesirable, since it is largely determined by self-aggrandizement and a denial of self-expression to others.

Creative needs. Creative needs are highly significant forms of the motive of mastery. In creativeness a person not only satisfies self-actualizing needs but a high degree of individual autonomy and freedom. It may be expressed in work or play, in love and procreation, in humble productivity or highly imaginative constructions. What we are saying is that creative needs are found in everyone, and that their expressions are not necessarily special and unusual. We have discussed the issue elsewhere, and we can do no better than to quote from that discussion:

. . . A person can feel or think creatively without ever producing a tangible manifestation of his freedom and spontaneity. He can *live* creatively when he actualizes his own potentialities, when he re-creates his immediate environment by his own intellectual and emotional powers, and when he strives to make his own personality into a work of art. Man is noncreative when he becomes alienated from others and himself, represses or inhibits his own spontaneity and freedom, and acts on the basis of neurotic self-deception. Neurotic behavior is fundamentally nonproductive behavior, behavior dictated by crip-

[23] Bonner, *Group dynamics,* pp. 47–48.

pling fears and stultifying defenses. It cannot transcend its personal inhibitions or surmount the inescapable barriers of daily living. Creativeness means freedom, and freedom consists of the spontaneous activity of the total self.[24]

THE STATUS MOTIVE. The need for status is a uniquely human motive. Although it is apparently not universal, it is found practically everywhere. The question of universality may be largely a problem of definition. The Zuñi Indians, as we have shown, and the Arapesh of New Guinea, do not seem to seek it, preferring inconspicuousness instead. The model of a Zuñi Indian, which gives him acceptance and security, is modesty and self-abnegation. Therefore he strives for these virtues, for they endear him to his fellows and his community. However, to the extent that he shuns conspicuousness he gains *recognition* from others, by whatever term we describe it. He gains "prestige" through modesty. He achieves "status" by means of humility. He is accepted or rejected on the basis of self-renunciation. If this is the correct assessment of the Zuñi's attitude, then he, too, seeks status in the eyes of others, and like human beings everywhere he evaluates himself on the basis of an ascribed position.

Without more ado, therefore, let us say that every individual seeks and possesses status—high, intermediate or low, with varying degrees of each. With this status is bound up an individual's social self and his esteem in the eyes of others.

Prestige. As suggested above, prestige is a psychological intensification of the need for status. The sources of prestige differ widely from culture to culture. In our own society it is most generally achieved through economic position and power. A powerful motive in the lives of most North Americans is success in economic and vocational aims. We are judged, and we judge others and ourselves, in the light of pecuniary achievement and the prestige value which it confers upon us. Our personalities are influenced by the position which we occupy in the status hierarchy.

Self-esteem. A satisfying self-image is a powerful motivating force in the lives of most people. Every normal individual desires, and in order to preserve his normality needs to have, a satisfying image of himself. Self-esteem is derived from mastery, or the successful pursuit of an end, and from a person's attitude toward other people's opinion of himself. In contrast to security, which is largely derived from belongingness, especially from love and acceptance by our parents, self-esteem is a sense of adequacy—even of superiority—dependent mostly on mastery and achieve-

[24] Bonner, *Social psychology*, pp. 425–26.

ment. A person may strive for and attain one without seeking or achieving the other. Security does not guarantee self-esteem, nor does self-esteem assure one of security. A wholesome personality is motivated by and seeks to secure both.

The achievement of self-esteem is an important source of self-confidence. Since self-esteem is bound up with public evaluation of a person's success or failure, the individual strives to achieve those values which society holds in high esteem. Failure to realize them begets self-depreciation and a sense of inferiority. The disesteem of others is a threat to the self, and many cases of pathological behavior are induced by a thwarted desire for recognition by one's fellows.[25]

CONCLUDING REMARKS. The four groups of motives—security, affiliation, mastery, and status—differ in their magnitude and urgency in different individuals and in different cultures. They differ also in accordance with the goals toward which they are directed —in other words, in accordance with the specific object or situation which relieves or satisfies the need of the individual. A discussion of the goal-objects cannot be undertaken in this chapter; and in any case, these objects are more appropriately treated by sociologists and anthropologists.

Again, a scientific account of the nexus between the inherent physiological drives and the complex socially acquired motives has been barely begun. So little progress has been made in this area by experimental psychologists, whose task it really is, that the little we know about it has been largely furnished by anthropologists. So true is this that the acquisition of motives in a cultural matrix has become a major concern with those personality psychologists who believe that learning theory as such is an unsatisfactory instrument for investigating the role of motivation in the human personality.

Furthermore, the complexity of personality cannot be understood and described unless we also know the role of the self in transforming basic biological drives into socially acquired motives. We thus come around once more to a frequently reiterated statement, namely, that unless we know a person's self-image we cannot know why he tirelessly strives to satisfy some motives, is indifferent to others, and rejects still additional ones.

Finally, viewed from the perspective of the total person, all the motives which we have so briefly discussed must find some

25 The need for self-esteem was considered a basic factor in the psychology of motivation by Koffka, at least a quarter of a century ago. See K. Koffka, *Principles of Gestalt psychology* (New York: Harcourt, Brace and Co., 1935).

degree of fulfillment if the individual is to live a normal and satisfying life. While each person will to a great extent create his own hierarchy and render prepotent those motives which best satisfy his needs, all normal people will strive with some energy for the satisfaction of each. The psychological well-being of both the individual and his society depends on the opportunities which life affords for the gratification of the needs which we have discussed in the preceding pages.

The organization of motives in the foregoing paragraphs may be criticized on the ground of incompleteness. We plead guilty to this charge, but promptly add that we do not propose an exhaustive list of motives. Dozens of them may be found scattered through the literature, but every classification thus far has been severely criticized and promptly rejected. When one looks at the taxological proposals of psychologists, psychoanalysts, sociologists, and anthropologists, not to mention those of biologists, one finds the list of motives growing and becoming more confusing. Maslow's classification has the great merit of being founded, more than any other theory, on an increasing amount of research on normal and healthy people rather than on neurotic individuals, and on human beings rather than on animals. We believe this to be also true of our own classification. Even the physiological drives in our system have relevance to personality only when they are viewed in the light of their transformation by individual and cultural preferences. Since we do not classify them on the hierarchical and prepotent principle, future research will less likely invalidate our principal categories. The important question for us is not which categories come first and next, but what they are and what contribution they make to a better understanding of human personality. We do not suggest that an integrating principle for the organization of human motives is unnecessary; on the contrary, we are keenly aware of its desirability, but we cannot overlook the fact that no classification, including our own, is based on sufficient empirical evidence.

MOTIVATION AND PERSONALITY

Clearly, in all that we have thus far said about motivation we have been interested in personality, not in motives as such. The varieties of motives, we have argued, are always those of a person, not abstract concepts or concrete processes flowing in a vacuum. Motives *as such* may be of interest to those who approach human behavior segmentally and mechanistically, but of themselves they have little value to the student of human personality. It is always a *person* for whom security, affiliation, the desire for mastery, and the need for status are daily urgencies. Personality is to a great extent, but not completely, defined as a configuration of interlocking needs and desires. While it is more convenient to say—as we ourselves have said—that motives seek fulfillment, it is always a person who strives to relieve tensions, satisfy needs, and reach out for desired ends. If this were not so, and until a better explanation is given, we could not account for the fact that (1) different people may behave similarly even though the motives determining their behavior may be markedly different; and (2) people with similar motives may engage in different forms of behavior. The unifying principle governing these dissimilarities is personality—or, as some prefer to describe it, the dimension of the total person called the self, or ego.

In order to show more clearly the inseparability of and mutual interaction between motives and personality we shall briefly examine the following problems: the functional autonomy of motives, unconscious motivation, the self and motivation, and being and becoming. In so doing we shall also touch some of the liveliest issues in contemporary theories of motivation and personality.

FUNCTIONAL AUTONOMY OF MOTIVES. For over twenty years now, the theory of the functional autonomy of motives has stood up as a serious challenge to the hegemony of childhood experiences in the formation of personality. The challenge is in some ways an old one, having been suggested by William James' conception of instinct. Some years later it was explicitly formulated by Woodworth who conceived the problem as the transformation of *means* to an end into *ends* in themselves. However, its current and best-known form is Allport's theory of functional autonomy.[26]

Allport regards adult motives "as infinitely varied, and as self-sustaining, *contemporary* systems, growing out of antecedent systems, but functionally independent of them."[27] He goes on to say that, just as a child becomes independent of his parents and grows into a self-determining person, so adult motives break away from their "seed-forms" in infancy and childhood. "The tie is historical, not functional."[28]

Of the types of evidence which Allport gives in support of the functional autonomy of motives, we shall choose only three ex-

[26] See W. James, *Principles of psychology* (2 vols.; New York: Henry Holt & Co., Inc., 1890), Vol. I, Ch. 10; R. S. Woodworth, *Dynamic psychology* (New York: Columbia University Press, 1918; G. W. Allport, *Personality: a psychological interpretation* (New York: Holt, Rinehart & Winston, Inc., 1937), Ch. 7.

[27] Allport, *Personality*, p. 194. Italics added.

[28] *Ibid.*, p. 194.

amples—one from everyday experience, one from experiments in miniature social situations, and one from psychopathology.

An excellent illustration of the first is the maternal feeling. It is a fact too well known to be denied that many women bear their children reluctantly, and even hate them after they are born. The "parental instinct," whose existence was for a time widely accepted by psychologists, or the "maternal drive," which has replaced it in the modern laboratory, is certainly absent in many mothers. Maternal behavior, though commonplace, is too complex to be explained by physiological factors alone. The force of custom and public opinion also enters into its expression. The attitude of others toward the mother's response to the child, coupled with her own image of herself as a mother, may gradually change her sentiment for her unwanted child to a feeling of love and the enjoyment of its care. As her love for the child grows her former sentiment abates and completely disappears, as far as any tangible evidence goes. Henceforth, nothing that her offspring does, not even the disgrace that he might heap upon her as a heedless and irresponsible adult, can diminish her affection for him. Her attitude of rejection or hate has been transformed into a tenacious sentiment of love.

The second example, the Zeigarnik phenomenon, is already familiar to the reader. The resumption of interrupted tasks does not require for its explanation a motive of self-assertion or competition. The desire for its completion itself has become a need with a dynamic push of its own; it has acquired an autonomous motivation independent of its original frustration.

The third example, that of neurosis, illustrates the condition where neurotic symptoms defy all therapeutic measures and become independent or autonomous systems of motivation. A symptom which was originally put into the service of allaying anxiety, or to escape the agonizing discomfort of a fear or a sense of guilt, has become an independent activity. It is now a phobia, a compulsion, or an inhibition which controls an important area of the individual's behavior. A neurotic symptom, in other words, is more than a defective coping mechanism; it is an autonomous motive persisting along a line of behavior which is functionally divorced from its origin. A neurotic individual's symptoms are means by which he defends himself against further anxiety. His mode of behavior has been learned; it has become a new motive; and we can truly say that he *wants* to be ill because his neurotic symptoms reduce his internal tensions, even though they do not resolve them. It persists as a motivating factor in the person's life, not because it was already established by earlier experiences, but for the reason that whenever it occurs it is reinforced because it mitigates his neurotic suffering. The habit of fear, or anxiety, or compulsion persists without the original external support.

The superiority of functional autonomy to mechanistic conditioning in explanation of the persistence of acquired motives lies in its dynamic character. Personality is a changing and growing being, and like the motives of which it is compounded, it is endlessly renewing itself. At every stage of its growth its motives and interests are contemporary; "whatever drives, drives now," as Allport expressed it.[29]

This is not a way of explaining personality as the end-product of archaic drives or impulses, but as a form of life endlessly seeking fulfillment. It is a way of explaining personality, not as a consequence of cross-conditioning merely, but as the person's determination to complete his incompleteness without in reality ever succeeding. It is this determination to find fulfillment which renders man, in contrast to the beasts, divinely discontented. What else but this thrusting impetus makes man, often in the face of unbelievable odds, pursue an interest beyond the bounds of "reason" or of mere hedonistic satisfaction? No automatic habit has such a fiercely impelling power.

Unconscious Motivation. Nothing in the foregoing discussion commits us to the view that all motives are rational and conscious processes; but neither does it compel us to view them as blind or undirected urges, which is often the way unconscious motives are interpreted. Likewise, our view of unconscious motives does not permit the popular form of psychologizing in which hidden meanings are imagined where none exists. Unconscious motives are, stated quite simply, impulsions of which a person is not aware, thus causing him to behave in ways which he is unable to explain. That an unconscious dimension of personality exists cannot be doubted, for its existence has been both experimentally and clinically demonstrated.

Every person has motives or impulses which he dare not at all times face. The tendency to repress them, or make them unconscious, has unfortunately too often been interpreted as unhealthy and even pathological. This is a grave error. Unconscious motives, like conscious ones, have healthy functions to fulfill. They are an important aspect of psychic economy, for they render many inescapable pains and frustrations bearable. Unconscious motives,

29 *Ibid.*, p. 206.

thus, have a purpose, and their purpose is to maintain the security and integrity of the person. While every healthy person is able to face his problems realistically, he cannot do so at all times and completely. Repression, or the involuntary relegation of consciously unacceptable ideas and impulses to the unconscious dimension of the personality, is a universal process. Accordingly, knowledge of the ways in which it takes place gives us additional insight into the nature of the normal personality.

Repression of impulses into the unconscious occurs to some extent in all people, since no one, presumably, can go through life and live a truly effective life without experiencing conflicts. Only those persons, if such there be, who are wholly insensitive to life's values, and mentally defective individuals possibly, are without disturbing conflicts. These people probably do not need to repress impulses. In normal people, however, repression not only is a means of coping with conflicts but in turn tends to produce conflicts. We have already suggested that highly complex personalities are subject to more conflicts than simple ones, since their choices and challenges to action are more numerous. Repression of unacceptable impulses seems to be associated with increasing humanization of the biological individual. Explanations of behavior in terms of unconscious motives are invalid only if they exaggerate the latter's importance, as in most psychoanalytical theories of personality. Recognition of the importance of unconscious conflicts is not to deny that most conflicts are conscious and intelligible to the healthy individual.

Defense mechanisms. Repression is effected and unconscious conflicts are mitigated or resolved by *defense mechanisms.* These mechanisms are now discussed in practically every book on personality, mental hygiene, psychology of adjustment, and general psychology. Hence it is not necessary to describe them in detail here.[30]

1. *Fantasy.* This is the most common technique of adjustment. It is especially common during childhood, when it serves as a means of controlling and manipulating the environment. Every adult daydreams and finds solutions to many of his problems by means of it. Not only the work of psychoanalysts but also that of experimenters in miniature social situations shows that people use fantasy as a means of adjustment. The experiments on inter-

---

[30] Confusion often arises from the fact that repression is itself treated as a mechanism of defense. To avoid this confusion it might be helpful to think of repression as a general, over-all technique of mitigating conflict and of the defense mechanisms as specific techniques of adjustment.

rupted tasks, which we discussed in Chapter 4, reveal the importance of fantasy solutions of adjusment problems. Fantasy solutions of problems are inescapable, since no one is psychologically competent to meet all conflicts and frustrations on a plane of higher reality, that is, realistically and effectively. The individual protects his self-image through fantasy. Fantasy may serve no other purpose than as a temporary escape for some persons; for others it may be so beguiling that they substitute it for reality, as in the case of mental disorder; whereas for still others it may be a technique for creating constructive and culturally acceptable solutions, as in the case of constructive and creative activities in art, science, or philosophy. In the latter case the solutions may be described as works of genius. In this case genius is indeed, as Santayana said, controlled madness.

2. *Rationalization.* The term "rationalization" has become a household word. It is essentially a method of self-justification. It is motivated by the fear of criticism and disapproval by others, especially for real or fancied failure. It is a way of achieving some degree of mastery, and in more severe cases, for appearing superior to what we are. It is not only socially induced, as is obvious in the foregoing statements, but also very often socially condoned. Society apparently does not tolerate complete sincerity in its members, especially when it might be inimical to social harmony. Thus, people in our society would be dismayed by a woman's frank admission that she pursues men for sexual reasons. Instead she rationalizes her motive by ascribing her interest in them to their fascination and charm. Rationalization is thus a means whereby the individual is helped to resolve two sets of conflicts, namely, between (1) his individual desires and the cultural imperatives of the group, and (2) his basic impulses and the sentiment of self-regard.

Rationalization is not, normally, a particularly constructive technique of mitigating conflict. It encourages self-deception and fosters illusions about one's fellow men. Still, "the vices of rationalization contain its only virtue: it enables the person to avert his gaze from his feeble self and so find sporadic relief from distressing anxiety." [31]

3. *Projection.* This technique is closely related to rationalization. In projection, instead of rationalizing his questionable motives the individual ascribes them to others. His faults are perceived to be not in himself but in another. Instead of justifying them, as in rationalization, the individual denies their presence in

[31] Bonner, *Social psychology,* p. 137.

himself. The person who habitually suspects evil in others probably has the evil himself. When projection becomes chronic and
all-encompassing it is known as paranoia, a personality disorder in
which projection is a dominant characteristic.

4. *Compensation.* By this important means, a person makes up
for weaknesses and failures by emphasizing his strengths and assets.
The woman who lacks physical beauty can stress her good character; the poor scholar may take pride in his physical prowess;
and a father may sacrifice pleasure and comfort to send his son
through medical school in order to compensate for his own thwarted
ambition.

The self-enhancing character of compensation should not be
minimized. It can be constructively utilized in changing an individual's attitudes toward himself. Overcoming a weakness by
achievement in another direction fosters self-confidence. Frequently it impels a person to increase his motivation along desirable
lines and creates a basis for substantial achievement. His achievement may in turn enhance his social status and decrease the need
for excessive self-defense. In reducing his need for self-defense
he may find it easier to relate himself constructively to others. His
constructive relatedness to others increases their acceptance of him.
Finally, their increased acceptance of him enhances his self-
confidence and augments his personal well-being. Thus what was
initially a mechanism of defense has become a technique of self-
enhancement. The historical bond between them has not been
extinguished, but their *functional* connection has been effectively
broken.

5. *Identification.* Adjustment here may be conscious or unconscious. Identification refers to the act of making oneself similar
to or like another person. It plays an important role in empathy
with or concern for other persons. The ability to play the role
of another, of putting oneself in another person's position, is a
significant characteristic of all socialized persons. In conscious
identification we erect a model of an ideal person, or imitate another
whom we admire. In unconscious identification we model ourselves after an ideal without being aware of our intention. Most,
if not all, personality psychologists believe that identification with
another, especially with a loved or highly esteemed person, is essential to the health and stability of the self.

6. *Fixation and regression.* These terms are closely related and
may be discussed together. Fixation refers to the *arresting* of
motivational development at an immature level. It may be temporary and nonpathological or permanent and pathological. In the

latter case the individual, irrespective of his chronological age, remains an immature and childish personality. Regression refers to the *return* to an earlier mode of motivational expression after maturity has already been attained. In normal persons it may be no more than a symbolic return to an earlier and more satisfying level of development. Hence, in a moment of crisis or other emotional distress a person may violently tug at his left ear because that was the way in which he responded to trying situations in his childhood. Regression in normal people is thus a retreat to a position which provided them with safety at an earlier period.

7. *Sublimation.* It is not always easy to distinguish this mechanism from compensation. In some respects an individual who sublimates an impulse or desire may be experiencing a compensatory expression of it. It is a means through which individually and socially unacceptable motives are diverted into personally and socially acceptable forms of expression. Since the rechannelization is almost invariably toward sanctioned and rewarded forms of behavior, sublimation is considered as one of the healthiest and most constructive expressions of human energy. It is probably safe to say that every normal individual can trace his constructive behavior to some degree of sublimation of his elemental impulses.

This does not exhaust the list of adjustive mechanisms. Our purpose has been to select for discussion some of the more common and probably universal unconscious means for preserving the integrity of the self. The person who wants to acquaint himself with other mechanisms and a more detailed discussion of all of them can easily find references in which they are discussed.[32]

Motivation and the Self. The relation between motives and the self will become more meaningful when the self is better understood. Since we shall consider this subject in detail in Chapter 16, our present discussion can afford to be brief. We shall here touch only the rather neglected problem of self-motivation, or the relation of motives to self-awareness.

Individual motives and previsioned goals are always the motives and goals of someone—of an ego or self. A person's image of himself, as we have already said on numerous occasions, and not only his biological energy, are functionally joined to the goals for which an individual strives. One person sets up goals that to others are hardly worth striving for; another sets his goals so manifestly out

[32] We recommend the following: L. F. Shaffer and E. J. Shoben, *The psychology of adjustment* (2d ed.; Boston: Houghton Mifflin Co., 1956), Chs. 6–7; H. P. Laughlin, *The neuroses in clinical practice* (Philadelphia: W. B. Saunders Co., 1956), Ch. 3. Laughlin's book is both comprehensive and detailed.

of reach that failure to attain them is written in the cards. Whatever the goal and whatever the magnitude of the motives, each individual perceives them in the light of his self-image. The level of aspiration is always in great part a function of the person's awareness of himself. Whether a person's level of aspiration is high or low, whether it is distorted or realistic, is dependent upon the image of the person at the moment of performance. This explains why goal-striving differs not only with persons but with different occasions in the same person. One person may want to be the world's best prize fighter, an aspiration which leaves another person cold. A person may have high aspirations as a chess player but only modest or no aspiration to become a Greek scholar. Psychologists and teachers know only too well that the same person shows differential aspiration levels on different tests. These differences cannot be fully explained on the basis of "strong" or "weak" drives, but in terms of the self-involvement of the person in the task which he is performing. Whatever an individual seeks or strives for is not a physiological hunger, a physical pain, an abstract idea, or an affective need, but *his* hunger, *his* pain, *his* idea, *his* love. We are justified in doubting that any human motive or disposition exists apart from the individual's perception of himself as a person. Love, however self-engrossing, is the love of a *person* for another; hate, however self-destroying, is the hate of one *self* for the self of another. Many of the most important motives in human life possess an intimate quality which is impossible to dissociate from the self. The love which I feel is *my* love, the hate, *my* hate. It is *I* who strive with my full being to reach the pinnacle of success; and when at last success is momentarily tasted, the taste is *mine*.

In our analysis of the learning process and the role of the self in learning in the preceding chapter, we called attention to the neglect by learning theorists of the acquisition of moral behavior. Moral or social conscience, the "generalized other," or whatever one prefers to call it, is a powerful motivating force in human life. But it is always a striving self who is good, or moving to become better. Moral conscience is more than a set of learned responses. It is a striving or urgency which in many people is prepotent over all other motives. It is a learned response which has become a motive force in its own right. Yet even in its own right it obviously does not exist by itself; it is an expression of the image which an individual has of himself as a moral person. The desire to be just, loyal, or good may become a more powerful motivating force than the desire to eat or drink or have coitus. The self, and not pleasure only, are in control.

BEING AND BECOMING. To most psychologists, being and becoming are malodorous terms, historically associated with metaphysics and mediaeval psychology. This is a grave error, and has deprived the psychology of motivation and personality of significant concepts. The ideas implicit in these terms are found in the works of only a few psychologists, namely, of Wertheimer, Murray, G. W. Allport, Goldstein, Gardner Murphy, and Maslow, to mention only the most prominent.

The reason for the neglect of being and becoming is not hard to find, at least in American psychology. The latter, like the whole American philosophic tradition, has been basically a pragmatic, adaptive, means-to-an-end description of man. Any behavior, any activity which is not in some way adaptive, which does not reduce tensions or restore equilibrium, which does not somehow satisfy a need or bestow a reward upon the individual, seems not to have caught the attention of the great majority of psychologists. American psychology has essentially been a psychology of adjustment, a coping and adaptive psychology. Instead of being a psychology of doing or of action, as it is often described, this psychology has been more static than is generally conceded.

On the other hand, the psychology of being-in-becoming, as we conceive it in this book, is not a view which denies motivation conceived as effort and purpose. "Effortless" activities, like gaiety, the enjoyment of beauty, or self-actualization, are not passive states. As conditions *achieved,* they involve exertion and striving. In contrast to the motives typically described in textbooks, which are for the most part deficiency motives, being and becoming are growth motives, motives of enhancement and development. From this point of view the state of *being* is not a form of passive existence, but a form of *expression;* and *becoming* is no metaphysical abstraction, but *an effort toward self-realization,* or self-fulfillment. Although it is characteristic of every healthy organism to strive for completion, it never fully achieves it. The psychological life of every being is thus a continuous process of change, since the attainment of completion is found only in death. Incompleteness is a dynamic condition, and makes room for psychological growth. "Personality is not what one has," as Allport phrased it, "but rather the projected outcome of his growth." [33]

[33] G. W. Allport, *Becoming: basic considerations for a psychology of personality* (New Haven: Yale University Press, 1955), p. 90.

The psychology of motivation must in the future place less emphasis on their homeostatic nature and more on the fact that many of its goals are unattainable. Man satisfies his wants, to be sure, but it is more accurate to describe him as being in a chronic state of need. Man wants not only to survive, but even more fiercely to grow. Personality growth is, in itself, a rewarding experience. Being in itself, conceived as sheer living, is a vital goal in healthy beings. Surely the enjoyment of life as *unqualified* living is a goal that needs to be placed on a level coequal with other human motives.

Thus, the concepts of being and becoming as motivational categories are not, like most classifications of motives, only instrumental or expedient, but central, orienting, and essential. They are ends in themselves. Being is the pattern of unique qualities which we call the person; and becoming is his self-propulsion into the future.

CONCLUSION

In this chapter we have reviewed the leading ideas regarding the psychology of motivation. We shall not summarize them here, for little would be gained from a mere summary of what we have discussed in detail. Instead, we stress those aspects of the problem which most psychologists either ignore or deny. Those aspects may be divided into two comprehensive criticisms. First, the psychology of motivation, having rescued the subject from a preoccupation with instinctual needs, has become similarly narrow in its excessive concern for homeostatic drives. Men are moved, as we have seen, by needs other than tension reduction. Man wants not only to preserve his being but to expand and enhance it. Man does not seek a state of rest, be it peace of mind or tranquility of the "soul." He wants not only to live, but to continue living better. It may well be that the basic law of animal life is self-preservation; but the human person wants to change and grow. While we are not prepared to agree with Goldstein that the maintenance of the existent state is a pathological phenomenon, it is truly not the dominant characteristic of the healthy personality.[34] Defense of the self is normal rather than pathological, but a more powerful tendency in all normal persons is toward activity and progress.

The second criticism of motivation theory concerns the neglect of the self in human aspirations. What men seek and strive for

---

[34] For K. Goldstein's view, see his book, *The organism* (New York: American Book Co., 1939), pp. 194–207.

is not chiefly determined by psychological deficits, but even more powerfully by how each perceives himself as a person. The person who strives primarily to be a good man cannot permit himself to be bad, not because he is devoid of base motives, but because in yielding to them he would contravene his image of himself as a moral person. A mature person is controlled in his behavior not by his motives alone, but even more critically by his central personality, by his psychological self. A striving, motivated self is never experienced through analysis and segmentation, except in pathological instances, but through self-regard and self-awareness. When viewed in this manner, motives and the self complete the picture of human personality. Anything less is tantamount to splintering the whole.

CHAPTER 10

Culture and
Purposive Behavior

John Dewey, whose fellow psychologists today have virtually either disowned or forgotten him, many years ago accounted for human desires, as well as mind or personality, by showing that they vary with the structure and operation of social groups.[1] As we ourselves have stressed the critical importance of the social environments in Chapters 6 and 7, the reader should by this time require no additional argument to convince him of their importance. He should now clearly see that personality, or any integral segment of it, such as motives and attitudes, are not antecedent or ready-made "givens," but represent the restructuring of original tendencies by social and cultural pressures. Motives are not data, but products and causes after they have been formed by a given environment. This is broadly speaking true even of physiological drives, for although they exist as biological data in their own right, as products and effective causes of human behavior they have relevance only when they have been transformed by a given social group. Man becomes a significant object of psychological study only when, through the process of socialization, he has transcended his organic heritage. What we are in effect saying is that whereas much of man's behavior has a basic biological source, most of his daily actions, especially his motives and at-

[1] J. Dewey, The need for a social psychology, *Psychol. Rev.*, 24 (1917), 266–77.

titudes, and most of all his essential selfhood, are molded by customs and cultural imperatives. Like most things human, these phenomena are culturally conditioned properties.

There is a great amount of evidence, much of which is presented in the pages of this book, that the structuring of personality, including its essential components, takes place in a cultural matrix and cannot be reduced to an inherited organic structure without falsification and distortion. As a biological organism, man is a puny animal; but as a socialized person, he is truly a constitutive and creative being. Thus, his psychological nature is vastly more a function of his place in a social matrix than a function of his biological inheritance.

CULTURAL PATTERNING OF MOTIVES

In one form or another we stated before that our motives are largely learned in the society in which we live. Desires and interests, and more particularly their satisfaction, vary from culture to culture, and from group to group in the same society. There are accepted and rejected ways of satisfying all motives, from the simple act of mitigating one's hunger to the complex performance of propitiating one's gods. This fact alone is sufficient to show the futility of setting up lists or categories of motives or drives, for any classification is bound to reflect the cultural bias of the taxologist as well as the expectancies of a given social group. While the claim cannot be critically demonstrated, there are many reasons for believing that beyond the inherent homeostatic drives there are no intrinsic human motives. Different people have similar motives even when they have been conditioned by different cultural values; and they have divergent motives although they have had similar social experiences.

Our problem, then, is not to account for the satisfaction of tissue needs, for these are easily explained in biological terms, but the more difficult question of the divergence of sociogenic or derived needs in different cultures. In order to account for these differences we must turn to the study of a variety of cultures and the motives which each reinforces or inhibits. Cultural anthropologists have amassed an enormous quantity of data on this subject, and we gratefully turn to them to round out our view of the nature of human motivation.

GREGARIOUSNESS. Like the desire for love or affection, gregariousness is an important expression of the affiliative motive. Early biologists and psychologists conceived it as an innate or instinctive form of behavior. Although social interactions exist in most animal species, especially in man, this process is not in itself necessarily a form of gregariousness, and it assuredly is not an explanation or proof that gregariousness is a basic and universal drive or need. There are many persons who display only a minimal degree of gregarious behavior. The extreme degrees of social attraction, ranging from simple interaction amounting almost to isolation to pronounced interdependence and interpenetration, must give us pause.

Certainly there is much more reliable evidence in support of the learned nature of gregariousness than of its universal and innate character. There are animals which exist singly or in sexual pairs, and there are human beings whose affiliation is confined entirely to their family group. Indeed, the latter fact lends credence to the view long held by some biologists, psychologists, and anthropologists that gregariousness is learned in the affective relations with members of one's family. This position has been taken by such diverse scholars as Darwin, Malinowski, and Klineberg.[2]

Regardless of the origin of the gregarious impulse, the anthropological evidence leaves little or no doubt in one's mind that it varies significantly from culture to culture. The people of Dobu Island in the western Pacific show no inclination toward gregariousness outside of their familial blood groups. Their hostility extends even toward their spouses, and true sociability, in the sense of a trusting and relaxed relationship, is confined to members of their own *susu*, that is, to the female line of descent and the brothers of these women in each generation.[3] Toward others, they not only have no social feelings but are distinctly and intensely antisocial and hostile.

The ungregariousness of the Dobuans contrasts sharply with the strong affiliative feelings of the Zuñi Indians. The latter are deeply attached not only to members of their families but also to all individuals in the community. The children "belong" not only to the biological parents, but to the whole village, and are tenderly ministered to by everyone. So completely are the Zuñis attached to one another that their individuality is almost completely sunk in the social whole of their society. This is gregariousness carried

---

[2] See C. Darwin, *The expression of the emotions in man and animals* (D. Appleton and Co., 1890); B. Malinowski, *The father in primitive psychology* (New York: W. W. Norton & Co., Inc., 1927); O. Klineberg, *Social psychology* (Rev. ed.; New York: Holt, Rinehart & Winston, Inc., 1954).

[3] R. Benedict, *Patterns of culture* (Boston: Houghton Mifflin Co., 1934), pp. 132–33.

to the point where individuality and isolation are practically obliterated.[4]

Similar contrasts may be found in many other societies. Gregariousness is by no means universally desired, and in many cultures where it exists, it is confined to very small groups, usually the family.

Americans are often described as a very gregarious people. They like to be with people, and fear isolation. The strong conformist tendency in our society is undoubtedly an element in our sociability and gregariousness. Group belongingness, as it is described, is a source of pleasure and security, and the proliferation of clubs, fraternities, and similar affiliative groups is probably a good index of the intense gregarious needs of most Americans.

Some recent writers have ascribed the gregariousness of Americans to the strong need for friendship and especially love.[5] Certainly the fear of rejection and disapproval is more pronounced in American than in European life. While it is difficult to document the assertion, it seems that the need to belong, to be socially accepted and loved, transcends even the desire to posses money or wealth so often attributed to Americans by many students of our social life. The desire for wealth may indeed be a hopeful means of vouchsafing love and social acceptance.

It is impossible not to note in the American's gregariousness a peculiar nonfulfilling quality. Instead of securing for him the feeling of security and belongingness or of warm companionship and relaxation which he eagerly—even nervously—seeks, its satisfaction becomes a compulsive need for more acceptance and greater social approval. Gregariousness thus increasingly becomes a self-defeating motive, rather than a self-fulfilling need. Gregariousness becomes a kind of compulsion toward ever increasing gregariousness without satisfaction, well-being, or effective self-fulfillment. As in the case of the achievement motive, which is effectively negated by anxiety, the gregarious motive is strongly neutralized by the fear of either not getting the love which a person wants, or losing it once it has been consummated.[6]

---

[4] *Ibid.*, pp. 104–5. More recent studies show that despite attempts to inculcate them with "new" ideas, the basic way of life has changed very little. See G. A. Reichard, The Navajo and Christianity, *Amer. Anthropologist*, 51 (1949), 66–71.

[5] See, for example, K. Horney, *The neurotic personality of our time* (New York: W. W. Norton & Co., Inc., 1937); E. Fromm, *Man for himself* (New York: Holt, Rinehart & Winston, Inc., 1947).

[6] For a discussion of the so-called achievement motive, which we have omitted, see D. C. McClelland, J. W. Atkinson, R. A. Clark, and E. L. Lowell, *The achievement motive* (New York: Appleton-Century-Crofts, Inc., 1953).

While this brief discussion can hardly be conclusive, it suggests that gregariousness is largely a learned disposition, and that it varies with the personality of the individual and with the specific customs of a cultural group. There is the further possibility, especially when we observe it in American society, that gregariousness is in some way related to the complexity of the person and the heterogeneity of the society in which he lives. Complex social structures, with their demand for collective action, the ubiquity of their mass communication, and the inescapable interdependencies of its members, stimulate and reward, however inadequately, the search for togetherness. In short, gregariousness has an important cultural dimension.

COMPETITION. We have already called attention to the fact that competition is not a universal motive, in our brief reference to the cooperative life of the Zuñi Indians in our Southwest. There is overwhelming evidence in many cultures that its presence or absence is culturally determined.

The Kwakiutl Indians on Vancouver Island are known for their fierce competition. Their competitive behavior largely stems from their conception of social rank, the chief prestige bearer in their culture. Competition for prestige conferred by rank is extraordinary by our own standards. Rank is achieved by means of dispensing or destroying property, during periodic feasts known as potlatches.[7] Possessions as such have no special value, but the prerogatives which they bestow upon the individual are of supreme value. Nobility titles are especially prized, and these are obtained through the destruction of blankets, coppers, and other valued objects. The main function of the potlatch is the humiliation of rivals. Through every potlatch a man obtains more prestige as well as more property with which to conduct more potlatches. These ceremonies are fiercely competive bouts in which every participant tries to destroy the prestige of every potential rival. The fear of having their prestige destroyed by the superabundant destruction of property by others is so intense that the humiliated person is not uncommonly driven to taking his own life.

Competition with others, and the status and ego-enhancement which it engenders, is carried to such lengths among the Kwakiutl that it accounts for many homicides. Death is the greatest of

---

[7] Kwakiutl competitive life has been described by many anthropologists, but the best sources are still the following: Benedict, *Patterns of culture*, Ch. 6, and I. Goldman, The Kwakiutl of Vancouver Island, in M. Mead (ed.), *Cooperation and competition among primitive people* (New York: McGraw-Hill Book Co., Inc., 1937), Ch. 6.

insults, and is redressed by the killing of another. The shame of death must be wiped out, and the bereaved simply kills another person in order to remove the humiliation which accompanies it. "Death, like all the untoward accidents of existence, confounded man's pride and could only be handled in terms of shame." [8]

Among the Ifugao of Northern Luzon, competition exists for the purpose of amassing individual wealth, for prestige is measured in terms of individual and family possessions. Competition is largely individualistic, for the culture lays great store by independence and individualism. Since property is held in very high esteem, prestige goes only to those who possess it. Because property invariably goes to the most aggressive individual, the Ifugao is extremely competitive and hostile toward his rivals, even to the point of destroying the latter by trickery or intimidation. Violent behavior is, accordingly, very common. Competitiveness is absent only in reference to a person's own family or other near kin. The Ifugao is thus characterized by a duality of motivational attitudes. Toward kinsmen he must be noncompetitive, but toward all others he must be ruthlessly competitive. His noncompetitive relations with his family often make competition with others more successful, for he can compete with others supported by his family unit. [9]

In the culture of the United States, competition is different still. Indeed, it pervades not only our economic and industrial life but reaches into the home, the school, recreation, occupation, and interpersonal relations. Competitiveness is conceived as a virtue, and the person who shows little of it in his behavior is considered unenterprising and lazy. Since we join it in our minds with the "capitalistic system," which in turn is mistakenly equated with democracy, competition is an extraordinary driving force in American life. Prestige is in no small degree measured by pecuniary standards and by the tangible possessions that money can purchase.

Thus, the desire for possessions, which may at one time have been no more than a means of assuring one a decent subsistence, has taken on the character of neurotic competition. The motive which began as a means of reducing anxiety in the economic sphere only creates more anxiety. The fear of failure which is aggravated by a pervasive competitiveness is a conspicuous mark of the American mentality. "From the parents' fear that their child might turn out to be a sissy, to the dread of being caught

---

[8] Benedict, *Patterns of culture*, p. 216.

[9] I. Goldman, The Ifugao of the Philippine Islands, in Mead, *Cooperation and competition*, p. 179.

not knowing the right answers in school, to the compulsion to keep up with, if not to surpass, the Joneses, the individual is hemmed in by neurotic competition and fear of failure." [10]

If competitiveness were the simple motive that drive-reduction theorists make it, it should carry more satisfaction and less anxiety to the individual than the evidence suggests that it does. But in American society competitiveness tends to produce more anxiety than personal gratification, especially in the middle classes. It generates fear of failure, of loss of status, and of one's competitors. A special quality of this anxiety toward competitors is the fear that they will retaliate. This fear of retaliation betrays not only a dread of losing status, but the suspicion that competitors will repay the individual in kind. [11]

The foregoing descriptions of the competitive motive in human society highlight the fact that it is differently conceived and expressed in different societies. Certainly the goals of competition vary noticeably with different cultural groups. This is not even to mention that competition is absent in many societies, which are motivated by cooperative pursuits instead. Competition differs also with class membership within a culture. In the United States it is, generally speaking, more pronounced in the upper and middle classes than in the lower classes. This is partly explained by the fact that profit in the form of economic goods goes much more to the capitalist than to the laborer. Since the laborer cannot successfully compete with the upper classes who own the means of production, he is more likely to be motivated by conflictual and aggressive behavior. In this he resembles in attenuated form the motivational structure of the poor segments of the Ifugao culture, whose only compensation for their balked wishes lies in any form of reckless behavior which serves as a problem and a threat to their upper-class employees.

COOPERATION. The motives of competition and cooperation have interested ideologists as well as psychologists, and the controversy over their priority have formed the basis of two sharply contrasting economic and political philosophies. So-called capitalistic societies, buttressed by the Darwinian principles of struggle and competition, make competition the cornerstone of their economic philosophy; whereas communist ideology, basing itself on the Marxian and Kropotkian principles of cooperation and mutual aid, perceives competition as the root of all individual and social

---

[10] H. Bonner, *Social psychology: an interdisciplinary approach* (New York: American Book Co., 1953), p. 414.

[11] See Horney, *The neurotic personality of our time*, Chs. 10 and 11.

evils. Ideological conflicts aside, it is a demonstrated fact that the moving force behind the behavior of many people is cooperation, not competition. This is so because, like competition, cooperation is a culturally induced disposition.

Margaret Mead has made the useful distinction between competition and rivalry and between cooperation and helpfulness.[12] This distinction is germane to our comparison of competition and cooperation. In competition the focus of behavior is the goal or end, the competitor being of minor consequence. This distinction no doubt accounts for the fact that economic competition in Western society is essentially impersonal. In rivalry, on the other hand, the center of interest is the opponent and the goal is of minor importance. In cooperative behavior the goal is shared by all in common; whereas in helpfulness the goal is indirectly shared through the relationship of the seeker to the helper.

In order to demonstrate the proposition that the motive of cooperation, like that of competition, is channelized by cultural values and expectancies, we shall describe its forms in a few different societies.

Let us first take a look at the interesting Arapesh people of New Guinea, as described by Mead.[13] These people are co-operative in person-to-person helpfulness. Most things in their society are shared. Children are loved not only by their parents but by all members of the community. No one shows competitive attitudes toward anyone else, so that even the assumption of leadership is made only because they consider it an inescapable responsibility. It does not, however, confer any power or privilege upon the person who is chosen to lead. In a cooperative society like the Arapesh, where status of any kind is nonexistent, it has no value and therefore men do not seek it. The ideal for which they strive is devotion to community welfare. When in the interest of community welfare they reluctantly assume leadership they do not compete with other leaders, for there is no hierarchy of power or status in the community.

While competition is nonexistent, rivalry between men of different localities is socially sanctioned. The Arapesh rivals will announce their intentions to each other, though they may never meet personally. Henceforth they will try to surpass each other in such activities as hunting, food-growing, or pig-raising. This shows that, despite the low esteem in which competition is held,

[12] M. Mead, Introduction, in Mead, *Cooperation and competition*, p. 17.
[13] M. Mead, The Arapesh of New Guinea, in Mead, *Cooperation and competition*, pp. 40–42.

a feeling of rivalry exists. While this behavior deviates from that of the "ideal personality," it is permitted, nonetheless. Here, as everywhere else, provision must be made for a certain amount of aggressive expression. However, this neutralized rivalry does not channelize all competitive aggression, and life is not devoid of anxieties and tensions. This observation is supported by the fact that sorcery against people with whom they are angry is socially sanctioned, and by the frequent quarrels with neighbors over trespassing pigs.

In Maori society of New Zealand, cooperation is combined with individual initiative. People cooperate in agricultural production, but each household owns and cultivates its own field. The products of their labors are deposited in a communal storehouse over which the village chief presides as executor but not as owner. Although cooperation and the promotion of the community's welfare constitute the highest good, each person obtains a high degree of personal reward in the form of recognition from others in the performance of his work for the community. At the same time, individual achievement is shared by all, and excellence in any skill is acclaimed by the entire community. Rivalry is approved when it contributes to the welfare of the entire group.

The blending of cooperation and individual initiative is again evident in the Maoris' provision for escaping the demand for conformity. Although everyone is expected to contribute to the well-being of the community, a person may, when communal demands become too oppressive, seek refuge in nonconformity. Notoriety is not criticized or denied. People may on occasion violate taboos, despite the fact that their violation is normally met with severe punishment. These safety-valves probably make it easier for the Maoris to work for the welfare of others without any serious feelings of antagonism.[14]

An interesting example of the dominance of cooperation over competition in our own society is found in the "communistic" society of the Hutterites in South Dakota. The Hutterites are a Christian religious sect which believes and practices true communism. They permit no private property, and no personal possessions. Everything in the community belongs to it and is used for the welfare of the community as a whole. They lead hardworking, austere, thrifty, and ascetic lives. They believe and practice their own precept: "We are not anxious for money and possessions but only desire godly hearts." In this atmosphere the motive of

---

[14] For a description of Maori society, see B. Mishkin, The Maori of New Zealand, in Mead, Cooperation and competition, pp. 431–53.

competition is never learned, and spirited rivalry is nonexistent. Instead, they are motivated by the need for self-abnegation in the service of their God and their community.[15]

AGGRESSIVENESS. One of the most universal and popular views of man describes him as innately aggressive. On this flimsy notion even wars have been explained and not infrequently justified. We know of no reputable psychologist who believes that warfare is a product of the innately aggressive nature of man. To attribute the cause of war to the inherent aggressiveness of man is to betray a shocking ignorance of its complex institutional character and of the social nature of man. The view that warlikeness is not innate was dispassionately expressed by a large group of psychologists more than fifteen years ago.[16] One writer over sixty years ago persuasively argued that warfare mainly characterizes advanced and complex civilizations.[17] Ethnological evidence tends to support this view, for warfare as it is commonly defined is relatively uncommon in preliterate cultures.[18]

Warlikeness, like most forms of aggression, is socially conditioned, and varies with the presence or absence of social sanctions regarding it. Ethnologists have shown that there are societies in which war is incomprehensible, or in which the language of its people does not even provide words with which to denote it. The aggressive violence which resembles war in the Western sense is often no more than a raiding party for stealing sheep or for capturing women and children to balance their population. In some cases it is a token activity or game, rather than a destructive act.

Since the publication of *Frustration and Aggression* the view has been widely held that frustration leads to aggression.[19] If this were indeed true, aggressiveness would be far more universal than the evidence leads us to expect. However, as we have already indicated on several occasions, not everyone reacts to frustration in the same way. Frustration, we have seen, may impel some people to redouble their efforts to surmount the source of their

15 For a detailed description of the Hutterite way of life, see L. E. Deets, *The Hutterites* (Ph.D. dissertation, Columbia University, 1939).

16 The psychologists' manifesto, in T. M. Newcomb and E. L. Hartley (eds.), *Readings in social psychology* (New York: Holt, Rinehart & Winston, Inc., 1947), 655–63.

17 C. Letourneau, *La guerre dans les diverses races humaines* (Paris: L. Bataille, 1895).

18 See L. T. Hobhouse, G. C. Wheeler, and M. Ginsburg, *The material culture and social institutions of the simpler peoples* (London: Chapman & Hall, Ltd., 1930).

19 See J. Dollard, L. W. Doob, N. E. Miller, O. H. Mowrer, and R. R. Sears, *Frustration and aggression* (New Haven: Yale University Press, 1939).

balked wishes, and others may find it an impetus to constructive solution of their problems, or to creative achievement. The people of Bali, who as infants and young children are deliberately frustrated by their mothers, develop not aggressive but "posturing" behavior, in which ritualistic dances and other graceful uses of the body are highly developed.[20]

The Zuñi Indians do not condone aggression and their life is mostly free of aggressive attitudes and behavior. Even the few crimes which are committed in their society are characterized by highly attenuated aggression. Examples of such nonviolent crimes are witchcraft and disclosure of the secrets of the masked gods to uninitiated boys. Homicide is practically nonexistent and self-mutilation and suicide are acts which not only do not exist but are baffling and incomprehensible. Even their ceremonial whipping is not punitive, but a form of ritualistic exorcism.[21]

The Kwakiutl Indians, whose daily lives are marked by a great amount of interpersonal tension, settle their disputes, as we have seen, in essentially nonviolent forms. The potlatch ceremony is a means of humiliating a rival by competing in the destruction of property. No overt aggression or violence is involved. They fight each other with property instead of fists or weapons.

The Eskimo of Greenland has an even less vigorous method of settling his disputes. He humiliates his adversary by mocking him with words or songs. The two "fight it out" by singing satirical verses at each other. Victory is declared by an evaluating audience, whose judgment is final. The foes abide by the decisions of the spectator and bear no further ill will toward each other.[22]

Among the Ojibwa Indians of Canada aggression takes still another form. Fear of being shamed by others is very pronounced among these people, and much of their violent behavior is a way of repudiating insults. While physical violence is practiced, the most common method of retaliating to insults is some form of shamanism. This consists of such practices as conjuring bad omens, or of petitioning the spirits to starve or paralyze the object of one's aggression.[23]

An instructive example of the cultural determination of aggressive behavior is found in the Comanche Indians. Originally a

[20] See G. Bateson, The frustration-aggression hypothesis, Psychol. Rev., 47 (1941), 350–55; G. Bateson and M. Mead, The Balinese character (New York: New York Academy of Sciences, 1942).

[21] Benedict, Patterns of culture, pp. 100–118.

[22] See A. Goldenweiser, Anthropology (New York: Appleton-Century-Crofts, Inc., 1937).

[23] See R. Landes, The Ojibwa of Canada, in Mead, Cooperation and competition, Ch. 3.

peaceful, unaggressive people, with important changes in their way of life they became extremely warlike.[24]

The Comanches came from the Montana plateaus and in the early eighteenth century were a peaceful and nomadic people. The introduction of the horse and the rifle in the early part of the nineteenth century brought about important changes in their way of life and eventually in their motivational and personality organization. Horses became important not only as currency and a source of prestige, but as riding animals which greatly increased the Comanches' physical mobility. They soon found that the horse could be used for cattle-rustling, a form of behavior in which they were encouraged by the English, French, and Spanish colonies which surrounded them. They thus became middlemen racketeers, killing and plundering the surrounding territory for loot to sell to the white settlers. The French they supplied with slave labor and horses; the Spanish, with cattle, for which the Comanches got guns which they used to eliminate competition from the warlike Apaches.

This warlikeness was in sharp contrast with their former peacefulness. In the Montana plateaus they were humble and harmless people, satisfied to spend their time hunting. Despite the difficult subsistence conditions, the Comanches did not punish anyone for trespassing on their land. Finally, the warlikeness stimulated by their changed conditions came to an end when they were placed in reservations by the expanding United States. Their predatory behavior had no useful function in the enclosed reservations, and they became once more a peaceful people.

The case of the Comanches demonstrates the validity of our central principle, namely, that motives and personality are effectively determined by changes in the cultural milieu in which people live their lives.[25] The changes in motivation from humble and unaggressive to predatory and warlike behavior and back again, can be explained neither by heredity, racial peculiarities, nor individual idiosyncrasies, but only by changes in cultural conditions in different periods of the Comanches' existence.

Not only does aggressiveness exist or not exist, but it is motivated for different reasons in different cultures. The ceremonial whippings among the Zuñis, as we have already indicated, are not expressions of aggressiveness, but are religious practices. The potlatches of the Kwakiutl, as we have shown, are not expressions of

[24] Our data are drawn from R. Linton, The Comanche, in A. Kardiner, *The psychological frontiers of society* (New York: Columbia University Press, 1945), Ch. 3.

[25] The case of the Tanala-Betsileo transformation of motives, briefly described in Chapter 7, is another confirmation of our view.

a basic cruelty, but rather techniques for maintaining their self-esteem by humiliating others who have shamed or humiliated them. The warlike aggressiveness of the Ojibwa Indians are an expression of magical beliefs rather than a desire to destroy their enemies. Their war parties are neither means of self-defense nor of destroying others, but are provoked by a member of their own group who has visions of success in combat. Thus, the person who has had a vision will send invitations to other men in the village to a "smoker." Here he informs them of his vision and asks the others to volunteer for training for war the next year. Those who perform well in these war parties receive feathers, and the bravest is given a virgin bride. An important aspect of this form of aggression is that the individual who has successfully led a war party acquires prestige and an opportunity for organizing a future one. This, then, is not a manifestation of "raw" aggressiveness, but a calculated means of obtaining a reputation and prestige.

Among the Eastern Crees of Canada aggressiveness seems to be found only as a temporary pathological condition in certain individuals. The Crees are an unusually gentle and peaceful people among whom bloodshed is rare and murder entirely unknown. But during frequent famines they show strong cannibalistic tendencies. Because of the gentleness of these people and because of a powerful taboo on human flesh, they experience considerable mental conflict. In severe cases individuals develop an abnormal craving for human flesh and the delusion that they have been transformed into *Wihtikos,* greatly dreaded cannibalistic spirits. During these "seizures" they may attempt to kill, and their behavior has to be restrained by others.[26]

Head-hunting, and other forms of killing, which are associated in the popular mind with cruelty and savagery in primitive man, are by no means always expressions of deep-rooted aggressiveness. Head-hunting may be either a religious practice or a means of securing a coveted trophy which will accrue prestige to its possessor. A man's standing in his community often depends on his heroic exploits in battle, in which the killing of men was incidental or unimportant. Among the Plains Indians, for example, merit was achieved not by destroying an enemy, but by striking him without killing him.[27]

A dozen additional illustrations from primitive societies could easily be furnished to show that aggressiveness is either attenuated,

[26] See J. M. Cooper, Mental disease situations in certain cultures: a new field for research, *J. abnorm. soc. Psychol.,* 29 (1934), 10–18.

[27] R. H. Lowie, *Primitive society* (New York: Boni & Liveright, 1920).

symbolic, or nonexistent. All of them support the view that aggressiveness varies with the culture in which it is practiced. They show that aggressiveness is socially patterned behavior and by no means always a spontaneous and inherent impulse. The combats resemble physical contests more than aggressive wars. They may very well be, as has been suggested, examples of what William James described as the "moral equivalent for war." [28] They are safety valves for the release of pent-up hostility, or forms of sport or amusement free of cruelty and destruction.

ACQUISITIVENESS. Although in Western society man's behavior is extensively regulated by the desire for money and property, in many other cultures this motive is either minor or nonexistent. We have already noted the attitude toward property in some other cultures and found it to be different from our own. The Zuñis, we showed in Chapter 7, have no interest in acquiring property beyond a few personal and household possessions. Again, the form which acquisitiveness takes must conform to the customs of the group. There is, in other words, an approved attitude toward property as there is toward competition, cooperation, aggressiveness, and the like. Even in American society, where the desire for money is paramount, it is not usually an end in itself, but an instrumental motive for the satisfaction of other needs, such as prestige, power, influence, a desirable mate, or a life of ease. Furthermore, as we have already noted, acquisitiveness may be either individual or collective. In competitive cultures, such as our own, acquisitiveness is intensely personal. The money or property for which we strive is for ourselves, or for our wives and children. In cooperative societies, it is distinctly collective. Wealth or property is sought to insure the well-being of the community. It is not to be possessed by one, but by all.

The argument which has been advanced from time to time, that acquisitiveness is inherent and hence universal because it is found in all animals, is happily in eclipse. Arguments for its biological nature rest on the confusion between acquisitiveness and the satisfaction of biological needs. What is posited is not acquisitiveness as defined by psychologists but the drive to satisfy such fundamental needs as food and sex described by biologists.

An illuminating attitude toward possessions is found among the Arapesh, whose cooperativeness we have already described. Almost everything among them is shared. An Arapesh kills an animal in order to give it to a relative. The individual who eats his own kill is by that fact outside the moral pale of the community.[29] Equally instructive is the fact that they not only do not own the land on which they gain their subsistence, but consider themselves as belonging to it. Accordingly, when a plot of land is no longer productive they feel that they must "give" children to the land who will toil upon it after the elders have departed.

To the Trobriand Islander in the South Pacific, food is not only a product to be eaten but an object to be displayed. His prestige in the eyes of the community is determined by how conspicuously his storehouse bulges with perceptible food.[30] To be regarded as a person with little or no food is the greatest of insults. This is in marked contrast to the Kwakiutl's frenzied determination to destroy his accumulated possessions and to be without property at the termination of a potlatch feast.

The profit motive, which is a typical manifestation of acquisitiveness, is lacking in some societies. For example, it is entirely absent among the people of Lesu. Although communal ownership is the rule in this society, certain types of private property, including pigs, are permitted. Pigs are traded, but always as part of a ceremonial feast. Payment for the pigs is made in public, so that in future transactions the seller can never exceed this price. No profit can thus accrue to any seller, for personal aggrandizement would not only violate the custom of communal ownership, but place the profiteer in a superior position in relation to the rest. Since all people live on the same economic level there is no incentive to compete with others for individual profit.[31]

As in the case of the other motives which we have analyzed culturally, acquisitiveness is fundamentally neither a biological nor an individual-psychological phenomenon. Even if it should have a biological basis—a claim that is difficult to establish—it is so thoroughly transformed or frosted over by social rules and expectations that it has for all practical and theoretical purposes become a culturally determined characteristic. An impulse which can be so radically changed by cultural influences can be defined neither in terms of biological structure nor on the basis of individual experience. It is neither an instinct, as conceived by McDougall, a sub-

[29] M. Mead, *Sex and temperament in three primitive societies* (New York: William Morrow & Co., Inc., 1935), pp. 29–30.

[30] B. Malinowski, *Argonauts of the Western Pacific* (New York: E. P. Dutton & Co., Inc., 1922).

[31] See H. Powdermaker, *Life in Lesu* (New York: W. W. Norton & Co., Inc., 1932).

limated libidinal striving, as defined by Freud, nor a secondary drive, as postulated by the radical behaviorists. It is very much a mode of behavior prescribed by a given society on the basis of its own history, traditions, and ideals.

THE SEXUAL MOTIVE. It would be absurd to deny, or even to minimize, the biological basis of sexual desire. We have made our position on this issue clear in Chapter 5. We there stated that the sexual life of man is intricately interwoven with his entire personality, and not only with his biological make-up. Since sex as a physiological drive is common to all animals, it does not tell us much about individual personality. We know that individuals differ in the intensity of their sexual interests and the specific goals toward which they are directed. If this is the case, there is no reason for not assuming that the sexual motive is also profoundly influenced by cultural values and ideals. Ethnological evidence in support of this assumption is enormous. We shall examine some of the evidence in this section.

Attitudes toward sex. Few things are more indicative of the cultural influence on the sexual motive than the institutionalized attitudes toward it. In fact, the impress of culture upon human drives is nowhere more pronounced than in the realm of sexual behavior. It varies from one extreme in which sex is taken for granted to the other where it is hemmed in by rigid and crippling taboos, that is, from a purely physiological act to a religious rite. In our own society the sexual motive is in the absurd position of being at once a degrading function and a romantic fancy.

Men everywhere condone some forms of sexual activity and condemn others. There are people who condone premarital sexual relations but who condemn marital infidelity. Others associate no shame or modesty with the sexual function, but are embarrassed if seen with their hair in disarray, even though they are seen fully naked by others.

The attitudes of the Trobriand Islanders differ remarkably from our own. Their children in play imitate their elders in the act of coitus, while the adults watch them in good-humored enjoyment, very much as Americans observe their children playing cops and robbers. Before marriage young men and women sleep together in bachelors' houses where they have opportunities for finding suitable mates for eventual marriage. After marriage this form of sexual experimentation gives way to monogomous relations which are violated less often than in our own society.[32]

[32] B. Malinowski, *The sexual life of savages in Northwestern Melanesia* (New York: Liveright Publishing Co., 1929), pp. 52–59.

Since nakedness is variously associated with sex it is interesting to note the large variety of attitudes toward it. Needless to say, the American attitude of shame or disgust is nonexistent in some other societies. "Normal" voyeurism and exhibitionism, though widely enjoyed, are nonetheless condemned in our society. On the other hand, in some societies people go about naked without self-consciousness or shame. In terms of their standards of conduct their behavior is normal.[33] In some societies shame may be experienced, not by exposing the genital organs, but of other parts of the body. Klineberg cites an interesting case of an Australian tribe in which the women were not ashamed to appear naked before white men but were exceedingly embarrassed to be seen with their headdresses in disarray.[34]

In our society sexual varietism and chastity are evaluated quite differently than in other societies. Attitudes toward premarital chastity have changed remarkably even in our country, especially since World War I. A number of studies give statistical support to the conclusion that premarital intercourse is considerably on the increase. This increase is particularly noticeable in the case of women, as documented in a number of good studies, extending from Katherine Davis' early investigation to the more recent studies by Kinsey.[35] In some cultures premarital chastity is admired, in others, condemned, and in still others, a matter of indifference. Trobriand women, as we have indicated, condone chastity only after marriage, whereas before marriage sexual intercourse is a sanctioned practice. Indeed, premarital intercourse is regarded as a natural prelude to eventual marriage. With other people still, such as the northern Bantu of Africa, premarital pregnancy is proof of a woman's fertility and increases her chances of marrying.[36] On the island of Dobu a boy freely moves about every night in search of a different girl for a sleeping companion. The only requirement is that he be out of her bed before daybreak.[37] It is not at all uncommon in primitive cultures for men to require proof of fertility before they will permanently attach themselves to a marriage partner.

[33] R. Briffault, The mothers (3 vols.; New York: The Macmillan Co., 1927).

[34] O. Klineberg, Race differences (New York: Harper & Bros., 1935), Ch. 15.

[35] See K. B. Davis, Factors in the sex life of twenty-two hundred women (New York: Harper & Bros., 1929); L. M. Terman et al., Psychological factors in marital happiness (New York: McGraw-Hill Book Co., Inc., 1938); A. C. Kinsey et al., Sexual behavior in the human female (Philadelphia: W. B. Saunders Co., 1953).

[36] J. Roscoe, The northern Bantu (New York: G. P. Putnam's Sons, 1915).

[37] R. F. Fortune, Sorcerers of Dobu: the social anthropology of the Dobu islanders of the Western Pacific (London: Routledge & Co., 1932).

In American society the sexual partner must always be of the opposite sex, and where the practice is otherwise it is condemned as a sexual abnormality. However, this is by no means a universal requirement. Homosexuality is widely practiced throughout the world, and even in the United States it is more extensive than is generally believed. Some societies institutionalize it, whereas others severely condemn it. It was highly esteemed among the ancient Greeks, and Aristotle even suggested its practice as a means of preventing overpopulation.[38] It has a high status in some Asiatic countries and in several Indian tribes of America. Transvestism, or sexual satisfaction obtained from dressing in the clothes of a person of the opposite sex, is accepted in men among the Sioux Indians. Indeed, men may form households together in this manner and greatly enjoy their relationship.

These and other examples too numerous to discuss here show that, while sex is no doubt a basic biological drive, it is modified, expressed, or controlled in accordance with the customs of the group in which it is exercised.

We have altogether omitted the important problems of monogamy, polygyny, and polyandry, all of which challenge the notion of a fixed mode of sexual expression. These are matters which are neither wholly sexual nor entirely moral, for what makes marriage attractive or moral is the manner in which it is defined by a society's customs. Jealousy, romantic love, preferences for sexual partners, and so forth, depend on the sexual attitudes which characterize a given group. They are much more dependent on social convention than most people in American society would be willing to admit. In fine, the sexual drive, like other organic drives, is inordinately modified by social pressures.

EMOTIONS AS MOTIVES. We have by no means exhausted the list of motives which are generated or modified by cultural imperatives. There probably are no functional human impulses which are wholly untouched by the prescriptions of a given culture. Human emotions, particularly, are insufficiently recognized as culturally directed motives. Psychological tradition has described emotions too narrowly as disruptive or disorganizing responses. This may well be a serious error. If motives are energizing agents in human behavior, then emotions, which are inducements to action, have motivational characteristics. Like motives, emotions stimulate and sustain action. This view has been

[38] See J. A. Symonds, A problem in Greek ethics (London: Privately printed, 1901), pp. 30–47.

proposed by Leeper.[39] We are largely in agreement with it, but we minimize the neurophysiological character of emotions and stress their cultural patterning instead.

From this point of view, emotions are fundamental motivating forces in the human personality. Man needs and strives for emotional expression just as he needs and strives to satisfy hunger, sex, or curiosity. Man is everywhere motivated to seek happiness and joy, to play and sing, to avoid sorrow and psychological pain. In omitting these human strivings we may, as Leeper remarks "be doing justice to the motivation of clams, but we are not doing justice to the motivation of human beings, or even to the motivation of chimpanzees or dogs." [40] The person who satisfies his desire to enjoy, to exult, to express grief at the misfortune or death of a loved one, is reducing tension—if that is the descriptive preference—as much as he does when he ingests food to reduce hunger, or cohabits with a given sexual object when he is genitally stimulated. So conceived, emotions have an *organizing* function in human behavior. If we conceive them only as disruptive elements, then such important human motives as love, tenderness, and other *positive* affective processes have no intelligible explanation. To conceive positive emotions as disorganizing, as one has to do in order to be consistent, is contradicted by the evidence of the role of emotions in adding zest and joy to life. It is to shut out a very large segment of behavior: the desire for joy and gaiety, for love, humor, and aesthetic enjoyment. Many human emotions must be perceived as states of being and becoming, as growth motivations, instead of disturbing functions. We laugh or play, sing or cry, because we need these emotions to attain our full being.

The satisfaction and expression of affective motives, like satisfaction and expression of other motives, is influenced by cultural expectancies. This point was clearly made in the brief discussion of the cultural determination of the affective processes, in Chapter 7. Whether or not a person will seek joy and laughter, and how much of each he will express, is stipulated by the customs of the group. Emotions thus add an intensity dimension to goal-directed behavior. The variations in the mode of expressing emotions are due to cultural patterning, as well as to physiological and experiential

[39] R. W. Leeper, A motivational theory of emotions to replace "emotion as disorganized response," *Psychol. Rev.*, 55 (1948), 5–21. Parenthetically, the emotions are a relatively neglected problem in American psychology. Perhaps if we conceived emotions as motivational dispositions they might get a better hearing. Leeper makes out a good case in showing that the standard theory of the emotions is partly cultural in origin.

[40] *Ibid.*, pp. 19–20.

conditions. Emotional reaction over the death of a loved one may be an expression of despair over the loss of a dear one, as in our society, or an intense feeling of anger over death's personal insult, as among the Kwakiutl. Neither the emotion as an affective quality nor as a motivational condition is the same in the two cultures. In the American it is normally a state of grief and a reluctance to surrender a love-object; in the Kwakiutl it is generally a state of resentment and a desire to wreak vengeance upon another who is thought to be responsible for the misfortune of the deceased. Love, grief, resentment, and revenge are not physiological states merely, but motivational conditions as well. Here, as in most things human, customs furnish the standards for individual behavior. Every human motive is intelligible when viewed in the light of social needs and uses.

PERSONALITY IN THE LIGHT OF SOCIALIZED MOTIVES

The preceding and present chapters have described the nature and kinds of motives, their biological origins, and their transformation by the cultural heritage. What do the facts and generalizations of these two chapters regarding motivation tell us about the nature and dynamics of personality? This is the problem to be examined here, though we can give only an incomplete account for the compelling reason that dependable knowledge is very limited.

It is probably true that, just as every event has a cause, so every act has a motive. But this is truistic and does not illuminate the problem of the relation between motive and action. It is partly because of failure to attend to this fact that so much theory and research in motivation and personality are inconsequential. If we take the current behavioristic explanations as models of motivation theory, we are led to believe that nobody does anything of consequence without prospect of a tangible reward. Reinforcement is the sole energizer of action. The companion of this mode of explanation, an integral part of the theory, is the assumption, based on physiological functions, that man acts only because his homeostasis has been disturbed and must return to a state of rest at all cost. Quiescence, rather than self-actualization, becomes in this view the driving force in all behavior. This way of conceptualizing the problem ignores the idiosyncratic nature of the individual and the powerful force of custom. It is a stick-and-carrot account of human action.

Few things in the psychology of motivation are more banal and trivializing than the implicit assumption that man is naturally a passive being, and that he is impelled to action only by an upsetting need. The truth is that while he is alive, action is a property of his being. We are just beginning to learn that nothing troubles an aging person so much as the prospect of becoming inactive. The observation of infants and children should have taught us that action is a law of their being. While he is alive man will engage in action, if only in aimless daydreaming. To say that a man seeks food because he is hungry is a tautology that can obviously explain nothing. Hunger and similar homeostatic drives describe active states of the organism, not impulsions or motives to action. They tell us nothing about a motivated person; and explanations of the foregoing types ignore the directive force of custom. No motive exists as such prior to an act; act and motive are inseparable elements in a behavioral continuum. Nevertheless, too many theories describe motives as if they were independent conditions existing in a kind of abstract vacuum. Our discussion, on the other hand, has consistently stressed the proposition that cultural expectancies pattern activities into ruling habits. Finally, current behavioristic theories of motivation resemble nothing less than a kind of higher and more rigorous theology in which man is conceived as an animal who is impelled to action only by expectations of rewards or pleasant outcomes which hold him in a state of action. It is not an accident that words like "drive," "need," "incentive," and the like, permeate every discussion of human motivation.

MOTIVATION, PERSONALITY, AND CULTURE. Everything that we have so far stressed in this book points to the conclusion that the individual, the group, and the culture of a given social space are three interdependent systems. While some motives unquestionably have a biological origin, they are all transformed by the demands of a specific group in a given culture. Man can choose and even create his own ends only within a social structure. His conations and his personality always mirror the dominant values and expectancies of his culture. Hence, the disputes between the exponents of the supremacy of the individual over his culture and the partisans of the supremacy of the culture over the individual are pointless dichotomizations of the wholeness of the person-in-society. Motive and personality, individual and society, develop concomitantly, not separately. The force of all that we have said in Chapters 6 and 7, and the evidence which we have adduced from comparative cultural studies in the present chapter, is that every individual mirrors within himself the preferred behavior patterns of his group and culture. Thus, in a highly competitive society the anticipation-of-reward account of motivation makes sense, whereas in widely cooperative culture, the same explanation is manifestly absurd. In a group that values economic wealth above all else, men will amass money or property; whereas in a society where the economic incentive finds no sanction, wealth will have no established position. Acquisitiveness, aggressiveness, premarital chastity, and so forth, vary in accordance with the degree of institutional sanctioning which is accorded them. The Arapesh are so unaggressive that they scarcely assert themselves to perform their ceremonies, whereas the Dobu are so suspicious of and hostile to one another that intrasocial tensions are held at a constant boiling point.

DIVERSITY OF SOCIAL ROLES. Differences in motivation between individuals and between cultures are also to be explained by the plurality and divergence of role expectations. In Chapter 7 we discussed the nature of roles and showed that they are extremely culture-bound. Role personality, we pointed out, is the structure of interrelated roles which a person is expected to enact by virtue of his status in his group. Here we wish to make the point that motives are also functions of the roles which a person plays in his group. Since in every society an individual enacts a plurality of roles, and rarely a single one, his motives will vary with the role that he assumes in a given situation. The plurality of roles and the variety of motives which are associated with them are in turn functions of the plurality of group memberships. The variety of roles, and the conflicting motives which they induce, are marked characteristics of complex societies like our own. Unless these facts are taken into consideration and understood, one cannot account for the many transformations of persons and their motives which occur in daily life. Thus, in one group, say his church, the individual will sincerely subscribe to the Golden Rule and be motivated to act according to its dictates. In another group, say his business establishment, he will with equal conviction subscribe to the dictum that "business is business," and crush his competitor. The sovereignty of one motive or impulse over another is a function of the dominance of one role over another, as these are prescribed by the different groups with which an individual is associated.

These forms of behavior are not necessarily instances of unabashed hypocrisy, but the natural consequences of plural and often contradictory group memberships. They show that human motives are inconsistent and contradictory because the cultural values which brought them into being are themselves highly divergent. Most of all, they highlight the fact that changes in social position and role tend to be followed by corresponding changes in the motivational and personality structures of the individual. With every change of group affiliation, corresponding changes in roles followed by correlative transformations of motives take place. This is the meaning of our oft-repeated assertion that motives and personality have no intelligible existence apart from their cultural milieu.

MOTIVATIONAL STRESSES IN CONTEMPORARY LIFE. A popular but well-founded theme of present-day students of American society is the psychological stresses that are the lot of almost everyone today. Man's security and self-esteem, we are told, are continually threatened by the changes and disequilibria of modern life. The anonymity and apparent self-sufficiency which characterize his daily life have given man the gratifying illusion that he is highly individualistic. Social distance seems to increase his desire for affiliation, and his readiness to conform is partly an expression of the need for belongingness. His emotional detachment from others has placed him in the unsatisfying position of being free from social involvements while desiring affiliation with his fellows. Since individuality and self-esteem are best obtained by means of economic success, his strongest motivation is often directed toward the goal of an ever increasing income. Should he be satisfied with but a modest wage or salary or return on his investment, he would very likely be considered as unenterprising and eccentric, characteristics which are easily joined in the minds of most Americans. His rating as a *person* is greatly dependent upon the degree of his motivation toward economic achievement.

This relentless struggle to get ahead involves frequent changes in group affiliations and in the performance of skillful role behavior. Frequently the changes in group membership and role enaction are accompanied by emotional and volitional stresses, reactions to which produce tangible personality characteristics. Aside from developing neurotic symptoms, which lie outside the limits of our interest in this book, the constant emotional and motivational shifts tend to produce definable personality structures. The most common personality organization, and the most highly esteemed, is the "flexible" individual who can adjust himself to almost any condition. This capacity of adjustment at a moment's notice has almost become synonymous with good mental health. The more self-actualizing person, who changes his personality color more in accordance with his self-needs, is often rated as resistant, uncooperative, and even queer. Yet the latter more frequently than not enhances the quality of the culture which too readily rejects him as a person. Some individuals orient their motivational and emotional life around negative attitudes of cynicism toward and distrust of the values and persons with whom they must perforce interact. Still others become shallow and insipid individuals without goals or character—the flotsam and jetsam of a confused and unintegrated life.

These are but the most obvious manifestations of motivational and personality structures in contemporary American life, but they are sufficient to illuminate the close relation between motives and their cultural stimulation and transformation. Whatever the biological structure in which the individual's motives may be embedded, as functioning processes which give him direction they are modified in accordance with the dominant customs and values of the culture in which he has his being. Society, culture, and the motivated person are inseparable and indivisible. Where they fail to touch one another, or where they have been torn asunder, or where they are damaged by a blind and senseless nonconformity, the result is invariably pathological or catastrophic.

These are the more or less factual aspects of the problem of the cultural determination of motives and personality. Only a few words of a speculative nature will be added. Summed up they form a rather dim prospect. Motives and personality are so disproportionately shaped by cultural demands that today the individual is all but lost in their all-embracing influence. The ideal man, the self-fulfilling individual, is no longer the center of social and psychological interest. Instead, society is determined, with a strong and generous nudge from psychology, to fit everyone into the mold of the "happy," "successful," and "well-adjusted" man, the man without problems, as Maslow has astutely described him. This is a pale substitute for the ideal man of other cultures and other times: the saint, the hero, the gentleman, or the mystic.[41]

CONCLUSION

In this and the preceding chapters we delineated those aspects of the problem of motivation and its relation to the psychology of personality which are essential to a dependable knowledge of both. If any reader still approached the problem of motivation from a nativistic view, we have supplied him with sufficient evidence to shatter his views. We have described the motivational process in terms of the individual's impulsion toward biologically, psychologically, and culturally determined goals. Whereas every human striving has a history, its satisfaction is determined by the integrated properties of the biological organism in a social field at the mo-

[41] A. H. Maslow, Personality problems and personality growth (Unpublished manuscript, 1954), p. 3.

ment. The "dynamics" of human behavior, of which we hear so much these days, is a description of the potent relations between the biological individual and his social-cultural heritage. Man's pursuit of desired ends makes up not only a large area of his personality but a significant aspect of his total culture. If there were no human motives there would be no culture; and if there were no culture our motives would be different from what they are. "We would still be hungry and thirsty, we would seek the release of other psychological tensions, but the manner of expressing them would be different. Society channelizes our basic drives into prescribed satisfactions and so transforms them into forms of behavior which, while historically connected with the organic urges, are markedly different from them. If behavior is predictable at all, it is predictable only when we know both the tensions which impel a person to action and the cultural situation in which the tensions operate." [42]

It is a mistake, however, to think of culture as only a channelizer of motives. It also creates new motives, just as the individual through various forms of self-discovery molds his own. Culture, no less than the individual, is a creative, not a static, force in human behavior. The desire for power, or wealth, or fame are motivating forces in individuals not only because society sets great store by them, but also because they are his means for actualizing himself as a person. The function of motives is not only to satisfy organic needs but even more to promote society's interests. Thus, biological self-preservation is transformed into social well-being.

The unremitting stress in this chapter on the cultural transformation of biological impulses may very well convince the reader that motives are wholly cultural. Such a conclusion would be a serious mistake. Not only does every society provide its members with a latitude of permissive behavior, thus allowing for individual differences, but every healthy individual resists enculturation. No creative person is ever completely formed by the molding forces of society.

Action, we said, is a property of man's being and does not account for human motives. The difference between action as such and action as a motivating force lies in the fact that motives are goal-directed actions. A goal is either set up by the customs of the group or previsioned by the individual himself. In other words, a motive is not a stimulus to action; action is a "given" which a motive directs along lines or toward goals desired by the individual or required by the culture.

[42] Bonner, *Social psychology*, p. 170.

CHAPTER 11

Language and Personality

The belief that human mental life and the organization of personality are reflected in, or effectively shaped by, the linguistic structure of a people is widely held, but the exact relation between them is difficult to establish with certainty. The relationship no doubt exists, for if it is true, as has been convincingly demonstrated, that social norms shape our attitudes and thinking processes, then personality, conceived as the organization of ideas, attitudes, emotions, traits and so forth, must likewise be significantly influenced by the linguistic norms of a culture. It is no accident that so many words in the Indo-European languages are self-referential. The personal pronoun looms large in the English language, and references to personal behavior and attitudes abound in common linguistic usage. Psychological and anthropological studies leave little doubt in one's mind that the relationship between language and personality is so close that the two terms cannot be intelligibly separated. An intimate knowledge of social behavior and the anthropological study of language, as well as an acquaintance with the personal idioms of literary styles, can only strengthen the conviction that the human personality cannot be understood apart from the linguistic structure through which every adult concepualizes and orders his experience. We would go further and state that the linguistic organization of experience is the supreme example of human behavior, of personality in action.

This view that personality is molded by language, while now almost commonplace in the psychology of language, emerged no more than fifty years ago. Before the turn of the century, and for

some time thereafter, language was almost exclusively viewed as
a vehicle of abstract thought, quite removed from the concrete
experience and personal make-up of the individual. Language was
an aspect of the larger process of thinking and reasoning, not of
total behavior. Thanks to the early investigations of Cooley,
Dewey, and Mead, and later of F. H. Allport, Markey, DeLaguna,
Sapir, and others, the role of language in human behavior has become an important dimension of the psychology of personality.[1]
Still more recently, the writings of the semanticists, like Korzybski
and Johnson, though largely oriented toward the misuse of language
in pathological behavior, and of Morris, dealing with the science
of signs and "behavioristics," have significantly contributed to the
psychology of language.[2]

Our purpose in this chapter is obviously not to cover the whole
area of the psychology of language, but to describe the role of
language in personality formation and personality expression. This
is the more difficult undertaking, since students of the psychology of
language have tended to apply their findings less to personality
organization than to behavior in general.

There now exist sufficient data to permit us to say that, although
language is a cultural product, it tells us a great deal about the
individual. Just as a person's attitudes, ideas, and ways of adjusting and solving problems tell us a great deal about him, so do his
linguistic habits and characteristic modes of verbal expression. In
a world where verbal symbols are effective ways for the individual
to relate himself to others and to the world around him, to learn to
grapple with his daily problems in an intelligent way, language is
not only an instrument for communicating thought but an important
determinant and expression of his total psychological being. Because language is commonplace, we tend, even in psychology, to be
unperceptive of the richness of the interaction between it and personality. Thus, in view of the evidence which we shall present
in this chapter, it is not too much to assert that a knowledge of

---

[1] See C. H. Cooley, *Human nature and the social order* (New York: Charles Scribner's Sons, 1902); J. Dewey, *Human nature and conduct* (New York: Henry Holt
& Co., Inc., 1922); G. H. Mead, *Mind, self and society* (Chicago: University of Chicago Press, 1934); F. H. Allport, *Social psychology* (Boston: Houghton Mifflin Co.,
1924); J. F. Markey, *The symbolic process and its integration in children* (New
York: Harcourt, Brace and Co., 1928); G. A. DeLaguna, *Speech: its function and development* (New Haven: Yale University Press, 1927); E. A. Sapir, Speech as a personality trait, *Amer. J. Sociol.*, 32 (1927), 892–905.

[2] A. Korzybski, *Science and sanity* (Lancaster, Pa.: Science Press, 1933, and later
editions); W. Johnson, *People in quandaries* (New York: Harper & Bros., 1946);
C. Morris, *Signs, language and behavior* (Englewood Cliffs, N.J.: Prentice-Hall, Inc.,
1946).

how an individual has assimilated and is using language to adjust himself to his problems, of how he handles his experience and actualizes himself verbally, gives us a knowledge of the nature of personality no less dependable than that of some other reliable techniques. Indeed, compared with many quantitative, analytical, statistical, and morphological studies of linguistic units, like phonemes and morphemes, for example, the "stylistic" investigation of language and personality often yields a more subtle picture of the total individual.[3]

NATURE AND ORIGIN OF LANGUAGE

When psychologists speak of the environment, they usually refer to persons, objects, and events external to an organism. An important part of this environment, implicit in all psychological descriptions but insufficiently expressed, is its symbolic or verbal content. This content may be denoted as man's *verbal environment*. We describe it in this manner because a large part—perhaps the larger part—of the environment is reached only through verbal cues, or language behavior. The verbal environment is the natural environment transformed by means of words or symbols. Customs, traditions, beliefs, and other nonmaterial social forms are crystallizations or fixations of verbal behavior, and verbal behavior is in turn conditioned or transformed by them. While this reciprocity is never absolute, it is ubiquitous. The capacity of verbal behavior is unquestionably inherent in man, and this truth is supported by the fact that no lower animal possesses it. As a system of sounds and symbols for communication, however, language is a thing of invention and culture. As such it forms the verbal environment of every individual, although it differs from culture to culture. It transforms the biological individual into a social person and it makes life for everyone intelligible and meaningful by providing him with a common universe of discourse. It is thus at once an individualizing and a socializing agent in the psychological life of the human person. An individual organism becomes a human person when his preverbal or elemental impulses acquire verbal direction. This is further confirmed in the instance of verbal breakdown in pathological behavior. Unlike the preverbal state of the infant, pathological behavior is a condition in which the individual creates new symbols, such as neologisms, uses the old ones in

---

[3] The latter problem will also be considered in the context of expressive behavior, in the next chapter. *Phonemes* are the speech sounds in a linguistic system; *morphemes* are its smallest meaningful units which remain constant in meaning, such as, "girl," "girlish."

idiosyncratic ways, or ceases to communicate symbolically altogether.

A NOTE ON THE ROOTS OF LANGUAGE. Recent psychology is increasingly less concerned with the unsolved problem of the origin of language and much more with its function in the present behavior of the individual. Nevertheless, a few words regarding its source, even though largely speculative, help one to appreciate the difficulty of the problem and highlight its perennial attraction.

Inasmuch as our aim is merely to suggest and not to explain the origin of language we need not go beyond the nineteenth century for illuminating insights. The lively—one might almost say acrimonious—controversy over the origin of language, initiated by Müller, the German philologist who taught at Oxford University, gave rise to several significant theories. Müller's view, which evidence and persistent criticism forced him reluctantly to modify, held that language is coextensive with thought. There can be no thoughts without words. We must assume, therefore, that language arose when thought was first initiated; or, more in keeping with Müller's view, thought had to wait for language before it could arise. Language is thus the indispensable condition of all human thinking and human consciousness.[4]

Herder, the German philosopher of history who explained man's development by means of a "law of progress," held the interesting but highly speculative view that human language is a product of man's practical need to denote objects of his experience. The denotation was made by imitation of the sounds which man heard in nature. Herder based his notion on the observation that the vocabularies of young children and preliterate peoples contain many words which imitate the sounds made by animals and natural phonomena, such as the barking of dogs, the "singing" of birds, and the splashing of water.[5]

Wundt, the German psychologist who founded experimental psychology, on the other hand, found the origin of language in gesticulation. He observed that the child, in trying to communicate his wants to others, would use bodily and facial movements, such as pointing and grimacing. Such gestures are, of course, also used by adults, especially when they do not possess a common language. Gestures are primarily expressions of emotions, but they may refer

[4] M. Müller, Lectures on the science of language (New York: Charles Scribner's Sons, 1862).

[5] J. G. Herder, Abhandlung über den Ursprung der Sprache, in Herder's Sämmtliche Werke (Berlin: Weidmannsche Buchhandlung, 1877–1913), Vol. 5.

to any form of nonverbal symbolic behavior.[6] In fairness to his predecessors, especially Lazurus and Steinthal, it should be added that like them, Wundt was trying to give a social-psychological account of language. All three held that language is determined largely by man's social needs, and that language in turn conditions man's social needs.[7] The universal laws of the mind, which all three were trying to formulate, are to be found in man's important social activities, especially in his language.

A plausible theory of the origin of language is found in the views of the French philologist Noiré and F. H. Allport, the American "behavioristic" social psychologist. They extend and confirm Wundt's view, but from different directions, namely, philosophically by Noiré and behavioristically by Allport. According to Noiré, language originates in the effect of objects on the sensory receptors, that is, in the ability of man to transmit his sensory impression to others. Language is thus the act of communicating, first, emotional gestures, and later, verbal symbols. This is in line with the now generally accepted view that laryngeal sounds preceded articulate speech in man's evolution. Expressions of fear or anger, for example, are means by which both men and lower animals control the behavior of others. This control of others by laryngeal sounds was the earliest stage in the growth of human language. Through laryngeal articulation man produced random symbols. He produced auditory-vocal responses through hearing them articulated in others. Whereas the articulation was at first random and accidental, it was soon duplicated deliberately. As Allport clearly explained it, the ear-vocal reflex of the spoken word was conditioned in the speaker by the sight of the object which was then evoked in another individual who was similarly conditioned. Success in this communication to and control of another with reference to the object would fixate the conditioned ear-vocal reflex as a permanent habit. Later, what was originally conditioned as a habit was used deliberately to create and adopt new words. In short, what was initiated accidentally was now achieved by design.[8]

From this view to the theory of G. H. Mead is but a small, yet important, step. He too begins with an analysis of gestures and physical movements, but goes beyond them to stress the fact that

[6] W. Wundt, *Elements of folk psychology*, trans. E. L. Schaub (London: George Allen & Unwin, Ltd., 1928), Ch. 1.

[7] This idea was basic to the founding in 1860 by M. Lazarus and H. Steinthal of the famous journal devoted to language and psychology, *Zeitschrift für Völkerpsychologie und Sprachwissenschaft*.

[8] See L. Noiré, *The origin and philosophy of language* (Chicago: The Open Court Publishing Co., 1917); F. H. Allport, *Social psychology*.

in human speech the gestures become *significant symbols*. In communication by means of significant symbols the individual not only responds to the gestures or symbols of another but interprets the meaning of his own gestures. This is communication through *conscious* meaning. In this form of communication or verbal behavior each person in the communicating act is conscious of what he is doing. Human language is thus a form of anticipatory or preparatory behavior, as we shall show in more detail later. Language, in short, is a form of self-communication as well as communication with others.[9]

The net result of the foregoing investigations, as well as of others too numerous to expound in these pages, is extensive agreement regarding the deeply social nature of language. Language, in both its origin and its function, is a technique of communication. It is at once a vehicle of thought and a means of influencing the thoughts of others. Thus, whether language is viewed through the eyes of a psychologist, anthropologist, linguist, or philosopher, it is invariably perceived as a social act in which the interlocutors mutually influence one another and themselves.[10]

NONVERBAL LANGUAGE. In the preceding discussion we were dealing with "true" language, or language as a conscious communicative act. However, language does not emerge full-blown in the simple behavior of a child. Months before he acquires the language and speech habits of his cultural group, a child engages mostly in what Piaget has termed "autistic," rather than verbal, thinking. This is the prelogical, rather than the logical, stage in the child's linguistic development.[11] Autistic thinking is pictorial rather than verbal, and is not communicated by overt language. It is in no way socialized, as true speech is, but is guided directly by the child's immediate and unconscious needs. Autistic thought is not adapted to reality, but is a "dream world of imagination." It is thus strictly individual and noncommunicable, and works chiefly by images.[12]

[9] Mead, *Mind, self and society*, p. 42 f. It is historically interesting to note that Socrates, as described by Plato, expressed the same view in his well-known remark: "When the mind is thinking, it is talking to itself." For the latter, see Plato's *Theaetetus.*

[10] See further B. Malinowski, *A scientific theory of culture* (Chapel Hill: University of North Carolina Press, 1944); O. Jespersen, *Language, its nature, development, and origin* (New York: The Macmillan Co., 1922); DeLaguna, *Speech: its function and development.*

[11] J. Piaget, *The language and thought of the child,* trans. M. Gabain (New York: Humanities Press, Inc., 1952). This book was first published in French in 1923, and although it has been criticized regarding particulars, it is still by all odds the most plausible account of the development of language and thought in children.

[12] *Ibid.,* p. 43.

Piaget's description of autistic or preverbal thinking is similar to Freud's analysis of unconscious mental processes. Early in his formulation of the unconscious mind Freud stressed the fact that much of adult thinking, and not only that of children, is archaic and pictorial rather than verbal. The language of imagery pervades much of our daily thinking. In this sense some of our thinking resembles dreams, and what is true of dream thinking holds for a sizable area of our ordinary thinking. Without words, thoughts are like dreams; and like dreams, nonverbal thinking is marked by *condensation* and *displacement*. In dreams and reveries thoughts are telescoped into new units; what is retained in the new unit is always material that will not challenge conscious and verbalized thoughts. This is condensation.

Displacement, on the other hand, is a "transference of accent," in which a latent thought or image is replaced by something not immediately connected with, or not recognized to be associated with, the complex of conscious and verbalized thoughts. This process renders the dream, or the dreamlike thought, acceptable to the individual's consciousness, for it makes the dream or the thought strange and unintelligible to the person experiencing it. What he cannot understand he cannot be held accountable for, and so unpleasant or threatening thoughts are made bearable.[13]

The gist of the foregoing discussion is that human thought always employs symbols, but the symbols need not be verbal. Indeed, much human thinking goes on in the form of pictorial symbols. Generally speaking, conscious or directed thought tends to occur in verbal symbols, whereas unconscious thought, whether in reverie, dream, or creativeness, proceeds by means of nonverbal or pictorial imagery.

The relation between language, thought, and imagery has interested psychologists for a long time. Just as rudimentary thought may take place without words, so thought processes may exist without imagery. Nevertheless imagery, defined as incipient perception, plays an important role in linguistic thinking. Incipient perception is a form of imagination, a symbolic process in which an absent stimulus can initiate a present response. It is a well-known fact that imagination is very active in children, especially in the period before they acquire an active vocabulary. However, the process of socialization curtails their imaginative activities, and compels them to substitute symbolic manipulation for them. In this way their thinking becomes increasingly organized and di-

---

[13] S. Freud, *New introductory lectures on psycho-analysis* (New York: Carlton House, 1933), pp. 33–39.

rected by the linguistic forms of their culture. There is great value in this, despite its inhibiting effect, for with the growth of verbal behavior children learn to cooperate with others and are prepared for the educative process required by their group.

Having recognized the great importance of learning the language of the group, we must return once more to the force of imagination in the lives of growing children. Socialization, we have said, tends to inhibit the free play of imagination by requiring children to substitute appropriate verbal symbols for their imagery. Now, while it is true that verbalization of subjective feelings, especially conflicts and anxieties, helps one to resolve them, nevertheless, nonverbal and imaginative activities are both therapeutic and constructive. Whereas adults handle their conflicts and anxieties by means of verbalization, the child with his limited linguistic skill must rely heavily on imaginative manipulation of his problems. In describing the imaginative life of the child, Jersild stresses its value as a means of dealing with reality, of overcoming vicariously the child's limitations, and of transcending the limitations of time and space, thereby enabling him to bring the world more into line with his own desires and wishes.[14]

Nevertheless, the imaginative, nonverbal life of the child is full of psychological dangers. Childhood is studded with insecurities and anxieties. It is not surprising, therefore, that, since these insecurities and anxieties are largely unverbalized and uncontrolled, they tend to persist in their original form. Indeed, evidence shows that unverbalized experiences are more resistant to extinction than verbalized habits.[15] They persist because in their formation they were not subject to the same symbolic control and extinction which characterizes adult behavior. An adult can literally talk himself out of learnings and memories.

LANGUAGE AS PREPARATORY AND INTENTIONAL ADJUSTMENT. In the past, students of language and thought based their conclusions too much on the observation of these activities in the abstract thinking of scientists, philosophers, and other professional thinkers. Too often verbal thinking on the part of these individuals was an activity engaged in for its own sake. Theories of language and thought were, accordingly, incomplete and one-sided. The basic functions of verbal thinking, those of adjusting the individual to his world, of adapting means to ends, and of manipulating his en-

[14] A. T. Jersild, *Child psychology* (4th ed.; Englewood Cliffs, N.J.: Prentice-Hall, Inc., 1954), Ch. 15. For his discussion of the development of language in the child, see Ch. 12.

[15] E. R. Hilgard and D. G. Marquis, *Conditioning and learning* (New York: Appleton-Century-Crofts, Inc., 1940).

vironment, were thus too often neglected. There was too little awareness of the indubitable fact that language is a precondition to establishing effective contact with the world. There was no conscious recognition by students of language and thought that both the child and adult make their wants known and satisfied largely by means of verbal communication. But the purpose of language, as of thought, is not only to understand the world abstractly, but to anticipate, modify, and redirect the events in it. Man has both survived and "progressed," not primarily because he has frozen the world into scientific and verbal images, but because he has used language as an instrument of adjustment and self-enhancement.[16]

On the other hand, recent students of language and thought have drawn their conclusions from a one-sided consideration of language development in children. Although this source, generally speaking, provides us with a better knowledge of a living language than the abstractions of professional thinkers, it is by its very nature largely limited to egocentric and unsocialized communication. Language as a functional instrument of communication is best exemplified in the adaptive activities of normal adults. Viewed from this standpoint, language acts primarily neither in the service of intellectual abstraction nor as an expression of childhood wishes, but in the interest of an effective mastery of the world around us. To this end, the anticipatory and preparatory function of language is of primary importance. At any rate, this aspect of language has an immediate relevance to human personality not characteristic of the other views. Psychology has committed the error of basing itself too much upon the behavior of geniuses, madmen, and children.

By language as a form of *preparatory and intentional adjustment,* we mean that it serves to anticipate the oncoming acts of another. By verbal indication to ourselves of the intentions of another we can adapt ourselves to his behavior. By verbal indication of our own intention to another person we assist him in anticipating our own actions. In this way communication between two persons is established. Verbal communication is thus a means of short-circuiting, compressing, or substituting for overt bodily behavior. It makes for economy in overt behavior, for instead of using gestures or other bodily expressions to arouse responses in another, we employ verbal symbols. In anticipating another person's behavior

[16] In fairness to the view here criticized, it must be pointed out that almost from the beginning of his career John Dewey, although himself a professional thinker, did not commit this error. In his view, the function of language and thought is to control and adjust one to the world of reality. See, for example, the central theme of his *Human nature and conduct,* which we have already cited.

through language, an individual becomes involved in that person's behavior. He can anticipate the other person's action because his own words affect him in much the same way they do the other person. Linguistic thinking always involves symbols which elicit the same response in others that they evoke in ourselves. "A person who is saying something," as G. H. Mead profoundly observed, "is saying to himself what he says to others; otherwise he does not know what he is talking about." [17]

Even animal gestures in a crude way exhibit anticipatory or preparatory adjustment, just as the glance of an eye or the stance of the body perform similar functions in human beings. When two hostile dogs approach each other, both growling and snapping, each tries to anticipate the other's action and to adjust himself to it in such manner that he will gain the maximum striking potential against the other. It is in some such reciprocal anticipation of each other's intention in a "conversation of gestures," in mutual physical adjustment that language arises and functions.

Language is thus seen to be a cooperative process in which the speaker's words and sentences reveal what he intends to do in relation to another person. In this process, when one person responds to the verbal cue of another he introjects the other's attitude within himself. This is what we mean when we say that two persons understand each other. Verbal behavior consists not only in stimulating others, but in self-stimulation. A word or a sentence is a communicative act not only when it affects or controls the behavior of others, but also when it affects or controls the speaker himself. "The act of addressing another person is the act of addressing oneself. We not only respond to another individual, but we use the apprehended stimulus from another by responding to it ourselves." [18]

The preparatory adjustment function of language is thus seen to be double-edged. It enables an individual to anticipate and prepare to meet and understand the acts or intentions of another person and his own acts and intentions at the same time.

THE PROBLEM OF MEANING. The nature of language, and especially the relation between language and thought, is illuminated by an understanding of the role of *meaning*. This problem, while extensively discussed by both linguists and philosophers, is tradi-

[17] Mead, *Mind, self and society*, p. 147. For a related way of viewing this matter with emphasis on perception, which we shall examine later, see R. Tagiuri and L. Petrullo (eds.), *Person perception and interpersonal behavior* (Stanford, Calif.: Stanford University Press, 1958).

[18] H. Bonner, *Social psychology: an interdisciplinary approach* (New York: American Book Co., 1953), p. 46.

tionally a psychological topic. There are numerous psychological theories of meaning, but none is completely convincing or widely held. Moreover, the problem of meaning has grown so complex with every formulation that only a cursory analysis is possible here. Before stating our own view of the meaning of meaning, it will be instructive to consider two or three others with which it is compatible, but which omit its rich overtones.

Substitution theory. This is a "behavioristic" explanation of meaning which utilizes the well-known principle of conditioned response. According to this view, a word or a symbol is a substitute for the object which is being symbolized. If an object is associated frequently enough with a given symbol, the symbol will in time evoke the same response as the object itself. The symbol now *stands* for the object. However, as Miller has recently pointed out, the very simplicity of this explanation has prevented its advocates from seeing its untenability. More sophisticated investigations have shown that symbols do not always elicit the same responses as do the objects they symbolize.[19]

A highly sophisticated substitution theory based on operant conditioning has been proposed by Skinner.[20] Through operant conditioning a symbol becomes a substitute for an object because it is reinforced or rewarded. Thus, when the child wants the ball lying out of his reach, he may utter cries for it to his mother. The mother picks up the ball, utters the word "ball," and hands it to the child. Since the mother's behavior of handing the ball to the child was followed by the pleasure of reward, he will ask for the ball by attempting to utter the word "ball" on future occasions.

This is not fully convincing, and it cannot be viewed as an explanation of the nature of meaning. For Skinner, the problem of meaning is not crucial, and in any case it can be accounted for only in the larger context of verbal and nonverbal behavior. Meaning is not a separate problem, and reinforcement, which accounts for verbal behavior in general, is sufficient to explain any form of behavior.

Dispositional theory. Morris' theory, like our own, stresses the *preparatory* nature of linguistic behavior. A word or symbol is not

---

[19] G. A. Miller, Psycholinguistics, in G. Lindzey (ed.), *Handbook of social psychology* (Reading, Mass.: Addison-Wesley Publishing Co., Inc., 1954), Vol. 2, Ch. 19.

[20] B. F. Skinner, *Verbal behavior* (New York: Appleton-Century-Crofts, Inc., 1958). In operant as distinguished from classical or respondent conditioning, the appropriate response to a stimulus is followed by reinforcement (or reward) which increases the likelihood that the appropriate response will occur on subsequent stimulation.

fundamentally a substitute for an object but a *tendency* or *disposition* to act in a certain way toward the object. Signs, which include "signals" and "symbols," control or direct behavior in the way objects would exercise control *if* they were present. Meaning is thus not an independent problem of language but is explained by the symbol-process and signal-process. Meaning lies in the substitution of a sign or a symbol, not for an object, but for another sign or symbol. Morris believes that the term "meaning" is not a basic concept in the science of language, for it lacks the precision necessary for scientific analysis. Like Skinner, Morris conceives meaning as part of the more general problem of behavior, and not of the psychology of language only. " 'Meaning', he says, "signifies any and all phases of sign-processes (the status of being a sign, the interpretant, the fact of denoting, the significatum), and frequently suggests mental and valuational processes as well." For these reasons the science of language would do well to dispense with the term altogether and to use "special terms for the various factors which 'meaning' fails to discriminate." [21]

Meaning as a phase in the total act. Although meaning cannot be adequately defined in scientific terms, the present writer cannot accept Skinner's view that it is a pseudo-problem nor Morris' belief that we can dispense with the term. Our own view is most akin to the views of John Dewey and G. H. Mead, and is as "objective" as any behaviorist could wish.[22] We believe meaning can best be defined in terms of the *significant symbol*—a symbol which arouses in an individual using it the same response it arouses in the individual toward whom it is directed. In this process—in this *social act*—the individual takes the attitude of another toward his own gestures or symbols. Every symbol comes to stand for a particular response, that is, for the response which it simultaneously elicits in the individual making it and the individual for whom the symbol is intended. All language is symbolic, even a dog's bark, but the symbol takes on meaning only when the individual reacts to it as he reacts to others who are using it. The symbol, we say, has become *significant*. The particular response for which the symbol stands is its *meaning* as a significant symbol. From this viewpoint, verbal or conceptual thinking is the act of internalizing in our experience the external symbolic conversation which we hold with

[21] Morris, *Signs, language and behavior*, p. 19.

[22] See Mead, *Mind, self and society*, pp. 75–82; Dewey, *Human nature and conduct*, pp. 82–94, and *Experience and nature* (New York: W. W. Norton & Co., Inc., 1929), Ch. 5.

another individual. The internalized symbol is a significant symbol —as distinguished from a signal or a sign substituting for an object or an act—because it has the same *meaning* for all persons in a given social group.

The meaning of meaning is thus found in the act of adjustment of individuals to one another by means of significant symbols. Meaning, in brief, always originates and is implicit in the structure of the total social act.

It should be noted that in this explanation of meaning both anticipatory or preparatory acts and imagery play important roles. "Meaning is the anticipation of an act not yet made, but which might be made, in response to objects or persons in one's environment. The person anticipates or 'imagines' the object not present or the act of another not yet performed." [23] Meaning thus originates and exists in the relationship of a given stimulus or symbol and the later phases of the social act of which the stimulus or symbol is an early, if not the initial, phase.[24] In this sense meaning is an *objective* relationship between phases of the social act. As Mead points out, it is not a mere psychic addition to the act, and not an idea as traditionally conceived.[25]

Whereas we reject both Skinner's and Morris' notion of the superfluity of the problem of meaning, we agree with their view that it is a part—but an *integral* part—of the more inclusive area of human behavior. Meaning is always a complex phenomenon, for it not only originates in the intricate social act but also gains breadth and inclusiveness from it. Meanings form associations with other meanings, as well as with objects and social relations. These associations give meaning to other meanings, and to objects and relations. The understanding of an object or event is enriched when we can connect it with other objects or events. A simple illustration of this is found in the formal definition of words, wherein one word is defined by another one and the latter by still another one, and so on. The cognitive and communicative character of language, however, lies not primarily in the relation of words to one another, but in their capacity of organizing human experience. The very nature of thought can be understood only in a context of meaning, and meaning alone can render human thought intelligible.

[23] Bonner, *Social psychology*, p. 67.
[24] See Mead, *Mind, self and society*, p. 76.
[25] *Ibid.*, p. 76.

CONCLUDING REMARKS ON LANGUAGE. Whatever may be the explanation of the nature and origin of language, there can be no doubt whatsoever that it has played a significant role in the evolution of psychological man and of human society. Although thinking may function without words—an assertion which cannot be directly established or disproved—mental behavior characteristically moves forward by means of verbal symbols. Thought is, indeed, as Angyal has expressed it, "the symbolizing function of the organism." [26]

One need only consider the familiar contrast between men and other animals to sense the vast importance of language in human behavior. In the absence of language or any organized system of symbols, an animal's behavior is confined to exceedingly narrow limits. By means of cries, gestures, or bodily expressions an animal can, for example, warn others of an impending danger. However, it cannot generalize this experience in such a way as to communicate danger in the abstract. It is limited to conveying to other animals only each specific danger. Having no words or abstract symbols an animal is limited to communicating specific experiences de novo, over and over. Every animal must learn to meet every novel situation for itself. To use Linton's illustration, a female animal can impress upon her young an immediate danger represented by men or guns by her terror or haste to hide or run, but she cannot communicate to them about men or guns in the abstract.[27] An animal's communications are always bound to the immediate situation. One animal may threaten another animal in a specific circumstance, but it cannot convey to still another animal a situation in which the act of threatening took place.

In concluding, we would only point out that the kind of knowledge which we have expounded in this chapter has not been obtained in the animal laboratory. And yet, for the study of personality it is the most crucial in the whole area of human behavior. As we shall see, personality largely grows out of the verbal or symbolic interaction of two or more individuals within a given cultural milieu. In man, the bond between the internal world of thought and the external world of objects and persons is effected by the symbolic system which we call language. Man's fulfillment of his stature as a person is thus greatly facilitated by the self-and-other references of his verbal behavior.

[26] A. Angyal, *Foundations for a science of personality* (New York: Commonwealth Fund, 1941), p. 58.

[27] R. Linton, *The study of man* (New York: Appleton-Century-Crofts, Inc., 1936), p. 82.

PERSONALITY AS VERBAL DISPOSITIONS

Although psychologists have written extensively on the nature of language, particularly concerning its development in children, and although social anthropologists have presented us with excellent studies of the structure of language systems and the variety of linguistic forms in human society, very few studies have explicitly bound language and personality together to form a coherent subject matter. Discussions of language and personality tend to follow parallel analyses, with too little precise indication of their convergence. Implications of their connectedness, to be sure, abound in the writings on the psychology of language, but explicit integrations are exceptional rather than usual. This is much less true of writers on general semantics, but their concern has been much more with the pathology of language and personality than with the healthy individual. However, even in the area of pathology their conclusions often outrun their empirical evidence. Thus, when writers like Korzybski and Johnson attribute personality disorders mostly to the failure to use non-Aristotelian linguistic or logical categories, their documentation remains inconclusive.[28]

There is no intention in the foregoing statement of minimizing the importance either of the role of language in children's psychological development or of its close connection with behavior disorders. There is substantial evidence establishing the fact that a child's thinking and progressive adjustment are enormously aided by language, and a knowledge of the nature of mental disorders quickly convinces one that they can be partially explained in terms of the faulty use of or reaction to verbal symbols. These conditions are inescapable in view of the fact that language is at once an agency for communicating behavior and a molding factor in psychological development. The structure of a language, as we have shown, conditions both our perception of the world and the course of our thinking.[29] Furthermore, in the face of much evidence, there is no question but that the thinking of mental patients, especially of schizophrenes, which has been studied extensively,

[28] See Korzybski, *Science and sanity,* and Johnson, *People in quandaries.* Non-Aristotelian categories stress relations of inference and implication, whereas Aristotelian emphasize the law of identity, noncontradiction, and the excluded midle, which have only a limited usefulness.

[29] For an extensive discussion of this dual nature of language see B. L. Whorf, *Language, thought and reality* (New York: John Wiley & Sons, Inc., 1956). Although Whorf's view of language is highly controversial it deserves careful study by anyone interested in the psychology of language.

is in no small degree a product of language disturbance.[30] Knowledge of this phenomenon is by no means new, for more than fifty years ago German psychologists investigated the role of language disturbances in both normal and abnormal people. As early as 1905 Stransky investigated the flight of ideas, or the withdrawal from reality, in normal people, in contrast to similar behavior in manic patients.[31] He found a close relationship between the flight of ideas as measured by distraction and a disconnectedness in verbal behavior.

We now turn to those aspects of the psychology of language which are crucial to the understanding of the relation between language and personality.

LANGUAGE AND PERCEPTION. Inasmuch as the role of perception in personality is widely discussed in contemporary research we shall begin our analysis with the relation between language and perception.

Philosophical students of language, such as DeLaguna and Cassirer, early emphasized the importance of language in the perception—indeed, the "construction'"—of the external world.[32] The collective determinists, like Durkheim, Lévy-Bruhl, and others, whose ideas were presented briefly in Chapters 6 and 7, believed that the world is perceived through the collective symbols of the group. So completely surrounded is man by the symbolic system of his group that his perception of the world of objects, persons, and events is significantly shaped by it. The symbolic or verbal presentation of an object articulates and sharpens its appearance.

Some experimental psychologists also early noted the close relation of language and perception. In an experiment requiring subjects to reproduce visual forms by means of drawings, Gibson found that when reproductions and visually presented objects diverged from each other, the differences were often due to verbal cues presented by the analysis of the form during perception.[33] McGranahan's early review of the psychology of language likewise calls attention to the importance of language in human perception, pointing out that language has the effect of giving objects greater individuality and causing "similarities to be seen in things similarly

---

[30] See J. Kasanin (ed.), *Language and thought in schizophrenia* (Berkeley: University of California Press, 1946).

[31] E. Stransky, *Über Sprachverwirrtheit* (Halle: Marhold Verlag, 1905).

[32] DeLaguna, *Speech: its function and development;* E. Cassirer, Le langage et la construction du monde des objets, in *Psychologie du langage* (Paris: F. Alcan, 1933). See also E. Cassirer, *An essay on man* (New Haven: Yale University Press, 1944).

[33] J. J. Gibson, The reproduction of visually perceived forms, *J. exp. Psychol.,* 12 (1929), 1–39.

represented," and influencing perception "in the direction of speech forms." [34]

The well-known experiments of Bartlett show a similar relation between verbalization and perception. He was able to show, for instance, that the recall of an object, such as three lines to form an inverted N, was increased by naming the object.[35] This is undoubtedly due to the need, of which we spoke in Chapter 6, of anchoring ourselves in a meaningful or categorizing manner in our environment. The effect of verbalization or naming on recall was even more pronounced in the case of more complex objects. For example, when as a stimulus two angles are placed together to form a square figure and the subjects name or label them "carpenter's square," or "picture frame," the recall of the stimulus figure is significantly improved. Verbalization of unstructured figures assures their recall because the attachment of words to them renders them meaningful by relating them to or identifying them with familiar objects. Thus, by labeling the two angles placed together in a certain way as carpenter's squares or picture frames, the subjects anchored them in a verbal framework with which they were familiar. An object that cannot be named or labeled by a familiar word or symbol cannot be rendered meaningful, and accordingly cannot be reproduced correctly, if at all.

At about the same time that Bartlett was conducting his experiments in England, Carmichael and his associates were doing similar research in this country.[36] They used a set of twelve line drawings with two names assigned to each drawing. Their experiment showed that, while the structural and other properties of the stimuli affected their recall or reproduction, naming or labeling them by means of words (in this case provided by the experimenters) was also a very important factor in both perceiving and remembering them.

These and other experiments objectively corroborate what has been known concerning the relation between language and perception on other grounds, especially anthropological ones, as we briefly indicated in Chapter 7. The study of both primitive and literate languages shows that our perception of the world is indubitably molded by our language structure. The structure of

[34] D. V. McGranahan, The psychology of language, *Psychol. Bull.*, 33 (1936), 178–216, on p. 202.

[35] F. C. Bartlett, *Remembering: a study in experimental and social psychology* (Cambridge: Cambridge University Press, 1932).

[36] L. Carmichael, H. P. Hogan, and A. A. Walter, An experimental study of the effect of language on the reproduction of visually perceived form, *J. exp. Psychol.*, 15 (1932), 73–86.

every language reflects the world as it is perceived by those who use the given language. We perceive the world through the verbal relations of our language. There is no other way of seeing it; for although our perceptions are obviously determined by the anatomical structure of our sense organs, our total perception of reality is also significantly molded by the structure of our language. While every object is perceived through our sense organs it is also modified and apprehended by many centuries of cultural verbalizations.

The role of categorizing. Perception, like conception, is strongly determined by the process of categorizing, and categorizing in turn is deeply affected by the language structure of a given culture. Bruner and his associates, who are responsible for some of the best recent insights into the process of categorizing, have pointed out that there is no logical distinction between perceptual and conceptual categorizing.[37] Since we have already discussed the relation between language and thought or conception, we shall here consider the process of categorizing in perception only.

In perceptual categorizing we seek to identify perceptual objects by placing them in a class of similar objects. Thus, an object of a certain size, shape, and color is perceived as a rubber ball. In this case there is a correspondence or identity between the set of stimuli which constitute the rubber ball and the class or category by means of which we, or our culture, have labeled this object on previous occasions. Although the individual perceives the object in terms of the anatomical structure of his sense organs and his private experience, thus making his perception partly an individual property, he sees it even more extensively on the basis of the verbal categories of his particular culture. An individual perception thus reflects the linguistic categories of the cultural group in which a person lives, as well as his personal history and the idiosyncrasy of his individual make-up.

One can hardly overestimate the significance of categorizing in human behavior. By means of it we render different objects or events of experience equivalent to or identical with each other. Again, by means of categorizing we simplify our environment, thereby making it more manageable. Moreover, categorizing reduces the necessity of learning every object or event anew with every experience of it. Furthermore, it provides direction for appropriate behavior. That is, it helps us to anticipate the actions of persons or objects without having to test each of our propositions

[37] J. S. Bruner, J. J. Goodnow, and G. A. Austin, *A study of thinking* (New York: John Wiley & Sons, Inc., 1956), Ch. 1.

regarding them separately. Finally, it enables us to classify objects or events into coherent and orderly systems, thereby making our experience intelligible and meaningful.[38]

The nature of a given personality is revealed in the manner in which an individual categorizes his experience. We understand a person better when we know that he perceives all women as stupid, or all men as untrustworthy, or every proffer of help by another as a means of making him beholden to the latter. An individual's manner of relating himself to others is largely influenced by his perceptions of them as these are formulated by his verbal categorizations.

LANGUAGE AND THE SELF. Although we have reserved a separate chapter for the discussion of the self, we have already described it sufficiently to permit us to show the role of language in its origin and development.

The self, including self-perception and the perception of others, is intimately bound up with language. As we pointed out in the section on the preparatory adjustment property of language, in linguistic thinking symbols elicit the same response in others that they call out in ourselves. The self, linguistically conceived, is the act of saying to oneself what one says to others. By means of verbal symbols one stimulates oneself in the same manner as one stimulates others.

Role-perception and the self. The act of producing the same response in one's self as one produces in others involves the act of taking the role of another. A person learns this mode of behavior as a child when he assumes his mother's bodily gestures, words, tone of voice, and so forth. He introjects the role of his mother, and this process of introjection is the act of role-taking. G. H. Mead, who has elaborated this process and made it an important building block in his theory of the self, vividly illustrates the process by contrasting the play of dogs and the play of a child. Two dogs in play, as everyone has observed, will act as if they are about to engage in combat. Each dog adjusts his own acts to the incipient acts of the other. He will bark, growl, and engage in simulated biting. Each animal adjusts his acts to the oncoming acts of the other. In the play of a child, unlike that of the dogs which stimulate each other to respond in certain ways, the child will stimulate himself and respond to his own stimulation. He will act out a role and respond to his own role behavior.[39]

---

[38] *Ibid.*, pp. 12–13.
[39] Bonner, *Social psychology*, p. 117.

In this process, in which the child talks to and acts toward himself in the same way that he talks to and acts toward others, he is being another to himself. As Mead describes it, the child will say something in one character and respond to it in another character, and his response in another character is a stimulus to himself in the first character, and so on. The organized structure which arises in this role conversation is the self.[40] Self-consciousness, in short, depends upon language or some other form of symbolic communication, in which one becomes aware of one's self as an object, or in which one acquires the ability to make himself an object to himself.

In the absence of linguistic self-and-other responses the self cannot arise. At the same time, in the absence of the act of a stimulus affecting the individual as it affects another, language as we understand it can likewise not arise. The self and verbal stimulation-and-response are inseparable. In the personality growth of Helen Keller the contactual experience which she could give to another as it was given to herself was indispensable in the growth of her self. As Mead pointed out, Miss Keller did not acquire a self until she was able to communicate with others by means of symbols which produced the same responses in herself which they aroused in others.[41] Writing of her own early life without symbols, she remarked that without a language one is not a complete human being.[42]

The emergence of the self is coextensive with the child's use of the personal pronouns. The self-reference of the child begins with the child's use of his own name, as everyone knows, and develops slowly into the use of "I," "me," "our," and so on. The pronoun "I" clearly indicates an important step in the development of self-awareness. This was demonstrated by McCarthy, who found a close relationship between the child's use of pronouns and his chronological age. At eighteen months only 10 per cent of a child's words are pronouns, whereas by the age of fifty-four months it will have increased to 20 per cent.[43] Fisher found a similar relationship in nursery-school children ranging in age from eighteen to sixty months. Her study revealed a high positive relationship

[40] Mead, *Mind, self and society*, pp. 150–51. See further, Markey, *The symbolic process*.

[41] *Ibid.*, p. 149.

[42] H. Keller, *Teacher: Anne Sullivan Macy* (Garden City, N. Y., Doubleday & Co., Inc., 1955), p. 61.

[43] D. McCarthy, Language development in the preschool child, in R. G. Barker, J. S. Kounin, H. F. Wright (eds.), *Child behavior and development* (New York: McGraw-Hill Book Co., Inc., 1943), Ch. 7.

between chronological age and the use of "we," "our," and "us." [44] Fisher's study implies what we know to be true on the basis of other evidence, namely, that awareness of one's self—of the "I"— develops hand in hand with the awareness of others—of "we," "our," and "us." The two studies confirm Piaget's observation of the growth of language from the autistic to the egocentric to the heteronomous. They also confirm his finding that "true" social speech, that is, speech in which the child uses words not wholly from his own point of view but from the point of view of those whom he addresses, is a function of age. In Piaget's own investigation, "true" social speech was seldom found to appear before the seventh year.[45]

We have entitled the present subsection, "Role-perception and the Self." We are suggesting by this that role-playing as we use the term is a *verbal-perceptual* process, not merely a mechanical assumption of another person's roles. Unless we perceive or understand the other person's role we may be able to assume it, but we cannot verbally indicate to ourselves how we should respond to the other person. The verbal indicator becomes a *significant* symbol; and the symbol becomes significant, that is, meaningful, when the individual not only indicates the object to himself but is *ready to respond* in certain ways to the object. Mead expressed the same idea many years ago when he said that it is through the ability of the individual to be the other, at the same time that he is himself, that the symbol becomes meaningful.[46] Role-taking involving significant symbols is the act of identifying, or verbally indicating to oneself, the responses one makes to his sounds as the kinds of responses that others make. This role-taking by means of significant symbols is a complex verbal process, for it requires the verbal signification of another individual and the imputation to that individual of a response tendency similar to that of the speaker, or role-enactor, himself.

LANGUAGE AND INDIVIDUALITY. A large portion of the theory and research on the relation of language and human nature has been devoted to the socializing effect of language, and rightly so, for language is indeed one of the greatest—if not the greatest—socializing agents in human life. The fact of a common language makes for social solidarity among those using the same speech. Common interests are strengthened by a common language. The induce-

[44] M. S. Fisher, *Language patterns of preschool children* (New York: Columbia University, Teachers College Bureau of Publications, 1934).

[45] Piaget, *The language and thought of the child*, pp. 99 ff.

[46] G. H. Mead, A behavioristic account of the significant symbol, *J. Philos.*, 19 (1922), 157–63.

ment to cultural coherence by language is sometimes so powerful that it arouses strong ingroup versus outgroup hostilities. This is seen in the case of many European nations which distinguish political allegiances and sentimental attachments to their country on the basis of language. Czarist Russia did her best to Russianize the Polish areas in her empire, and after World War I Italy sought to eliminate German language and culture in the former Austrian territory ceded to her. The sentimental distinction between Croatian and Serbian bears out the same point. Though the languages are the same, to preserve their separate identity Croatians use the Latin alphabet whereas Serbians use the Cyrillic characters of the Greek Orthodox Church. The persistence of *Plattdeutsch* in northern Germany and of Provençal in southern France, and the establishment of the ancient Gaelic tongue as the official language of contemporary Ireland, illustrate the same unifying function of language and its effect on social, political, or sentimental distinctions.[47]

Individualizing force of language. While the socializing character of language is more clearly evident, its individualizing quality is also demonstrable. On the basis of comparative studies Sapir concluded that speech habits are complex indicators of individual personality. Perhaps most people can—or do—empirically or intuitively form impressions of others by the quality of the latter's speaking voices, their phonetic patterns, the length and structure of their sentences, the quality and extent of their vocabularies, the speed and evenness of their articulation, the appropriateness of their language to the language habits of the persons whom they address, and the stylistic consistency of the words which they employ.[48] In view of these differences in linguistic habits it is clear that one of the most important clues to individual personality is a person's verbal behavior. Language is not only an enculturating factor but also an isolating or individualizing process. We shall now briefly consider the important individualizing factors in language.

1. *"Stylistic" Indicators.* The individuality of a person is reflected in the "style" of his speech. Although French literary critics have overgeneralized the importance of style in written and spoken language, there is a profound truth in their dictum that *le style est l'homme même.*

Some years ago Sanford investigated linguistic style quantitatively. A statistical analysis of linguistic style sometimes deprives it of many subtle nuances, but its utility should not, as Sanford

---

[47] See E. Sapir, Language, *Encycl. soc. Sci.*, 5 (1933), pp. 167–8.
[48] *Ibid.*, p. 160.

has himself argued, be ignored. While there is reason to believe that the calculating machine "misses a great deal that would register on the human brain," and that "the delicate texture of style appears to be easily injured by our crude analytical devices," [49] there is sufficient evidence in the writings on the psychology of language to warrant the conclusions that verbal behavior is closely bound up with personality, and that this relationship can be usefully analyzed in quantitative terms. [50]

Sanford's investigation has been experimental and quantitative and, while open to legitimate criticism, has produced interesting and fairly reliable results. His aim was to determine differences in personality as revealed in individual oral and written styles. His procedure may be described as follows.

From a group of twenty male undergraduates who were being used in a related investigation, Sanford selected two sophomores, twenty years of age, who had approximately the same grades in their college work. These subjects were designated by the names "Chatwell" and "Merritt." Their verbal habits were very different, except that they were both verbally productive, and their personalities were markedly different. Preliminary work with written composition suggested to Sanford that a student's writings reflect far less his own individuality than his high school teachers' ideas of grammar and rhetoric. In order to eliminate this conventionality in writing, Sanford used samples of his subjects' oral speech, which were elicited by prearranged stimuli and recorded phonographically without the subjects' knowledge. In a second session different but "equivalent" stimuli were used, and in addition the subjects were required to reconstruct a seminarrative piece of writing which they had read before the previous meeting with the experimenter. To these samples of speech were added two specimens of eighty clauses each from the written autobiographies of Chatwell and Merritt.

All in all, there were eleven samples of speech from each subject

[49] F. H. Sanford, Speech and personality: a comparative study, *Char. & Pers.*, 10 (1941–42), 169–98, on p. 169.

[50] A few pioneer quantitative studies are the following: D. McCarthy, Language development, in C. Murchison (ed.), *A handbook of child psychology* (Worcester, Mass.: Clark University Press, 1931), pp. 278–315; G. K. Zipf, *The psycho-biology of language* (Boston: Houghton Mifflin Co., 1935); B. F. Skinner, The verbal summator, a method for the study of latent speech, *J. Psychol.*, 2 (1936), 71–107; B. F. Skinner, The alliteration in Shakespeare's sonnets: a study in literary behavior, *Psychol. Rec.*, 3 (1939), 186–92; J. B. Carroll, Diversity of vocabulary and the harmonic series law of word-frequency distribution, *Psychol. Rec.*, 2 (1938), 379–86; D. P. Boder, The adjective verb quotient: a contribution to the psychology of language, *Psychol. Rec.*, 22 (1940), 310–43; F. M. Young, An analysis of certain variables in a developmental study of language, *Genet. Psychol. Monogr.*, 23 (1941), No. 1.

—two specimens of *comments on pictures,* two *three-word stories,* two *ten-word stories,* two of *description,* one of *retold story,* and two of *autobiography.*[51]

Style was analyzed by means of grammatical and lexical categories. Although Sanford was fully cognizant of the limitations of grammatical rules, since they are to a greater extent than is commonly acknowledged intellectual artifacts, he employed them in the absence of a better alternative. With these limitations clearly in mind Sanford used over a dozen linguistic categories which had a good intraindividual and interindividual reliability.[52] In other words, the individual differences found in the study were differences between the experimental subjects and not differences imputed to them by the experimenter.

The results of the foregoing method of investigation bring out the linguistic individuality of Chatwell and Merritt. Merritt's speech is characterized by complexity, thoroughness, caution, uncoordination, and similar traits. The intricacy of his responses is shown in the use of many detours into subordinate clauses and of interpolations, especially by his parenthetical inclusion of one clause within another, and by his habitual "parenthetical formulas such as 'so to speak,' or 'as I said.'" He seems to be incapable of going rapidly from one response to another, but returns over and over to examine a previously made response, repeating it, rephrasing it, and repeating it once more in a slightly different form. In commenting on Merritt's perseverating and complex discourse, Sanford attributes this state of affairs to "a marked inability to get ahead with the business of responding." Merritt "does not release any idea until he has examined it from all sides, explained it, elaborated or qualified it in some way." When there seem to be no more elaborations or explanations to add, he repeats the idea. "He covers relatively little psychological territory in his verbal productions," Sanford points out, but tends rather "to worry each idea at great length before proceeding to another." [53]

The personality of Merritt is deeply etched in his verbal behavior. He is a person who, as Sanford describes him, "assiduously avoids the end of the limb . . . rarely making a statement for

[51] Sanford, Speech and personality, pp. 170–72.

[52] Examples of linguistic categories are as follows: *mechanics of speech* (interval between presentation of stimulus and initiation of response, total words in each story, speed of speaking, etc.); *grammatical categories* (sentences, clauses, verbs, etc.); *composite categories* (complexity of clauses, sentence distribution, copulas, verb-adjective ratio, etc.). For a complete listing of all the categories the reader should consult Sanford's article, especially pp. 173–82.

[53] *Ibid.,* p. 187.

which he may be challenged or held accountable. He leans continually toward indirection and caution. A characteristic sentence involves a copulative clause and a noun clause—'It appears that he might graduate.' The 'certainty-uncertainty' ratio shows that he much prefers 'it seems,' to 'it is.'" His modal constructions show the same general trait, for in his speech nothing happens overtly; instead they "might happen" or they "could happen." "This relatively extreme degree of caution," Sanford concludes, "suggests that Merritt is on the defensive in his speech, always deferent lest he displease his auditor, always insuring himself against possible censure." [54]

Chatwell's style, and the personality which breathes life into it, are markedly different from those of Merritt. It is almost totally devoid of the conventional and tortured qualities of Merritt's style. Rather it is picturesque, colorful, and lively. The rarity of repetition of content makes his mode of expression almost free of monotony. His many short, brisk sentences and his varied vocabulary cause his verbal behavior to be intense and emphatic. Unlike Merritt, Chatwell is simple and direct in his speech and writing, free of tortuous subordination and qualifications which make Merritt's style involved, hesitant, and timid by comparison. The dynamic quality of Chatwell's style is derived in large measure from the fact that his characters engage in active and overt behavior. Verbs of action abound whereas copulas and psychological verbs are infrequent.[55] Where Merritt might say, "He decided he might go," Chatwell would say, "He went," or more characteristically, "He went rapidly." This is further illustrated by the fact that Chatwell seldom uses the static copulative expression, "it seems."

Again, Chatwell's verbal responses are forward directed. "One response leads directly to another, and they all lead toward the proper completion of the task at hand. He rarely turns back upon a statement to rephrase it, to qualify it, to enlarge upon it, or to explain it," and he rarely repeats it. In contrast to Merritt's hesitant speech, Chatwell's is marked by coordination and smoothness. Chatwell plans his responses before he speaks, and, once started, they go smoothly and efficiently toward the designed end. "One gets a picture," Sanford writes, "of a strong determining

[54] *Ibid.*, pp. 189–90. Using conventional psychoanalytical terms, Merritt might be described by internal conflict, indecision, anxiety, hypersensitivity, guilt feelings, submissiveness, and compulsiveness, all of which characterize the rigid and anxiety-ridden individual, in whom doubts and scruples abound.

[55] Psychological verbs are words indicating cognitive, sensory, and affective behavior, such as thinking, seeing, and loving.

tendency in any situation, resulting in the relatively effortless and ordered concatenation of the separate phrases, clauses, and sentences, each leading smoothly and immediately to another." [56]

Another contrast between the verbal behavior of Merritt and Chatwell is in the area of evaluation. Merritt, we noted, is hesitant in making up his mind, and he is afraid of passing judgment lest he incur the displeasure of his auditor. Chatwell, by contrast, passes judgment freely and "readily impresses himself upon his utterances." However, there is an important shortcoming in this quality, for too frequently his adjectives express his own feelings and predilections rather than serving to communicate with others.

We have already called attention to the halting and uncertain linguistic style of Merritt. Chatwell's style, on the other hand, is almost never uncertain or diffident, as shown in his strong disinclination to explain, justify, or belittle his own judgment. He creates no impression of "conditionality or doubt." He prefers the confident and even dogmatic "is" to the tentative copulas "seems" or "appears." "With respect to this trait of confidence," writes Sanford, "Chatwell and Merritt are at opposite poles." [57]

The description of Chatwell as a person is already implicit in the description of his speech. If the relation between language and personality is as close as we have hypothecated, then it is clear that Chatwell is a dynamic and colorful individual, relatively free from inner doubts, even to the point of dogmatic certainty. His cognitive and affective responses are well organized and closely interconnected. He is bored by details, prefering the larger sweep of the imagination to precision of reference. He is confident, unconventional, and independent. Language for him is less an instrument of communication and description of the external world than a means of expressing his own individuality and impressing his auditor. [58]

The foregoing description of stylistic indicators illustrate the psychodiagnostic value of verbal behavior. It adds to our belief that verbal behavior is an integral aspect of the total behavior of a person. It supports our view that there is no sharp break or discontinuity between verbal and other forms of behavior. The detailed study of the linguistic habits of Merritt and Chatwell add credence to Sanford's over-all conclusion: "When we have char-

---

[56] Sanford, Speech and personality, p. 193.

[57] Ibid., p. 196.

[58] Psychoanalytically, Chatwell may be described as well-integrated, ascendant, secure, and self-accepting.

acterized the person's speech we have gone a long way toward characterizing the person." [59]

2. *Voice and Personality.* A person's speaking voice is no simple "mechanism," for it is a product of the combination of anatomical, cultural, and individual factors. The dependence of the voice on the anatomical structure of the throat, larynx, nasal cavities, and so forth, is too obvious to require proof. The human voice is also molded by cultural demands and expectations. We unconsciously imitate the voices of people around us. One need only consider local and sectional differences in voice habits to confirm this point. Intonation, for example, is socially conditioned. If our voices are criticized because they vary too much from the cultural norm, or because they are considered unpleasant by others, we strive to improve them. On the other hand, such vocal characteristics as intensity and vigor are largely determined by the personality structure of the individual.

The relation between voice and personality has long been suspected, but rigorous investigations of the relationship are relatively recent. Sapir, a pioneer student of the cultural and psychological nature of language, was deeply cognizant of the relationship. His observations were based on comparative studies of language and upon astute and sensitive analyses of the linguistic habits of different people. [60]

One of the earliest, if not the first, attempts to investigate the relation between voice and personality experimentally was made by Pear. [61] In one experiment he asked a number of radio listeners to describe the physical appearance of nine speakers solely on the basis of their voice. He found their descriptions of the speakers on the whole surprisingly accurate. In a few cases, the listeners were even able to identify the vocation of the speakers. [62]

While Pear's observations are interesting and point the way to an objective investigation of the relation between vocal expres-

---

[59] Sanford, Speech and personality, p. 197. It is not saying too much that a man is as he writes and speaks. The integrated verbal behavior may thus be called, following Ellwood Murray, *the speech personality.* See E. Murray, *The speech personality* (Philadelphia: J. B. Lippincott Co., 1937).

Sanford's study, though important, seems somewhat overdone. The results are in part impressive more for their subjective evaluation by Sanford than for their objective corroboration. Conclusions and correlations are in need of more supportive evidence.

[60] See E. Sapir, Speech as a personality trait, *Amer. J. Sociol.,* 32 (1927), 892–905.

[61] See T. H. Pear, *Voice and personality* (London: Chapman & Hall, Ltd., 1931).

[62] In these instances there were no doubt nonvocal cues, such as vocabulary and speech content, which aided in the identification.

sion and personality, they are not highly reliable. They do not inform us whether individuality in speech and voice is a dependable index of personality or only a peculiarity unrelated to it. Likewise, they give us no dependable knowledge of the degree or extent of consistency of the vocal expressions of the subjects, and hence their relation to personality is problematic. However, despite these strictures Pear's investigation is a first attempt to advance the study of the problem beyond intuitive and impressionistic observations. What it lacks is a reliable scoring technique and a dependable definition or measurement of the subjects' modes of vocal expression. Accordingly, it is practically impossible to compare his results with chance expectancy.

A few years after Pear's pioneer investigation, Allport and Cantril performed a similar study but with more rigid and reliable procedures.[63] Their method and results we shall briefly describe in a few paragraphs.

The major part of the research consisted of six experiments at the Harvard Psychological Laboratory and two experiments at a radio broadcasting studio in Boston. In the laboratory experiment 302 students, in six groups ranging from 32 to 85 members each, acted as judges. In the two studio experiments the radio listeners were asked to mail in their judgments. Two hundred and eighty-five replies were received. Thus, altogether, 587 judges participated in the eight experiments.

Measures of personality of the speakers consisted of both physical attributes like age, height, appearance in photographs, and appearance in person; and psychological traits like introversion-extraversion, ascendance-submission, vocation, political preference, and dominant values. In the six laboratory experiments the student-judges were furnished with written information concerning the personality features of each speaker. They were then instructed to match each of the voices with the correct description of the speaker's personalities. In the final part of the laboratory experiment they were instructed to match the voices with summary sketches characterizing each voice.

In the studio experiments the announcer instructed the listeners how to make out their reply cards, and gave them the necessary information concerning the speakers.

Finally, in four of the lab experiments the students were asked to submit free descriptions (as contrasted with those furnished by the experimenter) to supplement their matchings.

[63] G. W. Allport and H. Cantril, Judging personality from voice, *J. soc. Psychol.*, 5 (1934), 37–55.

For brevity's sake, we shall omit the judgments of physical characteristics, a high percentage of which were surprisingly accurate, and turn instead to the results of the "inner," or psychological, characteristics of the speakers as judged by their vocal expression.

Introversion-extraversion was successfully matched with voice above chance. Ascendance-submission was likewise accurately judged in a statistically significant way. In one experiment the majority of incorrect answers were due to the fact that the submissive college professor had cultivated an ascendant manner of speaking for teaching purposes. In the judgments of dominant values the results were definitely positive and significant in half the experiments. The matching of political preferences with vocal expression was surprisingly successful. Finally, in the summary sketches, which were used to determine whether or not the voice reveals *"a complex pattern* of personality better than a single feature," the results again were positive, indicating that a *"pattern of qualities seems, on the average, rather more correctly matched with voice than does any single quality."* [64]

Some important features of the results of the foregoing experiments deserve our attention. Statistical analysis of the data showed that 74 per cent of the coefficients of correlation were positive, 47 per cent *significantly* so, and only 14 per cent fell within the range of ± 1 P.E. Thus the judgments, even when they were erroneous, were not mere guesses. A significant fact is that the "inner," more deep-seated traits, were judged *more consistently and more correctly* than physique and appearance. Even more successful than the matching of voice with any single feature was its matching with summary sketches. The total portrait, in other words, yielded better estimates, thus giving support to the argument against "segmental" research upon isolated variables in personality. "Studies which deal with the interplay and patterning of qualities," the investigators write, "are closer to the realities of organized vital processes, and for that reason yield more positive results." [65] Apropos of voice and personality only, the results show that vocal expression reveals a *complex pattern* of personality significantly better than it does a single feature.

Again, in those experiments (which we have not mentioned) in which the subjects spoke behind a curtain instead of over the radio, the average results were approximately 7 per cent higher. This finding, according to the authors, suggests that the voice is slightly distorted by mechanical noise.

[64] *Ibid.,* p. 46. Italics in the original.
[65] *Ibid.,* p. 51.

Finally, it must be remembered that, except for records of physical characteristics, the criteria for the experiments were *objective,* even though their validity and reliability were not perfect. The results of the experiments are nonetheless both dependable and remarkable. The authors' comments best sum up their general conclusion, and we can do no better than to quote them in full. They write:

. . . Those who are familiar with the complexities of the task of measuring personality will find it rather remarkable that the human voice can be so accurately matched with results from the available tests for ascendance-submission, extroversion-introversion, and personal values. Such a degree of success with these objective criteria constitutes a peculiar kind of validation for the tests themselves and an encouragement to their further development. At the same time, since the criteria are imperfect, it must be borne in mind that the human voice may reveal even more concerning personality than our results indicate. *In our desire to keep the investigation objective and quantitative, we may have minimized the degree to which the voice expresses personal qualities.*[66]

There is a phase of recent research on language which would require another chapter for a satisfactory exposition. We should be remiss, however, if we did not make at least a passing reference to the recent contributions of Osgood and his associates on this all-important subject. These contributions are important particularly because they show how empirical work is forcing behavior theory into a corrective direction, and because they deal with some of the most crucial problems in an empirical fashion.

CONCLUSION

We have presented but a fragment of the extensive theoretical, anthropological, and experimental research on the psychology of language and the relation of verbal expression to personality. Unfortunately, research on language and personality is lagging today, so that, relatively speaking, formulations and conclusions must be based on early investigations. Current investigations of the psychology of language are largely concerned with problems of communication, especially communication in small groups, publics, and masses. Information theory is also engaged in research on com-

[66] *Ibid.,* p. 52. Italics in the original. The following references are also recommended: H. Herzog, Stimme und Persönlichkeit, *Ztschr. f. Psychol.,* 130 (1933), 300–79; G. W. Allport and P. E. Vernon, *Studies in expressive movement* (New York: The Macmillan Co., 1933); W. Wolf, *The expression of personality* (New York: Harper & Bros., 1943); L. Zucker, Psychological aspects of speech-melody, *J. soc. Psychol.,* 23 (1946), 73–128. See C. E. Osgood, G. J. Suci, and P. H. Tannenbaum, *The measurement of meaning* (Urbana: University of Illinois Press, 1958).

munication. Many studies are centered on the pathology of speech and the misuse of language in abnormal behavior. Accordingly, the study of the relation between language and personality is still relatively neglected.

Throughout this chapter the focus of attention has been on the individualizing character of language, not on its socializing force, even though the latter is pervasive in any study of the psychology of language. The researches and the data which they have presented, while hardly sufficient to justify statistically reliable generalizations on a large scale, are important indicators of personality characteristics and underline the psychological significance of language and verbal expression. They confirm what every person who is sensitive to modes of speech and the individual qualities of verbal behavior often perceives intuitively. As Sapir vividly phrased it some years ago, a very important function of language "is to be constantly declaring to society the psychological place held by all of its members." [67]

The importance of language as a psychological index is sometimes minimized as being based on data provided by testing a few verbose and verbally fluent individuals. But such criticism fails to recognize that this very condition of linguistic facility may be indicative in itself of an empty and superficial personality. To describe the verbal deliverances of another as *mere words* is to betray a surprising obtuseness regarding the relation of language to personality. "'Actions speak louder than words' may be an excellent maxim from the pragmatic point of view," as Sapir remarked, "but betrays little insight into the nature of speech." If language is, as the evolution of man and lower animals shows, the most human and civilizing of all human activities, then language and its relation to man are profoundly important for many practical as well as theoretical problems of human behavior. The human character of personality is largely due to human language. "It is unwise," therefore, according to Sapir, "to speak too blithely of 'mere' words, for to do so may be to imperil the value and perhaps the very existence of civilization and personality." [68]

We have omitted discussion of the ancient and fascinating problem of metaphor in verbal behavior. There is a great deal of philosophical, literary, and psychoanalytical evidence indicating that metaphor is an important psychological indicator, and that it

[67] Sapir, Language, p. 160.
[68] *Ibid.*, p. 161.

particularly reveals unconscious verbal associations. Like other linguistic habits it expresses the speech personality of an individual.[69]

[69] For an interesting and introductory view of the place of metaphor in language behavior see E. F. Sharpe, Psycho-physical problems revealed in language: an examination of metaphor, *Int. J. Psychoanal.*, 21 (1940), 201–13. A useful and nontechnical treatment of the subject of this chapter is found in P. Chauchard, *Le langage et la pensée* (Paris: Presses Universitaires de France, 1956).

CHAPTER 12

Expressive Behavior

Although we have not labeled some aspects of language, speech, and voice as forms of expressive behavior, they may in fact be so described. The individual characteristics of speech, voice, and linguistic style are expressive of the human personality. The personalities of Merritt and Chatwell, described in the preceding chapter, were expressed in their written and spoken styles. Speech habits, we have said, are complex indicators of the individualizing force of language. It would have been logical and appropriate, therefore, to have discussed expressive behavior in the preceding chapter on language. However, because it has been so little dealt with in spite of its importance, we are devoting a separate chapter to the subject. While its validity in the study of personality cannot be accurately established, it cannot be lightly dismissed. Psychologists tend to pay little attention to it. A survey of the sections on "Personality" in the first ten volumes of the *Annual Review of Psychology*, reveals that only one paragraph of eight lines by McClelland is devoted to the subject.[1]

The reasons for this neglect are not too difficult to ascertain. Since psychology, like other sciences, is subject to fluctuations of interest and to styles of thought and subject matter, it has neglected expressive behavior partly because it is largely out of fashion. For this reason, many psychologists either lack interest in the subject or are too timid to investigate it.

The second reason for its neglect by psychologists is the important historical fact that the subject has been a favored target

[1] D. McClelland, Personality, in *Annu. Rev. Psychol.*, 7 (1956), 39–62, on p. 43.

of charlatans, "character analysts," and dilettantes whose real interest has been the exploitation of a gullible public. However, responsible psychologists need no more be deterred by quacks in psychology than bona fide physicians are by those in the field of medical practice. The study of expressive behavior by competent and recognized psychologists would, in fact, effectively aid in the war against fraud in this important area of human behavior.

A third and more telling reason for the paucity of interest is the unfortunate fact that very few dependable experimental data have been amassed to confirm the important claims of workers in the field. Moreover, the results of leading investigations have been inconsistent. However, while the latter is always to be deplored in scientific investigations, inconsistency in results is by no means peculiar to the investigations of expressive behavior; as a matter of fact, it marks a great deal of psychological research. The answer to the charge of inconsistency and paucity of experimental results lies, first, in a far greater concentration of interest in the problem and increased awareness of its importance, and second, in the recognition that it is, as Allport put it, the " 'wave of the future.' " [2]

THE NATURE OF EXPRESSIVE BEHAVIOR

The study of personality can proceed along two broad dimensions. It may concern itself largely or exclusively with adaptive or adjustive behavior. In this approach the center of interest is the individual's adaptation of means to ends; the achievement of goals by the performance of appropriate acts. The subject investigated in this approach is the large variety of more or less observable and "measurable" overt acts, such as what a person does and says. The person is conceived in the context of problems and the way he goes about solving them. He is described as an organism striving to satisfy basic needs. Hence, any act which he performs is transacted in order to protect himself and to aid him in satisfying important wants. This way of describing human behavior is deeply entrenched in the "functionalist" tradition of American psychology, and comprises the great bulk of our instrumental and adjustment psychology. From this point of view, most behavior is stimulus-bound, habitual, and for the most part automatic, once it has been set in motion.

The second, but largely neglected, approach is to study those aspects of behavior whose basic function is not adjustive or defensive, but expressive. There seems to be no determinable goal or

[2] G. W. Allport, in a personal communication.

"purpose" in this form of behavior, for it does not *seem* to consist of the adaptation of means to ends. It is not trying to solve a problem, cope with a life condition, or adjust to a disturbing situation. Indeed, it is a form of behavior in which an individual is not trying to achieve anything, but is only expressing his personality. We thus take issue with McClelland's definition of an expressive trait as "the characteristic way in which a person learns to adapt to certain recurrent problems." This is a definition of coping or adjustive, not expressive, behavior. Using McClelland's own example of walking, we should argue that, while walking is adaptive for all individuals, walking in a *certain way* is *expressive* of the walking individual's personality.[3] We hold, rather, with Maslow, who says that expressive behavior does not try to do anything. Thus, a "stupid man behaves stupidly, not because he wants to, or tries to, or is motivated to, but simply because he *is* what he is."[4]

Stated in this sharply contrasted way, however, our meaning is open to misinterpretation. We are not dichotomizing behavior into adjustive and expressive. On the contrary, we are fully cognizant of the fact that most forms of behavior have both adaptive and expressive features. We mean only to call attention to the extreme likelihood, based less on experimental investigation than on astute observation and clinical insight, by writers like G. W. Allport, Murphy, and Maslow, that some human behavior is primarily nonfunctional rather than instrumental. Expressive behavior reflects the unique inner disposition of a person which, while it is difficult to establish by means of objective, mensurative criteria, is often accurately established by clinicians and others whose minds are uncluttered by preconceptions and formal rigidity.[5]

Inasmuch as the distinction between adjustive and expressive behavior is fundamental to the understanding of the latter, it will repay us to examine each in some detail.

ADJUSTIVE BEHAVIOR. Adaptive behavior is to a surprising degree a product of socialization—of instruction, learning, and enculturation. Although beneath most instrumental or adjustive behavior is found a bedrock of needs, drives, and purposes, the

[3] See D. McClelland, *Personality* (New York: The Dryden Press, Inc., 1951), p. 156. McClelland is really defining adaptive, not expressive, behavior.

[4] A. H. Maslow, *Motivation and personality* (New York: Harper and Bros, 1954), p. 103.

[5] Expressive behavior has also been "measured" by means of such objective devices as handwriting, body-build, linguistic style, myokinetic diagnosis, and others. These and others will be described and analyzed in this chapter.

direction which the behavior determined by it takes is largely conditioned, as we saw in Chapters 6–10, by cultural and situational conditions. Furthermore, adjustive behavior is the act or process of adaptation of the individual to his environment as a technique of securing his survival or the achievement of his ends. Adjustive behavior is thus seen to be a practical technique, an instrument for the achievement of individually desired or socially desirable ends.

Determinants of adjustive behavior. There are three broad determinants of adjustive behavior, namely, the physiological, the psychological, and the social. The physiological determinants are all those conditions in which the biological organism strives to preserve itself and to maintain a state of equilibrium. The gratification of hunger and thirst is an obvious example. Seeking food when hungry and water when thirsty is a universal coping mechanism of the physiological type.

Psychological and social mechanisms of adjustment are closely related. Psychological mechanisms are the techniques by which the person handles his anxieties, reduces his tensions, defends the self against criticism or rejection, eliminates frustration-inducing conflicts, and the like.

Social modes of adjustments inhere largely in the mores. Thus, whether one sublimates or rationalizes certain features of one's experience is in no small degree dictated by the culture. In a society where one need make no excuses for his behavior, rationalization is superfluous; and in a society where there are practically no sexual prohibitions and frustrations, sublimation has no reason for being.

Learning plays a large part in the acquisition and use of adjustive techniques. Indeed, most of man's adjustive behavior is learned. There is added confirmation of this in the fact that adjustive behavior has to be continually reinforced. If it is not periodically rewarded it tends to become ineffectual and finally extinct. This condition is due to the fundamental fact that adjustive behavior is instrumental, goal-directed, and need-reductive.[6]

Adjustive behavior is not necessarily passive. People adjust themselves to their world not merely by submitting to it, but by means of efforts to change and control it. Enculturation is seldom an unopposed process. Every healthy individual resists enculturation and achieves some measure of individual autonomy. Adjust-

---

[6] Since the nature and role of learning in the formation of personality was examined at length in Chapter 8, it is unnecessary to discuss further the learning component in adjustive behavior.

ment is thus also an effort by the individual to control others and to change his environment. This is adjustment by reconstructing the environment, and is found to some degree in every individual in some circumstances. It is more or less successful because culture is far less coercive than it is directive. Adjustment is always a compromise between the cultural pressures acting on the individual and his own adaptive mechanisms.

In summary, the adjustive approach to human personality conceives the latter largely in terms of its behavioral content. This behavioral content is manifested in the adjustive apparatus of every individual—in the strivings, purposes, need satisfactions, environment control, and other instrumentalities of adaptation and of fostering the well-being of the individual.

EXPRESSIVE BEHAVIOR. While it would be misleading to say that every assertion concerning adjustive behavior is untrue of expressive behavior, roughly speaking this is largely the case. Whatever we say about adjustive behavior is almost, but not quite, the opposite of expressive behavior. The latter seems to have no discernible purpose or direction. If there is unmotivated behavior in human beings, expressive behavior is certainly the best, if not the only, example. It exists neither for the purpose of need-reduction, control or change of the environment, the attainment of a previsioned end, nor the adjustment to a physical or social environment. It seems to exist for and is an end in itself.[7] Sheer being or existence is its basic, perhaps only, determination.

The nature of expressive behavior may be summarized as follows.

1. *Expressive behavior is largely unlearned.* This is, as we pointed out before, in sharp contrast to the nature of most human behavior, which is invariably couched by most psychologists in terms of a species of learning theory. Expressive behavior is seldom as stimulus-bound as other forms of behavior, and the stimulus-response mechanism does not adequately describe it. *Its essence seems to be spontaneity.* Accordingly, training, conditioning, and social influences play a negligible role in its origin. Instruction

[7] In saying that expressive behavior seems to have no purpose but exists for itself, we do not imply that it is capricious and "uncaused." We simply wish to point out that its determinants are unknown or obscure, and that it is unmotivated by need-reduction. Some typical references in which purpose is attributed to all behavior even in the absence of supporting data are the following: P. M. Symonds, *The dynamics of human adjustment* (New York: Appleton-Century-Crofts, Inc., 1946), p. 4; R. Stagner, *Psychology of personality* (New York: McGraw-Hill Book Co., Inc., 1948), p. 260; D. Krech and R. Crutchfield, *Theory and problems of social psychology* (New York: McGraw-Hill Book Co., Inc., 1948), p. 32; O. H. Mowrer, *Learning theory and personality dynamics* (New York: The Ronald Press Co., 1950), p. 79.

may intensify it, in the sense of instruction in *more* spontaneity, but it cannot itself generate it.

2. *Expressive behavior is basically unmotivated.* By this we mean that the satisfaction and reduction of needs, which are essential to the acquisition and change of behavior—in current learning theory, at any rate—do not account for expressive behavior. Handwriting, bodily posture, dancing, walking, and similar activities do not satisfy any palpable need of the individual, but are performed because there is no other way for him to express them. They are his own uniquely organized ways of behavior, and are largely free from his own wishes to write better, stand more erectly, dance more attractively, and walk more gracefully.

This does not mean that these forms of behavior cannot be changed or improved by means of training and practice. They can; but the resulting behavior is less spontaneous, more contrived by deliberate motivation, and less truly expressive.

3. *Expressive behavior is little subject to direction and control.*[8] This fact is closely related to the preceding one, for controlled behavior implies the incentive to inhibit action, the motive to check an act in the interest of a specific goal. Expression is not, as Maslow points out, voluntary behavior.[9] For the same reason socialization and enculturation have very little influence on the manner of expression. A unique component of the individual survives every effort to channelize it along prescribed lines, even though in other respects it may resemble the expressions of others who were socialized by the same cultural demands. Its unsusceptibility to control is also due to its largely unconscious character. Unlike much of our adjustive behavior, which is subject to control in proportion to our awareness of its existence, expressive acts are deeply embedded in man's character structure, do not readily come to the surface of consciousness, and hence are not easily controlled. By its very nature spontaneous behavior cannot be easily managed. In the very act of trying to control it, we destroy its spontaneity and transform it into conscious and even mechanical behavior. In their pioneer investigation of expressive behavior Allport and Vernon found that, try as an individual might to control his posture, gait, handwriting, and similar acts, in the long run, when fatigue, distraction, and forgetting intercede, the individual returns to his original modes of expression.[10]

[8] See Maslow, *Motivation and personality*, p. 180.
[9] *Ibid.*, p. 185.
[10] G. W. Allport and P. E. Vernon, *Studies in expressive movement* (New York: The Macmillan Co., 1933).

4. Cultural conditioning plays only a minor role in expressive behavior. Since impulse and spontaneity are dominant features of expression, the effect of cultural norms is held to a minimum. Although the social group imposes a mincing gait on the Chinese, and Balinese society induces a dreamlike posturing in its people, neither the Chinese nor the Balinese perform their acts in a rigidly stylized manner. Each brings to his particular action the unique attributes of his individual personality. Just as no two fingerprints are alike, so no two persons express themselves in identical fashion, even in the same culture.

5. Expressive acts find their most characteristic outlets in unstructured situations. For this reason free associations and productions elicited by projective tests are among the most characteristic modes of expression.[11] It is indeed fantastic, as Maslow points out, that in the voluminous literature and therapy of psychoanalysis the foregoing relationship has scarcely been investigated or even speculated about. When one contemplates the expressive nature of free association it is easy to see the validity of the relationship. In projective tests the subject can freely and spontaneously complete an incompleted act, or give himself with complete abandon to the unstructured reality. The individual's perceptions are determined primarily neither by the structure of the presented stimulus nor by the pressure of external reality, but almost wholly by the inner organization of his psychological disposition. This is but another way of phrasing Maslow's statement that, while adjustive behavior is largely determined by cultural and other environmental variables, expression is determined to a great extent by the state of the organism.[12]

6. Expressive behavior does not strive to change the environment. In this respect it differs markedly, as we pointed out earlier, from adjustive behavior, one of whose chief functions is to control and change reality.[13] When at times it does affect the environment, this fact is adventitious and unplanned. The purpose of a lecture, for example, is to add to students' knowledge, change their beliefs, and make them more enlightened human beings. The lecture has a purpose, or a variety of purposes, all of them aimed at the goal of producing educated individuals. But the manner of expounding its subject matter, the peculiar stance and manner of expression used by the lecturer are expressive, not controlling and adaptive.

[11] Maslow is one of the few psychologists who has explicitly recognized this relationship. See *Motivation and personality,* pp. 195–98.

[12] *Ibid.,* p. 180.

[13] *Ibid.,* p. 180.

If these characteristics aid in bringing about desirable changes in the hearers, this fact is unpremeditated and coincidental. "The environmental effects of expression, when there are any at all, are unmotivated and epiphenomenal."[14]

7. *Expressive acts are properties of the total individual.* A strain of consistency runs through them, so that an individual expresses his essential being not in his gait alone, nor in his laughter, posture, handwriting, voice, and similar features, but in his entire organism. Even so apparently trivial a mode of behavior as the manner of holding a pencil or the amount of pressure applied to it in writing is consistently related to other features of the total personality.[15]

The foregoing statement is an answer to the question frequently asked, sometimes with an undertone of pleasant mockery: What does expressive behavior express? The answer is: It expresses the individual as a relatively consistent total self. In his expressive acts the total individual often reveals himself more truly than in his adjustive behavior, for the process of adjustment often entails a large repertoire of defenses and deceptions which may be wholly absent in expressive behavior. Whereas adaptive behavior may reflect the way a person wants to appear to others, expressive behavior is usually a reflection of the way he is.[16]

The foregoing description of the nature of expressive behavior, when contrasted with our observations on the adjustive and instrumental processes, clearly shows that, while the two modes of behavior are related, they are nevertheless very different. We make no special plea for their differential importance; on the contrary, we firmly believe in the crucial place of both in any full-bodied description of the human personality. We devote this chapter to expressive behavior in an attempt to remedy the lack of attention it has received in the psychology of personality.[17]

[14] *Ibid.*, p. 186.

[15] W. Wolf, *The personality of the pre-school child* (New York: Grune & Stratton, Inc., 1946).

[16] It should be added, however, that in a well-integrated individual the discrepancy between one's self-picture and the ratings by others is relatively small. However, this statement can be legitimately challenged in the light of some recent research. See, for example, A. H. Hastorf, I. E. Bender, and D. J. Weintraub, The influence of response patterns on the "Refined Empathy Score," *J. abnorm. soc. Psychol.*, 51 (1955), 341–43; Hastorf *et al.*, in R. Tagiuri and L. Petrullo, *Person, perception, and interpersonal behavior* (Stanford, California: Stanford University Press, 1958). See also L. J. Cronbach's statement, *ibid.*

[17] It is highly significant that of the leading American psychologists of personality only five have given us more than a cursory discussion of the subject. These are G. W. Allport, A. H. Maslow, Gardner Murphy, H. A. Murray, and Werner Wolff.

SOME FORMS OF EXPRESSIVE BEHAVIOR

So far we have briefly expounded the general characteristics of expressive behavior, and have briefly contrasted them with the adaptive or instrumental features of the human personality. In this section we shall present in considerable detail some of the kinds of expressive behavior. Some of these, such as style of handwriting and psychomotor expressions, have been extensively investigated; whereas others, such as posture, gait, and dancing, have been given insufficient attention.

The forms of expressive behavior are used in two related ways in this chapter. On the one hand, as forms of behavior they reveal qualities of personality, both segmentally and holistically. On the other hand, they serve as "measures" or methods for the psychological study of the total personality. Thus, handwriting not only projects the inner psychological organization of the personality, but serves as a measuring stick for its investigation. While as techniques they lack the rigor which is characteristic of the well-established psychological methods, they have value in supplementing the latter. Moreover, the better-established methods of assessing personality leave very much to be desired. The well-known quantitative methods, particularly statistical analysis, never uncover more than a small segment of the total personality. The limited view of personality which quantitative methods present us rests on limitations inherent in them. Experimentation, for example, inescapably oversimplifies what is in fact a complex phenomenon, and neglects features of the personality which do not show up in an experiment. Statistical measurement, dealing fundamentally with representative samples of behavior, loses sight of the single individual. It cannot investigate him directly because he is well concealed in the representative group. The person as a unique individual is beyond the pale of direct quantification. Finally, it is very doubtful that the quantitative method in psychology has contributed any truly *fundamental* ideas to the study of human behavior.

The foregoing remarks are made not to disparage the quantitative methods in psychology, but to call attention to the fact that though as useful tools they have a valuable place in psychology, they should not be used to the exclusion of expressive and other techniques. While the study of expressive behavior is admittedly imprecise, we should not forget that quantitative techniques have been disappointingly sterile. Perhaps the judicious use of both, and the rejection of unsupported claims by each, will give us a better picture than we now possess of the complex unity of the total personality.

GENERAL FEATURES OF GRAPHOLOGY. While ostensibly scientific investigations of the relation between handwriting and personality is relatively modern, it has fascinated philosophers and writers for many centuries. Rose Wolfson tells us that as early as the second century "Tranquillius saw peculiarities in Octavius Augustus' handwriting; and in the eleventh century the Chinese were noting the relationship between handwriting and character." [18] It is of course well known that the British scientist Sir Francis Galton interested himself in the subject and believed that handwriting is a reflection of mental traits. With the publication of Klages' painstaking work, the subject of handwriting gained undoubted respectability, more particularly in Europe than in the United States.[19] In our own country the subject was given a strong initial impetus by the researches of June Downey and the meticulous investigations of Allport and Vernon.[20] And from Klages' claim that no two people write exactly alike to Murphy's assertion that contemporary graphology makes sense the problem of handwriting and personality has persistently obtruded itself on the psychological scene.[21]

Rudiments of graphology. The "science" of handwriting is intricate and highly specialized. We shall present in this section only those elements of the subject which are essential to our main problem, which is the relation between the style of an individual's script and various qualities of his personality. Any concern with graphology as a diagnostic tool is only incidental.

Today, practicing graphologists employ about two dozen variables in various combinations. Among them are, typically, the following:

[18] R. Wolfson, Graphology, in H. H. Anderson and G. L. Anderson, *An introduction to projective techniques* (Englewood Cliffs, N.J.: Prentice-Hall, Inc., 1951), p. 416.

[19] For his well-known discussion of graphology, see L. Klages, *Handschrift und Charakter* (Leipzig: Verlag von Johann Ambrosius Barth, 5th to 7th editions, 1923).

[20] See J. E. Downey, *Graphology and the psychology of handwriting* (Baltimore: Warwick and York, 1919); *The will-temperament and its testing* (Yonkers, N.Y.: World Book Co., 1923); Allport and Vernon, *Studies in expressive movement.*

[21] For the latter's views, see G. Murphy, *Personality: a biosocial approach to origins and structure* (New York: Harper and Bros., 1947), pp. 688–94.

letter form
letter size
width of stroke
curvature of stroke
pressure of stroke
space between letters
space between words

direction of line
space between lines
fluctuation of line
degree of slant
variation of slant
width of letters
connection between letters [22]

Equipped with data regarding his subject's age, sex, nationality, and the like, the graphologist examines a specimen of the writer's script.[23] Interpretation of the integrated variables is made on the basis of four major categories. These are overcontrol, undercontrol, midway control (that is, an equal distribution of overcontrol and undercontrol), and rhythmic control.[24]

Overcontrolled handwriting is characterized by a configuration in which the performance of such variables as size, degree of slant, width of stroke, and size of letter are restrained, retarded, and inhibited. The slant of the letters is toward the left, the letters are very narrow, the spaces between words are wide, and the stroke is irregular and thin.

In undercontrolled script the small letters vary considerably from very small to fairly large, with a preponderance of small ones. All letters are wider, the stroke is thicker, the lines fluctuate up and down, the slant turns to the right, and the curves are enlarged.

In the midway type of control, there seems to be a rivalry between overcontrol and undercontrol, with neither one in the ascendancy, but with a constant fluctuation between them. Thus, the slant of the letters are both left and right, the curves are both irregular and enlarged, the spaces between letters are both wide and narrow.

In the rhythmically controlled type, the writing moves from overcontrol to undercontrol but in such a manner that the script is predominantly steady, balanced, and stable. The width of the stroke, the size of the letters, the spaces between them, their slant, and the spaces between the lines are rarely exaggerated.

[22] See, for example, T. S. Lewinson, An introduction to the graphology of Ludwig Klages, Char. & Pers., 6 (1938), 163–67; R. Saudek, The psychology of handwriting (New York: Doran Co., 1926); T. S. Lewinson and J. Zubin, Handwriting analysis (New York: King's Crown Press, 1942). The latter is highly recommended for its unflagging determination to establish objective measurements of graphological variables.

[23] It is generally agreed that a single specimen of a subject's script is usually sufficient, for the form of his writing does not change significantly, except over long periods of time.

[24] Wolfson, Graphology, in Anderson and Anderson, An introduction to projective techniques, p. 416.

An important and instructive fact about the four categories of script is that, although the graphologist looks to separate features (such as width of stroke and size of letter) in his analysis, in actual practice he approaches a specimen holistically. His analysis is guided not only by single components but even more by the configured specimen. He begins with an impression of the whole as it is determined by the dominant characteristics, a distinct pattern which stands out even to the individual who has no technical knowledge of graphology. He proceeds from the dominant features to the separate and discriminable particulars. He observes tendencies and patterns long before he makes minute analyses and diagnoses. By the time he has completed his analysis he has taken account of the entire sweep of a person's writing experience.

The value of the holistic impression is clearly demonstrated in Eysenck's study of the relation between handwriting and pathological states. On the basis of his study of the handwritings of fifty psychiatric patients he confirmed the conclusions of Allport and Vernon that the correlations between personality and specific graphological features were usually low, whereas the correlations for patterned or holistic features were well above chance.[25]

Other features of graphology. Although graphologists have established norms, such as those discussed above, they have found that within the limits of these central tendencies there are individual differences and deviations. Persons vary in speed and directional movement. McAllister, for example, found that writing movements go either toward the body or away from it, and that the speed of these movements differs.[26] The degree of pressure is certainly different in different persons, as has been demonstrated by Saudek.[27]

In her original work on family resemblances in handwriting, Downey found a relationship between handwriting and heredity and intelligence. Although her conclusions have not been clearly established, they suggest the existence of factors that may very well be important determinants of people's handwriting.[28] Espe-

[25] H. J. Eysenck, *Dimensions of personality* (London: Routledge & Kegan Paul, Ltd., 1947).

[26] C. N. McAllister, *Researches on movements used in handwriting*, Yale Psychological Laboratory Studies, Vol. 8 (1900). See also, G. V. N. Dearborn, Kinaesthesia and the intelligent will, *Amer. J. Psychol.*, 24 (1913), 204–5.

[27] R. Saudek, *Experiments with handwriting* (New York: William Morrow & Co., Inc., 1928).

[28] J. E. Downey, *Preliminary study of family resemblances in handwriting* (Laramie: University of Wyoming Press, 1910).

cially interesting is Marum's predictions of intelligence ratings, in which she was successful largely with persons of superior intelligence.[29]

Again, although the results are quite inconclusive, there is more than a glimmer of possibility that handwriting may be affected by learning and practice. It can also to some extent be disguised, as Osborne has shown, although expert graphologists report that they are not easily deceived by the results.[30]

Not to be discounted is Downey's early discovery that handwriting is effectively determined by the writer's mood. This is true not only of the total configuration of the script, but of such specific variables as regularity and slant.[31] The effect of mood is probably indirect, in the sense that emotional states cause changes in general muscle tonus as well as the contraction and expansion of the muscles.[32]

HANDWRITING AND PERSONALITY. Our discussion thus far clearly points to an intrinsic relationship between handwriting and personality. While the exact correlations are seldom quantitatively impressive, this does not justify the extreme criticism sometimes leveled against research in this area. It is not in the interest of the scientific study of this problem to perennially cite the statistically low correlation of −.016 found by Hull and Montgomery, for these investigators measured the relation between graphic signs, or fragmentary parts, and specific personality variables.[33] Psychological use of graphology, in any case, has shifted away from the exclusive consideration of specific variables to an emphasis on patterns of graphological traits and configurations of personality characteristics.

Representative studies. In recent years the trend of investigation has been toward the experimental form, often with the willing collaboration of professional graphologists who in the past were not sympathetic with this approach. A fairly recent example of this procedure is the use of ranking on tests and scales. Eysenck's use of matching technique illustrates the determination to obtain

[29] O. Marum, Character assessments from handwriting, *J. ment. Sci.*, 91 (1945), 22–42.

[30] For the limits of disguisability, see A. E. Osborne, *Questioned documents* (Albany, N.Y.: Boyd Printing Co., 1929).

[31] Downey, *Graphology and the psychology of handwriting.*

[32] K. G. Roman, Studies in the variability of handwriting, *J. genet. Psychol.*, 49 (1936), 139–60.

[33] C. L. Hull and R. P. Montgomery, Experimental investigation of certain alleged relations between character and handwriting, *Psychol. Rev.*, 26 (1919), 63–74.

dependable measures of the relation between handwriting and personality.[34]

In this experiment a graphologist analyzed the scripts of fifty neurotic patients. These analyses were matched with such personality indexes as brief personality descriptions sketched by a psychiatrist, clinical diagnoses of the patients by their psychiatrists, questionnaires returned by the patients consisting of self-measurements of temperamental traits, and intelligence scores. The graphologist's sketches, finally, were matched to the patients' handwritings.[35] In this way, the graphologist's assessment of the patient's personality was derived from the latter's script validated against the psychiatrist's rating and the patient's self-assessment as indicated in the questionnaires.

The results obtained in this manner were considerably above chance. Eysenck notes that by chance, 50 per cent of the questionnaire responses of both patient and graphologist should have agreed, whereas actually 62 per cent ± 1 per cent agreed. If only those judgments on which the graphologist felt very certain were taken into consideration, the amount of agreement rose to 68 per cent ± 3 per cent. Eysenck concluded that inasmuch as these percentages are derived from 1,350 comparisons, one is justified in placing a high degree of confidence in the accuracy of his results, and adds that "graphology does to some extent at least, succeed in correlating handwriting and personality traits." [36]

Comparing the patients' graphological characteristics with their psychiatric symptoms the following relations were found in Eysenck's experiment.

Depression: falling or fluctuating lines; very heavy or very thin, timid, and irregular pressure; small and slow writing; heavy or irregular pressure; slant often to the left.

Anxiety: narrow spaces between words, and between lines; abrupt ending of words; either heavy or irregular pressure; small and slow writing; slant may be to the left.

Hysteria: irregular height, width, and slant of letters; fluctuating lines; indistinct and mixed connections of letters. In addition, there were grotesque slants to the left, exaggerated flourishes, heavy pressure, and lack of proportion in the accentuation of some letters, particularly initials.[37]

In a much earlier study, Land matched graphological traits with emotional reaction scores on the Pressey X-O Test. While

---

[34] H. J. Eysenck, Graphological analysis and psychiatry: an experimental study, *Brit. J. Psychol.,* 35 (1945), 70–81.

[35] *Ibid.,* pp. 73–75.

[36] Eysenck, *Dimensions of personality,* p. 240.

[37] *Ibid.,* p. 241.

lacking the holistic character of most recent investigations, Land's study disclosed a significant correlation between the subjects' emotional state and such graphic variables as normal slant, downward alignment, and extreme backhand.[38]

Perhaps the best known and most frequently cited investigation of the relationship between handwriting and personality is that of Allport and Vernon, which we have already cited. Their experiment was not aimed to study specific graphological formations and the correlations of these with single features of personality; rather, it tried to determine to what extent the form-quality, or total impression made by the script as a whole, reflects *configurations* of personality.[39] In this holistic view of the problems, the authors early recognized a feature of psychographological analysis which is only now the prevailing approach.

The experiment aimed to match specimens of handwriting with case studies of the personalities of the subjects made by three psychologists. The subjects were ten male adults, from 21 to 45 years of age, the average being 32. Three of the subjects were graduate students, two were members of a university faculty, two were college graduates engaged in business, one was a college student in good standing who had withdrawn because of emotional difficulties, one was a postmaster, and one a barber. Of the whole sample, two were foreign-born, one an Italian and one a Korean. All had received either the entire or greater part of their education in this country.

In the experiment, each subject copied a passage of forty words, which included the letters and punctuation marks whose formations are considered of graphological significance. The subjects were not informed of the use to which their script was to be put.

The judges in the experiment consisted of 143 male undergraduates, most of them sophomores, 25 members of the college faculty (including some faculty wives), and 17 professional graphologists of many years of experience. The results are given in the accompanying table.

The mean scores, or numbers of correct matchings, as calculated by Edwin Powers in the chapter cited, are 1.77, 1.80, and 2.41 for the three groups, and 1.83 for all the judges combined. This means that 339, or 18.3 per cent, of the total 1,850 trials were correct. As Powers observes, according to the theory of probability an

[38] A. H. Land, *Graphology, a psychological analysis* (University of Buffalo Studies, 1924).

[39] Allport and Vernon, *Studies in expressive movement*, Ch. 10. The matching of sketches of personality with script was performed by Edwin Powers.

NUMBER AND PERCENTAGE OF CORRECT MATCHINGS [40]

Correct Match- ings	Under- gradu- ates N = 143 No. %		Faculty N = 25 No. %		Graph- ologists N = 17 No. %		Com- bined N = 185 No. %		Chance N = 185 No. %	
0	24	16.8	4	16	1	5.9	29	15.7	68	36.8
1	44	30.8	7	28	2	11.8	53	28.6	68	36.8
2	34	23.8	7	28	7	41.1	48	26.0	34	18.4
3	28	19.6	5	20	4	23.5	37	20.0	11	6.1
4	10	7.0	1	4	2	11.8	13	7.0	3	1.5
5	1	0.7	1	4	1	5.9	3	1.6	0	0.3
6	2	1.4	0	0	0	0	2	1.1	0	0.1
7–10	0	0	0	0	0	0	0	0	0	0.0

average of 1.0 correct matchings could be obtained by chance. Accordingly, each average is somewhat superior to chance. Computation of the statistical results revealed that the probability of obtaining 1.83 correct matchings by chance was about 1 in 4.5 times. For the graphologists the probability of getting 2.41 correct by chance was about 1 in 8.5 times. The chance of getting 6 correct, the score which was achieved by two students, is 1 in 1,920 times. When the judgments of the combined groups were considered, it was found that in 5 out of the 10 choices, the judgments most frequently made were correct, and in 7 out of 10 cases the modal scores exceeded chance.

An interesting and significant confirmation of handwriting as an indicator of a deep-lying personality configuration, is the case of multiple personality recently described by Thigpen and Cleckley.[41] Samples of handwriting made by graphologists of both Eve White and Eve Black—this was before a third "personality" was discovered—while in many ways different, established beyond doubt that they had been written by the same human hand. No indications whatsoever were found to indicate a deliberate intent to disguise the writings of either one of the personalities. This example, while only a single case, adds further evidence to the hypothesis that style of handwriting is a deep-rooted dimension of the human personality.

More recent researches have neither materially increased nor challenged the main conclusions of the earlier studies. Unfortu-

[40] Adopted from Allport and Vernon, *Studies in expressive movement*, p. 217.

[41] C. H. Thigpen and H. Cleckley, A case of multiple personality, *J. abnorm. soc. Psychol.*, 49 (1954), 135–51. The full report is now in book form by the same authors: *Three faces of Eve* (New York: McGraw-Hill Book Co., Inc., 1957).

nately, as we have already remarked, disappointingly few investigations of the kind here described have been made during the last two decades. However, the better ones, such as those of Lewinson and Zubin and of Pascal, support the case for a dependable relationship between handwriting and personality, and employ similar concepts and methods of measurement. Pascal's careful validation deserves special mention.[42] To be fair, however, we must note that Lorr and Fields, who factor-analyzed their inventory scores, found no reassuring validity in their own results.[43]

However, it is questionable whether the piling up of more validation studies will further illuminate the subject here under consideration. The weight of evidence, though admittedly slight, is in favor of a positive relationship between handwriting and personality above the chance level. Perhaps the relationship is too subtle and complex to be adequately measured by the crude tools which have been used. In any case, Wolfson's estimation seems eminently reasonable when she writes that "research findings appear to favor as psychologically most tenable and fruitful the hypothesis that handwriting *expression* and personality functioning are intricately related, but the problem of handwriting as a testing device persistently raises obstacles to quantification and interpretation." [44]

ARTISTIC TASTES AND PRODUCTIONS. It is a commonplace fact that students of the arts—of painting and music in particular—easily recognize the productions of well-known artists. Styles of art, even more perhaps than of handwriting, are clues to the individual's personality. While literary analysts have seldom succeeded in communicating the psychological meaning of artistic style, there is some objective evidence that it is subtly related to the total personality. Although artistic productions are partly motivated, as when the artist in his productions is trying to communicate with and stimulate others, they contain a large component of purely expressive experience. All healthy beings have the impulse to

[42] G. R. Pascal, The analysis of handwriting: a test of significance, *Char & Pers.*, 12 (1943), 123–44; G. R. Pascal and B. Suttel, Testing the claims of a graphologist, *J. Pers.*, 16 (1947), 192–97. In the first study, in which he correlated 14 objective handwriting scores with 21 measured personality traits, he found significant correlations in 37 instances and chance expectations in only 15.

[43] M. Lorr and V. Fields, A factorial study of body types, *J. clin. Psychol.*, 10 (1954), 182–85. For a similar assessment, see P. F. Secord, Studies in the relationship of handwriting to personality, *J. Pers.*, 17 (1949), 430–48 and W. R. Birge, An experimental inquiry into the measurable handwriting correlates of five personality traits, *J. Pers.*, 23 (1954), 215–23.

[44] Wolfson, Graphology, in Anderson and Anderson, *An introduction to projective techniques*, p. 427.

enjoy beauty and many have intense desires to express their aesthetic feelings in overt ways. If writers use artistic and other special-skill examples in their discussions, it is only because they know more about the creativeness of a da Vinci, a Beethoven, or a Goethe than about the spontaneous artistic impulses of the masses of obscure individuals.

Although the *subject matter* of artistic productions may be deliberately chosen as well as determined by prevailing public tastes, the *style* of their execution is uniquely personal and without clearly discernible causal determination. Despite the latter limitation on empirical investigation some experimental evidence has been accumulated to establish a relationship between style of production and personality variables. The chief barrier to the discovery of positive relations between them has been the variety of criteria for objective analysis. One workable set of criteria is that developed by Precker.[45] These criteria are (1) content, or subject matter, (2) use or avoidance of color, (3) use of space (in size of product, format, and relationship of elements within the picture), (4) form and pattern (shapes and their arrangement within the picture), (5) use of the media (characteristic ways of handling materials, quality of lines and strokes, pressure, etc.). That the five categories here listed are differentially managed by various artists cannot be denied by anyone who is familiar with the creative productions of well-known artists.

Some years ago Waehner investigated pictures made by children and college students by which she was able to differentiate statistically several psychiatric categories and the personalities of college girls. In one study she analyzed 760 pictures drawn by 38 children ranging in age from 8 to 11.[46] In another study using the paintings of 55 college girls she was able to establish a close relationship between the "style" of the paintings and the personalities of the girls, as revealed by Rorschach protocols and handwriting analyses.[47] Wolf, utilizing multiple expressive features, such as the drawings, brush paintings, finger paintings, posture, and balloon-play motion pictures of three children, found a positive relation between these factors and the children's behavior as reported by their teachers. Alschuler and Hattwick performed what is easily

[45] W. Wolf and J. A. Precker, Expressive movement and the methods of experimental depth psychology, in Anderson and Anderson, *An introduction to projective techniques*, pp. 474–75.

[46] T. S. Waehner, Formal criteria for the analysis of children's drawings, *Amer. J. Orthopsychiat.*, 12 (1942), 95–104.

[47] T. S. Waehner, Interpretation of spontaneous drawings and paintings, *Genet. Psychol. Monogr.*, 33 (1946), 3–70.

one of the most thorough and exhaustive quantitative studies of the relation between artistic expression and personality. They analyzed the paintings of 149 nursery-school children and compared them with the materials of case studies and with teachers' ratings. They found a close relationship between the formal characteristics of the paintings and personality variables.[48]

A recent study, utilizing the experience of Alschuler and Hattwick, was made by Stewart.[49] In this study 31 variables were studied in the self-portraits of eighty high school students of both sexes. The ratings of the expressive variables fell into five clusters for boys and seven clusters for girls. The correlations between these variables and behavior characteristics differed noticeably for the sexes. An over-all relation between artistic performance and personality factors was clearly established by Stewart's investigation.

Numerous other investigations deserve consideration in a survey of the problem, but we have cited at least enough to show that a positive and generally dependable relationship between artistic productions and personality has been established.

GESTURE, POSTURE, AND OTHER BODILY MOVEMENTS. These forms of behavior have been of interest to many students of expressive behavior, but we have very little reliable evidence of their relation to personality. Krout's interesting study of autistic gestures has not been replicated by others. Krout recorded more than three hundred common human gestures, such as shuffling one's feet, adjusting one's glasses, and yawning. While such gestures appear trivial on the surface, according to Krout they are expressions of inner dispositions toward external reality. Thus, yawning, which initially may have been an expression of sleepiness or fatigue, may come to express boredom in the company of others. Adjusting one's glasses, which originally may have been a normal response to the discomfort of wearing them, may later symbolize annoyance by another person.[50]

Posture seems to be related to personality, but it is difficult to say whether the relations one observes are based on well-known stereotypes or on basic personality characteristics. As a response of the total organism, posture probably expresses a diffused psy-

[48] R. Alschuler and L. W. Hattwick, *Painting and personality* (2 vols.; Chicago: University of Chicago Press, 1947).

[49] L. H. Stewart, The expression of personality in drawings and paintings, *Genet. Psychol. Monogr.*, 51 (1955), 45–103.

[50] M. H. Krout, Autistic gestures, *Psychol. Monogr.*, 46 (1935), No. 208. See also his earlier study, A preliminary note on some obscure symbolic muscular response of a diagnostic value in the study of normal subjects, *Amer. J. Psychiat.*, 11 (1931), 20–71.

chomotor state.[51] Without benefit of scientific evidence, most people tend to associate a slouched posture with lack of confidence, and a straight position and erect shoulders with self-confidence and a readiness to face the challenge of experience.

Gait is closely related to posture. Eisenberg and Reichline were able to establish above chance expectation the relation between gait and the attitude of dominance in a study of 238 women.[52] In this experiment the authors showed a thirty-second motion picture of the gait of each woman to one hundred students and asked them to match each gait with the presence or absence of dominance-feeling. The judges were correct in 63 per cent of the cases. This is, as we have remarked, above chance discrimination. Whatever the relationship may be, there can hardly be any doubt that every individual has his own rhythm and tempo of walking, and it is to that extent an expression of his individuality. In his youth the present writer knew a boy whose gait was described as "the million-dollar walk." This same boy was generally recognized by others as a self-confident, even cocky, youth who seldom failed in projects he undertook.

German psychologists used gait as a criterion for officer selection in World War II, as did the American OSS Assessment Staff.[53] Some years before, Enke established a relation between gait as well as other psychomotor traits and constitutional types.[54] These, as well as other studies, have made out a strong case for the claim that gait is an expression of personality.

The importance of posture and gait as expressions of psychological traits is very widely recognized by teachers and students of physical education. Through the body design and its movements the person reveals his inner self. The "stuff of the ages goes into man's thinking, is interpreted and comes out in movement and posture again. Personality goes into structure—by denial or affirmation into person again." [55] In his gait and posture man expresses a whole gamut of feelings and emotions. "Guilt, craft, vision,

[51] E. J. Kempf, *The autonomic functions and the personality* (New York: Nervous and Mental Disease Publishing Co., 1921). See also W. H. Blake, *A preliminary study of the interpretation of bodily expression* (New York: Columbia University Bureau of Publications, 1933).

[52] P. Eisenberg and P. B. Reichline, Judging expressive movement. II. Judgment of dominance-feeling from motion pictures of gait, *J. soc. Psychol.*, 10 (1939), 345–57.

[53] See E. Mira, *Psychiatry in war* (New York: W. W. Norton & Co., Inc., 1943); OSS Assessment Staff, *Assessment of men* (New York: Holt, Rinehart & Winston, Inc., 1948).

[54] W. Enke, Die Psychomotorik der Konstitution-typen, *Zeitschr. f. ang. Psychol.*, 36 (1930), 237–87. See further, W. Wolf, Involuntary self-expression in gait and other movements, *Char. & Pers.*, 3 (1953), 327–44.

[55] M. E. Todd, *The thinking body* (New York: Paul B. Hoeber, Inc., 1937), p. 2.

meanness, ecstasy, and lure appear in certain arrangement of arms, hands, shoulders, neck, head, and legs." [56] Rathbone points, out with good reason, that good posture in sitting and standing is esteemed not only for its hygienic value but for its psychological value as well. "The habitual postures each assumes," she writes, "are aspects of his general health and general state of mind. If he is buoyant and happy, his usual postures . . . will be erect and extended; if he is ill or depressed, his body will tend to be slumped, because the extensor muscles will not have sufficient tone." [57] It seems that every gesture of our bodily behavior reflects the inner individual.

DANCING AS EXPRESSIVE BEHAVIOR. One of the most fascinating of human expressions which illuminate the nature of man is the act of dancing. While it is amenable to change by instruction, the personal idiom of dancing transcends training and the demands of a particular situation, and each dancer's body, as Agnes De Mille remarks, is a unique instrument with individual modifications.[58] In great ballet dancing the performer expresses more than superficial feelings. Every motion and movement, every nod and gesture, is quintessential: there is in each subtle and vibrant act an irrevocable necessity and finality; none can be performed otherwise than it is. De Mille shows this in describing the dancing of Diana Adams by saying that "every gesture is absolute, as though there were no possible other gestures." [59]

That dancing has a fundamental individual component is attested to by the fact that, even though the performers are trained in the same way by the same teacher, they express in their dancing their unique personalities. This is as true of the creators of the dance—the choreographers—as it is of the performers themselves. Agnes De Mille has an uncontrollable preference for diagonal movements, with figures entering at one corner of the stage and leaving at the opposite one. George Balanchine has an affinity for single male figures "embroiled with two to six females one of whom either blinds or strangles him. The bodies of the dancers become entangled with each other in endless ropes or chains," and so forth. "One might build an interesting picture of Balanchine, the man, from these points of style. They are as natural to him as his sniff." [60] Jerome Robbins has still a different style, revealing

[56] *Ibid.*
[57] J. L. Rathbone, *Corrective physical education* (5th ed.; Philadelphia: W. B. Saunders Co., 1959), pp. 84–85.
[58] A. De Mille, *And promenade home* (Boston: Little, Brown & Co., 1958), p. 61.
[59] *Ibid.*, p. 76.
[60] *Ibid.*, p. 181.

his exuberant personality and his inexhaustible energy. He makes a free-limbed use of the body, as in sports. Whether his gesture is gay or anguished, all resources are put into play, and the strength and vigor of the movement communicates with the gusto of an athlete. Reflecting on the art of choreography, De Mille poses a thoughtful question. "Is it not likely," she asks, ". . . that certain space relations, rhythms and stresses have psychological significance, that some of these patterns are universal and the key to emotional response, that their deviations and modifications can be meaningful to the artist in terms of his own life experience, and that these overtones are grasped by the spectator without conscious analysis?" [61] Each individual as a psychological being, then, has his own symbols in space and rhythm. "If idiosyncrasies of expression constitute a key to others' understanding," De Mille adds, "they serve the artist in much the same way, as a means of self-revelation and a technique for reaching his emotional reservoir. They determine his work habits and of course the character of his expression." [62]

One of the most revealing facts about dancing—more specifically ballet dancing—is its transmutation of the sexual impulse. "Dancing represents sex in its least costly form, free from imprisonment and free to a great extent from emotional responsibility . . . it means freedom *from* sex. The forces which impelled women to the austerity of the church operate to form the great dancer. In a strange transmutation dancing is a form of asceticism—almost a form of celibacy." The genius with which certain women dance, De Mille continues, "derives from faculties and needs beyond any mere act of compensation," for talent is compounded of the entire personality and is as much a sign of exuberant health as of sickness. "Dancing has become a kind of sexual limbo whose inhabitants identify their own flesh with their purpose, a confusion not equally true for women artists whose bodies are not their life work. Dancing is, in a deep sense, the only physical union many of these women know, a sort of automarriage." [63]

Dancing as a form of human expressive behavior, while voluminously described and analyzed by professional dancers, has not attracted much attention among psychologists. However, the investigation by Franklin, Feldman, and Odbert deserves mention. In this experiment the authors observed each of eighteen high school girls, 15 to 17 years old, dancing in their stocking feet for

[61] *Ibid.*, p. 183.
[62] *Ibid.*, pp. 187–88.
[63] *Ibid.*, pp. 226–27.

thirty minutes. Their "style" of dancing was assessed on the basis of 22 movement-factors, such as position of the arms, degree of rising on the toes, and flexibility of posture. When the 22 variables were correlated with trait scores on Guilford's Inventory of Factors, STDCR, and other tests, significant relationships between certain personality variables and dancing behavior were discovered. The shy and inhibited girls tended to move slowly, held a rigid posture, held their arms down for the most part, held their trunks straight, and seldom rose on their toes. The spontaneous and sociable girls moved more rapidly, used their legs more, and held their shoulders down. Of the 22 movement-factors which the investigators examined, six were found to be significantly related to personal traits, namely, position of arms, shoulders, trunk, legs, feet, and degree of speed.[64]

Dancing may thus be described as a form of direct expression and fulfillment, the actualization of covert as well as overt dispositions of temperament. "It is a physical release," according to De Mille, "as no other performing art can be, because it is practiced on the whole body; the body is the instrument, the medium itself, and the exposure is total and voluptuous." [65]

"MYOKINETIC" BEHAVIOR. In 1940 Mira y Lopez published the results of a method of determining expressive behavior which he called "myokinetic psychodiagnosis." This has been recently published in book form, and deserves the careful study of every student of expressive behavior.[66] Although it measures a subject's control over his temperamental impulses, it "leaves impulsivity in virtually full command." [67]

The test materials of the myokinetic diagnosis are unusually simple. They consist of models of six drawings of geometric figures. These are lineograms; zigzags; stairs and circles; chains; parallels and U's in one position; and parallel's and U's in a second position. The subject is asked to draw the various forms without being able to see the paper and pencil in each hand, without resting his elbows, and in a horizontal position parallel to the table. While the tests measure characteristics other than expression, such as extratension, intratension, constitutional affectivity, depression, schizophrenia,

---

[64] G. H. Franklin, S. Feldman, and H. S. Odbert, Relationship of total bodily movement to some emotional components of personality, *J. Psychol.*, 26 (1948), 499–506.

[65] De Mille, *And promenade home*, p. 221.

[66] See E. Mira, Myokinetic psychodiagnosis, *Proc. roy, Soc. Med.*, 33 (1940), 173–94; and *Myokinetic psychodiagnosis* (New York: Logos Press, 1958). Translated from the Spanish by Mrs. J. Dubois.

[67] G. W. Allport, Foreword to Mira's *Myokinetic psychodiagnosis*, p. xv.

and intelligence, we are here concerned with them only as indicators of expressive movement. When the M.K.P. test was given to a sample of two hundred normal adults of both sexes, certain characteristics were found. Linear length in left-hand drawings exceeded that performed by the right hand for both sexes, and this length was distinctly greater for both hands in the female subjects. Maximal and minimal lengths of the zigzag drawings were practically equal in both sexes for both hands, although length of lines tended to be somewhat longer in the drawings of the females than in those of the males. "This," says the author, "suggests a constitutional predisposition to excitation which is relatively greater among women than among men." [68]

Inasmuch as the psychological interpretation of the several drawings is technical and time-consuming, we need state here only a few of their expressive meanings. Generally speaking, when lines are drawn in a direction away from the subject, they indicate aggressive tendencies; when they are drawn toward the subject, they reflect self-aggressive or suicidal trends. Strokes that are directed upward reveal elation or euphoria; whereas strokes that go downward generally show a depressed state. Constancy between left-hand and right-hand drawings is believed to indicate intrapsychic coherence: that is, the relative absence of intrapsychic tensions.

CONCLUDING REMARKS. The scientific study of psychological phenomena requires that experimental work be tested regarding its reliability and validity. The reliability of a measure is assured when it consistently measures what it purports to measure. A measure of reliability, then, establishes a relationship between the same phenomenon at different times and different phenomena at the same time. It must give similar results every time it makes a measurement of the same trait. A measure of validity is obtained when an instrument measures what it purports to measure, and not some other factor. A measure is thus valid when it has demonstrated the existence of a relationship between the results of an experiment and the psychological variable which is being investigated.

Now, practically all the experimental investigations which we have described in this chapter are both reliable and valid, although the coefficient of correlation of none of them is reassuringly high. Allport and Vernon, who made reliability studies of their results, found an interconsistency correlation of $+.75$ in 75 per cent of their experiments. Waehner and Wolf, in their studies of different forms of expressive behavior, were able to predict personality variables

[68] *Myokinetic psychodiagnosis*, p. 97.

from measures of expressive behavior, particularly in paintings and drawings, with dependable accuracy.

The comments of Allport and Vernon on their own tests of expression generally apply to most of the forms which we have described in this chapter, but in varying degree. "The great majority of tests, diverse as they were," the authors write, "show not only reliability but also significant statistical and logical inter-relations with other tests. . . . For those measures which are less satisfactory there almost always seems to be an explanation in terms of inadequacy of technique, rather than in terms of specificity in the performance of the subjects." [69]

Lest the reader form the impression that the subject of expressive behavior is only crudely empirical, or that it is wholly unmotivated, it is only fair to point out that this is not entirely so. Whether it is entirely unmotivated depends in part on how we interpret motivation. If we conceive the latter in the language of stimulus and response and interpret it entirely in the conceptual language of homeostatic needs or painful behavior, then expressive behavior can be said to be unmotivated. However, if we view expressive behavior in terms of perceptual and cognitive controls based on comparison of inputs left by the residue of past experience—the apperceptive mass of Herbart—then it obeys lawful controls. This is the kind of lawfulness posited by Berlyne on the basis of rigorous experiment. His experiments lead in effect to a remodeling of stimulus-response theory in the very direction suggested by our discussion in this and other chapters. To be sure, Berlyne is less concerned with personality and expressive behavior, than he is with creative behavior, but it is very relevant to our own discussion of expressive behavior, especially in the sense that creative behavior is truly self-actualizing.[70]

CONCLUSION

The experimental investigation of expressive phenomena is in need of a renaissance. For the reasons enumerated in the intro-

---

[69] Allport and Vernon, *Studies in expressive movement*, p. 120. For tests of the predictive value of other expressive techniques, see the following: T. S. Waehner, Interpretation of spontaneous drawings and paintings, *Genet. Psychol. Monogr.*, 33 (1946), 3–70; W. Wolf, Projective methods for personality analysis of expressive behavior in preschool children, *Char. & Pers.*, 10 (1942), 309–30; W. Wolf, *The personality of the pre-school child.*

[70] See D. E. Berlyne, The influence of complexity and novelty in visual figures on orienting responses, *J. exp. Psychol.*, 55 (1958), 289–96; Uncertainty and conflict: A point of contact between information theory and behavior theory, *Psychol. Rev.*, 64 (1957), 329–39.

ductory paragraphs of this chapter, the subject has not received the amount of professional attention warranted by its real and potential value for the study of personality. Thus it is necessary, for example, to investigate more thoroughly than Maslow has done the nature of self-actualization as expressive behavior. It might be particularly fruitful to investigate the expressive nature of sexual behavior in women which, when uninhibited by the crippling demands of conventional expectations, is predominantly expressive in character—an emission of something within the depths of a woman's being.[71]

The very warp and woof of contemporary self-theory, psychological growth, self-actualization, and becoming—the views of such seminal psychologists as Allport, Angyal, Goldstein, Maslow, Murphy, and Rogers—have a close affinity with the problem of expressive behavior. With Maslow, one may say that all behavior is expressive in addition to being other things.[72] The researches and psychological observations of these men lead to the conclusion that expressive behavior and similar original dispositions like drives and instincts, are not primarily, if at all, mechanisms for securing the organism's survival, but represent potentialities for attaining health and adulthood. Through expressive dispositions the individual has the opportunity, as Allport phrased it, "to become something more than a stencil copy of the species to which he belongs." There is an urge in every healthy individual to become increasingly individuated and, out of the complex web of his continuing experience, to develop a life-style characterized by self-awareness and self-enhancement.[73]

Expressive, in contrast to adaptive, behavior may very well be determined by laws which do not now adequately account for it. Spontaneity cannot be easily contained within a formula; like all fugitive behavior it eludes rigid formulation. To regard expressive behavior, then, as an important aspect of the total personality without recognizing that it is considerably autonomous is to see only part of the picture. To the holistic psychologist the content of behavior, which makes up the larger segment of the psychology of personality, is to a great extent a social artifact. He thinks that the basic nature of human personality is to be found as much in the individual's life-style as in what he says and does. To infer the nature of personality from forms of expression requires as much

[71] The expressive nature of woman's sexuality was suggested to the author by A. H. Maslow in a personal communication.
[72] *Ibid.*
[73] See G. W. Allport, *Becoming: basic considerations for a psychology of personality* (New Haven: Yale University Press, 1955), pp. 27–28.

aesthetic sensitivity as empirical knowledge and methodological skill.

The student of expressive behavior is forced to the conclusion that the behavior scientist must concern himself with the whole of behavioral reality, not only with a specialized segment. He must concern himself with all the relevant problems of behavior, from "color-theories to defense mechanisms, from the functions of a white rat's vibrissae to the mystic's sense of unutterable revelation, from imaginary playmates to partial correlations." [74]

[74] G. Murphy, *An historical introduction to modern psychology* (New York: Harcourt, Brace and Co., 1930), p. 1.

CHAPTER **13**

The Attitude-Value
Complex

Individual and social attitudes were among the earliest and most widely investigated psychological processes, especially in the fields of personality and social behavior. Most of our socialized responses to others are in the form of attitudes toward them. When we say, for example, that we like or dislike a certain person, or that we approve or disapprove of his actions, we are expressing an attitude. These responses or attitudes toward others, as well as toward any other object or situation in the social environment, are learned tendencies to act in expected ways. An attitude is thus a dispositional reaction of an individual to his perceptual environment. Since attitudes are constant potentials to act in certain ways, a knowledge of their nature, origin, and role in human behavior is a matter of great importance for the psychology of personality.

If attitudes are ways of responding to one's perceptual environment—to the persons, objects, and situations in the perceptual world—they imply a general or specific directionality. The objects toward which they are directed have a degree of attractiveness to the individual. They are desired or desirable, unwanted or rejected. Accordingly, most, if not all, attitudes are directed toward or conditioned by a value, or a complex of values. Attitudes and values are thus inseparable. This inseparable attitude-value relationship we shall call the attitude-value complex.

However, our chief objective is not to study attitudes and values as such, even though we shall discuss their structure at length; rather, it is to show their place in personality formation, and more particularly the extent to which they illuminate the nature of personality. We believe that in knowing an individual's value-complex we can learn to understand him in the same manner and to the same extent that we can by studying his motives, learnings, thoughts, and perceptions. Instead of approaching the attitude-value complex as if it were autonomous, we shall examine it as an integral part of the total personality.

Again, we shall omit any discussion of the methodology and techniques for measuring attitudes. These problems, while very important, are not immediately relevant to the psychology of personality. They belong in the field of general social psychology. The reader who wishes to study such problems as methods of data collection and scaling techniques will find a voluminous literature on these subjects in a large variety of sources.

THE NATURE OF VALUES

In view of the enormous amount of research performed on the nature of attitudes, one might expect to find varied and not too consistent definitions of these human dispositions. However, this is not true. The definitions are very much at one in declaring them to be tendencies or dispositions, rather than overt acts.

A similar unanimity does not exist regarding the nature of values, and the subject is both vague and confused. Nevertheless, the subject must be thoroughly examined, for the attitudes which cause us to choose between different forms of behavior are always value-bound. Goals and ideals are not only motivated, but are crucially determined by the value system which serves as a guide to their realization. Most behavior rests to some extent on presuppositions which direct it along desired lines. Our attitudes toward Negroes, communists, or the Catholic church presuppose a value system which renders them meaningful. Attitudes as such are only tendencies to act; it is the scheme of value that makes them future-oriented.

Since values both condition and direct most of our attitudes, we shall consider them first.

VALUES: ELEMENTS AND SCHEMA. Human values are perceived both singly and in patterns. Children's wants consist for the most part of separate or loosely connected desires and wishes. They want candy or ice cream, to watch television or go to the movies. The process of canalization establishes such wants in accordance with cultural expectations, and the child's internal tensions will make certain that appropriate behavior will lead him to their satisfaction. In many adults, likewise, there is only a tenuous relation among the separate values which they pursue. One gets no clear picture of a dominant value system, but only of many values with no particular strain of consistency among them. Their values are characterized more by discontinuity than order, so that it is virtually impossible to describe their personalities by a consistent value pattern.

On the other hand, some individual's can be recognized and described by a dominant value system. On the basis of such a value system it is possible to classify personalities into fairly consistent types. Spranger devised such a classification more than forty years ago, and Morris more recently.[1] These are discussed in detail in Chapter 3. Each based his classification of personalities on the basic value patterns by which each individual ordered his life. Spranger's styles of life, or systems of value, are theoretical, economic, aesthetic, social (that is, sympathetic), political, and religious. Morris' value patterns, or "paths of life," as he calls them, are moderation, self-sufficiency, affection, sensuousness, sociality, activity, and a balanced integration of the other six.[2]

Psychological studies of value-schemas point up the fact that maturity, consistency, and integration of personality are greatly dependent on the possession by the individual of a relatively harmonious set of personal and social values. These value systems serve as directing agencies which give meaning to his life. One need not be a psychologist to observe that much of the individual's behavior consists in striving for desired objectives. It is a commonplace fact that people differ in the objects they value and the ends which they set up to achieve. The individual who strives mostly for physiological satisfactions is different from the person who is mostly involved in aesthetic or moral concerns. Another one is different still because he will sacrifice his own well-being for the welfare of others. In each case the value complex has saliency in the individual's personality because it holds a central and dominant position in his daily life. Because what is important to a person motivates him in many ways, he comes to perceive

---

[1] See E. Spranger, *Lebensformen*, trans. as *Types of men: the psychology and ethics of personality*, by P. J. W. Pigors (Halle: Max Niemeyer Verlag, 1928); C. Morris, Individual differences and cultural patterns, in C. Kluckhohn and H. A. Murray (eds.), *Personality in nature, society, and culture* (New York: Alfred A. Knopf, Inc., 1948).

[2] For a valid and reliable scale for the measurement of values, based on Spranger's work, see P. E. Vernon and G. W. Allport, A test for personal values, *J. abnorm. soc. Psychol.*, 26 (1931), 231–48.

people, objects, and himself in the light of his value system. His perceptions are colored by his ruling values. The latter determine his subjective accentuation of experience and of the world around him.

We have already referred to the future-orientedness of values. This forward-directedness of values gives to attitudes, which are subjective tendencies, their forward thrust, and keeps the healthy individual from becoming a completed and static product. We come to understand persons by the kind of future they are producing for themselves and others.[3] Spranger's uncompromising stress on the future orientation of the individual is an attractive as well as a veridical feature of his view of value-relation and personality. The six value systems he posited and the kinds of persons who pursue them are, of course, ideals which an individual can only approximate. Should he in some unimagined way attain the ideal— a possibility which by definition is denied in Spranger's schema— the individual would cease growing as a psychological being. From the point of view of a value schema, whether Spranger's or anyone else's, personality is neither a possession nor a product, but an unceasing act of becoming. Death alone puts a quietus on the unending process.

However, a note of caution must be injected into this analysis. There are upper limits to the possibilities of growth in every person, as Allport has pointed out; but the limits can be moved by reflection, self-objectification, and breadth of education. While this is true from the psychological point of view, from the standpoint of ethics, "the stretching toward this limit, whatever it is, is as much of a triumph for a life of slight potential as for a life whose potentials are great."[4]

A problem of great psychological import is the identification of the value schemas which guide the individual's behavior. In one sense, psychologists have made a variety of attempts to classify human desires, but their work has concerned itself with the classification of motives, not with the systematization of values. To be sure, motives conceived as ends are value-oriented, but these are not identical. Again, any classification of values into a schema must reckon with their cultural determination. There may be universal schemas, but we know too little about them. White has given us a comprehensive classification of basic values which could

---

[3] For a penetrating discussion of the creative force of personal values, see P. Weiss, *Man's freedom* (New Haven: Yale University Press, 1950).

[4] G. W. Allport, *Becoming: basic considerations for a psychology of personality* (New Haven: Yale University Press, 1955), p. 88.

serve as a provisional schema. He divides them into physiological, social, egoistic, fearful, playful, practical, cognitive, and miscellaneous.[5] Examples of physiological values are food, sex, and health; of social, love and friendship; of egoistic, independence, self-regard, and aggression; of fearful, emotional security; of playful, new experience and creative self-expression; of practical, economic value and work; of cognitive, knowledge; and of miscellaneous, happiness.[6]

Empirical investigation of values. The scientific study of values has been seriously hampered by two serious drawbacks, namely, (1) the fallacious belief that values lie outside the domain of scientific inquiry; and (2) the paucity of empirical research. That these drawbacks need not be permanent has been demonstrated by recent objective studies of the role of value in human behavior.

Recent experimental investigations of perception and cognition suggest rich possibilities for the study of values. The theoretical researches of Brunswik and Wolf, and the empirical investigations of Murphy and of Bruner and his associates, are a few examples.[7]

In their investigation of the differential perceptions of coins in children from the Boston slums ("the *poor* group"), and from a progressive school in the Greater Boston area ("the *rich* group"), Bruner and Goodman established the validity of three important general hypotheses regarding the relation between values and perception, and thus indirectly between values and personality. The hypotheses are as follows:

(1) The greater the social value of an object, the more susceptible will it be to organization by behavioral determinants.

(2) The greater the individual need for a socially valued object, the more marked will be the operation of behavioral determinants.

(3) Perceptual ambiguity will facilitate the operation of behavioral determinants only in so far as ambiguity reduces the operation

---

[5] R. K. White, *Value-analysis.* Copyright 1951 by the Society for the Psychological Study of Social Issues, p. 12. The category of *miscellaneous* has little functional value, for behavior is not regulated by miscellaneous values, except in very poorly organized individuals. It is one of those categories which is a confession of helplessness and defeat in the attempt to simplify complex psychological phenomena.

[6] The reader should compare these with the classification of motives given in Chapter 9.

[7] E. Brunswik, *Wahrnehmung und Gegenstandswelt* (Vienna: Deuticke Verlag, 1934); G. Murphy, *Personality: a biosocial approach to origins and structure* (New York: Harper & Bros., 1947); J. S. Bruner and C. C. Goodman, Value and need as organizing factors in perception, *J. abnorm. soc. Psychol.,* 42 (1947), 33–44; J. S. Bruner and L. Postman, Symbolic value as an organizing factor in perception, *J. soc. Psychol.,* 27 (1948), 203–8; W. Wolf, *Values and personality: an existential psychology of crisis* (New York: Grune & Stratton, Inc., 1950).

of autochtonous (i.e., indigenous) determinants without reducing the effectiveness of behavioral determinants.[8]

The experiment of Bruner and Goodman revealed that the "poor" and the "rich" children did not see the same coin as the same size, and their judgment of coin size varied with the individual's *need* for whatever it symbolized. The difference was highly significant, for an analysis of variance showed that the source of variance was significant beyond the probability level of .01.

The general conclusion indicated by this and other experiments is that the individual tends to maximize the reward value of an object. Value, in other words, is a determinant of subjective size, and the direction and magnitude of accentuation of size may be a function of the particular values involved.[9]

Sorokin has recently undertaken, under the auspices of the Harvard Research Center for Creative Altruism, a comprehensive investigation of the role of values, particularly love and altruism, in the determination and growth of personality. Basing his conclusion on the voluminous data published in his *Social and cultural dynamics*, Sorokin shows that creative, that is, unselfish, love for other human beings is the most constructive feature of the healthy personality and the sane society. Love is a factor in increasing the longevity of individuals and organizations, and deficiency in *the vitamin of love* is responsible for many mental disorders and social disorganization. Citing the examples of the longest existing organizations, namely, Taoism, Confucianism, Hinduism, Buddhism, Jainism, Christianity, and Mohommedanism, Sorokin attributes their durability to their altruistic education of millions of people in unselfish love.[10] Sorokin's data constitute a powerful argument for Spranger's social man, Morris' life-styles of sociality and affection, and White's social or friendship category.

It would illuminate our human nature if we could adduce similar evidence for the molding force of other values, such as ethical, religious, and the aesthetic. Psychologists pay all too little attention, for example, to the role of beauty in molding personalities. Psychoanalysts, of course, have written voluminously on art and beauty, but their conclusions are mostly negative; they deal too

---

[8] Bruner and Goodman, Value and need, pp. 36–37.

[9] Bruner and Postman, Symbolic value, p. 207.

[10] P. A. Sorokin, The powers of creative unselfish love, in A. H. Maslow (ed.), *New knowledge in human values* (New York: Harper & Bros., 1959), pp. 3–12. For the documentation upon which his conclusions are based, see his *Social and cultural dynamics* (4 vols.; New York: American Book Co., 1937–41), Vol. 3, Chs. 9–14.

much with their defensive functions and with their pathological aspects. The love and experience of beautiful objects, persons, and situations is as civilizing as love, and may well be an important aspect of it. Weiss, the philosopher, expresses this fact eloquently. He writes:

The experience of beauty is a crucial experience; to have undergone it is to have begun to change one's ways. He who sees beauty is transformed; under its influence his behavior becomes subtler and more appropriate than it had been before. As an effect of it he acts with others more harmoniously than he did; he treats things as being more precious, as being of greater import, as deserving to be worked over more, to be cared for more than they had been. No one can be said to have had a vision of true beauty, to have a genuine grasp of a true work of art, to have the gift of tongues, to have seen a value beyond the reach of those immersed in a given epoch, unless he shows in his acts that he is sensitive and concerned with the rights and needs of others in and of themselves.[11]

Our brief analysis of the nature of values shows that all mature men live by intentions and presuppositions. These intentions and presuppositions are probably unique for each person, and they mold the individual's character in important ways. They serve as guides to action; they make every personal history coherent and meaningful because they subordinate the minor component of a value system to its larger matrix. This is the meaning of a hierarchy of values, wherein one value is placed before another, and first things come first. Accordingly, in knowing an individual's hierarchy of values we learn to know him as a person. By studying man as a self-perfecting individual we come to see him as one whose "passion for integrity and for a meaningful relation to the whole of Being is his most distinctive capacity."[12]

Values and norms. Although the intentions and presuppositions by which a person guides his life are probably unique for each person, as we said in the preceding paragraph, they do not originate in a vacuum. Being human constructions, they arise in and are modified by a cultural milieu. These social values are called social or cultural norms; they are the more or less binding and accepted rules of a group or a larger society. As anthropologists have shown and as Sherif demonstrated some years ago, they function as anchorage points, or frames of reference, which guide the attitudes, judgments, and overt behavior of people in groups.[13] The child learns these norms through the influences of others, by means of formal

11 Weiss, *Man's freedom*, p. 176.
12 G. W. Allport, *Becoming*, p. 98.
13 See M. Sherif, *The psychology of social norms* (New York: Harper & Bros., 1936).

and informal instruction, by imitation of the behavior of others, and earliest of all, through the normal process of canalization. Once the norms have been established through canalization they tend to persist because behavior congruent with them is rewarded and acts in their defiance are punished. Thus, although values may arise from individual wants, they are also in many instances antecedent to them. They often direct the course of wants, as when we want things because they have social value, because they are valued by others, or because they confer prestige upon the individual.

Although values and norms are closely related, they are not identical. Values are more akin to motives, since they are based on human wants and desires, and not only on the expectations of members of a group. Their individual nature, in contrast to their social origin, is what makes them unique for each person. They are also intimately linked with attitudes, as we have already made clear. Indeed, motives, attitudes, and values commingle in well-nigh endless ways; when they are canalized and organized into relatively consistent forms of behavior, they form personality. As we shall see, personality is in a very important way the coherent value system of the individual.

Contrasting these concepts further still, we wish to point out that both motives and attitudes are more specific than values; values are, however paradoxical it may sound, at once more universal and unique. They are universal because they are found in all mankind as norms of behavior; they are unique because every individual internalizes them in accordance with his own disposition. "Unique" does not mean apart from the group or culture; it signifies either an individualistic internalization of culture-bound norms, or the primacy of individual over group goals. Norms are culturally established categories of action; motives are individual strivings toward desirable objects; attitudes are tendencies to act toward the objects; and values are the personal-social impulsions toward approved and desired ends.

The difference between norms and values can be indicated in another way, with particular reference to the alleged neutrality of science. The norms of Western society do not approve the wholesale extermination of peoples, either in peace or in war; and the norms of contemporary science are in agreement with this moral principle. Nevertheless, an individual scientist, while accepting society's dictum in principle, may in fact close his mind against it—under the guise of scientific neutrality. He dichotomizes between society's norms and his "scientific" values. Thus he might say that, as a good citizen he does not approve of destroying whole communities of people, but if you want him to instruct you in how to perform the task efficiently, he can spell out the details of how to effect it. Moral schizophrenia results from the inconsistency or clash between cultural norms and individual values, just as ethical behavior is a consequence of their congruence. Atomic scientists, however, perhaps more than others, are concerning themselves with this problem.

Universal and unique dimensions of values. We have said that values are both individual or unique and culturally determined. Uniqueness is a term that describes both individual value dispositions and cultural norms. The divergence of cultural norms for different societies has been pretty well established by such cultural anthropologists as Ruth Benedict and Margaret Mead.[14]

However, the thesis of a unitary and integrated culture is open to question, and has recently been challenged by Florence Kluckhohn.[15] There is more similarity in cultures than the cultural relativists admit. She maintains that there are common value orientations in all societies, and that the various cultures practice individual variations of these orientations.

Kluckhohn bases her classification of value orientations on two basic assumptions. These assumptions are as follows:

(1) There is a limited number of basic human problems that all peoples at all times and in all places have had to solve.

(2) While the solutions have varied they have done so within a range of possible variations.

There are five such basic human problems, according to Kluckhohn: (1) the view of basic human nature; (2) the view of man's relation to nature; (3) the significant time dimension; (4) the preferred activity orientation; and (5) the dominant modality of man's relation to others.[16]

In Kluckhohn's view, individuals differ in their solutions of these culturally defined problems. Thus, a person may conceive human nature as unalterably evil, or as evil but perfectable, or as a mixture of good and evil. An individual may conceive man's proper relation to nature as a form of submission to it, or as in harmony with it,

---

[14] See for example, the following: R. Benedict, *Patterns of culture* (Boston: Houghton Mifflin Co., 1934), and *The chrysanthemum and the sword* (Boston: Houghton Mifflin Co., 1946); M. Mead, *From the south seas* (New York: William Morrow & Co., Inc., 1939), and *Male and female* (New York: William Morrow & Co., Inc., 1949).

[15] F. Kluckhohn, Value orientations, in R. R. Grinker (ed.), *Toward a unified theory of human behavior* (New York: Basic Books, Inc., 1956), pp. 83–93.

[16] *Ibid.*, p. 85.

or as being capable of exploiting and subduing it. In his time orientation, a man may look to the past, the present, or the future. His activity orientation may be in the form of being-in-becoming, which is a creative orientation; or in the form of doing, which lies essentially in the field of action and performance. By knowing the range of variability in these orientations, we can better understand the culture which subscribes to it; and by knowing an individual's preferences for one or another solution of them, we can gain knowledge of his personality. Thus, for example, a person who thinks man is by nature evil presents us with a different impression from that of the individual who believes that man is fundamentally good; the individual who rejects the past and believes that change is desirable differs markedly from the person who feels most comfortable with the status quo; and so on. While these orientations may be idealized and formalized in a theoretical analysis, there can be no doubt that all people approximate them to some degree. As cultural and behavioral approximations they are both valid and useful in the study of the relationship between value systems and personality. All in all, although we recognize the limitation of infering personality characteristics from value schematas, a knowledge of their existence and function in human actions aids us in better understanding the meanings which govern a man's behavior, and brings us closer to making dependable predictions of how he will act in concrete situations.

THE NATURE OF ATTITUDES

Judging by the prodigious amount of theoretical, methodological, and experimental research that has been performed on attitudes during the past two decades, we can still say, as Allport said in 1935, that the problem is central in the field of social psychology. Today, the study of attitudes is increasingly investigated with reference to its place in personality. The recent volume by Smith, Bruner, and White is an excellent demonstration of the intimate relation between attitudes and personality, and it makes out a valid case for the use of attitudes, or opinions, as a method of assessing personality.[17] Our objective in this section is the systematic understanding of attitudes and the light they throw upon the human personality; we are not concerned with the techniques of measuring them.

The psychology of attitudes, despite its important place in the

[17] M. B. Smith, J. S. Bruner, and R. W. White, *Opinions and personality* (New York: John Wiley & Sons, Inc., 1956).

study of social behavior, and despite the enormous labors spent on its investigation, is still considerably vague. The very abundance of published works on the subject has probably materially contributed to this state of affairs. This situation has been aggravated by the variety of interests and approaches and by the great stress on quantitative measurement. Fortunately for our purpose, the problem can be simplified by examining only those aspects of the subject that have direct relevance for the study of personality. We shall not be detained by consideration of the origin, change, and measurement of attitudes, important as these are for other areas of human psychology. We are free in this chapter to disregard the somewhat fruitless controversy over the question whether attitudes and opinions are or are not identical; for from our point of view opinions are expressed or verbalized attitudes. We can safely ignore the relation or similarity of attitudes, motives, traits, beliefs, and sentiments. They are doubtless related, but their interrelation is not here a crucial issue.

DEFINITIONS OF ATTITUDE. The fact that writers have not tended to define attitudes in exactly the same way only compounds the existing confusion. Yet, from the early concerns of German psychologists, to its introduction into American psychological thought by Thomas and Znaniecki, to its sure establishment in contemporary investigations, the term "attitude" has, at bottom, meant the same thing. While the terminology, or the preferred statement of its meaning, has varied in the writings of different psychologists and sociologists, the concept of attitudes has had an enduring and fundamental meaning.[18]

Attitude as a determining tendency. Probably the earliest definition of attitude is that given by Thomas and Znaniecki. It is also the meaning given to it by the German psychologists at the turn of this century in the term *Bewusstseinslage*. From this point of view an attitude is a *preparatory* action; as such it may be defined as a predisposition to act toward or away from an object or value. Being a *preparatory* act, it is always a potential adjustment toward an object or situation. Once the attitude is expressed a desired adjustment has been made, and it ceases, for the time being, to

[18] A small sample of references dealing with the subject, is the following: J. Orth, *Gefühl und Bewusstseinslage, Abhand. Geb. Pedagog. u. Psychol.,* 1903); W. I. Thomas and F. Znaniecki, *The Polish peasant in Europe and America* (5 vols.; Boston: Badger, 1918–1920), Vol. 1; F. H. Allport, *Social Psychology* (Boston: Houghton Mifflin Co., 1924), Ch. 13; G. W. Allport, Attitudes, in C. Murchison (ed.), *A handbook of social psychology* (Worcester, Mass.: Clark University Press, 1935), Ch. 27; G. Lindzey (ed.), *Handbook of social psychology* (Reading, Mass.: Addison-Wesley Publishing Co., Inc., 1954), Vol. 1, Ch. 9.

have an activating effect upon the individual. However, it may persist in the individual's memory in the form of a habitual "set." An attitude is thus not an isolated disposition, but the preparatory phase of a behavioral continuum of which adjustment is the end-product. The writing of these lines, for instance, is an adjustment to the wish to express certain facts and ideas. The writer's attitude is the *intent* to write, but the *act* of writing is the realization of an attitude in overt behavior. When he stops writing, the attitude as a form of anticipation or trial response endures as a potential act, as a disposition to write.

Attitude as a postural response. This is essentially Floyd Allport's view, and is one of the earliest strictly psychological formulations in America. A postural response in early American psychology was conceived as an organic state of readiness, and is deeply embedded in stimulus-response theory. Neuromuscular adjustments arise in the interstimulations of individuals. Attitudes are thus not only responses to stimuli, but also "the *preparations for response* set up in the neuromuscular system." [19]

Although this definition is couched in stimulus-response and neuromuscular language, it is clearly the same in principle as the definition in terms of determining tendency. Like the latter definition, Allport's view conceives it as a *preparation for action.*

Attitude as an anticipatory response. The definitions by Gordon Allport and by Krech and Crutchfield, both of which have been widely quoted, are good examples of this kind of definition. In his early formulation Allport defined an attitude as "a mental and neural state of readiness exerting a directive influence upon the individual's response to all objects and situations with which it is related." [20]

The definition by Krech and Crutchfield is more comprehensive in that is recognizes the relation of attitudes to other psychological variables. They define it as "*an enduring organization of motivational, emotional, perceptual, and cognitive processes with respect to some aspect of the individual's world.*" [21]

Common features of definitions. In a preceding paragraph we stated that, despite the difference in terminology used in various definitions, the views on attitudes boil down to roughly the same thing. The foregoing and other definitions too numerous to state here, without exception stress the preparatory, anticipatory, inten-

[19] F. H. Allport, *Social psychology,* p. 320. Italics in the original.
[20] G. W. Allport, Attitudes, p. 810.
[21] D. Krech and R. S. Crutchfield, *Theory and problems of social psychology* (New York: McGraw-Hill Book Co., Inc., 1948), p. 152.

tional, and relatively enduring characteristics of attitudes. All of them implicitly or explicitly recognize the motivational, affective, and cognitive properties associated with attitudes. Without exception, they conceive attitudes as traits, factors, or latent variables, to use the more recent terminology.[22] Each of them without exception views attitudes as *latent* variables; or, phrased in our own language, as *determining tendencies* or *dispositions* to act with reference to a value. Under ideal conditions act and attitude would be inseparable, so that an act would be what the attitude means, and the attitude would mean what the act does.[23]

ATTITUDES AND VALUES. In earlier pages of this chapter we emphasized the fact that attitudes and values are correlative. A value, we have variously said, refers to the concerns and interests of human beings; so that any object which acquires interest and meaning for someone is a value. Attitudes and values tend to form a relatively consistent system—the attitude-value complex, which forms the subject matter of this chapter—and serve as a *Verankerungspunkt*, or anchoring point, for the personality.[24] This complex serves as a frame of reference by means of which a person's perceptions of the world are organized into a fairly consistent and meaningful experience. Every individual organizes his experience by means of a pattern of functionally related perceptions; and he responds to new situations in terms of his frame of reference. Common sense tells us that of the large variety of social objects which compose our daily experiences we respond to some and are indifferent to others. One object derives its meaning or value from other objects with which it has come to be associated. To a person who has neither heard of nor tasted caviar, the latter has no meaning; to the individual who likes it but can only rarely have it, it is a delightful luxury; while, as Shakespeare said, it "is not a delicacy to the general," who can have it whenever he wishes. Each individual perceives the caviar through the screen of his own attitude-value system, frame of reference, or anchoring point. The behavior of each toward caviar is influenced by the attitude-value complex,

---

22 For uses of some of these terms see the following: G. W. Allport, *Personality: a psychological interpretation* (New York: Holt, Rinehart & Winston, Inc., 1937); L. L. Thurstone, *Multiple factor analysis* (Chicago: University of Chicago Press, 1947); P. F. Lazarsfeld, The logical and mathematical foundation of latent structure analysis, in S. A. Stouffer *et al.*, *Measurement and prediction* (Princeton, N.J.: Princeton University Press, 1950), pp. 362–412.

23 See H. Bonner, *Social psychology: an interdisciplinary approach* (New York: American Book Co., 1953), p. 175.

24 See K. Koffka, Perception: an introduction to the *Gestalt-Theorie*, *Psychol. Bull.*, 19 (1922), 531–85; S. Rogers, The anchoring of absolute judgments, *Arch. Psychol.*, 1941, No. 261.

or by the frame of reference in which he makes his selections and judgments.

The attitude-value complex affects not only man's daily behavior but his scholarly and scientific ideas as well. While scientists like to think of their investigations and conclusions as entirely objective, it is now pretty well agreed that this is not altogether true. Like any human activity, science and scholarship are subject to the influence of value-relationships.[25] The salient values of the scientific world as well as politico-economic ideologies shape the attitudes of scientific workers. They direct the scientist's interests, determine the choice of his investigative techniques, and affect his conclusions.[26] The contemporary emphasis on nuclear and other operationally-directed research, is a reflection of the dominant concern of scientists with the problems of national defense. The ethos, or peculiar values of our time, impels them to become ego-involved in problems which did not trouble their minds a generation or more ago.

The persistence of many attitudes regarding race, religion, and politics, for example, can be explained in the same manner. Race prejudice, to consider a widespread and well-investigated example, is not due to the depravity of human nature, but to the powerful pressure brought to bear upon men by the value-system of a group. Since attitudes and values are deeply anchored in a normative frame of reference, they are widely shared and mutually reinforcing. Studies of race prejudice show that our attitudes are acquired less through our interaction with prejudiced individuals than from the pressures of the ethos and the reference groups of our society. Social values, or frames of reference, much less than interaction and contact with the objects of our prejudices, determine our attitudes toward rejected people. The frames of reference of the group are internalized by the individual; he becomes self-involved in them and acts in accordance with their claims. This self-involvement in the values of the group, especially when it is emotionally toned, as it usually is, adds to them the features of irrationality and invulnerability which are prominent in human prejudices.

A value-system, or frame of reference, then, is a more or less

---

[25] See the Introduction.

[26] For early considerations of the relationship between science and the dominant values of the times, see R. Müller-Freienfels, Studies in the social psychology of science, *J. soc. Psychol.*, 4 (1933), 26–41; E. Schrödinger, *Science and the human temperament* (New York: W. W. Norton & Co., Inc., 1935); K. Mannheim, *Ideology and utopia* (New York: Harcourt, Brace and Co., 1936), especially Chs. 2 and 4; G. L. De Gré, *Society and ideology* (New York: Privately printed, Columbia University Bookstore, 1943).

consistent body of standards which give meaning or direction to an attitude. An attitude, on the other hand, is an internal tendency to respond to an object. When the object becomes desirable, or when it is conceived as satisfying a wish or need, it becomes a value. In fine, attitudes and values are inseparable, and together they form the attitude-value complex which guides an individual's behavior.[27]

THE ATTITUDE-VALUE COMPLEX AND PERSONALITY

In the preceding pages of this chapter we already directly or by implication disclosed something of the bond between an individual's attitude-value complex and his personality. We showed that an important characteristic of human behavior is the selection of ends which will best secure an individual's adjustment and survival. Indeed, all human living is a succession of choices between alternative ends. These choices have a motivational function, for they impel the individual to act in such a manner as to aid him in reaching a desired end. A man's attitude-value complex is his chief psychological instrument for understanding human reality—perhaps of physical reality, as well. Look deep enough into an individual's attitudes and values and you discover no mere fugitive beliefs, but an expression of his total personality. While the values and attitudes of an individual are many and even diverse, the personality which they help to mold is not fractionated except in deviant cases; and the more consistent they are, the more truly do they give coherence and unity to it.

ATTITUDE-VALUE COMPLEX AND THE SELF. Inasmuch as we discuss the self at great length in Chapter 16, we omit a description of its nature here. Also, while the self is defined divergently in the literature of social psychology and the psychology of personality, a preliminary delineation of it will adequately serve our purpose. Even a brief analysis shows that the self is fundamentally an organization of attitudes and values.

Role-perception. The self is most clearly seen in role behavior. In role behavior the individual acts as an object to himself. The

[27] We believe that psychologists generally would take issue with the contention that value judgments differ from moral judgments, as is done by some philosophers—most recently by W. D. Lamont. According to this view, a value judgment always refers to the cognitive activity by which we impute value to things; whereas a moral judgment is an assertion regarding what ought or ought not to be done. However, from the social-psychological point of view, all values are characterized by "ought-ness"—by the force of social, as well as personal, pressures to act in certain ways. For the allegation that value judgments and moral judgments are dissimilar, see W. D. Lamont, The value judgment (New York: Philosophical Library, 1955).

child first perceives himself as an autonomous being when he introjects the role of his mother. He plays her role in his perceptions of her bodily gestures, her words, the sound of her voice. Later, in playing with other children he will play their roles in such a way as to stimulate himself and respond to his own stimulation. He enacts one role and responds to his own role-enactment. When he has reached adulthood he will have mastered the enactment of many roles in accordance with his perception of the world around him. In his perception and enactment of roles he is making choices among alternative ways of behaving. If he is truly socialized, he will be able to synchronize the various roles into a relatively consistent set of roles—the role of the "generalized other." [28]

The enactment of roles depends on the individual's perceptions, and these perceptions are, as we saw, bound up with his attitude toward himself and others. The variety of roles which he is called upon to perform differ, so that every individual comes to perceive himself in different ways. Each of the roles represents a different aspect of the person, so that in reality a person is as many "selves" as there are roles for him to enact. However, since the need for integration is strong in everyone, every individual will, through learning and necessity, combine them into a relatively consistent and dynamic configuration. This dynamic pattern is what we are able to identify as the self of a person.

The human self is, thus, at once public and private. It is public in the sense that the roles which the individual plays are social expectations. He is what he is because others perceive him through the roles which he enacts. It is private in the sense that he plays his roles in keeping with his own perception of what others expect and anticipate. The public self is the totality of role-expectations; the private self is the individual's uniquely organized ways of regarding himself; it is the individual as he appears to himself. Stated differently, the public self is the pattern of roles imposed upon the individual by others, whereas the private self is that pattern of roles which is selected largely by himself. The integration of these selves into a coherent person is made possible by the frame of reference, or attitude-value complex, which we have already described.

It should be noted in the foregoing phrasing that the self is not an organization completely determined by the expectations of others, or by the culture demands of the group. The self as here described is different from both the current behavioristic accounts

[28] See G. H. Mead, *Mind, self and society* (Chicago: University of Chicago Press, 1934), pp. 135–51.

of reinforcement and the psychoanalytic view that man behaves because of fear of punishment. We have stressed the importance of individual choices on a "scale" of values. Man behaves as he does, not only in expectation of rewards and fear of punishment, but because of his own perception of the course of action he should take. From this point of view, then, it is a fallacy to attempt the reduction of selfhood and self-directed behavior either to allegedly more elementary functions, or to cultural imperatives. The self has a degree of autonomy which is largely denied by both psychoanalytic and behavioristic accounts of human behavior. Although the attitude-value complex, which serves as a framework for every self, is culturally conditioned in part, it transmutes the anticipation of reward and the fear of punishment, which weaken or destroy autonomous behavior, into individual perceptions of right and wrong. The individual internalizes the values of his community, to be sure, but every internalization is unique, so that, in effect, culture can never compel a person to act rightly or wrongly. The choice between these important values is the individual's alone. The choice between good and evil are autonomous properties of the person who possesses the capacity to anticipate the proper course of action.[29]

The integrated self. We have said that with the exception of deviant cases, or in cases of immaturity, the self is a dynamic pattern of roles. The unified self is the reference point for all attitudes and values; it is an organization of these psychological variables. Inasmuch as neither attitudes nor values live in isolation, and since persistence is a fundamental property of the attitude-value complex, they make for the continuity and identity of the self. The "feeling of selfhood" is maintained by the involvements of the self in abiding attitudes and values. When the attitudinal system in which the self is involved radically changes; or when the value system for whatever reason becomes dysfunctional; or when the frame of reference in which both attitudes and values are embedded collapses, as sometimes happens in extreme cases, the self becomes disorganized. A disorganized self, then, is one in which the attitude-value complex no longer serves as a dependable guide to action.

Attitudes, values, and the self, thus, cannot be separated. De-

---

[29] This is discussed in detail in the next chapter. *Gestalt* psychologists, like Wertheimer and Köhler, have described the capacity to prevision the right course of action by the idea of *requiredness*. Thus, a person's ethical behavior is a product of his ability to perceive the requirement of the situation. See M. Wertheimer, Some problems in the theory of ethics, *Soc. Res.*, 2 (1935), 353–67; W. Köhler, *The place of value in a world of facts* (New York: Liveright Publishing Corp., 1938).

scriptions of value-behavior in the language of reinforcement, and of attitudinal behavior in terms of the force of cultural imperatives, are not false but irrelevant. The fragmentation of attitudes into measurable units, practiced by the methodologists, and the denigration of values to the dimension of reward-and-punishment, which the reductionists try to effect, have not helped to perfect self-psychology and the psychology of attitudes and values. They have weakened not only the study of personality, but the other areas of the science of psychology as well.

PERSONALITY AS AN EXPRESSION OF A VALUE-COMPLEX. Earlier in this chapter we referred approvingly to Florence Kluckhohn's analysis of human behavior by means of its value-orientations. This value-orientation is synonymous with our own attitude-value complex dimension of personality. We believe that when we know an individual's attitude-value complex we know *him*. It is a human characteristic that makes accessible to study and understanding the social and individual nature of man. Insofar as man is everywhere molded by what seem to be universal value-orientations, he is very much the same in every culture; but insofar as he internalizes the value-orientations in accordance of his own inner dispositions, he is unique.

This is a paradox but not a contradiction. With unfailing eloquence, Allport has stated the dilemma clearly. "Each person," he writes, "is an idiom unto himself, an apparent violation of the syntax of the species. An idiom develops in its own peculiar context, and this context must be understood in order to comprehend the idiom. Yet at the same time, idioms are not entirely lawless and arbitrary; indeed they can be known for what they are only by comparing them with the syntax of the species." [30]

It may be argued that the presence of unique and universal properties in man is both obvious and in accordance with intelligent common sense. However, the apparentness of the manifest is often illusory, especially regarding those features of reality which are complex and elusive. The illusory impression that we are saying something which everyone already knows is a *post facto* observation, "the consequence," as Ichheiser starkly revealed, "of taking implicit awareness (immediate experience) to be explicit knowledge." [31]

We return now to Kluckhohn's universal value-orientations to discover what light they throw upon human personality.

[30] G. W. Allport, *Becoming*, p. 19.
[31] G. Ichheiser, Misunderstandings in human relations; a study in false perception, *Amer. J. Sociol.*, 55 (1949), Pt. 2, p. 3.

1. *Basic human nature.* Since the dawn of consciousness, man has formed impressions of other men. Many primitive people do not impute the property of humanness to persons outside their own group; they recognize only themselves as people or human beings. In wartime few civilized men ascribe qualities of decency to their enemies, and even many cultivated people join the throng to excoriate their foes. Other men show a superior attitude toward human frailties by viewing people generally as wretched, helpless beings who need the benefit of their strength and wisdom. Still others have a basically accepting attitude and recognize the indisputable fact that human decency is compounded of many elements in which goodness, on the whole, prevails.

It may very well be the case that recent rethinking, based on experimental investigations, will eventually present us with a broader and more adequate mechanistic view. The change in this direction is already discerned in the attempts of some psychologists in revising stimulus-response theory by means of the findings of stimulus-response method. In this revision, habit is not conceived as a mere connection between an afferent process and an efferent process selected, no one knows how, by drive reduction. K. H. Pribram, in a review of physiological psychology in the *Annual Review of Psychology* (1960) conceives a more active mechanism to replace the stimulus-response arc. Nevertheless, while one of the basic problems of psychology is to determine how the human physiological machine works, the current physiological and biochemical accounts of human behavior have not helped us to explain man's value-bound character. Whether psychology can achieve this kind of explanation, even granting such revisions as those of Pribram and others, is a question that cannot be answered here.

In any case, man's view of human nature gives us an introduction to his basic character and personality. In his views of the character of man, each individual expresses or betrays the character of his own being.

2. *Relation of man to nature.* In man's attitude toward nature—or toward the entire cosmos—we get still another glimpse of his personality. We are not here concerned with the metaphysical question of the place of man in nature, but with the psychological relatedness of man to physical reality. Philosophers have professional views of this relationship, but ours is the simpler problem. We wish to know whether man considers the universe as devouring of all life, or sees it as something to be controlled by man for his own advantage. The person who feels small and insignificant as he gazes at the powerful sea beating against the rocks, or as he

watches the stars in the heavenly firmament, differs from the person
who identifies himself with the vastness and power of the universe;
and both in turn differ from the individual who is bent on harness-
ing the world's untapped energy, or is challenged to ascend the
highest mountain peak. These attitudes, while not mutually exclusive, express feelings of dependency or powerlessness, humility
or meekness, self-confidence or defiance.

3. *Time orientation.* This attitude-value complex has occupied
the minds of philosophers for centuries, but not all contemporary
psychologists have grasped its significance for the understanding of
man. Kluckhohn's analysis of the temporal dimension recognizes
three forms of orientation, all of which have been held in high esteem in the history of human thought. They are the past, the present, and the future. An orientation toward any one of them reflects a difference in attitude and values and consequently of
personality. The person who gazes to the past and evaluates present actions in terms of ancient values tends to be conservative.
There have been whole peoples and entire cultures that found
solace and tranquility in the golden age of a dead past. Much of
their energy was absorbed in reproducing the imagined splendor
of a former epoch in the living present. Society abounds—and always has abounded—with people who look backward to what they
quaintly term the "good old days," when the world and its people
were better, happier, and more contented. In order to convince
themselves of the verity of their own beliefs they have found it
necessary to condemn the reality of today. Whether as dreaming
idealists or rebellious malcontents, they see the world degenerating
and its people and customs destroying everybody. They echo
Cicero's plaintive cry: *O tempora! O mores!*

To some persons there is no time more auspicious than the present. Like Omar Khayyam, they want to drink deeply from the
cup of life, before the day has turned into night and the night into
the dim past. There is no solace in the pleasures of yesterday, for
they are dead; and there is no hope for the morrow, for tomorrow
we die. The pleasure principle reigns supreme, and the sensualist
and the epicure are its best-known manifestations. Of course, not
all present-oriented individuals fit this description. The realist,
the practical-minded, the builder of today are also motivated by
the urgency of the present and the immediate. Much of the world's
work is performed by those whose minds are so geared to the present. They are successful in proportion to their refusal or inability
to be hampered by the past or intimidated by the future.

The future-oriented individual, while scorning neither the past nor the present, is essentially forward-looking, amenable to change, and guides his actions by selected prospective goals. He has a clear *Lebenslauf*, a life plan, a purposeful directionality.[32] There is a propulsive energy toward anticipated ends in this type of individual which is often remarkable. It is too well known to need elaboration that some people, in the face of insurmountable obstacles, will persist along a chosen line no matter what the odds against achievement may be. Even in defeat their indignation over their failure impels them to persist in the same direction.

4. *Activity orientation*. Philosophers' concern with this orientation is well known and well founded. People in all cultures are oriented either along the dimension of being, being-in-becoming, or doing.[33] Persons who are oriented toward the being dimension are fundamentally expressive in their behavior. "The essence of the Being orientation," writes Kluckhohn, "is the spontaneous expression of what is conceived to be 'given' in the personality . . . a spontaneous expression of impulses and desires. . . ."[34] She cites the case of the Mexicans in whom the being orientation is dominant. Their *fiestas* alone show the importance of sheer being, of spontaneous existence.

However, the stress on being does not resemble the sensualist's unhampered gratification of impulses. On the contrary, as Kluckhohn relates in the case of the Mexicans, the demands of the other orientations, namely, their conception of man's relation to others and to nature, their view of human nature and so forth, give rise to codes which restrain the individual in positive ways.

The being-in-becoming orientation resembles the being orientation, yet is also different from it. Its major stress is less on spontaneous being as such and more on unconstrained development. It passes beyond spontaneity into creativity. The individual who is motivated by this orientation tends to be self-actualizing, or to become more and more what he has the capacity of becoming.[35] While it may be found in any person, it is probably most highly developed in aesthetically minded people and intellectuals.

The doing orientation, which is often ascribed to the American individual, is characterized by energetic activity. Success and achievement of goals set up by the competitive pecuniary and class culture of American life, are powerful motives. The person's goals

[32] See C. Bühler, *Der menschliche Lebenslauf als psychologisches Problem* (Leipzig: S. Hirzel, 1933).

[33] See Kluckhohn, Value orientations, pp. 85–87.

[34] *Ibid.*, p. 86.

[35] The self-actualizing personality is described in detail in Chapter 3.

are much less his own than ends deemed important by others; and accomplishment is evaluated more by the standards of others than by one's own.

5. *Man's relation to others.* This orientation, like the others, varies from culture to culture, and not every person internalizes it in the same way. There are three ways in which man relates himself to others: lineal, collateral, and individualistic.

In the *lineal* orientation man strives for goals with members of his family line, or blood group. It is therefore characterized by strong family solidarity and individual security. In the *collateral* orientation a person joins with many others in seeking the goals of his whole community. In the *individualistic* orientation individual goals take primacy over group goals. It does not mean egoistic self-seeking, for most individualistically oriented people have due regard for the rights of their neighbors. Its sociality is characterized by *relatedness* to others, rather than *togetherness.*

A generally dependable index of an individual's personality can be constructed from a knowledge of how the five orientations function in his daily living. While there are no formal tests of these orientations, there is no reason why they could not be devised. Such a test, or tests, supplementing the well-known Allport-Vernon "A Study of Values," would tell us as much about the personality of an individual as some of the standardized tests currently in use. Indeed, since the Allport-Vernon test implies some of the foregoing orientations, the two might be integrated into a single assessing instrument.

FUNCTIONS OF ATTITUDES AND VALUES: AN EMPIRICAL STUDY. Our aim in this chapter has not been to measure personality through the study of people's attitude-value complexes, but to try to understand it by means of a theoretical formulation. Nevertheless, a number of the studies which we have cited are empirical, not speculative. An interesting and promising theoretical analysis of our problem, derived from detailed case studies of ten men, was recently made by Smith, Bruner, and White.[36] These intensive case studies are presented, say the authors, "in an effort to trace out the lines of development and maintenance of opinions *in vivo* as a test of the utility of our conceptual model." [37]

The authors do not make an artificial distinction between an attitude and an opinion. They think of each as "a predisposition to experience, to be motivated by and to act toward, a class of objects

[36] Smith, Bruner, and White, *Opinions and personality.*
[37] *Ibid.*, p. 3.

in a predictable manner." [38] As "adjustive" instruments, attitudes or opinions are, in their view, both expressive features of personality and major techniques for dealing with reality. In this, the substance of this chapter concurs.

The Smith-Bruner-White "experiment." The individuals whose attitudes and personalities were studied were ten adult men, all but one of whom were married, and living in the Greater Boston community. They were in no sense a representative sample, but were chosen on the basis of "sufficient intelligence to be verbally productive" and "a wide variety of social backgrounds and walks of life." Their age-range was from 27 to 48; their intelligence quotient on the Wechsler test ranged from 113 to 142; their education varied from six years in grade school to college graduation; their annual income ranged from $2,500 to $20,000; and in their religion, with the exception of a single Jew, they were almost equally divided between Protestants and Roman Catholics.

The authors followed the pattern of using multiple procedures and investigators, and of entrusting valuations and interpretations to a Diagnostic Council, after the manner of Murray's well-known procedure.[39] This Council consisted of seven senior members of the staff—three social psychologists, three clinical psychologists, and one social anthropologist. Seventeen investigators, including graduate students and outside consultants, administered the 28 procedures which were used to study the relation between the subjects' attitudes and personalities. The "procedures" were such items as interviews on childhood memories, health and sex history, abilities, views on Russia, stress interviews, intelligence tests, and Rorschach and TAT tests.[40]

Although only a very careful reading of the ten cases can give the reader full insight into the relation of these individuals' attitudes and their personalities, we shall present in the next few paragraphs only a brief description and analysis of one of them. He was called John Chatwell, was 28 years old, married, the father of twin boys, a law clerk, and a student.

His *system of values* was certainly influenced by his own place in society. His self-picture was that of a well-born, well-endowed, and well-educated individual. In nonmaterial values—that is, values aside from economic wealth—Chatwell saw himself as a member of an aristocracy of brains. Owing to contacts with Asian

---

[38] *Ibid.*, p. 33. This definition clearly implies values as objects of the predispositions or attitudes.

[39] See H. A. Murray, *Explorations in personality* (New York: Oxford University Press, 1938); also Chapter 4, above.

[40] For the full description of all the procedures see *ibid.*, pp. 52–60.

civilian populations during his military experience, he was convinced that "the American system, for all its faults, operated effectively to preserve the dignity of the individual." Although he acquired from his parents such important values as freedom, enterprise, rationality, and high standards of personal conduct, these values were tested, confirmed, and recreated in his own personal life history.

In his *views on Russia,* Chatwell was rational and objective, believing that Russia should be permitted to experiment in the direction of a nationalized economy, and that people should be given a free choice to accept or reject her theories and practices. While he granted Russia the right to preach and practice her politico-economic doctrine, he did not himself agree with it.

Chatwell's *time perspective* was a long-range one. He believed that given time, developments in Russia favor peace; for neither Russia nor the United States want war. His orientation toward Russia was an accepting one, favoring approach rather than avoidance. He believed that we should neither fear nor be awed by her. Although he was confident that skillful diplomacy would avert a war with her, he was prepared to be hostile toward her if war should be the only outcome of the current tensions. His policy stand, therefore, was the proposal to strengthen the United Nations in favor of limitation of armaments. "Russian leaders," he believed, "must be educated to understand our willingness to live and let live in freedom."

Chatwell's *capacities and traits* were singularly high. His IQ on the Wechsler-Belevue Adult Intelligence Test was 142, the highest of the ten individuals. This placed him in the highest one per cent of the general population. The Vigotsky Test revealed that he had the capacity for the 'highest level of abstract thinking' and 'elegant precision of performance.' Two Rorschach tests, administered nearly eight years apart, both showed "zest and energy in the production of many excellent responses," and both indicated a flexible and versatile manner of handling details. In both tests there was "a certain lack of emotional warmth and depth. Both the Rorschach and the Thematic Apperception Test gave evidence of "the dominance of intellectual control."

The pressure of his *basic strivings* was toward independence and individual accomplishment coupled with stress on investigation and discussion. Owing to his slight build and lack of skill as a football player, he directed his assertiveness into discussion and debate. His drive toward intellectual goals was maintained and intensified by the need to receive recognition and praise from others, by the need to surpass rivals and disparage their irrationalities, and by the need to inquire and to understand.

Chatwell's *adjustive techniques* were initiative and enterprise. He performed all sorts of work while he was in college; and his military career was marked by initiative in volunteering for assignments. He was not modest regarding his own value to prospective employers; and both in law school and in legal practice "he was energetic and forth-putting, leaving few stones unturned when interested in a case."

Opinion maintenance and furtherance were strong in Chatwell. His opinions were not easily swayed by arguments, wide reading, and contact with others. "To most sources of information he felt equal if not superior." However, his mind was not closed to differences of opinion, provided these were presented on a high intellectual level. "Verbal competitive aggression was probably his prepotent motive in relation to peers of the same sex. His opinions were therefore part of his equipment for obtaining the kind of social adjustment that he most craved. For this purpose it was all the better if they did not agree with those of others; the only requirement was that he have opinions and that they be defensible. He used the same technique in working over the offerings of authorities and thus establishing his place in relation to them." [41]

SOME CONCLUSIONS. The investigation by Smith, Bruner, and White shows that attitudes and values are an integral part of the total personality. It shows also that attitudes and values serve the individual as strategies for coping with and mastering the world in which he has his being. By knowing his attitude-value complex we can better understand the individual. The study of an individual's attitude-value complex is a way of "testing" his personality, and can thus serve as a "measuring" device superior in some ways to the Rorschach, TAT, and other techniques. An interview in which a person's value-attitude orientations are tapped can be more revealing of the configured personality than the use of standard tests. The authors note the fact that their two-hour interview on "Personal Values and Religious Sentiments," which asked the question "What things really matter to you most in life?" and covered the individual's philosophy of life, was the most revealing procedure in their entire repertoire. Their study shows, furthermore, what was made clear by our own analysis of the problem, that attitudes enable us to infer a person's value system with encouraging success. Since a person's value system is his way of perceiving and evaluating himself, other people, and the ambient world, it tells

[41] *Ibid.*, p. 111.

us a great deal about him as a *person*. Thus, while individuals will sometimes make evasions and prettify the records, as they tend to do in many other personality tests, tests of attitudes and values, the authors point out, can give us "a picture of the person that was consistent with and in some ways more revealing than later information obtained by more conventional projective techniques." [42]

Another advantage of the attitude-value complex as an indicator of the personality is its elicitation of the more creative strategies of the individual's behavior. Unlike so many conventional test protocols, which elicit deficient and crippling coping mechanisms, such as sexual conflicts, depressed feelings, and impairing defenses, the tests of attitudes and values bring out the individual's strengths and capacities. "The planful, value-guided aspects of personality functioning" did not come through on the projective techniques in the study by Smith, Bruner, and White. Worse yet, quite often in the projective tests "the liabilities of a person's adjustment were amplified while his assets were dampened by the nature of the instruments employed." [43]

The use of interviews or tests of an individual's value-complex can also rectify the current conception of ego-defense, as the authors point out. The conventional, psychoanalytically oriented defense measures are, they rightly aver, "techniques of defense used *in extremis*." But Chatwell and the others never permitted themselves to get into such dilemmatic situations in many spheres of their lives as to require the defensive aid of reaction formation, repression, undoing, denial, and similar mechanisms. Knowledge of people's attitude-value complexes shows the great importance in human behavior of "constructive strategies as a means of avoiding the vicissitudes that make crippling defenses necessary." [44] Insight into a person's attitude-value complex can thus often give us a better view, or serve as a corrective of the traditional view, of ego-defense. Too many tests of personality lead one to believe that human beings are burdened by self-impairing defenses. Tests of what a person believes, how he relates himself to others, and how he feels about people and the world, which are basically attitudinal and evaluative, as well as conventional or standardized probing techniques, should be used in order to gain a more balanced assessment of his personality. Attitudes and values express positive and constructive mechanisms for manipulating the world; they reveal the creative ways in which a person makes the most of his capacities

[42] *Ibid.*, pp. 281–82.
[43] *Ibid.*, p. 282.
[44] *Ibid.*, p. 283.

and limitations. If only half the time and energy that is spent on administering and devising still more projective techniques were devoted to an examination of an individual's attitude-value complex—and also of expressive behavior—we might more nearly come to grasp the full stature of the creative potentialities of individuals. This would be a signal achievement for the science of man.

CONCLUSION

Our exposition of the nature of attitudes and values—or as we prefer to call them, the attitude-value complex—has centered on three areas: (1) the nature of attitudes and values; (2) the relation of the attitude-value complex to personality; and (3) the use of the attitude-value complex as an instrument for assessing personality.

Clearly, attitudes and values are of central concern in the study of personality. Much of what every person is, is the outcome of his attitude-value complex. While attitudes and values are for the most part social, they are not altogether so. Every person also develops highly individualized responses to objects, people, and situations. These are products of his own unique experience, biological bent, or temperamental disposition. It is commonplace that most people have special tastes, likes, and aversions concerning a variety of physical and social objects. Again, no two people internalize the socially induced attitudes and values in identical ways; their perception of the world and people leads to individual, even eccentric, responses. Attitudes and values, like personality as a whole, have an individual as well as a social dimension. This is well to remember in view of the widespread tendency to over-stress the stimulus-value and conforming nature of attitudes.

The foregoing caveat does not imply that attitudes are inherent dispositions, but only that their organization in the person's behavior is determined by the person. This is especially true of their motivational and affective aspects. Attitudes are, in other words, individual motives toward and feelings about reality, as well as social perceptions. This is inherent in our definitions of atttitudes as *tendencies to act toward or away from* objects, people, and situations. An attitude is thus not only a predisposition to act with reference to an experience, but also a *motive* to realize an end, accompanied by a positive or negative emotion or sentiment toward it.

Finally, although the larger function of the attitude-value complex is to adjust the individual to reality, to control its various features in the interest of his security and survival, it also has a very important expressive dimension. An individual's style of thinking about the world, his manner of interpreting experience, the intensity of his responses to the values of society—these and similar attitudes are modes of expression as well as techniques of adjustment. While we discussed the expressive nature of man in the preceding chapter, we made no effort to relate attitudes to the subject as a whole. The expressive component of the attitude-value complex, like expressive behavior generally, is a neglected stepchild of modern psychology.

CHAPTER 14

Character and Moral Behavior

From the study of the attitude-value complex to the investigation of character and moral behavior is but a short step. This is the more true if one believes, as we do, that consistency is a property of every healthy personality. In every sound and effective personality, attitudes, values, and character are highly congruent. In our brief reference to the moral dichotomy in contemporary life we called attention to the divided character of men's beliefs and acts. The scientist who assures us that he does not believe in the wholesale slaughter of entire populations but is ready on order to devise the instrument that will accomplish it, may show moral cleavage in his thinking. His intellective capacity is divorced from his moral values, with a resulting conflict in his personality.

The study of character and moral behavior, like the investigation of expression, is a neglected problem of American psychology. This fact is paradoxical, for in view of the practical bent of American psychology, the study of moral behavior should be one of its greatest concerns. What is more practical and useful than ethics and character? What other science than psychology, committed as it is to the study of *all* behavior, is better qualified to examine man's moral life? Although philosophers and theologians have wrestled with ethics and the moral dilemmas of man for centuries, they have not given us the insight into human character commensurate with their efforts. Like other forms of human behavior, moral conduct will be adequately understood by the use of the techniques and insights of psychologists, rather than by the speculations of theologians and philosophers.

All this is not to imply that the contributions of philosophers and theologians have been sterile and ineffective. The nature of character and the problem of moral behavior are too complex and difficult to be handled by a single discipline. While the observations of philosophers and other thinkers are often striking and illuminating they all too often are not rooted in human reality. As "bloodless categories," to use F. H. Bradley's arresting term, they live *in vacuo* with little effective relevance to human living. Character is thus too often conceived as a depersonalized and disembodied entity, rather than a living reality. We are concerned with the nature of man in his moral choices and adjustments, not with the goodness of God in an abstract universe. The obligation of psychology is to dispel mysteries, not to create them. While it may be philosophically appropriate to base goodness on truth, and even to identify the one with the other, it is psychologically more veridical to base it on human motives and attitudes. A categorical imperative, like Kant's, attractive as it is by virtue of its stern command, tells us much less about the moral nature of man than the latter's self-image, or his obligation to place himself in constructive relationship with others. But man's self-image and social cooperation are problems peculiar to human psychology, not to the philosophy of man.[1]

SOME OBSERVATIONS ON THE STUDY OF CHARACTER

We can increase our understanding of the moral individual by considering moral development in its evolution, by the attempts of earlier scholars to give an account of egocentrism and the moral order, and by the different scientific models which have been invented to delineate moral behavior.

SOCIAL EVOLUTION. The process of socialization provides a fundamental clue to the origin of moral behavior in man. Car-

[1] The foregoing strictures do not apply to the philosophy of John Dewey. His empirical inquiry into the psychology of ethics, especially his emphasis on the role of motivation in moral conduct, deserves the thoughtful consideration of every psychologist. See J. Dewey, *Human nature and conduct* (New York: Henry Holt & Co., Inc., 1922), especially Sections III and VI. This recognition of Dewey's empirical approach to moral behavior does not commit us to the acceptance of his theory of values, in which ends are only means to other means, with no terminus. Of the utmost relevance to the psychology of character is Dewey's conception of motives as *possibilities,* as aspirations for ends that can be gratified. For both his view on values and the concept of possibility, see his *Theory of valuation,* International Encycl. Unified Science (Chicago: University of Chicago Press, 1939), Vol. 2, No. 4.

penter's study of the social behavior of nonhuman primates, as well as similar investigations, shows that primates below man, despite their many resemblances to the human species, do not form a "true" social group, but only an organization of tenuously related individuals. Their "social instincts" may herd them together, but this fact of itself does not produce the kind of social reciprocity which we find in human groups. They respond to one another as more or less separate individuals, not as *complexes of stimuli*. Their social behavior lacks the coordination and integration which evidence shows is found only in human societies.[2]

The act of symbolic communication is a basic feature of human integrated social behavior, as was made abundantly clear in our discussion of language in Chapter 11. By means of language man can transmit to his fellows his private images, and thus condition each to make fitting responses to others. Social conditioning, or the whole process of socialization and the resulting higher level of integration, is an evolution which no creature below man has experienced. This higher level of integration is found in the self, which is discussed in detail in Chapter 16. The self is the integrative axis, the dominant organizing center, of all meaningful human actions. A unique feature of the integrative self is that, as G. H. Mead has so well shown in his *Mind, Self and Society,* it enables man to become an object to himself. The capacity to be an object to himself is what makes man, in contrast to the nonhuman primates, a self-conscious, self-directing, and self-evaluating being. In the absence of these characteristics moral behavior—which is to say, behavior engaged in for the sake of others and not only oneself—would be impossible. Moral behavior so conceived is predicated on the existence of an integrating center—of a self. If every society holds man morally responsible for his own actions it is because every society recognizes, if but dimly, that he is a self-directing agent. Through self-awareness man not only relates himself intelligibly to himself, but to the larger society of conscious people as well. In this dual awareness, man and society are integrated into a moral structure.

In our view, man's superego is thus a conscious as well as an unconscious and defensive set of attitudes. Freudian psychology has overemphasized the element of fear in moral behavior. In fact, it may be argued that a morality that is as extensively an outcome of guilt and anxiety as Freud seems to imply, is not in our view a healthy morality, for it is a morality directed by disabling defenses.

    [2] C. R. Carpenter, Characteristics of social behavior in non-human primates, *Trans. New York Acad. Sciences,* 4 (1942), 256.

Available evidence seems to indicate that moral behavior stemming from an integrated superego is less self-defensive and more self-directing. It is behavior in which the self-conscious, self-evaluating individual can simultaneously foresee and take the consequences of his own acts. The individual is not *driven* to be good by a cruel superego, but by a conscious choice of that act which generates the greatest amount of individual and social harmony. The resulting concord is not mere conformity, as in conventional and compulsive behavior, but a self-imposed, self-directed, and free moral activity. Character and morality have their origin, but not necessarily their complication and refinement, in the symbolic interactions of men in integrated groups.

EGOCENTRISM AND THE MORAL ORDER. For a long time, especially in the seventeenth and eighteenth centuries, the dominant theme in individual and social psychological speculations was the goodness of man contrasted with the depravity of society. This dichotomization of man and society led to an exaggeration of the binding and humanizing force of a "social contract" between men. Rousseau's sentimentalization of the innate goodness of man had to be supplemented by the coercive power of customs, laws, and institutions. This was an undoubted improvement upon the dictum of the "war of all against all", of Thomas Hobbes, but it still omitted the force of self-directing behavior in men. It ignored, as do most theories of character and of ethics, the seeming paradox that behavior cannot be socially ethical in the absence of individual choice. When it is made in response to blind custom and the directives of fossilized institutions, it degenerates into forcible constraint. We hold this to be true even in those circumstances when an action is the enforced will of a plurality, if there is no general desire to abide by its dictates. It is this failure to bridge individual and social interests that has led to the construction of the fiction of a "general will" which is alleged to arbitrate in moral disputes.[3] Little do some social scientists realize the fallacy of overemphasizing the all-encompassing power of Durkheim's "social constraints," or society's controls and directions, as discussed in many of his works, particularly his *On the division of labor in society* and *The rules of sociological method.*

From our point of view, moral behavior, while being a response to external coercion in the form of social constraints, also arises from the individual's conception of himself as a moral person.

[3] See J.-J. Rousseau, *Contrat social* (Paris: M. Dreyfus-Brisac, 1896), Bk. I, Chs. 1–3. This book was first published in Amsterdam, in 1762.

Character and moral goodness are expressions of man's image of himself as acting in the interest of others as well as of himself.

MORAL BEHAVIOR AND PSYCHOLOGICAL CONFLICT. Psychoanalysis has almost from its inception explained moral character as the resultant of unresolved conflicts among the id, ego, and superego. We surmise that no psychologically oriented student of character and morality denies the undoubted fact that much of what we commonly designate as moral behavior arises from the conflict of individual impulses with the demands of the social group. Child training and the entire process of socialization are replete with demonstrations of the truth of this observation. No doubt, too, a man's character develops in the crucible of individual and social conflicts, but only in the sense that "strength of character" represents their successful resolution. The weakness of this mode of explanation lies in the fact that it not only makes conflict the overriding force in all moral behavior, but, in the view of some writers, "the *necessary basis or ground* on which conscience, the moral sense, and our system of ethics grow and develop." [4] This goes beyond the evidence and omits the *desire* of people to act in the interest of moral ends. Even children, as a consequence of positive socialization, act in ways designed to bring satisfaction to others and not only to themselves. Altruistic behavior, for example, is substituted for selfishness, not because of a conflict between egoistic and altruistic impulses, or out of fear of punishment, but because the child in his interaction with his parents has learned to identify himself with them. The image of his parents or other "ideal" selves is incorporated into the child's personality and becomes internally reinforcing. The child's self-image is often sufficient to cause him to behave in morally acceptable ways. A great bulk of social learning, including the acquisition of morally acceptable habits, is not a simple process of conditioning and reinforcement, but the action of the psychological *person*. In this mode of explanation we concur with Allport's emphasis on the central position of the *self* in human learning.[5]

Clearly, then, the view that moral behavior is an outcome of conflict is based on views which, while valid as far as they go, are too largely patterned after psychoanalysis and reinforcement learning theory. While these two make strange bedfellows, they are

[4] T. H. Huxley and J. Huxley, *Touchstone of ethics, 1893–1943* (New York: Harper & Bros., 1947), p. 4.

[5] G. W. Allport, The ego in contemporary psychology, *Psychol. Rev.*, 50 (1943), 451–78; also, Effect: a secondary principle of learning, *Psychol. Rev.*, 53 (1946), 321–34.

both based upon a mechanistic model of learning. However, this model is inadequate for the explanation of many forms of human behavior for, as Gibson has astutely remarked, it does not account for the astonishing prevalence of moral behavior among human adults.[6] The mechanistic model applied to the study of man fails to take into account the fact that, although he is an animal, man is uniquely human. To be sure, to say that man is uniquely human does not deny that he is a complex mechanism, nor that he can be studied like any other part of nature. But unlike other living organisms that he resembles in numerous ways, man is a symbol-producing and symbol-employing being. His capacity through symbolic interaction to identify himself closely with himself and with others gives him a range of moral responsiveness possessed by no other creature. Because of his unique socialization, as distinguished from bare animal conditioning, man develops a self-process through which he sets up standards of behavior which are not only self-referential but other-minded as well. This other-directedness of his impulses comprises an important part of his character and moral behavior.

RESEARCH MODELS AND MORAL BEHAVIOR. The brief reference to the mechanistic model for human learning deserves a more detailed discussion. Since some kind of model guides all important scientific investigations, it will help us to account for both the neglect and the one-sided view of moral behavior if we consider the leading models in contemporary psychological research. These widely used models do not convincingly represent man's moral nature, for they either neglect or do not pretend to account for man's future-pointed behavior. "Addiction to machines, rats, or infants," as Allport remarks, "leads us to overplay those features of human behavior that are peripheral, signal-oriented, or genetic. Correspondingly it causes us to underplay those features that are central, future-oriented, and symbolic."[7] The rigid emulation of the physical sciences which seems to prompt the creators of most of the current models in psychology is frequently of little help.

In the above-cited article Allport describes three paradigms that have guided most psychological thinking about personality and related problems. They are the mechanical, the phylogenetic, and the genetic models.

The *mechanical model* has its origin in the conception of the

[6] J. J. Gibson, The implications of learning theory for social psychology, in J. G. Miller (ed.), *Experiments in social process* (New York: McGraw-Hill Book Co., Inc., 1950), p. 152.

[7] G. W. Allport, Scientific models and human morals, *Psychol. Rev.*, 54 (1947), 182–92, on p. 190.

psychology of man stemming from reflexology, particularly the behavioristic psychology of John B. Watson. This view, though now in eclipse, is too well known to require extensive delineation. Briefly, it conceived personality—when it showed any interest in the latter at all—as a compounding of stimulus-response processes. Recent behaviorism, while it is vastly more sophisticated than Watsonian psychology, and although some forms of it (such as Tolman's purposivism) recognize the forward-directedness of human actions, has not taken us appreciably farther in accounting for moral behavior.

All contemporary behaviorism accounts for both animal and human behavior in the language of reinforcement. *Reward* is the central fact in all behavior, particularly learning. Unless an animal, usually half-starved, is rewarded it will not learn. This all-inclusive paradigm is believed adequate to explain all human actions, from gratifying hunger to sacrificing for the welfare of others. However, the telling and fatal weakness of this mode of explanation is its failure to account for forms of behavior which are performed for no hidden or tangible reward. It does not account for actions performed in the interest of sheer expression, essential being, self-sacrifice, unrealized potentialities, and the perseverating quality of moral intentions. Worse yet, this point of view is insensitive to what is most human in all human action, namely the moral nature of man. This despite the fact that increasingly more scientists, particularly biologists, without denying that man is a part of nature, perceive him as "an animal unlike any other" and "with no values to revere except those of its own making." [8]

Moreover, once we admit the existence of self-oriented behavior, in which the ego is involved in the choice of moral ends, the deficiency of the mechanical model becomes evident.[9] Self-psychology views moral behavior as a function of the *personality*, not of reaction tendencies.

The *phylogenetic model* explains human, like other behavior, as a function of the developmental history of the individual as a part of the animal species. It is a model derived from the study of animal behavior. It is thus quite similar to the mechanical paradigm.

[8] This situation is attractively discussed in J. Rostand, *Can man be modified?* trans. J. Griffin. (New York: Basic Books, Inc., 1959).

[9] We disposed of the charge that the concept of the self—or ego, as some prefer to call it—implies the existence of a mysterious or mythical inner man, in an earlier chapter. To those who prefer a qualifying term in order to avoid an implied entity inside the human organism, we suggest our own term of *self-process*, or Mowrer's "ego process." See O. H. Mowrer, The law of effect and ego psychology, *Psychol. Rev.*, 53 (1946), 321–34.

The essential difference is that it depends less on the all-encompassing effect of reinforcement. When Tolman, for instance, expands his "sign-*Gestalt*" theory to embrace what he calls "need-cathexis," he is moving in the direction of a developmental psychology of behavior. It explains human behavior, including moral choices, by tracing the attachment of physiological drives to objects in one's experience. A man who behaves morally "cathects," or attaches, a drive to socially acceptable actions. Primary drives are converted into secondary drives, in which a hedonic investment is made in that form of behavior which is approved, and no such investment is made in behavior which is disapproved. Moral behavior from this point of view is nothing more than need-cathexis.[10] Shed of the technical language, and simplified more than may be advisable, this view accounts for human behavior—and by implication human morals—by means of drive-directed processes.

The *genetic model*, most firmly established in psychoanalytical investigations, is an antidote to the animal-type of explanation. It aims to account for human conduct by infantile and childhood experiences. So widespread is this approach that many psychologists, especially in the field of child development and the psychology of personality, habitually account for man's present behavior and future-oriented striving in terms of early conditioning and socialization. As Allport facetiously phrased this preoccupation with childhood conditioning, a man's character is, in all essentials, "determined by the time his last diaper is changed." [11]

The genetic model is based on the questionable premise that motivation in human infants and children—indeed, of people throughout the entire trajectory of their lives—is fundamentally similar to that of other animals. To be sure, this assumption makes for convenience and economy, but therein lies its inescapable weakness. When science forces complex phenomena into tight formulae for the sake of preserving its principle of economy, it must inevitably distort or falsify the complexity of human aspirations. The genetic model suffers from this overadherence to an important but very limited scientific directive. A psychology that aims to explain human morals by means of infantile fixations and need-cathexis can hardly take us beyond the level of immature imperatives. It makes adult morals but a recapitulation of the moral acts acquired during, and perceived through the screen of, childhood. It makes

---

[10] This is, of course, the familiar Freudian explanation of behavior, and antedates the views of Tolman and others by a good many years. Cathexis is a grotesque substitute for Freud's term *Besetzung*, which refers to the individual's investment or attachment of affect to preferred objects of his experience.

[11] Scientific models and human morals, p. 185.

other moral-like acts basically reactive instead of intentional.[12] It rejects any explanation of moral conduct in terms of potentiality and becoming. It cannot account for what is popularly called conscience—that is, man's active character—for this cannot be defined in the narrow language of operationism. Those psychologies, like Freud's, which deal with the problem of conscience conceive it in terms of the fear of punishment, anxiety, the moral "censor." Despite all his preoccupation with the ego, Freud never followed his own insights of explaining human morals through the powerful force of a person's own self-image. He continued to explain conscience and human morals as ways of acting in response to fear of punishment and the coercive power of cultural imperatives. Thus, the superego, instead of serving to reveal man's essential humanity, only highlights the cruelty of society's constraints.

As we shall see, in a moral act based on intention there is a feeling of creativeness in performing it; in an act discharged because of the fear of punishment there is a feeling of strain and of blocked impulse. In this connection, the writer vividly recalls the *intimidating* effect of the word *Verboten* in his youth. While this command controlled his behavior in expected ways, there was no feeling of self-fulfillment in the act of obeying it. On the contrary, it was marked only by relief from anxiety in having chosen the expected course of action. This was moral behavior of a sort, to be sure, made in response to a vague but awesome authority; but it lacked the freedom and intention which are the marks of a full-grown morality.

This kind of moral behavior can be conveniently explained in terms of some brand of current learning theory, to be sure. Thus, in our childhood we acquire expedient ways of satisfying our needs. The simple gratification of our needs tends to reinforce these ways, causing us to choose them on future occasions. The proper ways are further strengthened by the rewards and punishment of vigilant parents. As we mature, this fear of punishment somehow becomes transformed into the *need* for punishment after bad behavior and becomes a form of self-punishment. The process is complicated by the fact that the fear of wrong-doing, because of anticipated punishment, develops both guilt feelings and the desire for self-approbation. In this way the moral self is born, for the in-

---

[12] We are using this term in the sense initially employed in the *act psychology* of Brentano and his followers. It refers to the forward impulsion of human action even when no clear goal is perceptible. The goal is "immanently" there, but the striving individual may not be aware of it. Human motives at any age may scarcely do more than reach "forward hungrily into the future like the tip of a scarlet runner bean groping for a goal it does not know about"—G. W. Allport, *ibid.*, p. 184.

dividual now performs an act which "yields a primary satisfaction only to someone else."

This explanation by Gibson, couched in the language and concepts of learning theory, is typical of the mechanical paradigms of both Freudian and reinforcement theories. The valuable aspect of Gibson's explanation is that in self-initiated moral behavior "the reinforcement process no longer needs to be initiated by another person but can be aroused by a concept of, or attitude toward, one's own act." [13] However, in this statement Gibson virtually deserts the learning model of moral behavior and conceives the latter in the form of self-propulsive, or intentional, acts.

The *intentional model*, which underlies not only our own discussion of human morals but that of all purposive behavior in this book, differs markedly from the paradigms so far discussed. The fundamental idea of this mode of explanation is *foresight*. In the realm of morals it refers to an individual's capacity to foresee tomorrow's consequences of today's deeds. In moral choices and discriminations we do not always act on the basis of social coercion, but on the basis of the capacity to foresee the consequences of our own acts. The more refined and mature a person's moral acts, the more he moves on the plane of future orientation. Moral man acts not only in response to the stimuli of social imperatives, but in his highest moral reaches follows complex intentional dispositions. Moral habits are not mechanical responses merely; nor are they largely instrumentalities for the satisfaction of needs; they are both. But we cannot rest the case of ethical discrimination on the impelling force of habit, either instrumental or socially driven. The moral conscience of man is unique in being basically self-propelled. Until a man has an image of himself as a moral being his habits will be insufficient to impel him to act in response to long-range planning. Thus, when we know how an individual views himself, when we grasp the intentional dispositions which cause him to choose between different moral acts, we are in a good position to predict his oncoming behavior. Man reveals his characteristically human nature in his moral character. His character, integrated with his self, his temperamental dispositions, and the other components already discussed, constitute his total personality.

We thus take issue with those writers who see a dichotomy between character and personality. McClelland has made this distinction. He uses the term "character" to refer to an evaluation of a person in terms of some standards, and the term "personality" as

[13] Gibson, The implications of learning theory for social psychology, p. 164.

a "scientific conceptualization." [14]   In our own view, McClelland's
definition of character is in fact a "scientific conceptualization" of
the social self, which is described in detail in Chapter 16. We hold,
further, that character is not wholly the evaluation of a person by
someone's standards; it also represents highly individualized—even
unique—intentional dispositions and preferences of the person.
Character is always distinguished by integrity to one's image of
one's self, as well as by adherence to the image held of us by others.

"SCIENTIFIC" STUDY OF CHARACTER

Can character and morality be studied scientifically? The answer to the question hinges largely on the view of science which
one holds. If empirical investigations of honesty and deceit, for
instance, such as those of Hartshorne and May and Piaget; or of
altruism and self-control by Hartshorne, May, and Maller; or the
multiple-conditions of character development investigated by
Ligon, are admitted into the category, then we have no less than
the beginnings of a scientific study of moral behavior.[15] On the
other hand, if we demand that the study of human morals be a
closely integrated synthesis of empirical data with a rigorous system of theory underlying it, then we have not even taken the first
step toward a science of human character. Further, there is a tendency to disguise such studies by a show of science. Yet no matter
how objectively one studies the nature of human character, both
the procedures and the results are inevitably colored by the character of the scientist, his portrait of man, and the dominant ideas of
his time. Claims to the contrary, love and hate, malice and good
will, avarice and generosity, and the like cannot be experimentally
investigated—not yet, surely.

Various psychoanalytical investigations of character have been
too preoccupied with its negative qualities. The literature of psychoanalysis is replete with overemphasis on social anxiety as the
basis of the moral conscience; at its worst, it exaggerates man's obsession with guilt. As if to atone unconsciously for making man a
prisoner of his fears, psychoanalysis proceeds in its therapy to remove consciousness of fault from it patients. For the impairing

---

[14] D. McClelland, *Personality* (New York: The Dryden Press, Inc., 1951), p. 63.

[15] H. Hartshorne and M. A. May, *Studies in deceit* (New York: The Macmillan
Co., 1928); J. Piaget, *The moral judgment of the child* (New York: Harcourt, Brace
and Co., 1932); H. Hartshorne, M. A. May, and J. B. Maller, *Studies in service and
self-control* (New York: The Macmillan Co., 1929); E. M. Ligon, *The Union College
character research project* (Schenectady, N.Y.: Union College, 1953); E. M. Ligon,
Dimensions of character (New York: The Macmillan Co., 1956).

quality of guilt it substitutes an equally unacceptable moral forget-fulness. Apparently the psychoanalysts are not yet aware of this moral contradiction after their more than sixty years of concern with the superego of man.

Again, long before psychoanalysis came upon the psychological scene, man knew of his incapacity to acknowledge the evil in him-self, and of the imperious need to project his guilt upon someone else. He has perhaps always ascribed his own moral lapses and evil intentions to others, to adverse circumstances, to the corrupt-ness of his time. Moral self-exoneration and scapegoating are as old as mankind.

EARLY STUDIES OF CHARACTER. It is well known to scholars that the origin of ideas is difficult to trace. No doubt most important ideas have antecedents which are generally either forgotten or go unrecognized. In any case, a survey of widely cited literature re-veals that Fernald deserves recognition as one of the early empirical investigators of moral behavior. Most revelant here are the tests he constructed for classifying criminal and other offenses according to their gravity.[16] These were verbal tests with no particular re-lation to the respondents' real life situations. Basically, they were tests not of moral behavior but of moral judgments. It is hardly necessary to point out that a child or an adult may judge an act as morally right without performing it in his own behavior. Moral discrimination and moral behavior may be far apart in actual situa-tions. An act and an attitude, we pointed out in the preceding chapter, are not always congruent; and this holds with equal force in the moral realm. It is this confusion between a moral judgment and a moral act which led Fernald to the negative conclusion that morality cannot be adequately measured by verbal or other tests.

The reason for Fernald's pessimistic conclusion lies not in his use of tests, but in his unawareness that he was measuring, not moral traits, but intellectual perception and social sensitivity. His sub-jects answered the questions within the framework of their intelli-gence and social expectancy, rather than on the background of their personal character.

However, Lowe and Shimberg, more than a decade later, did not commit the same error, although their conclusion was equally nega-tive. Using fables illustrating moral situations, their subjects were asked to judge the rightness or wrongness of various moral acts.

---

[16] G. G. Fernald, The defective delinquent class: differentiating tests, *Amer. J. Insanity,* 74 (1925).

The tests were obviously *judgments* rather than tests of morality and character, as the authors clearly recognized.[17]

A series of tests simulating real life situations devised earlier by Voelker, and later modified by Cady, has considerable interest for the study of character.[18] In Voelker's ingenious tests a number of boy scouts and camp girls—to whom we are accustomed, parenthetically, to impute good moral character—were subjected to various tests of honesty by placing them in situations where cheating was easily possible. Thus, the subject could accept or refuse work-credit not due to him, accept or refuse help from another when he was instructed to work independently, or keep his eyes open or closed in performing a task which required the use of the eyes for effective results.

In Cady's modification of Voelker's tests, subjects were to keep their eyes shut and insert crosses in circles, trace lines with pencils around squares, and perform similar tasks. All the tests offered many opportunities for cheating. The subjects' honesty was thus tested by giving them a high score for cheating and a zero score for refraining from it.

These and other early tests, while displaying considerable ingenuity, were, like many later ones, essentially atomistic. They tested specific moral traits, but did not come to grips with a subject's total character.

CHARACTER EDUCATION INQUIRY. About thirty years ago Hartshorne and his associates undertook a study of character, covering a period of six years.[19] This inquiry is well known and was the first large-scale investigation of the nature of character. Several hundred children in grades five to eight served as subjects. If the careful control of data is a test of scientific dependability, the Character Education Inquiry, with all its faults, is a reliable scientific investigation.

The Inquiry sought data regarding three areas of moral behabior: (1) the subject's moral knowledge, (2) his moral attitudes and opinions, and (3) his actual moral behavior. We might add, parenthetically, that of these three the first is of little importance in gauging a person's character; for as we said before, there may be

[17] G. M. Lowe and M. E. Shimberg, A critique of the fables as a moral judgment test, *J. appl. Psychol.*, 9 (1925), 53–59.

[18] See R. F. Voelker, The function of ideals in social education, *Teachers Coll. Contrib. Educ.* (1921), No. 112; V. M. Cady, The psychology and pathology of personality, *J. Delinq.*, 7 (1922).

[19] See the appropriate references in footnote 15, above. To those should be added the following: H. Hartshorne, M. A. May, and F. K. Shuttleworth, *Studies in the organization of character* (New York: The Macmillan Co., 1930).

considerable variance between the morality which a person knows and understands and the moral acts and values which he displays in concrete situations.[20]

For information concerning the subjects' moral knowledge and moral attitudes and opinions, the investigators used questionnaires, particularly inventories on cheating in concrete situations. For the study of moral behavior in concrete situations they designed techniques which were not open to the criticism that applies to their other methods. The tests were objective, well controlled, and their purpose was well concealed from the subjects. The latter characteristic is highly important, for the subjects' knowledge that the tests aimed to elicit their honesty, for instance, would have immediately changed their behavior in the "right" or expected direction.

A few examples of tests of overt honesty in the Inquiry as well as in other studies may give the reader some idea of both their nature and objectivity.

Possibility of cheating on an examination
Possibility of cheating in a game in which the subjects were blindfolded
Self-scoring of papers on an information test
Returning money when subjects were overcharged by a storekeeper
Checking titles on a fictitious book list that subjects claimed to have read
Claiming to have knowledge on which subject was later tested [21]

The tests of honesty were analyzed for reliability and validity and were found satisfactory, although the authors fully recognize several types of error. In general, and test for test, they report, deception may be measured "almost as consistently and with almost as little error as we are able to measure intelligence." [22] Validation was tested by means of three criteria: ratings, records, and the subjects' confessions. Specifically, this was accomplished by (1) getting the opinions of teachers, parents, and other children concerning the deceitfulness of a child; (2) gathering the conduct records on the children tested; and (3) asking the children themselves what they thought of certain types of conduct—such as whether they believed that getting help from a dictionary is cheating when they were admonished not to seek such help. Assuming that a true picture of children's opinion regarding honesty is about what one would expect in the general population, and supposing that this assumption is correct, then in about 90 per cent of the tested sub-

[20] See G. L. Grace and H. A. Grace, The relationship between verbal and behavioral measures of value, *J. educ. Res.*, 46 (1952), 123–31.

[21] The methods of measuring deception are discussed in great detail in Ch. 3 of *Studies in deceit*, pp. 47–103. See further, H. E. Brogden, A factor analysis of forty character tests, *Psychol. Monogr.*, 52 (1940), No. 234.

[22] *Studies in deceit*, p. 135.

jects the scores represent not only deception but also the feeling that the act is a genuine case of dishonesty. The authors accordingly felt that their tests did in fact measure what they were designed to test, namely, dishonesty, deceit, unfairness, and so forth.[23]

The trait of *self-control* was also investigated by the Character Education Inquiry. It was measured by the techniques of inhibition and persistence. The technique of inhibition consisted of the use of various forms of temptation and distraction. The child who did not yield to these intrusions received a high rating for inhibition, and vice versa. The child who performed the largest number of such tasks as solving puzzles had a high measure of persistence; the child who accomplished the least was given a low measure on the scale of persistence.

Another important moral quality which the Inquiry investigated was the trait of *cooperativeness*. Some of the tests of this trait consisted of decisions by the children to give prize money to a philanthropic institution, to the most successful performer in a competitive exercise, or for classroom and play equipment.

A few years later Maller reported in a brief paper the results of a factorial study of the correlations among the four composite measures of character in the Character Education Inquiry described above.[24] Although he found a low magnitude of intercorrelation among these factors, Maller was convinced of the existence of a general or common factor, which he called factor C. This factor is "the readiness to forego an immediate gain for the sake of a remote but greater gain."[25] This conclusion confirms our own previous stress on the importance of long-range, future-oriented intentions as an essential mark of character and moral behavior. It is also confirmed by a later study by Cattell, who has found a general factor in his own researches, which he has designated as the "stable character" factor.[26]

Finally, the notion of a common or general factor, of a stable character, is supported by common experience. When we judge a man's character we note not only his honesty, or benevolence, or self-control, but a set of fairly consistent principles that regulate his conduct.

The existence of a general factor of character was posited some

[23] *Ibid.*, p. 137–40.

[24] J. B. Maller, General and specific factors in character, *J. soc. Psychol.*, 5 (1934), 97–102.

[25] *Ibid.*, p. 101. Maller attributes the low magnitude of intercorrelation partly to the imperfection of the tests in their experimental forms.

[26] R. B. Cattell, *The description and measurement of personality* (Yonkers, N.Y.: World Book Co., 1946).

years before Maller's analysis of the Character Education Inquiry data, and at least two decades before Cattell's formulation of a stable character. In 1915 the English psychologist Webb demonstrated—at least to his own satisfaction—the existence of a generalized "will" factor, which he called the W-factor. This W-factor he considered to be the essential part of an individual's character.[27]

Webb's will-factor was based on the intercorrelation of the judgments of the behavior of some two hundred college students. Factor analysis disclosed an undoubted persistence of striving, or will-character, which corresponds to what common usage designates as persistence in a course of action, self-control, or an upright character.

Much later Brogden established several general factors, especially self-control, which added credence to Webb's W-factor. Using forty different tests, including intelligence ratings, tests of persistence, and some of the tests of honesty of the Character Education Inquiry, Brogden found that self-control, persistence, conscientiousness, and resistance to suggestion—traits which popularly describe the "strong" character—were particularly pronounced in the morally "good" individual.[28] In a later analysis of character-trait intercorrelations, he found similar clusters, although the primary aim of his study was not to corroborate his earlier findings.[29]

STUDIES BY PIAGET. At about the same time that the results of the Character Education Inquiry were published, Piaget in Switzerland was engaged in the study of moral judgments of children.[30] His investigations are widely known and deserve our serious attention. Like the studies just reviewed, Piaget's investigation is a good example of the genetic paradigm in the study of character. The main stress is on the developmental stages in the growth of moral life. Although the stages inevitably overlap, as in all genetic growth, there are, nevertheless, three distinct phases.

The first stage in the growth of moral life is the stage of *moral realism*, beginning in early childhood and terminating at about the age of eight or nine. In this stage the child acts within the framework of parental authority; he is moral in the sense that he obeys the rules imposed upon him by adults. The second stage, overlap-

---

[27] E. Webb, Character and intelligence, *Brit. J. Psychol.*, 1915, Suppl. 1, No. 3, 1–94.

[28] H. E. Brogden, A factor analysis of forty character tests, *Psychol. Monogr.*, 52 (1940), No. 234.

[29] H. E. Brogden, A multiple-factor analysis of the character trait intercorrelations published by Sister Mary McDonough, *J. educ. Psychol.*, 35 (1944), 397–410.

[30] Piaget, *The moral judgment of the child*.

ping considerably with the first with respect to the children's age, is the stage of *incipient cooperation*. Here he begins to make judgments on the basis of some awareness of the feelings of others and the effect of his own behavior upon them. Each child, especially in games requiring cooperation, gives some thought to mutual control and unified action. Nevertheless, what rules exist are still rather vague. The child begins to take the attitude of another. He acts more and more on the basis of the norms of his reference group. Rules are no longer completely felt as constraints imposed upon him from without; there is a glimmer of self-imposition in following the rules of his group. The child usually achieves the third stage by the time the child reaches his twelfth or thirteenth year; he now makes moral judgments that are based on the *codification of rules.* Here every detail of playing the game is fixed, and the rules are known by and are binding on the whole group. The rules of the group are now his own rules.[31]

OTHER STUDIES. Not all studies of moral character, by any means, are developmental in their approach. While we can learn a great deal concerning moral behavior by observing stages in children's growth, there are other aspects that throw light upon character, even when the subjects are children.

The relationship between moral judgment and intelligence has received considerable attention. While the correlations vary in different studies they are, on the whole, reliable. In administering the Stanford Binet and the Thurstone Proverb Test to two groups of women offenders in a state reformatory, Harriman found a high correlation between the median IQ and the median score on the Thurstone Test.[32] One group of women scored a median IQ of 96.2 and the other of 76.2. The more intelligent women made a median score on the Thurstone Test nearly twice as high as the less intelligent group. The correlation between IQ scores and moral judgment scores was .92.[33]

An earlier study of seventh-grade children by Lincoln and Shields yielded similar, but lower, correlations. Using the Stanford-Binet and the Shields Moral Judgment Examination they

---

[31] Piaget was not concerned with the moral judgments of adults. By the time a child reaches the stage of the codification of rules he already exhibits potential adult moral behavior. By implication, adult moral judgments are scarcely more than complications and refinements of "the rules of the game" emerging in adolescence. This hardly accounts for the subtle and altruistic nature of the adult intentional moral self.

[32] This test, consisting of well-known proverbs regarding moral aspects of life, was designed to reveal an individual's moral proclivities.

[33] P. L. Harriman, Ethical discrimination as a function of intelligence, *Sch. & Soc.,* 38 (1933), 812.

found a correlation of .54 which, though rather low, suggests a positive relation between intelligence and moral judgments.[34]

Chassell, basing his conclusion on the examination of several studies, concluded that the relationship between intelligence and moral behavior in the general population is somewhat below a correlation of .70.[35]

Not least important is the relation between morality and the socioeconomic status of a child's parents. This is a relatively neglected problem in the psychology of character; only occasionally have students of moral behavior examined it. Lerner's early study, which deserves more attention than it has received, has not been replicated.[36] Using two age groups of six to eight and nine to eleven years, he divided each into one group of "good" socioeconomic environment and another group of "poor" family background. To the children in each group he told stories concerned with lying, and recorded their responses to them. Generally speaking, the children from the good backgrounds showed superior moral discrimination to the children from the poor home environments. The former tended to be more "idealistic" regarding moral behavior, whereas the latter betrayed the type of practical, moral insensitivity which is often noted in people who since childhood have been exposed to the harsh realities of material existence.[37]

A serious difficulty in measuring the relation between home background and moral conduct—more specifically honesty and similar virtues—is the control of other factors. In the Hartshorne and May study, for instance, the factor of intelligence was not held constant, because their data did not permit the use of the technique of partial correlation. In any case the correlations which they found were somewhat spurious. From considerations other than the data themselves, the investigators estimated that, if intelligence were held constant, the correlation between home background and deception scores for persons in an unselected population would be about −.30.[38]

[34] E. A. Lincoln and F. J. Shields, An age scale for the measurement of moral judgments, *J. educ. Res.*, 32 (1931), 193–97.

[35] C. F. Chassell, The relation between morality and intellect, *Teachers Coll. Contrib. Educ.*, 1934, No. 607.

[36] E. Lerner, *Constraint areas and the moral judgment of children* (Menasha, Wis.: Banta Publishing Co., 1937).

[37] The Character Education Inquiry, of course, investigated this problem, as well as the relations between moral conduct and such factors as race, nationality, religion, and education, in some detail. What the psychology of character now needs is replication of these and other studies, with particular reference to the present somewhat unconscionable scene, and with more relevance to a man's character as a whole. For the CEI's findings, see Hartshorne and May, *Studies in deceit*, Chs. 8–12.

[38] *Ibid.*, Ch. 9.

A significant study by Barkley, especially since it was performed with college students rather than children, is worth noting in connection with the relation between moral judgment and socioeconomic status.[39] In this investigation students in a Southern woman's college were drawn from two groups of freshmen designated as "commercial students" and "liberal arts students." Although the two groups engaged in all the academic and social activities of the college, they were segregated in their own dormitories. After certain drop-outs from the experiment were eliminated, the commercial group consisted of 79 subjects and the liberal arts group of 95.

The instrument for measuring changes in moral judgment was the Shields Moral Judgment Examination, a test designed to measure the ability to make moral and ethical discriminations. The reliability index of this test was .81, but its validity index was not given.

The other measuring devices used in the study were the Carnegie Mental Ability Test, the Clark Revision of the Thurstone Personality Schedule, and Form A of the following three scales: Katz's Attitude Toward the Law; Attitude Toward God, by Chave and Thurstone; and the Chave-Thurstone Scale for Measuring Attitude Toward the Church.

The home backgrounds of the subjects were classified on the basis of the type of work in which the father was engaged at the time of the study. These occupational ratings were classified according to ranking on the occupational ladder, from I, or high-ranking, to V, or low-ranking.

Barkley's results showed that in the two highest occupations there were more fathers from the liberal arts group, whereas in the third- and fourth-ranking occupations, there were more from the commercial group. The two groups were about equal in rating on the fifth occupational group, but none of the fathers were in occupations rated lower than the fifth group. Furthermore, it was found that the liberal arts students whose fathers were in occupational group IV (next to the lowest in rank) made the lowest average score on the test, but made the largest gain in average score achieved by any group during the year.

Two important conclusions are strongly indicated by Barkley's data. The first is that "moral judgment is associated with socioeconomic status as indicated by the occupation of the breadwinners in the homes from which the subjects came." The second conclusion is that the liberal arts program seems to have had a greater

[39] K. L. Barkley, Development of the moral judgment of college students, *Char. & Pers.*, 10 (1942), 199–212.

influence than the commercial course upon the development of moral judgment. The latter is shown by the fact that the liberal arts students made an average gain of 3.7 points, whereas the commercial students made an average gain of only .90 of a point. The first figure is a statistically significant gain; the second is not.[40]

An interesting study of Turkish children by Ugurel-Semin, confirms the role of socioeconomic factors, but in a somewhat different direction. Like the Barkley study it shows that the culture in which socieconomic classes are embedded plays a determining role.[41] In general, the children from poor homes were as frequently generous as those from the homes of the rich, were more often equalitarian, and were less frequently selfish.

CONCLUDING REMARKS. With the exception of Barkley's study of college students, the researches of the Character Education Inquiry, and the investigations using its data, all exclusively employ the genetic model. We have recognized the value of this approach on preceding pages of this chapter; but we must reiterate that the study of moral development in children has not taken us far in the attempt to account for the nature of the morally mature individual. Character, we have said in various ways, is not action based on childhood conditioning and reinforcement alone, important as these are in the earlier stages of moral development; it lies more deeply in a person's image of himself, or in his intentional strivings toward moral excellence, which are the essence of a mature character.

A second, and more unsupported as well as damaging, conclusion of the studies we have reviewed is the doctrine of moral specificity. Having been disillusioned by their discovery that the practice of honesty in one situation did not transfer to another situation, Hartshorne and his collaborators, as well as many other investigators, took refuge in the notion that morality is highly specific. Their subservience to the criterion of predictiveness blinded them to the holistic and future-pointed nature of the consistent and integrated character. Prediction from a consistently organized whole is considerably more certain than expectancies based upon knowledge of unrelated particulars. Generalization is much easier when we have insight into *dynamic patterns* of moral or any other kind of behavior. If we assume that all situations in moral behavior are independent, so that every ideal or virtue must

---

[40] These findings accord well with the claim of humanists and many educators, that a liberal arts education is a highly "civilizing" force.

[41] R. Ugurel-Semin, Moral behavior and moral judgment of children, *J. abnorm. soc. Psychol.*, 47 (1952), 463–74.

be acquired separately, then we can never hope to understand human character, which is essentially a whole. Parenthetically, it is interesting to note that Allport's book on personality is still the most convincing proof of the fallacy of the doctrine of specificity.[42]

It may well be that, had Hartshorne and his associates used more mature subjects in their research, the results might have lent support to a more holistic view of human character. This conclusion is dimly implied in the fact that the Inquiry found evidence of increasing consistency of moral traits with the increasing age and maturity of the children. The implication gives added support to our view that generalization of traits in young children is weak, and that children, on the whole, are not the best subjects for the study of character and morality. The investigations by Hartshorne and his collaborators are, as the title of their book makes plain, studies in *deceit*, not of character as an intentional whole.

The tendency toward consistency of moral traits suggests the urgency of longitudinal studies of character growth. Cross-sectional studies, such as those we have briefly described, do not give us knowledge of the actualization of moral potentials. One can feel confident in saying that in the investigations reviewed, no child even approximated his maximum moral growth.

Underlying most investigations is the fallacious assumption regarding basic drives, a fallacy that characterizes most contemporary research on motivation. This assumption, based almost exclusively on the study of animal drives in the laboratory, is that whatever we do, we do to satisfy a craving or need. However, as we tried to show in our discussion of expressive behavior, human beings engage in many activities that satisfy no palpable "basic" needs. To base the whole psychology of motivation on need-gratification is to go far beyond the evidence, and to give us an account of many forms of behavior, such as self-sacrifice and altruism, wholly in terms of self-seeking. Thus, the parent who sacrifices for the needs of his children is allegedly satisfying his own needs rather than the needs of his children. This is an old argument, of course, but it has never been scientifically demonstrated.

The main points of the foregoing remarks are simply these: attitudes, values, moral traits, and the like, function not in isolation, but in relation to the total personality. Moral behavior, like any organized and consistent behavior, is a function not of separate

---

[42] See G. W. Allport, *Personality: a psychological interpretation* (New York: Henry Holt & Co., Inc., 1937). To this book should be added the recent volume by Ligon which, though conceived in a different frame of reference from Allport's, also serves as a strong argument against the specificity of moral acts. See E. M. Ligon, *Dimensions of character* (New York: The Macmillan Co., 1956).

needs but of the *personality*. An attitude, or a value, or a moral act functions in a variety of other attitudes, values, and moral acts, not by itself.[43] The only way to truly understand them is to see them in their interrelatedness. To attribute a coherent system of moral—or any other—values to young children is to endow them with a capacity for abstraction and generalization which they do not possess. It does not require an elaborate scientific investigation to discover not only that children—certainly up to the age of seven or eight—have a very flexible scale of values, but that their values lie almost exclusively in the realm of sense pleasure. Children's moral values change both with current demands and with their age levels.

Finally, although it is generally agreed that children are born into a society of ready-made moral standards, no research has yet been able to determine when and how these are internalized by the child. Most psychologists are aware of the problem, but they do not always admit ignorance regarding it.[44] In any case, it is certain that neither experimental nor clinical psychologists have thrown much light on this problem.

Piaget's investigations only emphasize the child's egocentricity. A child's acts, he has demonstrated, are perceived in the framework of their hedonic consequences, not by the kind of moral intentions which we have been talking about in this chapter. Regard for others comes later in the youth's development, but Piaget has not spelled out the manner in which this comes about. His emphasis on stages of moral development has received the criticism it deserves, but its critics have been equally unsuccessful in accounting for the origin of moral obligations in morally mature people. Rogers comes closest to giving us a hint regarding the awakening of the moral consciousness, although his concern has been not with moral conduct but with psychotherapy. When, as the result of therapy, the client comes to see himself in the light of values and intentions, instead of individual desires and neurotic defenses, he acts on the plane of maturity instead of childish fears and frustrations. He has begun to form an image of himself as a

[43] See W. A. Koppe, Attitude measurement by use of worksheets, *Union College Studies in Character Research* (Schenectady, N.Y.: Union College, 1954), Vol. 1, No. 11; W. A. Koppe, A report to co-scientists, *Adventures in Character Education,* Union College Character Research Project. (Schenectady, N.Y.: Union College, 1955), Vol. 8, No. 7.

[44] Thompson, Hutt and Miller are a few who have verbally acknowledged it. See G. G. Thompson, *Child psychology* (Boston: Houghton Mifflin Co., 1952); M. L. Hutt and D. R. Miller, Value interiorization and democratic education, *J. soc. Issues,* 5 (1949), 31–43; D. R. Miller and M. L. Hutt, Value interiorization and personality development, *J. soc. Issues,* 5 (1949), 2–30.

mature person, and henceforth his behavior is being guided by long-term goals rather than immediate fears and desires.[45] In psychotherapy, as in real life, the individual develops an awareness of himself as a moral being. When this takes place depends upon the locus in the person's growth where he perceives moral and other values in the context of his perceptual field. Moral reality, like psychological reality generally, is a perceptual phenomenon. When the individual perceives himself as lovable, or honest, or morally good, this image of himself serves as a strong pressure upon himself to be loving, just, and morally excellent. But this perception of oneself as moral, like one's perception of one's self as an individual, differs from individual to individual.

UNION COLLEGE CHARACTER RESEARCH PROJECT (CRP)

For a period of over twenty years Ligon and his associates have been investigating the development of character in children. He recently compressed the prodigious amount of material into a single volume, which we have already cited.[46] The study has many admirable qualities, but the most important is that, unlike most of the studies which we have reviewed, it seriously challenges the doctrine of moral specificity, and stresses throughout the conception of the integrated moral character.

Strictly speaking, the research of the CRP was performed not only by experts but by other people as well: parents, teachers, camp counselors, clergymen, and the subjects themselves. Ligon refers to this teamwork form of research as the skills of the *co-scientist*. While recognizing that some forms of research require special or technical skills, Ligon found that many people not specially trained in scientific methodology were able to contribute knowledge and information that contributed to a better understanding of moral education and character growth.

Besides enlisting the aid of coscientists in the accumulation of his data, Ligon utilized the stupendous body of published research in child development which has been accumulated in psychological laboratories and clinics, and in investigations of educators, psychiatrists, sociologists, and mental health experts.

SOME WORKING PROPOSITIONS. Underlying Ligon's project are specific hypotheses or "theoretical decisions." These hypotheses that directed the course of his research and determined the major conclusions of the study, may be stated briefly.

[45] C. R. Rogers, *Client-centered therapy* (Boston: Houghton Mifflin Co., 1951).
[46] Ligon, *Dimensions of character.*

1. *The important role of* positive *goodness.* Much of the research in human behavior tends to magnify the negative features of behavior and trivialize the positive ones. This is true not only of traditional psychoanalysis but of much experimental and clinical psychology as well. However, the CRP emphasizes positive features. From the CRP's standpoint, a good child is one who performs good acts, not one who simply refrains from doing that which is bad. All the educational goals in CRP are positive. Stress is placed on "service for mankind," "sensitiveness to the needs of others," and determination "to see that every man gets his full chance at happiness and success."

2. *The child's contributions to his own growth.* It is astonishing to find how little psychology and education have outgrown the traditional theory that the child resembles plastic clay. In this situation the child is "a bit of molding clay at the mercy of his elders." Yet, as we argued, on the basis of evidence in various places in this book, the child himself plays the major role in becoming. The process of learning, for example, is not merely the mechanical responses of a child to external stimuli; the learner himself plays an active role in its accomplishment. Even commonsense observation convinces one that the healthy child approaches a learning situation, like most other situations, with determination and energy rather than passivity.

3. *The need to emphasize psychological health.* A great deal of clinical and personality psychology works within the framework of maladjustment. Efforts to improve the individual as a person operate on the premise that he must be divested of his weaknesses and maladjustive behavior. We do not deny the vital importance of curing a person of his psychological ills; rather, we deplore that a person's determination to grow and to become as "good" as he can is for the most part neglected. In the mentally healthy individual the positive far outweigh the negative and destructive features of behavior. Hence to be preoccupied with the fears, angers, and defenses which occasionally plague everyone, often is to be blinded to the prevalence of heroism, good will, and fortitude in most of us. "It is significant," writes Ligon, "that the emotion which is the opposite of anger, magnanimity, is an almost forgotten word in the language;" and calling attention to the psychologist's engrossment in the fears of children at various stages, he asks, "Where in the literature will you find studies describing the forms of courage common to these same age levels?" [47] Although there

[47] *Ibid.*, p. 52.

is a dearth of research evidence in favor of the positive elements in human character, the wise and intelligent observations of healthy individuals unquestionably confirm the belief that human beings respond to challenges more often than to crippling defenses.

4. *The limitations of the behaviorist approach.* We have already referred to this situation in current motivational theory (see p. 255 above). No psychologist is so imprudent as to minimize the importance of the basic animal drives in human behavior; and we have stressed their importance in Chapters 5 and 9. In most instances they probably are prepotent. But this is not the whole story; there are many instances in the lives of human beings, and even of animals, when other needs take precedence. The hungry rat will often explore his cage before he seeks the food that he smells; the unfed baby will dawdle over his porridge long before he consumes it; the loving parent will deny himself pleasures and comforts in order to vouchsafe the happiness and welfare of his children. These are not isolated cases; they are as frequent as their opposites. All through their history human beings have aimed at and achieved levels of moral grandeur that one would never suspect solely by examining their basic needs. In the realm of character, as in the healthy personality as a whole, an individual's conscious and intentional dreams and aspirations predict his future behavior more adequately than his basic needs. This conclusion has not been established in the laboratory and the clinic, but it is confirmed by the lives of morally great men.

REQUISITES IN CHARACTER EDUCATION. Since the chief aim of CRP was chiefly practical, namely, to devise means by which children's character could be improved, from kindergarten through high school, its conclusions must be viewed in the light of this effort. The techniques consisted of the use of many thousands of curricular elements, such as workshops, projects, and discussions.

Stories and biographies were used widely. Ligon was aware, however, of the ineffectiveness of this technique, for which published evidence exists.[48] Consequently he was governed by the hypothesis that stories and biographies must be adapted to the child and made meaningful to him by their relevance to the latter's daily life. The purpose of the curricular elements was to stimulate and challenge the young people who were used as subjects. However, Ligon was fully conscious of the fact that the techniques of character and religious education which he employed did not challenge even a small fraction of the maximum capacity of the

[48] See V. Jones, *Character and citizenship training in the public schools* (Chicago: University of Chicago Press, 1936).

adolescents involved. However, this is a shortcoming of every·
educational curriculum, from kindergarten through university.

1. *Evaluating the curriculum.* The curriculum was evaluated
by studying every element of the curriculum impersonally. Such
evaluations varied from almost purely subjective opinion, with
every effort to be honest and realistic, to carefully analyzed investigations complete with tests of significance. For example, the
Parents' Reports were studied to determine which lessons did or
did not contribute to the success or failure in achieving desired
objectives; a listing and evaluation of the motivations stimulated
by the parents and teachers and how these motivations operated
in the children; an analysis of the misunderstandings and impediments encountered by teachers, parents, or children; an evaluation of the effectiveness of additional materials and methods which
were used by the parents and teachers.

A second method of analyzing curricular materials was more
quantitative. The reports of parents and teachers were rated on a
seven-point scale, on which the average rating of the reports on
any one lesson was used as an approximate measure of its effectiveness. Sampling errors were minimized by using stratified ran-
domization in the choice of the groups which were tested. "With
all its shortcomings," Ligon writes, "this is the most objective
measure we have been able to use extensively in CRP." [49]

2. *Dealing with differences in motivated capacity.* No matter
how good the curricular materials for testing and teaching character may be, much depends on how they are employed by parents
and teachers. These groups, therefore, must be challenged to carry
them out effectively. Ligon calls the limits within which parents
and teachers can be challenged by the curricular material, *motivated
capacity.* People differ widely in the possession and use of this
capacity. Ligon believes that some curricula were designed largely
for people at the lowest level of motivated capacity, and have
failed to challenge the best; whereas the CRP has tended to go
to the opposite extreme, challenging the ablest but leaving the
less able in a "hopeless confusion." Techniques somewhere between these extremes are urgently needed but are yet to be devised.

3. *Recognizing the child as an individual.* In character training
and development, the child must be treated as an individual whole.
Accordingly, a basic principle in the evaluation of character training is to study its effectiveness with the individual. This is done
both cross-sectionally and longitudinally. The cross-sectional tech-
·nique observes the effect of a particular lesson on all the individuals

[49] *Ibid.,* p. 384.

in a group; the longitudinal method consists in accumulating all of the evidence regarding individual children over a period of months or years.

4. *Reflecting realities of the social order.* Any effort in character education must be deeply conscious of the culture in which the child lives. This is too often forgotten by both parents and teachers, but the child is deeply conscious of the disparity between what he is taught and what is actually practiced in the world at large. "The fact of the matter is," as Ligon expressed it, "we are asking our children to live lives we could not live. We often preach to them with our tongues in our cheeks." [50] Turning the other cheek in a cutthroat world can be very unconvincing, especially if the parents themselves are more concerned with social status in the community than with the discriminating and fine points of moral rectitude.

5. *Integrating the child's experiences.* This is already implied by the preceding conclusion, but differs from it. It refers to the fact that we must recognize not only the total social experience of the child, but also the interrelationship of home and school with other agencies in the community. More particularly, we must eliminate needless duplication of effort among the institutions of the community, and integrate them to prevent waste and harmful competition.

The stupendous labor of more than twenty years involved in the CRP makes consistency of both method and results impossible to attain. Nevertheless, the study gives a fairly uniform idea of how character can be investigated, how it is formed, and the means by which it can be changed for the better. Ligon has performed a commendable job. It is impossible to evaluate the study in the space of a few pages; but a shortcoming which has impressed itself upon the present writer deserves mention. The flaw is the more difficult to understand in view of Ligon's unfailing emphasis on the positive features of a child's moral aspirations. Perhaps in his zeal to effect collaboration among many individuals—the group of co-scientists—he has insufficiently stressed the role of *self-education.*

Ligon does not carry through sharply enough the implications of his own fruitful concept of *positive potential* in the individual child. A child learns to be good not only because of the ministrations, concerns, and teaching of others (including ideal and biographical figures), but also because of his own desire to be as good as he can. The intentional, self-propelling features of character development are given much less space than they deserve.

[50] *Ibid.,* p. 395.

Basing our own conclusion not only on the voluminous literature on character and moral conduct, both philosophical and psychological, but also on the fascinating observation of people in the matrix of moral choices and predicaments, we observe in both children and adults a powerful need for *liberation* from the constraints of conventional morality to the freedom of individual ethics. Character is the process of moving away from the pressures of the moral situation to the internalization of ethical values to form conscious moral conduct and understanding. Ethical conduct at its finest is a species of moral autonomy, in which parents, teachers, and others no longer exercise a crippling constraint upon the individual's moral behavior.

CONCLUSION

The preceding pages of this chapter are but a propaedeutic to a fullgrown essay on the moral nature of man. It is not intended to be more. We have virtually omitted, except by implication and occasional suggestions, the vital topic of conscience, without which character remains morally anemic and half-known. We do not believe that beyond its feeble beginnings it is scarcely more than a learned response to punishment. As we have said on several occasions, mature ethical conduct transcends the narrow limits of guilt associated with wrongdoing. If learning theory and Freud's notion of recapitulation were the important instigators of conscience and moral conduct, it would be hard to understand how we progress beyond the adolescent level. The functional autonomy of the moral conscience is as much a reality as the functional autonomy of motives. A time comes in the life of every individual when his image of himself is a more powerful determinant of his moral actions than the threatening admonitions of parent, teacher, clergyman, or policeman. The sense of guilt in the act of wrongdoing is not a reaction to the threat of punishment; it is rather, as Allport discerningly phrased it, "a sense of violated value, a disgust at falling short of the ideal self-image." [51]

We have described the process of the transformation of external constraints into internal sanctions at various places in this chapter. We recapitulate the substance of the process here. In the process of socialization the child identifies himself with his parents or other significant persons in his environment, making them truly a part of himself. The more affectionate and nurturent his early relations

[51] G. W. Allport, *Becoming: basic considerations for a psychology of personality* (New Haven: Yale University Press, 1955), p. 73.

with his parents are, the more likely is the introjection of them going to be positively and affectionately toned. The fear of admonitions and prohibitions, next, gives way to self-acceptance and individual choices. The process, however, is largely facilitated by the self-image which the individual has already established. Finally, truncated, unrelated, specific moral reactions are integrated into a consistent and forward-thrusting scheme of values. Conscience, then, is the generic *ought*, "the monitor of growth," impelling the individual to forsake tribal ways for moral individuality—a process of growth from "opportunistic to oriented becoming." [52] Character, to repeat once more, is the expression of intentional behavior.

Stated more concretely but prosaically, moral conduct is a *liberation movement* from (1) the external situation to internal transformation of the parental "must"; (2) present-bound needs and desires to future-oriented objectives; (3) specific needs and values to general principles of behavior; and (4) egocentricity to altruism. In this process morality becomes *self-directed and purposeful action*.

Character, thus, is not a mechanical response to the impositions of society. Current learning theory and traditional psychoanalysis, as we have said before, do not adequately account for moral behavior as we have described it. If the individual were scarcely more than a set of responses, or a submissive individual cowering in the face of cultural imperatives, he would have no character at all. At the same time, the moral conscience is not inherent at birth; for then character would be but an unfolding of inner capacities in the manner of earlier developmental theories. It is rather a novel product of man's interactions with other men from which, as in all creative human relationships, man emerges as an individualized person. Character is the continuous realization of the self in moral action.

[52] *Ibid.*, p. 74.

CHAPTER **15**

The Total Personality:
Its Structure

We have frequently emphasized the view that the human personality is a totality, a *Gestalt*, an organized whole. This stress on the wholeness and relative consistency of personality does not blind us to the discrepancies, even the contradictions, that exist in the behavior of the normal individual; nor does it mean that we are unmindful of the fragmentations often found in the abnormal personality. However, the behavior of the normal individual is characterized by dependability and some predictability. The more organized and integrated a person's psychological traits and processes are, the more must his personality be described as a psychophysical totality.

The relative consistency of motivational strivings, the attitude-value complex, speech and voice, character and moral behavior, and so forth, add to the organization of the personality. These dimensions, together with the self which is discussed in the following chapter, constitute the total personality. Personality, in short, is a *structure* or *organization* of psychological, biological, and social substructures.

The division of the total personality into "parts" or substructures itself calls attention to the organized nature of the personality. Parts presuppose wholes; and if we must for analytical, experimental, or diagnostic reasons divide the personality into various substructures or dimensions, we do so on purely heuristic grounds. Division has a legitimate and necessary function in scientific research; it distorts psychological reality only when we forget that we are dealing with segments whose character we can understand only in the light of the whole from which they are disjoined.

The term "structure" can be—and has been—misleading, especially since it was originally associated with the structuralism of Wundt and Titchener. However, Wundt's concept of *creative synthesis* and Titchener's view of mental *processes* imply that not even they conceived psychological structures as completely static. When we speak of the structure of the personality in this chapter we conceive it in terms of *dynamic relationships,* or changes among the various dimensions that make up the whole. Our definition, then, must be modified to indicate that personality is a *dynamic structure or organization* of various traits and other substructures which themselves, while relatively enduring, are constantly changing. When the change is in the direction of the realization or actualization of intentional ends, we speak of the dynamic process as the *growth* of personality.

The concept of structure or organization has interested psychologists for many years, but it is only in the last few decades that it has achieved a significant place in empirical psychology. The interrelations among the id, ego, and superego has been a problem in psychoanalysis almost from its inception. Structure is the fundamental concept of *Gestalt* psychology. Today's extensive investigation of perceptual organization is but the latest concern with an old problem.[1]

The most up-to-date research in the field of perceptual structure not only points to the great significance of structure for psychology, but implies a revolutionary revision of the concept of psychological law. Not all psychological variables can be measured in terms of quantitative equations alone; they must be described by means of *qualitative* laws, as well. In a penetrating analysis of the problems of perception and structure, based upon a great amount of empirical evidence, F. H. Allport has stated the matter emphatically and clearly. He states that "the proposition that structures are neither random, endlessly varied, inexplicable, nor amenable only to quantitative laws" is erroneous, for, he notes, "there is such a thing as unique *structural* law *sui generis.*" Structures, he adds, "are as lawful as quantitative relationships; but they are lawful in a different way—in a way that quantitative formulations are quite unable to state." Structuring, Allport as-

---

[1] Witness, too, the philosopher's concern with the organization of knowledge, with its paradoxical situation in which, because everything is related to everything else, in knowing anything we must know everything.

serts, is "a primary fact of nature" and follows some lawful principle different from the quantitative laws of traditional science.[2]

It does not detract from the stature of Allport's ideas to say that this view was fundamental in *Gestalt* psychology from the beginning, and that it is a basic idea in field-theoretical physics. We are referring to the concept of the relative, transposable form —that which could change and yet remain the same.

THE STRUCTURE OF TRAITS

A widely acceptable theory of traits has yet to be formulated. Much has been written on the subject, but the sheer bulk of these expositions only points up the lack of consensus. To this must be added the confusion of identifying traits with other personality dimensions, such as attitudes, to which they are closely related. The careless equation of traits and personality types but further confounds the issue. To avoid the latter error we have devoted a separate chapter to typology.[3]

To help the reader escape these and other pitfalls, we stress at the outset that, because traits and trait-complexes are *realities within* every psychological being, they are not open to direct observation, but are inferences. Their very generality, as opposed to specificity, makes them unamenable to immediate perception. However, this does not mean that there are traits in general; on the contrary every trait is deeply embedded in the psychic structure of the individual. Nor does it mean that there are no common traits—that no two people have the same trait. Two or more people may have very similar traits, because they were conditioned by the same set of cultural imperatives; but the place of these traits in the psychological economy of each is determined by the respective individuality of every person. Hence, when we use the term "general" in describing individual traits, we are referring to the extent or magnitude of its appearance in an individual's behavior.

TRAIT CLUSTERS. Although like other human characteristics, traits may function singly, thus accounting for their inconsistencies in individual personalities, they usually form clusters or substructures. The more mature and integrated the individual, the more his traits form relatively consistent systems. They tend to be *unitary* rather than segmental. It is this fact, seemingly, which is partly responsible for the confusion of traits and types. The tend-

[2] F. H. Allport, *Theories of perception and the concept of structure* (New York: John Wiley & Sons, Inc., 1955), pp. 621–29.

[3] See Chapter 3.

ency to form clusters or trait-structures challenges the tendency of some psychologists to multiply traits needlessly. The problem of trait-names has largely arisen from the need to designate the proliferation of single traits.

Nevertheless, a word of caution is important. Although traits tend to form structures, their relation to one another within each structure has a graded order. Some traits are more dominant than others and tend to take precedence in overt behavior. Thus, there are *primary* and *subsidiary* traits.

The primary traits are those by which we come to know the dominant disposition of an individual, his ruling or pre-eminent self. They are the traits by which anyone who knows him will describe him, for by the very strength of their organization they stand out in bold relief. Thus, a person may habitually be ascendant, submissive, or self-assertive. Ascendance, for example, is not an independent trait, but a cluster of such separate traits as self-confidence, security, and self-esteem. We recognize a person by the fact that in many more circumstances than not his relations with others are marked by one of these trait clusters.

Subsidiary traits are those that play a less controlling function in the total personality. They do not reveal as boldly the style of the individual's life as do the primary traits. They lack the persistence of the primary clusters; indeed, they are less likely than the primary ones to form consistent structures. External observes are less likely to perceive these traits, for they do not obtrude themselves upon their attention.

However, lest the foregoing distinction imply a division which does not in reality exist, we hasten to add that primary and subsidiary traits exist in a continuum. There is no objective device for measuring the degree of separation between them. We use the distinction as a conceptual tool, and not to assert a fundamental distinction between them. The primary and subsidiary traits may be *theoretically* perpendicular to each other, but in actual experience they probably never are. Thus, a person may be motivated by sociability and self-assertiveness at the same time, even though they represent different trait dimensions. Valid criteria for distinguishing primary from secondary trait-structures have thus far been designed only for those that are closely related. Thus, Guilford and Zimmerman succeeded in differentiating fourteen closely related trait variables by means of factor analysis.[4] Among these were such affiliated variables as social leadership, social poise,

[4] J. P. Guilford and W. S. Zimmerman, Fourteen dimensions of temperament, *Psychol. Monogr.*, 70 (1956), No. 417.

gregariousness, social initiative, desire for conspicuousness, self-defense, and standing up for one's rights.

The foregoing distinctions also conform with common-sense observations and clinical diagnosis. It is a rare personality in whom a single primary trait is all-determining. When it exists it is usually found in exceedingly narrow and highly focalized individuals, such as certain types of limited geniuses, fanatics, and madmen. In most individuals primary and subsidiary traits mingle to make what Allport described as *central* traits—traits that are "usually mentioned in careful letters of recommendation, in rating scales where the rater stars the outstanding characteristics of the individual, or in brief verbal descriptions of a person." [5]

In the foregoing analysis of trait clusters, two points stand out clearly. First, traits are not normally independent of one another, but merge more or less to form a larger matrix or substructure within the total personality. Second, while trait clusters, like other psychological variables, merge in various ways, some patterns, nevertheless, stand out more sharply, serve as fairly dependable descriptions of personality structure, and assist us in securing a better understanding of the personality as a whole.

CONSISTENCY OF TRAITS. Closely related to the problem of trait organization is the question of the consistency of traits. The concept of trait structure would imply sufficient interdependence among the separate traits to justify the belief that they are also consistent. But here we encounter a difficulty, for there is discouragingly little agreement among the experts. It seems that different circumstances and diverse motives alter the behavioral manifestations of various traits. Furthermore, there is clear evidence that some consistencies are artifacts of investigational procedures, whereby one method of research will reveal consistency while another will contradict it. To compound the difficulty, it is not improbable that occasional consistencies are due to the subjective interpretations of the investigator himself.

This pessimistic view of the situation is dispelled, however, once we agree to regard a measure of absolute agreement among traits as an unobtainable ideal. In the realm of psychological phenomena men have to be content with approximations. The quest for certainty and complete dependability is an illusion born of a too zealous emulation of physical science at a time when physical science is itself plagued by many uncertainties.

Furthermore, since no trait functions alone, one trait is bound

[5] G. W. Allport, *Personality: a psychological interpretation* (New York: Holt, Rinehart & Winston, Inc., 1937), p. 338.

to affect and modify another, thus making them incompatible. Variation in circumstances, changes in mood, conditions of physical and mental health, confrontation by novelty, demand for split-second decisions, and the like, make for unpredictable inconsistencies.

However, just as one swallow does not make a summer, so a single incongruity does not make for personal disharmony. Inconsistency is less a matter of discontinuity than a discrepancy between the primary and subsidiary trait structures. It is erroneous to interpret variance between these major clusters as a disharmony among individual traits. Viewed from the perspective of the total personality, the traits reveal greater harmony than is evident in their independent functioning. As in all things psychological, trait-consistency is not only relative, but a function of many variables.

Traits as factors. The consistency of traits has been extensively studied by means of factor analysis. While this is at present the most powerful tool in psychology, it is well to recognize the limits of its validity. Factor analysis is based on a premise that has not been wholly established, namely, that unified behavior is fundamentally an *additive* process. This additive process consists of determining the weighted effect of several independent variables, or factors, on human behavior.[6] It is a fair criticism, we believe, to say that factor analysis takes us perilously close to the discarded faculty psychology of the nineteenth century. However, without committing ourselves to the additive explanation of human behavior, let us briefly review the study of traits as factors.

In addition to the pioneer work of Thurstone, to which we referred in Chapter 4, the best recent factorial investigations of traits and personality are those of Cattell, Guilford, and Eysenck.

In a factorial study of the 17,953 trait names originally compiled by Allport and Odbert, Cattell succeeded in reducing the list to 160 contrasting traits.[7] To this list Cattell added eleven other terms, thus making the total reduced list 171. Using samples from this list of items and the correlations between the ratings of several groups of subjects, Cattell chose twenty clusters whose intercorrelations were above +.5. These clusters were then in-

---

[6] See Chapter 4.

[7] R. B. Cattell, *Description and measurement of personality* (Yonkers, N.Y.: World Book Co., 1946). See also R. B. Cattell and A. R. Baggaley, The objective measurement of attitude motivation: development and evaluation of principles and devices, *J. Pers.*, 24 (1956), 401–23. For the original study and list of trait names, see G. W. Allport and H. S. Odbert, Trait-names: a psycho-lexical study, *Psychol. Monogr.*, 1936, No. 211.

creased to 35 traits, and Cattell tested over 200 men on them and had each group of 16 of the entire sample ranked by one subject on a five-point scale. Correlations between these rankings were next factor-analyzed to discover the basic factors of personality.

The basic factors, while "technically" established, are disappointingly vague. Traits like cultured-boorish, Bohemian-conventional, or cyclothymic-schizophrenic are reminiscent of earlier, but less involved and less technical, investigations. A similar judgment can be passed on the factorial study of traits by Eysenck.[8]

It would take us beyond the limits of this chapter to engage in a critical analysis of the factor analysis of psychological traits. However, certain points should be noted. First, there is no objective evidence that the factors which have been so laboriously and quantitatively investigated measure what the various claimants believe they have investigated. Are the traits or "factors" realities embedded in the personalities of the subjects, or are they verbal artifacts? Do they describe the subjects measured, or the subjective opinions of those who rated or ranked them? Have the investigators uncovered primary personality factors, or only confirmed earlier typologies? A generous answer to these questions is that there is no certainty, and surely no agreement, among investigators of the subject; a harsh opinion is that the factor analysts have been ingenious in inventing measuring instruments, but have not materially advanced the substantive study of personality structure.

We thus return to our original observation that traits and factors, though related, are not identical. Factor analysis commits the error of many quantitative formulations of personality: it forces individuals into rigid categories. Factors, like "faculties" and instincts, have been universally distributed, whereas traits are individual systems. Traits describe individual persons, not groups and populations. The psychology of traits must not be confused with the psychology of types.

Trait-consistency as persistence through time. The consistency of traits may also be studied genetically, observing their endurance or change throughout developmental stages of personality growth. Clearly, a person who exhibits in his behavior a trait, or a cluster of traits, which has persisted from youth to manhood shows more consistency than one in whom the same trait has changed or been superseded by another. Temporary fluctuations and lasting changes

[8] See H. J. Eysenck, *The structure of the human personality* (New York: John Wiley & Sons, Inc., 1953).

of traits are characteristics of every healthy human organism; but equally, if not more important, is their endurance. Self-consistency and self-identification would be impossible without enduring traits.

The persistence of traits may be studied for developmental periods or for the life-span of an individual. Gesell, who is well-known for his study of developmental stages in infancy and childhood, has made some interesting observations in this connection.[9] Using motion pictures of the behavior of five one-year-old infants, he had a pediatric nurse rank them on each of fifteen traits. This procedure was repeated four years later with new motion pictures of the same children being judged by the same nurse. The ranks of 48 of the 75 original traits were found to be identical; those of 21 were changed by one rank, 5 by two ranks, and one by three ranks.[10]

This study alone cannot give us reliable information on the persistence of traits, but it does serve to suggest that there is some consistency of traits within a span of several years as measured by persistence. However, it is important to note that about a decade later Neilon, using a larger sample of children and a longer time span, only slightly confirmed Gesell's earlier findings.[11] In view of the fact that Gesell's study has been seriously challenged, and his conclusions are somewhat doubtful, Neilon's superior study is probably much closer to the truth.

Is the same consistency, generally speaking, found in adults? The answer is in the affirmative, and to about the same degree. While systematic changes in traits are found in most adults, persistence has an appreciable edge over change. Roberts and Fleming, in a study of 25 women during their four-year college careers, found an 86 per cent persistence in one, 26 per cent in another, and a 60 per cent average for the total population sample.[12]

[9] A. Gesell, Early evidence of individuality in the human infant, Sci. Mon., 45 (1937), 217–25.

[10] By the 75 original traits we refer, of course, to the ranking of the five children on each of the 15 traits.

[11] P. Neilon, Shirley's babies after fifteen years: a personality study, J. genet. Psychol., 73 (1948), 175–86. "Shirley's babies" refers to the infants who were investigated in a study by Mary Shirley, the data on which Neilon's study was based. See M. M. Shirley, The first two years. A study of twenty-five babies. Univ. Minn. Child Welfare Monogr. Ser. (Minneapolis: University of Minnesota Press, 1932), No. 7.

[12] K. E. Roberts and V. V. Fleming, Persistence and change in personality patterns, Monogr. soc. res. child developm., 8 (1943), No. 1. See further H. M. Williams, Factor analysis of Berne's Social Behavior Patterns of young children, J. exp. Educ., 4 (1935), 142–46; C. Burt, Analysis of temperament, Brit. J. med. Psychol., 17 (1938), 158–88; A. Angyal, Foundations for a science of personality (New York: Commonwealth Fund, 1941).

Other studies of this problem generally confirm the foregoing conclusion. While personality traits, like other variables of human behavior, are subject to continuous change, there is in all healthy human organisms a strain of consistency by means of which we can identify a person for a considerable time span—indeed, quite frequently for an entire lifetime.

Universality as a measure of consistency. Are there more or less enduring traits common to all healthy personalities, or are they uniquely determined? If traits are universal then consistency from person to person, as well as within a person, can be expected. Common sense as well as psychological research shows considerable similarity in people even in the face of widely divergent environmental stimulation. This seems to be noticeably true of basic disposition or temperament. Bipolar temperamental traits are found in all peoples, thus strongly supporting their universality. These bipolar traits also function pretty consistently within the life span of single individuals.

Ascendance and submission seem to be universal characteristics. Either one or the other appears early in the development of a child and tends to persist through the period of maturity. An ascendant individual early shows social initiative, leadership, assertion of his rights, and related characteristics. Bass and his associates, in a study of this trait in sorority women, found a slight positive correlation between ascendance and leadership.[13]

Feelings of confidence and inferiority are also universally distributed. It is well known that in every group some persons meet their problems enthusiastically and some retreat from them. These feelings are found in children and adults, and their behavioral indicators are such traits as belief or disbelief in oneself, feelings of acceptance or rejection by others, faith or its absence regarding success in an undertaking, self-acceptance or guilt feelings.[14]

Stable and fluctuating moods are very widespread. Some people, in the face of irritations and frustration that upset others, are able to maintain an even disposition. Others, called cycloids by many psychiatrists, are moody, have frequent elations or depressions, and often feel "just miserable." [15]

[13] B. M. Bass, C. R. Wurster, E. A. Doll, and D. J. Clair, Situational and personality factors in leadership among sorority women, *Psychol. Monogr.*, 67 (1953), No. 366.

[14] See M. Lorr and E. A. Rubenstein, Factors descriptive of psychiatric outpatients, *J. abnorm. soc. Psychol.*, 51 (1955), 514–22; J. P. Guilford and W. S. Zimmerman, Fourteen dimensions of temperament, *Psychol. Monogr.*, 70 (1956), No. 417.

[15] See E. M. Layman, An item analysis of the adjustment questionnaire, *J. Psychol.*, 10 (1940), 87–106.

However, it is unnecessary to describe still other traits, of which there are at least another half-dozen that are widely distributed. While no one has yet succeeded in establishing a normal distribution of personality traits, there is some evidence, though unconvincing, that they follow the "law" of the distribution of other psychological variables. As a convenient way of describing their commonality, the concept of normal distribution has its value; as a final word on the subject it is highly problematic. Personality, including the trait structures which are important components of it, is too complex to be ranged on a curve, normal, bimodal, or skewed. If most people's traits follow the normal curve, or are "average," this is to a considerable extent a function of cultural pressures to conform to a given standard. Finally, and not to be minimized, is the presence of the "vested interests" of test designers who not infrequently wish to symmetrize the distribution of their scores.

Consistency as a function of personality. E. Lowell Kelly, in a survey of significant studies in the area of personality traits, as well as data derived from his own investigation, has shown that consistency is a function of personality. We can do no better than to quote him at some length, because his conclusions strike us as insightful and well-balanced. He writes:

. . . Absolute changes in personality scores tended to be small but similar in direction and magnitude for men and women. We found evidence for considerable consistency of several variables, in spite of fallible tools and a time span of nearly 20 years. But we also found evidence for considerable change in all variables measured. These changes were shown to be relatively specific rather than reflecting any over-all tendency to change. . . . The intensive study of any aspect of growth and development cannot but serve to increase one's respect for the integrative capacities of the human organism. Beginning with the complex structures and functions provided by its unique genetic constitution, each organism, while maintaining its organic integrity and a considerable residue of its original nature, moves through its maturational cycle adapting to and permitting itself to be modified by selected aspects of the immediate environment. These adaptive changes, occurring most rapidly in the years of infancy and childhood, are so appropriately timed that they do not threaten the organism either physiologically or psychologically. Our findings indicate that significant changes in the human personality may continue to occur during the years of adulthood. Such changes, while neither so large nor sudden as to threaten the continuity of the self percept or impair one's day-to-day interpersonal relations, are potentially of sufficient magnitude to offer a basis of fact for those who dare to hope for continued psychological growth during the adult years.[16]

Traits, like personality as a whole, are not only persistent but plastic as well. Otherwise, neither changes in traits nor in per-

[16] E. Lowell Kelly, Consistency of the adult personality, *Amer. Psychologist,* 10 (1955), 659–81, on pp. 680–81.

sonality would be possible. This is the dual nature of traits: they change as they remain the same; and this is the dual nature of personality: it persists in the very act of transformation. Again, although the same trait is not identical in two individuals, it may be very similar. Unless we assume some stability in traits, we cannot intelligibly describe them; and if we do not assume that they vary with age, circumstance, social pressure, and the central needs of the organism, we cannot characterize them by the principle of growth. Change and persistence alike are functions of the total personality.

Finally, traits, like personality as a whole, form larger structures, since they are invariably interdependent. They form integrations, and do not remain isolated. The integrations differ in degree, from correspondences to coordinations to relative fusions. They correspond when they are integrated by the force of a common structural principle; they are coordinated when they form a graded order in which one takes a determining precedence over the others; they are fused when they functionally coincide.

THE STRUCTURE OF PERSONALITY

This is a good place to remind the reader of the warning we gave at the beginning of this chapter. We stated that, although the term "structure" in the early period of psychology described a static condition, we are now using it in a dynamic sense. Structure is the dynamic, moving relationship among the parts that constitute a constantly changing whole. When we use the term in describing personality we refer to the manner in which traits, trait-clusters, and other interrelated components, such as motives and attitudes, interests and values, form the total personality. But it is well to remember that when we study separate characteristics independently, we tend to break up the unity of personality. As we said before, we can learn a great deal from the study of separate variables, but in doing so, we must be aware of the fact that the segments give us only a partial knowledge of the whole.

Personality structure, then, refers to the relatively consistent organization of all the psychological phenomena which we have already described (learning, motivation, symbolic and expressive behavior, attitudes, values, and traits); *and* emotions, feelings, perceptions, habits, etc., which have been largely peripheral to our mode of treating the subject of personality; *and* the self which we discuss in detail in the next chapter.

Again the separate structures are also organized systems, and may be called the "broader" units of personality organization. This is, admittedly, a very imprecise way of denoting personality units; we use the term primarily to distinguish it from such smaller units as reflexes, stimulus-response couplets, and the like.

Finally, not only the logic of our position but the empirical facts themselves demand that we conceive the broader units as interrelated and mutually modifying. Clearly, unless they are interrelated there is no point in speaking of an organized personality. Personality structure *is* the organized relations among the distinguishable units.

KINDS OF PERSONALITY STRUCTURE. A rather obvious feature of all wholes, especially the structured personality, is that the kinds and degrees of organization vary. Clearly, individuals differ in degree of maturity, rigidity, spontaneity, constrictiveness, and stylistic expression of personality. These and similar forms of organization are sometimes so conspicuous that we can easily identify them. The personality of the child, the mentally defective, and the emotionally unstable can easily be recognized, even by the psychologically untutored individual. We can know an individual by the organization of his personality.

The last statement does not refer to personality types. When we describe a personality as rigid, for example, we are not saying that he is an "introvert," for example, even though rigidity is often a trait of introversion. Introversion refers to the dominant mode of a person's adjustment, of which rigidity may be but one element. Rigidity refers to the weakness of communication between systems within the total organization.

It is regrettable that Stagner's classification of personality structures has not been more widely used. It has the merits of simplicity, clarity, and comprehensiveness. It is confirmed by empirical and clinical evidence. It is a purely descriptive device and makes no pretense of being fundamental; in any case, we doubt that a fundamental classification can be made at the present stage of personality inquiry. Because of its relevance it may be helpful to turn to a detailed consideration of Stagner's five-fold classification: complexity, fluidity, accessibility, resistance, and centralization.[17]

Complexity. This varies markedly from the simple and slightly differentiated actions of an infant to the manifold behavior of a well-integrated adult. Children and feeble-minded adults are

[17] R. Stagner, *Psychology of personality* (2d ed.; New York: McGraw-Hill Book Co., Inc., 1948), pp. 67–70.

characterized by a small degree of differentiation. It is not difficult to show that an adult's interests and needs are more highly diverse than those of a child. His interactions with others are both more numerous and intricate than those of a simply organized individual. The latter, whether adult or child, is more "primitive" in his personality organization, his thinking is largely concrete, and the boundaries separating different aspects of the personality structure are poorly defined. With maturation and growth, a person is sensitive to a much larger number of stimulus situations, he interprets and perceives them in more numerous ways, and he encompasses more social interests and desires. To a child, the environment, judging by the paucity of his discriminatory responses, appears to be simple; to an adult, whose discriminations and alternative courses of action are multitudinous, the world is very complex.

We do not wish to imply that differences in complexity are exclusively, nor even primarily, quantitative. Indeed, in the present stage of our knowledge of personality structures, it is more prudent to say that they are fundamentally *qualitative*. Complexity, like other aspects of personality structure, is a *configuration*, not a multiplication, of individual traits. Even the term "degree," which we have used, is somewhat misleading. Degrees of variation in complexity are manifested more in patterns than in amounts, in configurations more than in numbers. This is an important reason why, without minimizing the importance of the quantitative description of personality, we are obliged to define it as the qualitative organization or arrangement of individual traits. Thus, although traits of personality vary from person to person, and individuals differ in the degrees of their personality structures, the differences cannot be meaningfully described in numerical terms. When a person changes from childhood to manhood, he has not "lost" or "gained" any personality characteristic; what has happened is that his personality has changed, or its structure taken on a different form. Likewise, when a person becomes psychotic, he has not "lost" his mind, but his personality has changed.

If one prefers to describe the complexity of the personality structure, one may do so in rather general terms by saying that the greater the number of intersections or converges of individual traits, or the greater the communication between them, the greater is its organization.

Fluidity. This differential refers to the degree of rigidity or flexibility of the personality structure. The term "fluidity" was used extensively by Lewin and other field theorists, and it was apparently introduced by Brown.[18] Its meaning is implied in the above description of complexity in terms of intersections, convergences, and communications between individual traits. Field theorists define it as the ease of locomotion from trait to trait and from part to whole. It is better described as the freedom with which communication between traits and trait-systems is established; or the ease with which changes take place in and between them. Evidence from clinical and child psychologies tends to support the view that, where fluidity is "adequate," both change and consistency of traits and systems are greater. When fluidity is weak or absent, which is to say when rigidity exists in traits and systems so that communication between them is reduced or blocked, the individual tends to be both inconsistent and unadaptable.

Social psychologists describe the same condition by means of role-anticipation and role behavior. A rigid person is one who is deficient in anticipating the roles of others, and hence is unable to play his own role in relation to them successfully. He tends to persist in certain types of role behavior even when conditions have substantially changed. He is unable to anticipate the other person's role; he does not readily put himself in another's place; and he does not easily perceive a situation from another individual's perspective. We call him a rigid, unadaptable, or maladjusted person.

The foregoing analysis is somewhat oversimplified, for there are conditions which challenge its accuracy. The most important of these is the fact that it does not apply well to young children, who seem to contradict it. They appear at once to challenge and confirm the principle of fluidity. Children are known to be highly impressionable, inconsistent, or contradictory in their behavior. They are described as both flexible and rigid. Their undifferentiation as persons makes them more pliable; but the same weak differentiation may also account for fixations in their behavior. Every parent is familiar with children who are inconsistent and stubbornly unyielding. No amount of effort to compel or persuade them to change their attitudes or habits yields the desired results. Having once established a certain mode of behavior, a child often persists against threats and punishment to continue his course, *quand même*. In this he reminds us of certain types of neurotics, psychotics, and mental defectives.

Lewin stressed this paradoxical condition some years ago.[19] How-

18 J. F. Brown, Die dynamischen Eigenschaften der Realitäts- und Irrealitäts-schichten, *Psychol. Forsch.*, 18 (1933), 2–26.

19 See K. Lewin, *A dynamic theory of personality* (New York: McGraw-Hill Book Co., Inc., 1935), especially Ch. 7.

ever, his explanation is not altogether convincing. He is fully aware of the inconsistency of arguing for both the child's fixation on certain habits and the latter's "generally greater plasticity." Nevertheless, he prefers on general biological grounds to maintain the hypothesis that the psychological structure of the small child is fluid rather than rigid. In any case, present experimental findings are not sufficient to yield a satisfactory answer to the question.[20]

We think a simpler hypothesis presents itself. The young child's personality structure is *both* more rigid and fluid for two specific reasons. It is rigid because differentiation of traits is still "primitive," or neuropsychologically uncoordinated; it is fluid because associations among the individual elements are few and impoverished; and because experiences have not yet been indelibly stamped into the child's mental organization to form enduring systems. This is the more plausible in view of the well-known fact that rigidity and flexibility in children are largely functions of circumstances. In some situations a child is unyielding and inflexible; in others, he is pliant and amenable to control and influence. Apparently even undifferentiated structures have individuality. This uniqueness might well be a genetic property of the human organism.

Accessibility. This term refers to the degree of disposition to react to external situations and the readiness with which an individual exposes his inner life. Some persons erect few barriers against communication with others, whereas some are characterized by inhibition and lack of self-expression. Some receive new stimuli readily, even exultingly, while some resist them automatically. The two resemble the well-known extraverts and introverts, respectively. The terms "open" and "closed" have been used by a number of writers to describe them. Thus, the "open" personality is marked by traits such as emotional expansiveness, sociability, ascendance, and expressions of optimism and self-confidence. On the other hand, the "closed" personality is described by characteristics such as emotional constriction, seclusiveness, and uncommunicativeness.

Differences in degrees of accessibility make for marked variance in our capacity to assess the two structures. Although projective tests may succeed in evaluating both, the "closed" personality is much more difficult to study and understand. The self lies more deeply buried in the inner regions of the personality, for the boundaries between it and other areas are not only more numerous, but more "solid" and semi-impenetrable. The "rich inner life" which is often attributed to the closed personality is inaccessible to satisfactory measurement or evaluation. It is well known that

[20] *Ibid.*, p. 229.

ratings by competent judges disagree most on the "enigmatic" personality structure; whereas the degree of agreement on the open personality is much greater. It is not necessary to rely upon testing devices to tell us that it is easier to understand the open personality; his ease in communicating his inner life makes him more readily understandable. On the other hand, one seldom feels certain of one's estimation of the "inner-directed" individual. While both presumably wear masks in order not to reveal themselves completely—the mores and social imperatives see to that—the mask of the closed personality conceals much more than it reveals.

It would be a mistake, however, to hold that the closed personality necessarily withholds his inner life from *all* those about him. Stagner is guilty of this error.[21] A more accurate assessment of the closed personality structure is that like the open personality he can give himself to others, but the number of people to whom he opens his inner life is very much more restricted. He is no enigma to those who have access to his inner life, but the number of persons who have ingress to it is exceedingly small. A clinical bias has resulted from preoccupation with the overinhibited, unexpressive, and overcontrolled symptoms of inaccessible neurotics. The difference between the open and the closed personality structures is one of degree, as in most personality distinctions.

Finally, it is well to bear in mind that ratings are often biased by personal preferences. We tend to describe the open personality in more positive, even flattering, terms, because he produces fewer frustrations in our assessments; and we are inclined to delineate the closed personality negatively because we are more easily repelled by his "strange" and "enigmatic" unresponsiveness. And to this one must add the well-established fact that in our judgment of people we not infrequently value positively those traits which we think are desirable (our own?), and devaluate those which we consider to be objectionable (those of others?). This is especially pertinent in those societies, such as our own, where extraversion and other-directedness are highly esteemed, and where introversion and inner-directedness are generally unadmired.[22]

Resistance. This personality structure overlaps with rigidity and inaccessibility, but it would be a mistake to identify it with them. Not all closed personalities are marked by excessive resistance, nor are all open ones unresistant. The need to keep the world at

[21] R. Stagner, *Psychology of personality*, p. 69.

[22] The terms "inner-directed" and "other-directed" are used in Riesman's popular analysis of life and behavior in the United States. See D. Riesman, *The lonely crowd* (New Haven: Yale University Press, 1950).

arm's length from the private self characterizes every normal individual. As in the case of the other structures, resistance is always a matter of degree. For reasons not yet demonstrably clear, every individual is characterized by self-involvement and the determination to retain his familiar image of himself. Any force in the world outside himself which threatens to change this self-image is strongly resisted. Although the universal experience of enculturation is inescapable, it is differentially resisted. This condition partly accounts for the fact that despite the levelling effect of socialization upon the individual, he emerges from the process as a differentiated person.

Extremes of resistance and submission belong characteristically to immature individuals, children, abnormal persons, and defective persons. Their resistances betray the inability to internalize the normal social restraints of community life. The much-decried rebelliousness of youth, if it really exists in contemporary American life, is often no more than a determination to maintain its own individuality. With experience and maturity, rebelliousness gives way to a discriminating assessment of social custom and self-respect. Even many "revolutionists" modify their recalcitrance when they achieve personal success and realize that others are not too different from themselves.

In several places in this book we call attention to the need for growth and self-realization. This need for self-enhancement is associated with resistance to enculturation and other influences. Therefore, not all resistance is a sympton of rigidity and self-containment. In fact, oversuggestibility and prompt compliance to the influence of others are marks of immaturity. In the normal adult resistance is selective; whereas in the child it is variable, undiscriminating, and inconsistent. All in all, whether the motives, attitudes, and traits are easily changed or not is greatly contingent upon the self's involvement in them. Resistance is less a function of the degrees of fluidity and accessibility than of the extent and intensity of a person's adherence to his self-image.

Centralization. Not only does every normal individual form and maintain a self-image, but his self becomes attached to many persons, objects, and experiences. The attachment is a form of identification with these referents. Accordingly, he will feel toward them as he feels toward himself, for they are psychologically a "part" of himself; and any threat to them is unconsciously construed by him as a menace to himself. The more numerous and intense his attachments are the more self-importance they acquire. He takes over the ideas and values of objects, persons, and events and

makes them his own. Praise or criticism of any of them thus tends
to become praise or criticism of himself. Whether he is pleased
by flattery or angered by criticism of any object depends upon the
degree of his self-involvement. Thus, a person may be quickly
moved to anger toward criticism of his church and remain unaffected by aspersions against his local club; or he may well up
with pride at the fame of his college, but feel unresponsive to the
good reputation of his high school. When the self is deeply involved in many persons, groups, or institutions we say that his
personality is *centralized*, or that the self serves as a focus of many
ego-involved objects and events.

In considering the foregoing kinds of structures it is well to
remind ourselves again that they are not distinct and separate.
Human behavior is always most accurately described as a continuum, with no sharp breaks among its numerous components.
Our description of the five qualitative structures has brought out
their interpenetration. As we said before, they are convenient,
rather than fundamental, ways of indicating dominant structural
tendencies.

DIMENSIONS OF PERSONALITY ORGANIZATION. It is possible to
vouch for the connectedness of traits and the unity of personality
by demonstrating that personality is organized along distinct but
related dimensions. The many components of the personality which
we have already described in detail separately, combine to form a
relatively organized whole. The integral parts or smaller regions
of the personality do not function by themselves but, as we have
repeatedly stressed, in close association with one another. Thus,
for example, the basic dispositions known as temperament, our
perception of others and ourselves, the forward striving of motivational forces, attitudes, and values, and our cognitive awareness of
ourselves as persons are dimensions along which personality structure can be fruitfully analyzed.

The most comprehensive and yet clear-cut dimensions are three
in number: *temperament* or the psychobiological structure, *psychological* disposition, and the *psychosocial* dimension.

Temperament. A scientific account of the nature of temperament has yet to be written. Although it is one of the oldest concepts for describing personality, going back at least as far as
Hippocrates, more than three centuries before the Christian era,
we have little dependable knowledge regarding it. The investigations of Kretschmer and Sheldon on somatotypes have given us
interesting information on the subject, but there is little tendency

in American psychology to accept their conclusions as convincing. (See Chapter 3.) Substantial progress has been made in the last decade, however, particularly by those who use factor analysis. Among the latter, Cattell, Eysenck, and Guilford are most prominent.

Temperament and personality have often been used synonymously in the history of modern psychology. This identification is not justified by the evidence. From our point of view temperament is a psychophysiological system within the personality, but not its totality. More important still is the fact that temperament is predominantly an affective and genetically determined segment of the personality. To this extent Kretschmer and Sheldon are surely right—at least to the extent that temperament has its basis partly in biochemical systems. We say "partly," because there is yet insufficient evidence to support the view that temperament depends largely on constitutional predisposition.

In the face of insufficient evidence for the constitutional determination of temperament, we leave the matter an open question. We do not deny the hereditary source of temperament; we question only the tendency to regard it exclusively as a biophysical system.

Constitutional explanations of temperament are probably in large part suggested as well as confirmed by three important facts. First, temperamental traits can be observed in very young children, before socialization has crucially affected their development. Second, temperamental traits tend to persist, and this persistence adds credence to their hereditary origin. Third, temperament is invariably defined as an emotional disposition and an enduring mood, and these are largely determined by glandular and other biochemical processes. Thus, both common usage and psychological opinion make temperament fundamentally the unique biophysical organization which directs the course of an individual's thinking, feeling, and overt behavior in a more or less permanent manner, without excluding the role of experience and learning. From this point of view temperamental traits like self-confidence and feelings of inferiority, carefreeness and conscientiousness, excitability and composure, are largely hereditary in origin. On the other hand, such characteristics as friendliness and hostility, ascendance and submission, dependence and self-sufficiency are socially determined.

We can get a clearer picture of the dimension of temperament by briefly examining some of its leading traits. We select only a few, for a discussion of all those which have to date been described would require a separate chapter. These traits, we might add, have been objectively confirmed and measured and are, accordingly, more firmly based than popular discussions would lead one to expect.

Emotionality is strongly bipolar. Thus the prevailing moods of persons are either *elation* or *depression*.[23] Some individuals are inveterately cheerful and optimistic, whereas others are habitually anxious and depressed. The first type is less easily depressed by upsetting events, but reacts to them with hope and affirmation. He is usually in good spirits and finds depressed people too somber for his tastes. On the other hand, the depressed individual is characteristically gloomy, and is usually abashed by the happy individual's pleasantness.[24]

The emotional dispositions may also be described as *stable* or *fluctuating*. Some persons display a marked equanimity in their life style. In others, moods seem to follow an "all or none" tendency: that is, when the person tends toward either an elated or a depressed mood, he usually goes to the limit of either pole.

Another emotional polarity that has been extensively studied is *tension* versus *composure*. The tense person, if we may speak redundantly, is incapable of relaxing, is easily excited, and is given to chronic anxiety.[25]

Emotions are also *mature* or *immature*. The emotionally mature person is characterized by emotional control, especially as it refers to overt behavior. The emotionally immature individual is self-centered, easily upset, and self-commiserating. Conventionally, he is pictured as exceedingly childish in his affective responses.[26]

The psychological dimension. Personality traits are also distributed along a primarily *psychological dimension.* In contrast to the emotional traits (temperament), which are deeply embedded hereditary predispositions, the psychological dimension is the level on which our motivational, perceptual, and cognitive traits are organized. Thus our motives, as we saw in Chapter 9, are individual intentions, whereas the direction of our drives, since they serve the interest of adaptation and survival primarily, are fundamentally expressions of temperament. As long as we heed our own warning against positing an absolute break between them, we may distinguish between these two dimensions. Furthermore, the psychological may be distinguished from the social dimension in that

---

[23] We are not using these terms in their psychiatric forms; they refer, rather, to the enduring dispositions of normal people.

[24] See Guilford and Zimmerman, Fourteen dimensions of temperament, for a detailed discussion of the above and other trait symptoms.

[25] Lorr and Rubenstein, Factors descriptive of psychiatric out-patients.

[26] *Ibid.*

the latter is primarily descriptive of interpersonal relationships. Thus, psychologically, an individual may be hypersensitive, but socially, hypercritical. In the latter case the traits point to the person of another; in the former, to the individual himself.

A few traits of the psychological dimension are here briefly presented. Like the temperamental traits, they are essentially bipolar.

Intentional and *impulsive behavior* is a well-established polarity. Some people are deliberate and cautious, whereas others are quick and fitful; some plan their actions carefully, whereas others make snap decisions about them; some act first and think later, whereas others calculate their words and actions with forethought. But this does not mean that there is any significant relationship between, say, speed of response and mental agility, or between deliberateness and impoverishment in verbal fluency. Correlations among most traits and deliberateness-impulsiveness have not been determined, and in the few where correlations have been studied, they have been relatively low.[27]

Self-confidence and *inferiority-feeling* have received an inordinate amount of attention, and have become bywords of the proverbial man on the street. Inventories, ratings, and factor analyses abound with testimony of their existence and their effect on human behavior. Among the best recent investigations are those of Lorr and Jenkins and Lorr and Rubenstein.[28]

There can be no doubt that individuals differ, often markedly, on this trait dimension. Some persons habitually feel and act self-confident, believe in themselves, and are confident of their acceptance by others. On the other hand, some people are plagued by self-doubt, self-depreciation, feelings of guilt, and the conviction that they are unaccepted by others.

It would be interesting and instructive to go into a detailed study of the sources of self-confidence and self-doubt. Apparently the social conditions which are most frequently cited as determinants of these attitudes do not satisfactorily account for them. Psychologically poor home conditions, for example, are less important than is commonly believed, especially by purveyors of popular psychology and mental hygiene. Perhaps this fact can be explained in terms of our own distinction between the psychological

[27] See J. P. Guilford, P. R. Christensen, J. W. Frick, and P. R. Merrifield, The relations of creative-thinking aptitudes and non-aptitude personality traits, *Rep. psychol. Lab.* (University of Southern California, 1957), No. 20.

[28] M. Lorr and R. L. Jenkins, Patterns of maladjustment in children, *J. clin. Psychol.*, 9 (1953), 16–19; Lorr and Rubenstein, Factors descriptive of psychiatric out-patients.

and social dimensions of personality. Being highly individualized traits, they are more closely related to temperament than to interpersonal contacts. Indeed, they may very well be more temperamental than strictly psychological. However, we describe them as psychological rather than temperamental because they are fundamentally expressions of *attitudes* toward the external environment, rather than their direct consequence. Thus, it is not the poor home or the inferior neighborhood that counts so much, as the attitude of the person—especially the child—toward the adverse social conditions.[29]

People differ remarkably on the traits of *impersonality* and *hypersensitivity*. Some persons are easily upset by the unfavorable attitudes of others, whereas others react with a characteristic aplomb. The latter view experience in the light of objective criteria and are not generally upset by personal reverses. They are extraverted and normally unworried by untoward events and the attitudes of others. The hypersensitive individual is characteristically egocentric, easily upset, and troubled by feelings of unworthiness. He resembles the person plagued by inferiority feelings, and cannot be sharply distinguished from him. In the same way, the impersonal and realistic individual is not always distinguishable from the self-confident person. However, the resemblance is general, rather than specific; that is, the self-confident and the impersonal individuals are similar in that both meet their environments positively and joyfully; whereas the hypersensitive and self-doubting individuals tend to recoil from reality. The latter resemble the introvert in various ways.[30]

The psychosocial dimension. The psychosocial dimension of trait distribution refers to the manner in which interpersonal contacts are expressed. While they are related to the psychobiological and temperament-dimensions, there is insufficient evidence in support of the view that they are either hereditary or purely psychological. They are indicators of the manner in which the individual relates himself to others. While in his relations with others it is still *he* who relates himself, the crucial fact is *the character of the relationship* itself.

The most obvious polarity on this dimension is the degree of *independence from* and *involvement with* other people. One

[29] See L. Ackerson, Inferiority attitudes and their correlations among children examined in a behavior clinic, *J. genet. Psychol.*, 62 (1943), 85–96.

[30] The factor of hypersensitivity has been established by several investigators. See especially L. V. Gordon, Validities of the forced-choice and questionnaire methods of personality measurement, *J. appl. Psychol.*, 35 (1951), 407–12; Guilford and Zimmerman, Fourteen dimensions of temperament.

hardly needs personality inventories to discover that some persons are characteristically self-sufficient while some are dependent on others; or that some prefer solitude while some must have affiliation with others. Nevertheless, the traits have also been empirically established, which makes our knowledge of them more dependable and certain.

The independent individual is not uneasy in a state of solitude, in contrast to the highly sociable individual who dreads it and in extreme cases is actually terrified by it. He not only enjoys his own company, but often prefers it to association with others. The sociable person feels deserted and lost unless he has people about him. His dependence on others for association, enjoyment, and entertainment is his dominant and conspicuous characteristic.

Another bipolar social dimension is *self-assertion* and *retractiveness*. These traits are sometimes confused with dominance and submission, respectively. Self-assertion is not necessarily characterized by the wish or need to dominate others, but may be a positive effort to maintain one's social initiative. Similarly, a retractive person is not socially submissive or fearful but, like the independent individual, likes to maintain his freedom in interpersonal contacts. The self-assertive person has social initiative and stands up for his rights when interacting with others. The retractive individual is socially passive and self-conscious.[31]

Receptiveness and *intolerance* are important social dimensions of personality. They are manifested respectively in the acceptance or rejection of others. The receptive person is in most things regarding his fellows tolerant, sympathetic, and accepting. He either minimizes or is indifferent to the faults and shortcomings of others. Being neither defensive nor critical, he establishes rapport with others easily. Basically he trusts human nature.

The intolerant person, on the other hand, is overcritical of others, and more likely than not will suspect their good intentions. While he is normally not positively unfriendly, he is typically so critical of the ideas and actions of others that his relations with them are usually strained, if not conflictual.

The foregoing clusters of traits are sufficient for our purpose. We have tried to show that there are three structures or dimensions of personality, namely, the temperamental, the psychological, and the psychosocial. The temperamental is fundamentally psychobiological; its diverse traits are probably hereditary, and its mode of expression is primarily emotional. The psychological dimension is an organization of attitudes, motives, and perceptions, and it is

[31] Guilford and Zimmerman, Fourteen dimensions of temperament.

largely "person-centered." The psychosocial dimension is an organization of interpersonal experiences, and it largely reflects the quality of the individual's relationship with others.[32]

THE UNITY OF PERSONALITY

Every attempt to organize traits and structures into dimensions is either implicitly or explicitly a search for the unity of personality. Despite many valiant and praiseworthy efforts in this direction, we still know very little regarding the wholeness of personality. Worse yet, premature generalizations have produced incompatible conclusions, neither of which is supported by sufficient evidence. At one extreme is the overemphasis of the wholeness of personality; and at the other, an insufficient appreciation of the "urge" toward individuality which is characteristic of every healthy personality. In the first case we see only its totality, and are blind to its vital components; in the second, we focus so intently on its segments that we forget the reality of the whole. We shall pursue this subject in more detail in Chapters 16 and 17, hence only a general statement of the problem need be given here.

THE MEANING OF UNITY. One can look at the problem of unity from two perspectives. We may describe it first in its most fundamental form—the *undifferentiated* whole of infancy and young childhood. Before experience and learning have had much influence on the psychological structure of the infant and young child his personality is simple and unified. The simplicity and unity are derived from the paucity of communication between the fluidity of the psychical systems. More than at any time later, the infant responds as a whole. In this respect his behavior is but a step, albeit an important one, from the mass reaction of the fetus before the infant was born. If at this time the child is a personality, which we strongly doubt, then his personality is a simple and uncoordinated totality, and undifferentiated unity is its fundamental characteristic.

A second way to picture the unity of the personality is to describe it as the integration of differentiated traits and psychical systems. Wholeness is a function of the intercorrelatedness of traits.

---

[32] Our manner of organizing traits into three more or less related dimensions is by no means the only one. There are several others. For a factor analysis of the problem and one quite different from our own, Eysenck's integration, as usual, is very good. See H. J. Eysenck, The organization of personality, *J. Pers.*, 20 (1952), 101–17. However, it seems that what Eysenck presents us with is less a model of personality dimensions than of personality types. Besides, his model is built, even more than those of the studies which we have cited, on psychiatric rather than normal, cases.

No trait, we have said, exists in isolation, but forms an overlapping and coherent system through congruence, convergence, and functional interdependence. Although we have numerous statistical and other quantitative descriptions of congruence, convergence, and functional interdependence, they do not adequately account for the unity of personality. Personality is not an additive process. It is not even supersummative, for this word suggests an entity apart from the separate traits, and results in a mystical view of personality. Quantitative descriptions have the scientific virtue of precision, but they do not give us a convincing account of the nature of personality unity. Despite their undisputed usefulness, statistical, factorial, and experimental models are still too crude to penetrate the internal psychological organization of personality. The unprecedented development of clinical techniques has yielded little more than subjective criteria for judging its unity. However, we hasten to add that no other mode of studying the unity of personality has succeeded in explaining its wholeness either. Not modesty, but paucity of evidence, impels one to admit that it is still an unsolved problem.

Nevertheless, both logic and clinical evidence point to the operation of a central principle, an agency of organization, which would account for the unity of personality. Even intelligent common sense can discover functional connections between traits and other personality variables. Psychologists are aware of all this, but they have yet to come up with a model of organization that is acceptable to most investigators in the field. Every psychologist who has exposed his views to public examination has probably felt the shafts and stings of professional criticism—criticism which, we hasten to add, is usually well deserved.

We do not offer still another organizing principle of personality. However, we strongly feel that personality cannot be described without assuming the operation of a central principle. We believe that every vital segment of human behavior throbs with the controlling power of the total personality. Not every psychologist will agree on what this principle might be, and some will prefer to ignore it on the ground that it is closed to rigid scientific investigation.

Be that as it may, we prefer to account for the unity of personality by positing a *self-process*, or more simply, a *self*. We have already warned the reader that the self is not a homunculus hiding in the inner life of the individual. The concept of the self, discussed in detail in the next chapter, enables us to account for the functional organization of the separate aspects of personality, from sensory experience, bodily behavior, and motivational striving, to the most abstract attitude-value complex, self-image, and social self—in brief, all the regions or subsystems which each person regards as peculiarly his own.

The study of the self thus in no way relegates the "segments" of the personality to an unimportant status; on the contrary, it recognizes their existence but tries to account for their interdependence by means of an organizing principle. Self-psychology thus enables the psychology of personality to enlarge its narrow boundaries without forfeiting its scientific character.

CONCLUSION

The problem of the organization of parts into larger systems is an old one in scientific thought. However, it is easier to get on with one's important work either by deferring this issue to a more auspicious occasion, or by disregarding it altogether. Yet, the sheer recurrence and persistence of the problem is a *prima facie* argument for its importance.

The structure or organization of the personality may be viewed bilaterally yet symmetrically. Along one axis we may order into a functional system such regions of the personality as attitudes, motives, traits, and values; along the other, we may unify these systems into comprehensive description of the personality as a whole. The process is a movement from larger to larger *Gestalten* until we reach an all-inclusive whole at its terminus. It is an overlapping of one region with other regions which at last emerges in a dynamic totality which, while including them, is withal different from them. Every ingress into a larger whole results in the modification of the separate parts by their dynamic relationships to one another. The organic pattern thus formed from the interpenetration of the various parts is an indivisible whole.

More specifically, our description of personality structure was made by examining traits, trait clusters, and the consistency of traits. We concentrated on the consistency of traits, for in this we can most clearly see their interdependence. Consistency may be "measured" by means of factor analysis, by trait persistence and universality, and by the degree to which traits are functions of the total personality.

We have described the subsystems of the personality structure by means of three important dimensions—the temperamental, the psychological, and the psychosocial. These dimensions are not existential realities, but convenient abstractions by means of which the separate subsystems may be suitably combined into a consistent whole.

Personality structure may be conveniently and fruitfully classified into five dissimilar but related forms, depending upon the degree of connectedness or communication among the subregions of each, particularly the sensory-motor, peripheral, and central areas of the more inclusive region. Individual structures are characteristically, but not exclusively, simple or complex, rigid or flexible, open or closed, resistant or submissive to external influence, and highly or poorly centralized with reference to self-involved attitudes and values. These axes of differentiation must be *qualitatively* conceptualized in the present stage of our inadequate quantitative and experimental knowledge. Though derived largely from indirect clinical evidence, until they can be more directly measured, they must remain abstract but useful inferences. Even their distribution is inferential and uncertain. Like most psychological phenomena, their distribution may follow the normal curve.

The unitary personality is at once a system of psychophysiological and psychosocial events. To describe personality exclusively in terms of one or the other system is to court unnecessary confusion, for it immediately revives the ghosts of psychophysical and psychosocial parallels or dichotomies. The unitary personality is a more or less integrated totality of psychophysiological and psychosocial systems of sensory-motor, peripheral, central, and external cultural events. To neglect one while inflating the significance of the other is to do violence to the essential integrity of the whole.

Finally, while the unity of personality has not been explained to the satisfaction of all interested investigators, some proposals are more promising than others, even though all are partially defective.

The view of integration proposed in this book is gaining increasing support from personality theorists. We have already indicated its main outline. It only remains to add that the self-process which we propose as an explanation is embedded in the fundamental principles of *Gestalt* psychology, especially in its current form of field theory, in the fruitful ideas of contemporary theory of perception, and in the conclusions of present-day phenomenological research. In fine, the view proposed in the following chapter and in Chapter 17 is founded on the results of perceptual experimentation, dynamic theories of personality, and clinical imagination.

CHAPTER **16**

The Total Personality: The Self

A French philosopher once remarked that if God did not exist man would have to invent Him. In the same vein, one may point to the need for a self in the psychology of personality. While the analogy is literary rather than scientific, it nevertheless calls attention to the indispensability of an organizing principle in the study of personality. It helps us to account, even if unsatisfactorily, not only for the unity of personality but also for an individual's only dependable criterion of his personal identity. Regardless of the paucity of experimental data for establishing a self-system, one has to assume it in order to account for our psychological existence from moment to moment, and from childhood until death.

With the advent of classical behaviorism in 1913 the concept of the self was virtually banished from psychological inquiry. Boasting that he was writing psychology with the human animal in front of him, John B. Watson, the founder of behaviorism, made clear that he would entertain no nonsense regarding "mentalistic" phenomena, self-consciousness included.[1] With this point of view, which then became dominant in American psychology, Watson and his followers shut out for a generation the insights of earlier self-psychology, notably those of William James.[2]

[1] J. B. Watson, *Psychology from the standpoint of a behaviorist* (Philadelphia: J. B. Lippincott Co., 1919), p. xi.

[2] We surmise that for some psychologists it is still pleasant and instructive to return periodically to James' broad and trenchant discussion of the consciousness of self. For that delineation see W. James, *Principles of psychology* (2 vols.; New York: Henry Holt & Co., Inc., 1890), Vol. 1, Ch. 10.

However, interest in the psychology of the self was revived about thirty years ago, and today personality psychologists are no longer apologetic regarding their interest in it. In this connection it is pertinent to observe not only that the self is a central problem in books on personality, but that two presidential addresses before the American Psychological Association, in less than fifteen years, were made on the subject of the self.[3] Today the literature on the self is enormous.

The chief weakness of a large segment of contemporary psychology is not what may well be an exaggerated emphasis on the learning process, or on animal behavior, or on the problem of adjustment; these are important areas of study, and the experimental investigations of learning, in particular, have aided in making psychology more scientific. What is significantly lacking in much psychology, even when it concerns itself with the problems of *human* behavior, is the feeling or awareness of ourselves as persons. It often fails to account for the relatively consistent and unified character of our motives, attitudes, values, emotions, and moral behavior. Their unification, and their persistence through time as a functional unit, requires some central agency to hold them together and make behavior harmonious. This functional unit, like every integrative agency in human behavior, is not an "entity" but a *process*. It is the *self-process*, the subjective and intimate feeling that each of us is an enduring individual, a *self*. Accordingly, those personality psychologists, of whom there is an increasing number, who work on the assumption that every normal individual functions as a psychobiological whole, are constrained to hypothesize a functional integrative center.

Furthermore, the existence of such clinically established processes as self-consciousness, self-evaluation, and self-identification; the indubitable fact that every person above the age of three or four can become an object to himself; and the transformations of the inner "core" of personality observed in successful psychotherapy, attest to the self-process. Rogers and others have found that changes in behavior are not solely consequences of learning, but are also modifications of the individual's picture of himself. Rogers has found over and over that the individual's perceptual changes are more bound up with the self than with the external world. In psychotherapy, as the perception of one's self alters, behavior alters.[4] This observation makes change of behavior as much a func-

[3] C. R. Rogers, Some observations on the organization of personality, *Amer. Psychologist*, 2 (1947), 358–68; E. R. Hilgard, Human motives and the concept of the self, *Amer. Psychologist*, 4 (1949), 374–82.

[4] Rogers, Some observations on the organization of personality, p. 359.

tion of the self-process as of reinforcement and learning. Reinforcement and learning theory generally to the contrary, character and moral behavior remain unaccountable in the absence of man's capacity to be an object to himself, to view himself in the light of loyalty to his value system and to his sense of responsibility to others.

ORIGIN AND DEVELOPMENT OF THE SELF

The problem of the origin of the self is a fascinating one, but no one has given us a scientific explanation of how and when the self arises. Since it is not a physical entity, its rise and evolution cannot be observed. Like the electrons and protons of the physicist, the self can be investigated only indirectly. Like other psychological processes and events, the primal self no doubt arises from the undifferentiated whole with which the individual begins his postnatal existence; but this is hardly yet the complex structure which we associate with the psychological self. Still, as the faint first glimmer of its origin, this primal self may well be the "seed" from which the mature self-conscious individual gradually emerges.

THE "BODILY" SELF. The place of the concept of a bodily self in the study of selfhood may very well be challenged. Nevertheless, it is hard to believe that the infant lying in his crib is completely oblivious to the sensory impulses, visceral processes, and muscular movements that characterize his bodily movements. We are not saying that the infant is *conscious* of these activities, but only that he *feels* them. The child who sucks his thumb or stuffs his toes into his mouth may very well be perplexed by their proper ownership, but in this very confusion or doubt, if such indeed it be, he must dimly feel a struggle between his mouth and the respective bodily parts. This division between himself and his body implies an incipient self-process.

Again, the young child is vaguely aware of many bodily processes, and when they become exceptionally focalized, as in the experience of sudden or sharp pains, he feels them as his own. Vague bodily perceptions are experiences of adults as well as children. Everyone has on some occasion found it difficult to localize a pain minutely; except for a general fixation, such as in the stomach, for example, it seems to be free-floating within the boundaries of the organ involved. This is profoundly more true of the very young child, whose perceptual functions are rudimentary and crude. The sense organs by means of which he perceives objects around him are the same sense organs by means of which he perceives his own body. His body is as real to him as are other objects in his environment; and by the same token, it is as much a part of him as the external objects which he has not yet learned to discriminate.

Since his body is the only object of experience that the young child "really" knows, it should not surprise us that it occupies the most important place in his perceptual field. The child staring at his closed fist, feeling the sensory impulses flowing through his body, startled or pleased by the sound of his own voice, enjoying the kinesthetic sensations running through his muscles—in these experiences the child comes to know himself as a physical body, his bodily self.

In view of the growing importance of psychosomatic processes in contemporary psychology, it is a little hard to account for the neglect of the bodily self in discussions of the psychology of self-experience. That the view of oneself often affects bodily health has been established in many cases of psychosomatic disorders; but that one's perception of one's body is intimately tied up with one's image of oneself is a neglected problem.[5] The boy next door is painfully conscious of his large protruding ears. His image of himself has for several years been profoundly affected by his reaction to their size. The middle-aged woman down the street has suffered considerable distress over her red, bulbous nose, which all the doctors whom she has consulted are powerless to change. In each case there is a vital bodily identification, and this association serves as a focal point of fixation for each self. It is commonplace, but nevertheless significant, that from infancy to old age our body is an important focus of our experience. Therefore, it would be odd, indeed, if it did not play a vital role in defining the individual's self.

However, in a young child the point of fixation of the bodily self is not a segment with which pleasure or pain is necessarily associated. One child will locate his self in his abdomen, another in his face, and still another in his jaw; and so on.[6] Admittedly, the segment of the body which the child selects for the localization of his self is often influenced by his parents' unconscious gestures; but

[5] Of course, we are fully aware that Adler built his whole earlier psychological position around the idea of body—or organ—inferiority; but his views have not been incorporated in the body of academic psychology. Besides, his objective and ours are not exactly the same.

[6] See E. L. Horowitz, Spatial localization of the self, *J. soc. Psychol.*, 6 (1935), 379–87.

this is not always decisive. For reasons that are obscure, the child may select some parts of the body because they are important to him. These parts come thus to represent *him*, rather than the mimicry of his parents.

The growth of the bodily self, especially the part of the body which comes to be identified with the child's psychological self, is also a function of his age and intelligence, although very little is actually known concerning these variations. In this connection, conclusions are based more on general developmental principles than on established facts. In view of what we know of developmental differentials in children, it is safe to conclude that age and intelligence, which largely determine the range of a child's experience, make for differences in the perception of bodily surfaces and physical characteristics. The size of the child's vocabulary for symbolizing bodily features differs in accordance with his age and intelligence. The wider and more suitable his vocabulary of bodily terms the earlier his body recognition tends to appear.

Again, the selected bodily parts often became centers of affectional discharge. Different children love or hate different parts of their bodies. Some of these fixations are apparent in infancy. Thumbsucking is the most frequently observed instance of this phenomenon. Oral and anal "fixations" are other well-known examples. Any part of the body that becomes a source of emotional satisfaction serves as a focus for self-attachment. In time the child comes to have attitudes toward these parts, or the entire body, in much the same way as he does toward objects and events external to himself. A twelve-year-old hates himself because he perceives his face as ugly; a nine-year-old is unhappy with himself because he has a marked growth on his right ear; and a fourteen-year-old is sure that no one likes him because he has buck teeth. In his youth, the writer knew a boy who shaved the hairline of his forehead to make him look more "intelligent." Likewise, children love the shapes of their noses, or the colors of their eyes, or the sounds of their voices just as they appreciate these things in others. Little do we realize how much of what we like or hate in another's appearance is a reflection of what we love or hate in ourselves. The child's crude self-image rests upon body attractions and repulsions.

Objective evidence for this line of argument is admittedly trifling, yet the argument is not based entirely on speculation. Also, psychoanalytical explanations, while sometimes too speculative, have given us insights into the problem. Freud and Abraham have given us plausible accounts of this development; Erikson has confirmed them in his description of play in children; and Schilder's empirical observations give it additional credence.[7]

The typical narcissist is unquestionably fixated upon and overvalues his body; equally obvious is the opposite trend of self-contempt in the person who devalues his body. Probably every normal individual dimly perceives his body as part of his personality structure. Thus, if his body does not come up to what he conceives to be the physical standard, he feels self-conscious and embarrassed about it. On the other hand, another individual may dissociate his body from his self, and even "disown" it. This condition has been noted among many prostitutes who, because men seek only their bodies, tend to dissociate the latter from the rest of themselves.[8]

THE SOCIAL SELF. The self is not an inborn organization; like so many other aspects of personality, it is acquired in association with others. Awareness of oneself is not wholly dependent on consciousness of others, but their attitudes toward oneself are, nevertheless, important determinants. The child's differentiation of himself from others—first from his mother and thereafter from other family members—is dependent upon their attitudes toward him. The perceptual self, which is discussed in the next section, is effectively shaped by how we think others perceive us. The child early forms an image of himself as he appears to others and by the way they judge or evaluate him. Before long he reacts in specific ways toward their judgments and conducts himself in accordance with his understanding of their evaluations.

Security and self-esteem are intimately bound up with the social self, and some forms of neurotic stress are undoubtedly dependent on the way others see us. Insecurity and self-devaluation are largely ways in which an individual reacts to other people's opinions of himself. The need to keep up appearances is largely an expression of the fear of other people's judgments. Sometimes, as in the case of neurotic individuals, the need to keep up appearances is so powerful that renouncing it is therapeutically more sound than attempting to satisfy it.[9]

[7] See S. Freud, Some character-types met with in psychoanalytic work, Collected papers (London: Hogarth Press, Ltd., 1950), Vol. 4, pp. 318–44; K. Abraham, Selected papers (London: Hogarth Press, Ltd., 1927); E. H. Erikson, Studies in the interpretation of play: I. Clinical observation of play description in young children, J. genet. Psychol., 22 (1940), 557–671; P. Schilder, The image and appearance of the human body (New York: International Universities Press, 1950).

[8] S. Cousins, To beg I am ashamed (New York: The Vanguard Press, 1938). For similar recent evidence, see H. Greenwald, The call girl (New York: Ballantine Books, Inc., 1958).

[9] K. Horney, New ways in psychoanalysis (New York: W. W. Norton & Co., Inc., 1939), p. 231.

We have said that self-esteem is fundamentally social. It is normally acquired in the child's interaction with members of his family. If the child's parents express a favorable view of him; if they are free of the self-righteousness which impels some parents to demand that the child accede to their every expectation, the child has an excellent chance of developing self-confidence and self-respect. If the opposite condition prevails, the child learns to mistrust and devaluate himself, and in time to mistrust and devaluate others.

A knowledge of a person's self-esteem illuminates our understanding of him. Clinicians and child psychologists agree that both excessive and deficient self-esteem are detrimental to healthy adjustment. An exaggerated or a deficient sense of self-importance implies a distorted perception of our status in other peoples' eyes. The distortion results in misunderstanding and conflict or in neurotic efforts to fortify a feeble self. In extreme cases, the need to maintain a favorable image in the eyes of others drives men into self-deceptions ranging from paranoid projections to grandiose schizophrenic delusions.

All this underscores the fact that, although our self-attitudes are largely produced by others' attitudes toward ourselves, a significant factor in our self-conception is the manner in which we internalize the attitude of others toward ourselves. A person's self-esteem is thus not entirely socially bound, but is dependent on his own perception of his relation to others. Changes in himself, or in his behavior, are changes in his perception of his relation to others.

William James long ago had this thought in mind when, in a characteristically expressive manner, he described his self-involvement in Greek and psychology, and in his perceptive analysis of the pugilist's attitude toward success and failure. "I, who for the time have staked my all on being a psychologist," he writes, "am mortified if others know much more psychology than I. But I am contented," he adds, "to wallow in the grossest ignorance of Greek." In other words, having no pretension of appearing as a linguist in anybody's eyes, his deficiency in that language caused him no feeling of humiliation at all. Writing of the defeated pugilist, he refers to "the paradox of a man shamed to death because he is only the second pugilist" in the world; and to the fact that though he is "able to beat the whole population of the globe minus one," it means nothing to him. But, James continues, another but puny fellow, "whom everyone can beat, suffers no chagrin about it," for he has no ambitions and pretensions along that line. "So our self-feeling," he concludes, "depends entirely on what we *back* ourselves to be." [10]

Again, basing his conclusion more on perceptive observation than on established evidence, James noted that our social selves depend upon the opinions held of us by various social groups. Membership in clubs, lodges, or college fraternities molds a person's attitude toward himself. Each group forms an image of its members, so that we may say that a person "has as many different social selves as there are distinct *groups* of persons about whose opinion he cares."

This view has been confirmed by recent social psychological studies of membership groups, reference groups, and other forms of social organization.[11] Adults as well as children will go to great lengths to identify themselves with their group, solicit its approval, and perpetuate its image of the individual member.

The objection of some psychologists to the concept of the self, whether social or perceptual, may well be based on semantic differences. Even a few who prefer not to use the self-concept recognize its operation in human behavior. They may substitute other terms for it, but in reality they are referring to the same process. Thus, in his systematic analysis of social learning, Rotter regards an individual's expectancy of the outcome of his own behavior as the anticipation by a self. To be sure, he quickly adds that if we substitute the word "person" for self, "there can be no objection to the term." [12] *The self, then, is the set of attitudes that a person has toward his own behavior.* When Rotter rejects the notion of a self as an *entity* we agree, of course, for we have already relegated this notion to the realm of reified and mysterious forces.

A major difficulty in Rotter's rejection of the self-concept lies in his formulation of social learning and of the person too exclusively in terms of the subject's expectancy. Surely, not all social learning is an attitude of expectancy regarding the outcome of a person's acts in a given situation. Personality can also be described in terms of the individual's *intentions.* The self is not simply a set of reactions resulting from past experience, but it is even more an

[10] James, *Principles of psychology,* Vol. 1, pp. 310–11.

[11] See, for example, the works of Newcomb, Sherif, and Whyte, among others, particularly the following: W. F. Whyte, *Street corner society* (Chicago: University of Chicago Press, 1943); T. M. Newcomb, *Social psychology* (New York: The Dryden Press, Inc., 1950); M. Sherif and C. W. Sherif, *An outline of social psychology* (Rev. ed.; New York: Harper & Bros., 1956).

[12] J. B. Rotter, *Social learning and clinical psychology* (Englewood Cliffs, N.J.: Prentice-Hall, Inc., 1954), p. 240.

effective mode of action toward the future. The self, as we have said or implied in various places in this book, is not a static structure, but a dynamic striving; a *becoming*, with a legitimate scientific meaning. It is directional as well as reactive; future-oriented as well as adjustive. There are no major psychologists who do not conceive most, if not all, human behavior as goal-directed. While many learning theorists conceive the directional aspect of behavior as an inference from the effect of reinforcing conditions, it may also be defined as a property of the person. Striving for consistency is an important property of the self, and cannot be exclusively described in the language of reinforcement. This partially accounts for the fact that such diverse theorists as Freud, Hull, Lecky, Lewin, and Rotter agree more than they differ on the need for a self-concept, whatever their preferred terminology may be.

THE PERCEPTUAL SELF. The social aspects of the self are always interpreted by the individual in the light of his own experience and intentions. The views which others hold of him are continually transformed by him in accordance with his own perspectives. Thus, when we say that the self is the view of other persons regarding oneself, we are stating only a partial and even less important truth about the self. The most important fact about an individual's self is that it is *his way of perceiving himself*. This perception of one's self in the light of one's own interpretation of his behavior is called the *perceptual self*. The perceptual self is, thus, an organization of self-attitudes. It is the only self which an individual can truly and intimately know; all other aspects of the total self are partially removed from direct perception and are inferred by others.

Some of the very best work on self-psychology in contemporary behavioral science has been performed on the perceptual self. The language used to describe this self may differ, but the self-process to which it refers is substantially the same. Thus, Combs, in his recent revision of a perceptual approach to behavior developed by him in an earlier collaboration with Snygg, describes the concept as the "phenomenal self." [13] To quarrel with this term is to cavil. Nevertheless, we prefer the term "perceptual self" for three reasons. First, the term "phenomenal" suggests something extraordinary, which Combs does not intend. Second, the term derives from phenomenology, the important philosophical system of Husserl.[14] While this fact in no way detracts from its importance, it does not suggest the extensive empirical and clinical evidence which has

[13] A. W. Combs and D. Snygg, *Individual behavior: a perceptual approach to behavior* (Rev. ed.; New York: Harper & Bros., 1959).

[14] E. Husserl, *Logische Untersuchungen* (2 vols.; Halle: Niemeyer, 1921).

helped to confirm it. Third, the concept of the self as used by
Combs and others, as well as ourselves, has been chiefly developed
within the framework of organismic psychology and extensive research on the perceptual process.

Because of the great importance that we attach to the perceptual
self it is necessary to examine the matrix in which it arises and functions. This matrix is the *perceptual reality* in which the individual
experiences himself as a person.

Perceptual reality. A basic concept of all holistic psychology,
particularly of such influential personality psychologies as those of
G. W. Allport, Goldstein, Lewin, and Murphy, is some variant of a
psychological environment. For our own purpose we have chosen
the concept of *field*. A fundamental property of all fields, whether
physical or psychological, is mobility or change. A psychological
field is a dynamic pattern of individual and interacting persons.
Causation in this field is instantaneous rather than lineal. Consequently the behavior of a person, while historically connected with
the past, may be functionally independent of it. No one can experience the past of his perceptual field, nor its future, but only its
immediate present. Accordingly, the perceptual field of every
person is inescapably unique. This perceptual field of the moment
is the individual's only psychological reality; it is where his experience derives its meaning. Consequently, behavior is not simply a
function of the impact of external stimuli upon the individual, but
more profoundly of his perception of them in an organized field.
Indeed, his perception of it *is* the organized field.

One of the startling things in everyone's experience is the marked
contrasts in his perception of the field at different instances of its
occurrence. Yesterday's imperative may be today's trifle. The
reason for this state of affairs we have reiterated at several places
in this book. A *Gestalt*, or a perceptual field, we have said, is
undergoing transformations while remaining the same. We referred to this, in the manner of the physicist, as the transposable
absolute—the form that is forever changing while yet remaining
stable. Without flexibility of the perceptual field, the individual
could not modify his behavior in the face of changed circumstances;
but without a degree of stability personality could never achieve
structure, organization, and duration.

The last term may sound inconsistent with the belief in discontinuity and functional autonomy which we have expressed at several points. However, this is not so; in all discontinuities something of a former condition remains. While we may never be able
to step into the same river twice, it is still the same river. This is

the meaning of the relative, transposable form. This is a common-place phenomenon in the physical sciences. In chemistry, for example, a substance may undergo continuous variations in physical and chemical properties, and yet maintain the same crystal structure. Without organization and stability experience would be chaotic, unpredictable, and meaningless. Surely, our discussion of personality structure and organization has made this abundantly clear.

Organization of the perceptual self. The individual, we said, perceives himself as immersed in perceptual reality. This perceptual reality, like all wholes or *Gestalten*, is characterized by organization and relative stability. The stability of the perceptual self is only as great as the steadfastness of the perceptual reality in which it has its being. An organized perceptual reality tends to produce a consistent perceptual self. The healthy individual seeks both change and stability; but change and stability are effected by unity of organization and consistency. Thus, an important mark of the perceptual self is consistency.

There is no empirical proof of the validity of Lecky's postulated *need* for self-consistency—certainly not as the sole basic need of the human organism. Nevertheless, its importance in self-psychology is enormous. It is not a need, as this term is usually employed, but a practical device for making human experience orderly and intelligible. Just as, for instance, man rationalizes his failures in order to cope with them, so he organizes his perceptions in order to find his way about in a maze of individual experiences. This is the "substitute world" which he can understand and from which important standards of behavior are derived. This world he alters or maintains to the degree that it serves his goal of organization, unity, and consistency.[15]

The consistency and stability of the perceptual self are not biological properties. No amount of neurophysiological explanation can account for them. As properties of the perceptual self they are outcomes of an individual's experience. Thus, a child who is severely scolded for every inconsequential transgression may come to look upon himself as unwanted. It is easy thereafter to interpret every disapproval, however slight, as an act of parental rejection. Having formed an image of himself as an unwanted child, he continues in his belief, even in the face of contradictory evidence, because it is the only perception which he knows. Since everyone

[15] P. Lecky, *Self-consistency: a theory of personality* (New York: Island Press, 1945).

interprets his own experience in the light of his perceptual field, the child perceives himself in the light of the only image which he has.

We have already shown how this takes place in the description of the infant's development from undifferentiated responses to the adult's highly discriminating behavior. Socialization, particularly the growth of language, plays an important part in the process. (See especially Chapters 6 and 11.)

Cultural aspects of the perceptual self. If the perceptual self is the only image of himself which a person has, how can one account for the similarities among perceptual selves? Why is it that, although unique, every self nonetheless resembles other selves, sometimes to a startling degree? Common or similar experience has long been known to account for similarities. However, no less important is the influence of a common social heritage and cultural expectancies. This begins with the effect of the family, particularly its mode of child-rearing, and the role of the school and other institutions, and continues through life in contacts with the dominant customs, class membership, and prevailing cultural values and norms. To this must be added the social self, which, as we have shown, is determined by the social attitudes of others toward our own conduct. Since no human experience of any consequence takes place outside a cultural setting, it is not surprising that the cultural matrix in which the self originates and develops should make us very similar. This has been discussed in such great detail in other chapters that it is unnecessary to add more.

Changes in the perceptual self. Our stress on the consistency and stability of the self may well mislead the reader into believing that it is rigid and unchangeable, despite our frequent warnings to the contrary. The number and degree of changes are largely a function of modifications in the perceptual field of the individual. As the perceptual field changes, we have said, the person who organizes his experience within it also changes. We can illustrate this change by means of a real and vivid example.

Hans, as we shall call him, came to the United States as a boy fifteen years of age. In Europe he was considered bright and scholarly, had performed well in a *Gymnasium,* and was highly esteemed by everyone who knew him. He was cheerful and ascendant, sang habitually, and was unusually self-confident. Not knowing English when he settled in the United States, he was placed in the first grade long enough to learn it. Sitting at his desk with the other first-graders he felt deeply humiliated, especially because the other children constantly stared at him. They laughed at his odd pronunciation of English words. Even the teacher seemed to be amused. In the third grade, to which he was promoted three weeks after entering school, his teacher admonished him before the entire class to change his handwriting because it was, as she described it, "too German." On the playground he was teased and annoyed because of his clothes, which had some buttons on the pockets and others to tighten his knee breeches. Frequently some of the local bullies accosted him after school, challenged him to fight, and often beat him. On these occasions he was afraid not only of the bullies, but of what his parents would say when they discovered that he had been fighting, since they considered violence of any kind as an evil. However, one day in anger, fear, and desperation he tore a limb from a tree with the strength that comes of desperation and struck at one and then at the other of his assailants. Both quickly ran out of his sight. Thereafter he was no longer molested.

Two important changes took place in Hans' perceptual self. First, he changed from a self-confident and even overproud boy (he was often called *der Stolze* in his native community) to a fearful and submissive person, in reaction to other people's perception of him as a "Hun." His three-weeks' sojourn in the first grade was utterly humiliating in the light of his former image of himself as an excellent student. The teasing and bullying confirmed his unpleasant image of himself. However, his success as a "fighter," his rapid advancement in school, and the developing reputation as a writer of excellent "American" prose, not to mention the recognition of his artistic talent, changed him once more into a confident, buoyant, and self-accepting individual.

The case illustrates the principle which we have stressed on several occasions. When an individual's perceptual reality, or more specifically his perceptual field, changes, his perception of himself also changes.[16]

Is a science of the perceptual self possible? On several occasions we use the term "unique" to describe the perceptual self. In so doing, are we not lost in subjectivism; and if so, how can we arrive at lawful conclusions regarding the self?

---

[16] It is easy to illustrate and confirm by many other examples, the effect of one's self-image upon one's attitudes and achievements. The apologetic and resigned comments of people that they were always poor at "figures," or that they were never able to spell, is too well known to require comment. One need in no sense subscribe to the false doctrine of Émile Coué to admit that the picture one has of oneself tends to strengthen and confirm it. Instead of ascribing this condition to autosuggestion *à la Coué*, we account for it on the basis of the person's total reaction to his perceptual field. This stricture also holds for the current doctrine of "positive thinking."

Three answers present themselves. First, our question applies to other sciences as well. Lawfulness is not an objective fact, but an assumption of the scientist. Scientific experience has shown that before we can organize and understand what we have observed we must assume that the universe is not capricious but lawful. Initially this is an act of faith, but with the observation of many uniformities it becomes a principle of increasing certainty. Psychologists work on the premise that the more thoroughly they understand the individual and the biological and social conditions which have molded him, the more meaningful—that is, uniform and consistent—will his total behavior be. Thus there are "laws" of human behavior as there are laws of falling bodies or the ebb and flow of the tides. The crucial difference is that the principles governing human behavior do not permit the high degree of certainty and predictiveness which characterize those of the natural sciences. Human beings show an individuality which characterizes no other creature. While their behavior is often predictable it is not fully dependable.

In the second place, the perceptual field imposes its own laws upon the individual. He does not merely pick and choose his actions randomly. Completely random selection of his perceptions would make for chaos instead of organized behavior. But once the selections have been made the individual's perceptual world becomes established, and his actions are determined by it. From then on, changes in perception depend upon changes in the perceptual or psychological field. The stable organization of the self which has been noted by all students of the subject is a product of the lawfulness of the perceptual environment.

Third, neither the physical nor the psychological universe is a closed system. Nothing in either universe is absolutely and irrevocably determined. The psychological, like the physical, field has the property of randomness, only more of it. As we tried to show in the Introduction, randomness in the universe makes change and transformation possible, and prevents the universe from falling to pieces by permitting it to bypass or surmount disturbances. In the face of the recurrent changes in the universe, it is hard to account for its stability during the long course of its existence unless we attribute the property of randomness—that is, *limited* determinism—to it.

Uniqueness thus means that events are not *absolutely* determined. In the psychological field, events are determined only at the instant of their occurrence; at other times they are "free" to enter whatever region is accessible. At the moment of ingresss into another field they are subject to the "forces" of that field and behave in accordance with its structure. Psychological causation can only be understood as a form of interrelatedness of events. When the events are interrelated they do not determine each other, but form a field in which they become connected. The connectedness of events is what makes prediction possible, even though we may be ignorant of the source or cause of their sequence or association.

Unpredictability, and hence uniqueness of human behavior, can be described in still another way. While the field as a scientific *inference* permits predictability, to the perceptual self it is not an inference but an undisputable reality. But prediction from an inference to a reality is subject to limitation and error; hence we cannot "really" anticipate the behavior of an individual over a period of time with confidence. Uniqueness may thus be roughly equated with unpredictability, but not be described as scientifically meaningless.

OTHER FRAMES OF REFERENCE AND THE SELF. In our review of the nature of the perceptual self we leave no doubt regarding its crucial importance in the organization of personality. However, the perceptual field is not the only matrix in which the self originates; it is only one field in which it operates. It is the matrix in which each person views things as he thinks they really are. There are two other matrices, or frames of reference, in which the self is formed. One of these is the realm of moral judgment and behavior; the other is the domain of ideals and aspirations.

The moral self. The psychologist's indifference to the role of ethical attitudes in human behavior has pernicious effects on the study of the self. Nowhere more than in the sphere of self-psychology is the concept of character—or of moral behavior, if one prefers—indispensable. The "superego," which is the moral dimension of the self, is the "conscience" that directs the individual's conduct toward morally desirable ends. This moral self is a system of inner checks which impels the individual to act on the principles of altruism, justice, and other-mindedness. A person with a well-organized moral self does not act on the basis of external constraint or fear of punishment. He is ethical because he has a well-developed image of himself as a moral person. He remains loyal to this image as long as his self remains enmeshed in the frame of reference of moral values. He becomes evil when he enters a frame of reference where his self is transformed into acceptance of wrongdoing.

The ideal self. Of all the animals, man alone has the capacity of setting up ideals and striving for their realization. Man is a myth-maker, and among the myths which he creates is the ideal self. It would be a mistake to think of this self as an ineffectual fantasy, for it is a dimension of the total self which affects the behavior of the individual "possessing" it. However, despite the extensive psycho-analytical literature on the ego-ideal, we have little reliable evidence regarding its effect upon the personality. Self-enhancement and level of aspiration are often identified with it, yet they are not the same. The ideal self is the image which a person has of the kind of person he would like to be. The ineffectuality of the ideal self in directing a person's behavior, especially in the face of harsh reality, is that too often it is composed less of dynamic striving toward a previsioned goal, and more of poorly motivated wishes and of what the current ideals of the "good" man happen to be. Moreover, the idealized self-image frequently serves as a tyrannical agent, as in the case of those distraught neurotics who strive for perfection.

Nevertheless, while these things may be readily granted they do not give us a full account of the striving individual. A wholesome ideal self is frequently the only psychological agency by means of which man may surmount the tribalism of his age. When the ideal self is founded on a realistic assessment of one's own capacities and limitations it can serve as a compass to guide the individual's behavior. It also has the additional merit of aiding in the individual's long-range goals and planning, which we discussed in Chapter 14. In some people it is what Allport calls "a criterion for conscience." [17] In some cases, by striving to implement his ideal of what he wants to be, man not only may change himself but may aid in the trans-formation of the moral environment in which he lives. Although empirical documentation for this assertion is meager for the general population, that it describes well-known historical instances cannot be gainsaid.

Thus far we have described the nature, origin, and development of the self, with particular emphasis on the perceptual self; and the frames of reference, in the form of the moral and ideal selves, which serve as guides to prospective actions. Although it has taken us many pages to describe these features of the psychology of selfhood, we have in reality presented only an incomplete picture of the total self. We shall now remedy this deficiency in part by examining

[17] G. W. Allport, *Becoming: basic considerations for a psychology of personality* (New Haven: Yale University Press, 1955), p. 97.

the equally complex problem of the self's manifestations in concrete behavior.

EXPRESSIONS OF THE SELF

Psychologists of adjustment sometimes have difficulty attempting to account for the mechanism of adjustment largely by means of motivational categories, for the motivational patterns which concern them also require explanation. Motives are not free-floating, and the adjustment needs of the human organism are incomprehensible apart from a self-process. The continuity of motives, like the enduring actions of other aspects of human behavior, presupposes a unifying agent; otherwise they could not be recognized from moment to moment and from day to day. The relation of past behaviors to present ones presupposes a binding and centralizing agent—a self.

It is interesting to note that most psychoanalysts—Anna Freud more particularly—long ago perceived the necessity for a self, or ego, to give meaning to the self's mechanisms of adjustment.[18] Hilgard, in the Presidential address which we have already cited, explicitly argues for the need for a self-concept around which to orient the various mechanisms. This thesis is that "all the mechanisms imply a self-reference, and that the mechanisms are not understandable unless we adopt a concept of the self." [19]

Similarly, a person's emotional and intellectual involvements, his aspirations, and his actualization of his personality, are comprehensible only if we adopt the self-concept to account for them. Therefore, we shall now examine the most important processes which require the existence of a self for their explanation. These are the following: self-involvement, self-defense, and self-enhancement.

SELF-INVOLVEMENT. This is an important psychological process by which motives, attitudes, and values are integrated and gain meaning. It is a vital factor in the organization of perceptual reality and the perceptual self. Self-consistency is virtually the degree or intensity with which an individual's self becomes attached to his own acts. The more his self is involved in his behavior, the more intensely he concentrates on what he is doing. Thus, a starving individual may think only of food, all his other interests being

[18] A. Freud, *The ego and the mechanisms of defence* (London: Hogarth Press, Ltd., 1937).

[19] Hilgard, Human motives and the concept of the self, p. 375.

either nonexistent or so completely subordinated that he is unaware of them. A writer may be so absorbed in his work that he forgets to eat. A spectator may be so engrossed in a football game that he is unconscious of the unseemly epithets which he shouts at the opposing team. For most of us most of the time, our involvements are less dramatic but equally important and real.

Self-involvement and attitudes. It is clear from other discussions in this chapter that the self is the organization of attitudes, values, and other psychological variables into a relatively stable and consistent structure. When attitudes and other psychological processes attach themselves to a particular experience, we call the process self-involvement. Self-involvement thus entails what Sherif and Cantril have called ego-attitudes.[20] Among the attitudes that every individual possesses are attitudes toward himself. The self is thus in an important way an individual's system of self-attitudes. The concept of self-attitudes confirms the existence of the perceptual self, for the latter, as we have noted, is an individual's perception of himself, or his self-attitudes.

The concept of self-attitudes also illuminates the modification of the self. Earlier we said that changes in the self are changes in a person's perception or image of himself. In attitudinal terms, this means that the self changes as one's attitudes toward himself change. Broadening this statement, we can assert that as any system of an individual's attitudes changes, he himself changes. Changes in self-attitudes are changes in self-perceptions, because self-attitudes and self-perceptions are deeply interwoven.

The foregoing statements do not imply that an attitude, motive, or value, each by itself, produces self-involvement. Involvement in a task, attachment to a friend, and loyalty to an institution are not expressions of motives, or attitudes, or values alone; they are manifestations of an active self. The psychology of learning, despite its unprecedented success in explaining other psychological phenomena, cannot account for our daily self-involvements. Yet these self-involvements are vital aspects of human behavior. Only by assuming a self-concept can these phenomena be meaningfully elucidated. A person "loses" himself, or becomes involved in, other persons, objects, or situations because he refers them to himself; they are *his*. They are not simply learned responses or habits, but the self's investment in them. The more he invests his motives, attitudes, and values in them, the more focal they become for him.

[20] M. Sherif and H. Cantril, *The psychology of ego-involvements* (New York: John Wiley & Sons, Inc., 1947).

A condition in which the self has no concern holds no interest for the person. The person whose self is not involved in the affairs of others is unaffected by them. If their activities are perceived as frivolous, their triviality is a product of the self's noninvolvement; if they are extraordinarily important, it is because the individual is profoundly engulfed by them.

This condition of self-involvement is operant in all individually important acts and attitudes, and helps to account for an individual's selective responsiveness to experience. The highly self-involved person functions more effectively in a circumscribed situation than a weakly self-involved individual. Mozart was a musical genius, not only because he inherited a generous share of musical talent, but also because his self was largely involved in a life of music. It is very doubtful that talent alone nurtures a Shakespeare, a Beethoven, or an Albert Einstein; such men create because their selves are singlemindedly dedicated to realizing themselves in the creative act. It is not difficult to name exceptions, of course. Goethe, for example, was not only a poet, but a courtier, statesman, and amateur scientist. However, his years of creative passion were not consumed in the latter activities, but in the writing of beautiful poetry, including his poetic drama, *Faust*. Compared with his poetic writings, the other activities were but interludes—episodes, some of which, by the way, provided the very opportunities which made his sustained creativeness possible.

In the same way, men are honorable and good, not simply because they have *learned* to be virtuous, but also because their self-attitudes are deeply involved in the value of moral goodness. Goodness is a value that is achieved by a striving and intentional self who is deeply immersed in the pursuit of moral ends. For a man profoundly involved in moral values, amorality has little or no meaning; there is no moral neutrality in ethically-involved attitudes and behavior. The "fanatic" in any human enterprise may indeed be cripplingly narrow, but this is not the central truth about him; the important fact concerning him is his uncompromising attitudinal and motivational involvement in a selected venture. Tolstoi and Gandhi were not simply fanatics in the opprobrious sense; rather, they were so deeply involved in the pursuit of preferred ways of life that other interests and values became peripheral to their main themes. Not much psychological insight is gained by describing such behavior as "narrow-minded," "rigid," and "maladjusted"; any psychology which thus describes it is at least partially wrong. Its explanation lies more appropriately in the process of self-involvement.[21] The value to which a person adheres depends on the intensity of his self-involvement in it. All self-involvement is characterized by degrees of intensity; and all attitude-value judgments and all behavior are affected to some extent by the degree of its intensity.

Self-involvement and motives. Motives, like attitudes, do not exist in isolation; they are always functions of the person. Even the rat, driven by hunger to seek the hidden food in its cage, is seeking it not with its stomach but with a dim general striving toward a goal. Its visceral and olfactory sensations combine with its perception of the path it must choose to form directional behavior. Its desire for food, or its hunger drive, is involved in its propriate striving. All other drives at the moment of food-seeking behavior become subordinate and peripheral.

Accustomed as they are to experimenting with animals, some psychologists seldom go beyond the concept of tension reduction. The inadequacy of this approach in human psychology becomes apparent when we turn to an explanation of man's behavior in similar terms. One would be hard-pressed to account for the lifestyles of Tolstoi and Gandhi in the language of tension reduction. Tolstoi renounced his aristocratic living, and Gandhi chose to suffer persecution and imprisonment, not to relieve tensions, but because their self-attitudes and self-involvements precluded any other choices. As soon as the self enters the arena of motivated behavior we are constrained to postulate self-involved, as distinguished from tension-reducing, motives. Self-involved behavior is not performed in the interest of tension reduction; on the contrary, the greater the self-involvement the less is the tension reduced. Self-involvement preserves and continues tension, instead of reducing it.

Again, the segmentalized drives which characterize most animal psychology are incapable of accounting for the unity of the self and personality. These drives are marked by an absence of the long-range goals which typify human motivation; whereas the reduction of animal drives is usually described in terms of past events.

This criticism also applies to some psychologists who make adjustment the central principle of human behavior. Adjustment to them is not so much a future-oriented process as it is dependent

---

[21] A fair question in this connection is whether an experience has meaning to a person because his self is deeply involved in it, or whether he is deeply involved in it because it has meaning and importance for himself. We believe that in the present stage of our knowledge they are mutually reinforcing. This answer is implied in the concepts of self-attitude and attitude-value complex.

upon past conditioning. Thus, a person tends to adjust to the present or future situation in terms of previous stimulation. Like the drive reduction theory—although in fairness, less so—some adjustment explanations neglect the striving, intentional, and self-involved character of human motivation.

The upshot of this brief comparison is this: goal-seeking when viewed from the perspective of self-involvement at its greatest intensity has no terminus; it is not, strictly speaking, need-reductive, for its goals are unattainable. The satisfaction it gives to the self-involved person is not one of fulfillment. The parent whose self is involved in the welfare of his children does not cease to have concern for them when they reach maturity; his self-involvement is a lifelong process full of satisfactions, but seldom of repose. Like perfection devoid of its neurotic element, the satisfaction of deeply self-involved motives is always around the corner. Like William James' caption on his portrait at Harvard, self-involved motives are "always not quite."

The motives in self-involved behavior thus act as integrative and enhancing functions in the human personality. They serve at once as stabilizing and transforming agents in the growth of personality. They give stability to personality by serving as an anchorage for a person's wants and needs; they aid in his change and growth by their future-pointedness. In this respect motives and attitudes serve the same function in self-involved behavior. An attitude is always a tendency to act in the direction of a goal or value. Self-involved attitudes bind the individual to the goal or value in such a way that they serve as directive agents, while providing him at the same time with consistency and stability by their tenacious adherence to selected ends.

DEFENSE OF THE SELF. We have stressed the human organism's striving for consistency and stability. This struggle for self-maintenance is an effort to maintain one's self-image, one's perception of oneself as an enduring person. This may be either normal or neurotic. Normal self-defense is the desire to maintain one's integrity and self-esteem without utilizing crippling mechanisms. Neurotic self-defense, which concerns us only peripherally, consists in the use of self-deceptive techniques which serve to hide from the person, and presumably from others, his real or imagined defects and weaknesses. Defense mechanisms are self-impairing only when they lead to false perceptions of oneself and others and when they distort and damage interpersonal relationships. They are normal and inescapable techniques of adjustment which, if their employment is not abused, contribute to personal equilibrium. Thus whether we conceive the defenses as normal or neurotic depends largely on whether they contribute to constructive or creative adjustments. Clearly, this is a matter of degree, and in any case depends considerably on the person who employs them. The meaning of rationalization, for instance, and its effect on a person's self-esteem, may differ remarkably in different people. One person, upon discovering his propensity for giving excuses for his shortcomings, may feel embarrassed or guilty, whereas another one may be positively affected. In the first case the person suffers; in the second, it may serve as an impetus for surmounting it in the future. Rationalization by one individual may progressively impair his effectiveness as a person, while by another in similar circumstances, it may support his ego sufficiently to make rationalization no longer indispensable.

The implication of the foregoing remarks is clear. They suggest what we know to be true, namely, that the means by which the self seeks to maintain its integrity are not necessarily bad. When used constructively as pointers to the future, as aids in attaining important long-range goals, they are constructive and useful. Stripped of its negative associations, self-defense serves as a stabilizer of the personality. In this sense self-defense is, indeed, as Murphy remarked, "a central concept personality study." [22]

We shall now examine the leading mechanisms of self-defense.

Compensation. This is one of the most widely used and in many ways the most positive and satisfying, modes of adjustment. It represents on the psychological dimension what is well known in the field of physiological processes. A blind person develops acute tactual perception; if one kidney becomes diseased or dysfunctional, the other will take over its labor; if a lung is infected or removed, the other will perform the functions of both.

In like manner, the mediocre scholar may find a substitute gratification in athletic achievement, the homely woman may pride herself on her exceptional character, the man of small stature may develop an overassertive bearing. It should be noted in this connection that it is not the physical feature that impels a person to make up for a deficiency, but *his attitude toward it.* Clearly, in a society where neither physical beauty nor athletic prowess is valued, there will be no need to compensate for lack of these attributes.

Compensation is in some ways the most positive and satisfying mode of adjustment. This is the more true the more the compensating individual utilizes his assets instead of relying on extraneous

[22] G. Murphy, *Personality: a biosocial approach to origins and structure* (New York: Harper & Bros., 1947).

powers such as rank or social position. Productive compensation is a way of defending the self by exploiting one's assets and abilities to offset one's failures and deficiencies. It is valuable, too, because all men must at times employ it. There is no person in the world who can meet all life's problems and frustrations, all its short-comings and deficiencies, with complete success and equanimity; indeed, there are times and occasions when he can maintain his composure only by compensating for his defects and inferiority feelings. There are occasions when life presents threats to each of us for which we must compensate according to our abilities and needs. Life itself precludes universal satisfaction of wishes, and failure and insecurity are burdens of us all.

The lives of great men, men of unusual accomplishment, are often marked by compensatory needs which were instrumental in their achievements. No one fully knows the magnitude of Franklin D. Roosevelt's agitation over his physical handicap, nor the profound role it played in making him an immortal figure. History is replete with examples of the force of compensation in the lives of great men and the events which it produced. Daily life is filled with men's efforts to overcome balked wishes by unconscious artifices and compensatory stratagems. From the day the first member of the human species became dimly conscious of himself, he has erected protective mechanisms to preserve his newly found regard for himself as a person. One can scarcely fathom the compensatory striving of Adolf Hitler that brought nought but wrack and ruin to contemporary civilization. This is compensation of pathological dimensions, but in principle it varies not at all from that which has produced some of civilization's greatest miracles.

These facts in no way detract from the place of human capacities and positive intentional acts. It would be an egregious mistake to attribute all greatness to compensation for balked wishes, or the determination to conquer a profound feeling of inferiority. Surely, it is clear in the pages of this book that man is moved even more urgently by growth motivation than by deficiency needs.[23] Man strives and achieves, not for compensatory reasons alone; on the contrary, being a purposive and intentional individual, he is even more profoundly propelled by ideals and previsioned ends which have no connections with failures and defeats. His ideal self-image acts as a sovereign guide that is far more powerful than his need to conceal his deficiencies. In a preceding paragraph

[23] *Growth* and *deficit* motives have been described in detail by Maslow. See A. H. Maslow, Deficiency motivation and growth motivation, in *Current theory and research in motivation: a symposium* (Lincoln: University of Nebraska Press, 1958).

we distinguished between constructive and neurotic compensations. The latter, we said are basically self-deceptive. Unfortunately, too much contemporary psychology magnifies the neurotic mechanisms at the expense of those which are productive. We write voluminously about the crippling mechanisms, but we have little to say concerning the mechanisms of forward movement and self-affirmation. This is true, let us face it, because our knowledge regarding the latter is almost trifling. Despite the compensatory character of Franklin D. Roosevelt's striving, we venture the opinion that the substance of his basic character was formed long before his impairing illness. The latter served as the most crucial occasion for Roosevelt's "struggle to classify" himself as a person, to use Murphy's adroit phrasing.[24] It was the strongest impetus to find himself as a person.

The chief value of normal compensation is that it aids in changing an individual's image of himself. It helps him to conquer deficiencies by enabling him to make achievements in other directions; it promotes self-confidence and self-esteem by dulling the sharp edge of his feeling of inferiority. Because it tends to heighten his determination to succeed in another enterprise, it may serve as a goad to substantial achievement. Once this circle of attitudes has been initiated it increases its own acceleration. Thus, achievement tends to increase a man's status in the eyes of others, which reduces his self-defensiveness; the reduction of self-defensiveness make his communication with and relatedness to others easier; his more confident relations with them makes him socially more acceptable by them; and this in turn increases his self-confidence.[25]

Rationalization. While this technique differs from compensation, it is motivated by the same need to defend the self against criticism and failure. Just as one person compensates for a real or fancied deficiency in order to bolster up his self, so another one will unconsciously use emotionally satisfying instead of true reasons to account for his psychological deficits.

In rationalization, a person does not compensate for a weakness by exploiting his strength, but by concealing his weakness. The failing student, for example, may not make up for his shortcoming by displaying an artistic gift or athletic prowess, but by believing that his failure was due to the incompetence or ill will of others, or by denying the value of excellent scholarship. Thus, if the teacher had not had a grudge against the student, or if the latter

[24] Murphy, *Personality*, p. 534.

[25] For experimental investigations of compensation, especially the compensatory value of substitute task, see the references in Chapter 4.

wished to be a "greasy grind" like his neighbor, he too would have received superior grades.

The mechanism of rationalization is so well known that it hardly requires detailed description. The mechanism of "sour grapes" is almost universally understood, and has been known for centuries in the fable of the fox and the grapes. The important thing to note is that it is pressed into the service of defending the self against perceptions which, if recognized, might have demoralizing and even disorganizing effects upon the rationalizating person.

Whether rationalization is helpful or not depends on how extensively it is used and on how much it reinforces the self-deception implied in its use. There are no satisfactory experimental data by means of which its effect on the self may be evaluated. Psychoanalytical interpretations indicate that, generally speaking, it is an unsatisfactory mechanism of adjustment. Inasmuch as it is fundamentally self-deceptive, it distorts one's perception of himself and of perceptual reality. Since it tends in time to weaken one's capacity to face life realistically, its value is chiefly negative. Yet its use is not wholly lost upon the individual, for "the vices of rationalization contain its only virtue: it enables the person to avert his gaze from his feeble self and so find sporadic relief from distressing anxiety." [26]

Identification. In this form of self-defense, the individual erects a model for the self to imitate, or gets emotional support by vicariously experiencing the joys and triumphs of another. The person who is "selected" for identification is always one who is highly regarded by the self-defending individual, even if the model is socially unacceptable. Thus, one person may identify himself with a great statesman or businessman, whereas another will imitate the ways of a racketeer or a gangster. Generally speaking, however, the object of identification is someone who is admired for his virtues rather than for his vices.

In most healthy individuals identification begins in the home, especially between parents and children. By virtue of the child's dependence upon his parents and their ministrations to him, he comes to regard their characteristics as his own. Much of what we know as character formation, as was shown in Chaper 14, can be attributed to the child's assimilation of his parents' moral attitudes and making them his own. Identification is unquestionably an important molding force in the child's character formation.

Obviously, the model that a person imitates need not be a known

[26] H. Bonner, *Social psychology: an interdisciplinary approach* (New York: American Book Co., 1953).

or living person. Many Christian saints are known to have patterned their lives after Jesus Christ. While Hitler regarded no one as superior to himself, his acts and utterances betrayed a Napoleonic self-image. A man of the writer's acquaintance fashioned his life in his youth after Emerson's philosophy, especially the latter's doctrine of self-reliance. Quite possibly human conscience and the superego are fundamentally products of the process of identification. In that event, identification is not only a means of defending the self, but an instrument for its integration. In his identification with others, and with ideas and values, the individual is enabled to orient his own conduct around a central agency, and thereby achieve unity and consistency. Even though initially identification is enlisted in the interest of self-defense, with growth and maturation it can serve as an autonomous expression of self-confidence. We have here one more confirmation of the principle of functional autonomy: what was originally a purely defensive maneuver has become a positive strategy. In short, some forms of identification are not merely defense mechanisms but stimuli to self-enhancement.

Identification is also an agency in human socialization. This should be clear from our discussion of social participation in Chapter 6. Selfhood, we saw in earlier sections of the present chapter, is derived in the process of making oneself an object to himself. Self-objectification is greatly facilitated by assuming the role of another. This consists not only of anticipating another's role, but of behaving in response to the other person's perception of oneself. The degree of man's sociality—his capacity of relating himself to others—is partly a function of his ability to be other-minded, to put himself understandingly in the position of another. Identification is in great part the individual expression of this important process. Cooley has referred to this process as "the looking-glass self," G. H. Mead as the "generalized other," and Washburn as the "ejective consciousness." [27]

In phrasing identification in the language of role behavior we call attention to its *active* feature. Unfortunately, conventional discussions of identification unwittingly often convey the idea that it is primarily a passive condition. Preoccupation with its unconscious character is probably responsible for this situation. Patterning oneself after one's image of another may also be a conscious and intentional act. Role-playing is at once the conscious anticipation of the act of another and the process of *enacting* his role. To

[27] C. H. Cooley, *Social organization* (New York: Charles Scribner's Sons, 1911); M. F. Washburn, Ejective consciousness as a fundamental factor in social psychology, *Psychol. Rev.* 39 (1932), 395–402; G. H. Mead, *Mind, self and society* (Chicago: University of Chicago Press, 1934).

the extent that identification is the act of playing the role of another, it is a dynamic process. It is a transaction between what we are and what we hope to be.

Projection. It is not always easy to make a sharp distinction between this mechanism and rationalization. Both are basically forms of self-justification and the incapacity for facing one's own weaknesses. However, whereas the rationalizing person uses pseudo-rational accounts of his deficiencies, the projecting person ascribes his faults to others. He protects himself from exposure, criticism, and disapproval by projecting his faults upon another. It is a means of defending one's self by *denying* one's weaknesses.

There are compensatory as well as rationalizing elements in every form of projection. Indeed, it is remarkable how closely related the processes of compensation, rationalization, and projection are. The dynamic function of each form of these adjustments is to explain away a person's sense of inferiority. In each case the individual shuts out whatever item of reality does not confirm what he wants to believe. Also, there is in each of these modes of adjustment a tendency to form what Wernicke, more than a half-century ago, called *überwertige Ideen,* or exaggerated ideas, of one's own deficiencies.[28] This exaggeration or overemphasis leads to anxiety and oversensitivity concerning them. The anxiety renders them intolerable, and so they must be denied by attributing them to someone else. The deficiency is now not in oneself, but in another. "Thus the mother who has an exaggerated concern about her daughter's sexual morals is probably falsely perceiving in her daughter her own repressed erotic interests." [29] The fanatic who rails against pornography or drinking may very well himself be tempted by these activities. It serves as a kind of scapegoating against those who indulge in behavior which is a temptation to himself.

There is ground for believing that "normal" projection begins in infancy. The undifferentiated nature of the infant's activities is probably its earliest source. The small child cannot sharply differentiate his own sensations from those of another. As he responds to his mother's ministration with anticipation and pleasure he cannot discriminate between those which are his own and those of his mother. Since the distinction between them is blurred, he easily and inevitably ascribes some of them to her. As he grows older and becomes conscious of traits that his mother condemns, it is simple to yield to an already established habit and ascribe them

[28] C. Wernicke, *Grundriss der Psychiatrie* (Leipzig: Verlag von J. A. Barth, 1906).
[29] Bonner, *Social psychology,* p. 137.

to someone else. By projecting it on another person he allays his anxiety and keeps his self-image intact. When his discovery of his projection increases and exposure is imminent, it may result in serious anxiety and, in extreme cases, psychotic breakdown. Paranoia, in which projection is a major symptom, is a good example.

Insofar as projection enables an individual to manage his tensions, it is useful. Though it is not a constructive resolution of conflicts nor an effective reducer of anxiety, it has a limited psychological value. However, most of the evidence regarding it impels one to devalue its over-all effectiveness. Since it is always a function of lack of self-knowledge, its excessive use but further impairs an individual's self-insight. It thus closes the door to the growth of insight and, instead of aiding the individual to get out of his predicament, tends to make his dilemma more engulfing.

Concluding remarks. We have selected for delineation only a few of the mechanisms of self-defense. What we have said concerning the value of those discussed generally holds true for the others as well. In a circumscribed way, and when not excessively used, they have a useful function to fulfill in maintaining the equilibrium of the self. Since no person is competent to master every situation in his life adequately, and since everyone is subject to failures and disappointments as he is to bodily ills, everyone will use such psychological devices as are accessible to him in the light of his personal history and in the face of his individual needs. In all of us some of the mechanisms become generalized and utilized in particular life situations. We come to know a person by his use of them, for they form an integral part of his style of life. They serve as coping mechanisms, aiding the individual in his search for self-consistency and the preservation of his self-picture. For this reason alone it is erroneous to describe them with an undertone of disapproval. Up to a point they are useful; and their usefulness depends largely on the manner and extent of their use by each person. Beyond that, they are crippling deceptions, and in this sense their use is obviously detrimental.

Moreover, as we pointed out earlier in this chapter, the sheer fact of the existence of coping mechanisms in human behavior is a powerful argument for the existence of a self-process. Every mechanism of adjustment is used by a person; it implies a self-reference. The self-referential aspect of the defense mechanism in turn implies the existence of other selves, for we defend the self only against the opinions and evaluations of other selves. The mythical isolate who has no interaction with anyone else would hardly need to invent techniques for preserving his self-image.

Like a lower animal he would have no self-consciousness, and no self that needed defending.[30]

SELF-ENHANCEMENT. Up to this point, our discussion of the self, despite warnings to the contrary, may imply that the self is largely concerned with preserving its equilibrium. The search for stability is, to be sure, an important activity of the self; and the mechanisms which we have just described attest to the significance of that fact. It is a commonplace in biological science that every organism upon being disturbed by its drives attempts to return to its former position of repose. This return to stability is known as homeostasis, and it operates in men no less than in lower organisms.

However, many forms of human striving cannot be described in the language of homeostasis. There are human aspirations which have no discernible terminus, as we said before. Man wants not only safety but the satisfaction that comes from adventure, novelty, growth, and self-expansion. In order to approximate his ideal image man will abandon his present security in order to achieve a higher level of self-integration. It is well known that when the healthy individual reaches a desired goal his standard of performance is correspondingly heightened. He is constantly reaching for a higher level of achievement. This striving for increasingly higher levels of self-realization is not altogether a function of social pressures and cultural values, although they play an enormous role, unquestionably; it is also a psychological property of the healthy person. A self that has ceased to move forward is not a healthy self. Complacency is not a quality of the normal self. Although death will eventually overtake it, while it lives it cannot accept stagnation: *"a resigned self is a sick self."* [31]

Since the foregoing observation is confirmed by many forms of evidence, it follows that self-enhancement is a vital factor in the psychology of the self. It takes its place—perhaps on an equal basis—with self-defense. In any case, self-defense is not *the* central concept in personality study, but shares the spotlight with self-enhancement. Self-enhancement refers to that aspect of the total self which is, as Murphy so well phrased it, "clearly or dimly glimpsed as *something to be realized."* [32]

---

[30] The reader who desires a comprehensive and detailed treatment of all the adjustment mechanisms should consult the following: L. F. Shaffer and E. J. Shoben, *The psychology of adjustment* (2d ed.; Boston: Houghton Mifflin Co., 1956). For a sophisticated and penetrating discussion of the mechanisms, see Murphy, *Personality*, Chs. 22–24.

[31] Bonner, *Social psychology*, p. 140. Italics in the original.

[32] Murphy, *Personality*, p. 539. Italics in the original.

Level of aspiration. A fruitful approach to the study of self-enhancement has been the concept of aspiration level. An individual's aspiration level represents him not only as he is at any particular moment, but also as he would like to be at some point in the future. It is a "measure" of his intentional disposition, an important element of his long-range behavior. By knowing a person's level of aspiration we learn a great deal about *him*.

Because a person's level of aspiration gives us insight into his ideal self—the self that he would like to be—it is important to discuss it here. Inasmuch as we described it at some length in Chapter 4, including some of the important experimental work which established and measured it, we shall be very brief.[33]

An individual aspires for things out of immediate reach for two reasons: (1) as a social self, he is impelled by the standards of society to compare himself with others in the realm of achievement; and (2) it is in the nature of every healthy human organism to reach out beyond the limits of its current attainment. Without pursuing this distinction further, it is sufficient to point out that, because the individual unavoidably compares his performances with those of others, he experiences either elation or dissatisfaction with his own accomplishments. As an intentional, purposive individual, he sets up goals and values whose attainment is essential to his well-being. But success or failure in human aspiration has meaning only in the context of our knowledge of the ends which impel the individual to action. In striving for previsioned goals, the individual self constantly undergoes restructuring in the light of the level of success that he has set up for himself to achieve. This restructuring is either pleasant or painful. It is pleasant because it brings reward in the form of admiration by others, or enhances his status, or augments his self-esteem. It is unpleasant because it always involves a change from the security of homeostasis. Nevertheless, the greater the success in achieving a given end, the more pronounced the rise in the level of aspiration, and the greater the accompanying satisfactions. To the extent that aspiration toward a goal is successful, it adds to the defense of the self; but to the extent that it impels the individual to raise his horizon to greater heights, it is self-enhancing.

There are two classes of determinants of the level of aspiration,

---

[33] The level of aspiration has, of course, been known in different verbal guises for a long time, and William James considered it an important factor in his discussion of the self. (See James, *Principles of Psychology*.) The term "level of aspiration" was introduced by Tamara Dembo.

namely, those stemming from the cultural norms of a group, and those which are associated with the individual's self-image.[34]

The cultural determinants of aspiration level are all the cultural pressures upon the individual to raise his sights toward higher achievement. Group standards are the most obvious cultural factors. The excellent and much cited experimental study by Chapman and Volkman demonstrates the strong effect of group standards upon the aspirations of an individual. For example, they found that when, in the act of pursuing a goal, a person compares himself to a group of inferior performers, he will raise his standard. Cultural norms not only bring pressure upon the individual to achieve a certain level, but to keep the level rising. Cultural pressures not only determine the level of achievement to which we aspire but also the level of performance with which we are satisfied.[35]

A person's level of aspiration is also markedly determined by his self-image, especially his ideal self-image. He strives and achieves, not only because of external pressures in the form of group standards and other people's opinions, but also because of his loyalty to his conception of himself as a person. Thus, some individuals maintain a high aspiration level with little or no thought of the opinions of others, and despite repeated failures. Such persons' goals are strongly self-oriented and are not too easily swayed by the pressures of cultural expectations.[36]

Nuttin interprets this persistence in the face of failure too negatively. In ascribing it to poor integration and structural rigidity he overlooks the driving need to hold on to one's image, a persistence which is often more satisfying than the expectation of success. It also ignores the well-known fact that the negative view persists only when the aspiring individual is still failing, and ignores the accolades which are heaped upon him when he becomes a great success. The history of many great men bears this out quite clearly. While they were struggling and failing they were considered ab-

[34] This should be compared with the classification of Lewin and his associates. They divide them into temporary situational factors and general cultural factors. The temporary situational factors seem to correspond to those associated with a person's self-image. For the view of Lewin et al., see K. Lewin, T. Dembo, L. Festinger, and P. S. Sears, Level of aspiration, in J. McV. Hunt (ed.), Personality and the behavior disorders (New York: The Ronald Press Co., 1944), Vol. 1, Ch. 10.

[35] D. W. Chapman and J. Volkman, A social determinant of the level of aspiration, J. abnorm. soc. Psychol., 34 (1939), 225–38; P. S. Sears, Levels of aspiration in academically successful and unsuccessful children, J. abnorm. soc. Psychol., 35 (1940), 498–536.

[36] See J. Nuttin, Tâche. Réussite et échec. Theorie de la conduite humaine (Louvain: Editions Université de Louvain, 1953).

normally stubborn and pigheaded; when they finally succeeded, they were acclaimed as geniuses. The self-involvements of Mozart, Beethoven, and Einstein appeared superficially as expressions of inflexibility, but we all admire their persistence in the light of their extraordinary achievements.

However, whichever interpretation is put on the foregoing remarks, it seems to be a fact supported by empirical data that an achievement motive exists in practically all normal individuals. Striving for leadership, fame, prestige—indeed any forward movement of the self—characterizes every healthy individual.[37]

Self-actualization. We reiterate here an oft-repeated statement in this book: *every healthy human organism has the attribute of self-extension.* This attribute has been variously denoted, and it is an old idea in human thought. Aristotle made the concept of self-realization a basic attribute of the good life. The goodness of man, he believed, consisted in the realization of his essence, that is, in his self-realization.

We use the term "self-actualization" to describe roughly the same process. We do this for two reasons. First, the term "self-realization" implies the attainable, an end to be reached, more than active striving. Second, the term was central in the ethics of Aristotle, with its stress upon happiness as an accompaniment of virtuous behavior. Self-actualization is the process in which an individual is continuously externalizing himself in whatever activities are characteristic of his being. In contrast to the act of self-defense, which is the process of preserving a certain state of existence, self-actualization is the effort of an individual to multiply and extend his self-activities. While we do not agree with Goldstein that self-actualization is the sole motivating force in human behavior, we can accept his definition of its nature. "*Normal behavior,*" he writes, "*corresponds to a continual change of tension, of such a kind that over and over again the state of tension is reached which enables and impels the organism to actualize itself in further activities, according to its nature.*"[38]

In regard to the self, this form of self-extension stresses the dynamic, tension-producing, and tension-enjoying aspects of the total personality. Conceived in this manner, self-actualizing per-

---

[37] D. C. McClelland, J. W. Atkinson, R. A. Clark, and E. L. Lowell, *The achievement motive* (New York: Appleton-Century-Crofts, Inc., 1953); J. P. Guilford, P. R. Christensen, N. A. Bond, and M. A. Sutton, A factor analysis study of human interests, *Psychol. Monogr.*, 68 (1954), No. 375.

[38] K. Goldstein, *The organism* (New York: American Book Co., 1939), p. 197. Italics in the original.

sons "seem to be fulfilling themselves and to be doing the best that they are capable." [39]

On the basis of an expirical study of about 49 individuals, some contemporary, some historical and public figures, and others who gave evidence of falling into the category of self-actualization, Maslow concluded that this characteristic marks every mentally healthy individual. In mentally ill individuals it was either weak initially or became perverted and emasculated by a faulty socialization. It seems to be present in all healthy children before the stultifying effects of a repressive enculturation have had an opportunity to take effect. Those persons who survive the constrictive effects of a rigid socialization display many self-expressive tendencies in adult behavior. They are recognized for their constructive adjustment to and creative alteration of reality, by spontaneity and non-defensive relations with others. (See Chap. 3.)

Self-actualization is not the selfish pursuit of one's own interests; it is neither egocentrism nor self-glorification. These are neurotic characteristics, and the self-actualizing individual is not neurotic. The self-actualizing person enhances his self, not by considering other people as inferior, as is done by the insecure and defensive individual, but by the actualization of his potentialities. His self-assurance and unaffectedness are the expression of his independent spirit.[40]

Inasmuch as self-actualization is in essence a pattern of traits marked by independence, self-sufficiency, the ability to enjoy privacy and aloneness, and both the capacity and preference for working things out alone, we have other evidence than the biological theory of Goldstein and Maslow's limited number of cases. We believe that self-actualization is similar to the trait of self-sufficiency which we already described in the preceding chapter. Self-confidence, independence, and self-understanding characterize the self-sufficient temperament, as they do the self-actualizing individual.[41]

Our knowledge of self-enhancement is far inferior to and less certain than our understanding of self-defense. We have attempted

[39] A. H. Maslow, *Motivation and personality* (New York: Harper & Bros., 1954), pp. 199–234.

[40] These traits have been found in most independent and self-sufficient individuals, and they contrast sharply with the conformity behavior of nonself-actualizing persons. See R. S. Crutchfield, Conformity and character, *Amer. Psychologist,* 10 (1955), 191–98.

[41] For the verification of these traits in the self-sufficient temperament, see C. Morris and L. V. Jones, Value scales and dimensions, *J. abnorm. soc. Psychol.,* 51 (1955), 523–35.

to present as reliable a description of self-enhancement as our present knowledge permits. This description has been drawn in terms of two strong activating dispositions, namely, level of aspiration and self-actualization. The intellectual challenge of these characteristics is at the moment far greater than the evidence which supports them. Until such a time, however, when our empirical and experimental knowledge is greater than it now appears to be, they will serve as a vital impetus to further investigation.

CONCLUSION

From the quantitative point of view our discussion of the self may appear vague and unconvincing. Some psychologists, we know, see no scientific need to posit so elusive a psychological structure as the self. This is especially true of the "radical" behaviorists, of whom Skinner is the most typical.[42] However, we have given a few plausible arguments to show why the self-concept is necessary in the psychology of personality. Among these, two are most important: (1) the concept of the self is necessary to account for the consistency, unity, and perdurance of the personality; and (2) it is required in order to give to the mechanisms of self-defense and the process of personal enhancement a point of reference. These processes and dimensions of individual behavior, which make for consistent and unified conduct, make possible that organized totality which we call personality. Without a self, a person has no map to consult when he tries to understand himself, especially in moment of crisis or difficult choice.[43]

It is difficult to understand how man could either understand or solve his own problems in the absence of an organizing principle: *the self-principle*. For as Murphy has discerningly observed, most of our problems and difficulties are self-problems.[44] Conceived as an integrating concept, the self-concept, or self-process, has a scientifically justifiable place in the study of personality. Without a self, man would be an impulsive and uncoordinated behaving animal. While lower animals are characterized by coordinated behavior, their behavior is mostly an expression of instinct and deeply conditioned habits. Man, not being a creature of habit

---

[42] See B. F. Skinner, *Science and human behavior* (New York: The Macmillan Co., 1953).

[43] V. C. Raimy, *The self-concept as a factor in counseling and personality organization* (Ph.D. dissertation, The Ohio State University, 1943).

[44] Murphy, *Personality*, p. 562.

to the same extent, needs a map in order to steer him to his previsioned goals. For this directionality, he depends upon his organized selfhood.[45]

[45] We have not done full justice in this chapter to the complexity and psychological "richness" of the psychology of the self. More specifically, we have omitted an extensive discussion of the self-psychology of Carl Rogers, who has written some of the very best conceptualizations of and insights into the nature of the self, as these emerged from his therapeutic work.

Part IV

CONCLUSION: SUMMARY AND INTERPRETATION

CHAPTER **17**

Toward a Unified View of Personality

Throughout this book we have in one way or another described personality within a unified, three-dimensional framework. By means of this framework we have tried to show that personality is a dynamic structure of biological factors, interpersonal contacts, and cultural values. In other words, man is a *biopsychosocial being*. He comes into the world equipped with a relatively undifferentiated set of actual and potential psychobiological characteristics. These characteristics are developed, deflected, or inhibited by the kinds of controls imposed upon the growing individual by the persons in his environment. The process of personality patterning is furthered by cultural pressures, especially those of the class structure of the child's parents. Having experiences similar to those of others in his group, the growing child tends to develop the same traits as others who are molded by the same cultural expectancies. Stress is placed on both the individual and institutional aspects of the molding process without committing us to decide the relative importance of either, since no dependable choice can be made in the present stage of our knowledge.

The systematic approach to the psychology of personality in this book has been holistic and field-dynamic, which we conceive as a single, unified point of view. This approach does not blind us to the possibility that other points of view may also be valid, for in the psychology of personality, as should be clear, there is no *true* theory, but only more or less dependable proposals. As we have pointed out, science is many-sided, and the study of personality, more than any other phase of the science of human behavior, is highly personal. In our reasoned judgment, the under-lying unifying concepts of this volume, and the view of personality briefly stated in the remaining pages of this book, carry a conviction that opposing positions have thus fair failed to undermine or challenge.

Furthermore, in our judgment, the well-entrenched views of psychology, when they deal with the problem of personality, have produced rather static and atomized pictures of the human indi-vidual. In their predilection for causal explanations of human be-havior they have overlooked the thoroughly dynamic character of human personalities. In their search for operationally definable units, they have atomized the holistic structure of personality. We believe that the holistic, field-dynamic view, by whatever other label it may be described, does more justice to man's essential wholeness and his fundamental uniqueness. Finally, it is a view expounded in different phraseology and from the unique perspec-tive of each, by such well-known and gifted psychologists as Gordon Allport, Kurt Lewin, Gardner Murphy, A. H. Maslow, and Kurt Goldstein; and it does not differ fundamentally from the views of Prescott Lecky, Carl Rogers, and Arthur W. Combs.

Having surveyed the psychology of personality, it is now neces-sary to pull together the separate strands into a conceptually coherent system, and to postulate basic principles for the organiza-tion of motives, traits, attitudes, and values into a unified per-sonality. In this effort, it is not necessary to engage in a discussion of the biological nature of man, for we accept it as a "given," the importance of which only a narrow and rigid environmentalism can minimize. The student of personality must also remember that the biological individual is not a passive recipient of external cultural stimulations. The healthy human organism resists socializa-tion and actively works to transform his environment. Encultura-tion is not easy; it is always confronted by a unique and recalcitrant biological nature. On the other hand, it is equally important to note that, despite the individual's effort to resist the molding force of culture, the customs of society will inordinately, if slowly, pound him into their own image. Biologically based psychologies have the merit of pointing up the difficulty of shaping the individual in accordance with the cultural norms of a society; but our own discussion in this book has confirmed that the job can be done.

THE INTERPERSONAL REALITY

Personality psychologists have not always distinguished cultural pressure from *interpersonal* conditioning. We have shown that cultural conditioning is the process whereby the cultural influences of a group shape an individual in accordance with its norms and values. To the extent that each individual is subject to the impress of the culture he becomes more or less like every other individual in his social environment. We analyzed the process of cultural conditioning in detail in Chapters 6 and 7. Accordingly, it is unnecessary to recapitulate the process here. However, it is necessary to take at least a glance at the important process of interpersonal conditioning, for a knowledge of it illuminates the study of personality.

INTERPERSONAL CONDITIONING. While the interpersonal influences cannot in fact be disentangled from the cultural forces, they are distinct enough to help us to account for many individual differences in persons who have been subject to the same cultural pressures. Interpersonal conditioning is the process whereby the individual's personality is influenced by person-to-person relationships. These interpersonal relationships involve the influence of another's sex and age differences, temperament, character, style of life, and personality as a whole. The temperaments and characters of the influencing parents, quite apart from the cultural norms which they bear in their behavior, play vital roles in shaping the personalities of their children. A tyrannical father has a markedly different effect upon a growing child than a kindly, or permissive, or indulgent one. An overprotective or a rejecting mother has a noticeably different effect upon a child than a mother who aids her child to become gradually independent of her control over him. An emotionally unstable or neurotic parent tends unconsciously to transmit his instability or neuroticism to the developing child, no matter what the cultural matrix in which both function may be. The presence of older or younger siblings with whom a child interacts makes a difference in the quality of his socialization. There are different latitudes of behavior in every society, which affect individual development, and this difference in latitude is especially potent in individual families.

Character of the parents. We have been saying that a child is conditioned not only by the culture of his group but by the personalities of its members. The parents affect the child earliest and sometimes most permanently, and they have already received our attention in Chapter 6. There is a wide range of personalities found in American families, and the individual differences of family members is in part responsible for the differences in the personality structures of the children. A son growing up under the influence of an amiable tyrant, as in the story of *Life With Father*, will be a different person from one reared under the influence of an arbitrary and cruel despot. A daughter influenced by a generous but determined mother, as in the play *I Remember Mama*, will have a different character from one conditioned by sentimentality and indulgence.

It is easy to find families in the same culture, socioeconomic class, and educational attainments who nevertheless produce very different children despite the sameness or similarity of cultural conditioning. In one family the son was permitted to have a free choice of companions and the freedom to pursue his own career. The father was a highly successful businessman who had little interest in "cultural" matters. From childhood on, the son was given opportunity to absorb whatever educational and aesthetic experiences he desired, and the father encouraged him in his interests. When the boy had grown up he wanted to go to an art school. The father was interested in his son's ambition and helped him wisely in every way he could. The son has exhibited creative talents since his childhood. He was never dissuaded by his practical father from his artistic interests. The boy is a stable, happy individual who is making a good adjustment to life and progressively realizing his ambition to become an artist.

Another boy, reared in accordance with the same cultural norms by an intolerant and domineering father and an indulgent mother, turned out to be a quite different individual. The father, a successful furrier, had failed to satisfy his strong desire for a medical career. His son wanted to become an athletic coach, but his domineering father, whom he feared, had other plans for him. He wanted his son to become a doctor, a form of compensation through one's children not uncommon in our society. The son, knowing that his father would not support him financially in getting a degree in physical education, acceded to the father's wishes and enrolled in the premedical course in the state university. After two years of unsuccessful struggling the boy had to leave college at the advice of the resident psychiatrist. He was a picture of utter dejection and of repressed resentment toward his father.

In still another case a boy, the product of an overprotective and overambitious mother and a "self-made" father, developed into a submissive and dependent individual who was still leaning, even at the age of thirty-two, upon his forceful and determined mother. Driven by his mother's insatiable ambition for his career and overawed by his father's rise to a position of prominence, the boy was overcome by a sense of inadequacy and a chronic fear of failure. While the father never gave cause for the son's unconscious comparison with himself, the mother continually reminded the helpless son of his father's achievement, which she urged him to emulate. This constant admonition by the mother only aggravated the son's feeling of helplessness and inferiority, and he became progressively more isolated and withdrawn. At thirty-two years of age he still lived with his parents, held on to an inferior position, and seldom ventured forth from the protection of his domineering mother.

Cases like these can be multiplied a thousand times, but each shows the same forces at work. The personality, character, or emotional disposition of parents or other adults who condition the growing child can leave an indelible impression on his developing personality. Cultural conditioning, with all its power of molding the individual into a standard matrix, does not account for his total personality. Every individual must be understood in terms of his own biography as well as the social mold into which he is cast. Individuality or uniqueness, if so understood, can be empirically validated. Thus, to repeat once more, the individual is not only a biological being or the product of a cultural group, but an individuated person significantly influenced by the emotions and personalities of others in his early environment.

Much of what is recognized as individuality in the mature personality stems from the quality of the interpersonal contacts here indicated, as well as from the person's native predispositions. Our brief remarks concerning interpersonal conditioning underscore the fact that no normal individual is completely at the mercy of his culture. Man has in every group various degrees of psychological autonomy; nowhere does he follow cultural imperatives and expectancies completely. Certainly those aspects of the total personality which have a strong biological basis have a high degree of persistence and self-direction. Man is a part of society, no doubt; but he can also transform and transcend its customs when they threaten his self-integrity, no matter how strongly they are reinforced by cultural influences. In short, individual differences have a partial origin in the basic temperamental dispositions and attitudes of the adults with whom the child has his early interpersonal contacts. Thus, such personality characteristics as self-confidence and its opposite, ascendance and submissiveness, gentleness and aggressiveness, anxiety and serenity, can usually be traced to parents who approach their children with these attitudes.

PERCEPTUAL PATTERNING. In Chapter 16 we stressed the importance of the perceptual frame of reference in which the self originates and develops. We described the perceptual self as that dimension of the total personality which emerges from the manner in which the individual views himself. Although self-perception is limited by the basic neurophysiology of each individual, it is much more determined by the slow process of growth and maturation, and by the interpersonal experiences which a child has in his primary groups. What we are saying is that perception of oneself and of others is initiated in the early social interactions of the child. The social self, as we saw, arises from the manner in which we perceive other people's relations to ourselves. The adult who is habitually suspicious and distrustful of others was not born with this perception of people, but acquired it in his early relations with others. The distrustful people who conditioned him to become suspicious served as models for the growing child, and by a normal process of stimulus generalization, he learned to perceive them as untrustworthy persons who only confirmed the image which they helped to create.

This process of perceptual patterning should not require further analysis, as our discussion of the perceptual self has made its importance in self-formation very clear. It is so patently evident in the life of every individual that one needs little formal argument to convince one of its role in a person's daily life. Perception is the modality through which we come into contact with both the external and internal environments.

DYNAMICS OF PERSONALITY

The conception of personality presented in this book has already been stated in different ways and in different places. It shows that the person is a dynamic agent in the sociocultural process. He not only is conditioned by the established values of his social environment, but also transcends them and creates new ones as well. He is an active force in his own development. He sets up his own goals and achieves them. He is frustrated by society's barriers and prescriptions, but he can also renounce and prevail over them.

This reciprocal process, as well as the resistance to enculturation and the search for personal autonomy, can be formally described by means of organismic, or field-dynamic, principles. These we shall now state and elaborate.

FIELD-DYNAMIC PRINCIPLES. Our informal holistic, field-dynamic analysis of personality and its formation supports a fundamental proposition in this book, namely, that personality is an organized complex of interrelated motives, traits, attitudes, and values. The question now facing us is this: *What are the underlying principles governing the organization and structure of personality into a more or less coherent whole?*

Before considering these principles it is well to indicate that they govern all functional wholes, all energy systems, be they physical, biological, or psychological. They show that part and whole are mutually modifying, even though, as Lewin and others have shown, the direction of change is more often from whole to part. In every organismic whole there are centers of high potential with varying degrees of autonomy. As we have said many times, individuals can control or restructure their own environmental fields. They are not passive or helpless creatures of society, but effective molders of its structure. As Murphy observed, "it is only by not accepting culture as it is that new cultures are made." [1]

We proceed now to a brief presentation of the basic holistic, field-dynamic principles.

1. *Personality is a dynamic field or integrated whole.* This follows from the principle in physical science that every system of energy is a dynamic unity. This conclusion is also forced upon us by the fact that all human behavior is interactive, that no experience exists in isolation, or without being influenced and modified by all other experiences. An integrated whole is not a mere summation of parts, but a dynamic unity which, though it includes the parts, is different from them. Personality as a whole possesses properties that are not found in any of its constituent parts, such as perceptions, ideas, and attitudes. Personality conceived as a patterned whole cannot be perceived or understood by any individual trait as such, but only as a unit.

On the other hand, personality is not self-sufficient; it does not exist in isolation. Personality is a part of a whole called society. This has been stressed often enough not to require repetition here. The person and society together constitute a complex organization which may be called *the continuum of universal human nature.*

[1] G. Murphy, *Personality: a biosocial approach to origins and structure* (New York: Harper & Bros., 1947), p. 905.

Insofar as the division of labor in science requires some isolation of subject matter, society may be said to be the subject matter of sociology and the individual the subject matter of psychology. The fundamental datum, the irreducible element, of psychology is personality as a unit. On the basis of this canon and its implications it can be asserted that the central subject matter of psychology is personality.

2. *Personality derives many of its properties, or its "nature," from the group in which it has membership.* This principle is derived from the *Gestalt* view that the part derives its properties from the whole. Accordingly, there is no personality outside a social group. In isolation from a social group the individual does not become a fully developed person. Furthermore, personality differs with the properties of the group to which an individual belongs. Our analysis of a number of preliterate groups has shown a large variety of personality structures corresponding to the dominant values, feeling-tone, or ethos of each society. Similar correlations have been found to obtain between the personalities and cultures of Western civilization.

The derivation of personality traits from the character of the group is also seen in the more individualized interpersonal relations which we discussed earlier in this chapter. The personality and character of the parents, the attitude and treatment by other adults and siblings, leave their impress upon the personality. A "nervous" parent tends to produce a "nervous" child. The imposition of the customs and mores, the inculcation of basic disciplines, the impress of class status, the influence of the educational and religious institutions of the group upon the developing individual—all these processes give testimony to the complicated network of factors which mold the individual into the type of person which he gradually becomes.

3. *The group restricts or controls the activities of the individual.* This principle is derived from the field-dynamic criterion that the whole determines the actions of the parts. It is also implied as the converse of the preceding principle of derived field properties. No individual, no matter how much a center of high potential he may be, no matter how free, is wholly independent of the group of which he is a part. This is in keeping with the field-dynamic principle that causation takes place not from part to part but from whole to part. While he is able to influence society the individual is also deeply influenced by it. We have seen this principle operating in practically every phenomenon that we have studied in these pages: the effect of customs and mores on the individual, the

development of attitudes, the cultural expression of motives, the acquisition of language. Everywhere we find the individual hemmed in, restricted, controlled, suppressed, punished, and rewarded by the rules and customs of his group. Individuality and freedom are, paradoxically, biosocially determined.

4. *Individual differences are products of the effect of group variation and biological differentiation upon the person.* This idea derives from the *Gestalt* principle that the parts are derived from the whole by a process of differentiation. The investigations of Coghill have shown that the development of the organism proceeds from mass action to differentiation. The human organism develops hands, fingers, eyes, ears, internal organs, by a process of differentiation from a mass of undifferentiated protoplasm. Differentiation means the individuation or relative segregation of specialized units within a larger whole.

In a similar fashion the human person becomes gradually and relatively differentiated from his membership group. The process begins in part in the differential attitudes of parents and others toward different members of the same family. Interpersonal influences differ in the same cultural group. Some persons, by virtue of the interplay of heredity and environment, become higher potential centers than others. They are more individuated or free than others. Not every person is affected in the same way by the same set of customs, expectancies, and individual attitudes. There are differences in the way in which each person internalizes the external culture. Culture does not have exactly the same meaning to different people, for every person sees his culture through his perceptual frame of reference. The relation of each individual to his culture is not duplicated exactly in every other individual, just as not every organ of the body fulfills its function similarly in other bodies, and not every potential in a gravitational field assumes the same dynamic relationship to the whole. Every individual, every bodily organ, every physical event acquires through differentiation specific structures and functions in the total psychobiosocial field in which it has its being.

5. *Personality develops and changes as a whole.* It moves from simple differentiation to progressively higher or more complex levels of organization. Generally speaking, a person is not timid or insecure, say, in only a single situation. Insecurity or timidity characterizes his whole personality. If he overcomes his social timidity, for example, it is usually because he has become *generally* more self-assured. It is not an isolated characteristic that changes but a whole configuration that undergoes differentiation and modi-

fication. The reason why the chronic alcoholic is not "cured" is that, while he may vow never to touch liquor again, he has not in fact experienced a change in his personality. He is psychologically ill because his personality lacks sufficient integration to prevent a trait or action from becoming isolated from the rest of his behavior. His excess drinking leads a life of its own, like some aspect of a dissociated personality. Just as physical growth is a function of the organism-as-a-whole, so personality organization is a function of the total psychobiosocial individual. Personality structure is no more an addition or multiplication of separate traits or attitudes than the physical organism is an accumulation of discrete protoplasmic cells.

6. *Personality develops in accordance with the principle of psychological economy.*[2] Its correlate in physics is the law of least action, or what Bertrand Russell once described as the law of universal laziness. The *tendency* of every object in the universe from a falling apple to an individual madly in love is to arrive at a destination in the most direct way. This implies what we have already stressed on several occasions, that every object is moving toward a goal. Human behavior is fundamentally goal-integrated. Needs produce tensions and tensions must be either resolved or integrated on a higher level of organization. The individual who becomes a doctor by performing those actions which will enable him to achieve his goal is acting more economically than the person who daydreams about becoming one. But each is arriving at his goal in the only way possible to him at the moment on the background of his individual biography, value-system, and intentional disposition.

7. *Personality strives to preserve its integrity or re-establish it when it is disturbed.* This is another way of formulating Lecky's principle of self-consistency. By the integrity of the personality we mean its wholeness. This is an application in personality study of the well-known principle of *homeostasis.* According to this principle the human organism is self-regulating and self-preserving. It resists change, and when its equilibrium is upset it tries to re-establish it.[3] The example of the child's resistance to socialization and enculturation is a simple illustration. The obstinacy and resist-

---

[2] Psychoanalysts employ the term "psychic economy" to describe the same principle. Psychological economy seems preferable because of its wider connotation.

[3] For a discussion of the theory of homeostasis by its original formulator see W. B. Cannon, *The wisdom of the body* (Rev. ed.; New York: W. W. Norton & Co., Inc., 1932). Köhler proposed this notion even earlier. See W. Köhler, *Die physischen Gestalten in Ruhe und im stationären Zustand* (Braunschweig: F. Vieweg, 1920).

ance sometimes persist under the most threatening and disorganizing external conditions. Maslow calls attention to the examples of the maintenance of security feelings in emigrés who had undergone the most harrowing experiences.[4] In an earlier study of ninety victims of Nazi persecution, Allport and his collaborators noted the same persistence. They found that the disasters and catastrophes, the deprivations, cruelties, and indignities of life in concentration camps, did not radically alter the personalities of individuals.[5]

Many other examples, though usually far less dramatic, might be cited. Such findings testify to the persistency and vitality with which the well-integrated person maintains his individuality and integrity. Moreover, they show that field-conditioning is not a one-way process; for despite radical restructuring of the social field, as in the change from conventional modes of life to the life of concentration camps, individuals maintain their personal integrity. This can be explained by the fact that when the individual is threatened he mobilizes all his energies to resist change and to maintain his balance. This mobilization is a total process, so that when any integrated system is disturbed it is disturbed not merely in one part but throughout. When the individual is emotionally upset he is upset not only in his glandular system but in his total psychobiosocial make-up. He is not only "afraid" but his heart pounds, his respiratory system is accelerated, and he may fight or run. He is afraid "all over."

8. *Personality is the product of the organism's reaction to the total social field.* This principle asserts that personality develops and changes as a whole. The latter principle shows that insecurity, for example, is not an isolated individual trait but characterizes a generally insecure person. The present canon, on the other hand, asserts that because personality is a psychobiological unit, its reaction to a specific situation is part of a reaction to a larger situation. The person responds to a situation, or social field, as a whole. Thus, to borrow Wheeler's example, a person's defense reaction of boldness is not a reaction to a limited social situation, say the amused glances of other people at his small stature, but to this situation in its relation to many other situations. If the same people who are amused at the individual's diminutiveness also showed him respect and friendliness he would not resort to the defense

---

[4] A. H. Maslow, Dynamics of personality organization. I. *Psychol. Rev.*, 50 (1943), 514–39.

[5] G. W. Allport, J. S. Bruner, and E. M. Jandorf, Personality under social catastrophe, *Char. & Pers.*, 10 (1941), 1–22.

mechanism of boldness. He could maintain his equilibrium in active relation to an equal distribution of social situations.[6]

9. *Personality develops in accordance with its own potentialities.* No individual is merely the product of social and cultural pressures; nor is he bent only on preserving himself and maintaining a homeostatic state. We have repeated in different ways that the healthy person is marked by the determination to grow, to become more and more what he can potentially come to be—in short, to actualize his unique latent possibilities. When growth toward independence and autonomy is blocked, the individual strives to surmount the barrier, to redouble his effort toward the realization of his potentialities, often by deferring or sacrificing other satisfactions. He is not ordinarily a passive creature. He resists blocking forces and the pressures of enculturation by mobilizing his psychobiological energy with stubborn persistence. The mature person is thus one who, while internalizing the demands of the group —because this is inescapable—restructures them in the light of his own experience, value-system, level of aspiration, and intentional disposition. He wills not only as society wills, but wills to actualize his own potentialities. A healthy personality is thus the congruence of individual and social values and the aspirations of a unique individual.

The foregoing field or organismic principles are interrelated; each implies every other. No one principle is sufficient to account for the complexity and the unity of personality. Together they emphasize the relative consistency of the behavior of the person-in-the-environment. Together they imply the falsity of any atomistic, segmental, vitalistic, or mechanistic account of the emergence and growth of personality as a whole. With the psychoanalysts, *Gestalt*-theorists, and holistic psychologists we can affirm that the basic unit of psychology is the total personality.

Viewed holistically and field-dynamically man is, to use Murphy's phrase, "a nodal region," a structured field within a larger structured field, in which all elements interact. Beyond the structured field of the person are the structured fields of other persons in a continuous reciprocity; for man, as Simmel observed more than fifty years ago, lives his entire being in reciprocal relationship with others—"*in Wechselwirkung mit anderen Menschen. . . .*"[7]

[6] R. H. Wheeler, *The laws of human nature* (New York: Appleton-Century-Crofts, Inc., 1932).

[7] G. Simmel, *Soziologie* (Leipzig: Duncker u. Homblot, 1908). See also Murphy, *Personality,* p. 7.

in the direction of field dynamics and the concept of contempo-
raneous causation. Indeed, one can hardly be amiss in saying of
field dynamics that it is a more precise scientific restatement of
Sigmund Freud's doctrine of the basic urges as well as an extension
of this doctrine.

Again, both psychoanalysis and field dynamics, each in its own
terminology, assert that personality is greatly affected by the manner in which each individual reacts to the frustrations in his daily
life. Freud conceptualizes this process by means of the term "repression," whereas Lewin employs the term "frustration." Thus,
in the Freudian view, both constructive and neurotic behavior
are consequences of repression; constructive behavior being a
consequence of the unconscious sublimation of repressed material,
and neurotic behavior being the result of failure at satisfactory
repression. Allport describes the same process as the expression
or inhibition, respectively, of the individual's propriate strivings.
Murphy and Maslow, each in his own idiom, describe it in the
same manner. Goldstein conceives the process in terms of self-
actualization and self-preservation, respectively. Lecky accounts
for the same processes by means of the achievement of self-
consistency in the case of the healthy individual, and its breakdown
in the case of the abnormal person.

All modern personality psychologies postulate as an explanatory
principle some basic impetus or motive "force" to human behavior.
Freud posited the basic urges; Lewin, vectors in a field; Allport,
propriate strivings; and the others whom we have mentioned, some
variant of the same dynamic striving. In Freud's psychology,
creativeness and the mechanisms of adjustment aid in diminishing
or overcoming the inevitable personal conflicts; in Lewin's system,
the conflicts are controlled in the interests of the person by the
latter's performance on planes of "higher" or "lesser" (phantasy)
reality; in Allport's view, unification of personality is achieved by
future-pointed, or propriate, strivings. Goldstein, Murphy, and
Maslow, again each in his own individual manner, account for the
behavior and unity of man by some variant of the principle of
self-actualization; and Lecky's concept of self-consistency performs the same function in his own system. With some trepidation,
we also include Sullivan in this context; for, although his idiosyncratic language often leaves us in doubt, generally speaking he was
groping toward the same end—an explanation of the integrated
person through an active and dominant self-system. He resembles
the others, too, in his view that the personality is the unity of the
motivational, affective, and cognitive dimensions. While person-

ality is healthy, it functions as a unit; when the whole is in any way dissociated, the individual is overcome by anxiety, helplessness, and insecurity.

Furthermore, in all these psychologies, except possibly Allport's, which we discussed in Chapter 2, there are no serious dichotomies or discontinuities.[8] Murphy has found it necessary to write a fairly long chapter in his book, *Personality*, to stress the fact of continuity in human behavior. "Despite all vicissitudes of life there is continuity," he says.[9] While he admits that one cannot claim too much for the sources of continuity, at the same time one cannot claim too little. Furthermore, he was impelled to write another long chapter on discontinuity, not in order to establish any dichotomy between the normal and abnormal, or infancy and adulthood, but in order to stress the fact that no two persons are exactly alike. An important consequence of his concern for discontinuity is that, by means of this concept, he has made room for psychological types.[10]

Each of these psychologies is, in one way or another, a *self-psychology*. However, in none of them does the self resemble an isolable entity; on the contrary, it is conceived as a necessary principle of organization, consistency, and unity. The concept of the self in Allport's psychology thus again suggests the validity of our remark, that his position is not incompatible with the doctrine of continuity. His concept of propriate striving, and particularly his examples to confirm its existence, supports our conclusion. Roald Amundsen, the famous explorer, from the age of fifteen had one dominant passion: to become a polar explorer, as Allport points out. In the face of seemingly insurmountable obstacles, Amundsen's dominant propriate striving persisted. Allport states Amundsen's aspiration well when he writes of him: "Not only did he maintain one style of life, without ceasing, but this central commitment enabled him to withstand the temptation to reduce the segmental

---

[8] In the face of Allport's unfailing emphasis on the unity of personality, this is a puzzling feature of his psychology. He stressed in a variety of ways the gap between normality and abnormality, and especially the discontinuity between a child's undeveloped and his later mature personality. However, there is nothing in his theory of functional autonomy, for instance, to preclude the continuity from childhood to maturity. Certainly his emphasis on growth and becoming suggests a *gradual* transformation of infantile behavior into adult personality. Our own belief is that in his *strong* but valid criticisms of the animal and infant models when applied to human personality, he perhaps unwittingly suggests that there is an unbridgeable hiatus between earlier and later conditions of being and becoming. For his criticism of animal and infant models in the study of personality, see Chapter 14, above.

[9] Murphy, *Personality*, p. 714.

[10] *Ibid.*, Ch. 31.

tensions continually engendered by fatigue, hunger, ridicule, and danger." [11]

Similar corroborating data is found in the study by Allport, Bruner, and Jandorf of the persistence of personality in the face of social catastrophes, which we have already cited.[12] Indeed, Allport holds that a complete or adequate psychology "would in effect *be* a psychology of the ego," or self.[13]

Thus, despite the apparent vacillations and unwitting equivocations, Allport's psychology of the developing self implies the concept of continuity from infancy to adulthood. The prominence which he gives to the processes of self-identity, ego-enhancement, and ego-extension serves to stress an undoubted continuity of the personality. However, Allport is undoubtedly right in his unfailing belief that an adult personality is not the mere recapitulation of archaic functions. In this regard, his view is a much needed corrective of Freud's overemphasis on the role of infantile experience in adult behavior.

As for the other personality psychologies which we have discussed, all of them clearly are self-psychologies. Goldstein's motive of self-actualization is the impetus by which the human person becomes truly healthy and mature. Maslow's self-actualizing person implies a striving, aspiring self. Murphy has deemed the self so important that he gives it an entire section in his treatise on personality, consisting of six closely reasoned and illuminating chapters. Lewin was keenly concerned with the concept of self, or the self-system, as he called it in his earlier writings. He was convinced that some sort of self-concept is basic to the understanding of personality and character. He held strongly to the view that, if one is to describe personality as a whole, one must focus, not on its isolated properties or traits, but upon the larger unit or self-system.[14] Lecky's preoccupation with the self is clearly evident in the title of his book, *Self-consistency*.

The most encouraging feature of the self-concept is its basic similarity in the psychologies which we have discussed. While the phraseology differs, and while the emphases are not exactly the same, the concept has the same psychological meaning and performs the same psychological and heuristic functions in the views

[11] G. W. Allport, *Becoming: basic considerations for a psychology of personality* (New Haven: Yale University Press, 1955), p. 49.

[12] Allport, Bruner, and Jandorf, Personality under social catastrophe.

[13] *Becoming*, p. 55.

[14] See K. Lewin, *A dynamic theory of personality* (New York: McGraw-Hill Book Co., Inc., 1935), Ch. 2.

of the writers whom we have discussed. In none of them is the self coextensive with the total personality, but in all of them it is the reference point for personal experience. This agreement can be best described by Allport's term, "propriate striving." Not one of them views the self in a manner that warrants the widespread criticism of the self-concept as a being or soul that performs acts and is inaccessible to psychological investigation. They view it as that special aspect of the total person which has to do with "warmth, with unity, with a sense of personal importance," as Allport phrases it.[15]

The centrality of the self in the study of personality is emphasized in other important psychologies of personalities. The rich and insightful work of Carl Rogers is an important confirmation of this claim. We have not delineated Roger's work on the self extensively because it is therapeutically oriented, and ours is a discussion of the healthy personality. Nevertheless, everything of importance in Rogers' client-centered therapy strongly confirms practically everything we have said in this book concerning the wholeness of personality and the pressing need for every individual to maintain his integrity and actualize himself as a person. Indeed, Rogers' therapeutic work is the most convincing in a long line of proofs, of both the indispensability of the self-concept and the uniqueness of the total personality. The self, particularly, is prominent in Rogers' therapeutic researches, for in client-centered therapy the "cure" of psychological ills consists not merely in eliminating symptoms and restoring health, but in a form of reorganization of self-perceptions which result in *self-acceptance*. Everyone who has worked with "maladjusted" individuals knows that genuine improvement in mental health consists far less in social adjustment, in fitting oneself into the group in which one must live, important as this is, than in accepting oneself as worthy of respect. Furthermore, Rogers' therapeutic findings support the importance of wholeness, individuality, and uniqueness. This is shown in the demonstrated fact that in all of Rogers' many clients the most important consequence of his mode of therapy is their perception of their independence, spontaneity, and integration. The clients' deepest and most vital experience in therapy is their perceptual reorganization of themselves as free, independent, and self-actualizing persons.[16]

[15] *Becoming*, p. 55.
[16] See C. R. Rogers, *Client-centered therapy* (Boston: Houghton Mifflin Co., 1951), Ch. 11.

A VIEW OF THE PERSON

We have reviewed in this chapter the wide group of factors that comprise the personality as it is perceived by numerous important views in contemporary psychology. This review has stressed the molding force of interpersonal reality, especially the role of interpersonal conditioning and perceptual patterning. It has briefly expounded the field-dynamic principles by means of which the total personality may as a first approximation be explained. Finally, it has essayed a provisional synthesis of most of the important contemporary views of the nature of personality.

The question now before us is this: *On the basis of the approaches to the study of personality, what sort of view of the person emerges from them?*

In view of the proliferation of established views and the burgeoning of new ones, an answer to the question may appear presumptuous. However, we do not think so; and our efforts in this direction already point the way to a tentative answer. Let us see.

WHOLENESS AND THE PERCEPTUAL FIELD. Everything we have said in this book points to the conclusion that every individual is an organized whole, or total person, whose view of himself and of others is a product of his reaction to his perceptual field. This fact has been stressed in our discussion of the tendency of the biological organism to react as a totality and in the description of the self as a process of self-perception, self-identification, and self-maintenance. No stimulus-response account of personality and human behavior has yet succeeded in accounting for this "need" of the organism to maintain its integrity as a living being. No atomistic account of behavior, with all its excellent paraphernalia of experimentation, quantitative precision, statistical analysis, and operational definition, has given us an explanation that all personality psychologists find acceptable. The same is true of the point of view that is favored in this book. The reason for the inadequacy of the stimulus-response approach is that much important research in physiology and in the psychology of personality has demonstrated that in both the physical organism and the psychological person *total and organized, rather than atomistic and segmental, behavior is fundamental.* This is in line with our field-dynamic view that behavior, growth, and development are holistic phenomena, not atomistic chains of events.

The process of self-perception, furthermore, is directed by the perceptual field of the person. The only *fundamental* reality that any person can know is the reality which he infers from his own perception of the world—the world of events, objects, people. The philosopher's "absolute reality" has for centuries concealed from psychological thinkers the simple fact that for a living person his own perception of the world is the only world which he can "really know." If one retorts to this way of viewing reality by asking how knowledge of self and reality can be anything but solipsistic, the answer is that the personality psychologist is constantly relating perceptions to one another, analyzing and testing them, in order to increase their reliability.

PERSONALITY AND INTENTION. The data in this book, as well as others which we have been unable to include within the limits of our discussion, lead to an incontravertible conclusion: *Every healthy person directs his actions toward a goal, or a set of interrelated goals, the achievement of which is to him an absolute necessity.* Goal-directed behavior has been established in the animal laboratory as well as in the human community. But what distinguishes the goal-directed behavior of a person from that of a lower animal is that the latter is fundamentally drive-reductive, whereas the former also functions in the service of self-enhancement. While every person must satisfy his hunger and thirst, his appetitive and sexual needs, the crucial fact about these and other needs, especially of growth and enhancement, is that they are self-directed and self-oriented. A man strives to accumulate wealth, not because wealth of itself is satisfying, for it may in fact satisfy no "need" whatsoever, but because of the individual's perception of its meaning in the context of his individual style of life. Thus, to use a commonplace example, the miser and the spendthrift have different perceptions of the "meaning" of money.

Man, then, is an intentional, goal-setting being. He strives for ends which often have no drive-reductive value, for they satisfy no basic need, but only the determination of the individual to extend himself beyond his momentary existence. Personality is future-pointed, and the direction of its expression is self-determined.

SELF-CONSISTENCY. It is not enough to say, as we have just asserted, that man's goal-direction is self-conducted. *Man is determined to seek goals which cohere with his life-style and are consistent with his image of himself as a person.* Once the self-image has been established, the person's every need, every striving, every intentional act must be consistent with it. Self-consistency is a highly selective process, so that whatever violates the integrity of the self, whatever act is at variance with a person's concept of himself, must be either eliminated or redefined in such a way as to be congruent with his self-picture. No doubt much repressed and neurotic behavior is behavior that is incompatible with an individual's self-image. In extreme cases, as in some forms of hysteria and paranoid reactions, the "disowned" behavior, if it were accepted by the individual, would be so self-demoralizing that he is compelled to reject it and ascribe it to someone else. Projection is at once and extreme and an unsuccessful effort to keep the self intact.

While it is difficult to find corroborative evidence for our assertion, we believe that much of the resistance to enculturation and the normal rebelliousness of every healthy individual is due not only to the fact that socialization deflects his biological impulses but also because it endangers the integrity of his self. The lack of evidence for our assertion, we might add, is matched by the absence of evidence against it. Although we do not accept Lecky's all-encompassing claims for the sovereign force of consistency needs, we have no doubt whatsoever of the central importance of wholeness in the growth and maintenance of the self and personality.

CONSISTENCY AND CHANGE. The impulsion toward self-consistency is never absolute. If it were, growth and changes in personality could not take place. The healthy personality is a changing personality. Personality is, as we said before, a being-in-becoming: while it lives, it changes and grows; while it changes, it is reorganizing itself on a more effective level. We are generally less cognizant of this fact because much of our knowledge of personality is based on the study of neurotic and defensive individuals. The defensive individual is more likely than the relaxed person to interpret the acts of another as threats to his own integrity; therefore, he is much more determined to maintain his consistency. Consequently he, as well as the psychologist who observes him, is more likely to be impressed by the stability of the subject's personality and be less aware of the tendency of the healthy individual to grow and expand. Indeed, much of what we observe as a "cure" during successful psychotherapy consists of the subject's increasing acceptance of himself as a different person. On the other hand, the healthy individual has always accepted himself as substantially different from others, exulting in his knowledge and striving continually to renew himself—to grow, to change, to realize his potentialities.

SELF-ACTUALIZATION. Every person who is not hedged in by crippling defenses, who does not surrender to every social pressure and cultural imperative, is engaged in the never-ending process of self-enhancement and self-actualization. He is not satisfied to maintain himself, to retain consistency and stability only, important as these forms of striving are; he must perpetually differentiate himself and become more and more what he has the capacity and intention of becoming.

In view of the misinterpretation to which the process of self-actualization is subject, we hasten to say emphatically that it is not a form of self-seeking, egoism, or selfishness. On the contrary, existing studies of self-actualization are quite convincing in their demonstration that the self-actualizing person is in essence striving for increasing relatedness with others. This fact was made clear in Chapter 3, where we pointed out that, although the self-actualizing person likes detachment and privacy, he also relates himself easily to others, has great compassion for them, and accepts them as warmly as he accepts himself.

Self-actualization is by no means a psychological process only. Evidence of its existence has been found in biological research. Genetically, no better example of this exists than the process of constant change in organisms, from a lower to a higher phylogenetic level. The fundamental push of all healthy organisms is forward.[17]

Contemporary biological researches favor the view that a living organism is by no means wholly concerned with self-preservation, but with transcending its present state in order to attain a more complex, effective, and satisfying integration. This but reiterates Goldstein's assertion that self-preservation is basically pathological, whereas self-actualization is an expression of the organism's need for growth and enhancement. Although the process is never wholly smooth, the organism strives forward against all impediments to its achievement. The human being who is relatively free from neurotic inhibitions and defenses is guided by what Horney has well described as the *morality of evolution*. This morality is concerned with the question of what motives obstruct or induce human growth; or more precisely, it is a way of working at ourselves to transcend infantile and ineffectual modes of behaving and of achieving self-direction and self-understanding. In healthy self-actualization "we do not need an inner strait jacket with which to shackle our spontaneity, nor the whip of inner dictates to drive us to perfection." [18] Indeed, the search for perfection, like the quest for mastery and dominance, is a symptom of a sick self. The self-actualizing person strives for neither one, but only for the realization of his potentialities and for integrated growth.

[17] See H. S. Sullivan, *Conceptions of modern psychiatry* (Washington, D.C.: William Alanson White Psychiatric Foundation, 1945), Ch. 2.

[18] K. Horney, *Neurosis and human growth* (New York: W. W. Norton & Co., Inc., 1950), p. 15.

CONCLUDING REMARKS. The view of the person which we have just expounded should be fairly clear. We do not consider man as a passive being whose behavior is determined by need-reduction and automaton conformity. The morality of evolution impels us to view man optimistically. Despite his many tragedies in the form of sickness and death, and all other forces that constrict and minimize man's greatness, at his healthiest he is guided by constructive aspirations. Given full opportunity, man is basically an affirmative being. Pessimism is an attitude which results from the failure to appreciate man's capacity for affirmative striving, for love and compassion, for transmuting his destructive impulses into creative activities. Contrary to Freud's metapsychological pessimism, the researches which we have presented in this book affirm that love and creativity are not merely sublimations of libidinal urges, but positive forces used in the service of man's own transformation.

There is no pollyanna quality in this optimism. On the contrary, creative optimism is always cognizant of the tragic nature of life. Indeed, we hold that an important characteristic of the mature man is his perception of the tragic sense of life, to borrow Unamuno's appropriate phrase.[19] Creative optimism is what makes life's tragedies not only bearable, but a source of aesthetic enjoyment and poetic justification. To the neurotic person, ills are unbearable because he feels utterly trapped by them. For the healthy individual, they serve as one more means of putting his creative impulses to work in the interest of self-extension and self-affirmation.

PERSONALITY: THE CENTRAL PROBLEM OF PSYCHOLOGY

What is the main concern of the science of psychology? The answer to this question has long been disputed. Perhaps, if psychology were the objective science it is sometimes pictured this problem would not exist. But the whole history of psychology, as Boring demonstrated some thirty years ago, has been intensely personal.[20] If this is true of experimental psychology, it is even more true of the psychology of personality, which has not had the full benefits, real and questionable, of a rigid experimental methodology. The study of personality has had special appeal to the individualist in psychology, who often values creative thinking

[19] See M. de Unamuno, *The tragic sense of life* (London: Macmillan & Co., Ltd., 1926). Dover Publications issued a paper-cover edition of this earnest and passionate description of man, in 1954.

[20] E. G. Boring, *A history of experimental psychology* (New York: Appleton-Century-Crofts, Inc., 1929; 2d ed., 1950), pp. viii-ix.

and intuitive insights more than the demonstrations of quantitative experiments. As Hall and Lindzey point out, the study of personality has always been the province of the rebels and dissident individuals in psychology. Personality psychologists have been "rebels against conventional ideas and usual practices, rebels against typical methods and respected techniques of research, and most of all rebels against accepted theory and normative problems." [21]

However, this explanation is not the whole story. There is more than rebellion in the personality psychologist's attitude. He is convinced, on the basis of present results, that the conventional procedures are unable to account for personality successfully. There is yet no experimental procedure, no laboratory method, no statistical technique by means of which the student of personality can investigate *personality as a whole*. The conventional techniques have yielded dependable results only in those areas of psychology which deal with segments, albeit unified segments of the personality, such as "stimulus configurations," for instance.

It might be a good thing if the psychology of personality could be based on a rigid stimulus-response theory. Dollard and Miller made the attempt, as we tried to show in Chapter 8. However, as we indicated, in our judgment they have not succeeded; for not only have they failed to describe the *total* personality, but the measure of success which they have achieved has been largely due to their psychoanalytical and anthropological enlargement of the stimulus-response approach. Stimulus-response learning, for all its success and reputation, is not a simple process of drive-reduction or need-gratification. As we see the learning process, it is a function of the *person*. Irrespective of stimulus-response conditioning, need-gratification, or tension-reduction, learning is always a function of a person's intelligence, his degree of self-integration, his self-involvement, and his self-attitudes, such as self-confidence or its absence. The stupid, poorly integrated person, who is not involved in his task and whose attitude-value complex does not motivate him to acquire new knowledge, is a poor learner. It is generally agreed that the overanxious, overinhibited, and cognitively poorly organized individual does not learn as well as the relatively relaxed and self-confident person. Anxiety, fear, and the like tend to inhibit or disorganize the learning process. In either case, then, learning depends considerably upon the nature of the *learning person*.

Again, the principles of learning, while extremely important in their own right, are statistical formulations of the achievements of

21 C. S. Hall and G. Lindzey, *Theories of personality* (New York: John Wiley & Sons, Inc., 1957), p. 4.

population samples. Although they give us valuable knowledge of learning in general, they tell us very little concerning the learning of a specific person. In the nature of the situation, this is unavoidable, but from the standpoint of the individual learner it is a serious defect. It is unavoidable because of the uniqueness of every person. This uniqueness, as we have pointed out, is not only a psychological view, but is substantiated by numerous contemporary biologists. Dunn and Dobzhansky have long argued for the uniqueness of every individual. On the basis of important researches they conclude that biologists are impelled to "assert the absolute uniqueness of every human individual." Schrödinger, in one of his illuminating books, comes to the same conclusion.[22] Sinnott, whose ideas deserve wider discussion by psychologists than they have thus far received, has gone even farther. He holds that the very nature of protoplasm is such as to cause the organism to strive toward definite ends. While we are in no position either to affirm or to deny his claim that goal-seeking is *built* into the protoplasm of every organism, there is sufficient biological evidence for asserting that every organism conceived as a dynamic whole is pushing forward to the realization of positive goals.[23]

Sinnott's view is a biological argument for the importance of *intention* in directing human behavior, which, the reader will have noted, is the basic idea of the present book. We believe that man is seldom *driven* in the manner described by drive-reduction theory. He feels driven only in certain abnormal conditions, as in compulsion neuroses, for example. Man pushes forward toward a goal because he *wants* its consummation. Drives provide man with motive power, but they fail to account for the *direction* which his behavior takes. Psychological man is a unique system and therefore requires unique explanations for his behavior. If Sinnott is right in attributing uniqueness to every living system, then biology and psychology as we conceive them are loyal allies in portraying man as a unique, goal-seeking, and intentional individual. A theory of learning that is not geared to the uniqueness of the individual, and to the fact that it takes place in an organized system called personality, is short-sighted. Even the learning theorist does not claim that learning goes on in a vacuum; but by ignoring the learner as a person, he unwittingly leads one to believe that it does. This

[22] See L. C. Dunn and T. Dobzhansky, *Heredity, race, and society* (Baltimore: Penguin Books, Inc., 1946); E. Schrödinger, *What is life?* (New York: The Macmillan Co., 1945).

[23] See E. W. Sinnott, *The biology of the spirit* (New York: The Viking Press, Inc., 1955); also, by same author, *Matter, mind and man: the biology of human nature* (New York: Harper & Bros., 1957).

conclusion is strengthened by the fact that the main learning theories do not in their experiments take account of the fact that events *within* the learner—certainly the *human* learner—are a part of the series of events which determine the nature of learning. They minimize the deliberative aspect of human learning, the delayed responses that lead to individual choices. This deliberation, these delayed responses, are determined by the perceptual field of each individual, by his perception of himself as a person. *In a very profound sense, man is the cause of his own learning, his own individual behavior.* The learner is not a passive and receptive agent merely, nor simply a coping and adjusting organism, but an active, causal instrumentality. In short, man is an intentional and purposive being who not only adapts himself to, but creates and modifies, his own environment.

One cannot help but be struck by the fact that when man is deeply self-involved in a task or behavior, he restructures his own nature. A man is most truly himself when he can lose himself in his own purposive activities. While he submits to the demands and rights of another, he yet restructures them in the light of his own personality. No elaborate instruments of research are necessary to discover this fact; it is, in fact, confirmed by observation and intelligent common sense.

CONCLUSION

Our aim in this book has been to study personality as a whole. It is impossible, we believe, to study the whole person by investigating his separate parts. We cannot apprehend the nature of personality by discrete analyses of learning, motivation, language, the attitude-value complex, the folkways and mores of the community. At the basis of and implicit in every study of human behavior is the problem of organization—the problem of how descriptive units cohere to make a unified and dynamic structure.

The point of view implicit in every aspect of the psychology of personality expounded in this book is that, while we may theoretically isolate various elements of the total personality, and examine every individual apart from his social context—the *in situ* method permits us to do that—each is in fact only a part of a more inclusive whole. Again, the whole is not a summation of parts, but a *dynamic* unity—a moving and reciprocal relationship of parts to whole.

This mode of viewing personality requires a shift from atomism and elementarism to a more complex descriptive unit in psychology.

This descriptive unit is neither "mind" nor "behavior," but *personality as a whole*. The term "behavior" is itself best understood as the response of the total individual to the experimental field *as he perceives it at the moment*. Outside a perceptual frame of reference, behavior is meaningless.

Personality as a whole is the individual's organized perception of himself in his relation to others, or of himself in relation to the dynamic field of human nature. If accurate prediction of a person's behavior is ever to be achieved, its consummation will be effected, not on the basis of mechanistic cause-and-effect relationships, but through the knowledge of the exact relation of parts to the whole. Behavior science must aim to formulate dynamic rather than causal laws, functional interconnections rather than discrete bio-social events. It must be grounded in a coherent knowledge of the biological organism, the individual person, and the social group if it hopes to attain the status of a reliable behavioral science.

The individual who emerges from the standard tests, the laborious correlations, and the various scientific assessments is undoubtedly authentic, but at the same time he is colorless and lifeless in contrast to the vital being whom we know in our daily experience, in our conversations, in the searching and often agitated gropings of the troubled person, and, most of all in the *intentional* and *creative* activities of a healthy being.

The complexity and individuality of the human person may be lost, not only in the interstices of a nomothetic science, as Allport believes, but in the tenuities of ideographic principles as well. In this predicament lies the poetic tragedy of attempting, but not succeeding in, giving man's behavior a solid habitation and a legitimate name. As for ourselves, we feel the predicament acutely.

Nevertheless, there is no room for pessimism, and surely no need to declare a scientific moratorium on the rigorous pursuit of our subject. The history of science has shown that in the long run the road to truth, while divided by many pathways leading only to partial truths, lies in those methods which lead to testable and verifiable conclusions. When the psychology of personality has reached the stage of rigorous development, it will have attained the status of an exact science. Meanwhile, earnest psychologists will use whatever methods are available and such scientific imagination as they might be fortunate enough to possess.

Name Index

Subject Index

Abilities, and personality, 142–43
Acquisitiveness, 301–3
  absence of, in Zuñi, 301
  among Kwakiutls, 302
Adjustive behavior, as in the mores, 348
  determinants of, compared with expressive behavior, 348–52
Adrenal gland, 151
Aggressiveness, 297–301
  and frustration, 297
Ambivalence, 46
Americans, gregariousness of, 291
Anal disciplines, 166–67
Anchorage groups, 180–85
Anticipation, in transformation of drives, 264–66
Anticipatory response, in S-R learning theory, 237
Arapesh, and cooperation, 295
Artistic tastes and productions, as forms of expressive behavior, 361–63
Ascendence, as trait, 437
Assumption, hidden, in empirical procedures, 8
Asthenic, 155
Athletic, 155; see also Type, theories of, constitutional
Attitudes, 372–99; see also Values
Attitudes and values, 384–86
  as anticipatory responses, 383
  as determining tendencies, 382–83
  as postural responses, 383
  as preparatory actions, 382–83
  as tests of personality, 394–98
  common features of definitions of, 383–84
  definitions of, 382–84
  nature of, 381–86
  their functions, 393–98
Attitude-value complex,
  and personality, 386–97
  and the self, 386–89
  as *Verankerungspunkt*, 384–85
Autobiographical method, 122–23

Bali, people of, and aggressiveness, 298
Bantu, and premarital pregnancy, 304

Barriers, effect of, experiments on, 116–17
Basic disciplines, psychological effects of, 168–71
Basic urges, 45–47
  interdependence of, 46–47
Behaving self, in cognitive theory, 250–51
Behavior, learned, 225–54
Behavior, moral, 400–427
  and conflict, 404–5
  as a liberation movement, 428
  as purposeful action, 428
  research models in, 405–10; see also Genetic model, Intentional model, Mechanical model, Phylogenetic model; see also Character
Belief and conformity, as security motives, 268–70
Belief systems, 197–98
Being-and-becoming, 285–86
Belongingness, as affiliative motive, 270
Bewusstseinslage, 382; see also Attitudes

Canalization, 69
Categorizing, role of, in language, 330–31
Cathexis, in sign learning, 239–40
Cerebrotonic, 157; see also Type, theories of, constitutional
Character, 400–427; see also Behavior, moral
  child's contribution to his growth in, 423
  dynamic patterns, in study of, 419–21
  early studies of, 411–12
  general factor in, 414; see also Character, "will" factor in *and* Character, W-factor in
  limitations of behaviorist approach to, 424
  miscellaneous studies of, 416–19
  psychological health in, 423
  research in, 410–22; see also Character, "scientific" study of
  role of positive goodness in, 423

527